More than thirty countries.
Five continents. One mission:
To show American wars as they have never been seen before.

Praise for Andrew Carroll's extraordinary
***New York Times* bestseller . . .**

BEHIND THE LINES

"There are two vastly different ways of studying war. One has to do with the great story of history and of nations, the other with dying alone in a field hospital; with missing someone so much it aches; with wrestling down fear and shooting up courage; or enduring war's squalor and absurdity. Andrew Carroll studies the human side of war in this stirring, moving, and sometimes hilarious collection."

—Mark Bowden, author of *Black Hawk Down*

"This book is more than a collection of newly discovered war letters. There is something deeper, richer, and more intense at work here. Each letter is extraordinary in its own right, but together they illuminate war as it is rarely seen. Most important, *Behind the Lines* is the result of Andrew Carroll's unprecedented trip around the world to seek out these gripping, insightful, and, in so many cases, breathtaking letters. This is a book born of great passion. This is a book with tremendous heart and soul."

—James Bradley, author of *Flags of Our Fathers* and *Flyboys*

"From the American Revolution to Iraq, everything is here: the terror and exhilaration of bloody combat, love letters, funny letters, letters from civilians caught in the middle of war. *Behind the Lines* is worth savoring; you can dip into it at any page and find something fascinating."

—Joseph L. Galloway, coauthor of *We Were Soldiers Once . . . and Young* and *Triumph Without Victory: The History of the Persian Gulf War*

"This book is absolutely majestic."

"In all my years of military service, I don't believe I have ever read a book that has moved me as profoundly as this one. While it is often the generals and military leaders who receive the limelight, Andrew Carroll's *Behind the Lines* reminds us that it is the individual troops in the field and their loved ones at home who most deserve our admiration and attention. I cannot recommend this book more highly."

"There is nothing more powerful than words written when life as you know it hangs in the balance. From soldiers on the front lines writing to sweethearts and family, to resistance fighters and so many others in the midst of war, *Behind the Lines* has letters representing just about every race and many different cultures. This book is phenomenal and a must-read."

"The letters are, almost without exception, arresting in their earnestness, sincerity, and passion, and diverse in their sentiments—brave, fearful, amorous, angry, resigned, conniving, unbalanced, stoical. The result is captivating in its immediacy."

"Unique, both in scope and content. . . . This is a wonderful book."

"Carroll's book allows everyone to experience the rawness of war through words."

BEHIND THE LINES

*Powerful and Revealing American
and Foreign War Letters—
and One Man's Search to Find Them*

EDITED BY
ANDREW CARROLL

SCRIBNER
New York   London   Toronto   Sydney

For PETER LEHENY
February 14, 1970 to July 4, 2002

SCRIBNER
1230 Avenue of the Americas
New York, NY 10020

Copyright © 2005 by Andrew Carroll

First Scribner trade paperback edition 2006

SCRIBNER and design are trademarks of Macmillan Library Reference USA, Inc.,
used under license by Simon & Schuster, the publisher of this work.

For information about special discounts for bulk purchases,
please contact Simon & Schuster Special Sales:
1-800-456-6798 or business@simonandschuster.com

DESIGNED BY ERICH HOBBING

Text set in Adobe Garamond

Manufactured in the United States of America

1   3   5   7   9   10   8   6   4   2

Library of Congress Control Number: 2005042267

ISBN-13: 978-0-7432-5616-2
ISBN-10: 0-7432-5616-6
ISBN-13: 978-0-7432-5617-9 (Pbk)
ISBN-10: 0-7432-5617-4 (Pbk)

Permissions acknowledgments appear on page 473.

CONTENTS

I visited our old battlefield and was pleased to find it looked a quiet, contented area with people digging in the fields in the afternoon sun. Everything looked so peaceful and easy-going there this afternoon that I felt if this is what we are fighting to restore all over the world, it is right that we should do all we can to achieve it. Children were playing in the ditch where the German machine-gunner who shot Morgan had been lying. Nearby was Morgan's grave. It is strange that a young Irishman, living in England, should die for the freedom of Dutch children in Holland whom he never even saw and whose names he never knew. It seems to typify the tremendously generous spirit of sacrifice made by Morgan and so many others like him.

—*Irish soldier Major Charles Sweeny, with the Royal Ulster Rifles, writing to his wife on February 22, 1945, about one of his men who had been killed in the Netherlands five months earlier. Tragically, Sweeny survived combat but then died in an accident two days before the war in Europe was over.*

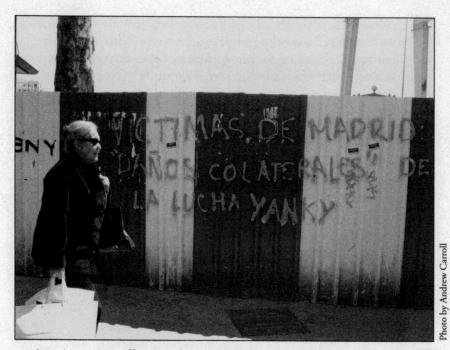

Anti-American graffiti near the Atocha Train Station in Madrid, Spain. On March 11, 2004, members of an al-Qaeda cell in Spain exploded several bombs on commuter trains in Madrid, killing nearly two hundred civilians. Many citizens blamed the US for the attack, which al-Qaeda claimed was a direct response to the deployment of Spanish troops in Iraq. The graffiti reads: VICTIMS OF MADRID: "COLLATERAL DAMAGE" OF THE YANKEE WAR.

INTRODUCTION

Before leaving, I had been forewarned to expect everything from indifference to outright hostility.

The purpose of the trip, which would take me to more than thirty countries across five continents, was to search for letters by soldiers and civilians from nations that had been wartime allies or adversaries of the United States throughout our history. My timing was not ideal. The invasion of Iraq was fueling anti-American sentiment around the world. People were burning the Stars and Stripes not only in Palestine, Cairo, and Tehran, but Berlin, Rome, and London. And in some of the places I would be traveling to, Americans were being threatened physically, kidnapped, and, in extreme cases, executed. Due to the brief amount of time I planned to stay in the relatively more dangerous regions, the risk for me was minimal, but some degree of concern was not unwarranted. (Indeed, only days before I checked in to my hotel in Afghanistan, a bomb placed by members of the Taliban or al-Qaeda detonated behind the hotel, shattering most of the back windows. Amazingly no one was seriously hurt. The day after the explosion I called to see if the hotel was still accepting guests. The clerk assured me cheerfully, "Oh yes, all is well! You come. Bring cash!")

The inspiration to seek out foreign letters came from an unexpected source—American veterans. In 1998, I launched an initiative called the Legacy Project that preserves wartime correspondences as a way to honor and remember those who have fought for this nation. Since then, people across the country have sent in tens of thousands of previously unpublished letters from all of our major conflicts, beginning with the War of Independence and continuing up to Operation Iraqi Freedom. The letters not only record extraordinary moments in time—the battle of Shiloh, the attack on Pearl Harbor, the storming of Fallujah—they capture the more human side of warfare and reveal the thoughts and emotions of the troops who have been eyewitnesses to these events. Although I had always admired those who served in the military, I had no real concept of all that they sacrificed, on and off the battlefield, until I began reading their letters home.

For two years I traveled throughout the US speaking with groups of vet-

1

erans about the importance of saving what they had written from the front lines. During these conversations we talked about wartime correspondences in general and how essential mail was to their morale, the tricks they used to evade the censors, the letters they dreaded receiving more than any others (rejection or "Dear John" messages from a sweetheart), and the ones that were the most gut-wrenching to write (condolence letters to the families of fallen comrades). We also discussed the changes in letter-writing from generation to generation, especially with the advent of e-mail, and how, while the tone has become less formal over the years, the emotions have remained fundamentally the same.

One question that initially surprised me was being asked with increasing regularity: was the Legacy Project collecting letters from other countries? I responded that only a few had trickled in over the years, donated primarily by stamp collectors and bargain hunters who had discovered them at estate sales and flea markets in the US and abroad. I was curious why these veterans were interested in foreign correspondences, and the history buffs replied that the letters would make for fascinating reading, providing a fresh perspective on familiar battles. But most of the veterans expressed the belief that these letters might contribute to our overall understanding of war and the larger impact of these conflicts on everyone involved—friend and foe alike.

An idea began to take hold. For years I had been yearning to go abroad and visit the places I had been reading about in the letters. I wanted to see the trenches of World War I that still zigzag through the French and Belgian countryside, walk along the Normandy coast where Allied forces had landed on D-Day, peer across the Demilitarized Zone marking the border between North and South Korea, explore the tunnels of Cu Chi outside of Saigon, and, if possible, set foot in Baghdad and Kabul. But instead of embarking on a mere sightseeing tour, I could give the trip a purpose and seek out war letters in every country I visited. All I had to do, I figured, was locate the main military archives and museums and dig through their collections. Ideally, I would also introduce myself to veterans and active duty personnel along the way and solicit letters from them directly.

Well-traveled friends and colleagues were more pessimistic about my plan of action. They alerted me that many of the institutions I expected to visit were government-run and notorious for their unwieldy bureaucracies. Upon arrival I would have to produce a letter of introduction just to secure an appointment with the archivists, and there was still no guarantee the staff would grant me access to their holdings. There was also the larger matter of the world's political climate at the time. Acquaintances overseas prepared me for the possibility that the veterans, military personnel, and other people I hoped to meet might distrust my motives or be unwilling to cooperate with an American. The very nature of the appeal was a delicate one, as I would be asking these individuals to share with me copies of their private letters. If a foreigner approached me with such a request, I'm not sure how enthusiastic my response would be.

After five months of planning and armed with an itinerary that weighed in at seven pounds, I was—out of stubbornness, naiveté, or perhaps a bit of both—determined to go. I had secured the necessary visas, gotten my vaccinations, cancelled my magazine subscriptions, reconfirmed all reservations, said my good-byes, fibbed to my mom about having no intention of traveling to Iraq, and then headed to the airport.

Gdansk was first. A port city on the northern coast of Poland, Gdansk is celebrated as the birthplace of the Solidarity movement, where, in 1980, a thirty-seven-year-old electrician named Lech Walesa galvanized his fellow shipyard workers to demand from Poland's Communist government the right to organize trade unions. The reason I began in Gdansk, however, had more to do with what happened there on September 1, 1939, when German forces pounded the city with artillery before launching a full-scale invasion of Poland, marking the beginning of World War II. (Arguably, the clash between Chinese and Japanese troops at the Marco Polo Bridge outside of Beijing, China, on July 7, 1937, which ignited a larger conflagration in the Pacific, represents the first shots fired in the war.) After Germany's assault, hostilities swept the globe like a virus, ultimately killing tens of millions of people. The Poles alone lost one-fifth of their population.

I arrived in Gdansk on September 1 curious to see where the war in Europe had erupted, but, more importantly, to find firsthand accounts written by Polish troops or civilians on that horrible day in 1939. The curators and librarians I spoke with were gracious but explained that they had nothing. They also thought it was doubtful that anyone in the city wrote about the invasion for fear of being accused by the Germans of spying. It was an inauspicious beginning to the trip.

With extra time on my hands, I briefly toured the city and wandered around Westerplatte, the site of the initial German bombardment. I watched as a steady procession of individuals, some alone, some with their families, quietly lit candles and placed flowers around the gravestones of Polish soldiers who were casualties of the attack. A group of German high school students crammed into the tiny History of Gdansk Museum and listened with rapt attention as their teacher narrated the events of that day and then described the hellish occupation of Poland that followed. One girl, apparently unfamiliar with this history, placed her hands over her mouth, aghast, and began to cry.

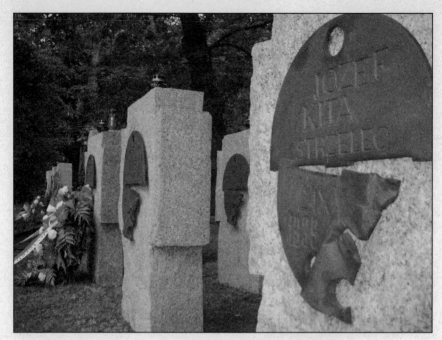

Graves of Polish troops killed during the German assault at Westerplatte in Gdansk, Poland. The metal nameplates have been created to look like soldiers' identification tags torn and fragmented in battle.

Man riding a bike on the Marco Polo Bridge outside of Beijing, China.

My next stop, Oswiecim, is better known outside of Poland by its German name—Auschwitz. I arrived late in the evening and, although I needed to get up early the next morning to take a tour of the former extermination camp, I was still on US time and couldn't sleep. The weather for the next day was forecasted to be warm and perfectly clear, and I knew that, being a Saturday, the place would be crowded with tourists. Recognizing it was an unusual request, I called for a taxi and asked the driver if he could take me over to the camp just to see the outside of the site under relatively more peaceful circumstances. I figured I could walk around the exterior grounds for a few minutes and take a picture of the infamous—and grotesquely cynical—*ARBEIT MACHT FREI* ("Work brings freedom") greeting that adorns the top of the camp's main gate.

As soon as the taxi driver and I pulled up to the entrance, I knew we were out of luck. The actual site was well behind a large parking lot and tourist center, and it would be impossible to see anything meaningful. The hour was getting late, and the driver had told me earlier that I was his last fare of the night. But sensing my disappointment, he seemed determined to find another entrance. Sure enough, after winding through a long, inconspicuous street off the main road, we came up to a dimly lit wooden guardhouse. The driver stepped out of the car and approached the night watchman, who looked understandably suspicious. The two men began talking, and I overheard the guard saying, "*Nie, nie.*" The driver was emphatic. Finally, the guard checked his watch, shrugged, and gestured to the entrance with a flick of his hand. The driver turned to me and said: "OK. We go in." He then opened his door, reached inside, and clicked the meter off. I told him I didn't think it would take us very long and that he should absolutely keep the meter running. "No, is OK." It was almost midnight.

All I could see until my eyes adjusted to the darkness were the tall black silhouettes of trees and the outline of what appeared to be row after row of barracks. We walked slowly and in silence. Occasionally the driver pointed to an important structure as we passed by. "Gas chambers," he said. "Here, crematoria." I would stop to look more carefully at a building or peek into a window and, every so often, blindly snap a photograph. Obviously the camp looked nothing like it did when, during the war, thousands of lives were extinguished within its walls every day. There was no sound of trains. No smell of burning flesh. No maniacal guards shrieking orders. No sense of human presence whatsoever. But the vast, shadowy emptiness of the camp worked its own kind of horror and was more haunting than any place I had ever visited before. As we drove back to the hotel, I stared out the taxi window, completely overwhelmed by what had just happened. I felt enormous gratitude toward the driver for going out of his way to make the visit possible. But mostly I remember thinking that this trip was going be intensely more emotional than anything I had expected.

One by one the letters were starting to accumulate as well. I located some remarkable correspondences by Holocaust survivors, and a museum in Warsaw had a poignant letter by a Polish pilot telling his parents that, since they had last seen him, he had fallen in love, married a British girl, and had a son. (But other than that, not much was new.) One archivist contacted members of his own family who were veterans to see if they had any letters, and although nothing came of it, I thought it was a rather thoughtful gesture.

After Poland I went to Russia. Through an American friend living in Moscow I met my exceptional guide, Olga, who mapped out the entire schedule for St. Petersburg. Our primary stop was the State Memorial Museum of the Defense and Blockade of Leningrad, and the staff could not have been more amiable. A quick, handwritten note from me requesting access to their archives was all that we needed to provide, and within minutes they were pulling from their files letters and other personal papers salvaged from World War II—or, as they call it, the Great Patriotic War. Leningrad, the city's name before it was changed back to St. Petersburg in 1991 after the fall of Communism, had endured one of the longest and most brutal sieges in history, lasting almost nine hundred days and claiming an estimated six hundred thousand lives.

The process of selecting letters was hardly a scientific one, but we worked out a relatively efficient system: the curator would skim through a file and summarize the contents for Olga, who then repeated it to me in English. Depending on my *"nyet"* or *"da,"* the item either went back into the pile or off to be copied. "This is a long poem by a soldier describing his sorrow," Olga said about the first document.

Me: "Um, probably *nyet*. I really just want letters."

Olga: "Well, this next one is very moving, too, but it's a journal, so *nyet?*"

"Nyet," I replied.

Olga listened to the next synopsis with growing, and then waning, interest. "It's a letter . . . from a husband telling his wife not to forget him if they are separated . . . but it does not seem to have a lot of emotion. I think we can find better." *Nyet,* she determined on her own. Sure enough, as the curator started describing a small stack of letters bound together, I could see Olga nodding her head and looking optimistic.

"These are a series of letters," she began to explain, "by a brother and sister orphaned during the siege who are telling their aunt all that has happened to them and begging her to come and save them."

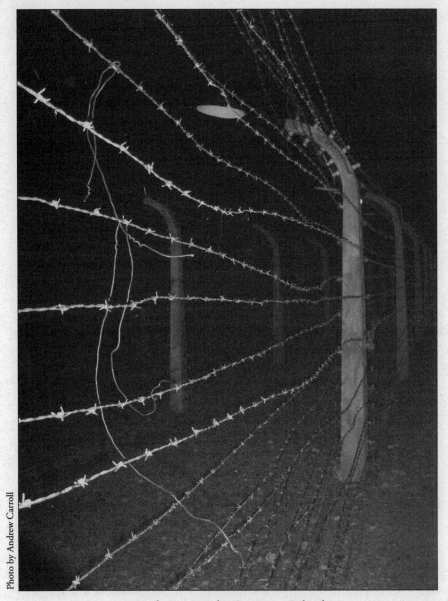

Auschwitz at night; Oswiecim, Poland.

"Da, da, da!" I exclaimed, and within minutes I had photocopies in hand. I would not have the letters translated word for word until I returned to the States several months later, but they were every bit as compelling as I had hoped.

The Balkans came next. My flight into Sarajevo landed late in the evening, so it wasn't until the morning that I discovered how stunningly beautiful the city is. I could easily understand why Sarajevo was selected as the site of the Winter Olympics in 1984. There is both a vibrant modernity and ancient patina to Sarajevo, where upscale hotels line the main avenues and cobblestone streets lead to the Old Market and its antique merchant shops. But intermingled with this beauty—and it is easy not to notice them at first, before you begin to see them everywhere—are thick clusters of luminescent white gravestones. Nestled among residential neighborhoods, in the city parks, next to schools, behind sports stadiums, and wherever it seems there should be an open space or field of grass, the cemeteries are an ever-present reminder of the terror that descended on Sarajevo beginning in the spring of 1992 when Serb forces declared war on Bosnia. Private homes and apartment buildings are still scarred and pockmarked with bullet holes and artillery blasts. And on the streets and sidewalks, shallow impressions in the shape of splattered paint mark where mortar shells exploded during the siege. The residents now call them "dragon's feet."

Thirty years old when we met, Amir Telebecirovic, my guide throughout Sarajevo, was still a teenager when the war erupted. It began, in fact, on his nineteenth birthday. Despite having no military experience whatsoever, Amir was forced to serve in the Bosnian army, which was massively out-gunned and under-trained compared to the highly skilled Serb troops. Many of Amir's closest friends, also just teenagers out of high school, were killed in the fighting.

As we walked the city on our way to meet with archivists and historians who had letters to show us, every corner prompted a sharp memory or horrific story. We crossed the bridge now named for Suada Delbrovic, the first person to die in the war. On April 6, 1992, as Serb forces began positioning themselves in Sarajevo, Delbrovic was shot to death on the bridge during a demonstration calling for peace. Just over a year later, on the banks of the River Miljacka below, two young lovers—Admira Ismic, a Bosnian Muslim, and Bosko Brckic, a Christian Serb—died in each other's arms after they, too, were caught in the crosshairs of a Serb sniper. Amir and I went to the Lion's Cemetery where the two are buried beneath a heart-shaped headstone. Later, when we passed the bustling open-air Markale market, Amir told me it was site of the infamous mortar attack of August 28, 1995. Almost forty people simply out shopping for groceries were blown to

View of Sarajevo from my hotel room.

*At the Historical Museum of Sarajevo, my exceptional guide Amir Telebecirovic
points out the kinds of makeshift and outdated weapons
they had to use against Serbian troops.*

pieces. The shelling of Markale was one of several atrocities against civilians that prompted the US-led NATO airstrikes on Serb forces around Sarajevo.

Amir recounted one story that, although relatively insignificant in the larger context of the fighting, was for some reason especially unsettling to me. At the beginning of the war staff members at the local zoo were unable to move the animals to safety, and Serb snipers situated on the hills overlooking many of the cages decided, for fun, to pick off the animals one by one. The lions were on the other side of the zoo and consequently were not at risk of getting shot. Their fate, however, would be much worse, as it was impossible for the animal keepers to make their way to the lions' cages and feed them without risking their own lives. Residents who lived nearby would later recall that one of the most unnerving sounds of the war was the roar—some described it as more like a dry scream—of the trapped, emaciated lions pacing their cages as they slowly starved to death.

Just hours before leaving Sarajevo, I asked Amir about the darkest moment of the war for him personally. There were many, he responded, but the worst occurred during the first winter of the siege. With no electricity or heating fuel, residents were freezing to death in their homes. Early one evening Amir's father went outside to collect firewood, which was becoming scarce throughout the city. (By the end of the war, virtually every tree in Sarajevo had been chopped down. Some individuals went to the desperate measure of digging up graves and dismantling the coffins, simply for the wood.) A Serb soldier or, more likely, sniper caught sight of Amir's father and shot him in the back. Neighbors were able to drag him to a car and rush him to the hospital. Before the siege, the drive would have taken only a few minutes. But the direct route was cut off by barricades and some streets were too dangerous to use, so they slowly had to wind their way through Sarajevo. The hospital itself was without power and overcrowded with other critically injured patients. Amir's father bled to death before any of the doctors could even examine his wound.

After hearing this, and with all the other stories of atrocities still fresh in my mind, I blurted out: "God you must hate the Serbs."

"No!" Amir responded firmly. "No, no. There's been enough hatred. I'm sick of it. My girlfriend is a Serb. Many Serbs in Sarajevo and throughout Bosnia suffered, too. Many people in Serbia didn't know what was going on because Milosevic lied to them. At some point it has to stop. There's been too much already. It has to stop." When I asked him how he could be so forgiving, he said, "Only people who have been through it can really understand how bad it can be." This sentiment would become one of the most dominant themes of the trip.

The subject was first brought to my attention during my visit to Volgograd just over a week earlier. During World War II, when the city was called Stalingrad, it was the site of what is considered to be one of the bloodiest battles ever fought. Tens of thousands of civilians were killed in the first thirty-six hours of the German bombardment that began on August 23, 1942. Disease flourished as bodies decayed in the streets and dogs fed on the corpses. Troops on both sides coerced young boys and girls into serving as scouts and runners, primarily to deliver messages or fill soldiers' canteens in the Volga river. And both sides shot the children they suspected of aiding the enemy. "For me, the philosophical question of whether violence is ever justified was once torturous," a Russian lieutenant named Joseph Maranov wrote to his beloved, Lola, from Stalingrad on August 29. "Now," he continued, "my dream, my aim is to rip apart, destroy, suffocate, and tear the enemy to pieces." Approximately half a million Russians and half a million German and Axis soldiers died in five months of savage fighting. "You do not understand the hatred," one Russian said to me after noticing I was reading a book on Stalingrad. "You have September 11 attacks in your country. How many killed? This was September 11 every day for almost two hundred days."

Memorial to the Fallen Heroes of Stalingrad. Three Russian soldiers sit at the base of the statue just under Mother Russia's left foot. They are smaller than her toes.

Photo by Andrew Carroll

A local guide took me to see the massive statue of Mother Russia, who stands majestically atop the highest hill in Volgograd and commemorates the resilience of the soldiers and civilians who defended the city. She is more than one hundred feet taller than the Statue of Liberty. Her right hand holds a sword, raised in defiance, and her left is outstretched in the direction from which the Axis troops invaded. Several hundred yards away is an indoor memorial with an eternal flame that pays tribute to those who perished. When my guide and I walked in, I heard tranquil but somewhat melancholic music playing. "Which Russian composer is that?" I asked.

My guide responded, "Actually it's Schumann."

I was incredulous. "They selected a *German* composer for the Stalingrad Memorial? Why didn't they pick a Russian?" The guide explained that when they built the monument in the 1960s, they wanted to send a message of reconciliation to the Germans who came to pay their respects to those who had died.

American veterans were also reaching out to former enemies. At the USS *Arizona* Memorial in Hawaii I met with two Pearl Harbor survivors, Dick Fiske and Everett Hyland, who, decades after the 1941 attack, befriended Japanese pilots who had flown in the raid. Fiske even put me in touch with one of these veterans, Zenji Abe, whom I met in Japan two months later. (In a terrible coincidence, the very morning I had lunch with Mr. Abe and his family in Tokyo, Dick Fiske passed away.) The two men had corresponded with one another before Fiske's death, but, regrettably, almost all of their letters have been lost.

Through a close friend named Mike Meyer who fought in Vietnam, I was introduced to Chuck Theusch, a veteran who frequently travels back to Vietnam to build libraries as a way to foster goodwill between our two nations. Chuck very kindly sent me copies of the letters he exchanged with a Vietnamese woman, Tran Thi Anh Thu, who worked at the My Lai Memorial. When they first met she wanted little to do with him. They are now friends, and with Thu's permission, Chuck provided me with a copy of their correspondences.

Whatever concerns I had about being confronted with resistance or a lack of cooperation on my trip proved completely unfounded. In every country people were going out of their way to be helpful—and often at a significant emotional cost. Many of the stories and letters they were sharing with me brought back painful memories of losing those closest to them. An Australian woman named Olwyn Green gave me a copy of the letter she wrote to her husband Charlie in 1992, fifty years after his death in the Korean War. "I always told you how much I loved you," she stated, "I probably didn't tell you: You are the finest human being I have ever known." A

Zenji Abe in Tokyo, Japan.

Dick Fiske, who died just months after I saw him in Hawaii.

Kuwaiti man named Abdul Hameed Al-Attar translated for me the last message he wrote to his son Jamal, who was unjustly imprisoned by the Iraqis during the 1990 invasion of Kuwait and then never heard from again. The uncertainty of Jamal's fate made the situation all the more unbearable for the family; "[Y]our mother is still keeping your personal belongings in your room," Al-Attar wrote to his son, "checking them every morning as if you will be coming soon (probably today or tomorrow) she says with tears pouring from her red eyes." Statistics can accentuate the enormity of war but not its humanity, and these letters are stark reminders of the individual stories behind the numbers.

Many veterans generously contributed letters that were especially intimate and candid. "I am fearing for my life for the first time," a Dutch private first class named André Dekker in Srebrenica confided to his girlfriend before passionately declaring his love for her. "You're everything to me," he wrote, "my shoulder to cry on, my love nest, and everything you give to me exceeds my expectations. I feel good when I'm with you, I can be myself and together we are invincible." (Dekker survived.)

The veterans who offered these more revealing letters hoped that they might have a cathartic value for the men and women in the armed forces now. No one can truly understand military life—the constant pressures, the separation from loved ones, both the thrill and terror of being sent into combat, the devastating shock of losing a buddy—like those who have already been through it. The older veterans empathize deeply with the current generation of troops and want them to know that there is solace in realizing that others have borne these hardships too.

A Korean War veteran named Alfred Puntasecca Jr. gave me a copy of a letter he had sent to his parents and siblings in 1953 before heading back to the States. Nineteen years old at the time, he wanted to prepare them for the battle-hardened man he had become, and not the boy they once knew: "I'm looking forward to seeing you again, but I'm in no hurry to see the expressions on your faces when <u>you</u> see <u>me</u>," Puntasecca wrote. "It is going to be hard being civilized again. What the hell ever civilized means." He then added, "I am going to tell you now. You'll need a lot of patience with me. Patience, and, understanding. We all will. See you soon." Fifty-one years later, a nineteen-year-old soldier in Iraq named Scott Curry mailed a letter to his mom that included the following:

Mother's Day is coming so happy Mother's Day. I wish I was there for the 2nd year in a row I've missed so much since I left for the Army. That's what makes coming home more scary than here. At least here we know what to do, shoot back. Home I will not know what to do, how to act, that's what worries me. Here we use violence to fix problems. I can't do that at home. So I have to re-learn how to live a normal life. I miss you so much and can't wait to see you.

What struck me about the majority of the letters that people were sharing was how graphic they were. More so, in fact, than anything I had ever read before. "I came across one of our boys—decomposed beyond all recognition," a Canadian chaplain named William Mayse wrote to his wife during World War I.

> [H]e lay just as he had fallen—the head was missing—but all the accoutriments was buckled on, his rifle & helmet lay close by—I cut the buckle off the belt as a momento, & we buried what remained of him—I tried to find something by which he might be identified but it was impossible—Poor boy—in some far away home in Canada someone is mourning the loss of husband—son or sweetheart—& the saddest of all is, they will never know how he died—or where he is burried, & even now they may be clinging to the hope, that he is still alive.

Both in the US and abroad, many of the people who were contributing letters voiced a frustration with how war is often romanticized in the popular culture. As evidenced in the letters themselves, this was not a new lament. "You say that you wish you were over here," Major Oscar Mitchell wrote to a friend named Sylvia Helene Hairston on April 15, 1944. Mitchell was serving in the China-Burma-India theatre of World War II, and he was quick to discourage Sylvia or anyone else from idealizing life on the front lines. "Although most people think that they are War Conscious, are they really?—so far removed from the far-flung battle fronts, can they be?" He continued:

> You are really War Conscious when you see the airplanes, in formation, early in the morning, flying to meet their rendezvous . . . and see this same formation returning in the evenings. But the number is not the same! Twelve went out, nine returned. You stand there, looking up, watching them fly into the distance; into and part of the horizon, then disappear. You wonder, what really did happen. Those that went down in flames. . . . Do they die as you see them in the movies? I do not think so. Not with a smile on their lips and a happy gleam in their eyes, rather painfully and regretfully with the knowledge that this is it! You'd have to see the wounded streaming back from the front after a battle . . . above all, to see the light go out of men's eyes. Young men shaking from nervous exhaustion and crying like babies.

Major Oscar Mitchell

Strong men they are, or were, who did not or will not have the chance, ever, to live normal lives. . . . People may think they know what War is like. Their knowledge is facts of the mind. Mine is the war-torn body, scared to soul's depth. When I was in the States, War was far away, unreal. I had read, I had seen pictures, but now I know.

Many individuals who provided letters that depict the harsh realities of war stressed to me that they do not regard themselves as pacificists. They believe that there is cruelty and brutality in the world—tyranny, genocide, slavery—and if the worst of these evils cannot be defeated through peaceful means, they must be destroyed by violent ones. The combat veterans I met, in particular, are fiercely patriotic and proud of their military service, and their letters speak with great conviction about the courage of fallen comrades and the importance of honoring the freedoms for which they gave their lives.

What they abhor is the glorification of war itself. They believe that sanitizing or concealing its ugliness only trivializes the sacrifices made by the men and women who serve. They want people to understand the toll it takes not only on combatants, but on their family members—and especially those who will receive a phone call or knock on the door informing them that their loved one has been killed. The wounds they suffer are every bit as traumatic and searing as the ones sustained on fields of battle, and they will last for the rest of their lives. The emotional aftershocks of war reverberate long after the peace treaties are signed.

And while many combat veterans recognize the allure of going off to battle and can well recall the intoxicating rush that comes from being under fire, they also know the exhilaration rarely lasts. It is tempered by exhaustion and hunger and endless hours of marching and waiting. It vanishes entirely when one sees a friend get shot to pieces or blown up and later shipped home in a flag-draped coffin. Civilians, too, often feel an initial sense of excitement when war is announced, and there is an undeniable electricity and tension in the air at the beginning of any conflict. Here again, the veterans are familiar with how easily that fervor can wane and how crippling it is to morale when troops suspect that support on the homefront has started to fade.

What they emphasize above all is that there is no greater decision a society can make than when or if it will declare war—and if it does, it must prepare itself for the consequences. What war demands of those who serve in the military, as well as the suffering it inflicts on so many who do not, is often much worse than what people who have not experienced it firsthand can imagine. This was the theme most commonly expressed, implicitly and explicitly, in the letters I found during my travels throughout the United States and around the globe, and it was the sentiment conveyed to me with the greatest urgency in the conversations I had with those who have been affected by war in some profound way. Individually, the correspondences they shared represent the private letters of troops and civilians writing to a spouse or a parent or a friend or some other loved one about what they have seen and felt and endured.

Collectively, these are their messages to the world.

—⁂—

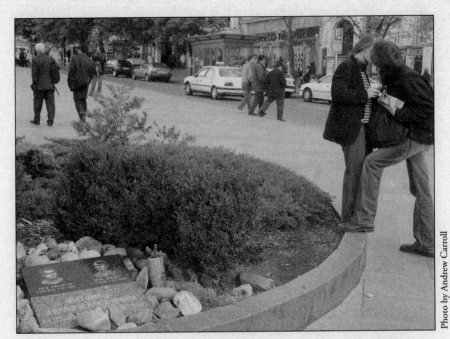

In 1969 two Czech students, Jan Palach and Jan Zajic, set themselves on fire in Prague to protest the Soviet occupation of Czechoslovakia. (In the weeks immediately before and after the March 2003 invasion of Iraq, six Czech citizens followed their example. Four died, and two suffered critical burns.) A few steps away from the plaque marking where Palach and Jazic immolated themselves, two Czech teenagers make out for a good several minutes.

Forever Yours

Letters of Love, Family, and Friendship

We have just arrived here after a most fatiguing March from East Chester—I got your letter at York Island—telling me I was a saucy fellow to kiss you before all the folks—Ah My Darling—I wish the <u>World</u> Knew you are to marry me—The Enemy are very near us & we are only waiting for the dawn to begin our Battle—Do not be uneasy about me—Please God—I hope to come out all safe tomorrow—The thoughts of your dear promise has nerved my arm so far & will again—The officers say I bear a Charmed life—They do not Know the talisman I wear next to my heart—My loved one—I am writing this on the head of a Drum & would you believe it with a pointed Stick—Remember me all my friends Darling & tell Mother not to feel uneasy about her son. I am my Darling your very Humble Servt—& Adorer

> —*Private John Eggleston, writing to his fiancée on October 27, 1776,*
> *while he and thousands of other American soldiers awaited*
> *an imminent British invasion of White Plains, New York.*
> *Eggleston would survive the battle—and the war.*

Your country needs you. Your four brothers have been killed in her defense. Unless you come, you are no longer a son of mine. I will have no coward in my family.

> —*A French mother from St. Pierre,*
> *writing to her son in November 1914*

Dear Brother, How have you been? Here, mother and the family are all fine. Your boys are playing and doing well, so do not worry about them. It's been so long since I saw you. I worry that we might not be able to recognize each other if we passed each other on the street. I also wonder if you might not be able to find your way back home after fighting for such a long time. Even right now, I am listening to the radio announcing news about your unit, Chung-Young, in Vietnam. Last time, we heard of so many deaths in the battle. Mother becomes so anxious whenever such reports come on. Brother, please take care of yourself. Let the Vietnamese respect you for your bravery but come back safely to us. There are lots of things to say, but I will end here. Be safe. I am always praying.

—*Lee Jung Ho, writing on February 2, 1966,*
to his older brother, Major Lee In Ho,
one of three hundred thousand South Korean soldiers
fighting with American troops against the North Vietnamese
and Viet Cong. The letter was found on Lee's body
after he was killed in action.

Thanks very much for your letter and even more for the picture you painted. It touched me more than you can possibly imagine. And not only me. My peacekeeping unit has gotten in the habit of sharing all packages and showing around any photos that come with the letters. So of course your picture, too, though not a photo

     was passed around

     in the semi-darkness

     of our dug-out

     as snow fell outside and the temperature dipped to 16 degrees below

     by all of us

     seated on sandbags and ammunition cases

     surrounded by empty ration cans and water bottles

     heavily armed

     with grimy hands

and barely warm enough, and I was asked over and over again what the girl looks like who can create such a beautiful and inspiring work of art. Our thoughts drifted toward another world . . . And so it was that your painting from far away Nuremberg reminded us of home and provided us with a few hours that the members of this illustrious crew will never forget. With sincere regards from a land that has become a part of our soul.

> —*Master Sergeant Michael Kaiser,*
> *writing to a female friend named Ines Dyba*
> *on February 2, 2000, while serving with*
> *peacekeeping forces in Kosovo. They represented*
> *the largest deployment of German troops*
> *abroad since World War II.*

An American Officer Named James Williams Explains to His Son Daniel Why He Is Fighting and Urges Him to Be a "Dutiful Son" in His Absence

In a nation of 2.5 million inhabitants, almost one in ten served in the American Revolution. Some were highly trained soldiers, but predominantly they were common tradesmen, farmers, and merchants who left behind family and loved ones to confront the well-equipped, professional British and Hessian forces. Those with children began a ritual that would be repeated in almost every generation for the next two hunderd and thirty years—writing a first letter home to explain why they have been called away and, most importantly, to remind their sons and daughters how much they love and miss them. James Williams, a thirty-eight-year-old native of Hanover County, Virginia, who later moved to South Carolina, was one of those quarter of a million troops called to fight. On June 12, 1779, Williams penned the following letter to his son, Daniel, gently encouraging him to be especially caring toward and supportive of his mother.

Dear Son:

This is the first chance I have had to write you. I am, by the cause of Providence, in the field in defence of my country. When I reflect on the matter, I feel myself distracted on both hands by this thought, that in my old age I should be obliged to take the field in defence of my rights and liberties, and that of my children. God only knows that it is not of choice, but of necessity, and from the consideration that I had rather suffer anything than lose my birthright, and that of my children.

When I come to lay down in the field, <u>stripped</u> of all the pleasure that my family connections afford me at home—surrounded by an affectionate wife and eight dear children, and all the blessings of life—when I reflect on my own distress, I feel for that of my family, on account of my absence from their midst; and especially for the mother, who sits like a dove that has lost its mate, having the weight of the family on her shoulders.

These thoughts make me afraid that the son we so carefully nursed in our youth may do something that would grieve his mother. Now, my son, if my favor is worth seeking, let me tell you the only step to procure it is the care of your tender mother—to please her is ten times more valuable than any other favor that you could do me in my person.

I am sorry to have to inform you of the melancholy death of Anthony Griffin, which took place on the 11th instant, while out with a scouting party. Alighting from his horse, and leaning on his gun, it accidentally went off, shooting him through the head. He never spoke after the accident. This is a fatal consequence of handling guns without proper care; they ought to be used with the greatest caution. The uncertainty of life ought to induce every man to prepare for death.

Now, my son, I must bid you farewell. I commit you to the care of Providence, begging that you will try to obtain that peculiar blessing. May God bless you, my son, and give you grace to conduct yourself, in my absence, as becomes a dutiful son to a tender mother and the family. I am in reasonable good health at present, and the regiment as much so as could be expected. The death of Griffin is much lamented. I hope in God this will find you, my son, and your dear mother and the children, all well. My best compliments to you all, and all enquiring friends.

I am, dear son, with great respect, your affectionate father,

Jas. Williams

Approximately five thousand Americans lost their lives in combat during the Revolution. (Up to twenty thousand more are believed to have died from disease, accidents, and the brutal treatment afforded POWs in the hands of the British.) James Williams was among the dead, killed in the battle of Kings Mountain in October 1780.

—⚊—

Thomas Drayton Warns His Brother Percival Not to Set Foot in Their Native South Carolina During the Civil War or They Shall "Face Each Other As Brothers Never Should" & Four Years Later, Percival Writes a Brief Letter to His Cousin Heyward Drayton on the Need to Help Thomas After the War

"Can you be so recreant and so unnatural as to aid in this mad attempt to impose the yoke of tyranny upon your kith and kin?" wrote the outraged father of William Terrill to his son after William announced he would fight for the Union. His brother, James, sided with his father—and their home state of Virginia. Both men would ultimately be killed in the war, and the family would erect for their two sons a memorial into which the words "God Alone Knows Which Was Right"

are carved. As the War of Independence represented a conflict that pitted a fledgling nation against its mother country, the Civil War was literally and symbolically a clash between brothers. Unlike the Terrills, fifty-two-year-old Thomas Fenwick Drayton and Percival Drayton, his younger brother by four years and a day, would both survive the war. But their relationship would be severely damaged in the years between as each held steadfastly to his convictions— Thomas for states' rights, Percival for the preservation of the Union. "[A]nd so Sumter is at last ours, and this too without the loss of a <u>single</u> life upon either side. To outsiders it would look like childs play," Thomas gloated in an April 17, 1861, letter to his brother after Fort Sumter surrendered to Confederate forces on April 12. But despite his rejoicing for the South's initial conquest, Thomas was well aware of the ruin and misery to come, and he continued his letter in a more somber tone, taking pains to remind his brother that the South was merely protecting itself against an encroaching federal government.

> *Before this dispute is over however, I look for abundance of death & blood—as I cannot for a moment suppose that the North will stop without sending other expeditions against us. I could hope that wiser & more pacific counsels would prevail and that we might be allowed to pursue our*

Percival Drayton   *Thomas Drayton*

ways in peace. . . . It is unfair to charge us with being the aggressors in this strife. Mr Lincoln who collected fleets and threatens assaults, is far guiltier than those who were provoked as an act of self defense into striking the <u>first blow.</u> . . . Behold the prospect before you and see whether I have been overstrained and fanciful in what I have sketched and stated. We are fighting for home & liberty. Can the North say as much? . . . If the Northern & Middle States allow the call of Lincoln & his shortsighted advisers, for men & arms to force us back into a hateful Union, then civil war is inevitable. So let all men set their houses in order "to die & not to live," and confess that self government is a cheat and that the American people have for 80 years been mistaking the phantom of liberty for the substance. Well may <u>we</u> <u>tremble</u>—who have children.

The brothers were originally from South Carolina, but their father, a prominent congressman named William Drayton, relocated the family to Pennsylvania after his retirement from public office. The brothers had friends and family in both the North and South, and Percival believed his fealty should be to their adopted home and, more importantly, the United States of America. In the following letter to Percival, Thomas emphatically advocated the Southern position once again and even questioned Percival's integrity for siding against his birthplace. (John Brown, whom Thomas refers to in his letter, was a white abolitionist hanged in 1859 for leading a raid on a federal arsenal in Harpers Ferry, which Brown had hoped would incite a slave rebellion throughout the South.)

Savannah 1st May 1861

My dear Percy

I returned last night from Montgomery—where I had been on some postal matters, in anticipation of the period when the Contracts at Washington, shall have been annulled by those who hold hateful dominion there. And how you Percival Drayton can consent to hold a commission under a Government—whom I know you cannot sympathise with—and whose vandal atrocity in the imitation of a most cruel war, clearly indicate what more atrocious & bloodthirsty attempts at <u>subjugation</u> will hereafter be attempted, such as stealing negroes, burning houses, John Brown raids to butcher helpless women & children, cut the dikes of the Mississippi and drown thousands of families "like rats in the hold of a ship" These & Such incursions & barbarities with which we are threatened by the northern borders—who already possess the reins of Government—if that can be called one,— where universal terror reigns as freedom of opinion is denied.

But enough—it wont do for you and I to quarrel—though in politics, we are divided. I had understood at our last interview—that although you would not take sides with the South—you would not do what you now have done,—take position against her, but that, you would resign and return to private life! But this is impossible—you cannot at such a crisis be a <u>neutral.</u> William Drayton—had he not died—would never have acted with you and retained a commission under an administration whose acts show it lost to all sense of justice, magnanimity and honesty, and in this hour of heartfelt sorrow, I pray Almighty God, that your convictions of duty—will never prompt you to set foot upon your native land as one of Lincoln's brutal cohorts, breathing fire & destruction upon a people who to repeated overtures of peace and earnest demands to pursue their own destiny in their own way, have been replied to with taunts and the sword brandished over their heads with the scornful division of presumptuous superiority, as from a superior race.

But henceforth, Percival Drayton, believe the South like yourselves a <u>unit</u>—and thus we shall enter upon this conflict <u>forced</u> upon us—in our faith—and relying upon God to maintain the justness of our causes, fighting manfully for our houses & rights;—and understand my brother that when the olive branch of peace is next offered, it will be extended by other hands than ours.—

Farewell Percy—and however much we may differ on the present issue—let no unkind word escape—to lacerate the heart of the other. Defend the soil of Pennsylvania if you will. Then, you and I will never meet as armed foes;—cross her Southern boundary—with hostile purpose—and we shall face each other—as brothers never should.

Love to my poor, dear old Mother—may God bless & sustain her at this terrible moment.—

Your affect brother
Thos F Drayton

Percival's response has been lost, but Thomas alludes to it in what would be his last letter to his brother for the duration of the war. "My dear Percy," he wrote on May 10, 1861, "I have just recd yours of the 6th inst. And cannot but lament that our political views are so widely different, and that your arguments should afford so convincing a proof that prejudice had evidently usurped the seat of sound judgment." Perhaps believing he had exhausted all possible arguments, Thomas kept his reply short and bid his brother adieu with these words: "I will keep this remarkable epistolary effusion of yours—for I am sure in less than a year, you will candidly disavow the assertions & opinions therein expressed." In less than a year, in fact, Thomas would be a brigadier general and Percival would be captain of the USS Pocahontas, and they would not be contesting their views through an exchange of words but through actual gunfire; Thomas and Percival Drayton would become the only two brothers in the war to command opposing forces in the same battle (Port Royal, November 1861). Percival would be the victor, but in a letter written after the confrontation to a cousin, Heyward Drayton, there was no sense of triumph. He wrote only vaguely and briefly of the sad period through which they were all living. The letter was dated January 10, 1862.

> *As you well say it is possible to go through the forms of Merry Christmas and happy new year but not these times at least to us they have no substance, as peculiarly to us this war has subverted the best formations of happiness and family union.*

Several lines later, Percival revealed the degree to which the inhumanity of slavery, which had been set starkly before him on occasion, influenced his perspective on the war. His remarks were apparently in response to a query by Heyward asking if Percival had been encouraging slaves to find haven on his ship, which some might consider beyond his first and foremost duty—saving the Union. Concerning the runaway slaves he aided, Percival replied:

> *The fact is that when the poor creatures come to me, frightened to death from having been hunted down and shot at, and I know if I sent them away it will be merely to expose them to a continuation of the same treatment, I cannot enter cooly into a discussion of the legal points of the question, and am obliged when in sight of a mother wailing over the loss of her child to look upon them as persons not things.*

Although Percival does not mention Thomas by name in his letter, his older brother could not have been far from his thoughts when he wrote the following:

> *As regard my serving here [in the South], instead of elsewhere, in my letter applying for service, I made no terms and simply went where I was ordered if my relations persist in this unholy rebellion. I am only doing a duty to my country, which should be higher than that even to my family, in assisting to put it down. One is to affect all time, the other only my generation which will soon pass away.*

At the end of the war, Percival's belief in the cause for which he had fought remained steadfast; it was Thomas who had grown disillusioned and humbled. His house had been burned to the ground by Union soldiers, and he was financially bankrupt. Upon hearing of his brother's plight, Percival sent him money and attempted to repair the breach that had for so long existed between them. On July 18, 1865, Percival wrote to Heyward about Thomas's condition and future prospects. (The identity of "Mr. Hipple" is not clear, but the "enviable position" Percival mentions is believed to be Thomas's former appointment as the president of the Charleston and Savannah Railroad. After the war, Thomas would become a farmer and then an insurance salesman.)

My dear Heyward

Mr Hipple sent me today a letter from Tom which goes out to you by same steamer as this. I will send him the money so soon as I can find out where he is. Have you not a balance in your hands belonging to him? If so you might send it also, I am sorry to see the remark about the negro, as it only shows that there is no real interior change yet. Why the mere talk of returning him to his former enviable position has almost caused violent outbreaks in some parts of the country, and the Cmdg Officer at Port Royal tells me, that several of the planters who have returned tell him that candor obliged them to admit that their slaves are in every respect in a better condition than ever before, better clothes, better houses, and better food.

I am as busy here as ever, and with the excessive hot weather wonder that I keep my health but I do, thanks I suppose to pretty temperate living and some horse exercise.

I hope Harriet has improved in health, and that you are enjoying yourselves.

Syl is quite well, and is going to Canada, to be among her dear English I suppose.

Love to Harriet and Millie and believe me,

Your Aff Bro
P. Drayton

In a four-page letter written on July 31, 1865, that focused primarily on his bleak fiscal situation, Thomas wrote with heartfelt emotion to Percival, "I am glad to see your hand writing once more, and I pray Almighty God that we may never be again so unfortunate as to be upon different sides. . . . I agree with you in thinking that we should 'set the past in the past.'" It is not known if Percival ever received the letter or knew his brother's sentiments; Percival died of natural causes four days after it was written.

Hessian Soldier Christian von Molitor Offers a Friend in Germany His First Impressions of America and Regrets That "Everything Will Be Destroyed and Ruined"

&

Henry Kircher, a Civil War Soldier Whose Parents Are German, Tells His Family That Despite the Beauty and Wealth of America, the People Continue to "Scuffle, Quarrel, [and] Murder" One Another

&

Sergeant Major P. Thomas Ferck, with the Little-Known Russian Expedition of World War I, Shares His Thoughts About His "Vacation" in Siberia and Its "Good-for-Nothing People" with Hester Hunt

&

Lieutenant Colonel Benjamin O. Davis, During a 1918 Visit to Japan—a World War I Ally—Expresses His Admiration for the Country and Its People

Wars, by their nature, are not only a clash of ideologies but often of cultures as well. And for many servicemen and -women sent hundreds or thousands of miles from home, their deployment marks the first time they have ventured beyond their city, town, or village. Suddenly they find themselves in a new land confronting mysterious customs, languages, and religious practices, prompting a range of reactions from curious fascination to outright disgust. During the War of Independence, it was America—in the eyes of thirty thousand German troops brought to the New World by the British to fight the colonists—that was the land of odd and unfamiliar sights and social conventions. (The three principal German commanders, as well as many of the regiments themselves, came from the Hesse-Cassel region of Germany. But not all of the troops were, technically, "Hessians," as they were commonly called—among other things—by the Americans.) The Hessians were ferocious, well-trained warriors, and they participated in almost every major military campaign of the Revolution after they landed in 1776. But they were hardly invincible. Nearly one in six deserted, and more than sixty-five hundred succumbed to illness—many because, from their perspective, of the inhospitable climate. One officer wrote in his diary: "Since the burning wind [in the daytime] and the cold spells are coming again [at night] . . . the men die like flies and the hospitals are filled." Captain Christian Theodore Sigmund von Molitor arrived in New York in June 1777 and was actually quite impressed with the country he and his fellow soldiers had come to conquer. While encamped in Amboy, New York, he wrote the following to a female acquaintance back in Germany on June 24.

Dear Friend,

This is the third letter that I have written to you since I have been in America. I do not know if you have received them. I wish nothing more than to know how you and your children are doing, and if you are still my gracious and good friend, and that you have not forgotten me. We are all well and it seems as if the strenuous duty makes your husband and me healthier and stronger.

We are now in camp outside Amboy, about seven and one-half miles from New York. Today five English and Hessian regiments came from Brunswick, which is about fifteen miles from here, and joined us in camp. How long we are to remain here and where we are then to march, I am unable to write. General Howe and the main army moved forward a few days ago to attack General Washington, who is not far from Brunswick. The rebels were so well entrenched that attack was impossible, even if our army were twice as strong. Our pickets were attacked twice by the rebels. Captain von Beust and I were ordered to the reserve. We had to move forward and drive the enemy, consisting of about 300 men, out of the woods. We had to withstand many bullets, before we forced them into the open, where we attacked with bayonets and drove them into flight. Only a grenadier of ours was wounded, and we killed three rebels.

I gave you a description of New York in my last letter, and also of Staten Island, where we landed. Amboy is an open city where many white people lived, who can now be locked out of beautiful houses which were well-furnished. At present there are not more than five families in all of Amboy. Most of the residents are with the rebels and have abandoned houses and property. Most of the houses are exceptionally well-built and furnished with the finest carpets. All the houses stand open and can be occupied by anyone who so wishes. We have a house near us, not twelve yards from my tent, which we took over. We cook and eat therein, and do with it as we please.

It is certainly a shame that everything will be destroyed and ruined. The land is extremely fruitful and everything grows in abundance. The very best soil in Germany does not compare to it. During peacetime it can be called a true paradise. Now however, everything lies in ruin and none of the villages with houses has a living soul. We find here in the beautiful gardens, which have now been destroyed, all possible vegetables, like we have in Germany, and, especially lots of asparagus. The wooded areas are extensive and consist primarily of nut trees, oak, and sassafras wood, of which we burn enough to supply all the pharmacists in the world. Here beer is brewed from the bark. It tastes very sweet, but is very light and healthy. Large juniper trees are plentiful, and most of the hedges and trees in the fields are almond trees. There are apple trees everywhere, often stretching out for miles and all of the best kind, but no pear trees. The fruit which hangs on the trees is still very small, and the shoots and buds are still grass green. I believe everything in Bayreuth ripens about four weeks earlier. All classes of domestic animals are here as in Germany, but the wild animals are different. The hares are small. They are a sort of rabbit. The birds are especially beautiful, some are quite red, green, blue, of various sizes. And canaries fly around as sparrows in Germany. No plum trees or fig trees are to be seen. We eat oysters daily and they are especially large. They are not considered special here. I often wish you might have some at your table.

My dear Ellrodt and I continue our close friendship. We are together the whole day and whatever one receives, he shares it with the other. During the evening we smoke tobacco and, if we are alone, talk about you and the dear children and wish you all the best a thousand times. May God keep all of you healthy. I will not allow you to suffer any need, nor that your life be shortened because of hunger.

My Ellrodt has promised me that he will send you twenty ducats with this opportunity. Therefore do not live so miserly as to ruin your health. Our daily longing and wish is to receive a letter from you. When I know that you and your dear children are healthy, I will be completely satisfied. Do not forget your true and constant friend and do not take your friendship, which I value above all others, away from me. There are few minutes when I do not think of you. How happy I would be if I were fortunate enough to see you and the dear children again. God grant us our health so that we can survive all the fatigue. The land is as wholesome as in Germany, if one can only hold on. During the day the heat is very great, and then at night again cold. You yourself know my dear friend that I was often sick while traveling. Here on land, not even a finger has caused me pain. Be so kind as to recommend me to your gracious married sister and her husband. Tell them I often think of them. I am sure that your sister and her husband will do everything possible for you. I am sending my journal to you, herewith. In it you will find of our entire trip, up to today. I know you will take time to read it. After you have read it, please be so kind as to send it to my father along with this letter. You will do me a service if you would write some lines to my father.

Do not allow any one but your brother-in-law and Lieutenant von Diskau to see this journal. It might possibly offend some people, as I am not a man of learning.

I recommend myself again to your favor, a million times, and kiss your hand. Write to me as to whether Fritz and Sophie still remember me. Whenever our recruits arrive here, I will take the opportunity to send you something from America. I have already written to you that Lieutenant von Weitershausen had the misfortune to lose his mind. A Captain von Weitershausen was also killed in America. Adieu my precious one. May God keep you in good health and bless you. Don't worry too much. God will watch over us here, also. And, regardless of what happens, I remain yours, with body and soul, as long as God and the rebels allow me to live.

Christian von Molitor

Molitor then added this postscript:

When we march, it may well be against Boston. When we again return to Ansbach, I will bring you a black slave. If you talk about me to good friends, you will place me in your debt, if you recommend me to them. Do not forget Major von Bose. I will bring you American feathers, pearls, and jewels. Kiss your scholars frequently for both of us. Adieu a thousand times. Write me often. I must always wear a mask before my face here so that my tender skin is not ruined and does not turn black.

Eighty years later, during the American Civil War, more than two hundred thousand German immigrants enlisted in the United States Army to help preserve the Union. When war was declared in April 1861, a nineteen-year-old machinist named Henry Adolph Kircher left his home in Belleville, Illinois, where his German parents had settled, and volunteered to serve with the 9th Illinois Volunteer Infantry. Believing Missouri to be in greater peril of a Confederate attack than Illinois, he joined with the 12th Missouri Volunteer Infantry several months later. Kircher was proud of the contribution he and his comrades were making to the cause, and due to their ethnic stock, he deemed them better suited for military life. On January 30, 1863, he wrote to his mother from Vicksburg, Mississippi:

Overall one finds that the regiments consisting of mostly Germans have better health than those consisting of Americans or Irish. First of all, the German stomach is better attuned to sauerkraut and root plants and therefore can stand pretty much everything. . . . And cleanliness is also much more in fashion among the Germans than in other regiments. This contributes no little amount to good health.

Lieutenant Kircher sometimes mused in his letters about America itself, and in March of 1863 he was inspired to write the following from Tallahatchie, Mississippi, as the natural beauty of nature began to reveal itself after a long winter.

Dear Everybody!

Now continuing, I must take up a new sheet of paper as well as a new subject, since the first was sufficiently filled and the latter was sufficiently blank.

In the near future, I don't think we will make any more attempts until the reinforcements are in place. I hope they will also speed up my correspondence up to now.

Spring seems to be coming on strong, as the sun is burning according to form, the birds are pleasantly chatty, the forest seems to be curtained with a magnificent green veil with a colorful pattern; everything, everything seems friendly, lively, and happy to have the cold, nasty winter behind it, but not the people, the pitiable creatures—they scuffle, quarrel, murder, and plunder in winter and in summer, in autumn and in spring. The beautification in nature seems not to arouse really good thoughts in mankind; continual hate, strife, envy and dissatisfaction are what man always find in it. How can it be otherwise? How else would people who live in such a great, spacious, and rich land get involved in such a terrible conflict as the one that has been raging for almost two full years among us, so many liberated from all the sufferings of this earth, but also so many and numerous torn from their pleasures (the few and meager ones of this world), and those pleasures turned into pains.

But what good is all my philosophizing. I can't change all of humanity, and that would have to happen first before it can be different here; therefore it is better that each one adjust and be satisfied with himself and his fellow man, even if all the rest are indifferent to me. You, my loved ones at home, are still dear and honored to me. It is peculiar, but very often, particularly on days like today, such thoughts come to me when the sun is shining so friendly, and everything seems so enlivened, then I am the saddest at heart because I have to spend the finest years of my youth with such boredom and inactivity. But I know it can't be changed. As long as there is war in the land, I will have to play soldier. If I only see a purpose that is really being pursued and that would really be legitimate, then I would allow it to suit me.

There is a boat going again today at noon. Therefore I must break this off.

The only newspaper that I saw here I bought from a paper carrier for 25 cents. It was the <u>Missouri Republican</u> of the 7th of March. It had various things in it, but only enough to lead one more and more into the dark.

Must close.

All well.

A thousand greetings to everyone from

Your Henry.

Henry Kircher later lost his right arm and left leg in battle and returned to Belleville, where, in 1877, he was elected mayor of the town. (Ironically, American soldiers would articulate sentiments almost identical to those in Kircher's letters while marching through Germany eighty years later in World War II. "Beautiful mountains, valleys, rivers, and lakes. Quaint little chalets, each and every one looking cozy and neat as a pin," wrote Robert Sherrard to his parents on June 26, 1945, "I have never in my life seen such beautiful country as So[uthern] Germany, California included. Why these people wanted to start a war is beyond me—they've got everything they need.") A little-known expedition to Korea in 1871, the Spanish-American War in Cuba and the Philippines at the turn of the nineteenth century, the 1900 Boxer Rebellion in China, the 1915 intervention in Haiti, and other, smaller military campaigns would bring US troops to exotic locations around the world. But no conflict, until 1917, had introduced so many Americans to so many different foreign countries as World War I. Since a significant percentage of the 4.7 million US servicemembers were the children of immigrants—if not immigrants themselves—predominantly from Europe, the culture shock was not overwhelming. Some troops, however, found themselves in less familiar surroundings. In one of the most forgotten military operations in US history, thousands of American soldiers were sent to Russia, initially an ally in the war, to fight against Vladimir Lenin's Bolsheviks, who were forcibly trying to gain control of the entire country. (The US troops were also responsible for guarding railroad lines, protecting Allied war materials stockpiled in northern ports, and helping to evacuate Czech soldiers who had been battling the Germans earlier in the war.) Forced to endure brutal Siberian weather for a mission that seemed increasingly quixotic, many of the Americans were, if their letters home are any indication, less than thrilled with the assignment. Sergeant Major P. Thomas Ferck wrote the following to a dear friend, Hester Hunt, in Denver, Colorado.

A.E.F. Siberia.
General Headquarters,

Dearest Hester,

I'm still in Siberia but can count the days that I will have to remain, for very soon I'll be on the deck of the old gray Transport, looking far into the distance toward Siberia. Just think I'll soon be on my way to dear old America, in a land of civilization, Hester dear, it seems almost beyond realization, but true. Then I'll see you and tell you all about my <u>vacation</u> in Siberia, the land of bears and Chinese. Won't Tommy be the happiest kid in the world the minute Denver is in sight? I am so anxious to see you Hester for it has been a long time since I said good-bye and it has also been long since I've received a letter from you.

Siberia and Russia is still in a condition almost beyond hopes of ever establishing a firm government. There are battles now and then but without any gain, it seems.

In our endeavor to guard the railroad we lost quite a number of men & in order to prevent the Bolsheviks from carrying out their plans of destruction. The Russian people lack the ambition and apparently have no desire of helping their country. They do not have the spirit that the

Hester Hunt and a US soldier whose identity cannot be confirmed (but he is not believed to be Sergeant Major P. Thomas Ferck).

Americans have. I have seen all classes and types of people and I hope I'll never see them again. Siberia is full of good-for-nothing people.

The rain has been falling all day and still raining. Winter will soon be here, but I'll be in dear old Denver, so let the snow fly.

I hope to show you many pictures of Siberia, my collection is quite good and I have about three hundred and fifty of them. Enroute to America, we are going by way of Nagasaki, Japan,—Philippine Islands—Guam,—Honolulu and at each stop I intend to take some pictures.

Do you ever see Jeannett White? I have written to her once but think my letter has not reached her. She is such a sweet little girl I always tho't so much of her for she was a real little lady.

This is the end of perfect day (rainy tho) and time for all soldiers to retire and time for Tommy to do likewise. I'll be so glad to see you, little girl, and we'll have the good old chats as before. I hope this letter finds you in the best of health and in as good spirit as I. Remember that I am your old pal.

Lovingly
Tom

Hundreds of the US soldiers would lose their lives in Russia, and the Bolsheviks would prove victorious, ushering in seventy years of Communist rule. (Thomas Ferck survived his deployment to Siberia.) Japan was also an ally of the United States during World War I, and for the American servicemen who traveled to the country during the war, it, too, introduced them to novel traditions and ceremonies. And for one American officer, they represented a refreshing change. Stationed at Fort Stotensburg in the Philippines, a lieutenant colonel named Benjamin O. Davis—who, in 1940, would become the first African-American general in US history—had the opportunity to visit Japan in the latter part of the war. On October 25, 1918, Davis wrote a letter to his future wife, Sarah "Sadie" Overton, to share his favorable impressions of the country. (Davis's use of the word "Jap" was merely an abbreviation and not meant in a derogatory manner.)

My own Sarah

You will note that I omitted to write you yesterday. It was due to the fact that I was too cold after my arrival here. I left Tokyo at 1:40 yesterday and arrived here about seven o'clock. Tokyo is practically a modern city. Except for its temples and parks it reminds me of Cleveland or Washington. The buildings are modern, the streets are wide. The Imperial Palace grounds cover a large area. Visitors are permitted only between the outer and inner moats. The Imperial Palace architecture is

Japanese and certainly is a thing of beauty from a distance. It was built in feudal times when the defense of the Palace seems to have been the principal thing governing the laying out of the grounds. I will write you more of these things from Stotsenburg or I hope that it will not be such a great while before I can tell you about them.

From Tokyo to Nikko is a steady climb. The country thru which we passed was well cultivated. This is the most beautiful spot I have ever seen. This hotel is situated high up on the mountain and is about a half hour by motor from the railroad stations. The surrounding country is filled with temples and shrines where the Japanese come from far and near to worship. The thing which struck me most was what an ideal spot for a honeymoon. I do long for you so much. I was rather blue when I wrote you on the 23rd. I feel much brighter today, yet at the same time, I can't help but think how happy I would be if you were with me. The weather is very cold. I have finally succeeded in getting warm. I do believe if I had had to go one half hour longer in the machine last night I would have been an icecycle (I guess that is spelled sufficiently correct for you to get my meaning) There was a good fire in the hotel, but it was like a camp fire, it heated only one side at a time, and I being cold all over, inside and out, I had a hard time. There are few folks here at this season. The hotel is under Jap. Management, and I like it very much. They are a great people. I like them the more I see of them. I can readily see why the white man dislikes them. They are not to be bluffed. What will not be ruled and run by the white man meets with his disapproval. The one great criticism I hear made by the white man is that the "Jap is too cocky." This is the one place where the white man is not supreme. He is treated with every courtesy, but at every time he is reminded that this is Japan the country of the Japanese, that is the bitterest pill for the Caucasian to swallow. I am very much afraid that there is a feeling being cultivated, mostly by Americans, similar to that which exists between Germany and England. It is too bad. I can see no reason for it and in my opinion it is due more to the "cockiness" of the white man than the Jap.

Now I suppose my opinion of the Jap. ladies is what will interest you. Well they are cute. That is about all I can say. I have seen them on the streets, in the hotels and in Yokohawa it was my privilege to dine with them. I have seen the celebrated Geisha dancing girls. Well they are cute, very dainty, but I don't imagine I would care for their love making. I suppose they can love the same as all women, but they are to me like any other piece of art. They are small, but then you know my type of woman. Just look at yourself. Possibly I do the Jap. girls a great injustice, but I am to be excused as I was already in love before coming to their country.

Well Sarah, I hope always to be in love. I hope always to be in love with the same girl and that she will always be in love with me. I am feeling more like my old self today. I am much encouraged. I was getting worried. I had begun to fear something real serious. However, I feel that the most serious thing against me was my longing for you and the effect of the climate on top of it. I am still longing for you, but instead of feeling depressed and hopeless, I feel just the opposite. I suppose that must be the effect of the climate. Well there is a mail leaving Yokohawa for the States on Sunday. So I'll get this in. With all of my love and the hope that something will turn up to bring us together soon, I am,

Your,

B.O.

—᠁—

Naubat Rai, the Hindu Father of an Indian Soldier Serving in France, Angrily Informs His Son How He Will Be Welcomed Home If He Brings Back a Christian Wife
&
Zbigniew Janicki, a Polish Pilot with the Royal Air Force, Writes to His Mother and Father About the Effect That Being Alone in a New Country Has Had on Him
&
Lieutenant Erma Meyers Explains to Her Parents That She Has Finally Gotten Married—but There Has Been a Surprising Development

During World War I, more than one million Hindu, Muslim, Sikh, and Christian troops from India served with the British Army in Europe. When given the opportunity to go on leave, many of these young soldiers found themselves surrounded by an abundance of temptations, and their mothers and fathers back in India worried that their sons would be corrupted by—from the parents' point of view—a relatively more licentious Western morality. One Muslim soldier, Mohamed Feroz Khan, received a stern warning from his father about avoiding brothels (euphemistically called "hotels") in France. Khan adamantly replied:

I swear to you that although I have been in France for two and half years, I have not even taken so much as a cup of tea in a "hotel." I swear also that up till this moment I have committed no evil deed in France. I am your true son, and your advice is plainly written on my heart.

For the parents of one Hindu soldier, however, a little concern might have been warranted. Although it is not clear to whom the soldier was writing, it was obviously someone he trusted, and on November 6, 1917, he sent the following. (The two hundred and fifty rupees he refers to is the equivalent of several months' pay.)

> *I am off to Paris which has been hitherto "out of bounds" to everyone but officers. Now we can go. Paris is a city of fairyland and God will now give us an opportunity of seeing it. I will write you all about it. I am taking Rs. 250 to spend. Whatever happens do not let anyone know about this. I intend to enjoy whatever pleasures there are. Do not let anyone know that Jai Singh is spending Rs. 250 in four days. If father heard of it he would be very angry. I should like to marry in France but I am afraid the family would be ashamed. You can marry very fine girls if you like.*

Another Hindu soldier considered doing just that. He wrote home asking for parental consent, and the reply from his father, Naubat Rai, was perhaps more extreme than he had anticipated. (The father's letter and the ones above were intercepted by British field censors and enabled the censors to gauge morale. The transcriptions do not include greetings or signatures.)

Consider, how could I possibly consent to your becoming a Musalman and marrying a Moslem wife, or embracing Christianity and marrying a Christian wife? Have you no shame? Do you think that I brought you up, so that you might marry a Christian wife? Could a man be so perverted as to lose his religion for the sake of a woman? You were one, who had a more promising future before you than any other man in the world, and yet you proceed to wreck your life by being a traitor to your faith!

Thousands of men have gone to France from here, but not one of them, except yourself has behaved in this unseemly fashion. There were 70 men in your own party, has anyone of them returned with a French wife? It is the greatest disgrace for a Hindu to become a Mahomedan or a Christian, do not therefore blacken your face before the whole world. I exhausted all my efforts to bring you up in culture and honour and endured all manner of trials and vicissitudes in order that your material and moral condition might be assured. Now, you proceed to disgrace yourself before the whole world!

Consider how from the commencement I strove on your behalf till in the end you became a <u>Gomestah.</u> Now I give you my last advice, viz. To put away this unprofitable idea from your mind, and never allude to a Christian wife in the future. And if you reject my advice, take care how you bring such a woman to my house, for she will be beaten on the head with a shoe a thousand times, and take steps also to provide for your mother and for your present wife. Why do you deal thus with me in my old age when I am past further work? Return home and take your present wife to you. If there is any fault in her, we can arrange another marriage for you here, four marriages if you like; but cease to think of disgracing yourself by taking a Christian wife.

Whether or not the soldier married the girl or dared to introduce any other young woman, for that matter, to his shoe-wielding father is not known. Nor is it clear exactly how his "present wife"—more likely, a fiancée—felt about the whole matter, although an awkward homecoming could certainly be imagined. Marriages between civilians and military personnel in both allied and enemy nations are common in times of conflict, and during World War II, well over one million servicemen proposed (oftentimes after only a brief courtship) to women they had met while stationed overseas. Zbigniew Janicki—a Polish airman flying with the famed Royal Air Force and defending England from waves of Luftwaffe attacks—was one of these lovestruck men. (The Kosciuszko Squadron, comprised of Polish pilots and air crews, was responsible for shooting down more German aircraft than any other RAF squadron.) Despite their heroics and the confidence airmen like Janicki exuded, they had been separated from their parents and siblings and were not immune to feelings of loneliness and homesickness. In the following letter to his parents, Janicki offered some insight into his emotions about the accelerated nature of a wartime romance.

November, 1941

Dear Mother and Father!

Following my departure from Poland, I wrote letters to you for a period of time, and then stopped, knowing that the chances were slim that you would receive them.

I am writing this letter for the sole reason of sharing my feelings with you. Years have passed since I have last seen you, and trust me, when I recall my last "invasion" of our home on the seventh day of the war, that moment is still vivid in my memory. Now, the third year has begun and time is passing very quickly. My last letter to you was written in Eastchurch in England, but of course, never sent. I decided to overcome what we call "sentimentalism," or maybe I didn't want you to get in trouble with the Gestapo. Anyway the letter you sent through the Red Cross in the spring of 1940 reached me in May and comforted me a little.

Since my arrival in England, I have changed a lot and so has my life. I must admit that not everything has happened the way it should have. After arriving in England we had to wait nearly eight months to fly and do real work. That period was difficult for me and my comrades, especially after our sojourn in France, and it had a depressing influence on my friends and me (weak consolation that I wasn't the only one). The English acknowledge our military ranks from Poland and this is why, as a young officer, especially during war in a foreign country, I let loose and lived the life without thinking about tomorrow, afraid that tomorrow would be too late. My longstanding interest in the English language and living among the English helped me quickly improve my vocabulary and enabled me to live an easy and pleasant lifestyle. But also I have to say that nothing demoralizes people as much as boredom, which I began to experience myself. Our urge to fly was restrained to the point that we had nothing more to do than wait and "learn" about England and its customs. Finally at the end of the summer, our group was sent to flight training. Believe me, after such a long period of inactivity, it was an incredible experience to climb back into a fighter plane. I felt like a person who had re-discovered his purpose and passion.

During the time in between training, a big change happened in my personal life. I met a girl by the name of Violet. As it turned out, she embodied everything I dreamed about in a woman. Being quite inexperienced in dealing with the other half of humanity, I was overwhelmed by this Irish-Englishwoman. Her personal charm and beauty caused me to fall for her in just a few days, like I had never before. Because of our mutual feelings (the best proof of which was her voluntary break up with a good and wealthy fiancé), after one month I was ready to marry her, but was still fighting a battle within me. I was afraid I might be confusing my affection for her with my loneliness here, along with my normal youthful feelings (I have Marysia on my mind).

This spiritual conflict between my desire for this English girl, in thoughts and in deeds, and my old principles, lasted for some time. Being as sentimental as I am, in the end I couldn't resist having somebody to fill the emptiness of separation from family and home, and having someone intimately close to my heart and body: a woman—a companion. I am sure that I could be a bachelor for a long time and resist all romantic ideas, but Violet was someone I couldn't lose. One month was sufficient to realize that there was no life for us without each other. Her breaking off of the engagement with her fiancé proved that my feelings were being reciprocated, and convinced me to propose and get married right away. This happened a few weeks later at a little Catholic church, without fanfare, but with a deep sense of mutual affection.

At that time I was stationed near New Castle in northern England, attached to an English fighter squadron. After training on Hurricanes, we were assigned to various English squadrons, before our own was formed. Overall I served in English squadrons for almost eight months (until May 1941), and after that I was assigned to Polish Squadron 302. Because military units often have to change locations, I have been all over England and Scotland, mostly with convoy patrols, or, as it happened last month, fighting Messerschmits over England and France. I have to confess that I have had very few opportunities to catch a Kraut in my sights, but my time will come . . . My recent success is of a very different nature. Most of all I would like you to know that you are . . . the grandparents and I am the father of a healthy son!!!

That is my greatest joy and, at the same time, my biggest worry because of the responsibility I am now facing. I hope you will be able to see my son (his name is Piotr) in the future, bless him, and watch him become a brave and honest man, as I do from the bottom of my heart. I want him to grow up to be a Polish gentleman, and have the best Polish and English qualities about him.

I would like him to appear in front of you and say what I am telling you now: I have the best and most loving parents a man could hope to have. In loving memory of you and my son, I would like to live honorably and never shame my family. This war is affecting thousands of people's lives, including my own. Life is precious to me as never before, but I know my duty, and I will avenge all the suffering Poland is going through and with God's help will kill more than one Kraut.

It is difficult for me to imagine what your life is like these days. I console myself thinking that all of you are carrying on with the hope for a better future. If you are suffering—sooner or later justice will come. Dad's hair has probably grayed, and Mom's is likely not as dark as it used to be. Dasia is probably married by now. She would be happy to know that we planned to give her name to our daughter. Even though I have my own so-called house, you are my family and my home forever. I dream of coming back one day with Violet and Piotr to see you all in a good health and receive your blessing.

Your loving son

Zbigniew Janicki would never have the opportunity to introduce his parents to their new grandson; Janicki was shot down and killed in June 1944. An American army nurse named Erma Meyers, who treated wounded and dying soldiers in the Pacific, also sought the comfort and solace an intimate relationship offered amidst the trials of war. In late 1942, Meyers had been introduced to a soldier named Bill (last name unknown), and they immediately fell in love. By early 1943, they were engaged. For her twenty-eighth birthday, Bill organized a surprise party that turned into a festive—and somewhat bawdy—affair, which Meyers related in a letter home:

> Dearest Mom and Dad. . . . I'm now the ripe age of 28—just imagine. The third birthday, away from my loved ones. I can't say that is exactly truthful—cause of course Bill was here. I had mentioned my birthday to Bill, but since he had made no further mention of it, thought he had forgotten it. On the morning of THE day, he casually wished me "Happy birthday", and I thought, that was that, and felt sort of hurt. Then, that evening, he said come on over to the officers club, and we'll have a drink on your birthday. I wasn't too enthusiastic, but went over,—and found half the outfit waiting for me, including the colonel. Sandwiches, drinks, etc, a real party. . . . Then came the trial by fire. The sons of guns, mostly Bill's roommates, had decided I needed some presents. Of course, it was impossible to obtain real presents, so heaven help me, they used their ingenuity. Most of them being doctors—you can imagine. A large box was put in front of me, and I was told to open it. Inside rested a variety of packages, large and small, each with a note written on it. I had to read each and every word, and then open the package, in full view of the hilarious audience. Now you know the sort of humour men stag parties have, so you can imagine with what qualms I started the process of reading. The first article was from a Dr. Lepsky, our GU man. This consisted of a slip of paper saying, "If its a boy, use this"—and inside was a razor blade. . . . Then my fingers picked up a jar of Tropical Butter, "Use this, in emergency", the sign said. By this time, my face was the color of beets, and all assembled were just about killing themselves, at my discomfort. But the worst was yet to come. At the bottom of the package, was a small banana, and typed upon it were the words, "This too may be used in an emergency,—may be eaten too". There were others too numerous to mention.

Later in the letter, Meyers discussed the obstacles she and Bill faced in getting approval from superior officers for their wartime wedding.

> Dad sent me a clipping from the newspaper, telling of a nurse in Italy being married, with the blessing of all concerned. If only I could make you understand how different the command is here. Marriage of nurses is looked upon with distrust, and severely condemned. All that is possible is done to forbid and prevent it [even] though I have the official permission

of a general. . . . If our marriage is prevented, Mom and Dad, and no matter what you may hear, let me tell you this. Our courtship has been no different, then if I were sitting on my own front porch. Bill has shown me every courtesy and respect, that I, as your daughter would expect and demand. Now, that you understand,—at least say a prayer or two for us. Just those few days [of a wedding] would make two people so happy, in the midst of this crazy world.

Less than four months later, Meyers notified her family that she was finally married. There had been, however, one minor change to the whole affair.

August 11, 1944

Dearest Mom, Dad and family,

By now you should have received the cable with the stupendous news within. If you've recovered from the shock,—I'll now try and explain.

Way last May just before I took sick, Bill and I broke our engagement. I would have told you at the time, but you seemed so happy and thrilled over the news, that I didn't have the heart to tell you.

Now why did I break off with Bill? Here's the answer. You of course remember his mother—who could forget her—the old battle axe—She was so insulting to me, so dead set against me it was sickening. To top it all off, Bill calmly tells me I must always obey her in every detail. SHE was his mother and ruler of all. That my loves, was the final straw. I began to think things over.

I realized I didn't really love Bill. I was so terribly lonely and depressed up there in New Guinea, that Bill took on added importance. He always was a cold fish, as you could tell from his letters. I just couldn't go through with it so broke it off.

By the way, the Borschts were secretly pleased over it. Bill is a nice lad, but just not my type, the old lady said.

Then I came down here on leave, and ran into Ralph.

I've known Ralph as long as I did Bill. He was in the original crowd that ran around with the Goldmans and Joe Allen. I've always thought a lot of him, but he never said anything—so never mentioned him in my letters.

My first week down here, Pearl gave a party at her house and Ralph showed up. Don't ask me what happened—all that I know is, that a month from then, I was a married woman. I still haven't stopped to catch my breath.

Of course you're worrying about what type of family he comes from.

Ralph himself is an industrial chemist by trade. He's a graduate from the University of Maryland. His people are old Litvaks, from Baltimore, his dad owning a Jewish delicatessen store. (At least we'll have plenty of cornbeef to eat.)

His Mom's maiden name was Glass from Baltimore—know them? I think my husband is a pretty swell person, and know you will too, when you meet him. Most important of all, I love him. And to me, that's pretty damn important.

Mom and Dad, dear I can't try to make you understand, but you always said anything that made me happy was OK with you. And this did.

Pearl knew about it before hand—but Mom Borscht was completely flabbergasted. We were married at the local temple by Rabbi Wolman. All of Brisbane knew about it at the last moment and just about turned up. Old Mrs. Borscht insisted on her wine being used for the ceremony, which was done. We were married under a canopy by the Rabbi, who was dressed in his Australian chaplain's uniform. Ralph was in his uniform, and I in mine. The best man was an American officer, and Pearle and her husband gave me away. Joe and Mina Solomon gave Ralph away.

I had given the Rabbi my Jewish name, and Dad's Jewish name. The ceremony was Australian Orthodox, and most of it in Hebrew. Since this is a British Commonwealth it had to be in accordance with British laws.

I recognized the words when the Rabbi named Dad's name, Benesh, and mine Esther. The whole thing is entirely different from an American wedding. They handed me a silver goblet twice to drink out of, and did the same to Ralph. The Rabbi placed a glass under Ralph's foot and he stepped on it. Then the next thing I knew, everybody was kissing me and congradulating me. Funny thing was, the groom isn't supposed to kiss the bride in that temple, but Ralph grabbed me and kissed me as soon as the Rabbi finished.

After the ceremony, we all went over to Mrs. Borscht's where a ten gallon keg of beer awaited us, and the party went merrily on. We spent our wedding night at Pearle's new home, its impossible to get rooms in hotels in town.

My CO extended my leave for two weeks, so am now on my honeymoon.

Frankly, Mom I'm gonna try like hell to have a baby, and get sent home, and out of the Army. How does that sound to you. Anyway it'll be fun trying.

Well thats about all my dears. Now you know the entire story. Give us your blessing.

Ralph's people live at Ruxton Ave., Baltimore Md. You can contact them and convince Mrs. Aarons that Ralph didn't marry a hussy, as she doesn't know anything about me. But for heavens sake, don't mention anything about Bill to them. Ralph himself knows all about Bill, they used to be pals, long ago.

So long for now. They're still holding all your letters up in New Guinea for me. I'll have to report back there you know. Ralph's full address is:

Lt. Ralph Aarons 0–2034376
Chemical Warfare Office
Base B.
APO 503—San Francisco California
Drop him a line.

Thats all m'loves   Your newly married daughter

Mrs. Ralph Aarons

(no less)

Despite the quick engagement and wedding, the deep love she felt for Lieutenant Ralph Aarons, who served with the Army Chemical Corps, was genuine and lasting. They went on to raise three children and were together until Erma's death in September 2000.

—⚌—

Through a Series of Increasingly Impassioned Love Letters, Captain Harry Kipp, Fighting in the Pacific, Attempts to Court a Young Woman Named Norma Clinton Back in the States

The two had never met. Norma Clinton was an exceptionally intelligent, attractive young honors student living in rural Georgia. Harry Kipp was a United States Marine Corps captain from Minnesota who had survived the attack on Pearl Harbor and was shipped off to the Solomon Islands to fight in the Pacific. In early 1944, at the request of her Aunt Jean (who had once dated Kipp), Norma sent him a letter and a photograph to raise his morale and simply let him know that people back in the States were thinking of him and all the troops in harm's way. Upon seeing her picture and reading her thoughtful and engaging letter, Harry was smitten. "Although Jean had told me that you might drop me a line I was nevertheless quite surprised and very pleased to receive your letter," he began his first missive to her, dated February 12, 1944. He continued:

When you said, "If you answer this letter I will send you another," did you mean another picture or another letter? I hope you meant both for I would enjoy looking at my pin-up girl in two different moods.

Your wish to become a nurse is a worthy goal to shoot at and I wish you success in realizing your aspirations. Might I hope to enjoy the priviledge of your services in the event I should ever need them?—or even though I didn't really need them? But since you are so proficient in chemistry you will probably be a labratory technician who does not personally attend patients. I knew there was a reason for my dislike of chemistry other than that I was too slow on the uptake to understand the elusive movements of the molecule.

It <u>has</u> been a long time since you saw Jean. You must have been a cute little tyke at that time. I haven't seen her either since nearly four years ago. Little wonder she married some one else. Would you wait that long for just an ordinary Marine?

Your hobbies are very akin to mine. I too enjoy movies and like to write letters. In that we are on common ground but I must admit that sewing holds very little fascination for me, that is if I am the one doing it but I do find pleasure in watching a good housewife sew.

Perhaps you believe that I deliberately delayed answering your ~~lettl~~ (sorry) letter but that isn't the case. You see I am in a very remote corner

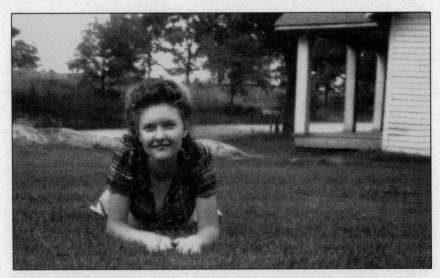

The photograph Norma Clinton sent to Captain Harry Kipp
that prompted their correspondence—and eventual love affair.

of the world and mail reaches us much more slowly than it takes to reach the States from here. Your letter arrived just yesterday. I hope that soon there shall be another (with a picture in it) and more to follow.

Goodnight sweets, won't you write again soon.

Yours,

Harry.

Capt. H.E. Kipp, U.S.M.C.
"A" Btry., 9th 55 MM Gun Bn.,
3rd Corps Arty., 3rd Phib Corps,

By summer, and after exchanging several more letters (most of which were lost or destroyed during the war), Harry had not just fallen, but plunged deliriously in love with Norma. Unable to contain his adoration, he expressed the depth of his emotions and addressed the question of how he would inform Aunt Jean that he was in love with Norma. Although—from his standpoint—there was no longer anything between them, it was still an awkward matter. (Aunt Jean's marriage had ended in divorce, and there was speculation that she was interested in Harry again.)

27 June, 1944

Dearest Norma;

Today your letters of 19 March and 1 May arrived, which makes four that I have gotten from you, and still leaves two unaccounted for. I am eagerly looking forward to their arrival.

Your pictures (I mean <u>you</u>) are heavenly. Now I do want to be two persons. Not so I could love you and someone else too, but so that both of me could love you. Looking at you lends meaning to the story of Mark Twain who when he first saw the picture of Veli?, gazed at it long and earnestly, then said, "This girl shall be my wife" I said those same words of you to your picture, Norma, and I pray that my words shall come to pass as his did. Heaven knows I meant them.

In my last letter I tried to explain my feeling for Jean, and why. I hope you will understand and forgive me, and realize that even though I had never known of you or never been thrilled by your loveliness it would still have been the same. It will be difficult, but tomorrow I shall tell her.

You cause me to believe that you exercise great care and much thought in writing to me. Norma, please don't compose letters to me. Just record your thoughts as they occur to you. Talk to me. Just as if you were here (How I wish you were!)

Must close. I can't write tonight. Your picture distracts me. I gaze at it continuously, marveling, hoping, imagining, fascinated—wondering if I can possibly ever be happy without you. Will write again when I recover a bit. In the meantime I'll be dreaming of you.

Love,

Harry.

The comment about marriage was not an offhand remark. Harry truly believed that Norma Clinton was the woman with whom he wanted to spend the rest of his life. But while he had seen a photograph of her, she had virtually no idea what he looked like. He was afraid she might not be attracted to him, and he offered a candid written description (he did not have a photo on hand) in the following letter on July 16—along with an official declaration of his intentions.

> *Am sorry I can't send you a picture now, but you did ask me to describe myself, and threatened me with your anger should I fail to comply. Remembering what you told me of your terrible temper, I hasten to tell you (and this hurts) that I am not at all handsome, am only five feet seven inches tall, have straight blond hair, blue eyes, weigh 170 pounds, and worst of all, have a childishly affectionate disposition. Now* you *tell me your reaction. As for your reserve in the letters you write to me, of course I understand. How could you write in any other way? You haven't even seen a picture of me, have never heard my voice, and know so little about me. There is something I do want you to know. Perhaps you will think me very naive and impulsive but I am sincere in the protestation of my love for you. I do love you. Norma, I want you to be my wife just as soon as I can possibly come for you. . . . Won't you tell me frankly, honestly, if you would marry me when I come home, should you find that you could care for me? . . . Considering everything I've already said more than you expected to hear, so "Goodnight", sweets. Will you answer just as soon as you recover from the shock?*

Shocked she was. It was only his eighth letter to her. She had not told her parents of the relationship, and she knew they would vehemently disapprove of the whole affair and accuse her of being impetuous and gullible for believing this far-away stranger honestly wanted to marry her. And if he did, based on a few photographs and letters, he was perhaps even more suspect. At the time, Norma still did not have an image of him. (She would later receive, forwarded by his uncle, a studio portrait of Harry in uniform. "He looked like a Roman God," she would say of his picture. "[F]rom deep blue eyes came a mixture of appraisal and curiosity, a man who viewed the world with interest and without reservation.") Norma entertained a number of doubts and reservations about his motivations, but after considerable thought, she penned her reply:

My Dearest Harry,

Yes, yes, yes, I will marry you! Just as soon as you can come for me. I want more than anything in the world to be your wife, forever! I love you with all my heart!

Your Norma

Norma did not tell her family; she would wait until Harry returned to the States. There was no point in worrying them now, and there was a far graver matter both she and Harry faced than her parents' reaction. It was not addressed directly, but broached only occasionally and somewhat obscurely. "One other thing, sweets," he wrote in a letter dated November 28, 1944,

please don't worry about my safety. I am as safe as you are and I will be for at least a couple of months. After that, if you must worry you may, but just a little bit, because I have a charmed life. If it were intended that anything unpleasant should happen to me, it would have happened long ago. We are not supposed to tell anyone when we go into actual combat until after we are aboard ship and on the way to make a landing on Jap territory and that letter doesn't get in the mail until several days or possibly weeks after we leave our base. To let you know that there will be no letters for a long time I'll end my last letter before leaving by saying, "Goodbye for a little while". Will you remember that?

Captain Harry Kipp, USMC

Norma would remember, and she could not refrain from sharing her anxiety. On March 4, 1945, as the war in the Pacific was becoming increasingly ferocious, Kipp responded to her concerns:

> *Norma darling, you mustn't feel badly when I say, "Goodbye for a little while." Even though it may be soon, I feel happy, and confident that everything will be all right. At other times in the past I used to wonder a little and my thoughts were not too cheerful but this time it's different because I know your spirit is with me and I'll always sense your presence. It will seem as if I can always reach back and touch your hand, and feel your reassuring answering pressure. Don't you see dear, that God didn't bring us together just to be torn apart? One day soon we'll be sitting hand in hand before our fireplace, silently dreaming as we gaze into the dancing flames while some little body near us in a little white crib stares in uncomprehending wonder at the new toe he has just discovered. Believe in that Norma dear, and it will come true.*

Less than three weeks later, after nonchalantly commenting about how beautiful Georgia must be at this time of year and his wish to be with her, Harry concluded his March 23 letter with the words Norma was dreading. "I must say 'Good-bye for a little while' . . . Don't worry, dear. I'm not afraid because I am taking you along and everything I do will be right because you are with me. Harry." Just over one week later, Clinton was listening to the radio when a news report broke into regular programming and announced that "United States Marines have invaded Okinawa, largest of the Ryukyu Islands on Japan's southern doorstep." Kipp was there, Clinton had no doubt, and she froze after hearing the bulletin. If he were killed, she might not know for months. She was not his wife, and only spouses and family members received official notification. The wait was unbearable. If Okinawa was anything like the battle for Iwo Jima, which had begun almost six weeks before and cost nearly seven thousand American lives, it would be a bloodbath. An estimated one hundred thousand heavily entrenched Japanese troops defended the island, which was ten times the size of Iwo Jima. Days passed, and then weeks, and still no word from—or about— Harry Kipp. And then, almost a month after his last letter, while literally waiting by the mailbox, she saw the postman driving down the road and heard him excitedly honk the horn. His beaming face told her everything she wanted to know, and after skidding to a stop, he waved the airmail letter with Harry's name listed in the return address. "My Beautiful Darling!," his letter began,

> *Turn your back to the mirror and look over your shoulder. Do you see wings? You must, because you are an angel. Today I received nineteen*

heavenly letters from you. Norma Mine, I hope I shall be deserving of your
wonderful devotion. You've done so much to make me happy, and I love
you more and more as time goes on and our wedding day draws nearer. I
can't possibly answer all of your questions or reply to your suggestions in this
one letter, but I'll try to catch up, sweets, in the near future. I'll write a few
lines every time I have a moment to spare and perhaps I shall be able to
send a letter at least once or twice a week. I think that from now on our
mail deliveries will be quite frequent and regular. . . .

Their correspondence resumed, and along with their exclamations of love and
longing, they wrote with growing enthusiasm about the day they would be mar-
ried. Finally, in August 1945 the war came to an end, and Harry was head-
ing home. On September 22, he landed in California, and, after he and Norma
were able to speak by telephone—which represented the first time they had heard
each other's voice—Harry sent the following letter.

8:30 Sunday evening

Darling,

I don't remember a word you said, but I still hear the sound of your
sweet voice echoing in my heart. How can I wait seven whole days to
hear you talk to me again? But this is the end of our long time of
waiting. Will you marry me soon? Monday? Tuesday? I've never loved
you more than at this very moment.

We didn't say much in our conversation, did we, honey? You were
simply breathless and I was nearly the same, and we could hear each
other so very faintly, but I wouldn't have missed it for worlds. The sound
of your voice went straight to my heart.

If my present plans carry through I will leave here Tuesday evening
and should reach Chattanooga sometime Sunday, and unless I let you
know otherwise, I'll call you at eight that evening. Do you suppose we'll
be as excited then as we were tonight? Well, why shouldn't we be excited?
Nothing as important as this has ever happened to us before. I can
hardly realize that so very soon the dearest, sweetest, loveliest little
darling in all the world will be my wife. We've waited nearly two years
now, and if we do find ourselves a bit embarrassed when we meet, it will
be no more than it is natural to expect and the awkwardness will
disappear in a moment, because deep in our hearts we understand each
other, and we know that our two individual lives are bound to each
other inseparably and nothing under the sun can ever change that.

Oh, Honeychild! Monday! Monday! Monday! I'm so happy I could
turn handsprings in the middle of Market Street. And Monday morning

I am going to give you the greatest, biggest hug you have ever hear about 'cause I love you, I love you, Norma, I love you and that's for sure!!

Harry.

One week later, Harry Kipp and Norma Clinton exchanged vows. Harry retired from the Marine Corps in 1953 after eight years of active duty in the States, primarily recruiting and training Marines. Norma finished college and became an elementary school teacher. The couple raised two children and remained together until May 1965, when Harry passed away from cancer.

—◊◊◊—

A Swiss National Named Werner Walti Carries with Him an Affectionate Letter from a Woman in California— Or So It Would Seem

The letter was like any other expression of love and yearning from a distant sweetheart, and Werner Walti, a Swiss national visiting Scotland, kept the missive with him at all times. Written by a woman named Marion (last name unknown) from Palo Alto, California, the brief but intimate letter fondly recalled wonderful days together between two people who were meant to be united once again. It is dated June 1, 1939—exactly three months before the outbreak of war in Europe.

Goodmorning, silent one! I have been wondering where you were, and have been afraid you would leave without saying goodbye. You may have gone already, but you can't be farther than my wishes for your happiness can travel.

Easter has come and gone without a word exchanged between us! I thought of you on Easter.

Will you forgive me for something? Do you remember the time I gave you the new penny? I was in very bad discipline that night. I was foolish as in the summer on Ridge Road and you brought me to my senses again. You are the strong wise one. And your help and affection have meant more to me than you can know.

Your Christmas letter—and the beautiful El Greco and Cathedral Sculptures are my treasures. Never will I forget that perfect Christmas day and your wonderful surprise.

Do you remember the little cow we had on Ridge Road and the little wooden Virgin and how you objected to their standing together? It was a funny little thing, or so I thought, that you should object. But since then it has showed me something deep in you that I was slow to appreciate. . . .

I love you for all that is fine in you, and for all your encouragement. I want to be worthy of your friendship.

My love goes with you—

Affectionately,
Marion

Not a word of the letter was true. It is not that Marion did not harbor these feelings, but that Marion did not exist, and Werner Walti was, in fact, a German spy named Robert Petter. The letter was believed to be part of Petter's cover in Scotland, where he had just arrived to investigate the strength of Royal Air Force units in the region. Caught in Edinburgh's Waverly train station with a fake passport and other incriminating evidence, Petter was later sentenced to die under the Treachery Act, and, along with another spy named Karl Drugge, was executed in August 1941. The Germans were not alone in manufacturing love letters for secret missions. In one of the most creative counterintelligence schemes in World War II, an anonymous corpse was dressed as a British major from the Combined Operations Headquarters, given the name William Martin, and, on April 30, 1943, dumped in the ocean off the coast of Huelva, Spain, where German agents were believed to be working. (Although Spain was officially neutral in the war, its fascist leader, General Ferdinand Franco, was pro-German.) Chained to "Major Martin"'s wrist was a briefcase containing what appeared to be highly sensitive documents indicating that the Allies were planning to invade Greece and the island of Sardinia, not Sicily as they actually intended. To substantiate that Martin was a real person, several love letters by a fiancée, "Pam," were included with the official papers. One expressed with persuasive anguish how much he would be missed after departing for his latest mission.

I do think dearest that seeing people like you off at railway stations is one of the poorer forms of sport. A train going out can leave a howling great gap in ones life & one has to try madly—& quite in vain—to fill it with all the things one used to enjoy a whole five weeks ago. That lovely golden day we spent together—oh! I know it has been said before, but if only time could sometimes stand still just for a minute—But that line of thought is too pointless. . . . Bill darling, do let me know as soon as you get fixed & can make some more plans, & dont please let them send you off into the blue the horrible way they do nowadays—now that we've found each other out of the whole world, I dont think I could bear it—All my love, PAM.

After Martin's body washed ashore, the contents of the briefcase made their way to Berlin and convinced the Germans to concentrate their forces closer to Greece and Sardinia. In July 1943 the Allies launched their successful assault on Sicily. The ploy, code-named Operation Mincemeat, was an extraordinary achievement. Decades after the war, the true identity of the corpse was revealed to be that of a thirty-four-year-old homeless Welshman named Glyndwr Michael who had committed suicide in a London warehouse. Michael's body remains buried in Huelva under a gravestone that now bears his name, as well as a dedication to "Major William Martin."

—∾∾—

**John Bateman Beer's Sweetheart, Ivy, Shares with Him
Some Unexpected News About Their Relationship
&
Union Soldier John C. Sellars Explains to "Miss Julia"
That, Although She Was Once the Only Girl for Him,
He Can No Longer See Her Again
&
Charlie, an American Soldier in England During World War II,
Assures His Girlfriend Back Home He Always Liked Her a Lot, but . . .
&
Captain Mary Ellen O'Connor, Serving in the Gulf War, Laments to
Her Sister, Erin, That She Barely Hears from Her Husband Back Home**

In September 1917, a British soldier named John Bateman Beer, serving in the 2/22nd London Regiment, received a long-awaited letter from his girlfriend. It was not, suffice it to say, the letter he was expecting.

My Dear Jack,

For the last month I have been endeavouring to pluck up sufficient courage to write and tell you that everything must be over between us. No doubt you will think me awfully unkind and perhaps fickle to write like this while you are away, but this matter has worried me a great deal, and I have been halting between two opinions, as to whether it would be kinder to let you know now, and let myself be called unfaithful, or to wait until you come home, although knowing all the time in my heart that I was untrue. When you went away, and I told you that I loved you best, I really meant it Jack, but such a lot seems to have happened since then. I really thought that I had forgotten Charlie in my love for you, and during the past nine months have been fighting against his love for me, wishing and longing for your return, but it is no use Jack, I cannot help loving Charlie best. I suppose it is because he was first. At first I made up my mind to fight it down <u>and be true to you, and if you still wish to keep me to my promise under the circumstances, I will do so.</u>

Don't take this too much to heart Jack. I am not worth it but don't think me altogether heartless. I would not hurt you dear unless I could help it, but unfortunately we cannot control our own feelings. Will you believe me when I say that I am very sorry, for I am, more so than perhaps you think. Anyway, forgive me if you can, and <u>I trust that you will still let us be friends,</u> whatever happens. Have not had the courage to tell your Mother yet, perhaps you will do so. Write back as soon as you can do say you forgive me Jack, shall wait impatiently for your answer.

One word about Charlie before I finish. He would have waited in honour bound until you came home.

All at home send their love to you.

Trusting this will find you in the best of health.

I remain,

Yours Very Sincerely
Ivy

Although the term originated in World War II, "Dear John" letters date back for centuries. (And with the advancement of electronic communication, troops can now receive "Dear John" e-mails.) Usually the message is from a girlfriend, fiancée, or, in the worst case, a wife who has fallen for someone else. As much as servicemen joke about the letters or try to make light of them, the effect of receiving one of these rejections in the mail can be devastating. "On the fifteenth of this month a german man in the 52nd Regt. P V commited suicide by shooting himself through the head," Civil War soldier Ephraim Shuey wrote to his sister in March 1864. "The cause of it was he got a letter that his wife got married and that troubled him so much." John Bateman Beer was markedly less troubled by his "Dear John" letter and—more defiant than hurt—wrote the following to his father on October 12, 1917.

> *Last week, I had a letter from Ivy, and I was surprised to know that everything between us was at an end. It seems as though a fellow named C. Hall, has been attending on her & of course in my absence, she has allowed herself to be talked over & change her mind. This is certainly a big surprise & of course I did not know what to do, so after thinking it over I have at present decided not to write to her at all, & let the affair finish up. I should like your advice on the subject. It is no good playing about on the matter, & I am not going to play second fiddle to anybody.*

Women, too, can find themselves on the wrong end of a rejection letter. During the Civil War, a "Miss Julia" (last name unknown) had been wooed by a Union private named John C. Sellars, who served with the Missouri State Militia Cavalry, Ninth Regiment. She initially disapproved of his overly flirtatious advances but later had a change of heart. It was, alas, too late. Sellars wrote the following to Miss Julia on March 4, 1865. (There are many misspellings and sentence fragments in the letter, as well as a hole in the paper near the end, which is indicated by a blank space.)

Miss Julia.

Dear girl I received your kind letter yesterday it gave me much pleasure to here from you. Such a kind friend as you seem to be. The tears started in my eyes when I read thoes preshes lines. But they came to late. I had give up ever hearing from you any more. I thought you did not care any thing a bout me or else you would not be so long a bout writing. You, don the same the other letter that I wrote. The reason that I did not write any sooner was I did not know how long you was a going to stay in the Bottom and I did not no where to direct to and I did not think about asking you before I left.

Miss Julia I thought you was the nicest little girl, that I ever saw. Your smiles had compleattey captavated me. Your purty black eyes and I reley <u>loved</u> you, and I thought at one time that you was the onley girl that I ever saw that was intended for me. I would of give any thing to bin with you after last summer. I wached meny a day for you to come to town. But did not git to see you but once or twice all sumer. and you was so carles about writing and when I saw you last December in the Bottom you appeard so cold and distent towards me that I did not know what to think you acted as thow you did not care whether you talked to me or not and I told you that it would be the last chance that you would have to talk to me that is what I meant in my other letter, and I did not write but a few lines and was very carles. I thought it would hurry you up if you cared anything about me, but it did not. I thought by you not writing it had ofended you and you was not a going to write a toll. And since that time I have promised to marry a young lady that lives a few miles in the country. I had just finished the bargen two days before I got your letter.

I am sorry that it is so but it can't be helped now. You told me that you did not like my way of doing I was sorry to here you say so. It was nature for me. When I love any one I can't keep my hands off of them. I like to hug the girls and kiss them and you say you did not like the way I don I had much rather talk to the girls than write them I can tell wether they mean what they say or not. You sayed that you hird some remarks about me I wished you had told me from what source it was from. I guess that thay had some object in view. Thay was interested themselves it was some of (Company A) you know what Sid and Ann sayed about Smiley. I care not what any one says a bout me it is without a caus. I ask no favors of such I try to be up rite and honerable all whiskey drinkers I scorn. You never hird me say any harm of any body. I do think it is a low pracktes to talk about others I have so much to do to tend to my own bisness. So Farewell dear Julia,

John C. Sellars

Sellars was not over her entirely, however. In a postscript, he asked: "Miss Julia I wish that I had your likeness so that I could see you in after days. I would prise it very hiley. I would keep it as long As I live." (It is not known whether she responded, but she did eventually marry another man, surnamed Smith, and they had twelve children together.) During World War II, British troops repeatedly complained that American servicemen courted all of the most attractive ladies in England. Women back in the United States who had been dating those American troops discovered that the grievance was not entirely a rumor. Gertrude "Trudel" Geschwill, a young nurse in Clifton, New Jersey, received the following from her American beau stationed across the pond in the fall of 1944.

England, 19 September

Dear Trudel:

The letter you wrote from the shore on the 25th of August arrived the day after the one you wrote on the 10th, and I was very glad to hear from you. Apparently you had a good time there, and I am glad it was a pleasant break in your routine, which seems rather strenuous. It was quite an idea to write your letter on a map—I have been around that vicinity, and it brought back some very pleasant memories. Several times I went out on fishing trips through that inlet, starting from the Manasquan side. One time, three days after the hurricane we had in 1938, I steered a forty foot cruiser for a half hour or so when we were about fifteen miles offshore and the skipper wanted to take a look at the engines, with all the other passengers seasick. I did not handle the boat as smoothly as an experienced helmsman would, and the seasick ones were loud in their suggestions that the captain should take over again. The sea was quite rough, but I did a fair job of steering toward a water tower somewhere south of the inlet, probably in Point Pleasant.

That picture of the ocean in the moonlight was really very beautiful; there have been times in England when I could see a similar scene, but the moon was setting across the ocean, rather than rising from it, and the point of view makes quite a difference.

I had a date with my Wren Sunday; it meant being away from camp over twenty hours to be with her five hours, as she is now stationed some distance away, but quite a lot happened in those few hours. We discussed those differences I mentioned in my last letter to you, and I discovered that Barbara was willing to make the concessions necessary to get around them; she has agreed to follow the rules set by the Catholic Church in such situations, and to come to the States with me. She probably thought, as you did, that I could be broken of the idea of being a confirmed bachelor, and she has been right. If the war had not started so soon after you and I met, and had not kept me here so long, things would have been different. I would have probably asked you the same question, although I always felt that you regarded your religion as highly as I did mine, and could not change or make any concessions any more than I could.

Writing to you, I can remember very well the night before Pearl Harbor, when we met, driving over the winter roads during the next two months between Jersey City and Clifton, and our most enjoyable dates together. War changes everyone, I guess, and I realize now that it has changed me more than I knew. I guess I'll never know now the method I once asked you about, but I suspect, that if we could have eliminated the obstacle in the way, it probably would have worked. I've always liked you a lot, and found you very attractive, which is a good start in any language.

Things are different now than I thought they would be when I last saw you and as a matter of fact look different than they did even one year ago. I made a decision in a situation full of unknown factors; in fairness to Barbara I cannot say I am sorry, but I can honestly say that if I had not come to England, and stayed so long, things might have been quite different.

Perhaps we shall see each other again, if this war ever ends; I hope things go well with you, and I hope you will write to me, if you don't mind.

Your friend,
Charlie

Geschwill was stung by the rejection, but not for long; almost a week later she met a handsome, twenty-four-year-old army technical sergeant named Henry Kempe, who asked her out. After four months of dating, Kempe proposed, and they married a year later. (They had two children and stayed happily married until Mr. Kempe's death in 1991.) The only thing worse for servicemembers overseas than opening a "Dear John"—or "Dear Jane"—letter is receiving virtually no words of affection at all. During Operation Desert Storm, US Army Captain

Mary O'Connor frequently wrote to her sister, Erin, in Wisconsin about the burdens of being away from her husband, as well as the challenges she faced as an American woman in Saudi Arabia. On April 2, 1991, O'Connor joked in a letter to Erin that a local Bedouin (desert nomad), "offered one of my guys two camels, 4 goats, 4 sheep, and a son for me. Now I have to have an escort when I do P.T." But later that same day, O'Connor brought up a much more serious subject she did not feel comfortable discussing with anyone else, including her husband. Indeed, he was the problem. (Names in this letter have been changed in the interests of privacy. Ummy is O'Connor's grandmother, and the term, "watches my 6," is the equivalent of "watches my back.")

Hello Erin,

Sure did enjoy your letter. Hawaii sounded so beautiful. Well as I chomp on my gam, sister-to-sister, let me try to be Mary Ellen instead of CPT O'Connor. I don't ask a whole lot of Brad other than to be there for me. He doesn't have to support me, fight my battles, etc. Over here I am called CPT Frosty because I hide what ever emotion I am feeling. The only connection any of us have with our personal selves is provided through mail. Quite frankly I am very hurt and disappointed Brad has not written. I have received only 4 letters since XMAS. 4. Yet I get mail from you, mom, and Ummy all the time. I get mail regularly from pen pals I have never met. I would write Brad everyday telling him about my day, what I feel, etc. I just got tired of the pain. No letters from him, yet everyone got one from a spouse.

I was very hurt to not have a letter describing what he felt when the war started. Damn it Erin I could have died! The only reinforcement to knowing if he cares are letters. I am so hurt that if we were not married, he'd be history even though I Love him very much. Since I can't function if I am emotional I have simply shut up that part of myself. I will deal with it when I return. You know the spouse support group wrote Valentine's greetings on a large banner and sent it over. I was embarrassed that Brad did not use the word <u>Love</u> anywhere in his greeting. I really needed to read that he loves me, or that he wants me to be his valentine—not watch my 6. Hell, everyone watches my 6—I just want my man. I have nightmares at night because I am afraid he can't deal with Mary and the Captain. He wouldn't be the first—although I pray he'll find the strength. I Love him very much. I poured my heart out to him—let him know me. I was vulnerable and I have had no response. Erin I hate this place, I hate the horrors I'll have to live with, I hate how old I feel. I don't want to hate Brad, I want to love him. But everytime I think of him and write as I am doing so now I end up crying because it hurts. I needed him thru letters, and he didn't or couldn't respond.

Everything else will need to wait. I can't write anymore.

Love you Sis,

M

Unfortunately, after Captain O'Connor returned from the Middle East, she and her husband could not reconcile their differences. They divorced a year and a half later.

—⁓—

**From 1942 to 1945, Kenelm Clifton Johnson-Hill,
an English Lieutenant Captured by the Japanese, Writes a Series
of "Letters" He Plans to Give to His Wife If He Survives
&
After Learning That Her Husband Has Been Reported
Missing in Action, Katherine Netting Continues Writing to Him
for Seven Months—but Does Not Send the Letters**

Taken prisoner by the Japanese after the fall of the Philippines in 1942, Major Horace Greeley was able to smuggle out an uncensored letter to his wife, Jeanne, in late November 1944, succinctly chronicling more than two excruciating years as a POW. American troops led by General Douglas MacArthur were swarming into the southern islands of the Philippines, and liberation seemed close at hand. (Greeley, however, would not be among those rescued; POWs whom the Japanese considered "healthy" enough to be exploited as slave laborers were forced onto transport ships and sent to Japan, and Greeley would not survive the journey.) In the final paragraph of his November letter, Greeley wanted to prepare his wife for whatever idiosyncratic traits or habits he might display when he returned. His appeal poignantly reflected the concerns of many long-term POWs who worried about the emotional aftershocks of their confinement and how they would be received by loved ones back home. "I realize that when you write it is like addressing a void—you don't know if I will receive your letters or not," he remarked.

You have kept up with the world and its change while I am thinking and living in terms of 1941.—here it is three years later. You say that nothing has changed, but when I come back, I'll show you the changes. Be patient with me—let me eat my fill—ride in elevators—walk the streets—have a cup of coffee, candy, ice cream—clean clothes—take a turkish bath to get really clean—read three year old issues of Time Life, etc . . and other fool things, like cooking at one or two in the morning. I'll have some peculiar ideas—will ask you if so and so took place and so and so said thus and so. Don't laugh too much. We have lived on rumor for years and some people have terrific imaginations. Yes, Honey, you have a difficult task ahead— to keep me educated and up to date. Time here seems like an eternity, but I never lose hope that it will soon be over and we'll be together again. Every day I thank a kind Fate that gave me you. I love you now and forever, with all my heart and soul, honey, so very, very much.

Kenelm Clifton Johnson-Hill was also imprisoned by the Japanese in 1942 and became one of tens of thousands of Allied POWs—along with hundreds of thousands of Burmese, Chinese, Javanese, and Tamil enslaved workers—forced to build the Burma-Siam Railroad that would extend for hundreds of miles through dense jungle and over large rivers. (The railway is the subject of the Oscar-winning 1957 film classic The Bridge on the River Kwai.*) English by birth, Johnson-Hill was living in Singapore with his pregnant wife Joyce, who was known by the nickname "Pooh," and their two-year-old son Brian. Six weeks before the Japanese invaded on December 8, 1941, Pooh and Brian left their home for Australia. Before the war, Johnson-Hill had enlisted as a second lieutenant in the Straits Settlements Volunteer Forces, which was attached to the 16th Defence Regiment RA. When the Japanese attacked Singapore, Johnson-Hill was immediately called up and ordered to man a gunnery position. Singapore fell on February 15, 1942, and Johnson-Hill was captured a week later with a piece of shrapnel embedded in his leg. In defiance of Japanese prohibitions against keeping journals (the penalty being torture and even death if they were discovered), Johnson-Hill began writing a series of short "letters" to his wife in a small notebook, knowing she might never read them. His first message, which was more of a general statement about his purposes, was dated April 23, 1942.*

It is difficult even to begin to put on paper one's thoughts, impressions, fears and hopes, and the hundred and one little events that make up the daily life of a POW. As for trying to finish this treatise, that is of course, beyond the bound of conjecture, no human being can foresee the horizon of events, or anywhere near the end of this little bit of world's history into which one has been flung as indiscriminately as bombs are dropped on civilian women and children. However, let us attempt a start anyway—and add a resolution to try and keep it up to date at least once a week.

That same day, he added another entry that acknowledged the gravity of the crisis but also emphasized his determination to ensure that the experience—"a

bad dream lived only by half a man with his other half in Australia"—would
fortify their love and strengthen their family in the end.

We have lost EVERYTHING and as far as I am able to ascertain,
stand little or no hope of recovering an iota of the wreck. At the age of
36, and with a wife and (I pray) two children, we have got exactly
nothing, that is in the material sense of the word. Spiritually on the
other hand, we have each other and our children, and being a prisoner of
war has most emphatically taught me to appreciate, and to love my wife
and children more deeply and more wholeheartedly than I ever thought
conceivable.

Johnson-Hill was intensely aware that they were not alone in their ordeal, and
he frequently wrote of all those who were going through the same agonizing sep-
aration:

Another pink letter day darling in that we were allowed to send off
another p.c. not that we were allowed to say very much or even hint or
put a date on it. Whenever you do receive it sweetheart mine at least
you will know that I am still alive. Several hundred who have died in
the meanwhile will only be able to leave their loved ones to guess by the
absence of a card that they are dead. What a terrible tragedy, it may take
years for the truth to come out definitively.

When Pooh left for Australia in November 1941, she was halfway through her
pregnancy. Ten months into his imprisonment, Johnson-Hill still did not know
whether Pooh had delivered a baby boy or girl, and he referred to the child as
"Blank." One year after his wife's evacuation from Singapore, he wrote the fol-
lowing from a prison camp called Tonchan, which he spelled "Tong Sha," in
Thailand (known then as Siam).

26th November 1942
Tong Sha. Even in the middle of the Siamese jungle I can not help
thinking deeper than ever of my sweet Pooh, my darling Brian and
Blank. This time a year ago, a whole year—more like a whole lifetime—
we said goodnight and goodbye on the steps of the 'Boysie Vain' How
little did we know or realise what fickle fate had in store for us. Hell, hell
and more hell. Wonder if we shall all 4 be together for the next
anniversary and even when I shall know what poor sweet blank is? Great
excitement this morning when large two engined planes flew over the
Camp. Rangoon is only 250 miles away by air and wonder if they were

British and if they are likely to bomb us thinking we are Japanese Troop Concentration.

Although there is not, unsurprisingly, much humor within the pages of Johnson-Hill's notebook, an occasional spark of levity comes to light. In one entry, he wrote simply:

Big discovery, sleeping partners say I am now cured of snoring. Won't my Pooh be pleased. Darlingest One.

Johnson-Hill and his comrades lived on rancid vegetables and paltry handfuls of rice. All of the delicacies in which he planned to indulge when freed were inventoried throughout the journal and with almost the same emphasis as seemingly more important matters. On December 10, 1942, he wrote:

Tong Sha. Another death, another Last Post, another grim reminder. Note—after war must try Golden Bells Preserving Victoria; most marvelous marmalade.

A year after the birth of his second child, Johnson-Hill still had not received one word about the baby's gender—or, more importantly, its health and well-being. On May 22, 1943, he wrote the following.

Received letter from Beryl in which she says "Glad Pooh, Brian and question mark are in Australia" so I have received congratulations today on our baby but am still in the dark with poor blank. Hello little blank. What happened to your letters darling there are lovely ones that count for me and any time. Her letter is dated 5th July 1942, nearly a year ago. However it was sweet of her to write and I ought to be and am grateful.

The much-anticipated news finally arrived.

10th June 1943, Thursday

Well, well here is a BIG date and a curious story. I will start at the very beginning. Major Watson Hyatt, you may remember him as a schoolmaster in Singapore, we went to their house, as he called in here the other day, I asked him to take Beryl and Cyril's letters up to Gerald as I knew they would interest him especially the bit about Pam. He duly went away with them. Two days later, today McGrath went south to Ta Sao where he met Watson Wyatt and handed him the letters back. He arrived back here soon after lunch and of course I opened the letter straight away inside was a chit from Gerald saying 'Congratulations on your second son, Alan.' Information gleaned from Eric Griffiths Jones letters!! Such are the ways of the world. Well, darlingest one I can't possible tell what a relief it was to know our child was born alive and that you must have recovered from it sufficiently to have him christened Alan, a name I like immensely and an initial which will not only not confuse him with any other Johnson-Hill but will put him first on O.R. lists. I wonder what other names you have chosen and if you had an easy time with him. What weight he was and whether he looked like our sweet Brian or whether there is a big difference like the Andre children. I am simply dying to get your first letter to hear all the details. As you can imagine what a hell it is to be a Prisoner of War under Japanese hands, not even allowed to know the sex on one's child until he is over 14 months old. Poor Boving does not know about his yet. I wonder on what date he made his appearance? Oh for your letter Beloved.

Holidays and anniversaries remained, emotionally, both the most agonizing and uplifting times for the prisoners, who found themselves awash in recollections of better days but then also used these memories to bolster their spirits. On Brian's birthday, he wrote the following:

It is quite unbelievable that our sweet child is 5 years old today, this making his 3rd birthday without his father while he is a POW. It is really rather tragic that he should be going through this interesting period without any paternal influence. I know darling that you will see that he does not forget me altogether. I am just literarily living for the day when we can all be together again and I can be introduced to Alan, sweet thing. I do hope he had as happy a birthday as possible in the circumstances and that lots of kind uncles and aunts remembered him.

On September 25, 1943, Johnson-Hill asked: "Further mail rumours have arrived in camp but nothing I hear from Australia. Wonder when I shall ever hear from my beloved Pooh again. Your last letter received was dated 2nd January 1942. Long before Alan was born and here he is nearly 18 months old and probably walking. Sweet thing!" Two weeks later he wrote ecstatically:

6th October, 1943 Wednesday
Darling, Darling at last after nearly two whole years—a letter from you, my sweet dated 4th September 1942. Such a great day today will

not write more until I have thoroughly digested your marvelous letter. Am far too excited and tired to write more tonight. Bless you all dear ones.

Mail was everything to the prisoners, and while on "rubbish duty" (i.e., cleaning up trash around the camp), Johnson-Hill discovered piles of letters sent to the POWs by their loved ones that the Japanese never forwarded but ripped up and threw in the garbage instead. Much to his own astonishment, he even found a torn-up photo of Pooh, Brian, and Alan. The mail that did get through was delayed by up to two years.

8th March, Wednesday, 1944

Another week over, another week nearer freedom. I have another go of malaria, my seventeenth in just over a year and as so often happens my ulcers on my heel and ankle have gone back on me and are far worse . . . Short letters—one in every 100 men have been allowed to be sent home. They convey no idea of the awful conditions in which we exist and no accounts of the hundreds of deaths. We are all rather depressed and tired after two years of it. A letter from my mother dated 24th June 1942 turned up yesterday, nearly two years old. She says let me know what you want though, through the Red Cross! I must start making out a list at once! Alan nearly two—how sad, they grow so quickly.

Throughout the entire journal, there is only one instance where Johnson-Hill expresses even the slightest frustration with his wife, and it came during a time when he was physically worn down, which understandably worsened his mood. (The malnourished and overworked men suffered from a host of illnesses, including cholera, fever, malaria, tropical ulcers, and dysentery.) Johnson-Hill had sent one of his allotted mailcards to his wife via England ("home"), thinking it would be faster. In fact, it only delayed the card's delivery, and Pooh made reference to this in one of the few letters of hers he ever received. He could not contain his irritation.

Denghi fever has left me thank heavens, but I am feeling rather weak and am suffering from lack of sleep, chiefly due to your letters darling. I hate rows and recriminations but let me quote from your letters first. "Did you imagine that I had gone home? I don't quite know when you thought I had been able to go, because you may remember that there was a little matter of having a baby which complicates traveling a bit", well darling I think that is hardly fair. I know I am only the father, but few fathers go through the torments of 14 months waiting to know if their wife is even alive or whether their baby is male or female. Enough jokes go on in peace time about fathers having to pace up and down the room for three or four hours, but how does that compare with 14 whole months under terrible conditions?

He then added pointedly:

When you complain darling of a rather dreary life of domestic duties with few parties etc you certainly make me laugh which is a good thing! Here we have all the fun that you miss my darling, work, work, work with 14,000 deaths of British troops and over 30,000 deaths amongst the conscripted groups of Tamils, Chinese and Malays.

All was forgotten by the time of the next entry, however, and Johnson-Hill focused on a much happier subject.

Yet another wedding anniversary darling with us not 'we' at all. It seems quite impossible to believe that we have been married 6 whole years. It seems much more like six months to me, so little have we seen of each other darling one. Have fever again, so will not add more to this now, but quietly think of you, Brian and Alan bless you.

Johnson-Hill could not know, of course, that the war would continue for almost another full year, but the ensuing months brought signs of hope. Allied warplanes were closing in on Japanese positions. Bombs could be heard in the distance like approaching thunder. As the Japanese tried to retreat further away from the air raids, they hurried the prisoners along from camp to camp, and it was harder for Johnson-Hill to keep up with his writing. The messages became increasingly sporadic, and entire months were skipped or summarized in hastily jotted sentence fragments. And then, after the atomic bombs were dropped on Hiroshima and Nagasaki, the word came that the POWs were finally free. In his last entry, Johnson-Hill's impatience to get home was palpable:

Wonder if there is any chance of us being together again this month. . . .
I suppose one shouldn't grumble about 30 days but Oh My God how I
long to see you again my darlingest one. . . . 1,100 officers left camp this
morning and some expected to leave today. Not me however.

Two months later, Johnson-Hill sailed on the USS Orduna *into Liverpool, England, where his family was waiting for him, and he was personally able to give his wife the three small notebooks of letters he had been saving for almost four years. At the same time that Johnson-Hill was a prisoner of war secretly writing messages he could not mail, ten thousand miles away in San Antonio, Texas, a woman named Katherine Netting was addressing letters to her husband, a fighter pilot in Europe, not knowing if he would ever see them. "Dearest Conrad: You may never read this, my darling, but I'm writing it because I want in some way to tell you all of the things that have happened since I got word of your being missing," Katherine began her first letter to her husband. Conrad J. Netting III was a twenty-six-year-old lieutenant in the 8th Air Force, US Army Air Corps who disappeared over France in June 1944, only days after the Normandy invasion. His wife went on to describe to him how she learned the awful news. "I heard those fateful steps on the porch," she wrote,*

> *I couldn't get to the door at all, it seemed. And when the man asked me "Mrs. Katherine H. Netting?", I knew for sure what I was about to read. I took the book and very carefully signed Mrs. K.H. Netting someplace. I'm sure I don't know where, but he handed the wire to me. I turned away from the door and tore open the envelope very carefully. And I didn't read it. I just looked to see Conrad J. Netting "Missing" "France" "10 June". I think I sat in the large chair then, but I'm not sure. I wandered around the room aimlessly for a few minutes then. I walked back to Grannie's room and I noticed, as though I weren't myself, but a third person watching myself in a dream, that I was shaking terribly . . . I can't think of you as any way but alive. And if they ever do finally tell me that you aren't I shall never be able to accept it. I shall never be able to remember you as anything but the most vivid, alive person I've ever known. They could even show me pictures to prove it, and I will never believe it. It will be my cross, my curse, and my joy forever, that in my mind, you shall always be vibrantly alive as you were when I had you with me. I'm tired now, my darling, so I shall stop for this night.*

Like Pooh Johnson-Hill, Katherine Netting was pregnant when she and her husband were separated by the war. Confident that it would be a boy, she and Conrad had already picked out the child's name before her husband left for Europe—Conrad John Netting IV. Lieutenant Netting even had his son's nickname, ConJon, painted on the side of his P-51 Mustang. On July 16, Katherine wrote to her husband about the birth of their first child.

Dearest Conrad—

Yes, my darling, Conjon came this morning at 5:50 ayem—O, Conrad, he is so much your son. His little nose is an exact duplicate of the one you arrived with according to your baby pictures. His hairline is the same and he has BIG feet and hands. They say at the hospital that he is the largest baby delivered that the night nurse ever saw—NINE POUNDS 4 OZ. I don't know how long he is but for comparison Butch weighed 6 lb, 12 oz and Barbara weighed 6 lb, and after a remarkable gaining tipped the scales a day or two ago at 9 lb, 2 oz. The nurses say he is going to be a very big man.

Just after I wrote a bit yesterday, the water broke. I called the hospital and they said I could wait until the pains (which hadn't started) were 10 min. apart. So the pains came and at about 6:45 I got Fanny and Mom and Dad and I went to the hospital. Fanny was expecting Tennille so she was to return. They got me all fixed and said the baby should be here about 12. About 10:30 the pains got a bit rough so I got some shot in the leg. That made me groggy and I barely remember seeing Tennille. About 11:30 they gave me the caudal and I immediately became numb from the waist down and sure enough, Conjon liked it that way so much he just stopped. I'm glad you weren't here for I'm afraid I wasn't nearly as brave as I planned to be. So they let the caudal wear off and I proceeded

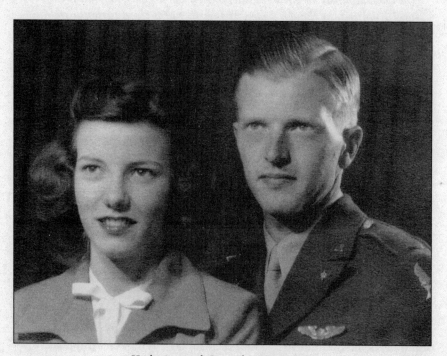

Katherine and Conrad J. Netting III

to urge him along the old-fashioned way. And it hurt! No kidding. Finally, it looked as though Conjon was going to be difficult so they gave me more caudal about 5. They waited for that to take effect good and then we went into the delivery room. As it is air conditioned, they had to wrap me in blankets. Major Seivers cussed and hollered and had to use emergency instruments. I asked him if the baby would be scarred. He nearly fainted. I got to hold him this morning, and he is the spitting image of you. If only I knew you were safe. How happy I would be. Thank you my darling for your son. I love you.

For almost seven months, Katherine waited for any word, any information whatsoever about her husband—whether he had been captured, critically injured, or killed, and, if so, whether or not his body had been recovered. The answer finally came on January 7, 1945, and one week later, Katherine wrote the following.

Dearest Conrad

Well, this shall probably be the last time I shall ever write these beloved words—Dearest Conrad—except perhaps to your son. Yes, I went to Corpus on the 7th and the next day Frances had word to call Charlotte. When she came out of the drug store, I could see she was upset. I immediately thought her father was worse. I was driving and I didn't say anything for a block or two. Then I asked if she wanted to stop for some bread. Then she sort of dropped her head and I reached over and patted her shoulder. She said, "but it's not about me." And I knew at once what it was. I drove on for a block or two—shocked and stunned and overcome—then I had a desire to be home with your son. I turned a corner and pulled over to the side and just caved in for a moment. It wasn't too long, darling, for uppermost in my mind was—and always will be—Conrad can see me now and I must make him proud of me. Fanny suggested I wait and talk to Tennille and so I stayed on and came home with them Saturday.

I feel so strange. I believe all the anguish—wild anguish—was spent when I first knew you were missing and might never return. Now I feel sad—empty—immeasurably lonely—and sick at the waste of so marvelous a life, the waste of both our lives together. I know you are dead. First the wire—then the letter—now a condolence card from General Marshall, Chief of Staff—each throws another spadefull on your grave. But above all, I am resigned. I haven't "cried" it out. I've shed tears, but not in abundance. And, although it is not what I prayed, dreamed, hoped for, I am making plans for my life—our lives without you.

I have talked to Charlotte regarding a 1/2 day job in her adv. agency. I will go to work as soon as she will take me on. I won't make much, but it will be something. But above all, I will be laying a firm foundation for a career. I could return to the govt but I want to take from my work more than money alone. I want security, a sense of accomplishment, a future, an interesting job, a pleasant one. As I learn, I can build something on my own hard work and I will. For I want Conrad to be proud of me and through me, of you. I also want him to have everything I can buy for him. I want to fill your shoes as I know you would have, if God had heard and answered my prayer that if one of us had to die, it would be me. So I shall work hard and long for our son, and I'll make him proud of all he has received from you. Before too long, I hope to put aside all your insurance and my pension and I will. On Tennille's advice, I will invest all the lump sum I receive over a $1,000 back in war bonds. I am going to write concerning that Socony Vacuum Policy, also. You left your family extremely well provided considering you were only 26 years and 3 days old.

I intend to see Sam in a week about a memorial service. Also, I will give something to the church in memory of the finest husband a girl ever had.

I intend to see about insurance on my own life for Conrad.

Darling, you know, I'm sure, how deeply I love you. I say love because I still do. I haven't stopped and I won't. Always, I love you as much as I did July 17, 1943, and all the days before and all the days since. I just can't stop. But, can you know the need I feel to marry again? When I look forward to emptiness after such happiness, I can't bear it. I hope God will let me be happy, not wildly, consumingly happy as I was with you, for I know I was amongst the chosen for having had you for a while. But quietly happy, the physical side is not so important, tho I will miss you so much—your hands, your kiss, your body. It is having no one interested in my life to the least detail that I miss tremendously. I want companionship—I don't want to live out my life—God knows, how beastly long I shall live—all alone for I'm afraid lest I be twisted, abnormally interested in Conrad or my work. I want a normal life, with a husband who knows my life was you. I believe if I ever should remarry, it will be long from now and to some older man who, too, has already known the greatest love. For me to marry a young boy—say Bob or Carl or anyone of that type—would be selfish. I believe all men are entitled to having a love such as I gave you. And I cannot give such love twice.

Well, my darling, from October 17, 1942 to June 10, 1944 or to January 8, 1945, really is a terrible, pathetically short time. Yet the love you gave me, the happiness, the joy, the magnificent son—could be copied in no one in a full lifetime. My dear, I am saying goodbye to you now—until we meet again. Please help me through the hard years to come, help me to do my best for your son and mine, help me keep alive your spirit by never being bitter. I need your help so—you may be dead to others, but you will live forever in my heart. I hate to stop writing for this is my last letter to you. O, my darling, how I love you.

Forever,

Your ~~wife~~

widow

In an extraordinary postscript to the story, fifty-eight years after his father was shot down over France, Conrad J. Netting IV received an envelope in the mail with a French postmark. "Dear Sir," a woman named Sylvie Grandin wrote, "My father is looking for more information about a brave soldier called Conrad J. Netting, killed in action, during the second world war in Normandy and buried in France." Grandin was trying to find anyone related to Lieutenant Netting because her grandfather had witnessed the crash and raced to the site in hopes of aiding the fallen pilot. Netting was dead when he arrived, so the grandfather, who happened to be a cabinetmaker, made the casket that was used to bury him. He then tended to Netting's resting place until he himself passed away. His son (Sylvie Grandin's father) was also profoundly affected by Netting's death and proposed that a memorial be created in his honor in Saint Michel des Andaines, the town nearest to where his plane had crashed. On June 8, 2002, Lieutenant Netting's son, Conrad IV, and his family (including Conrad V), stood with the Grandins in Saint Michel and unveiled the plaque dedicated to the American pilot whose sacrifice had touched the lives of so many people.

—∞—

Major Jim Colman Expresses His Love and Gratitude to His Fiancée, Mary Parkman, for Waiting for Him During His Three Long Years as a POW

For soldiers, airmen, sailors, and Marines who have been confined as POWs and are then suddenly freed, the feeling, of course, is one of sheer exuberance. "Dearest Mom and Dad: This is the second happiest moment of my life, at last a chance to write home," gushed Jim Norton on April 15, 1945, to his parents back in St. Paul, Minnesota. "The happiest moment came a few days ago when the greatest army in the world liberated me." Norton, a twenty-year-old private first class who had been taken prisoner during the Battle of the Bulge, went on to describe the moment he was rescued. (A "2nd Looie" is a second lieutenant, the lowest-ranking officer in the military.)

> *I've received nothing but the greatest of kindness from every one, and I never could put it in words what it feels like to be treated as a human being again. I am so happy I don't know whether to laugh or cry. Today we had the meal I've been dreaming about for 4 months—steak and french fries, and how—how I've been eating. I'll never forget as long as I live when I saw that first Yank. I always said I'd kiss the first one I saw who liberated us, even if it were a 2nd Looie, and you guessed it, he was. He was more surprised than I, and I imagine it's the first time in history an officer has ever been kissed by an enlisted man.*

For former POWs about to be united once again with a wife or fiancée, the knowledge that their sweetheart had waited faithfully for them, sometimes for years on end, only added to their sense of joy. It was the very prospect of these reunions that sustained many long-term POWs through a physical and emotional gauntlet it seems impossible to believe any person could survive. Homer James Colman, an American soldier from Salt Lake City, Utah, serving with the Fifty-seventh Filipino Scout Infantry Regiment, spent almost three years as a POW after US troops surrendered the Philippines to the Japanese in May 1942. After five months of brutal combat, Colman and ten thousand other Allied prisoners were forced on the infamous Bataan Death March—a sixty-five mile walk in the tropical heat without food, water, or medicine that proved fatal for many of the already sick and famished soldiers. Before he had embarked for the Pacific in May 1941, Colman became engaged to a young woman from Columbus, Georgia, named Mary Parkman. They would not see each other again until the spring of 1945. Safely back in the United States and recuperating at the Walter Reed Army Medical Hospital in Washington, DC (Colman had lost nearly half his body weight as a POW), he sent his fiancée the following letter reaffirming his love and devotion to her.

April 17

My darling Mary:

I'm going to take a day or so to finish this letter to you. It probably will be the last letter I'll ever write to Mary Parkman—although she will never cease to be my sweetheart, the next time I write, I'll address it to Mary Colman, my wife. Goodbye, Mary Parkman. You were the truest, sweetest girl who ever waited out the long, lonely, uncertain hours and weeks and years for a soldier who left you trying to hold back her tears— one of the thousands of brave women who have done the same thing in these last four, terrible years and who, unless the people of the world change their nature overnight, will continue to send their men off to fight against one another.

But I was lucky and I had your prayers to bring me back to you.

I could spend the remainder of my life telling you how much you meant to me during those long nights of waiting, and still I'd never be able to give you the entire picture. The nights and days that I had only you to live for and you to come back to. And the first moment when I realized in San Francisco that I could actually talk to you. And then the realization that I'd see you soon, not in a year or two years, but in a few short weeks I'd be able to hold you in my arms and kiss you and smell your hair and all the things that are you would be there—Those realizations that before had been my most pleasant dreams now are realities.

And my heart is filled with thankfulness, not for my being back alone, but for the fact that when I did return, I found you waiting. For that alone repays me a thousandfold for anything I might have given.

For all my heart and all my love is yours, has been and shall continue to be for as long as we both may live. God grant me the power and strength to make you happy.

And if I am able to bring you the peace and happiness that I want you to have, then I, too, will be happy, for we will no longer be just Mary Parkman and Jim Colman—two separate people. For you will be me, and I will be you, and there will be only one where two existed before.

In this, then, my last letter to my fiancé, as it will also be in my first and every letter to my wife, look and find all of the love that is there for you. And perhaps you may see somewhere the life together that will be yours and mine and our children's. Life that will be filled with tenderness and understanding and love, and that particular bit of happiness that we both have fought for so long to possess.

Goodnight, my sweetheart.

Forever, your
Jim

One week later, the two were married in the Walter Reed chapel.

—∞—

—————— **Featured Series** ——————

"Letters to Mom"

**After Receiving an Ominous Letter from Her Son's
Commanding Officer, Eula Owen Replies Immediately, Pleading
for Information as to Whether Her Son Is Dead or Alive
&
Thakur Singh, a Sikh Soldier Fighting in World War I,
Assures His Anxious Mother That He Will Return to Her
&
Private First Class William Smith Tells His Mother That,
with Four Sons in the War, She Is the "Best Soldier"
and Most Courageous Person He Knows
&
Lieutenant Junior Grade Joseph Ball Crallé II
Writes an Emotional Letter to His Mom on Mother's Day 1944—
the Year After Her Death
&
An Italian Soldier Named Fiorigi A. Contro Describes for His Mother
in Graphic Detail His Terrifying Escape from El Alamein
&
A Guilt-Stricken Iraqi Soldier,
Later Killed During Operation Desert Storm,
Confesses to His Mother That He Believes He Is Destined
for Hell**

The two-paragraph letter by Lieutenant E.C. Victorsen, informing Mrs. Eula Owen on April 22, 1944, that her son had earned a commendation for valor, was written with only the best intentions at heart. "I, as Commanding Officer of the Guard Detachment," the letter stated, "together with each and every man belonging to it wish to convey our deepest appreciation for that honor instilled in it by such action as taken by your son." The result could hardly have been more calamitous.

Abilene, Texas
May 1st, 1944

My dear Lt. Victorsen:
    Just a few hours ago I received your most gratifying letter concerning the commendations accorded my fine old boy—Richard Owen.
    My heart bursts with the utmost pride I have in him—<u>pride,</u> because

he has always stood for the best things, and <u>pride,</u> because he is capable and willing to do his duty in a fitting manner.

I am at a perfect loss, though, in knowing what happened. I have not heard from him since a letter written 3/12/44 and received on 3/19/44. He isn't usually negligent in writing, but I was growing quite uneasy about not hearing from him when your letter came, and now I am frantic. Naturally, I have conceived the idea that he was in some manner injured and unable to write. You see, Lt. he is all I have. He is my life; my heart; my <u>all</u>. All my people have been taken from me except him and my mother, who will soon be 93 years and is failing fast. I have not told her of this yet, until I can know definitely his safety.

Is it asking too much of you to let me know if he is safe and sound, also the details of his action. I can stand to know bare facts, but I cannot stand <u>silence</u> and <u>suspense.</u> Please, oh, please, Lt. let me hear from my boy at once.

I shall always treasure your letter. I expect to add below your message, an outline of the episode which sponsored it, frame it and hang it over the mantle. It came from your heart, your expressions held just the shade of meaning to show you were sincere in your appreciation and from the bottom of my heart, I thank you.

But <u>please,</u> oh <u>please</u>, let me know about my boy. I am enclosing a $1.00—will you please send a form cablegram. If he is alright mark No. 71. If he is ill, mark No. 82. If he was injured mark No. 79, but for God's sake let me hear of him.

With the deepest appreciation
Sincerely
Mrs. Eula Owen

In fact, Robert Owen was alive and well, and Lieutenant Victorsen would later express his regret for putting Owen's mother into such a state of alarm. Troops on the front lines are generally sensitive to the anxiety their own parents are experiencing and try to reassure them that they are not in danger—even if they are— and that there is no reason for concern. A Sikh soldier named Thakur Singh (whose fate is not known) sent the following message to his mother in Punjab, India, on June 7, 1916, while fighting with the British against German forces in Europe. ("Sirdar" is another term for an Indian officer; "ghi" is a variation of "ghee," a form of clarified butter; and "Khalsa" is the community of Sikh warriors into which males are initiated at puberty.)

Mother, the news is that once only in five months I have not received a letter from you. My thoughts are always with you.

Mother, put your ear down and listen to me, do not fret and I will soon be with you again. Put your trust in God, and imagine that I have merely gone to Lyallpur, think that I have been delayed there by the Sirdar or that I am not yet ready to return home. Mother, think of me always as though I were sitting near by, just as I imagine you always as being beside me.

Be of good cheer Mother, because there is nothing that I have done which is hidden from you. I tell you truly Mother, I will salute you again. Do not grieve, for I tell you confidently, that I shall bow before you again in salutation. I will come in the dead of night and knock at your door, and I will call loudly so that you may wake and come and open the door to me. With great delight you will open the door and fold me to your breast in a loving embrace. I will then sit beside you and narrate all that has happened to me of good and evil. Then, having rested the night in comfort, I will go out after daylight has come. Those brethren of the Khalsa whom I meet, I will salute. Returning home, I will eat my bread with pleasure and happiness. You, mother, will say to me "Shall I give you some ghi?" I will shake my head in refusal and say "Mother, I do not want any." You will press me to have some, and I will gently push my plate towards you. You will fill the plate with ghi, and I shall eat it with much delight. Believe Mother that this homecoming will take place, just as I have described it. I see you constantly before me. It seems to me as if it were but yesterday that I bent to your feet in salutation, while you placed your hand lovingly on my head. I am indeed a very fortunate man to see you again so, in imagination.

Some mothers have not one, but two, or even several, boys to worry about. Allie Smith had four; Floyd and Charles in the Marines, Fred in the Air Force, and William in the Army, all fighting overseas during World War II. Three of them would come home. On January 4, 1945, William was killed during Hitler's last major offensive of the war, the Battle of the Bulge, which came just months before Germany ultimately surrendered. Less than four weeks before he died, William sent a letter to his mother simply to express his gratitude for her strength and love over the years.

December 5, 1944

Dear Mother,

I hope this will find everyone well.

I wrote to you on the third of December but as I am thinking so much about home to-night, I might as well write again. I would like to be there very much. I miss everything that goes along when I am there.

Such as; talking about the old days, the good cooking, and all the love and little things that goes with a home. I miss all that very much.

I know you miss having all your children around too. Maybe it won't be long until we can all be together again. We can only keep praying for that.

I read in the papers about good soldiers but seldom read about the best soldiers. Those that are Mothers and Fathers of sons in the service. For my part, you are the best soldier I know. You fight a bigger problem than we do. You fight it with better courage too. With that courage in mind I will be able to fight my battles a lot easier.

I hope you won't worry too much about me. I am getting along just fine. I must close before I get too homesick.

Tell everyone Hello for me.

Love & best wishes,
Your Son,
William

Either of their own volition or at the urging of their commanding officers, American servicemembers overseas customarily put pen to paper and send a special message home to mom on Mother's Day. (The special day itself was promoted tirelessly by Ann Maria Jarvis, who established Mother's Day Work Clubs in the late 1800s to foster unity between grieving Northern and Southern women who had lost their sons in the Civil War.) What is unusual about the letter that Lieutenant junior grade Joseph Ball Crallé II, a twenty-seven-year-old Virginian serving in the Solomon Islands, wrote on Mother's Day in 1944 is that his mother had passed away the year before. The pain of her death was still raw, and he felt compelled to write the following:

My darling Mother,

Wherever you are, I have a feeling you are watching me on this day, the first Mother's Day I can ever remember us being apart.

And I want to tell you on this, your day, that I stand as I am a tribute to your moulding. You guided me through many crises, you steered me clean of many pitfalls, you formed my habits and my personality. My very life is a monument to your untiring efforts, your never-ending thoughtfulness, your tender love.

I shall always be thankful that you were spared the agony and uncertainty of this period, of weeks without news of my safety and whereabouts.

But today I want you to know that I face the future with confidence and without fear, knowing that we have a job to do, that our cause is just, and that we shall be victorious.

And so I send my love, wherever you are, and know that we shall meet again somewhere, someday!

Your devoted son
Joe

Fathers are often the ones in whom troops are most likely to confide about the graphic violence of war or the severity of their own situation, and they will often do so with the admonition, "Don't tell Mom." But whether they are afraid to show weakness to their fathers or have reverted to an almost childlike state of vulnerability, in times of great emotional distress, combatants—usually when they are out of harm's way—pour out their feelings on paper and appeal to their mothers for comfort and solace. (Fatally wounded soldiers on the field of battle are known to scream out for their mothers as they slip in and out of consciousness. It is a sound many veterans recall as one of their most searing auditory memories of warfare.) During World War II, an Italian soldier named Fiorigi A. Contro escaped the crushing defeat of German and Italian troops at El Alamein, Egypt, by General Bernard Montgomery's British Eighth Army. Of the almost seventy thousand casualties overall at the pivotal 1942 battle, more than fifty thousand were Germans and Italians, and Contro came within inches of being one of them. After he was far removed from danger, he wrote the following to his mother describing the harrowing retreat.

To my mother,

You do not know how many difficulties I have encountered in my life; I won't tell you the ones you don't know, so as not to make you any sadder, but one memory among many remains stronger than the others.

It was a gloomy April evening, Palm Sunday. After a sudden, brief alarm caused by a group of approaching enemy fighter planes, we tried to take off from a makeshift airport. We made it out but ten minutes later, a whole squadron of Junkers came flying in formation just above the surface of the water to prevent being detected by radar. We were attacked head-on by the planes, which were more nimble and better armed than we were, and in an instant we were completely overwhelmed and began to drop helplessly into the gulf one by one.

I felt bullets graze my back four times. Our plane was struck several times: in the engine, now on fire, in the nose, and in the tail.

A soldier in front of me became my shield and I got drenched in his blood. The pilot who gave the orders to jump had his intestines hanging out of his body.

The plane with its eighteen dead and wounded men on board was now on fire and losing altitude, and the only choice we had was to jump out as we had no parachute, just a life-jacket.

I was the first to get to the hatch and while I was hesitating about what to do I felt a strong push against my back, which knocked me out into the air and I fell into the water near Cape Bon.

I was terrified by the enormous danger I faced and still under the fire of machine-guns, I desperately struggled to reach the shore, which didn't seem too far away.

But when I got the water out of my mouth and caught my breath, I called out two names: "God!" and "Mamma!" I had never before been in such a situation.

By now I was exhausted and had no strength left. At that moment another plane was struck and crashed nose down with a deafening hiss right near me. . . . I closed my eyes and thought I was going to die. I gave myself up to whatever God had destined for me.

But it wasn't my time yet, and the fiery mass fell so close to me that the giant surge of the wave pushed me to land like a cork. I sought shelter in a sort of cave, and stayed there nearly dead and exhausted, listening to the horrible sound of the never-ending machine-gun fire from the airplanes.

I was found by the coast guard in very bad physical condition. Later I came to and woke up as though from a nightmare with my eyes full of tears. I described my long odyssey to the curious bystanders standing in a circle around me, who were stunned by what had happened.

But I really just wanted to be left alone so that I could replay in my mind a memory in which you, my dear, good mother, were the main figure.

You remember when I was little there was that big tank behind the country house, which we used for watering the neighborhood cattle? I was still in diapers, it was a beautiful spring day, and I went up to the tank to pick some little yellow flowers. I got close and stretched all the way out . . . and lost my balance and fell into the water. I screamed and you came running, my watchful and kind mother, and you carried me into the house and dried me off by the fire. You changed my little outfit and promised that you would stay close.

But your words and my promises were useless, because as soon as you turned around I ran out to the tank and fell in again. And you came running again and, gently, explained to me why I needed to be more careful and reproached me a little, and then told me to watch the chickens. One of them ran towards the tank, and I saw those little flowers that I had found so attractive, so, holding on to a reed,

I stretched out my hand, but the reed broke, and I fell in the water again.

You collected me again with so much patience, and decided to carry me to bed where I fell into a deep sleep, dreaming of those flowers.

When I woke up, my little bed was heaped with yellow flowers; who had gone to pick them? "Daddy," you said.

Life takes such strange turns.

When I woke up in that unknown land after falling into the sea, I did not have the sweet comfort of flowers, only sad reality.

When I was a little boy I had no fear, and when I was hesitating in the fuselage hatch, when only a push from a friend gave me the courage to confront the danger, I couldn't count on your help because you weren't physically there to reassure me. But I know it was your hand that saved me from the wreckage. Your prayers every day and your faithful spiritual presence are always with me, reaching out to me wherever I am. Souls communicate! The force of a mother's care extends very, very far.

So this memory, which I will never forget, is for you. To you I give all my affection and love, and all my care, above everything else.

Fiorigi A. Contro

At Capua, near Naples 7 May 1943

It is not known what the Iraqi soldier did to prompt such an outpouring of shame in the following letter-poem to his mother (though considering the atrocities committed against Kuwaitis in 1990 and 1991, there are numerous possibilities), but he clearly felt the need to confess that he had betrayed his faith and would be punished for it. His letter, however, would never be sent; it was found on his body during Operation Desert Storm, the American-led multinational campaign to liberate Kuwait from Iraqi forces. (The last two quotations are from the Holy Qur'an. There is no signature to the letter, and, obviously written in a state of great mental turmoil, it is incoherent in parts.)

Mother
What a lovely name!
Mother
How enchanting to hear your beautiful, calm voice. Will I hear your voice calling me once more?
Mother
I've never forgotten your face and your voice calls me each day in my sleep.
Mother

When am I to see your smiling face? Have mercy on me.
Mother
How I long to be embraced to your tender chest.
Mother
How much have you suffered and are still suffering for ten years.
Oh, Mother Mother Mother
Tell me about our home. How are my brothers? My longing and craving are increasing. Are they safe? Or have they gone to no return? to the day of my longing?
Oh, Mother
Please tell me because I know you are crying every now and then.
Mother
Please tell me. I hear crying, unable to sleep, longing so much for you.
Mother
Please tell me mother
Please pray to God to protect them.
I don't want him to protect me.
It satisfies me if he kept them safe for me.
Mother
Please have mercy on me. I know there is nothing you can do. Had it been in your hands you would have taken me out of hell.
Mother
Please ask God the Gracious, the Merciful to protect them. I don't want Him to protect me.
Mother
How is my poor father? I know he was burdened since the time we were born until this shameful black day. Any father would close a window that allows the wind to enter.
Mother
Tell me, is my father still waiting for me on the street corner, calling my name?
Give my regards to them until I see you once again, and if I don't, then it's sure I'll be in Hell. You will never see me. Our roads are different and God has no mercy on arrogant people.
If you don't see me, then this is God's promise Who has mercy on those who pray one day for them, another for me and to later on.
Mother
By God don't ask Him to have mercy on me. Don't ask Him to forgive my sins, because by doing that you'd hurt me. My God, since the day I was born until today, You denied me mercy and enrichment!
Mother

By God have mercy on me.

"In the Name of God, Most Gracious, Most Merciful. The sun and moon follow courses exactly computed . . . Then which of the favors of your Lord will you deny?" God, Most High, has spoken the Truth.

In the Name of God, Most Gracious. Most Merciful. "They don't forbid what God and His Apostle forbid."

Corporal Waverly B. Woodson Jr. Sends a Letter to His Father to Say "Thank You" for Everything He Has Given Him in Life

Mothers are not alone, of course, in receiving letters of admiration. Young servicemen and -women who have matured because of the discipline and sense of responsibility they have acquired from their military training often develop a greater appreciation for both their parents and the hitherto unrecognized sacrifices they have made for their children. An army medic corporal who went in with the first wave of the D-Day assault on June 6, 1944, twenty-one-year-old Waverly B. Woodson Jr. treated hundreds of men and saved numerous lives despite being shot himself. He would earn the Bronze Star for his actions under fire. Almost a year before his foray into battle, Woodson wrote the following letter articulating the values—which would later serve him well—his father had instilled in him growing up in Philadelphia.

June 21–1943

Dear Dad:

Sunday was Father's Day and by the time you get this letter, the day itself will have come and gone. But the day isn't important, Dad, when there are so many things I want too thank you for—the little things and the big things you have done for me.

I remember when you used too give me a dime or more too go to the movies. At the time I appreciated the sum but now that I look back on the past, I am even more appreciative of the things you have done for me.

I remember the time I wanted a bicycle and asked you too buy me one, for at the time there wasn't anything I wanted more than that. You told me too save up a certain amount and then you would get me it. After having worked and saved that amount, you added your money and obtained the bicycle. I really appreciated it as I have always appreciated everything you got for me.

I remember my first year at college, when you practically paid all the expenses, hoping that I would be able to receive a better education than you have. You always wanted too see that Lloyd and me, had more advantages than most fellows, so that we could start where you left off.

For all these things and many more, which you have done for me, I am deeply appreciative. For sometimes it was a sacrafice too do some things for me.

And I know, Dad that while we're here, you and all the other fathers are behind us. I know it wasn't easy too give up one son or possibly two, too the U.S. Army, but we are here too finish a job which was not done before so that we can make a world safe for future generations.

I don't think I've ever known you Dad, the way I do today. I never understood you as I do now. I thank you, Dad, for what you have been.

Tell Mom I said "Hello" and give her a big hug for me. Tell her I will write soon. But this is for you on Father's Day.

Love
Your son
Wave

—⁊⁊—

Corporal Waverly B. Woodson Jr.

Corporal William D. Taylor Asks His Newborn Daughter, Edith Ann, to Love Her Mom as Much as Possible While He Is Away— and To Be Especially Good to Her If He Does Not Come Back
&
Japanese Officer Yanagida Eiichi Confides to His Wife That He Becomes Distraught When He Thinks of the Innocent Children Who Might Lose Their Fathers Under His Command
&
Heather Ashline, the Wife of a US Soldier Fighting in Afghanistan, Tells Her Husband That Their Two Young Boys Miss Him Terribly and Are Always Thinking of Him

For military parents serving abroad for extended periods, the separation from their children becomes all the more difficult when they cannot be there for special family moments and their child's significant "firsts"—first steps, words, birthdays, etc. To nurture, as best they can, a presence in their children's lives, those far from home regularly send messages offering their affection, encouragement, and words of advice, even if their children are too young to understand or fully appreciate them. Corporal William D. Taylor, fighting in Europe during World War II, wrote frequently to his newborn daughter, Edith Ann, to express his love for her and to impart words of fatherly wisdom, all with the realization that any one of his letters could be his last. Taylor had never held or even seen his daughter, however; he was overseas when she was born. Edith Ann was still an infant when her father sent the following on January 14, 1944:

My darling daughter,

This letter is coming many miles away from you dear, but even tho miles do separate us I'm always thinking about you as I do your Mother. Now, your to young to understand this, but someday you'll be able to read it and understand what I mean. Your Dad was called away dear to do a job and which at present is being done very well. When I left home I left a million dreams behind me. The most important your mother and secondly even tho at the time you wasn't born yet, I left you. Its not easy for a fellow to leave things like that behind, take your father's word for it. What I'm trying to say is right now and forever your Mother is the swellest Mom alive. Chances are you may never see your Pop, so here's what I ask. Never leave your Mother. Always respect her and love her, she was made for it dear. I love Mom more than anyone or anything this world can offer. When I do come back your Mom, you, and myself are going away where we can be by ourselves. All the happy hours Mom and I use to spend will now be enjoyed by you also. For this reason alone your Mom and I fought. I'll sign off now dear, and before I do ask Mom to set this letter aside for you. Be a good girl and give my love to Mom.   Love and kisses,

Daddy

William Taylor returned home to Jersey City, New Jersey, after nearly four years abroad, but he would never speak of his war experiences and he kept his letters hidden. Edith Ann did not read the letter her father wrote to her in January 1944 until after his death in 1999 at the age of seventy-six. (Edith Ann was fifty-five years old at the time.) For many troops away from their families, the mere sight of other children is enough to induce a powerful surge of emotions. "Tasya, if only you knew how overjoyed I am when I see children the same age as Maya," wrote a Russian lieutenant named Sergei Galkin to his wife before he died in World War II.

> *I think about how I have a daughter just like them who hasn't seen her papa for 10 months already, and he hasn't see her. The children in liberated areas jump into the arms of the fathers who have liberated them from Hitler's cannibals. I guess Maya does the same—jumps into the arms of other soldiers and wonders where her papa is. That's why I write about Maya so much. My soul lights up when I meet a child here and he hangs from my neck asking where is our papa and when is he coming home.*

For a Japanese lieutenant who was also fighting in World War II, the responsibility he bore for the lives of his men, and the recognition that each death would inevitably traumatize a young son or daughter, weighed heavily on him. Thirty-three years old at the time, Yanagida Eiichi sent the following message, which is not dated and does not have a salutation, to his wife before he and his men embarked. (Eiichi himself was later killed in battle.)

Thank you for writing so often, and forgive me for not responding sooner. Mobilization and organization have kept me busy every day, from 5:00 in the morning until midnight.

Yesterday, most of the work was completed. Today was visiting day, and confusion reigned. Some of the soldiers were holding babies in their arms. Others were leading small children by the hand as they headed out, perhaps for a brief excursion. Will my men be separated from their families for only a short time, or forever? When I see the innocent children, I get a lump in my throat. The knowledge that I am responsible for the fates of several dozen subordinates weighs heavily on my shoulders.

Is Kyoko feeling any better? I may be asking the impossible, but please do all you can to ensure that her illness is cured promptly, no matter how much it costs. I worry about her all the time. Whatever the case, please take good care of her until I return.

Take care of yourself, too, and don't ruin your health by working too hard. Please take care of Kyoko.

Also, please write to my mother in the country once in a while (about twice a month). I've caused her a lot of worry. At least while I'm away, look after her on my behalf. Please be sure to take care of Kyoko.

Please convey my best wishes to your mother, brother and sister.

Spouses on the home front see firsthand the emotional impact the absence of a father or other family member has on the children, and they frequently emphasize to their loved ones how dearly they are missed. Elizabeth Barton, the wife of a Confederate soldier in the American Civil War, assured her husband that not a day went by that he was not in the family's hearts and prayers. "Willie says he won't kiss me but will kiss you when you come home," Barton wrote on September 10, 1862, referring to one of their two young sons. "I have kissed Harvey for you and he calls your name—Pap Pap a hundred times in a day." Just over a century later the wife of a South Vietnamese officer, who was serving with the Americans, wrote the following to her husband from Saigon to remind him that she and their children, Tram and Hao, were thinking of him always. (Her full name and parts of the letter have been cut for reasons of privacy. The letter was found in 2004 at an antiques store in what is now Ho Chi Minh City, and the officer's fate is unknown.)

> *My love, I miss you so much, I miss you so much my love . . . Tram speaks of you all day, making my soul feel lonelier. She misses you so much that she refuses to let anybody sit in your dinner chair and says, "Dad's chair is saved for him, so that when he returns he can sit there." If anyone made fun of her, she just replies "I'll tell my Dad, just you see." At night, she tosses and turns. Hao is no less than her, every evening he makes a fuss, asking to be taken out like Dad used to do for him. If I knew things were going to be so desolate without you, I would have never let you leave, even if your trip brings us many glories and benefits. . . . I had wanted not to write to you, I had wanted not to miss you, yet I still write and miss you. . . . Just a few lines to you, since I have not received my letters, so I know not what else to write. The children and I give you many kisses.*

In December 2001, Heather Ashline sent a remarkably similar letter to her husband, Jason, a private first class with the 10th Mountain Division fighting in the mountains of Afghanistan against al-Qaeda and Taliban forces. Their eldest son, Jason II, was two-and-a-half, and their youngest, Alec, was only three months old.

Hey Babe,

Jason is constantly thinking about you. He talks to you on the phone (pretending) and makes your mother and I do it too, he plays with you (pretend again) and he will ask about you. When we went home, he asked if we were going to go pick you up. When I said no, he said he wanted to. I don't think there's a minute when he isn't thinking about you. He's even trying to teach Alec to say "Dada." It's a little early, but we still try.

Tonight, Alec was staring at a picture of you on your mother's fridge. He was just fixated on it. Don't you worry about him knowing you, he'll remember. Now, let's talk about me. I love you, and nothing will ever change that. You have brought so much happiness into my life, and I'm not just talking about the two beautiful boys you gave me. I know in the past we've had some hard times, and there were moments when we almost let each other go, but our love was still there holding us together. That will stand true while we're apart and always. When we got married, I vowed to love you forever, and I plan to. We still have plenty of time to make our life together; we just have to wait a little while. Everyday I think about you coming home and how much I want to be able to hold you, touch you, see you come through the door after work. I miss cooking you your meals, dragging you out of bed in the morning, and kissing you goodnight at the end of every day. I need you in my life. Without you I would be lost, I wouldn't know how to carry on. If I ever lost you for any reason, my world would shatter. I'm going to go now; I'm exhausted. I love you.

Love Always,
Heather

During a major clash with enemy combatants, Private First Class Jason Ashline was shot in the chest. Fortunately, his Kevlar vest prevented him from being killed, and he returned to the States alive and well.

—⚏—

Lawrence Hoppner, an Australian Private Fighting in Vietnam, Exchanges a Series of Letters with His Sweetheart, Lorraine Woodward, Who Is Anxiously Awaiting His Return to Melbourne

Over a twelve-year period beginning in 1961, when President John F. Kennedy ordered two thousand military advisors to the region, the United States sent approximately three million troops to fight against North Vietnamese and Viet Cong forces in Southeast Asia. The Americans did not go it alone, however. Along with the native South Vietnamese and Montagnards (mountain people from the Central Highlands), hundreds of thousands of soldiers from South Korea, Thailand, the Philippines, New Zealand, and several other countries also participated in the war. (Thousands of Canadians joined up with US military units, although Canada itself was not an official ally. Some of the troops joked that they were filling in for the Americans who went to Canada to escape the draft.) More than fifty thousand Australian soldiers served as well, and one out of every hundred of them died. The conflict remains the longest war, to date, in Australia's history. In February 1966, a twenty-year-old private named Lawrence (nicknamed "Laurie" and then later "Hoppy") Howard Hoppner from the state of Victoria was called up for national service. While on leave during recruitment training, Laurie began dating a nineteen-year-old girl named Lorraine Woodward whom he had met in a café in Melbourne. (Actually, Laurie had struck up a conversation with both Lorraine and a friend of hers named Anne, and he decided to pursue Anne first. While literally in the process of writing her a letter, he received a birthday card from Lorraine and spontaneously decided to cross out Anne's name and scribble in Lorraine's instead. The relationship blossomed from there.) Laurie and Lorraine wrote regularly to each other after he left for Vietnam in April 1967 as a forward scout with the 7th Battalion, Royal Australian Regiment, A Company, and their correspondence is unique in that many of her letters ultimately survived the war. Frontline troops are rarely able to save even their most cherished letters from home, but Lorraine's letters endured despite the humidity and filth of jungle combat. A May 8, 1967, letter by Laurie offered a vivid reminder of how treacherous the conditions truly were.

Hi love. Well I have just come back from a 7 day exercise & have finaly realized just how dirty war can be. Our company came back all in one piece but don't know about the others. We killed 3 VC & wounded several others. . . . Our first night we were in an ambush on the edge of a river & we slept in the middle of a swamp. There were millions of mosquitoes & on top of that it poured rain all night. We walked through swamp for 5 days & were we cheesed off; we were covered in mud & wet through the whole time still not to worry. One thing is for sure we are far superior than they & as well we have them on the run. Any how darling never worry as we are never in any real danger as we have support of artillery & fighters which are available ~~wh~~ within a couple of minutes. . . .

Lorraine took him to task for the comments about his safety. *"You say not to worry,"* she wrote incredulously. *"<u>Not to worry!</u> You have to be kidding. I worry all the time, whether I know you are on an Op[eration] or not."* Her anxiety was growing with every report on the radio and television or mention in the news-papers about Aussie troops in Vietnam. On July 14, Lorraine sent the following. (Her expression *"going to the pack"* is another way of saying *"going crazy."*)

My dearest darling,

Hi darling. Have just read in tonight's herald about 2RAR 7RAR & the Yanks are all out on the biggest operation the Australians have been on yet. According to the paper it states you have been out 5 days.

I was beginning to worry why I haven't heard from you for so very long (over a week). I was starting to think that perhaps you were still in

Private Lawrence Hoppner

Saigon on leave and wouldn't hear from you again, or perhaps you had found yourself a nice little Viet. girl and had gone off. Terrible thoughts of mine don't you think?

Nothing much has happened around this place. All very boring really.

Tomorrow night, Sue & I are going to a Cabaret with Bluey & Jack for the Mordialloc Football Club. I suppose it should be quite good. Quite a lot of grog, probably too much. As for the rest of the weekend I probably won't be doing anything or going anywhere, so actually I will be having a very quiet weekend, and I will be able to lay around & dream & think of you.

I had a dream last night. It was about when you came home. It was really a beautiful dream. I can remember you kissing me for the first time since you went away & was I in heaven. The trouble was that the dream ended with a bump. Mum woke me up to tell me it was time to get up for work. I'm always having dreams like this. Hardly a night goes by without me dreaming something nice about you. It proves that I go to sleep thinking of you each night. And what better way than to go to sleep thinking of you.

I worried, really worried darling. More than ever, of you, if you're out on this big operation. I'm scared of how this rotten so called War will leave you. I don't mean physically, but more so mentally. If you get what I mean. You might come home too mature & think of things in different ways to what you thought of them when you left Me. You might change your mind about me too. If you haven't already.

Maybe, these are silly female thoughts of mine, but they are still worrying me. But more than ever, I worry about your health. I couldn't bear to have anything happen to you, so please darls look after & take care of yourself always. No matter where you are, please oh please, look after yourself.

I still haven't written to your Mum yet. She must think me terrible. I've really grown idle when I'm at home. I can't be bothered doing anything at all, except sit & watch T.V. I have two frocks cut out, waiting for me to finish, but I just can't be bothered. All I want to do is write letters to you and I'm even slipping there abit. I'm going to the pack I think. A real wreck. Not that I wasn't before you left, but more so now, & the trouble is I don't really care.

I've had a long black evening frock made up. It has black beading all down the front, a low neck line, a low back. I really think it's lovelly, as I simply adore black.

Have you received the fruit cake yet? If not you should have. It's been gone over three weeks now.

Well darling. This is it again. Please look after & take care of yourself always, as I will take care of myself. Only the good go young & I'm far from being good, as you know.

I love you so very, very, much & miss you just as much.

Will write again over the weekend. So until then, I close for now.

I remain,

Yours forever &
All my life
Lots, lots of love & kisses
Lorraine

xxxxxxxxxxxxxxxxxxxxxxxx

Laurie responded soon after to put to rest any doubts concerning his love for her, but the remainder of the letter would certainly do little to assuage her fears about the hazards he was facing.

My dearest darling

Hi love, received another wonderful letter from you last night so are taking the opportunity to answer it today. When you are not getting any mail from me darls you can be rest assured it is because I am out on an Opp, ambush or patrol I nor any one else is allowed to write to say what we are doing as sometime if mail gets into the wrong hands it can cause a lot of trouble.

That is why my letter may stop all of a sudden. So I have said before darls I will write every chance I get I hope your Cabaret at the Mordialloc football club went off O.K. Another thing darls I will would never go off as you say over any Viet girl or any one else for that matter you should know that darls

I quite often or actually nearly am always dreaming of you & me. of all the times we have spent together & of the times we will spend together

I was on that big opp & there were over 200 confirmed VC. killed but we didn't do very much it was a real easy opp. as for me coming home more mature well I am sure I will but it will be for the best that I can assure you darls.

Now for the not so good part. You say I might change my mind about you if I hadn't done so all ready.

I am very disappointed in you for saying that love You should know by now ~~the~~ that you are the only person for me now & forever. Those thoughts ~~nevr~~ never even enter my head I know they never will

I fully realize it is difficult me being over here & so much distance

between us but bear for a little while longer darls. its only another 18–20
weeks before I am with you again.

Well darling thats about all there is for now so until my next letter.

All my Love

All my life

Yours Forever

Laurie

xxxxxxxxxx

*On August 7, less than three weeks later, Lorraine received a phone call from
Laurie's mother. Laurie had been hit by shrapnel and shot during a firefight. He
had already been evacuated to a US military base hospital in Vung Tao, and
despite the severity of the wounds, the medical staff indicated that there was
every reason to believe he would pull through. Not knowing for certain his condition, Lorraine wrote him the following letter. (Jan and Bern are Laurie's sisters, and "Flinders St." refers to a railway station in central Melbourne.)*

My dearest, dearest, darling,

Your Mum rang early this morning to tell me the bad news, but alas, I
had left for work and so Mum had to talk to her and didn't catch
everything your Mum said. So Mum rang me at work at 9:00 am but I
hadn't arrived by then, & when I did get to work I got the message to
ring Mum back. I knew straight away that something was wrong either
with you or Dad. I ran her back straight away, and when she told me she
had a phone call from your Mum about you I just broke down.

Have just heard on the wireless that five boys were killed & later one
died of wounds and fifteen others wounded, but no names have been
~~real~~ released.

Oh darling, why did it have to be you to be one of the injured. Why. I
just can't understand it. How I hate the Army, the government & anyone
whom has anything to do with it.

I love you so very very much. I don't know what to do. I feel so sick
and upset, even worse since I've heard the news bulletin.

I met your Mum in Flinders St. and after we got her to "Traveller's"
Aid we rang up the Army where you can get news. He told me there was
no more news, but will ring either one of us, when he gets more news.
But I intend to ring him quite alot each day. He also said that there is
a good chance you will be sent home. I hope so, I really hope so. They
have got to send you home. We couldn't stand anymore of this. I want
to be with you darling & I cant be, when you are over there.

I feel so confused & sick, I can't think what to write. My stomachs all tied up in knots. I don't think your mother or I will be getting much sleep tonight, or any other night, until we know for sure, that you aren't too badly injured. Also Bern & Jan.

Please get well soon Darling, please. I want & need you so very, very much. Please get well. I love you so much & want you so much. They just have to send you home. They've got to. Just have to.

Get well please darling. I can't think straight anymore. You just have to get better. I've got to see you soon or I'll go mad.

The rotten, stinken' government & Army. I hate the bloody lot.

I am waiting for the news to come on the radio again to see if there's any more news. Also will watch the late news at 10 10 pm or Channel 2 as they might know more.

Sue has just rang me to see if I found out any more & she told me she has sent a telegram over to Ron to let him know that you were injured, so by the time you get this you should have had a visit from him. Have you seen Paul?

Don't worry about answering this letter darling as I know how things will be with you.

Please get well darling. I love you so very, very much & want you. I'll pray and hope with all my heart that you weren't ~~hert~~ hurt too badly and that they send you home soon.

I'll close for now, my love and only love. Hope to see you soon. My love, thoughts and wishes are with you always darling.

Please get well darls. I love you and am thinking of you always

All my love

All my life

I remain

Yours forever & ever

Lorraine

xxxxxxxxxxxxxxxxxxxxxxxxxx

PS   Please get well. I love and miss you very, very much.

A week after his injury, Laurie was finally able to attempt a letter home. (Lynn is Lorraine's younger sister.)

VIET NAM

13/8/67

My dearest darling Lorraine,

Hi darls this is my first ~~thr~~ try at writting. By now you will have received my tape I know it sounded shocking. I received your tape & cake yesterday I can not put into words how I felt when I heard you voice again

My right hand has been stitched up. There is 8 stitches on the back of my thumb is a bit of a mess I may not be able to bend it for some time a bullet went through a knuckle. I had 24 stitches on my right side of my head. 2 stitches in my cheek. 4–6 on my right shoulder.

I don't know what my back is like but I know there is quite a hole in it but don't worry darling I will be as fit as a fiddle in a few weeks.

They have just brought 3 letters & a card to me so will stop the letter & read them. Back again there was a card & letter from you & a letter from Lynn.

I will be very surprised if you can read this as it's hard to write. I was very lucky darling & have never come so close to death befor. We were pinned down for nearly 1 1/2 hrs it is one experience I will never forget.

Any how darling one good thing is I am coming home. I am due to leave here on the 28th of August so I should arrive back in Australia by the 1st Sept.

It will take up to a week before I am sent down to Melb. There I will stay until I am completely cured. You should see some of the Yanks here some are shot up real bad. There are about 50 patients in this ward I am the only Australian

The other Aussies are in different wards. 3 are being sent home today & rest of us are going in a fortnight, wont it be wonderful to be home again

We will be able to get engaged a lot earlier & married as soon as I get out of the Army. I saw Paul yesterday he was the one who brought your parcel in He is quite well & also looking forward to when he goes home.

Well my darling that about does it for now I doubt if you could read this. I love you darling & miss you so very much, hoping this finds you in the best of health & spirit.

> All My Love
> All My Life
> Your Forever & ever
> Laurie
> xxxxxxx
> xxxxxxx

Lawrence Hoppner was home in Australia within three weeks, and he and Lorraine married the following March. For his service in the military, Hoppner received one Australian Vietnam medal, one Vietnam Campaign medal, one Australian Active Service medal, and one Australian National Service medal.

—⁂—

Stunned by the Death of a Close Friend, Specialist Christopher Hurd Confides to His Mother How Profoundly He Has Been Hurt by the Loss
&
Sergeant Justin Merhoff Tells His Grandfather About the Assignment He Has Volunteered For and How It Has Affected His Perception of the Military and Those Who Serve

Despite the longstanding rivalries between the different service branches within the armed forces and the intensity with which troops can bicker and fight among themselves (not unlike real siblings), active duty personnel can develop a loyalty to one another that transcends family relations. When they go into combat, they put their lives into the hands of their fellow soldiers, Marines, airmen, and sailors, and this dependency creates a closeness unlike any other. And, notwithstanding the stoicism and reserved demeanor they tend to project in public, no individuals write with greater emotion about the sacrifices made by those who serve in the military than their comrades in arms. During World War II, Coast Guard yeoman second class Thomas Tuckhorn watched in awe as US Marines fought to the death at Iwo Jima. Tuckhorn had arrived on the island after it was (relatively) secure and personally began shuttling food from his ship to the Marines who had gone for days without sleep or sustenance. "I gave several fellows food who stood right in front of me and they ate the stew with their bare dirty fingers as they were so hungry," he wrote to his wife. "Honest Annette," he continued,

> *I'll take my hat off for the Marines from now on after seeing what they went thru. Yes sir, in my opinion the infantry regardless of whether being Marines or soldiers, that's the toughest branch of the service.*

Half a world away, Sergeant Bernard Paul Lyons remarked to his wife, Agnes, about the young soldiers he had witnessed battling entrenched German forces. "[The fighting] gets plenty tough up there at times," he wrote,

> *[and] calls for plenty of what it takes and costs heavily in precious life and limb. But soldiers of the line see it through. Guys who used to put gas in your car or clerk in the stores you bought your meats and groceries, who worked in the offices and factories, or who used to plough the good earth of our farms. . . . I'm talking about soldiers now—soldiers of the line— officers and men of the infantry regiments and those units attached to them as combat teams. All those men up there in the fox holes facing the enemy only a few score yards away. Say a little extra special prayer for those guys every time you can, too, will you?*

That sense of camaraderie is not limited to bygone eras; active duty personnel continue to express heartfelt sentiments about their fellow troops in their correspondences home. In the spring of 2003, a US Army specialist named Christopher Hurd wrote to his mom from Kuwait about the death of Captain Christopher Scott Seifert, who, like Hurd, was with the 101st Airborne. (Seifert's death was a stark example that relations between servicemembers are by no means immune to tension and outright hostility; on March 23, 2003, as American troops prepared for the ground campaign into Iraq, a US Army sergeant named Hasan Akbar, who had purportedly been overheard voicing anti-American statements before the invasion, tossed several grenades into the tents of other soldiers at Camp Pennsylvania in Kuwait and fired off numerous shots from his rifle. More than a dozen troops were seriously wounded, and, along with Chris Seifert, an Air Force major named Gregory Stone was killed in the late-night assault.) Seifert and Hurd had been close friends, and in his letter home, Hurd revealed both the depth of his pain and his attempt to forge something positive out of the loss.

Hey mom,

The loss of Cpt. Seifert has left a void, not only in our little group, but within our hearts as well. As soldiers and men we seldom if ever let our peers know how much they mean to us, until it is too late. I loved Cpt Seifert, as a soldier, as a man and as a friend. I remember the first day I met Chris, for some reason or another I was the only one running that morning when he first showed up. We ran together chatting and getting to know one another, right away I took a shine to him. Seldom in my travels or my life for that matter does one meet someone as special as Chris; needless to say I liked him from the first day.

I wept a great deal when I found out we had lost Chris. I was working late when it happened, I remember saying good-night to Cpt Seifert, and making some off handed joke, just to get one of those Chris Seifert smiles (anyone who knew him knows the smile I'm talking about); never once thinking that would be the last time I would ever see him. The events of that night will live with me forever, as well as the good friend that was lost to me . . . to us.

However if one flower sprung from the ashes of that night, it is for me this: never let the love you hold for someone go unappreciated, for life is too damn precious and short. Do not shelter that love until it is too late, for what good is a candle if you shield the light, instead let the light out feel the warmth and let it illuminate your way. Chris will live with me in my heart for the rest of my life, and so will the lesson of these events.

Love,

Chris

The bond between those in the armed forces extends intergenerationally as well. While serving in the Middle East during Operation Desert Storm, USMC Private First Class Raymond Ortiz received some words of support from a family friend named Edward J. Moore, a sixty-six-year-old veteran who had fought at Guadalcanal, Tarawa, and Okinawa during World War II. "Ray Sr. informed me of your being sent where you are and I wasn't surprised of that movement," Moore began his letter.

> *As I may have told you more Marines on a percentage basis go overseas than any other branch. Of course you remember the words from our Marine hymn "We have fought in every clime and place—that we could take a gun . . ." Your deployment bears that out very well. Needless to say I am proud of you and all your comrades-in-arms. I tried to be there but the "old man" told me to sit this one out. Damn it!! You carry on for me as I know you and all the other Marines will do an A-One job out there. As far as being scared and/or apprehensive, I understand very well. . . . Don't you and your buddies worry about your feelings. Those before you and me, that made Marine Corps tradition what it is, also went through their moments of doubt. Keep your butt below ground during an incoming attack and you'll be O.K. Take care dear friend and let me hear from you from time to time. Semper Fidelis.*

Conversely, younger generations of men and women who join the military often develop a greater appreciation for older veterans, particularly within their own families. In November 2004, a twenty-four-year-old sergeant in the US Army named Justin Merhoff handwrote the following letter to his grandfather, a World War II veteran named Hugh Merhoff. Justin had been designated the NCOIC (Non-Commissioned Officer in Charge) of an assignment that deepened his understanding of the sacrifices made by his contemporaries, as well as by those, like his grandfather, who had served before them. (Kari is Merhoff's wife, and Brandon is their newborn son.)

Dear Gramps,

I want to write you and let you know what I am doing these days. I found out that my unit was responsible for manning five of the twenty-two funeral honors teams that represent the 10th Mountain Division. I know this might sound a little morbid, but I really wanted to be on one of those teams so I volunteered myself, something you do not normally do in the Army, as you know from your own experiences in the military.

Since I've never been to a funeral before, I did not know what to expect. There were times that I had to try not to cry after seeing the family go through the turmoil that death brings. These emotions were new to me and were hard to take at first. All of the funerals are sad in their own way, but one in particular was for a Polish-born soldier who only had his sister there. A few times we were told that we were requested to perform honors and then told that the family members had changed their minds. I guess that it is either too hard for them to handle or they do not like the fact that the person who died fought in a war they don't agree with.

Every time I have performed honors for these fallen soldiers, I have gotten different degrees of response, from a handshake and a thank you to an invitation to eat with the family. These people thanked us for being there, and I thanked them for enabling me to honor their family member. I think that is why we are there—to help the families come to peace with the passing of these great men and women. What really got me was that there were guys who were not U.S. citizens but were fighting for our country. I might never have met these soldiers, but they are all my brothers and sisters in arms. We will forever, even in death, be bound to each other by our service to our country.

I know that not everyone agrees about war and the military, but my personal belief is that every man and woman who has fought for this country should be honored, both in death and in life. Before 9-11, there were people who did not respect those who serve. I did not even feel comfortable going off post in my uniform. Now I think the country as a whole has changed and most people I talk to respect us. Some questioned why I was serving with all that is going on over in Iraq, but most of the time the response is supportive.

During my time as the NCOIC of my funeral team, I have met a lot of people with great stories about their years in the service and the soldiers we are there to honor. I do not know which unit he served under, but I was also intrigued when I found out that one older veteran we buried was African American and had served during World War II. He fought for a country that at the time would only recognize him as a second-class citizen due to the color of his skin. In my eyes, if you are willing to fight for our great country, you should be treated as a hero, no matter your race, sex, or religious beliefs. I wished I were able to thank him in person, but I hope that by being there to represent the Army he fought in will be enough for the great sacrifice he made as a young man.

A lot of the funerals were for married men, and their wives were there mourning their death. With what is going on in Iraq and

Afghanistan and with the chances of me going over there soon being high, I thought of what Kari might feel if something happened to me. Brandon would be too young to understand. At another funeral for a Jewish veteran a man had to bury his father. Regardless of when I die, I hope Brandon will have kind words for me such as this man had for his father.

This whole experience has helped me better understand what happened during World War II, Korea, and Vietnam, and the sacrifices made by those who served honorably—and by their families. I know that you say you do not consider yourself a veteran because you were drafted and did not see action. You used the time you served to your advantage and became a doctor. You saved countless lives. Maybe you were not meant to fight. You are the reason I am in the Army today. You instilled in me the values that you learned during your service, and it has made me a better soldier. Most important, it has made me a better person.

Love,
Justin

—m—

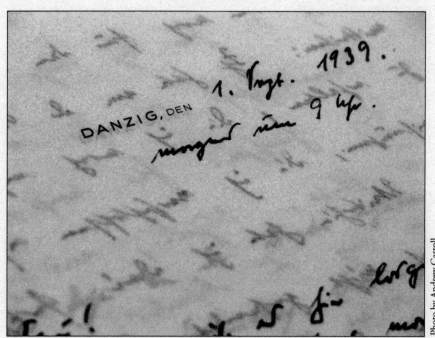

Letter by a German soldier, dated September 1, 1939, from Gdansk (Danzig), Poland. "In general, everything went along rather peacefully and orderly," he wrote to his wife. "The question is what will happen next. . . ." In the six years to follow, an estimated fifty million people would be killed, the majority of whom were civilians. More than twenty-five thousand men, women, and children would die, on average, every day until the armistice in 1945.

LINES OF FIRE

Letters of Combat

No doubt you must have thought that I have forgotten you altogether. If such thoughts have entered your head I hope you will forgive me, for I have been very bad even now my hand is all in a tremble. I have had some marvellous escapes   I got wounded in my leg with pierces of shell but only flesh wounds. I have had my hat shot off a couple of times and felt for the blood, but the nearest was when I got hit on my cheek with a bullet cutting it with the blood all over my tunic, and another bullet took all the hairs of my eye brow just leaving a little scratch, very strange it was just then when we see blood your own blood when you get right in the thick of it, of course I got into some scrapes and thank God that I am alive to tell the tale. It was simply dreadful at times Fancy living amongst shell and bullet nights and days with out sleep. It use to turn me sick at times to see the dreadful pieces of human bodys lying about, with a head rolling without a body legs and arms all over the place, often I have taken cover behind our own dead, as the Turk was having a shot at you, the bullet would plunk in the body in front of you; Oh Gill this was Hell on Earth for if Hell can be worse, but I really think it can't be worse.

> —*Frederick C. Trenne, a soldier from New Zealand,*
> *writing on January 12, 1916, to his friend G. Harry Gillespie*
> *about the fighting at Gallipoli*

Eleven o'clock had just struck, when my attention was attracted by repeated bursts of machine-gun fire. I soon saw three planes right above my head: one French, two German. The fight was going on for about half an hour when suddenly I saw the French plane turn all over, a black body came out of the plane and descended slowly. It was the airman falling, but I thought at first it was like a bird, so slowly was he coming down. Later on I understood my mistake: his coat had opened, acting somewhat like a parachute. He had his arms stretched out and hit the ground feet first. He had fallen in a small pond, not deep and frozen. The ice was broken but his body was not in the water. The Germans arrived soon, and with some hooks took him to the bank. Tuesday morning he was put in a coffin. On his grave they put a cross, made from a propeller. More than once I brought flowers, but the Germans forbade it, and always took them away. I don't know why.

—Jean Thuiller, writing on August 26, 1928,
to the parents of Flight Lieutenant Harry R. Wambolt,
describing the fate of their son during World War I

As the lone farmhouse was the only possible place for any Krauts to be, the Lieutenant sent out just one squad to clear it should it need clearing. Five of the six of us who went had never even seen a live German soldier. We ran into three Jerries in the farmyard one of whom tried to hide in a half-filled rain barrel, of all places. I'll never forget the neat triangle of holes Joe's tommy gun put in that barrel! I was almost hypnotized as I watched the water change gradually pink and then red as it spouted out the oaken bullet holes. As we started off across the fields I glanced back at the rain barrel. A dog sniffed warily at marshy ground around it. A large rooster, which had disappeared in a flurry of feathers such a short time ago, now crowed defiantly at the world.

—Maitland Livsey, an American corporal
writing from France on February 25, 1945,
to his father back in Portland, Oregon

Hello All! I'm sure your thoughts and concern are for us in Saudi, but we are fine. Keep watching the news and you'll see more action than myself. I'm sorry for not being able to call you but the first chance I get I will call. Please take care and don't worry. You don't realize that our unit is well out of danger. John

—*Twenty-six-year-old Sergeant John Madden,*
US Marine Corps Reserve, with the Eighth Tank Battalion,
TOW Company, writing to his parents and relatives
in Florida from Saudi Arabia during the Gulf War
on February 16, 1991

Dear Mike & Minnie! I've received a total of 3 letters from Ron & Louis from Canton, also I've received a letter from that lady who roomed with Sheila. I'm amazed at their concern. So far it is going fine. All is cool, and we train daily for our mission. I'll be honest in respect as to your concern. The flies are huge! Tell Mary K and Greg I said Hi! I should be home soon. See ya later, John This goes no further! <u>Seriously</u>

—*Madden, writing on the same day to his brother*
and sister-in-law. "The flies are huge!" was a prearranged code
Madden had given only to his brother—as he did not want
to worry their parents—to indicate that a land battle
against Iraqi forces was imminent. "Tell Mary K and Gregg
I said Hi!" was code for the fact that Madden would,
in fact, be near the front of the invasion
and very much in danger. (He survived the war.)

**Writing to His Father After the First Shots
of the American Revolution Were Fired, Samuel Bard Articulates
His Fears About the Bloodshed to Come
&
Expecting a Swift Victory, a British Officer Expresses How Much
He Will Enjoy Crushing These "Vile" American Enemies**

*"My Dearest Father, I am most sincerely sorry to confirm the afflicting reports,
which, before this, I suppose you have heard," wrote a New York physician
named Samuel Bard just days after the April 19, 1775, clash outside of
Boston between British troops and Massachusetts militiamen. "It is but too true,
that the sword of civil discord is at length unsheathed, and the horrors of that
worst of wars begun among us." It is unlikely that Bard knew just how prescient
his words would be. The Revolution was not America's first major conflict; the
French and Indian War, in which British and American soldiers served side by
side to defeat the French and their Native Indian allies in North America, lasted
nine years with thousands of casualties. But the Revolution would claim tens of
thousands of lives, and it would be a conflict of astonishingly brutal hand-to-
hand combat. Bard continued with his letter:*

Mr. Seagrove writes from Boston, that on Tuesday a body of eight
hundred troops marched suddenly from Boston, in the night, with
intention to seize a magazine which had been prepared at Concord, or,
perhaps, the delegates, who were there met. On their way they
encountered a company of minute-men exercising, and ordered them to
disperse, who refusing to do so, the troops fired twice over their heads,
and, as they still stood their ground, a third time, among them, and
killed eight; upon which the country was immediately alarmed by the
firing of cannon, and the troops intercepted on their return. General
Gage sent out a thousand men, under the command of Lord Percy, to
their assistance; these two bodies united, and made a kind of retreating
battle into Boston. Many officers were wounded; and between two and
three hundred private men killed. Seagrove adds, that preparations were

making, on both sides, as if it was to be very soon renewed. What number of the inhabitants was killed is not known; but all agree their loss must have been considerable. Other letters make the number of the troops killed to be near five hundred; but I suppose the truth is not exactly known; enough, however, is known, to fill every humane breast with the deepest affliction. We have had some commotion among us on the occasion, though, on the whole, we are remarkable quiet; and I am not without hopes, shall remain so, through the interposition of those who have interest among the common people.

I have ever preserved a moderate and temperate course, and you may be assured, shall, on this occasion, rather increase my caution than lessen it. God, and God only, knows where these unhappy disputes will end; it can hardly, however, be hoped they will subside before we have felt heavily the inconveniences of them.

Yet it is not impossible but that the resolution and spirit which have now been shown by our neighbors, may convince the British ministry that they have not much to expect from America by force; and in that way, will never get a revenue out of us which will pay the expense of collecting. God send that it may be so, and that we may again see our former happy days of peace and quiet.

Your affectionate son,
S. B.

Passions flared on both sides. British troops mocked the ragtag militia the Colonists had assembled and warned them that, as traitors to the motherland, they could expect no pity. (Many American soldiers, in time, would reciprocate that merciless spirit as well.) The sheer animus the British felt toward their enemy was evident in the following letter, written by an English officer (whose name was not recorded) just after General Washington and his men were forced to retreat from Long Island. The sentiments were shared by many in the British forces.

September 3, 1776

Rejoice, my friend, that we have given the rebels a d——'d crush. We landed on Long-Island the 22d ult. without opposition. On the 27th we had a very warm action, in which the Scots regiments behaved with the greatest bravery, and carried the day after an obstinate resistance on the rebel side. But we flanked, and overpowered them with numbers. The Hessians and our brave Highlanders gave no quarters; and it was a fine sight to see with what alacrity they dispatched the rebels with their bayonets after we had surrounded them, so that they could not resist.

Multitudes were drowned and suffocated in morasses, a proper punishment for all rebels. Our battalion out-marched all the rest; and was always first up with the rebel fugitives. A fellow they call Lord Sterling one of their Generals, with two others, is prisoner, and a great many of their officers, men, artillery, and stores.

It was a glorious achievement, my friend, and will immortalize us, and crush the rebel colonies. Our loss was nothing. We took care to tell the Hessians, that the rebels had resolved to give no quarters to them in particular, which made them fight desperately, and put all to death that fell into their hands. You know all stratagems are lawful in war especially against such vile enemies to their kind and country.

The island is all ours and we shall soon take New-York, for the rebels dare not look us in the face. I expect the affair will be over this campaign, and we shall all return covered with American laurels, and have the cream of American lands alloted us for our services.

—⁓—

A Continental Soldier Named Henry Johnson Sends a Short but Poignant Letter to His Parents Assuring Them He Is Well
&
In a Series of Letters Appealing to the Government for a Military Pension, William Hutchinson, David Welch, William Johnson, and Moses Hall Describe the Violence and Atrocities They Saw Firsthand

While there are countless letters, many of them stirring and eloquent, by the nation's aristocracy and commanding officers from the Revolutionary era, letters by common soldiers are harder to come by. The reasons are manifold. There were, compared to other major conflicts, fewer soldiers writing letters and, therefore, fewer letters to be passed down from one generation to the next. (An estimated two hundred and fifty thousand Americans fought in the Revolution; during the Civil War, upwards of two hundred thousand men could be fighting in a single battle. In World War II, more than sixteen million Americans served in uniform, and they exchanged literally billions of letters with loved ones back home.) Paper was hard to come by for the average soldiers in the field, and there was virtually no reliable postal service to ensure that their mail would be received. Correspondents primarily depended on acquaintances or an informal delivery network to drop off their personal letters at a public place, such as a tavern, to be collected later. And while officers were for the most part highly literate, many enlisted men were tradesmen whose reading and writing skills were modest. The letters of Henry Johnson (which he even misspelled as "Henery Jon-

son"), a young Continental soldier from New Jersey, are representative of what many young men wrote home from the front lines when they were able.

Febuary 25 1778

Onered perents

I am i Good helth Att present And I hope these will find you All the Same

The Situation of our Armey Is so that I dont Expect to Com home Very Soon You must Not look for mee till you See mee But if you Could Send me a Letter to Lett me no how you All Are It Would gave me grate Satsfaction to See the Same. But our ofisers have Left us without Money & Cloth and hear we are forsed to Stay Exposed to All Wether Let it Come As It will

Remember me to All my friends that Ask after me

So No More Att Present But I Remain your Dear and Loving Scion

Henery Jonson

On June 7, 1780, during the Battle of Connecticut Farms, Johnson was shot in the head, but the injury was not a mortal one; one week later, Johnson himself reported to his parents from the "Ospitreal" (hospital):

I have taken this opertunyty to let you know what misfortu[n]e I met with. A party of the Enemy Came to Elisebeth town [and] ma[r]ched to the Conecticut Farms We lay at Newark Mountain A Bout twelve oclock at Night we was Alarmed and Marched to the farms and about Sun Rise We [attacked] them . . . there was a Bout five thousand of them we kept up a a hot fire about fore hours and in the atack was wounded Col Ogden of the forth Regt and a number of Soldiers kild and wounded and I got a Wound in the head very Bad But I am in hopes With the Assistance of god that I Shall git wel again

Henry Johnson returned home after his recuperation and eventually became a shoemaker. While letters like Johnson's, which describe combat on a firsthand basis, are scarce, there are numerous correspondences written after the war by veterans petitioning the government, both state and local, for a pension. Within their appeals are often dramatic stories that reveal the true brutality of the violence these veterans and their comrades faced during the Revolution. (Applicants who could not write, often related their accounts to a third party, such as a lawyer or court clerk, who made a transcript of the narrative.) A native of Pennsylvania, William Hutchinson was in his early twenties when he fought with the Chester County Militia and, later, the Second Delaware Regiment at Trenton,

Brandywine, and Germantown. Hutchinson recalled the abuse that one man, who had been brought to their camp caked in blood and barely alive, suffered when British troops attacked—some used the word slaughtered—American soldiers at Paoli, Pennsylvania. (The selections below are from the letters of Hutchinson and other applicants, sometimes called declarants or deponents, and the originals do not include salutations.)

A Quaker, a stranger, came to our quarters & brought with him a man which he said he had found lying in the woods whose clothes coat, vest & trousers were stiff with gore & declarant believes they would have stood alone when taken off him. he was a virginian and had shared in the consequences of the massacre; had been singled out at the close thereof as a special subject for the exercise of the savage cruelty of the British soldiers. he told us that more than a dozen soldiers had with fixed bayonets formed a cordon round him & that every one of them in sport had indulged their brutal ferocity by stabbing him in different parts of his body & limbs, & that by a last & desperate effort, he got without their circle & fled. & as he rushed out, one of the soldiers struck at him to knock him down as the finis to the catastrophe in which only the front of the bayonet reached his head & laid it open with a gash as if it had been cut with a knife—he made, however, his escape & when brought to our captain, he had laid in the woods twenty-four hours. he had neither hat shoes nor stockings, and his legs & feet were covered with mud and sand which had been fastened to his skin by mixing with his own blood as it ran down his limbs.

Our Captain immediately dispatched his Lieutenant for a Physician who when he returned was so fortunate as to bring two with him. we then procured the means of washing & cleansing the wounded man & upon examining him there was found as our captain afterwards announced to the men forty six distinct bayonet wounds in different parts of his body, either of which were deep & sufficiently large to have been fatal if they had been in vital parts. but they were mostly flesh wounds & every one of them had bled profusely & many of them commenced bleeding again upon being washed. his wounds were dressed his bloody garments were burned and by orders of our captain he was waited upon with strict attention until he was able to walk & then was by Lieut Corry (our Lieut) taken somewhere not distant to an hospital.

In another reminiscence, Hutchinson recalled the appreciation shown to him by one general, Israel Putnam, for his devotion to cause and country. A seasoned warrior, Putnam was an early proponent of rebellion and had distinguished himself at the battle of Breed's Hill. Putnam was nothing if not a survivor; during the French and Indian War he was captured by a group of Indians (as they were referred to at the time), tortured, tied to a stake, and almost burned alive had it not been for the intervention of a benevolent French officer. After being freed, he was put on a British vessel that was shipwrecked and Putnam was one of the few to make it to shore alive. As Hutchinson's comments emphasized, Putnam admired perseverance and strength in the face of adversity.

Lieutenant Hops of Captain Evans's Company appeared at Col Montgomery's quarters bringing with him 9 or 10 men belonging to Capt Evan's Company who ought to have marched with us in October but did not & being young & in love with the cause I again joined the squad brought up by Lieut Hops & we were all attached to a company commanded by Captain James McDowell who with his company had a few days before joined Col Montgomery's Regiment, who still remained in command and rendezvoused in Philadelphia. I cannot recollect who was the general in command in Philadelphia at this time but after we had heard of the Hessians being taken we were reviewed by Genl Putnam on foot who addressed us as he walked close along the line. and as he came opposite to this declarant & a youthful fellow soldier who stood by his side and who in the struggle for Independence filled the grave of a brave man the General observing our youthful appearance, turned to us & laid his hand on the shoulder of each of us & remarked that he liked to see such young men turn out & that they would make men when their beards grew he then took off his hat & showed us his head which had been scalped by the Indians.

Indians fought for both the Americans and the British, but sided more with the latter. The Mohawks, Senecas, Cayugas, and Onondagas allied themselves with the British; the Oneidas and Tuscaroras with the Americans. David S. Welch enlisted at the age of sixteen and served for almost three years as a scout, but he was engaged in only one fight. It was, however, an almost fatal one involving two Indians he happened upon by chance.

It fell to my lot to be placed the most westwardly man of our party as we marched northward. In this way of marching about the middle of the day I had as I afterwards found become separated upward of half a mile from my companions when I discovered through a thicket of hemlock brush the appearance of a smoke evidently indicating the fact of there being a fire We were then in a wilderness some 15 miles beyond our then most frontier garrisons — Immediately on making this discovery I crept with the utmost caution toward the spot from whence the smoke rose — Presently I saw through the brush two indians sitting by a smoke that appeared to have been kindled to keep off the mosquitoes — I instantly laid myself flat down keeping my eye upon the spot to see if there were more than the two — In a few moments I become impressed with the belief that there were but the two — I was not more than eight rods distant from them —

After much hesitation as to what might be most proper I finally came to the conclusion that my companions were proceeding on & might perhaps soon be surprised as there might be more Indians within a short distance — I drew my gun & whilst lying thus flat on the ground I took deliberate aim at one of the Indians and shot him dead The other indian instantly sprung upon his feet seizing his gun & started to run — Without reflecting upon the consequence, I immediately run after him having my gun unloaded. The indian made but a few leaps after I started before he turned and fired upon me but his fire missed as I supposed by several feet. He then dropped his gun & came at me with his tomahawk. I encountered him with my empty gun — The first blow which he aimed with his tomahawk I warded off with my gun and in doing it I was so fortunate as to hook the deadly weapon from him — It fell upon the ground rather behind me — I was then encouraged and sprung to get the tomahawk in which effort I succeeded Whilst I was yet bent in picking up the tomahawk the indian who had drawn his knife gave me a cut giving me a deep but short wound upon my right leg a little above my knee — He then aimed a second stroke at me with the same weapon This blow I warded off with my left hand in doing which I received a wound upon between the thumb and forefinger About the same instant with the tomahawk I hit him a blow on the head which brought him to the ground And with another blow after he had fallen I made sure he was beyond doing me any further harm —

William Johnson was a teenager who volunteered for the New Jersey militia and fought, off and on, for almost the entire Revolution. One of his most vivid memories concerned a brief encounter between an Irish soldier serving with the Colonists and a fallen, though still living, redcoat.

The first marching service which this, and the other militia companies stationed at Newark, rendered was to cross over from Elizabethtown Point to Staten Island to attack the British troops who were stationed at different places on that Island, On our approach, the enemy retreated to their principal fortifications at the Narrows, and our troops then returned to Newark — Gen Wines commanded the American troops on duty on this occasion, who in all numbered about 1500 men, this must have occurred more than a year after deponent was first attached to the militia. In this skirmish some British were killed, one in particular he remembers, was lying on the ground mortally wounded, he had a green coat on, which one of our company (an Irishman) espied, and said, "Your coat is better than mine, I'll have it." he immediately took the coat off the wounded soldier and put it on his own back, and immediately run his bayonet in the body of the wounded soldier, who on his march back lay quite dead.

Moses Hall, who was only fifteen when the war began, also witnessed an atrocity committed by American troops, but he was not unsympathetic to the rage behind it. The troops had seized half a dozen British soldiers and were debating what to do with them when someone evoked the memory of Buford's Massacre. The fate of the prisoners was sealed at that moment. In May 1780, a British lieutenant colonel named Banastre Tarleton, already reviled by the Americans, purportedly disregarded a white flag of surrender offered by Colonel Abraham Buford and ordered his men to kill Buford's entire regiment, which they proceeded to do. A doctor familiar with the incident later wrote that the "demand for quarters, seldom refused to a vanquished foe, was at once found to be in vain." He continued:

> *—[N]ot a man was spared—and it was the concurrent testimony of all the survivors, that for fifteen minutes after every man was prostrate [Tarleton's troops] went over the ground plunging their bayonets into every one that exhibited any signs of life, and in some instances, where several had fallen one over the other, these monsters were seen to throw off on the point of the bayonet the uppermost, to come at those beneath.*

In his pension appeal letter, Moses Hall related what happened to the British prisoners they had caught, as well as the chain of thoughts and emotions he experienced afterwards.

The evening after our battle with the Tories we having a considerable number of prisoners I recollect a scene which made a lasting impression upon my mind. I was invited by some of my comrades to go and see some of the prisoners. We went to where six were standing. Some discussion taking place, I heard some of our men cry out, "Remember

Buford," and the prisoners were immediately hewed to pieces with broadswords.

At first I bore the scene without any emotion, but upon a moment's reflection, I felt such horror as I never did before nor have since. And returning to my quarters and throwing myself upon my blanket I contemplated the cruelties of war untill overcome and unmanned by a distressing gloom from which I was not relieved untill commencing our march next morning before day by moon light.

I came to Tarleton's camp which he had just abandoned leaving lively rail fires. Being on the left of the road as we marched along I discovered lying upon the ground something with appearance of a man. Upon approaching him he proved to be a youth about sixteen who having come out to view the British through curiosity for fear he might give information to our troops they had run him through with a bayonet and left him for dead. Though able to speak he was mortally wounded. The sight of this unoffending boy, butchered rather than be encumbered on the march, I assume, relieved me of my distressful feelings for the slaughter of the Tories and I desired nothing so much as the opportunity of participating in their destruction.

Such incidents would continue throughout the Revolution, with each side justifying its actions as fair reprisals for the "inhumanity" of the other. It was a vicious cycle that had occurred in previous conflicts, and one that would be repeated in wars to come.

—⁂—

In a Letter to James Porter, a US Army Captain Named F. M. Desha Recounts the Final Moments of Porter's Son, Andrew, During the War with Mexico
&
Captain Maschil Manring Writes to His Father About the Fate of a Beloved Friend and Fellow Soldier—His "Dear Brother George"

For most servicemen and -women—officers and enlisted personnel alike—few tasks are more emotionally demanding than writing to a fallen comrade's next of kin. Every word they put to paper will be read and reread by grieving relatives and will affect how that soldier, Marine, airman, or sailor is remembered forever. One of the earliest condolence letters in American history was penned by the Reverend John Ogilvie on July 21, 1759, during the French and Indian War. (Officially, the British campaign to gain control of North American ter-

ritory held by the French was not declared until 1756. Hostilities, however, had ignited two years before when a twenty-two-year-old lieutenant colonel named George Washington and a detachment of Virginia militia clashed with French troops at Great Meadows, Pennsylvania. British and American soldiers fought side by side throughout the conflict and were victorious in the end, but the financial costs to Great Britain were immense, and to help recover its losses it imposed heavy taxes on the Colonies. The war that had so unified the British and the Americans in the mid-1700s prompted the very fiscal policies that, twelve years later, would violently cleave them apart.) Except for the fact that he was shot during the siege of Fort Niagara in July 1759, little is known of the soldier's name or background, or of his friendship with Reverend Ogilvie. From the content of the letter, however, Ogilvie apparently knew his family quite well and was genuinely distraught by his death. He sent the following to the soldier's brother:

> I am extremely unable to express what I feel upon this melancholy Occasion: Nothing but the most perfect Resignation to Will of God, I am sensible, can support you under the loss of so worthy a Brother, who fell yesterday in his Country's Cause universally lamented by the whole Army: I sympathize with you, with the most intire Affection, & mingle My Tears with yours. But what shall I say to your dear Mother? I cannot write to her, you must therefore introduce the heavy Tydings in the most prudent manner. . . . I am persuaded that the Consideration of the Cause in which your brother fell & his own good Character thro the Course of his Life, will afford you Matter of Comfort under this Afflictive Dispensation. His Name will be embalmed to Posterity & always mentioned with Honour by every true lover of his Country. . . . I shall Commit his Remains to the Dust this Evening. Tell your Dear Mother how much I sympathize with her & that I bear her upon my Mind in my prayers.

Deciding what, precisely, to tell a family about their loved one's death is a sensitive matter and requires a balance between tact and honesty. Some writers, assuming that they even know the particulars, withhold specific information that might be considered too explicit, while others choose to disclose as much as possible, no matter how potentially unsettling. Captain Andrew Porter was one of the estimated seventeen hundred US troops lost in battle during the war with Mexico, a two-year conflict (1846 to 1848) that resulted in America's acquisition of land that would eventually become the states of Arizona, California, Colorado, Nevada, New Mexico, and Utah. A fellow captain named F. M. Desha had witnessed Porter's death firsthand and, in startling detail, described to Porter's father how it occurred.

La Encantada, Camp of
The Arkansas Regiment,
13 miles South of Saltillo,
Mexico
May 19th 1847—

Mr. James Porter:

       Dear Sir;

  Your letter of 17th Ultimo directed to Genl Wool, inquiring into the particulars of the death of your son, Capt Andrew R. Porter, who was killed in the bloody battle of Buena Vista on the 23rd of Feb. and also as to the practicability of having his remains brought to the United States, was received a few days since and handed over to the Colonel of this Regiment for information, who has handed it to me, in as much, as I now command Capt Porter's Company, and am knowing to the circumstances of his death, burial, etc. I was the 1st Lieut. of his company, and was close to him when he received his mortal wound. Four Companies of the Arkansas Cavalry, among which was Capt. Porter's, (the remainder of the Regiment being engaged with enemy in another part of the field) were formed in conjunction with the Kentucky Cavalry to resist a charge from the Mexican lancers numbering between 1500 and 2000 men. When they came within 75 or 100 yards of our line, we fired upon them and immediately charged upon their lines, they at the same time charging, and dividing so as to surround us. Here a bloody encounter, hand to hand, took place, which in a short time resulted in the dispersion of the enemy, though outnumbering us some 4 or 5 to 1. In this desperate charge your son fell at the head of his company, gallantly leading it on to victory.

  He and Col. Yell, who commanded the Arkansas Regiment, fell in a few paces of each other. When Capt. Porter was found on the field, his breast was pearced with a lance, his left hand half cut off with a sabre, and his face split from the left eye to the mouth, with a sabre. I saw the Mexican pearce him through the breast with his lance, and I immediately dashed at him with my sabre, remarking to Capt Porter that I would kill him (the Mexican) for him. He made me no reply but seemed to be bending over in his saddle as if in the agonies of death. The Mexican who killed him, and who had been dismounted, for he was on foot when he struck him with his lance, ran in among our horses, & I did not get the opportunity to slay him. These, sir, are the circumstances of your son's death, and you may rely upon their truth, as I was an eye witness to them. The sabre wounds I think he must have received whilst in the act of falling from his horse, as the wound in the breast was in itself mortal.

I was well acquainted with Capt. Porter, and had been for the last three or four years. We lived in the same town, and practiced law in the same courts. I deeply sympathise with you in his loss, and although he has fallen young, and in the midst of his usefulness, yet I know, that it will be a source of proud gratification to you, to hear that he fell as a brave soldier, in the ever memorable battle of Buena Vista, whilst upholding the honor of his country.

Immediately after the battle, and when all things had become quiet, I had his body interred along side of Col Yell's. When your letter was received, the company was making arrangements to have his remains carried to the United States. Every man of his company is anxious that it should be done, for no Captain was held in higher estimation by his men, or more beloved by them than was Capt Porter. I am now having a coffin prepared in Saltillo suitable for carrying his body back in, to the United States. Our Regiment will leave here on the 5th of next month, for New Orleans, there to be discharged at the expiration of its term of service, which is about the 1st of July. As the Regiment will leave here, and probably the army before this letter can reach you, and any one come here to get his remains, we have thought proper to take his remains as far as New Orleans with us, and there deposit them, from which place you can easily have them taken to North Carolina. It was our intention to take them back to the place of his adopted home, and where he had raised his company, but of course, we will abide by your wishes, and leave him at New Orleans subject to your order. When we get to New Orleans, I will write from there, and let you know where they can be found.

Capt Porter had been unwell with the rheaumatism in his ancles and knees for two or three weeks before the battle, and was advised by the surgeon, not to go out to the fight, but impelled by a love of glory, and a sense of duty to his country he determined to participate in the glory of the day, even though it cost him his life. Hoping that I have answered your letter satisfactorily to you, I remain with much respect,

Your Obt Servt,
F.M. Desha

Those who assume the somber duty of writing a condolence letter are often deal-ing with their own emotions over the loss as well, and their grief is all the more pronounced when the deceased is a family member. Maschil and George Man-ring were both officers in the Union Army, Fifty-sixth Regular Ohio Volunteers, A Company, and in mid-May 1863 they fought together at Champion Hill, Mississippi, under General Ulysses S. Grant. Champion Hill proved to be a critical victory in Grant's push toward the city of Vicksburg, "the nailhead that [holds] the South's two halves together," as Confederate President Jefferson Davis called it. But Champion Hill came at a high cost, with almost twenty-three hundred Union soldiers killed or wounded. (The Confederates had thirty-eight hundred casualties.) George Manring was among the dead, and on May 18, 1862, his brother wrote home to Ohio to break the news.

Edwards Depot, Miss.

Dear Father:

I am called upon to perform the mournful task of informing you of the death of my dear brother George W. Manring, who was killed in battle on the evening of the 16th of May near this place. The circumstances were as follows:

A fighting commenced at about eight o'clock in the morning. Company A was thrown forward as skirmishers. We fought till 10 o'clock in this manner, driving the enemy's pickets to his line of battle which he had formed as an eminence. I then ordered a retreat and informed the Commanding General where the enemy's lines were formed in order of battle.

We were immediately formed and ordered forward. The engagement soon became general. The portion of the enemy's lines with which our Regiment engaged, was formed along a line of fence in front of an opening containing about 40 acres. After a half hour's hard fighting, we started the enemy back, driving him beyond the field into the timber. We advanced across the field and made a stand at the fence, where we maintained our position for about half an hour. In the meantime the enemy were being heavily reinforced. The 28th Iowas being on our left, gave away and fell back without making a stand. In the retreat, we discovered the enemy coming both in our front and on each flank with a force of not less than ten times our number. We fell back about one hundred yards and made a stand right in an open field. We here checked their centre, but the Regiments on our right and left having retreated too hastily, we were compelled to fall back being flanked on our right and left. We made another stand in the field and tried to check the enemy who were advancing on us in four columns. Here is where my dear brother fell. He was shot twice, once in the right temple, and once in the left side of his chest. The last word which he uttered after he was struck by the ball was "O, Jesus." He died instantly. This was about three o'clock in the afternoon. My first impression was to stay with him, but considering that if I did so I would be taken prisoner or killed and thus the place of burial and the history of my brother would be lost to his friend, I concluded to rejoin my Regiment, which had retreated about one hundred yards beyond me, leaving me about half way between the rebels, who were pursuing us and my own Regiment. We tried to make a stand at the fence, but were too closely pursued by a superior force. We fell back to a ridge beyond the fence and made a stand at the fence, held the enemy in check till we were reinforced.

It was now half past three in the afternoon. At four, we succeeded in routing the enemy completely. I went immediately to where I had left my brother. The rebels had taken everything out of his pockets except a little blank book. They took his watch and all of his money, also his revolver, leaving his sword. Our Regiment was ordered forward in pursuit of the retreating enemy. I got permission to stay and take care of my brother. Sergeant Samuel J. Blake, Corporal Phail, of my company, stayed with me and assisted me in giving him and others of the company as decent a burial as the circumstances would admit of.

I had him conveyed to a shade by the side of the road, washed him, then selected a place for his burial. I set three men to digging his grave. I lay by his side on the battlefield all that night. Early next morning we finished the grave, I had him carried to it, and after impressing two kisses upon his cold temple—one for his aged father and one for myself—I laid him in his cold, silent resting place. I covered him up, and after offering a brief prayer that his remains might not be molested til such a time as they could be moved to Ohio, I left the grave. This was at seven o'clock in the morning. I overtook the Regiment, which was encamped two miles ahead at eight after performing one of the most solemn duties of my life. I shall never forget the manner in which he uttered the last sentence, so familiar as though he was addressing a friend. I have no doubt but they were the very words that he entered the final resting place of all good who have passed on before him. It is not unreasonable to suppose that those very words were heard by his sainted mother, brothers, and sisters, who have been at rest from their toils for a long time. There is scarcely a moment that passes over my head but I think of them. The verse which I often heard him sing comes into my mind frequently: "If happy in my latest breath, I may but gasp his name."

Surely if there was any person that was in possession of all virtues possessed in this life, it was him. I never knew him to be at fault in any instance. There was not an officer that knew him but respected him. All the men of the company loved him as they did a brother. He always did his duty well, his affections were divided between his God, his country and his friends. If I ever get home I intend to come after him. I wish you to select a place of his burial near where mother is buried, as I believe it would be his choice to be buried by her side.

From your affectionate son,

M. Manring

—⁓—

David R. Stevenson, a Scottish Immigrant in the Union Army, Reports to His Father About the Enormous Casualties at the Battle of Shiloh
&
Rebel Soldier Andrew DeVilbiss, Who Also Fought at Shiloh, Describes for His Wife the Aftermath of the Battle
&
James O. Cherry, Aboard the USS *Peosta,* Relates to His Sister a Violent Encounter Between His Captain and a Confederate Guerilla

There is no official tally of how many Civil War soldiers were immigrants, but the number is commonly estimated to be about one in ten, with most fighting for the Union. For reasons and motivations—pride, money, patriotism, fear of imprisonment, adventure—as diverse as those held by native-born Americans, hundreds of thousands of German, Irish, English, Scottish, Italian, French, Swiss, Dutch, Canadian, Belgian, Norwegian, Danish, and Cuban troops served the Northern cause. Germans represented the highest percentage, followed by the Irish. David R. Stevenson's motivations for enlisting are not known, but the young, Scottish-born Union soldier found himself thrust into the war's first truly catastrophic battle in early April 1862. There had been major clashes before, most notably First Manassas (also known as Bull Run) in July 1861 and General Ulysses S. Grant's campaign in the West, but these paled in comparison to the carnage of April 6 and 7 at the battle of Shiloh outside of Pittsburg Landing in Tennessee. (The name "Shiloh" itself referred to a nearby Methodist meetinghouse where much of the fighting took place.) With approximately twenty-three thousand casualties, there were more combat dead and wounded from this single battle than from the three prior US wars—the Revolution, the War of 1812, and the Mexican-American War—put together. On April 13, Stevenson wrote to his father.

Dear Sir

I take my pen in hand to write you a few lines informing you that I am in the land of the living and well and unhurt. I see by the Cincinnati Times that there was a tremendous battle fought here on Sunday and Monday the 6th and 7th. If you had been here you would thought so too. The rebles commenced the attack about day break. They drove us all to the river landing or closed us up till our army covered about one mile square when three gun boats opened fire up a ravine and they fell like grass before a scythe. This took place about 5 1/2 oclock the first day. The rebles and our army lay on the field where they hapened to be till morning. At daybreak our army opened fire on the enemy, Beulls force it was that opened the Ball the second day, his force having arrived during the night. Boath armies fought terrible during the second day till about noon when the rebles began to retreat which they kept up till four oclock when they started for Corinth every fellow for himself and the devil for all. They went like our men went from Manassas in great confusion.

Our loss is between seven and ten thousand killed and 30 or 40 thousand wounded. The loss of the enemy is larger than ours. Some of the dead rebles was not buried untill yesterday the job being a big one it took several days & the horses is unburied yet and smell very loud. Our camp contained a space of ground about 8 miles long by 4 wide before the fight it is the same now but better filled up than before the fight. The battleground is nearly all woods. Daton randall kill the first morning, forg michell wounded in the forhead by buckshot reported from the hospital dead. The musketry was at times as regular as hail falling on the roof of the house interrupted by cannon balls belching its insides out which cut off many limbs which fell on and hurt many off our men some of the balls going through trees two feet in diameter. The trees are all bulletmarked some having the balls in them.

I was not directly in the battle the first day. I was unloading the wounded all the first day till night when I went with a boat load to Savannah ten miles below. I waited on 20 men day & night untill Tuesday morning when I left and came up here on a boat. There was 185 killed & wounded in our regiment four of which was killed of my Co & 14 wounded. One since died. I wrote when in camp Dennison. If you expect any more letters from me you will have to answer this to insure it.

D R Stevenson

Andrew DeVilbiss was not an immigrant and he fought for the South, but he shared one thing in common with David R. Stevenson—he, too, made it through Shiloh alive. (Both Stevenson and DeVilbiss would be killed later in the war, however.) At about the same time Stevenson wrote to his father, DeVilbiss sent the following to his wife, offering his impressions of the battle's aftermath. (DeVilbiss self-censored his epithet concerning Northern soldiers.)

Corinth, Miss. April 16th 1862

Dear Mary

I hurriedly write you a few lines to let you know that I am well. I sent you an account of the battle, and eleven dollars a few days ago. The account of the battle by mail, and the money by Mr. Fuller of our company, who was wounded at the battle.

I am afraid the wounded man may have been detained at the Hospital at Holly Springs and mails are uncertain. I am anxious you should hear from me. It is given up to be the hardest fought battle on the American Continent.

The Yankee camps, that we took were beautifully located with fine springs running down in branches, but on Monday morning I saw those branches having their waters all colored with blood. O Mary you could never form an idea of the horrors of actual war unless you saw the battlefields while the conflict is progressing. Death in every awful form, if it really be death, is a pleasant sight in comparison to the fearfully and mortally wounded. Some crying oh, my wife, my children, others my Mother, my sister, my brother etc. any and all of these terms you will hear while some pray to God to have mercy and the others die cursing the "Yankee sons of b——s."

It is a grand and awful sight ~~to~~ and one that can never be forgotten.

My leg is yet a little black from the spent minnie ball that struck me, as I told you in my letter before. I am thankful to God for bringing me safely through. Go to the Church and thank him also, and pray for my preservation, and tell my boys to do the same. The man waits. Good bye. God bless you.

Andrew

P.S. Write to me by mail. I may have better luck here, and send otherwise, when you can. Your affectionate husband

A.D.

While the overwhelming majority of combat deaths in the Civil War occurred during major battles where great waves of men crashed violently into one another, smaller skirmishes and even guerilla fighting flared up throughout the country. Stationed on the gunboat USS Peosta, *which traveled up and down the Tennessee River, James Orville Cherry from Monroe, Ohio, wrote frequently to his sister Alice to share everyday matters and family gossip that any siblings might discuss. "Papa and Ma must have changed their minds about parties since last winter. They would not let you go to many then, but you seem to go to plenty of them now," Cherry wrote on February 12, 1863. He then promised to introduce her to some of his crewmates: "They say if she is as good look-*

ing as her brother they will go home with me [to meet you]. There is one good looking soldier here from Sabina, he says he has a good looking sister he will swap me for mine." (There is no indication from subsequent letters whether any sister-swapping ever took place.) But Cherry's letters also illuminated the darker side of his wartime experiences, and on June 21, 1864, he described an incident that accentuated how personal the fighting between Yanks and Rebs could be. (There is no signature to the letter, and it is most likely because, as the handwritten original indicates, Cherry had run out of room on the last page. His use of the most derogatory word possible for a black person was, unfortunately, spoken and written at the time even by those who opposed slavery and were, like Cherry, fighting the Confederacy.)

Dear Sissy

I have nothing else to do so I will commence a letter and finish it when we get to Paducah. We left Paducah over a week ago in company with a transport and four canal boats carrying government stores to Reynoldsburg. A railroad runs from that place to Nashville and most of the soldiers and stores for Nashville are taken this way because it is the nearest. We have been up the river as far as Chickasaw Ala. three miles

James Orville Cherry

above Eastfort. We have a union scout with us that is acquainted with everybody and every inch of ground from Paducah to the head of the Tennessee river. He is called Capt. Phillip's though he holds no Major's Commission. At nearly every place we stop, he takes fifteen or twenty of our men and scouts around the country. Yesterday at a place called Coffee's landing I went out with a scouting party. We went about three miles out into the country, and then went down the river seven miles to another landing where we met our boat. We found no rebs but we found plenty of places where they had been, we stopped at one house about an hour hunting for rebs, a nigger told us about forty had slept there that night but we found none.

Capt Phillip's has been with us nearly ever since we have been running up this river he did good service at the fight at Paducah watching the rebels and reporting to us all he saw. He hates the Guerillas and wants to kill every one he can. The Guerillas murdered his family, and came near doing the same with him. A year ago this spring five Guerillas captured him and each one of them put a bullet in him and left him for dead but he recovered and swore he would follow those men till he had killed all of them.

I saw him shoot one of them this morning at Saltillo, but I will tell you about it. We arrived at Saltillo about three o clock this morning and Capt Phillips took twenty men and went Guerilla hunting. He heard that a rebel lieut and private was in a certain house. He had the house surrounded and sure enough the rebs were there. Papers were found on them proving one to be lieut Watson of the rebel army he was sent aboard as prisoner. Phillip's recognized the other one as one of the five that tried to kill him. He brought the fellow down to the beach and then told him he had vowed to kill him and was going to do it now. He then raised his revolver, and the rebel started to run. Capt Phillips fired at him and so did two or three others but that poor fellow ran till he got onto our boat when he fell and cried that Capt Phillip's had shot him. He begged to see Capt Robith but our men took him and dragged him out to Phillips who shot him again through the head. This did not quite kill him and he was shot again. A hole was then dug and he was throwed in and covered up. He had six balls fired into him three went through his body and three through his head. I felt sorry for the poor fellow but it served him right. This make's two of the five that Capt Phillips has killed, and he says he wont be satisfied till the other three are in the same fix. He says he would rather kill each one himself than recieve twenty thousand a piece, and forego the pleasure of shooting them

—⁂—

**After Learning of the Execution of Defeated Black Troops
at Fort Pillow, Theodore Hodgkins Recommends to Secretary
of War Edward Stanton an Appropriate Response for the Massacre
&
Lieutenant Colonel Jonathan Singleton Mosby Informs
General Philip Sheridan of What He Has Done to Seven
of Sheridan's Men Responsible for Killing Seven
of Mosby's Rangers
&
Professor Francis Lieber Explains to Senator Charles Sumner
Why He Is Opposed to the "Retaliatory Resolutions" Favored
by Many in Congress**

*When war erupted in April 1861, citizens and soldiers in the North excoriated
the South for betraying their country and the ideals of freedom and democracy.
Southerners denounced the North for doing exactly the same. While genuine, the
acrimony was fueled more by regional pride than outright hatred for the other
side. This would change. By late 1861 and early 1862, tens of thousands of
households were receiving notification that their sons, husbands, brothers, and
fathers had been killed in battle. Soldiers passing through enemy lands often terrorized the local citizenry, further antagonizing already-raw nerves. After
surveying the damage wrought by Union troops on the land of his birth, one
Confederate soldier wrote to his family that the war had entered a new, more
savage phase. "We must fight to the death," he seethed,*

> *and lay low every invader that we can; the boy who knows naught of war
> must learn to glance his bright eye along the gun barrel, and strengthen his
> sinews to grasp the knife; and the young girl whose soul is innocence, whose
> thoughts are purity must learn to hurl the torch and with crafty hands pre-
> pare the subtle poison for the invaders cup. This must be a war of exter-
> mination.*

*Southern troops were not alone in their disgust: "I long for the day when we shall
attack the Rebels with an overwhelming force and annihilate them," wrote one
Union captain. "May I live long enough to see them running before us [and]
hacked to little pieces." The soldiers who frequently bore the brunt of this rage
on both sides were those who surrendered in combat. Cruelties were committed
by Union as well as Confederate troops, but one of the most infamous atrocities
of the war was reported to have occurred at Fort Pillow in Henning, Tennessee,
on April 12, 1864. After routing Union soldiers, Southern troops led by
Nathan Bedford Forrest went on a murderous rampage (according to Union*

Sources) against the members of the Eleventh US Colored Troops. Unarmed and begging for their lives, the black soldiers were said to have been shot in the face, set on fire, stabbed in the head and chest, and, if only wounded, buried alive. What became known as the Fort Pillow massacre prompted outrage throughout the country. Blacks were especially infuriated by what they considered not merely random instances of barbarity, but an official policy emanating from Confederate President Jefferson Davis's administration regarding the treatment of black troops. One gentleman, Theodore Hodgkins, wrote directly to the US Secretary of War, Edward Stanton, about the matter, offering what he believed to be a perfectly rational and simple proposal as to how the North should respond. (The word "grape" refers to small clusters of cast-iron balls that scattered over a large area when fired from a cannon. At close range, a single discharge could kill a dozen men.)

New York April 18th 1864

Sir:

Some sixty or seventy thousand of my down trodden and despised brethren now wear the uniform of the United States and are bearing the gun and sword in protecting the life of this once great nation With this in view I am emboldened to address a few words to you in their behalf if not in behalf of the government itself. Jeff Davis issued a threat that black men fighting for the U.S. should not be treated as prisoners of war and the President issued a proclamation threatening retaliation. Since then black soldiers have been murdered again and again yet where is there an instance of retaliation.

To be sure there has been a sort of secrecy about many of these slaughters of colored troops that prevented an official declaration to be made but there is now an open and bold murder, an act following the proclaimed threat made in cold blood gives the government an opportunity to show the world whether the rebels or the U.S. have the strongest power. If the murder of the colored troops at Fort Pillow is not followed by prompt action on the part of our government it may as well disband all its colored troops for no soldiers whom the government will not protect can be depended upon.

Now sir if you will permit a colored man to give not exactly advice to your excellency but the expression of his fellow colored men so as to give them heart and courage to believe in their government you can do so by a prompt retaliation. Let the same no. of rebel soldiers, privates and officers be selected from those now in confinement as prisoners of war captured at the west and let them be surrounded by two or three regiments of colored troops who may be allowed to open fire upon them in squads of 50 or 100, with howitzers loaded with grape. The whole civilized world will approve of this necessary military execution and the rebels will learn that the U.S. Govt. is not to be trifled with and the black men will feel not a spirit of revenge for have they not often taken the rebels prisoners even their old masters without indulging in a fiendish spirit of revenge or exultation.

Do this sir <u>promptly and without notice to the rebels at Richmond when the execution has</u> been made then an official declaration or explanation may be made. If the threat is made first or notice given to the rebels they will set apart the same no. for execution. Even that mild copperhead Reverdy Johnston avowed in a speech in the Senate that this govt. could only be satisfied with man for man as an act of retaliation. This request or suggestion is not made in a spirit of vindicativeness but simply in the interest of my poor suffering confiding fellow negros who are even now assembling at Annapolis and other points to reinforce the army of the Union Act first in this matter afterward explain or threaten the act tells the threat or demand is regarded as idle.

> I am Sir with great respect
> Your humble Servant
> Theodore Hodgkins

It is not known if Stanton even responded, but Hodgkins's proposal was not enacted. Unrelated to the Fort Pillow massacre, on September 23, 1864, six Confederate soldiers were captured and executed in Front Royal, Virginia, by Michigan cavalry troops commanded by George Custer. The men, including two teenaged boys, were "guilty" of serving under Lieutenant Colonel John S. Mosby, one of the war's most legendary and audacious characters. A short, wiry (he weighed only one hundred and thirty pounds), self-taught lawyer from Virginia, Mosby so impressed General Robert E. Lee with his lightning raids on Union supply trains and wagons and his sabotage of rail lines and bridges that Lee promoted the twenty-nine-year-old lieutenant twice within two weeks. By 1864 he had earned the rank of lieutenant colonel. Although Mosby and his Rangers were notorious for their guerilla tactics, they were not known for wanton cruelty. But the execution of his men enraged Mosby, and he was hell-bent on retribution. After hunting down more than two dozen of the troops responsible for the Front Royal killings, Mosby made them draw from a hat; those who picked a scrap of paper marked with an X would be shot. After carrying out what Mosby believed to be "a judicial sentence," he sent the following letter to the commanding general of the Shenandoah Valley region, Philip H. Sheridan. Mosby forewarned Sheridan he would exact even more severe measures if the circumstances were warranted.

Nov. 11, 1864

General:

Sometime in the month of September during my absence from my command, 6 of my men, who had been captured by your forces, were hung and shot in the streets of Front Royal, by the order and in the immediate presence of Brigadier General Custer. Since then another, captured by a Colonel Powell on a plundering exhibition into Rappahannock was also hung. A label affixed to the coat of one of the murdered men declared "that this would be the fate of Mosby and all his men."

Since the murder of my men not less than 700 prisoners, including many officers of high rank, captured from your army by this command, have been forwarded to Richmond, but the execution of my purpose of retaliation was deferred in order as far as possible to confine its operation to the men of Custer and Powell.

Accordingly, on the 6th instant 7 of your men were, by my order, executed on the Valley Pike, your highway of travel. Hereafter any prisoners falling into my hands will be treated with the kindness due to their condition, unless some new act of barbarity shall compel me reluctantly to adopt a course of policy repulsive to humanity.

Very respectfully,

your obedient servant,
Jno. S. Mosby,
Lieutenant-Colonel

Sheridan is not believed to have replied directly to Mosby, but he did write to General Henry Halleck, the US Army Chief of Staff, about his nemesis. Referring to those who hailed Mosby as a daring renegade, Sheridan decided the time had come to change that perception. "Mosby has annoyed me considerably," he admitted,

but the people are beginning to see that he does not injure me a great deal, but causes a loss to them of all that they have spent their lives in accumulating. Those people who live in the vicinity of Harper's Ferry are the most villainous in this valley, and have not yet been hurt much. If the railroad is interfered with, I will make some of them poor. Those who live at home in peace and plenty want this war to go on; but when they have to bear the burden by loss of property and comforts, they will cry for peace.

Mosby's popularity among pro-Confederate troops and civilians remained high for the duration of the war, and he evaded capture. (To the astonishment of his admirers, after the Civil War Mosby supported Ulysses S. Grant for president and became a Republican, the party of Abraham Lincoln.) As the rhetoric and animosity escalated on both sides in the final year of the conflict, US senators proposed sanctioning a "retaliatory resolution" concerning the treatment of Union soldiers in enemy prisoner of war camps; if an account surfaced of abuse in the South, an even harsher punishment would be meted out against imprisoned Confederate troops in the North. One of the most impassioned voices against the idea was a German-born law professor at Columbia University named Francis Lieber. Before the Civil War there was no comprehensive written code of conduct for the armed forces, and Lieber was asked by President Abraham Lincoln to draft such guidelines. In the spring of 1863, Lieber's General Order Number 100 was approved by the president and issued throughout the United States Army. The fundamental premise of the "Lieber Code," as it became known, was that civilians and enemy prisoners of war should be treated humanely regardless of "class, color, or condition." When the debate about retaliatory responses began in January 1865, Lieber wrote to his friend Charles Sumner, the senator from Massachusetts, to encourage a more just and moral resolution.

22 January 1865

My dear Sumner,

I return, once more, the London Times, with many thanks. I obtained the Letters of Historian in pamphlet form. Last evenings "Post" contained a very good article on it. Did you read it?

I am unqualifiedly against the retaliation resolutions concerning prisoners of war. The provision that the Southerners in our hands shall be watched over by national soldiers who have been in Southern pens, is unworthy of any great people or high-minded statesmen. I am most opposed to retaliation because it strikes those who ~~were~~ are not or may not be guilty of the outrage we wish to part an end to. That is the terrible character of almost all escalation in war. I abhor this revenge on prisoners of war, because we should sink thereby to the level of the enemy's shame and dishonour.

All retaliation has some limits. If we fight with Indians who slowly roast their prisoners, we cannot roast in turn the Indians whom we may capture. And what is more, I defy Congress or Government to make the Northern people treat captured Southerners as our sons are treated by them. God be thanked, you could not do it, and if you could how it would brutalize our own people! I feel the cruelty as keenly as any one; I grieve most bitterly that people whom we and all the world have taken to ~~have~~ possess the common attributes of humanity, and who after all are our kin have sunk so loathsomely low, I feel the hardship of seeing no immediate and direct remedy, except in conquering and trampling out the vile rebellion, but I maintain that the proposed (yet unfeasible) retaliation is not the remedy. Indeed calmly to maintain our ground would do us in the end far more good. Revenge is passion, and ought never to enter the sphere of public action. Passion always detracts from Power.

I believe that the ineffable cruelty practised against our men has been equalled in the history of our race by the Spanish treatment of the Indians and by the Inquisition, but counter cruelty would not mend matters. Those who can allow such crimes would not be moved by cruelties inflicted upon their soldiers in our hands. These cruelties therefore would be simply revenge, not retaliation, for retaliation as an element of the law of war and of nations in general, implies the idea of thereby stopping a certain evil. But no mortal shall indulge in revenge.

I am indeed against all dainty treatment of the prisoners in our hands, but for the love of our country and the great destiny of our people, do not sink, even in single cases, to the level of our unhappy, shameful enemy.

If I were in Congress I believe I would propose as a substitute, some resolution declaring our grief at the conduct of the South and our deepest sympathy with our sons and brothers in their hands; our knowledge of the truths of this cruelty; our firm resolution to put an end to this iniquity as soon as possible by putting an end to the rebellion, and our inability to retaliate in such a case, for the reason that all retaliation has with Christians and with men of honour, its limits prescribed by the morals of civilisation and by that God who supports heroic souls which are capable of withstanding the ~~feeling~~ indulgence of revenge when revenge is natural and might be indulged in.

It seems then that retaliations in this case is

impracticable, because, God be thanked, our people would not carry it out (the Northern man is immensely a kindhearted ~~man~~ being);

injurious, if it could be carried out, for it would barbarize our own people;

useless, because it would not affect the hard hearts which could indulge in the heaven-crying cruelties—a very shame to humanity itself; and therefore

immoral or criminal in turn because useless infliction of suffering no matter on whom is cruelty. It would be simple revenge, which does not belong to man.

If you could march out some ten thousand prisoners on our hands and say to the enemy: Either you treat our prisoners better or we execute every one of these ten thousand prisoners in our hands, and if you could make the enemy believe you, I would say, this is plain retaliation. But could you do it, would you do it? And as to starve those who have starved our sons—and by the thousand, why, every one knows the thing cannot be done, and Heaven be praised, it is so.

The only remedy for this bitter evil as for all others that beset us now is: Let us send men and men and men to ~~the~~ our Shermans and Thomasses that they may strike and strike and strike again. Let us place ourselves right before our own times and before posterity, and let the foul enemy see how he can place himself before the world and in history when lying has ceased. It is his affair.

Ever Yours
    Francis Lieber

Persuaded in part by Lieber's arguments, the Senate rejected the original resolution and passed another, more just version amenable to Lieber and his supporters. To the critics who accused Lieber of not understanding that the "realities" of war often compelled unpleasant but tough-minded actions, the sixty-five-year-old scholar reminded them that combat was not an abstract or theoretical concept to him; he had served in the Prussian Army as a young man and was injured during the Battle of Waterloo. Lieber also had a deeply personal stake in the Civil War—on both sides. His sons Norman and Hamilton fought for the Union, and his son Oscar fought for the Confederacy. Hamilton lost an arm, and Oscar was killed at the Battle of Williamsburg, Virginia, in May 1862. Lieber did not learn of his son's fate until months later. "I knew war as a soldier, as a wounded man in the hospital, as an observing citizen," Lieber said in reference to his boys, "but I had yet to learn it in the phase of a father searching for his wounded son, walking through the hospitals, peering into ambulances." It was an anguish that countless other parents—both in the North and the South—suffered during a war that claimed almost as many lives as all of America's other armed conflicts, from the eighteenth century to the beginning of the twenty-first, combined.

—⁀∾⁀—

An Indian Soldier Writes with Sadness and Amazement
About the Terrible Assortment of Weapons Being Used in World War I
&
British Soldier Ian H. Macdonnell Writes to His Mother
About Surviving a Gas Attack During the Battle of Passchendaele

Few of the weapons were new to warfare. The Flammenwerfer *was first proposed to the German army in 1901, but a crude version of the flamethrower existed in the fifth century BC. There are allusions to hand grenades in the fifteenth century, and references to landmines dating back to the eighteenth. In September 1776, the* Turtle *became the first submarine to attack, albeit unsuccessfully, an enemy vessel. Machine guns were tested in the American Civil War and later proved their efficacy in the 1898 Battle for San Juan Hill in Cuba. During the 1911–1912 Turko-Italian War, the Italians used airplanes—just eight years after Orville and Wilbur Wright's first flight in December 1903—for reconnaissance and bombing missions. But beginning in the summer of 1914, all of these instruments of war came together to form the components of an efficient killing machine that would decimate a generation of young men on a scale never before witnessed in history. Bullets, bombs, and bayonets would still account for most of World War I's fatalities, but the technologically "improved" weapons were particularly fearsome to the vast number of soldiers who had never heard of or seen such things before. "This war is very terrible," a Gurkha soldier named Shed Karn Das wrote home to India. "There is no safety for a man on the earth, or under the earth, in the air, or on the sea. Is this true warfare? . . . From all this it would seem that God is displeased with the peoples of the world." Of the estimated one million Indian troops—also known as sepoys—who fought with the British against the Germans on the Western Front, approximately ten percent of them were killed or wounded. An Indian soldier from Gujarat named Maganlal (last name unknown) wrote the following letter articulating the sentiments of many combatants, regardless of their country of origin. (A maund, which Maganlal refers to, is a unit of weight. There is no salutation or signature to the letter.)*

What a dreadful thing is this time of battle and strife, in which the most devilish weapons for the destruction of mankind, are being used by civilized and cultured nations of the Christian faith. Poisonous gases, bombs, machine guns which fire 700 bullets per minute, large and small cannon throwing cannon balls 30 Bengali maunds in weight, Zepplins, large and small flying machines which throw bombs from the air, land mining and the blowing up of sepoys located in the trenches, liquid fire that causes the clothes on the body to ignite, the firing of torpedoes under water without warning or giving any time to lower boats, and the using of star shells which turn the nights into day. Such are the modern and scientific processes by which nations seek to destroy one another. Every effort is being made to win over neutral countries. Alas! there is no God-like man who tries to stop this deadly war, but it seems that such must be the will of God for the punishment of sinners. That our benign Government may be victorious and that, once more, there may be peace on earth, such is my prayer.

One weapon, unleashed on a wide scale for the first time during World War I, caused particular alarm. In the late afternoon of April 22, 1915, after a ground-shaking bombardment by German artillery earlier that morning, a second barrage thundered throughout the farmlands of western Belgium. French and Algerian sentries on the Ypres salient watched with curiosity and then growing apprehension as a strange, smoky green vapor floated gently across the fields and into their lines. As it enveloped the men, some of whom had already started to flee, they clutched their throats and began gasping for air. It was chlorine gas. French and other Allied troops had used tear-gas grenades in the first month of the war, but this was the first time poison gas had been used by either side. Over the course of the war more potent gases were developed, and it is estimated that they caused almost one hundred thousand deaths—every one of which was excruciating. In addition, more than a million troops were injured by gas, including a British soldier named Ian H. Macdonnell who survived an attack at, it is assumed, the third battle of Ypres, also known as Passchendaele (named after the little village captured at the end of the campaign by British and Canadian forces). Macdonnell feared that his mother might hear that he had been gassed and wanted to assure her that he was fine and there was no cause for alarm—despite the obvious scare he and his men had just endured. (The "smoke" reference at the end of the letter was Macdonnell's not-so-subtle hint to his mother that, gassed or not, he wanted her to send him cigarettes.)

Dearest Mother,

I write this in bed from 15th Corps Dressing Station—I hope to heaven this will catch you before the war office list. <u>I am all right no danger at all,</u> but it will reach you as "gas poisoning." The Huns shelled our camp—which is about 2 miles between the lines—our 13th—most are pleasant—a lot of men were hit—we had most of our men out on working parties at night—up in the line—thank goodness they were.

We at the camp went to sleep & at 12.15 there was a yell, & I woke with my mouth full of a choking stench, to the tune of screaming shell—Gas!

We got masks on in the dark. Shells hitting everything. The Col. & I in our masks tried to get to the Brigade. We were lost in the dark & the shell holes. & came back to the hut under the sand bank. The rest is a night mare—an 8 inch gas shell hit the edge of the hut smashed it in & knocked us all endways broken glass, darkness,—& men, vomiting, & raving for air. Two had legs blown off. We wore our masks from 12:15 till 4. & the shell fell like rain. Ones' eyes were blinded even through the mask. However the net result is nothing to speak of—

All the food in the camp was poisoned of course. & the beautiful cake you sent had of course to be buried!

I was all right at about 10 o clock in the morning—barring dizziness, & runny eyes—but the doctor stethescoped me & said I had to go down. I didnt want to but they put me in bed when I got here. Mother dear I shall be out of hospital & going back in perhaps 4 day—thats all dont be anxious. All I have now is a filthy taste in my mouth & a little discomfort in chest & throat.

Already my eyes are better & I can read—& smoke! (please note)—so if you get a notice saying I am gassed you will know it is nothing & I shall probably be back to duty by the time you get it. I am not bad.

> Your loving son
> Ian

—◊—

After a Visit to the Western Front, British Artist Paul Nash Vows to His Wife That He Will Express the "Bitter Truth" of the War in His Paintings
&
A Canadian Clergyman Named William Mayse Writes to His Wife About a Battlefield Death That Profoundly Affected Him

The Passchendaele offensive, commanded by Sir Douglas Haig, was a prolonged bloodbath fought in knee-deep mud by exhausted troops that, in the end, achieved little. The Allied forces gained several miles of strategically insignificant land at a cost of three hundred and ten thousand casualties. (For the Germans, the count was about two hundred and sixty thousand.) A twenty-eight-year-old artist named Paul Nash was at Passchendaele, but not to fight; Nash had enlisted in 1914 but returned to England due to an accident unrelated to combat. He became an official war artist and, after recuperating and making numerous appeals to get back into the action as soon as possible, was sent to the Western Front. "My beloved," Nash began a letter to his wife from Ypres soon after his arrival, "This afternoon I go up the line to stay at a Brigade H[ead] Q[uarters] for a night or two from where I shall see wonderful things." Nash was filled with anticipation that he would be able to watch a battle in all its dramatic fury, but what he discovered was a spectacle of despair and annihilation beyond his imagination. Government officials had encouraged Nash and his colleagues to create uplifting and patriotic art, but, overwhelmed by the almost apocalyptic vision he had seen, Nash was emphatic that his work would be a testament to the war's barbarity, regardless of what the bureaucrats wanted or instructed. He wrote to his wife:

I have just returned, last night, from a visit to Bde HQ up the line, & I shall not forget it as long as I live. I have seen the most frightful nightmare of a country more conceived by Dante or Poe, unspeakable, utterly indescribable. In the fifteen drawings I have made I may give you some vague idea of its horror, but only being in it and of it can ever make you sensible of its dreadful nature & what men in France have to face.

We all have a vague notion of the terrors of a battle, & can ~~imagine~~ conjure up with the aid of some of the more inspired war correspondents and the pictures in the Daily Mirror some vision of a battlefield, but no pen or drawing can convey this country—the normal setting of the battles taking place day & night, month after month. Evil and the incarnate fiend alone can be master of the ceremonies in this war; no glimmer of God's hand is seen. Sunset & sunrise are blasphemous, mockeries to man; only the black rain out of the bruised & swollen clouds on thro' the bitter black of night is fit atmosphere in such a land. The rain drives on; the stinking mud becomes more evilly yellow, the shell holes fill up with green white water, the roads & tracks are covered in inches of slime, the ~~blacken~~ black dying trees ooze & sweat and the shells never cease.

They whine & plunge over head, tearing away the rotting tree stumps, breaking the plank roads, striking down horses & mules; annihilating, maiming, maddening; they plunge into the grave which is this land; one huge grave, and cast up the poor dead. O it is unspeakable, Godless, hopeless. I am no longer an artist interested & curious, I am a messenger who will bring back word from men fighting to those who want the war to last for ever. Feeble, inarticulate will be my message, but it will have a bitter truth, and may it burn their lousy souls.

No letters at all yet, I wish they would send them on. Be kind to your love & chide him not for writing so little, he had written to no one else yet. In a day or two he will have more to say & not so gloomy. I am longing to hear all about my darling. Tell me if you have sent John his Danae & my news of pictures generally.

For a little time, adieu, my sweet little baby

With a long long kiss the kind only we can give

From
Your most loving idolatrous lover
Paul

Despite the almost six hundred thousand casualties, Passchendaele was by no means the worst battle of the war. More than 1.2 million soldiers were killed and wounded at the Somme, and just under a million at Verdun. Soldiers in the field found it especially difficult to grapple with the enormity of the blood-shed, and they reacted in different ways. Some were emotionally cauterized by it all. "We all lay with our nerves strung up, waiting for the attack for which we supposed the artillery fire had been preparing," a German soldier named August Hopp wrote home. "But it didn't come. In spite of it all they would have found us at our posts, although they were still firing on our flank and killing and wounding many. But one gets by degrees so callous about death that one hardly looks round when anybody falls." Others could be shaken by a single death. William Mayse served with the Canadian Army as a clergyman, and in a graphic letter to his wife, Betty, he related a sight that emphasized to him the human cost of the war behind the incomprehensibly large statistics.

My Dear Betty:

I received you letter No 5 last eve in which you tell of Smalley's invitation—I guess I have already answered it, after reading your letter Pryor & I went for a ramble over another part of the battlefield, & we saw still more awfull sights than hithertoo—I would not be exaggerating if I said that we saw scores of unburried Germans in battered trenches & arround shell-holes, here & there what had been a French soldier & sometimes we would come across one of our own Canadian boys—when we found any remains that looked like a Canadian, we would bury them as well as we could—for there are all kinds of picks & shovels etc, lying around—I came across one of our boys—decomposed beyond all recognition but he lay just as he had fallen—the head was missing—but all the accoutriments was buckled on, his rifle & helmet lay close by—I cut the buckle off the belt as a momento, & we burried what remained of him—I tried to find something by which he might be identified but it was impossible—Poor boy—in some far away home in Canada some-one is mourning the loss of husband—son or sweetheart—& the saddest of all is, they will never know how he died—or where he is burried, & even now they may be clinging to the hope, that he is still alive, a prisoner, for he would be listed among the missing.

Talk about the "glory of war" there is no glory, it is hellish devilish. We saw places too where the trenches & ground arround was literally bloodsoaked & here & there shell holes with blood & water still standing in them. I must close this letter now, will write as often as possible. I have written to Rose & also the Bank about that money. Love & kisses.

Will

**Harold "Pompey" Elliott, Commander of the Seventh
Australian Battalion, Describes to His Friend J.C. Richardson
the Bloody Battle of Lone Pine During the Gallipoli Campaign
&
In a Letter Found on Her Husband's Body, the Wife
of a Turkish Soldier Bemoans Their Separation and Wishes
for His Safe Return**

*In no other conflict has trench warfare been as integral to the fighting as it was
during World War I. And while most of it occurred on the Western Front, which
stretched for more than four hundred miles, primarily through Belgium and
France, Allied forces in Turkey faced enemy troops that were, in spots, entrenched
a mere twenty feet away. On April 25, 1915, the first wave of approximately
sixteen thousand mostly untested soldiers in the Australian and New Zealand
Army Corps, or "Anzac," landed at Gallipoli in western Turkey as part of a
larger Allied operation to take over the peninsula. Their objective was to
secure the region, allowing the British fleet unimpeded passage to Constantinople
through the Dardanelles Straits, with the ultimate aim of knocking Turkey—
a German ally—out of the war. Due to poor planning, particularly on the part
of the British First Lord of the Admiralty, Winston Churchill, and the unexpected resolve of the Turkish soldiers, the Anzacs made little headway. Thousands
died during the initial invasion at what would become known as Anzac Cove
and the struggle to take the heights above it. A protracted stalemate—not unlike
the deadlock on the Western Front the Gallipoli landings were intended to cir-
cumvent—ensued, and the Anzacs ended up perched in a cramped area that,
at its farthest inland point, was only three quarters of a mile from the sea. In
August the Anzacs launched an ambitious, multipronged offensive, with the
biggest battle occurring at Lone Pine. Prominent in the action was the commander of the Seventh Australian Battalion, Harold "Pompey" Elliott, a
thirty-seven-year-old lawyer from Victoria. In January 1916, just over a
month after he and his men had evacuated the Gallipoli coast, Elliott wrote to
a friend and colleague, J. C. Richardson, about the historic confrontation at
Lone Pine between the Anzacs and the Turks.*

TEL EL KEBIR, EGYPT
25th Jan. 1916

My Dear J.C.,

Your letter of the 22nd Oct. reached me this day having been
apparently delayed in transit. I was very interested indeed to hear that
your brother was with the 7th. They are out on parade at present, but I
will see him when they return. With reference to my last letter to you

and my expectation of going out, I owe my deliverance to one thing, At the time I wrote I had orders to attempt the capture of a position with a totally inadequate force in my opinion. We were saved from meeting the fate of the 8th and 10th Light Horse, who were practically exterminated attempting a similarly hopeless task by the fact that we were urgently needed for another task, namely, to hold the position known as the "Lone Pine" which had been captured by our first Brigade. All these attacks were ordered with one object, viz., the distraction of the Turks' attention from the landing at Suvla Bay then in contemplation. My task was (with a Battalion counting cooks and all details, signallers, it did not amount to quite 700 men) to attack a formidable enemy's work known as "Johnston Jolly" We knew it was held by a large number of men with machine guns giving three tiers of fire. We have since ascertained that it was held by three complete battalions. You can guess whether my doubts were justified. However, just as we were making preparation for the attack by making blanket pathways attached to wooden poles to throw over the enemy's wire entanglements as we rushed forward; I was sent for hurriedly, ordered to cease all preparations for the attack and move at once to the support of the 1st Brigade whose remnants were being hard pressed in Lone Pine. Owing to the haste and to some of the men being engaged on fatigue carrying food and water from the beach to the firing line and to our machine guns being already engaged with the enemy, I had to move off with only 511 men and 16 officers. Our task here was comparatively simple compared to the previous attack which we were preparing for. Merely to hold a position already won, although only partially prepared for defence. Here we sustained the attack of some 3,000 Turks for about 20 hours practically without food and no rest.

The worst attack was made at dawn about 4.30 and kept up till nearly 8 o'clock. During this attack 344 rank and file and 12 officers fell, killed and wounded. I myself, my signalling officer and two other officers being the only unwounded officers and 167 men unwounded survived. My Adjutant had had his arm shattered by a bullet after a hand to hand fight with a Turk who jumped into the trench and tried to bayonet him but whom he shot with his revolver in the stomach. As he fell his friends threw a bomb over which burst and blew his head to pieces and so saved further trouble. Four of my boys got the "V.C." in this fight which is a record for one Regiment in one fight. I account for it by the fact that the Divisional Commander himself came down about 2 o'clock. He judged by the number of wounded streaming by his Head Quarters that we were getting a warm time and came down personally to tell me that we must hold the position to the very last man, and if necessary he and his staff would come and personally weld rifles and bayonets with the men if it became necessary.

He saw with his own eyes the trenches choked with the dead and dying trodden on by their comrades because they could not be removed from the narrow trenches, and torn to pieces by the bombs and shells the enemy were hurling over. Three times I, myself, thought it was all over and drew my revolver to do my little bit but each time the living never faltered as they reached the trench and it was only a very few, not more than six, who were brave enough to jump into the trenches on to the bayonets and in practically every case they were dead before their feet touched the bottom. In one place a line of dead men with their bayonets still over the parapet held about 20 or 30 yards of trench. In the early morning a machine gun swept that part of the line and killed every man at that spot—the trench sloped forward and as they died each man so suddenly that he simply leaned forward on the parapet and in many cases their hats and bayonets could be seen standing steadily behind the parapet and curiously enough that part of the line was avoided by the enemy.

I had supports in the rear ready to rush anyone who came in there but I did not replace the men owing to the fact that the trench was shallow and exposed to fire from the left rear of the position while the Turks still had a position with machine guns and these men were all shot through the back of the head but apparently the Turks in front of them did not know this nor that they were dead. After a few hours sleep we were again sent back and again lost men from bombs but no sustained attack was again made.

But these partial attacks were sufficient to prevent us attending properly to the wounded and from removing the dead. The weather was hot and the flies pestilential. When anyone speaks to you of the glory of war, picture to yourself a narrow line of trenches two and sometimes three deep with bodies (and think too of your best friends, for that is what these boys become by long association with you) mangled and torn beyond description by the bombs and bloated and blackened by decay and crawling with maggots. Live amongst this for days in spite of taking advantage of every night to work with respirators endeavouring to remove them this is war and such is glory—whatever the novelists may say.

The trouble was that the space of 100 yards over which we charged to take these trenches was after the first surprise swept continually with shrapnel and machine gun fire and it was impossible in the daytime to get across without enormous risk. By working night and day a narrow tunnel was put through underground connecting the new position, but it was often choked by parties bringing food and water and ammunition and bombs and the men were so fatigued that the labor of carrying out a few dead utterly prostrated them in the heat. Eventually we buried hundreds by the simple method of digging the fire trench a few feet deeper and covering them over but the smell still persisted. In one place we found a sort of underground cellar used by the Turks for disciplinary purposes. When I examined it, I found its occupant was a dead Turk chained to a stout post. In the first attack evidently some of our men had entered and in the semi-darkness had spotted an enemy and run him through with his bayonet without enquiry. I had over 30 corpses friends and foes alike fitted into this chamber, covered with chloride of lime and the entrance sealed with sand bags. Still the corpses did not diminish appreciably and we dug a huge tunnel back towards our own lines underground and packed in corpses in hundreds until it was full, then strewed lime over them and blocked them up. For over three weeks we labored night and day feverishly strengthening that position, erecting barbed wire entanglements and pushing them out in front night and day engaged in bombing and sniping at the enemy who had dug a new line a few yards from us burying corpses living and eating in a slaughter house. We were not allowed to have blankets or even overcoats lest we should be more likely to sleep sound and be hard to arouse in the event of an attack, but a few men at a time by reliefs were sent back to rest and then relieve others.

I got a chill from this developed a sort of fever and subsequently pleurisy, after three weeks of this sort of thing, was sent to Malta and subsequently to England. I managed to get back by the 9th Dec. and took part in the final retirement from Gallipoli and the fact that we were not simply decimated during the evacuation will always seem to me due to a special interposition of providence in our favor.

Looking back now I still cannot understand how, unless, their eyes were blinded, we could have eluded their vigilance for in many places the trenches were only a few yards apart.

All the Reserves and Supports were sent off gradually a few thousands each night for a week beforehand until there was only the firing line and supports we cleared and a few guns. Finally the last night they were gradually thinned out until all got away. One of my N.C.Os. suggested a plan (which was adopted by   for deceiving the Turks) was very successful; by means of two bully beaf tins so placed that water in the higher one would drop into a lower one and by its weight pull the trigger and fire the rifle. By adjusting the size of the hole in the upper one we found that we could fire a rifle at any interval up to an hour.

The plan was adopted and we gained a full hour by this dance before the Turks could suspect our departure from its trenches by the sudden cessation of fire along the line and it cost us only some 10 damaged rifles.

Your brother has just seen me. I have arranged for him to attend an N.C.Os' class. He will be useful as an officer later if he survives. I am only too glad to get hold of anyone who will likely make an officer for we use them up very quickly. I have had over 70 in my own regimental list since I left Australia and I am several under strength still.

We have orders to move from here very shortly, our destination is secret, don't know if there will be any fighting but I suspect plenty of sand and digging in.

Kindest regards to

Yours very sincerely,

Pompey

Anzac fatalities by the end of the entire eight-month Gallipoli campaign numbered more than ten thousand. (In total, approximately 40,000 Allied soldiers were killed. The Turks lost twice that many.) Although defeated, the Anzac troops had displayed, in the eyes of their countrymen in Australia and New Zealand, such valor and resourcefulness throughout their ordeal that April 25 was named a national holiday—"Anzac Day"—in both nations. (Within a month of writing his letter, Pompey Elliott was promoted to brigadier general, and after the war he was elected to the Australian parliament. Elliott was afflicted, however, with what would later be considered "post-traumatic stress disorder," and in 1931 he committed suicide.) Correspondences from Gallipoli by Turkish troops are rare, but a fragment of one letter by a soldier conveyed the sense of determination that made the Turks such formidable opponents. Writing to his mother, he recalled a moment of faith:

> *I opened my hands, looked up to the heavens and said: "God of Turks, Master of the Birds, the sheep, the leaves, the mountains. You have given all this to the Turks. Please leave it to the Turks. God, all this soldier wants is to keep this land from the British and the French. Grant me this wish."*

And just as the parents and spouses of Allied soldiers fretted about the well-being of their sons and husbands at the front, so did the loved ones of Turkish troops. The following letter was taken off the body of one Turkish soldier.

To my dear Husband:

I humbly beg to enquire after your blessed health. Your daughter sends her special salaams, and kisses your hands. Since you left I have seen no one. Since your departure I have had no peace. Your mother has not ceased to weep since you left. We are all in a bad way. Your wife says to herself "While my husband was here we had some means" since your departure we have received nothing at all. Please write quickly and send what you can. All your friends kiss your hands and your feet.

May God keep you and save us from the disasters of this war.

Your wife,

Fatima

There were an estimated two hundred thousand French, British, Indian, and Canadian casualties overall during the Allied operation in Turkey (in which the Anzacs played an essential part). The Turks sustained two hundred and fifty thousand casualties.

—∽∿∽—

Alfred Dougan Chater Shares with His Mother an Incredible Story of Humanity and Camaraderie from the Front Lines

"What would happen, I wonder," First Lord of the Admiralty, Winston Churchill, remarked in a November 1914 letter, "if the armies suddenly and spontaneously went on strike and said some other method must be found of settling the dispute!" For a fleeting moment one month later, this seemingly fanciful notion became a reality. On December 25, 1914, a British soldier named Alfred Dougan Chater, serving with the Second Battalion, Gordon Highlanders, sent the following letter home reporting on the momentous occasion.

Christmas Day.

Dearest Mother,

I am writing this in the trenches in my "dug out"—with a wood fire going and plenty of straw it is rather cosy although it is freezing here and real Christmas weather—

I think I have seen one of the most extraordinary sights today that anyone has ever seen—About 10 o'clock this morning I was peeping over the parapet when I saw a German waving his arms, and presently two of them got out their trenches and came towards ours—we were first going to fire on them when we saw they had no rifles. So one of our men went out to meet them and in about two minutes the ground between the two lines of trenches was swarming with men and officers of both sides, shaking hands and wishing each other a happy Christmas—This continued for about half an hour when most of the men were ordered back to the trenches.

For the rest of the day nobody has fired a shot and the men have been wandering about at will on the top of the parapet and carrying straw and fire wood about in the open—we have also had joint burial parties with a service from some dead—some German and some ours—who were lying out between the lines. Some of our officers were taking groups of English and German soldiers—This extraordinary truce has been quite impromptu—there was no previous arrangement and of course it had been decided that there was not to be any cessation of hostilities.

I went out myself and shook hands with several of their officers and men—from what I gathered most of them would be as glad to get home again as we should—we have had our pipes playing all day and everyone has been wandering about in the open unmolested but not of course as far as the enemies lines—The truce will probably go on until someone is foolish enough to let off his rifle—we nearly messed it up this afternoon, by one of our fellows letting off his rifle skywards by mistake but they did not seem to notice it so it did not matter—I have been taking advantage of the truce to improve my "dug-out" which I share with D. McBain the Scotch fellow—we put on a proper roof this morning and now we have got a tiled fire place and brushwood and straw on the floor—we leave the trenches tomorrow and I shant be sorry as it is much too cold to be pleasant at nights.

27th I am writing this back in billets—the same business continues yesterday and we had another parley with the Germans in the middle we exchanged cigarettes and autographs and some more people took photos—I dont know how long it will go on for—I believe it was supposed to stop yesterday but we can hear no firing going on along the front today except a little distant shelling. We are, at any rate having another truce on New Years Day as the Germans want to see how the photos come out! Yesterday was lovely in the morning and I went for several quite long walks about the lines—It is difficult to realise what that means but of course in the ordinary way there is not a sign of life above ground and everyone who puts his head up gets shot at.

With heaps of love and wishes to you and everyone for a happy new year.

Your loving son

Dougan

I'm so sorry I forgot to wish Father many happy returns—I do so now though somewhat late—

It was the first and last time such a Christmas truce would take place, both because the enmity between the British and Germans would intensify as time went on and because the senior officers ordered an end to unofficial cease-fires. "Divisional Commanders [must] impress on all subordinate commanders the absolute necessity of encouraging the offensive spirit of the troops," Sir Horace Smith-Dorrien, the British commander of II Corps, sternly instructed after the unsanctioned truce. "Friendly intercourse with the enemy, unofficial armistices (e.g., "we won't fire if you don't" etc.) and the exchange of tobacco and other comforts, however tempting and occasionally amusing they may be, are absolutely prohibited." But the memory could not be easily discarded by those on either side of the Western Front. "Christmas 1914 will remain unforgettable to me," a German soldier named Josef Wenzl wrote to his parents. "The British burst into song with a carol, to which we replied with 'Stille Nacht, heilige Nacht.' It was a very moving moment—hated and embittered enemies were singing carols around the Christmas tree. All my life I will never forget that sight."

—⁂—

A German Soldier Named Hans Fleischer Writes of a "Rare, Unforgettable" Experience That Allowed Him, Momentarily, to Forget About the War

Amidst the maelstrom of battle, combatants often seek out and cling to any vestige of civilization they can find—letters and photographs from home, books, music, delicacies, anything that is a distraction from the filth and turmoil of war and reminds them of calmer, more pleasant times. Feeling suffocated by his environs, a World War I German soldier named Hans Fleischer volunteered to go out on a patrol while stationed in the Alsace region of Germany, territory which is now in eastern France. While walking through the woods he made an extraordinary discovery. (The salutation and introduction to the letter are missing.)

"The man has to get out," I thought to myself, handing over the watch and going out on a reconnaissance mission. I wanted to know exactly where I was.

Through the thick underbrush, I meandered my way through a small path. Wonderful woods all around me. Not too long thereafter, I came upon a lighted area, and before me lay in the middle of a blooming flower garden, in peaceful silence, the castle of Baron de Turckheim. I stood struck in sight of it, and slowly I went closer to the gentle hills. Behind me lay Blamont. A wonderful picture, this little city with its red-brown roofs, built into a rolling valley, and marked by the old weathered ruins that Bernhard once destroyed during the Thirty Year's War, and the high, double towered gothic church. Like an old, good Swabian town,

Two Views of Verdun

Ossuary of Douaumont, which holds the bones of an estimated one hundred thirty thousand French and German soldiers killed at Verdun. The ossuary was constructed to look like a sword plunged into the ground, never to be raised again.

We grew old, all of us, dear mother, and, for a lot of us, our gray hairs will be the permanent mark of what we endured. No more laughter, no more cheer within the battalion. We're all carrying in our hearts a sense of grief for our comrades killed at Verdun. Should I be happy that I escaped? I don't know, but if I am killed later on, it would have been better for me to have been left here.

—Nineteen-year-old French soldier Gaston Biron,
writing to his mother on March 25, 1916.
He died six months later.

Parts of the area were originally wooded, and there is nothing there now except black trunks, not a leaf remains or a blade of grass, and despite everything, in all this horror, there's a wonderful sight: in the morning a lark sings and reminds us that beyond all this fighting, there's still a marvelous spring that will be there to lift our spirits.

—*Twenty-three-year-old German soldier Christian Brodeching,*
writing to his family on May 21, 1916.
He, too, was later killed in the war.

Photo by Andrew Carroll

Jewish grave at the German Military Cemetery in Verdun, France. Ten thousand Jews who fought in the German Army during World War I died or sustained serious injuries. Those who survived, no matter how heroic their wartime achievements, were later hounded, deported, and even killed by the Nazis.

there it lay, an image of freedom in the middle of the destruction of war. I went further through the garden and fields, past Weihern, and soon I stood on the terrace of the glorious construction. With astonishment, I climbed the stair and went in.

What a miserable image of destruction! The whole glory and wonder of this castle had become ruins and piles of rubble, everything cut down and in pieces, the wonderful chamber with its glorious library and its heavy, gold shrine, the woodwork covered room with its proud row of ancestor's portraits, the lovely living room with its uncommon furniture—everything forever demolished. With a shudder, I went through the rooms. There! In one corner in the back—was that not a grand piano? I stood in my tracks, and then almost fell down with shock. Right! A grand piano: Steinway & Sons and untouched. A miracle! Finally, finally, music! How painful and with what longing I had missed just this holiest of all arts, and now I find in the middle of all of this rubble a grand piano! The room became like a temple to me, and I sat down as if at an altar. I began slowly, my fingers gliding tremblingly over keys no different than others I have played on. All of my longings became swelling tones that went out into the summer morning. They were holy moments of the blissful memories of the world, when I was able to make music again for the first time. I awoke like out of a dream when I stopped.

But there! What was lying right under the piano? Did I see correctly? Right, sheet music! In haste I grabbed for the "The Valkyries." That was the culmination of my happiness, to find my Valkyries here! Soon, the sound rang out. Joyously and then more so. The old, raw soldier's playing became more relaxed, and seldom has a song of love and springtime and inner power emanated from me with more emotion. Outside, the destructive struggle between life and death, with all of its terrible incidents and gruesomeness—and here, in this moment, a German song of love. Rare, unforgettable hours! Feeling deeply fulfilled and happy, I had been taken back to my peaceful garden house. I was at home. I had made German music, and now I could go into war again. Blessed, I returned to my comrades.

Hans Fleischer

What is unique about Fleischer is that he is believed to have been one of an estimated ninety-five thousand Jews who fought in the German Army during World War I. It is not known if Fleischer survived, but even if he had, his life—like that of his fellow Jewish veterans—would have been one of harassment, and possibly even worse. Many Jewish veterans fled Germany after facing threats and persecution, including death in Adolf Hitler's concentration camps. Their years of service and sacrifice offered little to no protection against the anti-Semitic wrath of the Nazi regime.

—⁓—

In a Brief but Upbeat Letter to His Sister, Professional Baseball Player Eddie Grant Promises to "Knock Old Hindenburg Out of the Box in the First Inning"
&
Writing from France, William Guy Lamont Describes to His Wife and Daughter in the United States the Carnage That Seemed to Cover Every Piece of Ground

Americans were not indifferent to the conflagration abroad that began in 1914 and seemed to blaze more ferociously with every passing year. Tens of millions of United States citizens had either emigrated from one of the countries mired in the war or were the sons and daughters of those who had. Most Americans, however, felt it was not their fight, and President Woodrow Wilson successfully won re-election in 1916 by campaigning on the promise that he would keep the US out of the conflict. But after a steady accumulation of attacks and diplomatic developments—Germany's sinking of the British liner Lusitania, *which killed 128 Americans; repeated strikes on US merchant vessels; and the discovery of the Zimmerman Telegram, which revealed an attempt by Germany to form an alliance with Mexico—the mood of the country shifted dramatically. After a stirring speech by President Wilson, the US Congress officially declared war on Germany on April 6, 1917. "I don't know how much of a success I shall make of it," one American volunteer named Eddie Grant wrote to a friend, but, he went on to assert,*

> *I had determined from the start to be in this war if it came to us, and if I am not successful as an officer I shall enlist as a private, for I believe there is no greater duty that I owe for being that which I am—an American citizen.*

Grant's desire to serve was shared by many others, but his enlistment attracted more attention than most because Edward Leslie Grant had been the third baseman for the New York Giants (the team's name before they moved to San Francisco in 1958) and had played in the 1913 World Series. Grant was the first in what would become a long tradition of professional athletes who joined the military in times of conflict. Boxing champion Joe Louis and baseball legend Jackie Robinson were both in the army during World War II, although they were relegated to mostly stateside duties. Lawrence "Yogi" Berra, who would achieve fame as a catcher for the New York Yankees, was off the coast of Normandy on D-Day in a gunship providing antiaircraft fire. (Berra would later claim that he only had one, obviously accidental, hit—an American plane. After the pilot parachuted out, Berra said he could hear him cussing loudly the whole way down.) Future Baseball Hall of Famer Ted Williams flew combat missions in Korea, and football great Roger Staubach served in Vietnam. Writing to his sister Florence, Grant conveyed the patriotism and buoyant optimism shared by many who enlisted. He saw the war as the ultimate game, and he had no intention of losing. (Earle, mentioned in the letter, was his brother-in-law, and Paul von Hindenburg was the German Army's chief of staff.)

Dear Florence:—

I am an applicant for a commission in the Officer's Reserve Corps as you will see in a letter to father. The martial spirit of the Grants was bound to assert itself. But !!—don't allow Earle to get foolish. There are enough fellows in my position without others—he can do twice as much good right where he is. I cannot make this too strong—his garden and work is enough.

I want also to impress upon you that I am not the least bit pessimistic about this. And can't see why any of you should be. Why the Germans won't be able to win a game from us. We would knock old Hindenburg out of the box in the first inning.

There are seven of us in this house who are applying—maybe also probably all will not be accepted. McCormick my room-mate will not be accepted. He took his physical exam yesterday and had an accident—for when they took his chest expansion—he broke the tape-measure—he expanded seven inches.

Well will write Anon and let them all know that if necessary I will do all the fighting for all of us. <u>But don't think</u> it will be necessary.

With love

Les.

On October 5, 1918, five weeks before the armistice was declared, Captain Eddie Grant, serving with the 77th Division, 307th Infantry Regiment, H Company, was cut down by shrapnel while he and his men were under a furious artillery attack in the Argonne Forest. Grant's death marked the first of many to come among athlete/soldiers. Washington Senators outfielder Elmer Gedeon was shot down in France during World War II; Don Steinbrunner and Bob Kalsu, both professional football players, died in Vietnam; and Arizona Cardinals safety Pat Tillman, who had given up a $3.6 million contract to join the army after September 11, 2001, was killed in Afghanistan by friendly fire on

April 22, 2004. Although he did not do so professionally, a young man named Robert Carver, from Poplarville, Mississippi, played football, and his early letters also expressed an eagerness to fight. "[I would] just as soon go [into battle] as to go into a football game and you know how I like that," he wrote to his sister in October 1917. "Have been hurt, nearly killed once and am willing to play again. There is no more danger for me where I am than there would be playing football." But less than a year later, after seeing combat, his enthusiasm dimmed. Carver wrote:

> *We had several fellows with arms & legs off, one or two with consumption, several gased they looked awful and nine of ten shell shocked which caused them to loose their mind, to my notion the worst of all. Whatever they were doing when the shell exploded they do all the time. One or two with rheumatism and two Red Cross nurses one had lost her mind the other was taking care of her and returning to recuperate.*

The pattern would repeat itself. Troops deploying for Europe, where most US servicemen fought, began their "great adventure" overflowing with confidence—just as the British, French, German, Russian, Turkish, Italian, Serbian, and other soldiers had in 1914 before the war physically and psychologically ground them down. And the letters Americans sent home soon began to echo the horror of those written years before their arrival. Near the end of the war, a pastor from Russell, Kansas, named William Guy Lamont wrote to his wife and daughter after he and his men were relieved from the front lines. Safe from danger, he was able to relate the following account depicting life in the trenches "somewhere in France."

Oct. 25, 1918.

My Dear Dollie Girls—

       Today I received three letters from you, one dated Aug. 24th. one Aug. 28th. and No. Four dated Sept. 22nd.

Am very glad to get them for I was very anxious to hear from you as I have a little more chance to think just now. Our boys finally got out of the line and we had two days marching, one of them in the rain and slush, ~~one~~ a little ride in a box car then marching from one thirty a.m. until four A.M. Now we are in a little shell torn town but from under shell fire. I think we are surely the most talked of division in the army. If not we should be for what our boys did in four weeks is unexcelled any where on earth.

No doubt you to will rejoice to know we are out. It may be possible that I will take a run to Paris next week if so I am going to send you a cable so it will beat this letter there about a month. May be to busy to go if supplies get in for the boys are all crazy for just any thing they can get and there is no other place that they can get it around here.

Four weeks of trenches with out a house, newspaper, or bath has told on all of us. Our loss was heavy but light comparing it with the many towns and square miles taken.

In one shell hole I saw seven of our boys piled up. One was a 1. Lt. Heads blown off, one leg lying thirty feet away, arms blown away. For miles they were scattered along one or two in a place. There were in places dead germans thick enough to walk on, killed in all manner of ways. There would be strings of captured germans coming out continually. One dark night I was carrying up some cigarettes to the boys after they had come out of line for a few hours rest before going over again. I had a big gunny sack on my back, shells were flying but none coming my way but were bursting in a town half mile away and others whining over my head going to a town two miles behind us; well I was staggering along thru the dark and shell holes and behold I ran slam bang over a dead german. The feeling was not very pleasant. The cigaretts were delivered and appreciated in a way you will never know.

As I am writing such plesant things will go a little farther for these were our daily experiences There are no plesant things to write for there has been nothing for weeks but big guns roaring, shells flying and dead men and horses. If our division can only keep at it awhile this whole war will soon be over for we will have all the germans either dead or prisoners.

Oh yes, I was going to tell something else. One evening I was in a german trench on the Hindenburg line and was using a pick & shovel to square it up a little for my bed and when just good and started I dug into a german that had been buried in the edge of the trench so I moved down about ten feet and fixed it all right and stayed there three nights. Just to one side of this bed chamber about three feet on the bank two germans were burried and on the other side a few yards away was one not burried. When I left he was still lying out there. These are some of the worst things but there are many like them. Nothing can ever blot out of ones mind the memory of all this waste torn and devestated country and the aweful sights of death.

You wonder about sleeping under such conditions well, one gets so worn out that they become more dead than alive and one becomes more or less accustomed to every thing.

Hope I will be able to write of more cheerful things now for awhile. Hope my girls are well and happy. Lots of love. Dady.

—⚍—

After the Armistice Is Announced, a Chaplain
Named Melville Montgomery Tells His Family
That, Despite Being in Combat for Less Than a Day,
He Has "Seen Enough" of War to Last a Lifetime

With the infusion of fresh US troops in the final year of World War I and the climactic forty-seven day Meuse-Argonne offensive, the Americans and their allies were finally able to force the Germans into surrendering. On the eleventh hour of the eleventh day of the eleventh month in 1918, the war in Europe was over. The jubilation, as recorded in letter after letter, was palpable: "At about one minute past 11, a yell went up, and our boys and the Germans cheered till they were hoarse. It just echoed through the woods and over the fields," an American private named Maurice Barnett wrote to his family on November 14, 1918. He continued:

> *Five other boys and myself went over to the German lines to talk with the men we tried to kill and those that tried to kill us. They met us with a salute and a more tickled crowd of men then were those Germans. Some were fifty and sixty years old, some were only young boys.*

A French soldier named Maurius Maillet sent the following to his wife:

> *It's all over, peace has been signed—no more killing—the bugler is playing ceasefire. I'm in Ormont in the Ardennes. I'm leaving this moment for the border. Don't worry anymore. I'm out of danger now. Can't write any more today. A thousand sweet embraces for all of you. And a big kiss for you and see you soon.*

Back on the home front, the celebrations began almost immediately. Just after two A.M. (California time) on November 11, June Clevenger Miller sat down and penned a letter to her sister in Illinois:

> *The bells are ringing, the whistles are blowing, the guns are firing, every noise is doing, and every body is out. . . . My! What a peace! What a wonderful consummation. The scope! The millions it effects! . . . The whole world is shouting tonight, sick or well. And well it might, there never has been a brotherhood like this before.*

But amidst the excitement, there was also a somber realization of the staggering cost of the war to millions of families throughout the world. Lieutenant Frank Charles Miller (no relation to June, above), a Canadian who served with the

Royal Flying Corps, was in London recuperating from the flu when the postwar festivities began. In a letter to his mother, Miller shared with her a "pitiful sight" he noticed while walking the city streets.

> *There in Trafalgar Square where stands the Nelson Monument, I saw a merry mob having one hilarious time. . . . [Later] I was slowly wandering down Pall Mall about to turn into Trafalgar when something attracted my attention in the shadow of a door way. I naturally kept on walking but I curiously watched the object. It was a woman in mourning standing alone weeping softly. She was silently watching the merry making in the Square. Perhaps jealous of those living, enjoying freedom again, while she suffered the loss of her husband, boy, or sweetheart. Sad.*

Using an old typewriter and "liberated" German paper, a twenty-eight-year-old army chaplain named Melville Montgomery wrote to his family in Kansas two days after the cease-fire. "At the present sitting I am burning the last little piece of candle that I have," Montgomery noted in the beginning of his letter. Like many American troops, and despite the relatively brief amount of time he spent under fire, he was acutely aware of the incalculable toll the war had inflicted on so many nations. He had seen the detritus of battle scattered across the fields of France, and, as his letter indicated, the images had been burned into his memory. He continued:

At about six o'clock on the morning of the 11th two batallions of the 129th went into the front trenches. There was to be a "hop over." Five thirty is usually the zero hour. There was a delay in getting ready this time. At 9:10 the order was given. The men climbed over the trenches and started on a run out into a fog on no man's land. Soon Jerrie opened fire and the battle was on. At 9:15 the Adjutant of the Third batallion climbed over the top and shouted for the men to come back, but they were gone. He called a bugler and ordered him to blow recall. He blew recall three times and then blew assembly. The men came back. As far as we were concerned the war was over. It ended with our men going over the top.

One man was killed and several wounded. If the order had reached the line five minutes sooner they would have been saved. The order came to headquarters at 8:30 to stop all hostilities. Runners were sent to each batallion. The one to the third lost his way. Because of the delay they went over the top after peace was declared.

The Germans did not stop firing but increased their barrage. They

sent a large amount of shells into our line and into the village
headquarters. They sent over gas shells and we all had to don our masks.
Exactly on the dot of 11 o'clock Fritz stopped firing. The whole front
was as quiet as a country field. I went out and gathered together some of
the dead of the 130th in preparation for burial. Jerry came over into our
lines and we went over into his village. I talked about the reasons for the
war with a German Captain out in no man's land. He said he was glad it
was over and he was going back to his family.

The armistice is on. We are now praying that it may be a permanent
peace. We are all tired of it no matter how long or how short a time we
have been here, whether it is three weeks or four years. The eleventh
hour of the eleventh day of the eleventh month of the year 1918 was one
of the most important that the world has ever known. A great weight has
been removed from the hearts of people all over the world.

Since then I have been seeing the gruesome results of war. I buried a
man today who was killed in a swamp many days ago. He was a man
hidden with a machine gun in the tall grass and killed at his post. No
one knew he was there until some one happened to run across him today.

I have seen a German air plane crushed on the ground with the blood
of the driver sprinkled over it. I have seen graves torn open with the
remains of decaying men scattered about. I have seen wounded men and
dying. I have seen men who have marched all night, wet, cold, and
hungry go over the top with spirit. I have seen men suffering from gas. I
was at the battle front just one night and until eleven o'clock the next
morning. I have seen enough to do me. Others have been here for
months, some for years. Truly war is hell.

I do not know where we will go from here or what we will do. It is
hard to get transportation here for anything. There has been no mail
here since we came. It is hard even to get in town. Some are hopeful of
being home by Christmas. The boys want to get home by Christmas.
Good luck to them but I don't think they will make it.

I am in good spirits and still have a good appetite. I will be glad
whenever any mail comes for me. I have moved around so much it will
take it forever to come. I do not know when this letter will get out. I
hope quite soon. I wish I could send you all a Christmas present.

We are all glad the war is about over, aren't we?

With lots of love,
Melville.

Writing from the USS *New Orleans,* Ensign William Czako Gives His Sister an Eyewitness Account of One of the Most Fateful Attacks in American—and World—History

"Dear Sis: It is now 9:05 Sunday morning and we've been bombed now for over an hour," William Czako began a handwritten letter to his sister, Helen, on a winter morning from inside the USS New Orleans. *Czako, a young ensign from Fremont, Ohio, continued to provide his sister with a dramatic, moment-by-moment description of what he and his fellow sailors were experiencing as hundreds of Japanese Zeroes bombarded the unsuspecting US Pacific fleet at Pearl Harbor on December 7, 1941.*

Our anti aircraft guns are yammering and every so often a bomb strikes so close as to rock this ship. Again a bomb. We're helpless down here in the Forward Engine Room because our main engines are all tore down. We're trying to get underway if possible. We were just struck by a bomb near the bow. We're fighting back as much as possible because we have no power to load our guns, no power circuits to fire them. It is all being done by hand.

This seems to you like a nonchalant letter, but it's the straight dope. There is only a handful of us down here as most of our men are ashore on liberty. They really caught us sleeping this time. For a ship being in a Navy Yard for overhaul, we're putting up a good fight. The first officer has come down here now to take charge. We've lit off all the boilers that are not out of commission and are trying to get underway so that we will not be altogether helpless by laying alongside the dock and be a stationary target. Those bombs are getting closer—God grant that they do not hit that loaded oil tanker that is lying right across from us. Ten million gallons of fuel oil would bathe this ship in an inferno of fire. There are destroyers laying near us and three other cruisers. They must be the targets including us. I am on the interior communications telephone and I can hear the various stations screaming orders at one other. A man just brought us our gas masks. We have four engines but we can at the best only use 2. We're getting steam up though. The firing of the guns have abated somewhat but we've received orders to get underway as quickly as steam can be raised. The firing has continued. Wave after wave of bombers must be coming. We've figured that some aircraft carriers must be the source of these fast dive bombing planes. We've been struck several times now but fortunately there are no casualties as yet.

It seems funny to be writing like this when it may be your last. I've

never figured it to be like this. The next bomb may be our last but I will
keep writing until I am told to stop or am given another job. Some
Battleships that are tied up to the piers near the Fleet Air Base are
reported to be afire. It seems that the Airbase was their first objective and
the Battleships were just too close to that field. We were really caught
short this time. All the Battleships are in—they came in this week and
have been laying tied up. We have a few light cruisers that are out and
we hope they can keep that invading fleet at bay until our ships that are
undamaged and can get underway can get out of this trap. For a trap this
Pearl Harbor has become. If we can get out of here and to sea we've still
got a chance. We'll have our own power then. They can't get
ammunition fast enough to the guns because of no power to the hoists.
There has been a lull for a few minutes but there they go again. Strangely
Sis, I'm not excited but my heart is beating a little faster from all that
firing. I know that this is not a drill because the concussion of exploding
bombs is jarring the whole ship.

I don't know why I am writing this because if we are hit with a bomb
here—they won't find enough of me and the rest—let alone this letter. I
imagine it is to show myself that I can be calm under fire. A few of the
boys here are white faced and their voices hushed and choked. They too
know that this is no joke or mock battle—but the real stuff. For out of a
cloud studded blue sky and on a Sabbath morning death comes riding
unheralded to claim for its own the unprepared and unbelieving. Who
thought that they would strike in such a manner when most men were
ashore and spending their payday on those traditional Saturday night
sprees? They would not dare to attack us, let alone Pearl Harbor, the
mightiest and most fortified base in the world. They could not get
within a thousand miles of this place before we'd know it.—No they
dare not—but they did—Ah—there was one explosion—perilously
close—Yes—we were hit but not badly. The bomb struck between the
bow and the stern of another ship tied up just ahead of us. Comes the
report over my phones that there are no casualties but that there is a 40
ft hole in our bow and numerous small ones from flying shrapnel. That
was close and still our guns keep answering as fast as hands—and not
mechanical aid can feed those guns.

There is another lull and only sporadic bursts from our pom-poms.
Preparations to get underway are still continuing. It seems impossible
with all that machinery tore up but still we'll do what we can.—The
order has come now to secure from general quarters. We were under fire
for nearly two hours and I'm going to sneak up to topside to see what
happened—.

Although a short-term triumph, the attack on Pearl Harbor did not accomplish its primary goal of neutralizing the US Navy in the Pacific. Indeed, the American public that had wanted nothing to do with the Sino-Japanese conflict raging in the Far East was now out for blood. On December 8, Japan and the US were officially at war. Approximately twenty-four hundred Americans were killed at Pearl Harbor (almost a thousand of whom remain entombed in the USS Arizona, which sank to the bottom of the ocean). Forty-nine civilians were among the dead, including a three-month-old infant. William Czako miraculously survived and went on to fight in the Pacific. After the war, he remained in the Navy, working at a shipyard in Norfolk, Virginia, for more than thirty years.

—⁂—

In a Letter to His Family, Lieutenant Davydovych Zemchenkov Lashes Out at the "German Butchers" Responsible for Killing His Loved Ones
&
A German Soldier Named Bruno Kaliga Writes to His Family as the Situation in Stalingrad Reaches the Point of Utter Hopelessness

Claiming (falsely) that the invasion of the Soviet Union, an operation codenamed Barbarossa, was a preemptive strike to counter an imminent Soviet offensive, Adolf Hitler predicted in an address to his generals that Barbarossa would be a "battle of annihilation." German troops were convinced it would be, at the very least, a sound thrashing. "The war with Russia will last only four weeks!" one officer told his men. Well aware of the Russian capacity to stave off or outlast invaders, the Germans assembled an air and land force of unprecedented magnitude. The first of four million troops swarmed into the Soviet Union on June 22, 1941, catching Premier Joseph Stalin and his generals almost completely off-guard. "Today was a day of pride for us all," a German tank commander named Karl Fuchs, serving with the Seventh Panzer Division, wrote to his wife triumphantly from the Eastern Front on June 25. "The Russians are fleeing everywhere and we follow them. All of us believe in early victory!" Soon after, he expressed the contempt he and his fellow soldiers had for the Russian people as a whole, a prejudice nurtured by years of Nazi propaganda. "We're going to show those Bolshevik bums who's who around here," he crowed on June 28.

They fight like hired hands—not like soldiers, no matter if they are men, women, or children on the front lines. They're no better than a bunch of scoundrels. The entry of Spain and Hungary on our side against this Bolshevik archenemy of the world overjoyed us all. Yes, Europe stands under the leadership of our beloved Führer Adolph Hitler, and he'll reshape it for a better future.

It was not a future Fuchs would see; during a winter that even he admitted enveloped them in a "gripping cold not comparable to anything that we might experience at home," he was killed in action. And the Soviet troops he and his comrades had so disparaged turned out to be indefatigable soldiers fueled by righteous anger at having their country violated. (An estimated twenty to twenty-seven million Soviets died in the entire war.) The following letter, written by Lieutenant Davydovych Zemchenkov, offers a glimpse into the state of mind of one young soldier willing to sacrifice himself for his motherland. Zemchenkov was nineteen or twenty at the time, and he, too, would lose his life in the war.

Hello my Mama, Marusya, Nastya, Valya, Zoya and Ninochka!

Like a ray of sun, I send you a warm greeting from the front, where we are battling the German fiends. I wish you good health for many years, good spirits and strength to endure all the difficulties you encounter. Sweet Mama, I got a letter from Zhenya today. How terrible! The mental picture was shocking. Death bearing a fascist swastika has spread its wings over our family. It has torn our family apart and turned to ash the nest that we worked on for so many years. Death is red with the blood of those I hold dear and has destroyed all we have created and value. Can I possibly feel even the slightest pity or humanity for them after this? No! Only a bullet piercing the black heart of the German, only a pouring forth of a river of their foul blood, only their pitiless and complete annihilation can ease my soul and temper our grief.

Those damned fiends shot my beloved brother, sent my father to an early grave, burned my home and broke my mother's health. Words fail me. This grief is too great. I am crying and am not ashamed of my tears. My friends see them and grieve together with me. But I am not despairing or losing my strength. Quite the opposite: fiery hatred and revenge burn in my heart. I swear to wreak revenge on the enemy for the rest of my life. I will keep killing and killing Germans to avenge my brother's death. My comrades in arms swear to avenge my brother's death as well. We grip our weapons tighter and shoot even straighter. The damned fiends have already felt our blows. They've already tasted plenty of our lead and steel. We've already killed several thousand of the damned Germans and will kill thousands more. We've shown our skill at fighting and winning in bloody battles with the enemy. The government and the Soviet people have shown their appreciation for our deeds. We have received a great honor—the title of guardsmen. The enemy knows us and our strength.

Dear Mama and dear sisters, you are all I have left. I want all of you, especially Mama, to keep your spirits up. Don't lose the strength you have left and take care of your health. I understand how difficult it is to endure this grief, this great sorrow, but there is nothing else to do. We have to bear it. That is how life is, Mama. Your sorrow, our sorrow, is not the only one. I've seen worse during my travels. In the mines at Shakhti we found 4,500 people killed by the German butchers. There were babies and children, women and old men. The monsters didn't just kill them; they abused them and then put them down in the hole and shot them. In one of the prisons in Rostov the Germans shot 3,500 people. Wherever the Fascist monsters go, they leave behind them a river of blood and innocent Soviet dead.

Mama, be strong and believe that I will return. When I do, we will live happily again. We will rebuild what has been destroyed. It will come with time. Mama, I'm sending letters to the RK and the regional executive committee with a request that you and the girls be allowed to go stay with Zhenya. Go stay with her and rest over the summer. I will help you. I'm sending you one thousand rubles today, and in a few days will send more. Nastya, Valya, Zoya, help Mama. Don't worry about me. I'm alive and well. I'm beating the Germans mercilessly. The hour of total victory is near. We will crush the enemy and return to you victorious.

Mama, give my greetings and best wishes to all the communal farm workers. Tell them to keep their spirits up

Confronted with both an enemy filled with incandescent rage and the daunting reality of Russia's geography—a vast ocean in which conquering armies came to drown, as many have described it—the German hubris that had been so pervasive at the beginning of the offensive slowly disintegrated. Nowhere was this transformation more evident than at Stalingrad. On August 23, 1942, German warplanes blanketed the city with bombs and strafed civilians who tried to flee, killing an estimated forty thousand men, women, and children in two days. The Germans reached the heart of the city by mid-September but found themselves mired in street-to-street, building-to-building combat. Stalingrad itself became the battlefield, and the Russians knew that prolonging the fight into the winter months would give their reinforcements time to build up their strength and then surround the Germans. In December, General Friedrich Paulas and the men of his Sixth Army recognized that they were in a dire position. An urgent plea to Hitler requesting permission to withdraw was met with scorn: "Surrender is forbidden." As hunger plagued the troops and the subzero weather became as

debilitating mentally as it was physically, many lost hope. One German soldier,
Bruno Kaliga, wrote the following as the army was collapsing around him.

My dear ones!

It is New Year's Eve, and when I think about home, my heart breaks.
How miserable and hopeless everything is here. It's been four days since I
had any bread. I am subsisting only on soup, for lunch. In the morning
and in the evening, I have a swallow of coffee, and every two days I get
about 100 grams of meat or some sardines in oil or a bit of cheese. Hunger
hunger hunger—and all that lice and dirt. Day and night, we are attacked
by planes, and the artillery fire never ends. If a miracle doesn't happen
within the next few days, I will go down here. The only good thing is that
I know that a 2-kg. Packet with marmalade and cake is on its way to me
from you. Arsand Hede and Sindermann have also sent packets with cake
and other delicacies. I think about it constantly and have started to go
crazy thinking that these things will never reach me. Even though I am
completely exhausted, I can't sleep at night. Instead I dream with open
eyes of cake cake cake. Sometimes I pray, and sometimes I curse my own
fate. Everything is without purpose and without sense.

Photo by Andrew Carroll

The scattered remains of Russian troops who died at Stalingrad
are constantly being found and properly reburied.

When will salvation come? Will death come through a bomb or a grenade? Will it be sickness or chronic illness? All of these questions overwhelm us to no end. And with it comes the constant longing to go home, and homesickness does indeed become a sickness. How can a human being deal with all of this? Are all of these sufferings God's punishment? My dear ones, I'm not allowed to write all of this to you, but I have no spirit left in my body, and all humor has disappeared. One is merely a bundle of twitching nerves. The heart and brain are sickeningly overstimulated, and you shake like with fever. If they stand me up in court because of this letter and shoot me, I would like to believe it would be a good deed for my body. I am without hope, and I ask you, don't cry too much when you receive the news that I am no more. Be good to each other, thank God for every day that's given to you, because at home, life is sweet.

With heartfelt love,

Yours,
Bruno

Bruno's fate is not known, but it is doubtful he survived. Out of approximately six hundred thousand German and Axis soldiers involved in the battle for Stalingrad, half a million are believed to have perished. (The Russians lost at least that many.) The remaining ninety thousand who were sent to prison camps in the Soviet Union entered a world of immeasurable suffering. Only five thousand made it home alive after the war.

—⁂—

A Russian Sniper Named Natalya Kovshova Tells Her Mother How Much She Enjoys "Hunting" German Soldiers
&
Private Eddie Slovik, Scheduled to Be Shot for Desertion, Begs Supreme Allied Commander Dwight D. Eisenhower to Spare His Life

Nothing—not brute strength, bravado, nor impassioned declarations of patriotism—can accurately determine how a soldier, Marine, airman, or sailor will ultimately function in combat until he or she is actually under fire. The most physically intimidating and outwardly self-assured individuals can wilt in an instant, while those who seemed timid and unimposing in training can prove to be warriors of unmatched agility and aggression when the bombs and bullets start to fly. (One of the most decorated soldiers of World War II, Audie Murphy, was a baby-faced orphan from Texas who stood barely five and a half feet tall. Murphy joined the army after the Marine Corps rejected him for being too small.) Some troops not only perform confidently once in battle, they thrive on the rush of adrenaline. "[I]f you ever talk with either instructor jockeys or the jackpots [trainees] they are checking out and mention me, don't say I am a pilot, say I'm a _fighter_ pilot," second lieutenant Bill Fant, a farm boy from Kansas, boasted to his mother and father on March 25, 1943. Fant had enlisted in the army in September 1941 and was called to active duty three weeks after Pearl Harbor. Assigned to the 11th Fighter Squadron, 343rd Fighter Group of the Army Air Corps, he flew P-40s against the Japanese in the Aleutian campaign. The twenty-five-year-old Fant was killed six days after writing to his parents, but, as his March 25 letter attested, he was doing exactly what he wanted. He continued:

> I'd a thousand times rather be in the air than on the ground. And if I ever do get knocked off it will be sudden and final. I'd rather go out with a wide open throttle and two wings full of guns blasting than to sink into the slime of a fox-hole with a bayonet in my guts. Things happen fast in the air— you act but never have time to worry, which is just as well. I'm doing what I want and that's worth a whole lot to me. Up here more pilots die of old age than go down in flames. I'm safer here than driving a car at home, so don't worry about me—just forget it and I'll walk in and surprize you when you least expect me sometime.

Others drew all the inspiration they needed from the fact that they were defending their homeland. "Our detachment has moved to the other line in pursuit of Hitler's monsters," Natalya Kovshova wrote to her mother. "You can hear horrible stories from local residents who have been in the hands of the fascist pigs. The woman we live with had a guest come to visit who said that the Germans shot her brother and four of his friends, 14–15 years old, simply because they went outside after 4 pm." Kovshova was twenty-one when the Germans stormed into Russia in 1941, and within a year she became a highly skilled sniper with the 528th Infantry Detachment, 130th Infantry Division. (Although most modern armies still prohibit them from fighting in frontline infantry units, women have placed themselves in harm's way during virtually every armed conflict in history.) Few of her correspondences have survived, but the following letter to her mother, written only five weeks before Kovshova died in battle, reveals her genuine delight at tracking down and killing German soldiers.

July 7, 1942

My dearest Mama!

Please don't be angry that I didn't write to you about being wounded. But I didn't want to worry you for no reason, since nothing serious happened. Now I'm sorry that I wrote to Sverdlovsk about it. Everything ended up fine. My wounds have healed well, and, in addition to walking on the ground, I'm climbing trees as well.

The most serious wound was to my left arm above the elbow (where they stick the smallpox vaccination), and it has healed nicely. At first the scars were bright pink, but now my skin is getting thicker and darkening. My bandages are off, too, so that is that.

I've been back with my unit since June 2, 1942. Now Mashenka and I are working with the young snipers. Their statistics are looking good. In the last two weeks of June our students took down 3 Fritzes. Not bad! And if you consider that we haven't seen any fighting during this period, then it looks great. We didn't do any hunting in June, ourselves. My arm hurt, and Mashenka didn't have time. She's doing a great job—she teaches like a real professor. A few days ago five of us went on reconnaissance without saying anything to the company commander. We were under the Germans' very noses and they had no clue! They were talking, coughing, making phone calls and we heard everything. It was great. We found a whole line of reinforcements, and the location of a mortar and artillery battery. We thought, wonderful, we'll get praised,

Russian sniper Natalya Kovshova with her younger sister Veronika.

but we almost got put under arrest. "You shouldn't be running around on reconnaissance, especially without permission." What a nut. But we're not upset at all. Next time we get a chance we'll go again. Reconnaissance is an interesting business.

On June 5 we were read an order giving us the sniper badge— this one goes on the right side, but we'll get one for the left side, too!

Sweet Mama, don't be sad and don't worry. Everything will be fine. Kisses and hugs to all of you!

Nata

For other World War II troops, however, especially the "grunts" in the infantry, combat was less a sport than a prolonged, nightmarish succession of miseries, large and small. "[T]hat very sarcastic letter of yours demands a reply and eventually an apology from you," a peeved soldier named William Rigby wrote to his sister after she complained he was neglecting to correspond with her. (The letter was typed, and the mistakes and creative punctuation are in the original.)

> *You don't realize the effect that being in combat has on some men, ... some men can't take it and they break under the strain, others find another outlet for those emotions. You don't seem to realize that I've been living practically like an animal for the past seven months . . . . there is no glamour, or color, or dash to the life of the Infantrymen. All there is, is dirt and death. [. . .] I didn't write because I didn't want to write, all that I [wanted] to do, was to forget about what happened during the day and forget about what might happened tomorrow. I found an outlet for my emotions by not doing anything, by just relaxing . . . reading, listening to the radio, etc. Other wrote letters and obtained the same effect. I could say more, but I'll stop here and allow you to come to a new decision . . . . and please. stop pestering me about w riting.*

And in some instances, combatants decided they absolutely would not continue to fight. Serving with the Twenty-eighth Division in France, Private Eddie Slovik had spent only one night under fire, but it proved too much for him and he fled to safer ground. Slovik turned himself in, gambling that the worst possible consequence would be incarceration and a dishonorable discharge, a highly preferable alternative, he reasoned, to actual combat. But after being taken into custody and tried in November 1944, he was shocked by the sentence— death by firing squad. Slovik held out hope that the ruling could be appealed; it had been eighty years since the government had actually executed a soldier for going AWOL, and he repeatedly expressed remorse for his actions. When a month passed with no word of leniency, Slovik began to panic, and on December 9 he decided to plead his case directly to General Dwight D. Eisenhower, the Supreme Allied Commander.

Dear Sir,

I Private Eddie D. Slovik A.S.N. #36896415 was convicted the 11th day of November year 1944 Armistice Day by General Court Martial to be shot to death for desertion of the United States Army.

Dear Sir, The time of my conviction or before my conviction I had no intentions of deserting the Army whatsoever. For if I intended too I wouldn't have given or surrendered myself as I did. I have nothing against the United States Army whatsoever. I merely wanted a transfer from the line. I asked my C.O. when I came back if their was a possible chance of my being transfered cause I feared hazardous duty to myself, and because of my nerves. I'll admit I have some awful bad nerves, which no doubt in my mind we all have. I was refused this transfer.

Dear Sir, I must tell you more about my past. I assume you have my records of my past criminall life in my younger stage of life. After being released from jail I was put on a two year parole after spending five years in jail. In them two years that I was on parole I got myself a good job. Cause I was in class 4F the Army didn't want anything to do with me at the time. So after five months out of jail I decided to get married which I did. I have a swell wife now and a good home.

After being married almost a year and a half I learned to stay away from bad company which was the cause of my being in jail. Then the draft came. I didn't have to come to the Army when they called me. I could of went back to jail. But I was sick of being locked up all my life so I came to the Army. When I went down to the draft board, I was told that the only reason they were taking a chance on me in the Army was cause I got married, and had a good record after being out of jail almost two years. To my knowledge sir I have a good record in the past two years, I also have a good record as a soldier up to the time I got in this trouble. I tried my best to do what the army wanted me to do till I first ran away or should I say left the company.

Dear Sir, I don't believe I ran away the first time as I stated in my first confession. I came over to France as a replacement, and when the enemy started to shelling us I got scared and nervous that I couldn't move out of my fox hole. I guess I never did give myself the chance to get over my first fear of shelling. The next day their wasn't any American troops around so I turned myself over to the Canadian M.P.'s. They in turn were trying to get in touch with my outfit about me. I guess it must have taken them six weeks to catch up the American troops. Well sir, when I was turned over to my outfit I tried to explain to my C.O. just what took place, and what had happened to me. Then I asked for a transfer. Which was refused. Then I wrote my confession. I was then told that if I would go back on the line they would distroy my confession, however if I refused to go back on the line they would half to hold it against me which they did.

Dear Sir, How can I tell you how humbley sorry I am for the sins I've comitted. I didn't realize at the time what I was doing, or what the word desertion meant. What it is like to be condemned to die. I beg of you deeply and sincerely for the sake of my dear wife and mother back home to have mercy on me. to my knowledge I have a good record since my marriage and as a soldier. I'd like to continue to be a good soldier.

Anxiously awaiting your reply, which I earnestly pray is favorable. God bless you and in your work to victory.

I remain yours for victory,

Pvt. Eddie D. Slovik

It is not known if Eisenhower ever read the letter, but members of his staff did, and they saw no reason to overturn the military court's decision. American soldiers in Belgium and France were up against Germany's final major counteroffensive, the Battle of the Bulge, and the army could not afford a breakdown in discipline. Granting clemency to Slovik, many argued, would also be unfair to the hundreds of thousands of soldiers fighting under extremely hellish conditions. (Eighty thousand US troops were ultimately killed, wounded, or taken prisoner in the monthlong battle.) An example needed to be made. On the morning of January 31, 1945, in Sainte-Marie-aux-Mines, France, Eddie Slovik was tied to a post with his hands behind his back, and a black hood was placed over his head. A twelve-man squad took position in front of Slovik, aimed their rifles, and fired. Since Slovik's death there have been instances of men being shot in the field by officers for refusing to fight, but Slovik remains the last American serviceman tried and executed for desertion since the Civil War.

—⁂—

**Staff Sergeant Neil Schmelz Describes to His Parents an Unforgettable Religious Service He Attended During a Lull in the Fighting
&
In a Letter to His Parents, Lieutenant James R. Penton Includes a Sketch He Has Drawn Depicting Faith in Action**

Exposed to suffering on a breathtaking scale and often confronted with seemingly random deaths, especially of innocent civilians, it is not unexpected that some troops (regardless of the conflict) begin to question their faith or the existence of any divine, benevolent force in the universe. "Damn darling, I get so mad," an army lieutenant named Russ Merrell from Utah wrote to his wife, Betty, on July 5, 1944. Merrell had seen firsthand the utter viciousness of combat, and he was incredulous that human nature could be so wicked—or be allowed to be by a loving god.

> *I know for a certainty that this won't be the last war. There will be others. At the present state of civilization there just isn't any solution for all the difficulties. And yet very few people want to fight wars. Christ, a person is so damn helpless. I don't know why I worry about such things. I've lost confidence in everything.... If God's chief work has been the creation of this earth and man on it, to date He and His work have been a glorious failure.*

The same disintegration of social order that can throw an individual into existential despair, however, can also strengthen the connection many feel with God or whatever their concept of spirituality might be. This is more than wishful thinking; alongside the sadism and barbarity unleashed in all wars, there are heroic examples of selflessness and compassion. Servicemen and -women often risk their lives for total strangers, provide comfort to those who are sick or grieving, or act mercifully when vengeance might be their first impulse. Through these sacrifices and the close friendships they forge in battle, combat troops can experience a renewed sense of humanity. "Today I witnessed the most impressive sight I have ever seen," an army staff sergeant named Neil Schmelz wrote to his parents in September 1944. Schmelz went on to write:

We had Mass in a beautiful little church in this city and, honestly, the church seemed like a little heaven in itself. The soldiers filled almost half the church and the rest of it was filled with civilians. As usual our chaplain heard confessions first and then started Mass. Before he began reading Mass, though, the Belgian priest went to the pulpit and in their native tongue spoke to his own people. His sermon consisted of, as far as I could tell, a great big thank you to the American soldiers for coming to their country to give them the freedom they have long been waiting for. It was very impressive; the women were weeping and a hushed silence fell throughout the entire congregation. I almost had to cry myself. The priest also told the people that they should understand that we, the soldiers, were making a great sacrifice in that we were leaving behind our wives and families whom we greatly loved.

The chaplain then started Mass and it seemed like out of no where came the sweetest strains of the organ and the voices of the choir. All I can say is that it was indeed heavenly music. Then came the Consecration and the organist played the 'Star Spangled Banner': something none of us ever have heard before, but it just didn't seem one bit out of place. It gave us the feeling that we were really helping those poor people and that they deeply appreciated it. It made the shivers run up and down my spine. At the end of the Mass, to make the whole event as complete as it could ever be, the organist again played the 'Star Spangled Banner' and also the Belgium national anthem. Truly you could almost see the joy popping out of the people's eyes. If I live to be 100 years old I don't believe I'll ever see anything that will impress me more.

Neil Schmelz

At almost the same time that Schmelz sent his letter, a young Jewish officer named Joseph Portnoy described the following scene in a long letter to his wife from Holland (Bobby is their son):

> *Today continued with not too many events, but it gave me the opportunity of attending a Yom Kippur service. The service lasted all morning. I especially took note of the yizkor or memorial service. Death over here has become such a light matter that I've almost forgotten that it was supposed to be accompanied by sadness. But at the service, the Rabbi again gave us the theme of the old attitude of returning to God and everlasting life. It sunk deeply, and made me realize that the toughness of war can easily be erased once one returns home to the churches and synagogues, and begins building the stones of civilization all over again and removing us from the callous savagery that we find here in this war. There will be a successful returning. Don't be afraid darling. Gosh how I adore you. I can tell you that over and over again, and each time I mean it. It's marvelous to have a love that's always in springtime. Tickle Bobby's feet for me. Yours Ever.*

Also in September of 1944, Lieutenant James R. Penton, serving with a tank destroyer battalion in France that was pushing its way toward Germany, sent his parents a letter and sketch he had drawn that illustrated true grace under fire. It was inspired by a scene that deeply moved Penton, a self-proclaimed "argumentative and skeptical atheist." (Bill Penton, whom he alludes to, is his cousin, and the long ellipses are in the original letter.)

3 September 1944

Dear Mother and Governor:

In the "Reader's Digest" there's a monthly article entitled "The Most Unforgettable Character I've Known,"—or something of the sort. Well, not so long ago I met an unforgettable character myself . . . .

My guns were in position in a small farmyard in the recently-wrested town of Vire, along the crest of a beautiful ridge,—and but a stone's throw from the rubble-dusty-haze rising above the warm ruins of the cities' downtown business section.

There was no "Business As Usual" in Vire that night,—only "Nazi-Tactics as Usual" as the Butchers of Spirit and Property harassed the town from afar with artillery shells aimed at no one spot in particular. My platoon crept into town as dusk merged into darkness,—barely moving at all in the tortured streets so as to keep down dust - - - and resulting enemy observation.

And as the sun of early morning dissolved the fog, yawning faces appeared from the depths of holes in the ground, and the boys were moving about comparing notes about the night before. Considerable interest was shown in the truck,—which had suffered three gashed tires, a perforated radiator, and other numerous shrapnel holes.

In the light of day I noticed a sprawling, peaceful convent to the immediate rear of the position,—with its courtyard and spires almost miraculously untouched. And while I sat there,—in the protection of a bank, gazing at the convent and listening to the melodious chiming of its bells intermingle with the hideous wail of Jerry 88's,—a solitary nun made her way deliberately through the yard, a bucket of water in one hand. It was a shock to hear her address me in perfect English, show identification papers, and learn that she was caring for the livestock in the absence of the terrorized farmer and his family.

And that's the sum and substance of my story. All morning long, as the whine of Jerry artillery overhead kept the rest of us in our holes, that nun moved serenely and placidly about the skeleton of the burned-out barn,—and around the bodies of dead, bloated cows; - - - - - milking the swollen cows, feeding and watering the chickens, collecting eggs.

And I know that our most argumentative and skeptical atheist was duly fascinated and impressed by that display of the power and force of that Sister's faith——and complete fearlessness . . . . . . It was not the sudden, stimulated and short-lived courage which drives a man to risk hot lead on a daring dash to aid a buddy, to me, it was far more than that . . . . . It was the picture of a mellowed and complete faith,—it was serenity of mind and soul amidst man's savagery of arm and spirit. . . . . That nun hadn't spent two years of training, and "battle-conditioning" and crawling under gun fire . . . . . but her poise and expression and dogged pursuit of someone else's domestic duties in the midst of that inferno was something we will all remember;—as we will the quarter-hourly chiming of the convent bells, as if in patient, long suffering defiance of the high explosive shells which ripped the city . . . .

And as I sketched the nun,—some of the boys glanced over my shoulder . . . There was no title on the paper,—but every one immediately recollected . . .

Well, there is nothing new to say. We seem to be doing things rapidly here in France,—but don't expect that daily collapse . . . These Germans are either crazymen or madmen,—and the fact that they are being cut off into little "pockets" does not prevent their generals from driving them to the long drawn-out slaughter . . . . .

Received a letter from Bill Penton yesterday. Hardly seems possible he's been overseas two full years. Time flies here, though,—and I rarely know what day of the week it is.

Do not worry when I don't have time to write. You know in the army—"no news is good news."

Love to all,
Jim

More than two months later, Penton was shot through his right shoulder. "Well, how's this for my first southpaw letter?" he wrote in a short, surprisingly upbeat message to his parents on December 23. "My right arm is in a plaster of Paris cast,—I'm in Paris, too—France. . . . I'm O.K., though, and will soon be in England. Don't worry over me. Love to all, Jim." Penton would recuperate fully, return home, and continue to sketch and paint.

—⁓—

Second Lieutenant Thomas A. Edwards Writes to His Parents from Iwo Jima—but Says He Will Never Mention the Island Again
&
In a Letter from War-Ravaged Germany, Captain Roy F. Bergengren Shares with a Friend What He Hopes Will Be Achieved After So Many Years of Death and Destruction

"It is with great shame that I report that despite our efforts, we will not be able to prevent this strategic island from falling into enemy hands," General Tadamichi Kuribayashi, commander in chief of all Japanese forces on Iwo Jima, wired Imperial General Headquarters on March 17, 1945, before killing himself. "Please accept my most sincere apology for failing to fulfill my mission." Three and a half years after a crippling blow at Pearl Harbor, the United States had transformed the world's eighteenth-largest army into one of the most powerful, and now the full fury of its military was bearing down on the islands of Japan in preparation for a full-scale invasion of the mainland. (Code-named Downfall, the operation would have eclipsed the June 1944 Normandy landings in both size and complexity.) For five grueling weeks beginning on February 19, 1945, seventy thousand American troops, most of them Marines, confronted twenty-two thousand Japanese soldiers on the tiny but heavily fortified and booby-trapped island of Iwo Jima. Using flamethrowers, grenades, artillery, machine guns, and at times even bayonets and knives during hand-to-hand fighting, the Marines successfully captured the island, but at a cost of sixty-eight hundred lives and twenty thousand wounded. (All of the Japanese either were killed or committed suicide.) On March 13, a Welsh-born US Marine officer

named Thomas Alun Edwards sent his parents a letter from Iwo Jima that, although brief, said volumes about the strain the Marines were under.

Dear Folks:

Well here I am, still alive & well. Things are dragging out for a final showdown. The island has been pretty well secured, and we're all thankful. This place has been Hell and still is. It is just a hot dusty pile of sand and ashes.

It smells of death and is barren and desolate. Suribachi is bleak, and forbidding. The men sit about listlessly. Nobody is in any sort of mood for kidding. There is death all around. A lot of the boys that landed when I did, are dead. Every time the ambulance goes by, I say to myself, "There but for the grace of God, go I." It is the sight of our own dead that is terrible.

You see these youngsters, horribly mutilated by shrapnel, & artillery. There is no peacefulness in their death—it came on them too violently and viciously. Many of them had no idea why they fought. They were so young. I am humble and grateful for being spared.

I would rather not write anymore today, and I will not mention any more about Iwo Jima in any later letters because I am sick about my friends who died, and so please just tell me about things at home, & don't mention this campaign anymore.

All my love to you both
Alun

The battle for Okinawa, which followed almost immediately, had half as many casualties, but the combat was every bit as horrific. Describing the first influx of injured troops, a navy pharmacist's mate recalled the scene in a letter to his parents: "They were hurt bad, it wasn't pretty & they mumbled, those who could, first eye witness reports. 'Jesus Christ it's murder' said a Guadalcanal veteran, & another kid, not more than 18 kept repeating, 'Oh God, oh God . . .'" And some men were so traumatized they went truly mad. J. W. Foster, captain of the USS ATR 80, related the following story in a letter home (OOD stands for "officer on deck"):

Shortly after dropping anchor an incident occurred which left me in a physically weakened condition, and the likes of which I surely hope never happens again. I was standing out on the wing of the bridge when a Marine 1st Lt. came alongside in a small boat and wanted to take his casualties off. I told him that they had already been transferred to the hospital ship and everything had been taken care of, but this did not seem to satisfy him.

At first he seemed to be normal, but the longer he stayed, the crazier he began to talk, such as: "We're all going home;" "All of my men have been killed;" "The war is over;" "I want to go with my men;" etc. Then he asked again if I was or wasn't going to give his casualties back, to which I replied, "No." He pulled out his .45 pistol and fired point blank at me. God's Grace prevented him from hitting, I suppose, for a Marine doesn't miss at that close range. He took off toward another transport nearby, so I sent them an urgent message to investigate him. . . . About five minutes later, I got this message back, "The Marine officer came aboard, shot the O.O.D., then blew his own brains out." Well, I wasn't so scared until I heard this, and I'll admit my knees knocked together a few times when I realized what a close call it had been.

The Pacific war ended four months later in a crescendo of violence with the atomic explosions over Hiroshima and Nagasaki. As the world celebrated the news of Japan's surrender, frontline troops wrote more solemnly about the conclusion of hostilities. "Everybody around here had a wild time for a few minutes when the news first came through about the end of war," twenty-four-year-old Max Peters wrote to a friend back home. "But, although I felt just as jubilant about it as the rest, I still had the memories of the death and destruction I had seen in the last few weeks too fresh in my mind to feel like giving vent to any cheering and shouting." After providing a litany of gruesome memories from those past few weeks as a sergeant with the Tenth Mountain Division in Italy, Peters went on to write:

I can easily see that we can never expect the folks at home to understand what we've seen and done; so I'll skip all the rest of the things that I've done (or I'd rather say "things that the war has made me do") - - - I'm pretty sure I couldn't even bring myself to mention a great many of them anyhow - - - - maybe if I force myself not to remember them their meaning will gradually fade away. Now that at least partial peace has been obtained I only hope that all our statesmen and people at home as well as us overseas will see that the peace we form is a real and lasting one. I and all the rest of us over here will certainly do everything in our power to preserve that peace - - - We owe that much at least to our buddies who are gone.

Peters was not alone in his yearning for something positive and enduring to be born out of the sacrifices made by those who would not be returning home. Even before the armistices in Europe and Asia were declared, servicemen and -women who traveled through demolished towns and villages once bustling with life, or drove past the seemingly endless blur of homemade crosses on open fields, *reflected intently on the cost of their hard-won victory. Roy F. Bergengren Jr., a captain with the Seventy-eighth Fighter Control Squadron, Second Air Defense Wing, saw combat for over two and a half years in Africa, England, France, Germany, Italy, and Sicily. Writing to a friend in Madison, Wisconsin, Bergengren ruminated not only on the end of the war, but on the human condition itself and what its future would be in the shadow of such a searing and monstrous tragedy. He passionately hoped that his generation and those to come would learn from the years of slaughter and ruin he, like so many others, had witnessed first-hand.*

Dear Don,

Having entered Germany a while ago, I feel something like the coast-to-coast marathon runner must as he crosses the New York state line.

In 28 months, I've journeyed through 11 countries to get here. It was a rather round about route, but there's never been any doubt about where we're headed. I hope I shall travel right to Berlin—and then home.

So far, it has been an interesting, if unpleasant experience. I could certainly have done nicely without it, but since it has been necessary, I'm glad to be one of those taking a share in it.

There have been a few outstanding impressions. Obvious though they may be, they are none-the-less vivid.

First is the absolute futility of war. Seen at close range, it becomes so brutal and stupid that we have to rub our eyes to believe the world is capable of it. It can't be written; samples of the death, poverty, and destruction in war's wake must be seen to be appreciated.

In a Lyons café, a French journalist asked me,

"Why is it you Americans refuse to believe the Germans really tortured and killed so many innocent people in France?"

I couldn't answer. I guess it's because we live so far from such things and we must see to believe. Words fail to make such things real.

A second impression is the fundamental similarity of the peoples of the united nations. I've lived and worked with British, French, Australian, South African, New Zealand, Polish, and Belgian soldiers to name a few. I'm convinced that we all seek the same general sort of life. We criticize one another for our little individual eccentricities; each of us thinks his is the best nation; but fundamentally we differ little. When this war is won, we must remember only the fundamentals and get together in a big way.

A third impression is that of America's own capabilities. London, Algiers, Paris, Rome, Florence, Marseilles, and every other city and town in every liberated country teeming with American traffic. Huge depots of American supplies, throngs of American men everywhere. If we can put forth one half the effort for peace that we've expended in this war, because it was necessary, there should never be need for another war. We must realize that peace, now, is just as necessary as the war has been.

I'm now living in a half-wrenched miner's house. There's snow and there's cold in addition to other little worrisome things. I and millions of others like me aren't enjoying ourselves at the moment, but we're perfectly willing to live this way because we have faith that the peoples of the world this time are going to do a better job in fashioning the peace.

I greatly enjoyed your Christmas box which arrived before I left Italy—in fact the various pages of the "artist's sketch book" now gaily adorn the walls of this shack and greatly add to it's livability. When I pull out, they'll go along with me. They're quite the travelled little beauties.

I've rambled on at some length and must now get a bit of shut-eye. The lessons to be learned from war are so simple and so obvious, that they have to come out. This time, dammit, we've got to remember them.

My best to the gang,

Roy

—ɯ—

Writing from a Hospital Behind the Front Lines, Private Ted Brush Gives His Parents an Unsparing Report on How He Was Wounded in Action
&
Lieutenant James Van Veen, an American Pilot Flying in Korea, Laments to a Former Sweetheart That He Does Not Feel Close to Anyone—But That It Might Be for the Best

Even before the final surrender of Japan was signed aboard the USS Missouri *on September 2, 1945, marking the official end of World War II, the long-term global peace so many troops had prayed for was already threatening to unravel. The menace was not Japan, America's former enemy, but the Soviet Union, its wartime ally. The mutual distrust between President Harry Truman and Soviet premier Joseph Stalin at the Potsdam Conference in the summer of 1945 better reflected the relationship between the two nascent superpowers than the image of grinning Russian and US soldiers at the Elbe River several months earlier. As the Soviets imposed Communist rule over neighboring countries and, years later, tested their first atomic weapon, many in the West perceived a larger Communist conspiracy at work to dominate the world. Their fears were bolstered on June 25, 1950, when ninety thousand pro-Communist North Korean troops surged across the thirty-eighth parallel in a surprise invasion of the*

US-backed Republic of Korea. President Truman immediately mobilized the army and appealed to the newly formed United Nations for military assistance. By the end of July, American-led UN and Republic of Korea (ROK) soldiers were vastly outnumbered and clinging to the southeast corner of the peninsula. The tide suddenly turned, however, in September after General Douglas MacArthur, who commanded the UN forces, staged an ambitious landing behind enemy lines at Inchon. "I will be glad when we start pushing these Gooks back across the 38th Parallel," a young private from Ohio wrote to his family on September 15, 1950, the day of MacArthur's invasion. Like many of his fellow soldiers, he anticipated a swift conclusion: "After we start, it won't last long & I can get home that much quicker." The fighting would last another three years. Officially, the UN called the conflict in Korea a "police action," but for those on the front lines it was a full-blown war. On September 30, 1950, the North Koreans were in full retreat, and within weeks they had been driven back to the Yalu River, which marks the boundary with Manchuria. It was an astonishing reversal, and one that heralded the possibility of a unified, democratic nation. And then the Chinese attacked. In late October and early November hundreds of thousands of Chinese soldiers streamed into North Korea, and by January 1951, the Chinese and North Koreans had recaptured Seoul and other major cities. Three months later the tide turned again, and the UN troops were now on the offensive. The seemingly endless crisscrossing over the thirty-eighth parallel continued, with hundreds of thousands of lives lost in the meantime. "I arrived in Korea last night," twenty-year-old Private Ted Brush wrote to his parents in Richfield, Idaho, on August 14, 1951. Brush was stunned by the physical devastation of the country and the plight of the civilians.

> It is quite a site. Every town is shot up, and most of the good buildings are all ruined. The Seoul railroad yards are a mess. There are wrecked tracks with ruined cars all over. The Korean's are in pretty bad shape. They live in bombed out houses, grass and doby shaks, and burlap houses. I don't see how some of them can avoid freezing to death.

Brush's letters, like those of his fellow troops fighting in Korea, were not censored. Combatants were instructed to use their discretion, but their letters tended to be more forthcoming about locations and casualties than those from World War I and II. (Many servicemen and -women from the world wars related graphic combat accounts and sensitive information, too, but these letters were often written long after a battle or smuggled home by a friend returning to the States.) The Korean conflict had exploded too quickly for the military to implement an official procedure for checking all outgoing mail, and with the war's end always seeming imminent, such a mechanism was never put in place. There was *also concern that suddenly instituting censorship would dampen morale and suggest that the government had something to conceal. (Truman's popularity was already sinking in the US as a result of the war.) Less than two months after landing in Korea, Ted Brush sustained multiple wounds while fighting in Taejon. On October 6, he described his injuries to his parents in detail.*

Dear Folks,

I suppose you have already received a telegram saying that I was wounded in action. I am now in a hospital at Tajon, South Korea, about 30 miles behind the front line. I was hit by two grenades. We went into the assault up a hill and the Chinks just stayed in their holes and threw out grenades. I dodged around still keeping moving forward but slowing down cause grenades were all over. I was shooting at the chinks' holes to keep them from getting up and shooting and I knelt down to put a new magazine in my B.A.R. when a rocket shrapnell from a grenade behind me hit me right along the left jaw. I saw blood spurting and my face went numb so I called to my foxhole buddy (Kelly) to take my B.A.R.

I was just handing it to him when someone yelled "Grenade!" I started to hit the dirt and Kelly kind of fell away when I felt myself get hit in the right leg. A curious feeling went up my leg and then I got hit in the right cheek. I fell down and felt blood running in my boot and looked at Kelly, he was holding his hand and motioned for me to come back where he was but I couldn't make it. I just laid there praying, half afraid I was going to bleed to death. I was calling a medic but I couldn't see one. About 1/2 hour later, one showed up and bandaged me, another guy had tried to move me, but I couldn't hardly move. I laid there for about another hour and 1/2, hollering for a litter (I could hear my squad leader cussing and yelling to get one for me too, when I noticed bullets kicking up dust and found out a sniper was firing at me, so I crawled over the hill.)

They're about ready to put me on the train to Pusan so will close. I have a broken leg so maybe I'll get home. I am fine, but it still hurts a little. Will write tomorrow so don't worry. The medical corps is doing a good job on me.

Love,
Ted

P.S. We lost a lot of men on that hill. The # of the hill is 477.

In a foreshadowing of the Vietnam war, troops in Korea also began to communicate their frustrations about the conflict more openly. Griping about unpalatable rations, awful weather, and other inconveniences was nothing new, and combatants in previous wars expressed bitterness toward those responsible for starting them. But servicemembers rarely opposed the objectives for which they were fighting. In Korea, the aggravations were mounting. Many blamed the president for gutting the military after World War II, and they were further incensed when he fired MacArthur in April 1951 after the general's comments about wanting to wage a larger war with China. They were furious about the outdated equipment and inadequate gear they had been issued. And they found it maddening to seize, surrender, recapture, and then lose again the same territory time after time, especially as peace negotiations were started and then abandoned because of—from the perspective of those in the field—trivial squabbles and disputes. In an emotional five-page letter about the loss of a close buddy, Robert "Bat" Banuelos Madrid, a Japanese-American Marine named Robert M. Wada vented about the war's overall aims, which he argued should be more aggressive and include advancing "all the way to Moscow." The letter was dated December 21, 1951, a time when UN forces had, once again, penetrated into North Korea. (Wada self-censored one word in the text.)

> I loved ["Bat"] like my own brother and I never let him leave my heart and I never shall forget him—I think of him everyday and still can not believe he is gone—We are now waiting for the peace talks to either go through or blow up—We are preparing to move back 10–15 miles—Goddamn Rudy, we are leaving the ground we just took, the hill "Bat" was killed on and everything—F—— it, let's go on—It hurts me, It really does Rudy, to leave the ground so many guys died on—Especially "Bat."

Other troops were nearly despondent about being in Korea. Less than a month before he was killed in action, twenty-two-year-old Private James Arnold wrote to his family:

> If something don't happen to me I should get to see all of you people about Xmas or I'm going to be greatly disappointed. I guess all we can do now is to pray that the good Lord will see fit to stop this mess in the near future. It looks to me like he is the only one who can stop it now. I went upon the front lines & stayed alnight & one day. I did't see any action but some of my buddies did in fact one of them is missing now. Boy that really makes a fellow feel bad, to have to go & help carry the dead & wounded out on litters when he knows they died for some useless cause. The hills are so steep & rough that ambulances can't get in to get the boys so they have to be carried out by hand unless they can get them by helicopters they move a lot like that. You talk about hurting . . . if someone had of shot me it would have been a favor to me.

Even letters that articulated a sense of pride and determination revealed hints of an underlying gloom and ambivalence. James Van Veen was attending the University of Michigan's School of Business Administration on an ROTC scholarship when he was called up to fly combat missions in Korea with the 310th Fighter Bomber Squadron. On April 25, 1953, Lieutenant Van Veen wrote a short letter to a woman he had dated at school named Elise Kerlin. Van Veen believed his contribution to the war effort was valuable, but he also longed for home.

25 April '53
K-2-KOREA.

Dear Elise,

It has sure been a long time since I have written you. I hope you have not forgotten me completely.

I now have 20 missions. They have taken me from the front lines to near the Manchurian border. I have certainly been lucky so far, for fate has been with me and I have gotten home after every mission.

As a pilot quite a bit is demanded. Sometimes I think too much, but actually I wouldn't be doing anything else here. It seems your part in the fight is tangible. I do not mean to slight any of the jobs that go to support the flying end not a single jet could get into the air.

So often I think of the beautiful campus and the wonderful time I had at Michigan. I wish I was back again. It always seems that no matter what you are doing you wish you were doing something else. I remember in my last semester I thought how wonderful it would be to fly a jet fighter in the cause of freedom. So here I am and wish I back at school. Foolish isnt it?

I often think how happy you made my last semester for me. I shall never forget it. I hope you dont feel too badly towards me for breaking it off so abruptly.

As for my love life. I can truly say I have none. At present I am writing no one, and have no ties. Perhaps it is best this way. When one prepares to be far from home he should hold no ties, for so often it can only mean more loneliness for all concerned. Many men in my line have died here or have been killed in training in preparation for war. I have seen their wives and loved ones suffer sorrow which they will never get over.

I have been talking on and on about myself and have not asked about you. Hope you will write me and bring me up to date I will be looking forward to hearing from you.

Well I sure have run out of things to say. So until my next I remain your correspondent

> Love
> Jim

Kerlin responded to Van Veen's letter, but her reply was sent back with the word "deceased" stamped over his name. At the time of Van Veen's death, neither the Chinese and North Korean troops nor the UN forces were able to overpower the other decisively, and negotiations sputtered on and off again until July 27, 1953, when an armistice was declared. Neither side had, in the end, gained ground after the UN action successfully pressed the Communists back above the thirty-eighth parallel in September 1950. Millions of Koreans perished in the three-year war, along with thirty-seven thousand Americans (eight thousand are still listed as missing in action). The number of Chinese deaths is not known but is believed to be in the hundreds of thousands. Officially, the war is not over but merely in a state of cease-fire.

—⁓—

After a Crushing Loss, a Soldier Fighting in Vietnam Criticizes the Military Leadership but Praises His Fellow Troops for Their Courage and Tenacity

"Vu Ban is in the Muong country," Roger Micault wrote to a young neighbor curious about a soldier's life in Vietnam, "a country with very rough terrain, and there's only one way to handle it: When we leave on patrol, we either crawl on all fours along the sides of the mountains in order to climb them, or we march in the valleys where the rice fields are, where we're in mud up to our knees." He continued:

> *There's no road, trails are waterlogged by the rainy season, and you can't always use them because they're often mined by the Viet Minh. And the sun is always beating down! What a country! At night, the mosquitoes succeed in finding their way through the mosquito-netting and keep us from sleeping. Another big problem—safe drinking water. I mean there isn't any. We do have a spring beside the post with water that's nearly clean. But it's the only one, and you maybe have to go 50 km to get to the next one. So when we're on patrol we have to make do with river water or water from the rice fields (there's plenty of that) that we have to filter with a handkerchief and disinfect with chlorine. And since it's so hot and we're very thirsty, we make ourselves drink it.*

Micault then went on to share his thoughts about the war from both a military and political perspective. He was frustrated by the growing strength of the Communist leader Ho Chi Minh and his Viet Minh troops, and Micault lamented hearing about the antiwar sentiment—including accusations against the soldiers themselves—fomenting back home.

> *When will this war end? I admit that I don't see the solution. . . . Ho Chi Minh is getting organized and counts a lot on the Chinese Communists. As for us, we don't have enough personnel or equipment, and we're disapproved of by one segment of public opinion that doesn't hesitate to call us assassins and that glorifies Ho Chi Minh . . . We really wonder what's going to happen in the future.*

The future for Roger Micault and his comrades, in fact, was bleak. Micault was a French soldier fighting Viet Minh forces in 1949, and five years later the French would be soundly defeated at Dien Bien Phu. France had begun its colonization of Vietnam almost a century earlier, but after the French capitulated to Germany in 1940, Japanese troops—who were allied with the Germans— occupied Vietnam until 1945. (Ironically, during World War II the US Office of Strategic Services, which would later become the CIA, provided funding and weapons to the Viet Minh guerillas resisting the Japanese; the Viet Minh was the precursor to the Viet Cong, who would battle American troops years later.) When Japan surrendered to the Allied Powers in 1945, the French began to reestablish, with military force, their presence in Vietnam. Ho Chi Minh famously warned them, "You can kill ten of my men for every one of yours that I kill, but even with those odds, you will lose." By 1954, popular support in France for the war had plummeted, and the most devastating loss was yet to come. Approximately three hundred miles northwest of Hanoi in a strategically located outpost named Dien Bien Phu, the French had stationed fifteen thousand troops (many of whom were colonial soldiers from Algeria, Morocco, Thailand, Vietnam, and West Africa) commanded by Colonel Christian de Castries. On March 13, General Vo Nguyen Giap's Viet Minh soldiers unleashed a withering artillery barrage from the mountains encircling the valley, catching the French by surprise. Essentially surrounded, the French relied on airdrops for food, munitions, and other dwindling supplies. Much of it, however, fell into the hands of the Viet Minh, who were especially delighted by the chocolate bars, candies, and perfumed love letters they discovered. After being attacked and bombarded relentlessly for almost two months, the starving and shell-shocked French troops raised the white flag on May 7, 1954. More than three thousand had been killed, and ten thousand became prisoners of war. (Forced to march hundreds of miles through rugged terrain, many of the wounded succumbed to disease and mal-

*nutrition. More French soldiers died as POWs than during the siege at Dien
Bien Phu itself.) The Viet Minh suffered tens of thousands of casualties. On May
8, a military doctor named Jacques Aulong wrote the following letter from Hanoi
to his mother and father in France expressing the grief he and his comrades were
experiencing about the defeat. (General Henri Navarre, alluded to in the letter, was commander in chief of all French forces in Vietnam. When Colonel De
Castries became increasingly overwhelmed by the tragedy unfolding before
him, Major Marcel Bigeard assumed control of much of the tactical decision-
making during the siege.)*

Dearest Parents,

    Diên Biên Phu fell yesterday, after heroic resistance. A day of sorrow.
The atmosphere is that of a death chamber. We lived with the
imminence of this fall, but we cannot face the fact that it has actually
happened. It's like the long-awaited death of someone who has suffered a
terminal disease, and yet we are in a state of shock and cannot conceive
of this tragedy as irreparable and irrevocable

    You cannot imagine how admirably brave and clear-headed they were

Jacques Aulong

up until the very last moment, when the radio went definitively dead. The wire taps were recording up until 17H20; the last words were mixed with the roar of explosions. We heard "Ah, the bastards!" And then nothing. De Castries had the pieces of artillery blown up, along with their ammunition, before the onslaught of Viets. The last explosion of ordnance was more powerful than all the rest. They used the "Stalin's organs", six-tube rockets, for the first time.

We hear that Bigeard succeeded in getting through the lines with a few hundred men. To go where? Cost: twenty doctors and around twenty élite battalions. When I think that, day before yesterday, and the day before, the 1st BPC, our last paratrooper battalion, was parachuted in, it's insanity!

A catastrophe of this size involves immense and horrifying responsibility. Everyone here is in a state of agitation, against the government and our politicians to begin with, and against the high command, starting with Navarre, as well.

Our soldiers proved themselves blameless, and I say it without a trace of chauvinism. They maintained an iron morale, right up until the end, and there was an amazing flow of troops who volunteered to be parachuted in until the very last day.

And parachuted in under such conditions! It's the only remaining thing that we can be proud of. Shame and sadness for all the rest. And what will happen now?

We can't even hope to recuperate the wounded. When will they understand in France that we must have done with this at all costs, and rapidly, before we suffer a final catastrophe? I'm not talking about myself, I think I'll be capable of doing my duty up until the end, just as I volunteered for Diên Biên Phu on March 15th. I can tell you, now that it's over. The director didn't think it was up to me to do so. But I think of all that can be saved, human lives and moral interests, even material ones. We no longer have our place here, and this has been true for so many years, otherwise we should chuck the hypocrisy and send in the contingent. I'll leave you now, my heart full of immense sadness, and I embrace you tenderly.

Jacques

Two months after the surrender of Dien Bien Phu, an agreement was reached in Geneva that divided Vietnam at the seventeenth parallel, with the Communists under Ho Chi Minh ruling the North, and the anti-Communists led by Premier Ngo Dinh Diem governing the South. With the Cold War escalating and the possibility of Ho Chi Minh's forces overtaking all of Vietnam, Pres-

ident Dwight D. Eisenhower boosted military aid and ordered advisors to the region. On June 8, 1956, one of those advisors, Technical Sergeant Richard B. Fitzgibbon Jr., became the first casualty of the growing conflict in Vietnam. (Other Americans had already been killed in Southeast Asia, including pilots assisting with the airdrops to Dien Bien Phu, but Fitzgibbon's death is officially recognized as the war's earliest on the American side.) Less than nine years later, under orders from President Lyndon B. Johnson, the first ground combat unit—US Marines, Third Battalion, Ninth Expeditionary Brigade—came ashore at Da Nang on March 8, 1965. Fitzgibbon's son, twenty-one-year-old Lance Corporal Richard B. Fitzgibbon III, landed in Vietnam soon after. He, too, would be killed in the war.

—⁓—

Lieutenant John Abrams Explains to His Wife How the Fighting in Vietnam Differs from Past Wars
&
The Friend of a Viet Cong Collaborator Named Huynh Lan Khanh Tells Lan's Mother How Her Daughter Died

"Well this war is a lot different than any other war," Lieutenant John Abrams explained on an audiotape he mailed to his wife, Jane. (Although relatively more common in Vietnam, audio "letters" dated back to the 1940s. During World War II, Pepsi-Cola established canteens that, along with offering sandwiches and sodas, gave servicemembers the opportunity to make a 78 rpm record with a personal message for their family members.) Abrams was a Navy helicopter pilot originally from Milwaukee, and he frequently sent his wife audiotapes that recorded his stream-of-consciousness thoughts on everything from the snap decisions they had to make in combat and his disdain of the Viet Cong (nicknamed "Charlie") to his comparisons between Vietnam and past conflicts. "You could ask somebody from World War II or Korea if they ever killed anybody," he mused,

and they'd probably say, "Well, I don't know." And they're probably telling the truth. They were firing at long ranges, long distances, to emplacements, this type of thing. This isn't that kind of war. This is a people-to-people war. We're firing from 600 meters away. We fire, we hit, we see what we hit. We see the results of our hit. We see the wounded, and of course we oftentimes see the dead. Of course, Charlie gives it back to us too. We take a lot of hits in the aircraft. Occasionally one of us gets it too. We've had three door gunners wounded—one of which died—since I've been here. I've been shot at quite a few times, and

I think I've got a purple heart coming for a minor thing that happened here a couple weeks ago. There's nobody here that's not getting shot at, although this part of the war isn't as highly publicized as the part that's going on in the north. The part we're doing down here nobody wants to talk about. It's a dirty job. It's women, twelve-, fifteen-year-old boys and grown men that we're killing because they're killing Vietnamese and trying to kill us. Some of the atrocities that Charlie commits are unbelievable. It's really hard to believe some of the things that he does. In this thing the last few days we liberated a VC prisoner of war camp. Some of the people have been in the camp for two and a half to three years.

Abrams was interrupted by the sound of gunfire crackling in the background. "Wish that guy would stop firing," he muttered, "it's making me nervous." He continued his train of thought:

Yesterday, for example, we were cleared into an area where Charlie supposedly had an arms cache. We went into the area—sure enough, there was all camouflaged arms cache. So we went in, circled the area one time at high altitude, rolled into our strike. All of sudden, people started running out of the hootches—we call them hootches, they're grass houses—running out of the hootches that this material was all stacked around. And every one of them had a saffron robe on. A saffron robe is a bright orange robe—kind of the color of a flight suit, if you remember what that looked like—that the Buddhist monks wear, every one of them. Now, what were Buddhist monks doing where there was a large cache of Charlie equipment, and no Buddhist pagoda around the area? Charlie's not dumb, but he's not smart either, really. They ran out of the hootch, ran across the rice paddy, and they never got any further. Now maybe there were some Buddhist monks among them. Possibly there were. And Charlie was trying to escape along with them. But they all got it.

Although not a soldier, a Vietnamese woman named Huynh Lan Khanh aided the Viet Cong and was, similar to the situation Abrams related, caught between her comrades and US forces, with fatal consequences. A close friend and coworker of Khanh's wrote to her mother to describe as best he could how Khanh had died. Other than her name, exact details about her life and where she was working are not known.

Dear Tam,

    I just received your letter from comrade Dot. I know you are anxious to hear back from me, so I am responding to you now. Sister Kinh, I understand you must be very sad writing to ask about Lan Khanh, and it hurts me to write about her.

In my earlier letters, while you were at Lo Go, I enclosed personal items and photos of Lan Khanh, and when I saw brother Tam and took him to Lan Khanh's grave, I told him how Lan Khanh died, and the affection we all had for her. Her strength, frankness, ambitiousness, responsibility, and especially her courage will never fade in my mind. Lan Khanh was a great assistant in my office who I haven't been able to find for two years, and I want you to know how good she was!

Now let me tell you a story about her death. At 9 am of Jan 4th, 1968, Khanh and her 5 colleagues were delivering rice. It takes about 30 minutes to travel from the office to the depot. As soon as they arrived, they were ambushed and some were shot by enemy rangers (why did this take place? I will tell you in detail when I see you). Khanh was two meters away from an American ranger, thus unable to get away. She was accompanied by a comrade who was standing 10 meters behind and trying to return fire, but he was killed.

After the rangers had pulled out, we inspected the battle site and when her body was found, here is what we were able to determine: Khanh was wounded by a landmine, and was then immediately captured. She tried to resist but failed to escape. They took her to the helicopter nearby but couldn't get on because we had shot it to pieces. They had to call the jet fighters to protect their unit together with Khanh, and our force had run out of ammunition and was outnumbered. About 2 pm, they could communicate and were evacuated by another helicopter. When the helicopter started to climb, at about 0.5 km Khanh jumped to her death. I think she died at about 2 pm on 4 Jan 1968. It is so painful telling this.

I will tell you more when meeting you again as I can't say anything more!

Your brother
Kien

PS. It was not until 6 Jan 1968, that we found Lan Khanh's body and buried her properly.

—⁓—

Still Rattled by the Incident, Lieutenant Robert P. Mackey Describes to His Father What Happened to His Platoon After They Entered a Minefield

For American infantry units, the "close combat" ground warfare of Vietnam was relentlessly nerve-wracking. Much of the fighting occurred in dense jungles through which enemy forces could maneuver swiftly and stealthily. Snipers hid in trees. Seemingly quiet villages harbored Viet Cong soldiers pretending to be civilians. The enemy was nowhere to be seen and everywhere at once. Adding to the claustrophobic nature of the war were the ubiquitous booby-traps and landmines that could potentially be triggered at any moment. Some devices were as simple as the cartridge trap, which was a single bullet placed on top of a nail in a small hole; when stepped on, the bullet exploded through the victim's foot. Others were more elaborate, such as camouflaged pits with jagged spikes lining the bottom or crossbows set off by tripwires. On March 26, 1969, twenty-four-year-old Lieutenant Robert P. Mackey wrote to his father back in Chelmsford, Massachusetts, after several of his men walked into a minefield in Phouc Vinh. The casualties were so horrific that Mackey instructed his father not to tell his mother the specifics. (For reasons of discretion, one sentence near the end of the letter has been edited.)

26 MAR 69

Hi, Dad,

I thought I'd write to you this time, so you can tell Mom a bit easier. I do believe I might get a Purple Heart. Oh, it's nothing to worry about now. This happened on the 24th and after I wrote Vi, I couldn't write anymore because my arm hurt, and last night we had a Memorial Mass for one of my people that didn't make it. I've seen so many people bleeding and smashed open these past two days that I'm damn near sick to my stomach. I was hit about 2" below my right wrist, so you can tell I'm doing OK now. The wound was about an inch long and almost an inch deep. Here's what happened:

Replica of a Viet Cong booby trap in Cu Chi, Vietnam. The hole is about six feet deep, and some of the spikes are almost a foot long. When covered with branches and leaves, the pit is virtually impossible to detect.

Photo by Andrew Carroll

Monday, I had two projects going, a rocket fence and minefield clearing operations. In the morning, I spent equal time between the two, but in the afternoon, something made me stay at the minefield. I had 3 2-man teams spread out in the field, with an NCO with them. I was on the radio at the time, I had my platoon Sgt with me and my old platoon Sgt. and my driver. I remember I was smiling to my plat sgt. then I turned and looked out at the men in the field. Just then an explosion, two mines one on top of the other went off, booby trapped. I saw a shape blown in the air and the others hitting the ground, my arm was spun around me by some powerful invisible force. I grabbed my arm, then got on the radio and called for emergency help. God damn, men were laying on the ground, my men. As I climbed over the barbed wire fence, one of them got up, the medic had already given a pressure bandage to my plt Sgt and he administered first aid. The man, Cosme, got up and walked out of the field. I went down there and counted. Somebody was missing. Keeler was draped over the tall grass further into the minefield, hardly no head, no arms, one leg and a little bit of chest. there was no helping him. I was dripping blood, and quite capable of taking care of myself. By that time, help had arrived and every one was being moved from the field and to the small hospital facilities. By this time I had started to lose control of myself. I had one man holding his own guts in, and another with a very serious head wound with possible brain damage.

Dad, I tried to encourage them while we were at the hospital. I talked to four of them, the fifth one was in a semi-conscious state, I hope I did my best. But I was plagued by why did it happen? Was it my fault for not training them more carefully? Should I have been there and maybe I would have been the trap-wire? As far as I know, the five are still alive. I was the least hurt and returned to duty, more or less, a few hours later. The blood, and the bloodless holes in their bodies. Mine had since stopped and I saw a deep gash. It has never hurt me since I first was hit. they are the first I ever lost. One killed and five wounded and me. I've got four stitches in there and that's nothing compared to what they got.

Last night, or this morning, 0350 hrs, we had rounds come in. 3 dead, 11 wounded in the outfit 200 yds straight up from us. At 0555 hrs. we were hit again, this time about 75 yards on the other side of us killing 2 and wounding 8. I was fully clothed when the second barrage hit us because I knew they'd hit about 0600. I went over to help. Dad, I don't know if I felt sick or not, but this time I maintained my bearing. One of those 8 lost a kidney. I'll never be able to get used to it.

Tell Mom selected parts of this, I don't think she wants to hear it all. We expect to get hit again tonight. I'm scared stiff.

Other than that, everything is hunky-dory. The stitches should be coming out on Tuesday.

Be good, give my love to everyone.

Love,
Bob

Mackey recuperated from his wounds and returned home in September 1969.

—ɯɯ—

After Possibly Killing a Man in Combat, Specialist Fourth Class Ronald "Butch" Livergood Asks His Parents to Forgive Him

Witnessing the killing of other human beings, particularly enemy soldiers, can become so commonplace during wartime that some combatants grow almost non-chalant about it. "We were sitting around eating coconuts, sugercane, bananas and pineapple, plus a few other things I couldn't identify, and, in a general way, were relaxing and having a good time—waiting for orders to move on," twenty-year-old Robert Hughes wrote from Vietnam in a typed letter to his family in Columbus, Ohio. (ARVN is an abbreviation for the Army of the Republic of Viet Nam, who were allied with the Americans. The typos and spacing errors are in the original text.)

From out of nowhere there came some shots real close. We all jumped behind anything available and really didn't know what was happening— at least I didn't. I saw an A.R.V.N. running toward a clump of bamboo. There were more shots—from the bamboo—and the A.R.V.N. disappeared in the grass. I saw him again crawling toward the clump. The V.C. stood up and aimed his pistol right at the A.R.V.N. (we call him Number 10) and pulled the trigger—empty, just like in the movies. "No. 10" jumped up and let the V.C. have a full round in the head. Pretty gruesome, but that's what happened. ("No. 10" had borrowed the lieutenent's radio man's M-16, and had it full automatic. The 20 rounds were out before he knew what was happening.) Good thing he didn't miss; he didn't know how to reload the thing There was nothing left of the V.C.'s. head—just a lot of blood, brains and shattered bone. (burp) Number 10 was pretty proud of himself. Quite a brave little guy. The excitement over, we settled down to lunch again.

But some troops were notably less casual about killing when they were the ones firing the shots. "I'm so damn lonely, and I feel so helpless," a soldier wrote to a female friend in the States.

I know I can't change anything so what's the use in ever thinking about it. People killing people, that's all the whole damn world thinks about. Well they can go on killing, but I'm not going to. Do you know or have any idea how it feels to kill a person? I shot a gook 2 days ago and it really is a bad feeling.

Uncertain if he had done so or not, twenty-year-old Ron "Butch" Livergood was distressed by the mere possibility that he had shot an enemy soldier, even in self-defense. On February 14, 1968, Livergood sent the following letter from Ben Luc to his parents in Gary, Indiana, after debating with himself whether he should tell them or his wife, Linda, what had happened.

Dear Mom and Dad

Hi folks, Well I am sorry I havent wrote to you in quite a while, but if you been listen too news you could pretty well figer out. Sigon was hit heavy and we were to. So they have been keeping us busy during day and night. We were mortared last night and about 4 days ago. Two of the fellows in the Company were wounded but nothing to serious. Now don't you start worrying about me I am O.K. a little nervos but O.K.

I am not worried that much anyway I been reading the Bible off and on and it helps a lot. I think God is protecting me as much as he can. I finally got some film for my camra and I been taking pictures like mad. Mom I don't know if I should tell you this or not, but I have to tell somebody and I can't tell Linda because she would worrie to much, and I think you might be able to take it better than her. I think I might have killed a person but I am not sure, we were fired at and I seen some men running with rifles so I opened fire on them and one of them fell to the ground. I just pray to God for forgiveness.

It shook me up quite a bit but I am feeling better now, because we went out to where I seen him go down. We found blood but nobody. I am glad of that. Well I am glad I got that off my chest I feel better now. I just hope you can forgive me.

Mom I don't know if I should tell you things that happen over here or not because not to many of the guys write home about it. But the pressure builds up in me and I just have to tell somebody. If Linda ~~if~~ knew she might not be able to live with me knowing that her husband has killed a person. Well I change the subject. Hows all the kids back home fine I hope. Tell everyone I send my love and Ill be home in 327 days. I love you both, and I will write more later

Love

Butch

Your Son in Vietnam

P.S. Write as often as possible mail call is all I have to look forward to.

Love

Butch

The incident that Livergood, who survived the war, recounted in his letter occurred during the Tet Offensive, named after the Vietnamese lunar new year, which begins at the end of January. Viet Cong and NVA (North Vietnamese Army) forces launched a massive, coordinated blitz throughout the South on the eve of Tet, catching the Americans and their allies (many of whom were out celebrating) by surprise. Although militarily it was a disaster, failing to overtake and hold a single town or city or ignite a greater Vietnamese uprising as was intended, the attack was an enormous political victory for the Communists. Images of firefights in the US embassy compound and mayhem in the streets of Saigon, including the abrupt, point-blank execution of a VC officer, flashed on television screens throughout the United States, fueling the perception that Vietnam had descended even further into chaos. All of President Lyndon Johnson's podium-pounding arguments that the US was winning the war were silenced by the stark, photographic evidence many Americans believed proved the contrary. At the end of March, Johnson stunned the nation by announcing he would not seek reelection.

〜〜〜

Chaplain Ray Stubbe, Writing from Vietnam, Supports a Friend Back in the States Applying for "Conscientious Objector" Status

By the spring of 1968, American combat deaths in Vietnam were well above the twenty thousand mark with, in the minds of many, no end in sight. Antiwar demonstrations throughout the US were growing in size and intensity. The president was burned in effigy. Young men tore up their draft cards in front of the White House and the Pentagon. Groups of activists confronted government and military officials giving speeches on the war and attempted to shout them down. While some troops fighting in Vietnam lauded the protestors—"They are letting the 'brass' know what many people over here think too! . . . So more power to 'em," one soldier wrote to his father—others denigrated them for undermining morale and emboldening the enemy. "You mentioned the demonstrators back home," twenty-eight-year-old Sergeant Corbin M. Davis replied to his mother in Brooklyn, New York. Davis continued:

> *I think one of them things I would like most is to have them here in my platoon for about three or four days. . . . If they were here one of the things I would do for them is fall them in at attention, give them a 'left face,' and then march them about a mile and a half to the aid station. When we arrived there, I'd give them a 'right face' and then march them one at a time past each of the 32 bodies lying there. There is one sergeant by the name of Savage who is quite impressive in death. He has the entire right side of his head blown off by machine gun fire. Another kid of about 20 years old took a direct hit from a large gun and it blew his right hip and lower abdomen off. . . . I have it real good compared with some of these guys over here, and it makes me sick to my stomach to see them and know that back home there are animals allowed to walk the street and suggest such things as taking up collections to aid the Viet Cong.*

Combatants also had strong opinions about young men on the homefront who claimed conscientious objector status and refused to fight. Many servicemen accused them of lying about their moral opposition to the war simply to get out of being drafted, while others either shared their objections or respectfully agreed to disagree with their position. Chaplain Ray Stubbe, a twenty-nine-year-old naval officer from Milwaukee, was serving in Vietnam when he was asked to substantiate the claims of a friend in Massachusetts requesting conscientious objector status. What is striking about Stubbe's letter is not just the conviction with which he expressed himself, but the conditions under which he was writing: Stubbe was one of approximately six thousand American troops at the besieged Khe Sanh Marine Corps combat base in the northwestern corner of South Vietnam. On January 21, 1968, less than a week and a half before the Tet Offensive, the NVA launched a major attack against Khe Sanh that would last until the beginning of April. More than two weeks into the siege, Stubbe handwrote the following letter to the local draft board in Marblehead, Massachusetts.

MONDAY—05 FEBRUARY 1968—
KHE SANH COMBAT BASE

Dear Sir:

1. Please excuse this not being typewritten; we are under continuous mortar and rocket attacks, and it's quite hazardous moving across

to the office, whose typewriters are all busy typing casualty letters or forms anyway.

2. I am an ordained Lutheran minister of the Lutheran Church in America, and am a Navy Chaplain on active duty with a Marine battalion here in Khe Sanh.

3. I am acquainted with Mr. Geissmann, having been his roommate at the University of Chicago last year, for a period of one year.

4. I am familiar with Mr. Geissmann's views, and, although I myself, obviously, do not subscribe to them personally, he is most sincere in them himself. I would feel very sick indeed if all the men I see killed or injured here and in great pain—were it all for naught—because we are denied our right of dissent. ~~and therfre~~ We are Americans. We bleed for that right. Therefore, although I do not agree with Mr. Geissmann, I will uphold his right and recognize the sincerety of his beliefs as something for which we are dying.

Very respectfully,
Ray W. Stubbe

The situation in Khe Sanh had President Johnson's devoted attention. "I don't want any damn Din Bin Phoo," he exclaimed in his Texas drawl, referring to the French surrender in 1954. There was reason for concern. The NVA had surrounded the base with tens of thousands of soldiers, just as they had done at Dien Bien Phu, forcing the Americans to airdrop all supplies and munitions. And orchestrating the siege was none other than Vo Nguyen Giap—the same general who had defeated the French fourteen years earlier. The Marines and soldiers in the base were able to stave off an assault long enough, however, for thirty thousand American and ARVN troops to come to their assistance. After suffering approximately ten thousand to fifteen thousand fatalities the NVA finally retreated. American deaths were in the hundreds (estimates vary from about two to seven hundred), with up to twenty-five hundred wounded. Ray Stubbe was, fortunately, among those who made it out alive. He never found out, however, if his former roommate had been drafted or not.

—⁂—

In a Letter to a Friend, Specialist Fourth Class Jerry Hill Tries to Answer the Question: "Why Are Our Men [in Vietnam]?"
&
Former Peace Corps Volunteer John Pohlman Explains to a Close Friend, Carolyn Barber, How His Views on the War Have Changed Now That He Is Under Fire

"Since I've been in Vietnam I've flown many missions that were purely for paper purposes," a young airman complained in a letter to his family, written a year and a half before the 1973 Paris Peace Agreement. "While I like to stay away from war stories let me just say that a person resents risking his life for the sake of logging another combat sortie for statistical purposes." He was not alone; disillusionment was plaguing the armed forces in Southeast Asia as deaths climbed well past fifty thousand and public support continued to erode on the homefront. But what was particularly dispiriting to many combatants—and had been for some time—was the unconventional nature of the conflict itself. With the exception of the Tet Offensive, the battle for Khe Sanh, and the 1972 Eastertide Offensive, the war was mostly an unremitting campaign of firefights with few measurable objectives other than the killing of as many enemy soldiers as possible. Servicemembers could not point to a map and see the countries they had liberated or follow the approach of victory the way World War II troops, for example, could mark their drive across Europe toward Berlin or up through the islands of the Pacific and into the heart of Japan. In Vietnam, territory was more likely to be relinquished after a hard fight than secured. (Even Khe Sanh was deserted only three months after tens of thousands of troops had fought so doggedly to prevent its loss to the NVA.) Vietnam was a war of attrition and a test of wills, but as the persistence of an inexhaustible enemy seemed only to strengthen over time, many American and allied forces wondered what difference they, both individually and as a whole, were making. For some, a sense of meaning came from helping the civilian population. Gerald I. Nelson was a staff sergeant in the US Marine Corps, and after a visit to a village in Chu Lai, Nelson wrote the following to his wife, Victoria, back in Beaufort, North Carolina:

One time we went into a hamlet and our 'doc' wanted to fix up some of the little children. I said 'Hell yes. Let's do everything we can.' So I was the lead man on patrol because I had the shotgun. And I stepped from behind some trees into a small courtyard. There standing were three little girls, each about 10 years old. One started crying and just stood still, afraid, and the other two took off and hid behind a hut. I couldn't blame them after seeing me. Well, we stopped there for a break and one of the girls (I fell in love with her) peeked her head out and I motioned her to come to me. She finally came over after much coaxing and I gave her some dry milk in a pack. . . . I mixed the milk in water for her and she looked at me with those sad black eyes and drank. I couldn't help getting a lump in my throat because I think she knew (as a child does) how I felt, and yet she never said one word to me. . . . [A]s we left I felt in my heart that we had accomplished so much and yet we did so little. But maybe this is what has to be *done in this war. Show these people what we can do for them and how foolish the V.C. cause is, and then, and only then will there be peace in all of Vietnam. I pray for these people that it will be soon.*

Other troops viewed the conflict as integral to a larger global fight against Communism. Losing Vietnam would be a tragedy for the Vietnamese, they argued, and it would embolden the Soviets and other antidemocratic regimes. Specialist Fourth Class Jerry Hill was fully aware of the brutality of the war, but, in a letter to a friend back in Danville, Illinois, Hill tried to put their overall mission in the context of a more powerful struggle unfolding around the world.

Dear Gary,

So you want to know how it is over here in Viet Nam. I don't get to see an American newspaper very often so I don't know how bad they say it is over here but I'll tell you it's definitely bad.

Right now I have it fairly good myself but it wasn't like that when I first got here.

Had plenty of fighting in Quin Nhon but here in Ban Me Thuot where I am now things are pretty quiet.

I'll never forget the feeling I had when I killed my first man. After the first one it was easier but still not easy.

My best buddy who I've been with ever since two months in the army was killed fighting right next to me. I haven't made any close friends since for it's a hard feeling to get over.

I've seen dead Americans, some that were scalped and some that were tortured to death.

All in all Gary this is the dirtiest war of them all so the less the people back home know about it the better off they are.

The people here are friendly but you don't know who to trust. Your friend in the daytime might try to cut your throat at night.

Now I'll try to give you my feeling on being over here in Viet Nam.

To start out we do have a purpose over here and we are needed here very badly. This country has been hard at war for 12 years trying to defeat Communism without any winning results till the Americans came. From the long hard struggle these people have had, its put them in a state of poverty. There is much sickness in this country from the downright filth the people live in.

The big question everyone thinks about is "Why are our men over there?" In 1956 Hungary revolted against communism and asked for help which they definitely needed we didn't go there. When Castro turned Cuba communistic we didn't go there so why are we here?

All I can say is a person would have to be here to fully understand why we are here.

I'm no hero and I can't wait till I'm out of this army and back in the states but as long as there is a free America and there is communism there will never be world peace. Freedom and prosperity is something taken for granted back in the states but over here there is very little. Prosperity and freedom are what the Vietnamese are fighting for, and as long is there are people who want freedom I will try to fight and help them have it.

Jerry

For the average combatant in Vietnam (and arguably in most wars), there were two objectives that ultimately took precedence over any humanitarian, philosophical, or long-term geopolitical concerns: looking out for one's buddies and getting home alive. The troops were not uninterested in or oblivious to the domestic and international policies at stake or the larger ethical issues of the war, but their priorities in the field were simply much more pressing. In April 1970, just as overall troop levels were being reduced, Warrant Officer John H. Pohlman wrote a letter to a close friend named Carolyn Barber reflecting on his contribution to a war in which he had had, before being drafted, no desire to participate. The twenty-five-year-old Pohlman had left the beautiful island of Fiji, where he was teaching children as a Peace Corps volunteer, to hump through the oppressively humid jungles of Southeast Asia at a time when his own government was signaling its intention to pull out of the region. The perspective he articulated in his letter was shared, either in word or in spirit, by many of his comrades in Vietnam.

April 15

Dear Carolyn,

It would be interesting to know first what you're expecting me to have to say. Or what you want to hear me say. Either to confirm your suspicions that the army has begun to make a conservative establishment tool out of me, or else to bolster your own anti-war feelings by hearing first-hand that the whole mess over here is the royal shits. I'm afraid you're going to get neither.

My outlook, though not my actual perception, has narrowed considerably in the last month. It matters very little what my views are on the war. It doesn't make a bit of difference whether I feel it is just or unjust, politically or morally. The fact is that I'm here, and will be for the next eleven months. And as terrible as the war may be for you to contemplate, it is far more difficult, for me, to live with, and, as things look now, through. That is my own very selfish compulsive interest right now. Survival.

I developed this mental tunnel vision during a mortar attack the first night I was here. Something happens to your mind when you realize there are people out there who don't like you. And they aren't trying to make you get a haircut, or bust you, or pave your park. They're trying to kill you. It doesn't matter that it isn't me, it's what I represent that they want to stamp out. When somebody shoots at me, I take it personally. It's a weird experience.

To be continued.

Love + kisses, John

Pohlman was killed later that day.

―⚉―

———————————— **Featured Series** ————————————

"Last Letters Home"

Scottish Highlander William Paterson, "On the Eve of a Great Battle," Cautions His Parents That They Might Never Hear from Him Again
&
A Dying Australian Soldier Named H.W. Crowle Finds the Strength to Tell His Family How Deeply He Loves Them
&
Before Leaving on a Secret Mission to Kill a High-Ranking Nazi, Czech Soldier Jan Kubis Expresses His True Emotions to a Young Woman Named Marie Zilanova
&
A Japanese Kamikaze Pilot Named Ichizo Hayashi Encourages His Mother to "Cheer Up" and Accept What He Is About to Do
&
Sergeant Gene Vance Jr., Serving in Afghanistan, Exchanges a Series of Letters and E-Mails with His Wife Before He Becomes One of the First Casualties of "Operation Enduring Freedom"
&
Twenty-Three-Year-Old Sergeant Josh Harapko, Fighting the War on Terrorism with the Tenth Mountain Division, Sends an Unexpectedly Reflective and Emotional Letter to His Mother

Ideally, the letter would never have to be sent. But if the worst should happen, a young second lieutenant named William Paterson, from Wick, Scotland, wanted his parents to understand that he was fully aware of the peril he faced and would be thinking of them until the end. Paterson was serving with the Seaforth Highlanders in World War I, and in mid-November they were preparing to punch through the German line at Cambrai, France. From the very first line, Paterson chose to be as straightforward as possible.

France. 16/11/17.

My Dearest Father & Mother,

I feel it my duty to write you this last message of love, which will only reach you in the event of my death.

The fact is, we are on the eve of a great battle or advance, & with my platoon, I have been detailed to go to the furthest objective 3,500 yards from our own trenches. I need not tell you what this means—you know well enough.

Well, I hope this message never reaches you, because if it does not, then I come out of the fray alright. However, so many are bound to fall, & perhaps I amongst the rest. If such should happen, remember that the sacrifice has been made in a good cause. I do not want to leave you, far from it, but whatever happens, dear father & mother, I am prepared to go forth with a clear conscience, and the knowledge of always having followed your example of uprightness & purity of word & action, so don't worry about me; but think of me as having gone forth into a purer & more peaceful world, where I will meet you all some day.

And now I must thank you all for all you have done for me. My whole life has been centered around you, and any little success I may have made is the outcome of your generosity, so you deserve to reap the benefit. My one aim was to see if I could not help to get you settled down comfortably, and then, after that had been done, I might have thought of doing the same myself, so if anything should happen to me, I hope you may derive some little help from my unfinished work, & that it may continue to be successful. We have been a happy family, much thanks to the sacrifices you have made for us, & the many times you have gone without, yourselves, that we might be satisfied.

I look back on my life—mostly spent at home—and I feel that sometimes I have given you cause for regret, but I know, if such is the case, you will forgive & forget. I knew that when I joined the army I caused you much worry & anxiety, but I think you will admit I did the right thing. If I had not done so, I should never have been satisfied, & perhaps you won't think it credible, but I was satisfied & content when wading through muddy Flanders, & sitting under earsplitting shellfire,—satisfied, because I knew it was where I ought to be at this time.

Well, I sincerely hope Johnnie, Donnie, Alex & Eddie may get successfully through their careers, and it must be a great pleasure to you to watch their welldoings. I'm proud to be your son & their brother. I hope Lizzie & Bella, & Jeannie & her family may spend many happy days & be a comfort to you always.

Well, dear father & mother, I have written at greater length than I intended. Now, whatever you do, don't worry. I am not worrying— except for your sakes—, and ready to carry out the stern duty that is before me, prepared, & calm in body & mind.

So in wishing you goodbye, remember that life at best is one long journey of toil & strife, & that if I go under, I have reached the goal to which we are all passing day by day.

May God, the Father of us all, guide & comfort you, until the joyful day when we will all meet again in the Promised Land where all is joy & gladness, & where suffering & sorrow entereth not.

Your Affectionate & Ever Loving,
Willie.

A sniper's bullet ended Paterson's life only days later, and Mrs. Paterson received her son's letter along with a sincere expression of condolence from his commanding officer. (Mr. Paterson did not learn of his son's fate; he himself had died, presumably of natural causes, before the news was received.) For frontline troops, death is always a possibility and, depending on the hazards, even a likelihood. It is rarely, however, an absolute certainty—with one exception. Combatants who have been mortally wounded and realize they have little time to live will often dictate to a close buddy or the medic treating them a final message home. Those who are physically able will hurriedly write as much as they can before losing consciousness. Second Lieutenant H. W. Crowle, with the Tenth Battalion, AIF (Australian Imperial Force), was critically injured in Pozieres, France, on August 21, 1916. As gangrene ravaged his body and his strength began to flicker, Crowle tried to be optimistic but recognized, even as he was writing to his wife and son, that his time was all but finished.

Dearest Beat and Bill,

Just a line you must be prepared for the worst to happen any day. It is no use trying to hide things. I am in terrible agony. Had I been brought in at once I had a hope.

But now gas gangrene has set in and it is so bad that the doctor could not save it by taking it off as it had gone too far and the only hope is that the salts they put on may drain the gangrene out otherwise there is no hope. The pain is much worse today so the doctor gave me some morphia, which has eased me a little but still it is awful. Tomorrow I shall know the worst as the dressing was to be left on for 3 days and tomorrow is the third day it smells rotten. I was hit running out to see the other officer who was with me but badly wounded. I ran to far as I was in a hurry and he had passed the word down to return, it kept coming down and there was nothing to do but go up and see what he meant, I got two machine gun bullets in the thigh another glanced off by my water bottle and another by the periscope I had in my pocket, you will see that they send my things home. It was during the operations around Mouqet Farm, about 20 days I was in the thick of the attack on Pozieres as I had just about done my duty.

Even if I get over it I will never go back to the war as they have taken pounds of flesh out of my buttock, my word they look after us well here. I am in the officers ward and can get anything I want to eat or drink but I just drink all day changing the drinks as I take a fancy. The Stretcher Bearers could not get the wounded out any way than over the top and across the open. They had to carry me four miles with a man waving a red cross flag in front and the Germans did not open fire on us.

Well dearest I have had a rest, the pain is getting worse and worse. I am very sorry dear, but still you will be well provided for I am easy on that score.

So cheer up dear I could write on a lot but I am nearly unconscious. Give my love to Dear Bill and yourself, do take care of yourself and him.

Your loving husband,
Bert.

Just outside of Berlin in the scenic, leafy suburb of Wannsee, fifteen high-level German officials gathered together in an elegant villa on January 20, 1942, to coordinate the Final Solution, a euphemism for the genocide of Europe's Jews. (The Nazis had already begun murdering Jews and others—Gypsies, people with mental and physical disabilities, gays, Catholics—whom they regarded as "undesirables," but the purpose of the Wannsee meeting was to expand these efforts and ensure that the various government ministries were working in harmony with one another.) Every aspect of the proposal was carefully analyzed and discussed, from the legality of rounding up and killing innocent men, women, and children (many of whom were German by birth) to the precise logistics of executing them as efficiently and inexpensively as possible. Reinhard Heydrich, chief of the Reich Security Main Office, was tasked with leading the conference and directing the implementation of its proposals. Heydrich was nicknamed "The Blond Beast" and "Der Henker" (hangman), as well as "The Butcher of Prague" for the brutal means of oppression he employed as the Reichsprotektor *of Czechoslovakia, which had been seized by Germany in March 1939. Allied forces were determined to assassinate a leading Nazi in one of the occupied countries, and Heydrich seemed a deserving target. On May 27, 1942, two Czech soldiers—Josef Gabcik and Jan Kubis—approached Heydrich's chauffer-driven car as it slowed down through a sharp curve on a road near Prague and machine-gunned and threw several grenades at the vehicle. Both men were able to escape. Two weeks before the potentially suicidal mission, the twenty-eight-year-old Kubis sent a letter to a young woman named Marie Zilanova, whom he had fallen for several months earlier. Kubis could not in any way divulge what he was about to do, but, knowing he might never see Zilanova again, he wanted to express his fondness for her as discreetly as possible.*

Prague May 12, 1942

Dear Marie:

I have received many wonderful messages from you, and I have such fond memories of you. Please accept my cordial greetings and know that you are always in my thoughts.

I apologize for not responding to you for so long. I think of you every day, but I was unable to write to you because a friend of mine, without asking me, borrowed the book in which you wrote your address, and then he left for Moravia. So I had to wait for him to return, and I was

Jan Kubis

very glad that he brought the book back with him. I hope that you won't be angry with me because of this and will forgive me.

You will forgive me, won't you?

You have to, otherwise I won't be able to fall asleep at night if I know you are upset with me. . . . We soldiers also have our feelings and hearts that want to beat for somebody, but we have to hide it.

Marie, I'm not sure if it will be possible for you to write to me. I would like to give you the address of a place where you could send me a few lines, but it would not be possible for me to receive anything there now. I will send you the address next time.

Marie, I will finish even though I have more to say in my heart, but it is not possible to express it with words.

With best regards, you will forever be in my memory.

Yours

Initially it appeared the daring attack had failed; the shots fired at the car all missed Heydrich and the grenades exploded well behind him. But as it turned out, Heydrich had indeed been injured by flying shrapnel, which ripped into his back. He was rushed to the hospital and, due to an increasingly painful infection that spread throughout his body, died a week later. (After Heydrich's assassination, Jan Kubis and Josef Gabcik were tracked down by the Nazis and killed. An estimated thirteen hundred Czechs in all were executed in reprisal for Heydrich's death. One small village, Lidice, was wiped out entirely. Based on inaccurate reports that its citizens were protecting members of the assassination plot, the Nazis surrounded Lidice, just outside of Prague, and shot virtually all of the village's men and deported their wives and children to concentration camps. The Nazis then dynamited, burned, and bulldozed the village to the ground.) No warriors, as a group, are more associated with "last letters" than World War II Japanese kamikaze pilots. Even as the defeat of their country seemed inevitable in early 1945, thousands of these young pilots flew themselves into enemy warships in a last, desperate act of aggression. It was customary for them to write to their families before they embarked on their mission, and the language they used to convey their emotions was rich with metaphor and lyricism. They compared themselves to cherry blossoms that would be reborn at springtime and rays of sunlight that would forever warm the faces of their loved ones. "We are fifteen warriors," one pilot wrote simply, "may our deaths be as sudden and clean as the shattering of crystal." Like many of the suicide pilots, Ichizo Hayashi was young (twenty-three) and prepared to give his life for the Empire. But he was unique in that, while most Japanese are followers of Shintoism or Buddhism, Hayashi had converted to Christianity. His final words were addressed to his mother.

Mother,

The time has come for me to write you a sad letter. I have truly been happy in my life. I have been a spoiled son, haven't I? I know you will forgive me for being such a child.

I am glad that I have been chosen to be a Kamikaze pilot, but I cannot stop from crying when I think of you. You have raised me the best you could, and I am sorry that I must die before I can show my love for you in return and make you happy. How can I tell you to let go of me or be proud of my sacrifice to the country? Mom, I shall not speak of this anymore, since you know how I feel.

When I received your second letter regarding the girl you intended for me to marry, I could have refused because I already knew about my mission. But I wanted to be your little boy just like I used to be, and the letters I received from you made me so cheerful. I wish I could see you again and had enough time for a quiet talk with you and rest in your arms just once more, but Moji was the last place we could be together. I leave the day after tomorrow. The day after tomorrow I must die. I am looking forward to flying over Hakata, and I will silently say good-bye to you from above the clouds.

I am sorry I could not see Chiyoko to thank her. Everyone in our family was so supportive and helpful when I had my high school exams. I miss our house in Miyazaki-cho. Mom, I know you had great dreams for me and I have disappointed you. I wish I could say that I was right, but I should have listened to you. Please take comfort in knowing that I have been selected as one of the best pilots to accomplish the mission, and I am especially honored to lead other students.

After I die, you will still have my brother Makio, and although you may love me more than you love him, I know he will be able to provide anything you and our family might need in the future. You also have my sisters Chiyoko and Hiroko, and your grandchildren, remember? I promise I will always be with you in your heart. I want you to live in peace, and thinking of you being happy makes me happy, so please do not be sad.

From time to time I am tempted to come home to you. But I cannot because it would be cowardly. When I was baptized, the priest said to me, "Renounce your own life." I am committed to our Saviour, even if it means being struck down by the American bullets and sacrificing my life. Everything is in God's hands. Our life and death on this earth should not matter to us who live with God. Jesus has said, "Thy will be done." I have been reading the Bible every day now, because I feel close to you when I do. I will fly and crash to my death with the Bible and the

Book of Psalms in my aircraft. I will also take along the mission badge which the schoolmaster gave me and the charm I received from you.

Regarding marriage, I never intended to take it lightly, but it would be better if you explained the circumstances to the girl and her family. I really wanted to get married and please you. It is just not possible now.

Forgive me, and I know you will as you always have. Mother, I admire you so much. I could never be as good and courageous as you are. You have never hesitated to sacrifice yourself and you bear so many burdens, and I find it so difficult to do. The only fault I have found in you is that you loved me too much. But how can I blame you? For I needed to be loved by you.

I can die peacefully knowing that you, my sisters and brother, and my friends will always remember me. I will pray to you when I crash into the enemy, and pray for me after my death because all of your prayers are heard and accepted by God.

I have asked Umeno to deliver this letter to you. Please do not show it to anyone else. I am ashamed of it. It's strange, as it does not feel like I am the one who is going to die. It feels as if I can see you anytime again soon. I suppose it is because I am overcome with grief when I realize I will never see you again.

The vast majority of last letters do not, in fact, offer heartfelt declarations of patriotism or profound reflections on mortality—not because the writers did not harbor such feelings, but because combatants are more often than not blindsided by death and do not have an opportunity to put their sentiments into a single, enduring message. Although enormously meaningful to its recipients because it is the "last letter," they most typically record all the normal, everyday emotions that correspondences touch on, whether written in times of war or peace. (Some troops also refuse to write an "in case I die" letter for fear it will be self-fulfilling.) Married in the fall of 2001, Sergeant Gene Vance Jr. cancelled his honeymoon when his West Virginia National Guard unit was put on alert after September 11. Vance was sent to Fort Campbell, Kentucky, with the Nineteenth Special Forces Unit in December and then shipped to Afghanistan. On March 15, 2002, Lisa Vance concluded an e-mail to her husband with: "I love you and miss you lots! Mrs. Vance (Still amazes me that that's actually my name! That you actually married me! I'm sooooo lucky!)." He replied the same day:

Well Honey,

I feel pretty lucky myself. Us getting married was the best thing that ever happened to me! I feel pretty fortunate to have someone like you that I can rely on. I guess not everyone over here has someone to go home to. A few tried to stay because they know when they get back they're getting divorced or someone has already left. I'm glad I don't have to worry about that.

It would be cool if you found a company or two to drop ship stuff to me here. I had actually thought about it, but kept forgetting to mention it. One guy got a package sent from Cabela's full of meats and cheeses. It actually looked pretty good. I'll keep that in mind.

Love, Gene

On April 17, 2002, Vance e-mailed the following to his wife:

Lisa,

I had just a minute to run by here to send out a message. This terminal is MUCH more of a hassle to get to, but I just wanted to touch base.

Things kind of dried out for us today. We hope to get a heater installed before dark, we've froze the last two nights! But if you can stay in bed long enough, it actually gets hot pretty quick in the morning. It's strange, freeze at night, and bake all day. I took some pictures of the mountains this morning as I walked around with my coffee. It was really pretty with the snow covered peaks.

I'll try and stay in touch for as long as possible before we push out. Still don't know when exactly, but I can't say anyway. But it'll be pretty soon. Try not to worry too much though, we won't be by ourselves. There should be lots of help in the area. Again, I can't talk about specifics.

I hope you got the picture I sent this morning. I really miss you and I'll be in touch again soon.

Love,
Gene

It was the last e-mail Lisa Vance would receive from her husband. On May 19, Sergeant Gene Vance was killed during a firefight near the village of Shkin while patrolling for Taliban and al-Qaeda forces. Soon after learning of her husband's death, Lisa Vance received in the mail handwritten letters her husband had sent to her in late April and early May, including the following (Storm and Suzie are the Vances' dogs):

Dear Lisa,
Well, we're here! We are in SE Afghanistan very near the Pakistan border. The "compound" here is surrounded by walls and lots of barbed wire.

We can see for miles from here, so hopefully no one tries to mount an attack.

It was really weird the night we got here. We flew from Bagram to here in a British helicoptor. It was dark, but you could see the local militia types manning the check points. We drove through a huge iron gate (almost like coming inside a castle or something) into a large enclosed fort. (I've taken several pictures of things since we got here.) Anyway, it seems that the only "decent" room left was essentially an old stable or something. We had to sleep on the dirt & straw in a <u>very</u> dirty room. Luckily, it didn't seem as if animals had actually been kept there in a while. The buildings & compond itself are made from wood and mud and straw. It is impossible to stay clean! After 4 nights we finally got cots and I am <u>so</u> ready to sleep on that tonight! . . .

As for now, I feel safer now that I'm here. The buildings and surrounding area are better than we thought before coming.

It's been really strange. At each place I go to, I go through a phase I have to adjust to. First, I was afraid in Uzbekistan. Then a little more in Bagram. Then when I got here, I was really scared. But you adjust.

I can't wait to get home where all I have to worry about is Storm or Suzie sneaking up to lick me or something! And of course, I want to get back to normal with you!

I'm glad I stay busy, because I think of you and home enough as it is. I can't wait to get back! I just love you so much.

Love,
Gene

By the time of the invasion of Afghanistan in October 2001, American and Coalition troops had at their disposal more ways to communicate with the home front than any other generation of combatants. Although not everyone had access to the technology in all parts of the region, many troops could make satellite phone calls or send e-mails, text messages, faxes (although even those have become antiquated and are rarely used), and audio and DVD recordings to their loved ones. These transmissions let anxious family members and friends know almost instantaneously that their serviceman or -woman was alive and well. But when an especially intimate or personal message needed to be shared, many troops sat down with pen and paper and handwrote an actual letter they would later mail—or, in the event of a worst-case scenario, had instructed a buddy to do so on their behalf. In early March 2002, Coalition forces began to gear up for Operation Anaconda, a major assault on Taliban and al-Qaeda strongholds in the mountains of Afghanistan. Josh Harapko, a twenty-three-year-old sergeant and platoon leader with the Tenth Mountain Division, rarely sent letters to his mother back in Arizona or opened up much about his feelings under any circumstances. But with great care, Harapko neatly handwrote the following letter to his mom before advancing into what would be one of the worst firefights of the Afghan campaign. (Peg was a very close family friend who had died of cancer; Marcie and Dave are her children; Jake is Marcie's son; Nikki, Lauren, and Steve are Josh's cousins; and Sean is his brother and Heidi is his sister. She, too, was in the military and would go off to serve in Iraq two years later.)

Dear Mom,

    I'm writing this letter before I leave. I couldn't say what I wanted to over the phone. First I want to say I love you so much. You were always there for me even though I would never talk about my problems. Second you gave me the options to be a man giving me slack in the rope to try to make the right decisions. No matter what you always believed in me, no matter how much of a punk I was to you. We are leaving for Bahgram to flush out 600 Taliban soldiers from the mountains. This is the biggest battle of the war on terrorism. We already sustained 30 casualties and one KIA. I never thought war was fun. It's hard to see all the guys who were shot or wounded and to know your going right back in there. I thought you should know where I am.

    I don't want you to worry about me. (I know you will cause I'm your son). Mom I'm not afraid to die for something that is right. I'm more scared of being wounded like most of these guys and not being able to walk again. I just hope that I made you proud, and if I don't come home for any reason I just want you to know I'll always be with you. Really

Sergeant Josh Harapko

you shouldn't worry though. My guardian angel (Peg) is with me. I didn't get ahold of Sean, but please tell him I love him. I remember when I used to tell him to stop acting like my Dad. Well tell him I really respect him for that. I wish I could have told him myself. I wish we could have hung out together more and I regret not being able to.

I want you to know you raised the cream of the crop. I haven't been able to contact Heidi so please tell her I love her so much. I'm so proud of her. I want her to know that. I wish I wasn't such a brat when she was around. These are just some things I needed to justify before we move out. Tell Aunt Kathy my prayers are with her and Uncle Joe. Tell Nikki I hope to be there for her wedding. Tell Aunt Barb and Uncle Kevin I love them. The same to Aunt Sharon and the kids and Uncle Bob. If you go to Steve's graduation tell him how proud I am of him. For Lauren tell her I liked hanging out with her and her roommates. Also good luck and congratulations. To Marcie and Dave you were just like a blood brother and sister and I love them like family, and to little Jake happy birthday.

Well Mom I have to go now, all that I have said here are words from my heart and I mean every last one of them. Tell Aunt Joyce I said hi and I love her. I hope to see you soon but if that doesn't work out I just needed you to know how I felt. I Love you and Miss you. Take care your always in my thoughts.

Your Loving Son Josh.

Harapko survived Operation Anaconda and returned to the States alive and well. In an awful irony, however, he and ten other soldiers died one year later (March 11, 2003) when the UH-60 Black Hawk helicopter they were flying in crashed during a routine training mission at Fort Drum, New York.

In a Letter He Considers Almost a "Confession," a US Marine Writes to His Priest Back Home About the Opening Weeks of Operation Iraqi Freedom
&
Lieutenant Colonel David Bellon Provides His Father with a Graphic Depiction of the Fighting in Fallujah and the Ruthless Tactics Used by the Insurgents

"VICTORY!! As of 0800 our time it's over," Master Sergeant L. Vincent Francese declared triumphantly in a February 28, 1991, letter to his wife,

Rhonda, in South Carolina. Francese was a US Marine serving in Kuwait during Operation Desert Storm, and, like the other five hundred thousand troops in the region, he was elated that the war had ended swiftly and with minor American and allied casualties. The shortest major conflict in US history (after a forty-three-day air campaign, the ground assault lasted only one hundred hours), Desert Storm was not only a resounding military success, it ushered in a restored sense of confidence within the armed forces, as well as a new generation of highly sophisticated instruments of war. From the B-2 "Stealth" Bomber that was virtually invisible on radar, to laser- and satellite-guided missiles that could strike a target with pinpoint accuracy, not since World War I had there been such dramatic advancements in weaponry. Military planners envisioned future conflicts that relied less on live ground troops and more on automated and robotic weapons systems, including remote-controlled reconnaissance devices and unmanned tanks and warplanes. The US-led air strikes against Serb forces in the mid and late 1990s further demonstrated that battles could be won with minimal casualties—or, as with the Serbian campaigns, no combat fatalities at all—for the American servicemembers involved. During a February 1996 speech, Air Force Chief of Staff General Ronald R. Fogleman remarked that the US was on the verge of "a new American way of war" that focused more on air power and less on "placing thousands of young Americans at risk in brute, force-on-force conflicts." Advanced capabilities will, General Fogleman predicted,

> *help minimize casualties on both sides, reduce the "CNN effect" [i.e., bringing the horrors of combat into people's homes via live television], and allow us to wage war in a way that corresponds to what appears to be the values of American society—that is, what the American people are willing to accept on the battlefield. Air power will also provide tremendous leverage to resolve future crises—rapidly and at low cost.*

The earth-shaking "Shock and Awe" barrage launched against Iraq on March 20, 2003, demonstrated how overwhelmingly destructive a massive air campaign with technologically superior weapons could be. (More firepower was unleashed on Baghdad in the first twenty-four hours of Shock and Awe than during the entire Gulf War.) American and Coalition troops encountered pockets of resistance during the ground invasion that followed, but major clashes or a prolonged standoff with tens of thousands of Iraqi troops did not occur. The Iraqi army, in the eyes of many, seemingly melted away. But even in the first few hours and days of the war, US and Coalition servicemembers noticed that the paramilitary forces loyal to Saddam Hussein were employing unconventional tactics that unnerved some troops and infuriated others. One F-18 pilot, Captain Travis Russell, alluded to what the Coalition was up against in an e-mail to family members back home in Washington, DC.

> *We launched on a mission this morning where we found and employed on our targets. We did a tag team with a flight who was already working these guys over pretty good and we just added to the punch.... I had to pause there for a second to put on my gas mask and chemical suit, those silly Iraqis keep launching scuds this way. Anyway, we put a hurting on some guys earlier today and we hope it did some good. Amazing, they are certainly taking advantage of our humanity by faking a surrender to set up an ambush. You can bet those who were alive to start the ambush were not alive much after.*

Another combatant, a US Marine captain (whose name is being withheld in the interests of privacy), handwrote a short but emotional letter to his priest back home in the States about his first combat experiences in Iraq. Although he was heartened by the welcome response he and his fellow Marines received from many civilians as they advanced toward Baghdad, he was haunted by the retaliatory measures the Marines had to take against Iraqi forces who hid themselves behind innocent men, women, and children.

Easter
20 April 2003

Father Bob,

With religious banners flying, truckload after truckload of cheering Iraqis pass our position. After decades of religious oppression, the Shi'a muslims are now free to worship as they wish. Old men have tears of joy and the younger generation try to thank us the best they can in their broken English. "Thank You America" and "Mr Bush. . . good" are about all the Marines can understand, but the sight of the liberated people is an incredible gift to all of us on this most wonderful Easter.

What a difference a month can make. Thank you for your prayers during the darkest days of the war. Even though I had a front row seat to man's inhumanity to man, I believed that good would prevail. I never thought that man could be so cruel. My time in An Nasiriyah will hopefully be forgotten. Never have I felt so angry before, a kind of anger that I never knew existed. I never felt joy in my actions, nor regret. The paramilitary forces which we faced shielded themselves with civilians. The blood of the innocent was spilled and will forever stain my hands.

My actions were just and had to be done, but that doesn't make it easier and I will just have to live with it. This letter is turning into more of a confession than a greeting, but maybe that's what I need.

Thank you for watching over my family and the families of others who proudly wear the military uniform. Despite all the ugliness that I've seen, I still believe this world is beautiful. I look forward to standing before the St Rose altar with my fiancée in August. It will be a time that will only have room for love. Only through love will there be peace! Please continue to take care of St Rose. You are a good man, Father Bob, a very good man!

God Bless.

The Lord is my light and my salvation; Whom shall I fear? The Lord is the stronghold of my life—of whom shall I be afraid?

Psalm 27:1

(special words during a trying time)

On May 1, 2003, President George W. Bush announced that "major combat operations in Iraq have ended," but went on to say that he recognized there was still

> *difficult work to do in Iraq. We're bringing order to parts of that country that remain dangerous. . . . The transition from dictatorship to democracy will take time, but it is worth every effort. Our coalition will stay until our work is done and then we will leave, and we will leave behind a free Iraq.*

In the months to follow, the conditions became significantly more threatening as a full-scale insurgency began to take hold. Unable to match the air power or heavy artillery of the US and Coalition troops, the insurgents waged guerilla— also known as "asymmetrical"—warfare, both to kill their enemies and terrorize anyone associated with them. The United Nations closed its Baghdad office after it was partially destroyed by a car bomb on August 19, 2003, and many aid workers and civilian contractors fled the country after their colleagues were kidnapped and executed, either by a shot to the head or decapitation. The epicenter of much of the violence was Fallujah (also spelled Falluja), a city just west of Baghdad and in the heart of the Sunni Triangle, where Saddam Hussein remained a popular symbol of anti-American resistance. In November 2003, insurgents shot down a US Army CH-47 Chinook helicopter, killing sixteen soldiers. On March 31, 2004, in an incident that startled the world, four American civilian security workers were pulled from their car in Fallujah and beaten to death. Insurgents then set fire to their bodies and dangled the charred remains from a bridge over the Euphrates. "The Falluja fighting is intense, up close and personal," a thirty-eight-year-old US Marine Corps major named David Bellon e-mailed his family on April 13, 2004. Bellon, who was serving as the First Marine Regiment intelligence officer, was especially revolted at how viciously the insurgents were targeting other Iraqis.

> *I cannot tell you how many reports I have gotten about insurgents threatening civilians at gunpoint telling them that they will be killed if they try to leave the city or do not let the enemy use their land/homes for attacking us. The enemy takes over houses at gunpoint and tries to draw fire hoping that we will kill innocents so they can exploit it. I sincerely doubt that the Marines have passed by a mosque/minaret where they have not taken fire. We return fire and it is the lead story. The hypocrisy and lies are exasperating. . . . I could go on and on about the treachery of our enemy here, smuggling weapons in humanitarian rations under Red Crescent banners, moving arms and ammunition via ambulances, bombing civilian vehicles in order to alienate the people from the coalition. . . . However, the worst are reports that these foreign fighters have snipers in the city that engage the women and children as they try to escape the fighting. It sounds too horrific to be true but nothing is off the table to this enemy. Daily, they fire unguided rockets into the city and then get on the mosque loud speakers to blame the US. On, and on and on. . . .*

Bellon and his fellow Marines had been gearing up for an all-out assault on Fallujah that spring, but it was eventually called off. Seven months later, Bellon— who was now a lieutenant colonel—e-mailed his father to let him know that they were preparing, once again, to take over the city. (IED stands for improvised explosive device, and "muj" is short for mujahidin, a military force of fundamentalist Muslim warriors engaged in a jihad against those whom they believe to be enemies of their faith.)

Dear Dad—

As you have no doubt been watching, we have had our hands full around Fallujah. It would seem as if the final reckoning is coming. The city has been on a consistent down hill spiral since we were ordered out in April. It's siren call for extremists and criminals has only increased steadily and the instability and violence that radiates out of the town has expanded exponentially. If there is another city in the world that contains more terrorists, I would be surprised. From the last two years, I just don't see a way that we can succeed in Iraq without reducing this threat. The cost of continuing on without taking decisive action is too high to dwell on.

The enemy inside the town have come to fight and kill Americans. Nothing will sate their bloodlust and hatred other than to kill everyone of us or at least die trying. It is hard to fathom as a Westerner as rational thought would dictate that we will only be here for a relatively short blip in their history and while we are here, billions of dollars in investments will pour in and opportunity that is beyond comprehension will open up for anyone willing to work. This is not Kansas and this enemy does not think like that.

If we build a school or clinic, they destroy it. They would rather deny medical care or education for the children of the citizens who live nearby than to have any symbol of the West in general and America specifically among them. It is hard to comprehend. Frankly, we are done trying.

For eight months, we have been on our chain. The enemy has fooled itself misinterpreting our humanity and restraint for lack of will and courage. For eight months, we have watched Marines, Soldiers and Sailors maimed and killed by invisible cowards hiding behind some wall or in a canal as he detonates another IED. For eight months, we have been witness to suicidal sociopaths driving vehicles laden with explosives into crowds of Iraqis and into our own convoys.

Just last week, we lost another nine Marines killed and an equal number of wounded as the result of some ignorant extremist who was able to convince himself that killing himself and as many Americans as possible would send him to paradise where he could finally get his virgins.

Now, their own ignorance and arrogance will be their undoing. They believe that they can hold Fallujah. In fact, they have come from all over to be part of its glorious defense. I cannot describe the atmosphere that exists in the Regiment right now. Of course the men are nervous but I think they are more nervous that we will not be allowed to clean the rats nest out and instead will be forced to continue operating as is.

Its as if a window of opportunity has opened and everyone just wants to get on with it before it closes. The Marines know the enemy has massed and has temporarily decided to stay and fight. For the first time, the men feel as though we may be allowed to do what needs to be done. If the enemy wants to sit in his citadel and try to defend it against the Marine Corps and some very hard Soldiers... then the men want to execute before the enemy sobers up and flees.

It may come off as an exceptionally bellicose perspective but where the Marines live and operate is a war zone in the starkest reality. When the Marines leave the front gate on an operation or patrol, someone within direct line of sight of that gate is trying to kill them. All have lost friends and watched as the enemy hides within his sanctuary that has been allowed out of what one must assume is political necessity. The enemy has been given every advantage by our sense of morality and restraint and by a set of operational rules that we are constrained to operate under. The Marines feel like their time has come and we will finally be ordered to do what must be done and be given the latitude to do it. Even though the price will be high, there is not a man here that would chose status quo over paying the price.

Every day, the enemy takes more hostages, assassinates developing Iraqi leaders and savagely beats suspected collaborators. I will give you just one recent example that happened last week. One of our patrols was moving down a street when they saw what looked like a fight. The Marines closed with the scene. It was a family that had come to Iraq on religious pilgrimage that was taken hostage and was being taken into Fallujah. The muj stopped for some reason and the father began fighting. The Marines interdicted and captured two of the kidnappers. Two more ran and the Marines could not get a shot without fear of killing/wounding others.

Every day, insurgents from inside Fallujah drive out and wait for Iraqis that work on our bases. Once the Iraqis leave they are stopped. The lucky ones are savagely beaten. The unfortunate ones are killed. A family that had fled Fallujah in order to get away from the fighting recently tried to return. When they got to their home, they found it taken over by terrorists (very common). When the patriarch showed the muj his deed in order to prove that the house was his, they took the old man out into the street and beat him senseless in front of his family.

Summary executions are common. Think about that. Summary executions inside Fallujah happen with sobering frequency. We have been witness to the scene on a number of occasions. Three men are taken from the trunk of a car and are made to walk to a ditch where they are shot. Bodies are found in the Euphrates without heads washed downstream from Fallujah. To date we have been allowed to do nothing.

I have no idea the numbers of beheadings that have occurred in Fallujah since I have been here. I have no idea the number of hostages that have ended up in Fallujah since we have been here. I just don't know that Americans would be able to comprehend the number anyway. Unfortunately, the situation has only gotten worse. There is no hope for any type of reasoned solution with an enemy like this.

Once again, we are being asked by citizens who have fled the city to go in and take the city back. They are willing for us to literally rubble the place in order to kill the terrorists within. Don't get me wrong, there are still many inside the town that support the terrorists and we cannot expect to be thanked publicly if we do take the city. There is a sense of de ja vu with the refugees telling us where their houses are and asking us to bomb them because the muj have taken them over. We heard the same thing in April only to end up letting the people down. Some no doubt have paid with their lives. The "good" people who may ultimately buy into a peaceful and prosperous Iraq are again asking us to do what we know must be done.

The Marines understand and are eager to get on with it. The only lingering fear in them is that we will be ordered to stop again. I don't know if this is going to happen but if it happens soon, I will write you when its over,

Love,
Dave

With AC-130 Spectre gunships providing support from the air and Abrams tanks and Bradley vehicles leading the drive in, fifteen thousand US Marines, soldiers, Navy SEALS, and Iraqi security forces attacked Fallujah beginning November 7, 2004. During the weeklong, building-to-building battle for the city, an estimated twelve hundred insurgents were killed and wounded—some of whom, it was discovered, were not Iraqis but Afghans, Egyptians, Saudis, and Yemenis. US casualties totaled approximately five hundred, including more than fifty fatalities. Dave Bellon himself survived.

—∾—

An Iraqi Woman Describes for a Relative in Cairo a Fatal Encounter Between Her Family and a Group of American Soldiers
&
US Army Specialist Gary Chandler Assures His Aunt That He Was Not Injured by a Recent Bombing—but Reports on the Condition of Those Who Were

For innocent Iraqis who have wanted nothing to do with either side of the fighting, remaining neutral has still not guaranteed their safety. Many have been blown up by the same crude bombs meant to kill US and Coalition forces, and some have been shot by troops who have mistaken them for insurgents. In September 2003, an Iraqi woman named Shayma (last name withheld for reasons of privacy) was the victim of a misunderstanding that had tragic consequences for her and her family. In the spring of 2004, when she was able to establish e-mail communication with relatives in Egypt, she described the traumatic event, which had happened the previous fall.

Dear Aunt Khadija,

I was so happy when I received your message last week. We were all destroyed and hopeless after the incident, but Mother is better, and I believe she will overcome the pain. Faris is getting better, and the doctors say he will be able to walk in two months.

You asked me for details of the accident, and I am going to tell you about it, but it is painful. It is hard to remember, and I was trying to forget it all.

It started at 10:00 in the evening that night last September, and I was at my family's home with my two babies. You know about the continuous cutting of electricity, so we were all sleeping on the roof of the house. Father used to put his gun under his head since the situation was, and still is, dangerous.

We heard knocks on the door, and there was a noise out in the street. We heard people shouting, and we couldn't recognize what they were talking about. Suddenly we started to hear shooting in the air, and father got up and went down. Faris went after him. I told him not to go out, but he wouldn't listen.

It turned out it was an armed robbery from a gang in the neighborhood.

Father heard steps, voices, and thinking that they were from the gang, he began shooting at them with his gun. They weren't the gang, they were American soldiers, and when they heard the shooting, they fired at father. Their bullets struck him in his neck, lungs, heart, kidney, legs. Faris was shot in his right leg by three bullets. There were three holes in his leg, but he is better now.

I'm sorry to tell you all these things, but you asked me to.

Now we are ready to come to Cairo, because we cannot live here anymore; it is hard to do.

Yours,
Shayma

As the fighting intensified, many US servicemembers became less sympathetic with the plight of average Iraqis, whom they sometimes referred to as "Hajis" or—more disparagingly—"ragheads." (Conversely, many Iraqis privately began referring to all US troops, regardless of their faith, as "Jews.") But from the very beginning of the war, one of the sentiments expressed most commonly in letters and e-mails by American troops was how deeply affected they were by the Iraqi children they saw and the suffering these children have had to endure. When Sheri Travillian heard over the news that a bomb had exploded near a base outside of Baghdad, where her nephew Specialist Gary Chandler was stationed, she frantically dashed off an e-mail to make sure he was all right. Chandler e-mailed the following reply.

Im fine.the bomb was off post but there were a lot of civilian casualties.the bomb was at a school.a lot a little kids were killed.they brought the victims here and we helped them.it was bad.all these little kids missing hands and feet.one little boy had half his face missing.the dead ones were the worst.im not gonna go into detail about them.i still see their faces.eyes still open starring off into space.ill never forget that,ever.well im fine not hurt.there was a bomb on post but we found it before it exploded.they cought the guy and he told them that there are more bombs on the way.well we hope none make it here.weve had some firefights at election sights they were'nt very long but just enough to scare people.its getting warmer out so the enemy starting to come out of hiding again.well I gotta get back to work. love gary

Some troops found hope in the prospect of younger generations of Iraqis grow-ing up in a country free of Saddam Hussein. In the middle of an effusive love letter to his fiancée, Danielle, a US Army Ranger captain named Jason Ritter commented:

> [P]erhaps we are making a difference over here. I think that we are. I did have an experience the other day that helped put it into perspective. I watched as a dozen or so little girls hurried past us on their way to school. I would like to think that you and I are directly responsible for allowing them the opportunity to even go to school in the first place. And maybe when it is all said and done the place will be changed for the better. I think so.

Other troops wondered, with tensions and hostilities appearing to become more aggravated with every passing day, if the cycle of violence would ever stop. "Yesterday a kid, who couldn't have been any older than 4, pointed a stick at me like a rifle and pretended to shoot me," a US Marine named Stephen Webber wrote in a long e-mail from Iraq to classmates at Saint Louis University, where he had been a junior before being called up for active duty. "I wonder if someday my kids will meet him on some distant battlefield. I pray to God that if I ever have a son, he never has to go to war. That would tear my heart out." After describing the bloody aftermath of an explosion that killed twenty Iraqis, the twenty-year-old lance corporal reflected on life back home and the psycho-logical toll that the war was taking on his loved ones—and him.

I feel very bad for my family. I know that I am putting them through hell. Sometimes I feel guilty for not just studying abroad. If you get a chance, hug your mom—for me. My mom is 9,000 miles and six months away. I would do anything to give her a hug right now. . . . It feels that everyone back in the world is getting on with their lives, finishing school, getting jobs or internships, making friends, planning their future—and we are frozen in time. When I get back, friends will be gone, innocence will be lost, and things will have changed.

Webber concluded: *"I just want things to be the way they used to be."*

—〰—

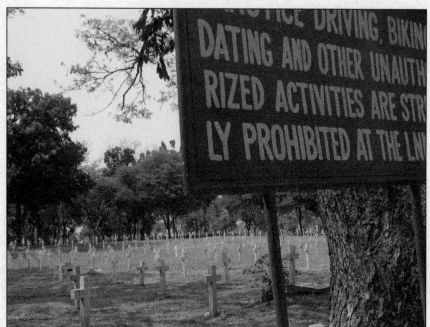

Although humor is not normally associated with military cemeteries, the sign above, at the National Filipino Cemetery in Manila, caught my attention because of its stern warning: PRACTICE DRIVING, BIKING, DATING AND OTHER UNAUTHORIZED ACTIVITIES ARE STRICTLY PROHIBITED. . . When I asked my guide why anyone would want to go on a date at a national cemetery, he smiled and said that "dating" was a euphemism for "something else." And apparently "something else" had been going on quite a bit there.

Laughing Through the Tears

Humorous and Unusual Letters

Just a wee note. I am "going over the parapet", and the chances of a "sub" getting back alive are about nix. If I do get back, why you can give me the horse laugh. If not this'll let you know that I kicked out with my boots on. So, cheer up, old dear, and don't let the newspapers use you as material for a Saturday magazine feature. You know the kind: where the "sweet-faced, grey-haired, little mother, clutching the last letter from her boy to her breast, sobbed, " 'e was sich a fine lad,' as she furtively brushes the glistening tears from her eyes with a dish rag, etc. etc." Your son is a soldier, and a dog-gone good one, too, if he does say it himself as he shouldn't. And if he gets pipped it'll be doing his blooming job. S'there y'are.

> *—Canadian soldier Hart Leech,*
> *writing to his mother during World War I.*
> *Leech was killed soon after.*

Every able bodied man who can hold a gun is now a parashot. I don't think, as a matter of fact, that the able bodied with the guns are going to be the only people to attack the parachuters, if they should attempt a landing here, for the country people are waiting for them with scythes and clubs. Myself, serious as I know the parachuter danger to be, can only find them funny. The thought of a German descending through the skies, disguised as a clergyman, even perhaps as a bishop, with his machine gun under one arm, and his bicycle under the other, is hard to take seriously. The wireless broadcast a description of how the parachuters will be dressed, and in spite of the fact that the country is grimly determined to exterminate the lot, everybody died with laughter. One of the comforts of war seems to be that when one horror piles on another there comes a point when a great deal of what is happening makes the public laugh.

—Noel Streatfeild, writing to "Binkie and Champion"
on June 13, 1940, about a possible German invasion
of England

I've got plenty of everything else (food). My assistants take care of me. We live well together. When I am gone they fall into a funk, but as soon as I appear they start working full steam. On holidays we drink 100 grams or so. As Markov always says, 100 grams isn't enough, but 200 grams is too much. Let's drink 150 grams. Twice.

—Soviet soldier Kotka Gofman,
writing to friends on November 3, 1941

Had a few scary weeks during the last days of November. Was it the AAA, surface to air threat, night tanking, night traps? Nope— we almost ran out of piddle packs. My squadron, in keeping with the theme that desperate times require desperate (i.e. moronic) measures, survived these dark days by adopting a completely unsafe dehydration plan coupled with the procurement of several emergency inflight relief vessels/urine storage devices—Gatorade bottles—for those times when bladder evacuation at 32,000 feet was just plain unavoidable. As an aside, donning the ever reliable DEPENDS undergarment was momentarily discussed but instantaneously dismissed. We were all in agreement that the image of a downed Navy fighter pilot in Afghanistan, paraded in front of the cameras of CNN, wearing only DIAPERS would only serve to heighten the fighting spirit and resolve of the Taliban and Al Qaida network worldwide.

> —*An American Navy pilot, e-mailing*
> *his family on January 2, 2002,*
> *in between combat missions over Afghanistan*
> *during Operation Enduring Freedom*

Tadeusz Kosciuszko, a Polish-Born Colonel Serving with the Americans in the War of Independence, Sends a Teasing Letter to His Friend, Major John Armstrong

Early American war-related humor manifested itself in many ways—satirical political cartoons (known then as caricatures), editorials, speeches, songs, and lines of verse. ("When perched on your charge on dress parade / You looked as brave a soldier as ever was made. / If you look but as brave when the bullets fly / Your Country will love you and so will I," reads one poem titled "The Colonel.") But levity was rarely evident in the letters of the common fighting man. Writing paper, especially in the eighteenth century, was a precious commodity for the average soldier, and when given the opportunity to send a letter to loved ones back home, necessity compelled him to report relevant war news and his own condition and well-being. Describing funny incidents or practical jokes played on comrades (which certainly occurred) was not a priority. Officers were more likely to be witty or facetious in their correspondences, particularly when it concerned, from their perspective, the imbecility of their superiors. The latter seems to be an especially timeless subject. "[L]ittle did we dream that it was still in the power of one blunderer to render all [our] favorable promising circumstances abortive," wrote Captain Charles Lee, with growing sarcasm, about General James Abercromby after Abercromby's failed assault on Fort Carillon in the French & Indian War. Lee continued:

> *[O]ur noble Leader soon convinc'd us that there can be no situation so disadvantageous [to the enemy], no success & victory so certain, altho' it is absolutely in your hands & only waits until you grasp it, but that a miscarriage may be brought about by the incapacity of a single person. I really did not think that so great a share of stupidity and absurdity could be in the possession of any man. Fortune and the pusillanimity of the French had cram'd victory into his mouth, but he contrived to spit it out again.*

Lee was just getting started.

There was one hill in particular which seem'd to offer itself as an ally to us[;] it immediately commanded the lines from hence two small pieces of cannon well planted must have drove the French in a very short time from their breast work, the consequence of which wou'd have been that the greatest part of 'em must have either surrendered or drown'd themselves in the Lake, for the Fort was not large enough to have contan'd half of 'em; but notwithstanding some of our Cannon was brought up & in readiness, this never was thought of, which one wou'd imagine must have occur'd to any blockhead who was not absolutely so far sunk in Idiotism as to be oblig'd to wear a bib and bells. So far, his behaviour cou'd only be call'd stupid, ridiculous & absurd.

Although unconfirmed, it is believed that Charles Lee, during the American Revolution, would later recommend to George Washington a young engineering officer he had encountered in Poland while advising their military. Regardless of how the introduction was made, Tadeusz "Thad" Kosciuszko (pronounced ko-SHOOZ-ko) came to America in 1776 and was greatly admired for his service to the Continental Army. He was also known for his sense of humor. When one American general complained that his name was difficult to pronounce, Kosciuszko retorted good-naturedly that "Knickerbocker" and "Schenectady" didn't exactly roll off the tongue for him, either. Writing on March 3, 1779, from West Point, where he was overseeing the construction of fortifications against a British attack, Kosciusko sent a short letter to his friend, Major John Armstrong, poking fun at Armstrong and his staff for neglecting him. (William Claijon and Colonel Troup, whose names Kosciuszko misspells, were aides to General Horatio Gates. "Bob" is most likely General Gates's son. "Priapus" is the Greek and Roman god of procreation, renowned for being endowed with a large phallus.)

West Point 3 March 1779

Dear Friend,

I do not tax you with want of Friendships in not writing to me knowing that you have a good reason to give, that the handsome Girls ingross the whole of your Time and attention and realy If I was in your place I should of Choise do the same. But you Col. Clairjon can give me no Reason but your Laxiness. I have ben told you are about Marying a Young girl and mean to exert yourself that the name of Clairjons may not be extinguished. You Col Troop as a good officer of Artillery will make use of you Activity and prove the Goodness of your Cannon on the wedding Day of Col. Clairjon. Your help Doctor Brown will be wanted with all your Surgical Faculties to promote so laudable a design for the interest of Mr. Clairjon and administere such Medicine as will make him Strong and Fameus as Priapus. You Bob will take exemple from the misfortune of Mr. Bucks and not be so imprudent as to get the clap. Send me one pound of green Tea. The Officer who bears this will pay for it.

Your affectionat Friend
Thad Kosciuszko Col.

—∾—

Disgusted by the Union Victory, Rebel Soldier Andrew O. Stoan Tells an Acquaintance What He Thinks of "Old Abe" and His Fellow Abolitionists

Governed by a strong sense of propriety, correspondents in the Civil War, like let-ter writers in the eighteenth century, were reluctant to use expressions deemed to be in any way offensive. Even words like "damned" and "devil," for example— tame to twenty-first century readers—were considered inappropriate by some and replaced with "d——d" and "d——l." But apparently there were exceptions. Lieutenant Sebron Sneed, a Rebel soldier with the Sixth Texas Infantry, did not employ such language himself in a January 1, 1863, message to his wife Fan-nie, but he was privy to a cache of intercepted Union mail whose contents shocked him and his comrades. "The letters, after being opened at the General's Head Quarters and the money and valuables taken from them, were distributed among the men," he explained. "All the mail was from home to the soldiers down the Mississippi River [and], Fan, I know it would amuse you to read some of them." Sneed continued:

> *Very few are from persons of education and the ridiculous composition, spelling and homely expressions have furnished me with food for merriment for many hours. I had no idea there was so much vulgarity in the letters of wives to their husbands—some of them are obscene and show filthy, lewd dispositions. Many important secrets are told. I intend to send you a bundle of them as soon as the boys quit reading them. . . .*

Confederate soldier Andrew Osborn Stoan is not known to have written or received any sexually explicit letters himself, but after the Union victory in April 1865 he did have some choice words for President Abraham Lincoln and the whole United States for that matter, which he seemed hell-bent on abandoning. Heartbroken by the South's defeat, Stoan dashed off the following letter to his friend George Coblentz to say good-bye—with explicit instructions on what he wanted Coblentz to tell their "abolishing [i.e., abolitionist] friends" after his departure.

June 12, 1865

Dear Sir:

It is with pleasure that I now write you a few lines to let you know how I am well. I'm all right yet and hope this will find you the same. Well Geo., Old Abe is dead and gone to hell where the whole race had ought to go. Well I would like to hear from you but I hain't got time to stay now. I am just on my way to regions unknown. I don't know where I will land yet it may be in hell with Abe but I hope not.

I shant be home for some time yet. I expect to go west from here and where I will land is not known to me. Tell my folks that everything is lovely and the goose hangs high. I shant come home til my place is sold. Now that I can take my folks with me the sooner they sell it the better for I shant come til it is sold. I wrote one letter to E. Snow but got no answer and I can't wait now to get it. So I haven't heard from home yet.

Well for some of my foolery now you tell them abolishing friends of mine that when I dye that I want to be burreyed with my face down so they can kiss my ass without turning me over. I spent more than five dollars when I heard the devil was dead and gone to hell where parting will be no more with him.

Well I haven't much to write now. I have lots of fun with the folks. Well I will have to bid you goodbye for this time. I would like to see my folks. It is impossible now to come home. Now tell not to fret about me. I shall take care of my own hide now and when I get threw with that then I can take care of them So good bye for this time.

Andrew Osborn Stoan

—◠◠—

Lieutenant Lewis Plush Describes to His Parents the Close Calls and Minor Disasters Experienced by Young Pilots in Training

Although initially skeptical that the double-winged contraption flown for twelve seconds in December 1903 by two eccentric brothers, Orville and Wilbur Wright, had combat applications, the US government recognized the airplane's military potential years later. (The British War Office expressed interest in the Wright brothers' flying machine almost right away. France, Germany, and Italy followed soon after.) In early 1908, the US Army officially contracted with the Wright brothers to create an aircraft specifically for the armed forces, introducing a new era in modern warfare. During World War I, thousands of planes were used for everything from reconnaissance and supply drops to troop support and aerial bombardment (early on, however, airmen pretty much had to drop the bombs by hand). Despite the impressive array of aeronautic advances in speed, agility, radio communications, and weaponry made in the years before and during the war, flying was still a relatively new science. Lewis Clifford Plush, who served in World War I as a first lieutenant in the Aviation Section, Signal Reserve Corps, became a first-rate pilot and would go on to receive the Distinguished Service Cross for his heroism in combat. But others were not so skillful. On February 10, 1918, Plush wrote a letter from France to his parents in Pomona, California, about the difficulties some trainees were having.

Dear Father and Mother,

I just came in from the flying field where several of the cadets are taking their first solo flight. The first trip alone is always a great event and furnishes plenty of thrills and amusements for the others on the field.

One fellow, in taking his first flight alone, had great difficulty in making a landing. He circled around once and tried to land. He missed the field by a quarter of a mile. He made another circle and tried it again. This time the field was so crowded with machines that he was afraid to try it. The next time he dove at the ground at a steep angle, hit on his wheels and bounced up in the air about fifty feet. He opened his throttle and made another circle. We thought perhaps we would have to shoot him down to keep him from starving to death up in the air. He made three or four more attempts and finally made a good landing. We found out afterwards that he had run out of gasoline and had to come down.

Lieutenant Lewis C. Plush

Since this incident took place, I have heard rumors of a very important invention. It is military information of a strictly confidential nature. I have been unable to secure any detailed information but this much I know according to the rumors: a biscuit gun is being designed to shoot biscuits to starving aviators who are unable to land.

You know what happens when an auto gets loose by itself and goes tearing down a street or jumping sidewalks? Well, try to imagine what a runaway airplane can do. Such a thing happened near here some time ago.

Engine trouble forced the pilot to make a forced landing near a little village where airplanes are an unusual sight. The whole populace turned out to welcome the American visitor. The pilot repaired his engine and picked out half a dozen sturdy peasants to hold the plane while he started the engine. He forgot and left the throttle about half open. The engine started with a bang and roar. The peasants ran for their life and left the plane to take care of itself. The plane chased the pilot. Then the pilot chased the plane. It performed remarkable feats all by itself. It started directly for a group of frightened peasants, swerved to one side, chased a dog for a hundred yards, jumped a ditch, and started up in the air. It banked to one side and barely missed a corner of a stone wall and smashed squarely into a large tree. An airplane without a driver can never be trusted. It is apt to do almost anything.

Funny incidents and incidents that are not so funny happen on the field every day.

> With Love, Lewis C. Plush
> U.S. Air Service
> American Expeditionary Force,
> France, Via New York

After the war, Lewis Plush returned to the States, where he grew apple trees and raised turkeys on a ranch in California.

— ⁂ —

**A Russian Soldier Mails a (Sort of) Heartfelt Letter to His Wife
&
A British Soldier Drafts a Multipurpose "Love Letter" for His—
or Anyone Else's—Spouse**

The letter, beautifully written in cursive handwriting, was tender and impassioned. Although not dated, it was sent by a Russian soldier during World War I.

My Dear and Beloved Wife!

I am sending you, my dear, a little note about myself from far away. I am, thank God, alive and well and feel good about myself. Write me about your health and the health of our dear children. If only you knew, how my heart longs for you and the children, if only I could hold you to my chest and kiss you from the bottom of my heart.

I ask you, my darling spouse, write me even more often. I live by your letters alone. As soon as I receive communication from you, I read it through and through several times, and it's as if I see you and the children, as if I am right next to you.

Every day I pray to our Good Lord above for you and for our children, and I ask Him, so that He, the Merciful, would let us meet again. And I believe, that happy day is not far off. Or, my dearest one, do not despair but instead as soon as you receive my letter, write me back about everything in great detail, for I eagerly await your note. I rely on the Lord, Our God, that I will find you and the dear children in good health and happiness.

I am sending heartfelt greetings to all our friends and family. Let them not forget me, for I shall not forget them.

I remain your loving and faithful husband.

What is unique about the letter is that the government, not the soldier, authored it. Recognizing the importance of mail to bolster spirits on the home front as well as the battlefield, the Russian government provided these prewritten letters, which soldiers could simply fold up and send to the designated recipient. (There were effusive letters for mothers and other loved ones, too.) The Russians were not alone, however, in encouraging their troops to write home—or "suggesting" topics for discussion. During World War I, the US military distributed mass quantities of Christmas cards to American troops for them to fill out and then send home: "NOTHING is to be written on this side except the date and signature of the sender," the instructions on the card exclaimed. "If anything else is added the post card will be destroyed." This was followed by a preprinted list of statements a servicemember could mark to update his family about his condition without accidentally disclosing information that might prove useful to the enemy. (One could select, for example: "I am well" or "I have been admitted to the hospital.") In 1917, a British soldier—or soldiers—created a tongue-in-cheek, preformatted "love letter" that poked fun at the impersonal nature of these messages and the limits imposed by censorship. The letter also revealed a cynicism and irony many soldiers had developed in response to a war they felt had reached the point of absurdity; the British lost approximately one million soldiers in World War I; the United States, by comparison, lost sixty-three thousand. (The Xs at the end of the letter are assumed to represent kisses.)

In the Field.
/ /1917.

```
    (dear,
My (dearest,
    (darling,
  I can't write much to-day as I am very  (overworked
                                          (busy
                                          (tired
                                          (lazy
        (CORPS )
        (G.O.C. )
and the (G.S.O.I ) is exhibiting intense activity.
        (A.A. & Q.M.G. )
        (HUN )
                              (quite well.
Things our way are going on (much as usual.
                              (pas mal.


We           ) put up a bit of a show (last night ) with (complete
The HUNS )                              (yesterday)      (tolerable
                                                         (-out any
                                                         (success


Our            The French      )
The Russian    The Belgian      )
The Italian    The Serbian      )
The Montenegrin The Roumanian  )
The Monagasque The Portugeese  ) Offensive appears to be doing well.
The United States The Japanese  )
The Brazilian  The Cuban         )
The Panama     The Chinese      )
The Bolivian )


                  (obviously   )
The German offensive is (apparently   ) a complete failure.
                  (we will hope)
```

```
                              (this year.
I really begin to think the war will end (next year.
                              (some time.
                              (never.

The (flies    )    (vile.
The (rations  ) are (execrable.
The (weather ) is   (much the same.


          (cheery.
          (weary.
The        is (languid.
          (sore distrest.
          (at rest.


                    (Chateau.
We are now living in a (ruined Farm.
                    (Hovel.
                    (Dug-out.


    (hoping soon to come on   )
I am (about due for           )                      (on.
    (overdue for           ) leave, which is now (off.
    (not yet in the running for )


I am suffering from a (slight )              (Fright     )
                    (severe)    wound (Shell-Shock)
          *   ...................................................


...............          (sent him        )
...............'s Wife has just (presented him with)....................


What I should really like is ....................................................


                    (letter.
Many thanks for your (parcel
                    (good intentions.
```

---

* Or state disease. If the whole of this sentence is struck out, the writer may be presumed to be well or deceased.

```
                (poultry (including Cows))
How are the (potatoes                        ) getting on?
                (children                     )


                (well.
                (better.
I hope you are (bearing up.
                (not spending too much money.
                (getting on better with mother.


Insert here protestations) ........................................
of affection—NOT TO ) ...........................................
EXCEED TEN WORDS. ) ...........................................


Ever........................... (State what ever)
..................................
```

XXXXXXXXXXXXXXXXXXXXXXXXXXXXXXXXXXXXXXXXXXXX

—m—

A German Wife
Urgently Appeals to a Senior Officer,
Insisting That Her Husband Be Allowed to Return to Her
and Provide the "Satisfaction" She Can No Longer Go Without
&
The Officer Replies

The absence of husbands from millions of homes during World War I left their wives with the enormous burden of maintaining their households by themselves, which often included raising children and, in more rural areas, tending to farmland and livestock. But there were other, more personal needs that required the presence of a husband as well. These matters were usually addressed euphemistically or delicately in the private letters between spouses, each stressing how much they "longed to be back in the arms" of the other or looked forward to "making up for lost time" once they were together again. And then there were those who simply could not hold out any longer and didn't care who knew about it. One German woman, whose name (as well as that of her husband) has been deleted in the interests of privacy, sent the following plea to her husband's commanding officer.

Treuen, January 2, 1917

Dear Leader of the Company!

I, the signer below, have a request to make of you. Although my husband has only been in the field for four months, I would like to ask you to grant him a leave of absence, namely, because of our sexual relationship. I would like to have my husband just once for the satisfaction of my natural desires. I just can't live like this anymore. I can't stand it.

It is, of course, impossible for me to be satisfied in other ways, firstly, because of all the kids and secondly, because I do not want to betray my husband. So I would like to ask you very kindly to grant my request. I will then be able to carry on until we are victorious.

With all reverence,
Mrs. S

The officer who received the letter, Kurt Zehmisch, was not unmoved by her plight, and responded on January 8.

Honorable Frau S   !

With this letter, I confirm the receipt of your friendly letter from January 2, 1917. I can certainly sympathize with you and understand that you would like to see your beloved husband come home, and I will do everything in my power to fulfill your wish. But you must also realize that I have many men in our company at the moment who have been away from their homes for nearly a year. To be fair to these men, I ask you to be patient for another 1–2 weeks. Then, I will be able to add your husband to our list of men going on leaves of absence.

With friendly greetings,
K. Zehmisch

—⚬—

RAF Captain George Huckle Records in His Logbook Excerpts from Actual Letters Sent to His Fellow Prisoners of War

"I wish you could picture the faces when letters arrive for us who are so far away from home," an American soldier wrote to his wife on March 27, 1944, echoing the sentiments of all servicemen and -women about incoming mail. "[E]verything stops so the letters can be read, each reading a portion of his letters to the others, telling something that a child or children said or did. Letters are

the breath of life." And when a month later he, himself, received letters, the reaction was rapturous: "Tonight I hit the jack pot! Mail! Mail! Oh, what sweet music to a home sick soldier." The significance of letters as a morale booster was especially great for those confined as prisoners of war. Letters were one of their few tangible connections to family and friends and helped break the maddening boredom of camp life. This made it all the more devastating when those back home seemed oblivious to the harsh circumstances, both physical and mental, prisoners endured. Shot down over Germany in August 1941, a Royal Air Force captain named George Huckle spent more than three years as a POW before returning home. During his imprisonment he kept a journal that recorded what he called "mespots"—letters to his fellow POWs from wives, sweethearts, parents, and siblings that included unwelcome information, ridiculous comments, or curt rejections. The following—again, all written to men being held in an isolated camp and subsisting on meager rations—represent just a sampling. (The succinct descriptions and dates before some of the letters were added by Huckle himself. The references to "5/-" [five shillings] and 5/6 [five shillings and sixpence] relate to British currency at the time.)

Darling I hope you are behaving yourself and not drinking too much.

—

Darling, I've just had a baby, but don't worry, the American officer is sending you some cigarettes every week.

—

Jan '44.—Darling I was so glad you got shot down before flying became dangerous.

—

Darling in your letter you ask for slippers. What colour would you like?

—

The words after lousy describing your new camp were obliterated.

—

To P.O.W. shot down '43—I'm sorry you were shot down so early in the war.

—

Darling, I hope you are staying true to me.

—

Can you buy beer anywhere or do they only sell wine.

—

Darling the first batch of repatriated prisoners arrived recently, they looked terrible. I hope you're on the second party.

—

Letter from fiancée to P.O.W.—Dear John, you were missing a month, so I got married.

—

I have a grandmother in Germany, have you met her?

—

From a wife—Dear, I'm going to have a baby by an American, brother has forgiven me, I hope you do.

—

From home—I find I can't get any sandals here so am sending out the coupons and perhaps you can get them in the shops over there.

—

If your skates have arrived, only go where it is shallow enough, so you can get out easily if you fall through.

—

From Best Girl—So you're in perfect health are you? Wait till I get you home. Then you'll know the meaning of bags under the eyes.

—

You will be satisfied to hear that I'm getting married next week, but you can look forward to our happy reunion when you come home. It will be too bad if my husband doesn't agree, because I'm going to see you anyway. If he's away you can stay at my home, and if he's at home we can go to mother's and not tell him. We can give the family 5/- each to keep their mouths shut.

—

Comparison—I'm on my honeymoon, so like you I'm in captivity.

—

From fiancée—I do appreciate your allotment as a chap I go with is only a private on 5/6 a day. Please increase it.

—

From girl-friend—Darling, I married your father. Signed, Mother.

—⁓—

Filipino Native Marcial Lichauco Describes in a Secret Letter to an Old Friend Some Lighter Moments During an Otherwise Fearful Time

"Dear 'Mother' Putnam," a thirty-nine-year-old Filipino named Marcial Lichauco began a letter to a close family friend on December 12, 1941, just days after the Japanese attacked the Philippines. "I am writing during a period of great uncertainty. I do not know whether or when I shall be able to contact you."

Unlike the strike on Pearl Harbor, which had occurred only hours before, the Japanese launched a full-scale invasion of the Philippines. Lichauco, a highly educated lawyer, knew that if his letters to Mrs. Putnam were discovered he risked being imprisoned, tortured, and even executed. But he wanted to record for his children an eyewitness account of the occupation, and the letter, written on scraps of paper, became a running narrative of the dangers he and his family experienced for almost three years. It also chronicled how many Filipinos used humor to alleviate the unbearable strain they were under on a daily basis. In early July 1942, Lichauco wrote of several bold actors who subversively mocked Japanese authority. (Fort Santiago, which Lichauco refers to, was a Manila prison notorious for its harsh treatment of inmates.)

Friday, July 10, 1942:

The few remaining American films which our movie houses still have on hand are being released at the rate of about one each month. They are, of course, very carefully censored. This shortage has been a god-send to the local vaudeville talent. Four comedians, however, have been recently taken to Fort Santiago by the Military Authorities who failed to appreciate the Filipinos' sense of humor. The scene which brought about the arrest of two of these men was as follows:

One comedian approached the other and, in a very respectful tone of voice, asked a simple question. The one addressed thereupon slapped him severely on the face. The audience burst into laughter because it reminded them of many cases they had witnessed in which Filipino civilians were slapped by Japanese sentries for no apparent reason at all. But the Military Police stopped the show and arrested the two men.

The other scene which occurred in another theatre was even more timely. After the Japanese entered Manila last January we soon found that they were very interested in wrist watches. The jewelry shops in town then still had a large supply on hand which Japanese officers were quick to purchase, but it was well known that many soldiers simply confiscated wrist watches from pedestrians whom they accosted on the streets and it was not uncommon to see a soldier with two, three or even four watches strapped around his wrist. In this particular scene, one of the Filipinos, dressed in khaki uniform but without any insignias on his coat to indicate his nationality, asked his fellow comedian to try and guess what kind of a soldier he was trying to impersonate. The conversation was more or less as follows:

"You are trying to simulate an Italian?"

"No."

"Russian?"

"No."

"Hindu?"

"No."

"Chinese?"

"No."

"Nazi?"

"You are getting warmer."

At this point the comedian dressed as a soldier scratched the back of his neck and, in so doing, his right sleeve was pulled up revealing three watches strapped around his wrist. There was no further need for his companion to say anything because the audience howled with glee. These two comedians also found themselves that evening in Fort Santiago.

In late January of 1943, Lichauco related an incident where an exchange of "letters" themselves played a crucial role.

Monday, January 25, 1943:

Here is the latest story that is sweeping the city concerning guerilla activities:

Jorge Vargas, head of the puppet government which the Japanese have organized here is said to have sent a letter through an intermediary to one of the most active guerilla leaders hiding in the mountains of the Island of Panay. "It is useless and cruel for you to continue your resistance," said Vargas in his letter. "Cruel because the civilian population in the villages near you suffer terribly as a result of the fighting that takes place around them. And useless because you will, sooner or later, have to give in. America cannot help you. What remains of her army here surrendered long ago. The Japanese fleet is master of the Pacific and no supplies from the United States can possibly reach these shores. American sovereignty is gone from the Philippines, never to return. If you and your men, however, will lay down your arms and report to the nearest authorities, the Japanese who are merciful and generous will pardon you for your stubborn resistance."

The guerilla leader did not reply in writing to Mr. Vargas. Instead he sent back a small package inside which were four juicy Delicious apples. As you probably know, apples do not grow in the Philippines.

In October 1944, the Americans, led by General Douglas MacArthur, initiated a ferocious naval, aerial, and then ground assault against Japanese forces in the Philippines as part of an overall campaign to retake the Pacific and, if necessary, invade Japan. Although Lichauco and his wife, Jessie Coe, watched with great anticipation as the Japanese were finally put on the defensive, they also feared that they—or, more important, their two children—could be killed by a stray bomb or artillery fire. In the following letter, Lichauco described a discussion with their youngest child about what life will be like after the occupation has ended. Like so many wartime correspondences that alluded to lighthearted moments, this one included a searing reminder of the terrible human cost of battle.

Sunday, October 15, 1944:

American dive bombers came over again today. The alarms sounded at 9.30 and, almost immediately afterwards, about three dozen fighter planes took off from Nielson field. This airport is about two miles from our house. The real show did not begin until an hour and a half later so that the Japanese had plenty of time to get ready. This time they were certainly not caught napping.

Photo by Andrew Carroll

A Filipino boy practices backflips near the site where General Douglas MacArthur left the Philippines after a full-scale Japanese invasion seemed imminent. (General Jonathan Wainwright was left to eventually surrender American troops stationed on the island.) MacArthur's famous "I shall return" statement is visible just under the boy's right foot. After the largest sea battle in history, at Leyte Gulf, MacArthur returned in October 1944.

When the guns were popping loudest we tried to amuse baby Cornelia.

"As soon as the war is over," said Jessie, "I will take a vacation in America. Wouldn't you like to come to America with me?"

Cornelia was pensive for a moment or two. "Is there candy in America," she finally asked. She has been getting very little of it here.

"Yes, plenty of candy," I replied.

Cornelia then looked at her locally made shoes which are pretty shabby and worn out.

"Do they have shoes in America?" was her next query.

I laughed and said, "Of course."

"Can I get two pairs of shoes there?" And when I laughed again and said she could have all she wanted, she very solemnly gave us her decision.

"All right, I go to America."

The worse part of the raid did not last more than forty-five minutes and we were out of our shelters in time to see the machine gunning of a helpless American flier who had bailed out over the city. He seemed to be heading for the river at first and to be making desperate efforts to avoid falling in the water. Then, when he was perhaps only two hundred yards away, a burst of machine gun fire was heard. The aviator who up to that moment had been kicking his feet and straining at the ropes suddenly went limp. The house-tops around us concealed him from view as the chute neared the ground. It was an awful sight to witness.

Marcial Lichauco and his family survived the war, and he had five more children (there are now eighteen grandchildren). After practicing law in the postwar years, Lichauco would eventually become a distinguished statesman, serving as the Filipino Ambassador to the United Kingdom, Denmark, Sweden, and Norway.

—⁂—

A California Man Insists to His Local Draft Board That He Really, Truly Wants to Serve—If Only It Weren't for a Few Minor Medical Problems

The December 7, 1941, attack on Pearl Harbor and Germany's declaration of war against the United States two days later ignited a patriotic fervor that prompted American men and women from coast to coast to enlist in the armed forces. There were, however, those who did not want to volunteer, and, if drafted, tried any number of pleas and schemes to secure a deferment. One young Californian assured his draft board that he absolutely wanted to join the military, but probably could not—or at least should not—for the reasons articulated in the following appeal. (His full name is not used in the interests of privacy.)

Draft Board No. 240
5507 Santa Monica Blvd.
Hollywood, California

Dear Sirs

This is to notify you of the symptoms I have Swelling of ankles & feet. Right eye effected & ear by bells paulsia. Right eye discharges white matter. Both eyes water on contact with wind.

Left great toe not active of operation from secondary infraction from bad case of athletic feet. Left great toe develops fever on too much pressure on it and fever's left leg to knee. Left chins bone pains from sunburn two years ago.

Left leg & arm cramps or rheuatism ashama and synus. Believe have touch of T.B. in lungs frequent coughing and spitting of matter and substance very gluey and color brownish black and vomatory in morning some times blood.

Stomack tender & pains. Burns like fire if drinkin orange juice for breakfast. Believe I have ulcers or cancer right large intestance have frequent pains. Have had doctor's treatment for it. Piles sometimes bleed.

Continus colds, and head pains. fevers. High or low pressure probably heart. spine in back pains & itches. frequent back of neck pains and severe headache.

All teeth ache very bad at times. Have infieorior complex and nervous conditions.

Perspirationn of forehead. Painful bunions on right foot & left bottom foot, right foot pains and have fever.

95% of my aquantancies claim that I'm mentally unbalanced. Worries me at times if its not so. Was kicked on head by a horse when very young.

James

P.S. am patriotick man & dont want you should think I'm trying to get out of draft. If was would exagerate a litle.

J.P.

The draft board's response, alas, is not known.

—▩—

**A Young German Soldier Named Willi Writes
of the "Fun-Filled Activities" That Keep Him
and His Fellow Soldiers Amused
&
Lieutenant Florene Thelma Keike,
US Army Nurse Corps, Shares a Somewhat Risqué Letter
with Her Family in Texas**

*Thrust into extremely stressful and often life-threatening situations, confronted
with the horrid sights and sounds of battle, and given enormous responsibili-
ties (most notably the power to take another person's life), many combatants
mature rapidly during their time of service. But the vast majority of troops,
regardless of the war, are in their late teens or early twenties, and it is not uncommon for them to talk of things that tend to amuse young minds—including, as
evidenced in the following letter by a young German soldier, deeply profound
discussions relating to bodily functions. (Please note: this letter is not for the
scatologically squeamish.)*

10, July 1943

Dear Magda and Bert!
    Please note my new address!
    Please do not be angry for not hearing from me in such a long time,
which really wasn't so long, because I'm always thinking of you all.
Perhaps you think that it's easy to say that and why bother coming up
with such lazy lame excuses. But you know, a soldier has very little time,
and I'll prove it to you straight away.

    05.30 wake up call, wash up, make bed, clean up sleeping
quarters, breakfast
    06.30 roll call
    11.30 lunch
    13.00 receive orders for the day
    13.15 line up for service
    17.00 clean and polish gear
    18.00 dinner
    19.00 clean weapons
    20.00 inspection of cleaned fire arms
    21.00 a letter to my wife
    21.45 blackout
    22.00 bedtime

From 22.00 until 05.30 air raid alarms whenever the Tommies feel like it. You see how day and night are packed with fun-filled activities.

In spite of all this, I'm fine and the boot camp drill has just brought me an advanced course in the bakery to fine tune me for a profession that I've been working in for the past sixteen years! Apart from that, I've become a real soldier. I can stand still, keep my trap shut, shout "shit" in a loud voice, behave like a "Johnny be good," and zap like a bolt of lightning about the parade grounds. In addition, they taught me not to steal any silver spoons and not to rape women, because this behavior is unworthy of a soldier.

I'm with twelve others in one barrack, and I'm probably the youngest. All are sacrifices for the total war. Among them, a doctor of chemistry, a middle-school principle, a diploma engineer, a blacksmith, a musician, farmers and craftsmen. In the evening, when we're all sitting around the table, the middle-school principal might tell us about something, and the blacksmith lets off a loud fart, purely out of excitement. The chemist mumbles a chemical formula and swears that there was some sulfur involved. The musician awards a B-major or a C-major, according to the tone of the fart. The engineer calculates the rate of dissolving in the air, and the blacksmith even thinks: "It smells just as if it came from a horse itself." I, however, think that it's a little "Johnny be bad" finding its way out again. Apart from all that, we get along just fine, because we're all struggling for one common goal—home leave. But up until now, the enemy proves stronger. I wonder who'll be the first to get through.

I like Bremen very much, but it would be even nicer if Tommy couldn't fly. Köln has been hit very badly. It's horrible how everything looks. I think the frontline isn't as bad as either of these cities. I heard from Mutz that you sent her two pictures, for which I thank you very much. I hope that you are all coping well under the circumstances, and hope for a quick peace for all of us.

Warmest greetings and kisses.
Your Willi

Women, not surprisingly, tended to be less uncouth in their letters, but they were not immune from enjoying the occasional bawdy story or joke. US Army Nurse Corps lieutenant Florene Thelma Keike, who served for more than two years in the Pacific during World War II, came across the following letter that had been passed around for amusement and shared it with her family in Austin, Texas. (Preceding the letter is a brief introduction explaining that a soldier, hoping to impress his beloved, bought her an elegant pair of gloves. His sister offered to help him shop for the gloves, and she purchased a pair of silk bloomers for herself. The two packages got mixed up, and the young man unknowingly sent the underpants and not the gloves with the letter. The typos are in the original.)

My dear sweetheart,

This little token is to remind you that I have not forgotten your birthday. I wish to express my appreciation of your friedship during the past year. I chose these becouse I noticed that you had not been wearing any when we go out evenings. Had it not been for my sister, I would have bought long ones with one button. These are very delicate, But the ladey in the store whare I bought them showed me a pair she had been wearing for three years and they were hardly soiled at all.

How i wish i could put them on for the first time, No doubt many other gentleman's hand's will come in contack with them before i can see you in them, But I hope you will think of me everytime you take them off and put them on again. I had the clerk put them on and they sure looked good on her, I wasn't sure of the size but i feel that I should be a complete judge if any one is. When you put them on the first time, Sprinkle a little powder into them and they will go on easily. When you take them off blow in them as they will naturally be damp from wearing.

I hope you will accept them in the same spirit they are given, And wear them to the dance saturday, when I come to see you be sure to have them on. I would like to count the number of times that I will kiss the back of them during the coming year.

YOUR'S AFFECTIONATILY,.

—◦◦◦—

Canadian Field Censors Report to Their Superiors About a Variety of Insulting and Prohibited Letters They Have Intercepted

"They are censoring our letters right here in Camp now so I will send this by civilian post," wrote a Canadian soldier from England during World War II, "as I don't want any fat son of a bitch reading my mail." Of the many bureaucratic and official procedures disdained by servicemembers in the First and Second World Wars, few inspired as much contempt and ridicule as censorship. Most understood the necessity of protecting sensitive information—indeed, their lives depended on it—but they nevertheless resented having their intimate correspondences read by total strangers and the seemingly willy-nilly manner in which letters were returned to them without explanation, cut to pieces, or, according to loved ones back home, delayed for months. Stories abounded as well about censors filching souvenirs and small gifts servicemen and -women

attempted to mail home and pocketing candy, money, cigarettes, and baked goods sent by family members to the front lines. (One censor even wrote on the bottom of an unsuspecting soldier's letter in the soldier's handwriting, "Hey mom, how about that fruitcake you promised me?" and then copped the fruitcake when the mom dutifully sent it on.) The censors, from their standpoint, were exasperated by the carelessness of the writers in revealing specific locations, ship and troop movements, casualty estimates, and other details that could prove useful if they fell into enemy hands. Field censors apprised their superiors of the overall mood of the troops, and, in one report compiled by Canadian censors in England during World War II, of how the different Allied troops were getting along with one another. The Canadian soldiers, for the most part, were less than complimentary about their British counterparts:

The Scotch like us better than the English do—the English don't like us much, and we don't like them either.

—

A lot of the people at home have been sending presents with the Limies, who are returning to England, for the Canadians over here. But oddly enough these presents never reach their destination. So that doesn't make us like them any the more. One of the chaps wife sent a wrist-watch over to her husband this way a few months ago, (it was a Bulova too) and he never got it . . . He says if he ever catches an English soldier wearing a Bulova watch he's going to lick the tar out of him.

—

The English call themselves reserved but I should call it hypocrisy. They are underhand. We have been warned not to mix too much with them because they are only trying to look down on the Canadians. There are, fortunately, Canadians here in large numbers. Also they (the English) are very slow to act and take a long time to make up their minds. Canada is heaven compared with England. They are very cold and consider us Colonials, coming from an uncivilized country.

—

I've always imagined the English army to be all military and neat but they're really the sloppiest slovenliest bunch I've ever seen. They never are neat or have any press in their clothes, just a bunch of bums, so we call them. The slouchiest Canadian is really tops compared to some of them.

One soldier wrote what might be the worst insult of all:

The beer here is rotten like everything else.

Sometimes the feelings were mutual, as indicated in the following British letter:

We are all in the barracks tonight, as we have had to scrub the place out today as the place is filthy, the Canadians have just left here.

Censors were also on the alert for letters that could affect morale, either in the field or on the homefront. The following nasty letter, supposedly from "a friend" sharing unwelcome news to a complete stranger, was held by the censors, with attached commentary stating, "Perhaps retention of this mail will eliminate further correspondence . . .":

Dear Mrs. Johnston,

Just a tip from a friend, as you know, no doubt, that your husband is in love with another woman, and I am afraid it is kind of heavy and I think that if you both want to be the happier, you will both go your own way. I am writing this, just from what I myself have seen, and I know how your husband is with this woman.

As a matter of fact he can hardly get away enough to see her.

tip from a
friend

Even if the grievances were true, letters that severely criticized commanding officers, military strategy, or anything integral to the overall mission at hand were also prohibited, as they could be used for propaganda purposes by the enemy. They could also dampen morale back home. Censors recognized the need for combatants to vent, and they often grappled with the question of what constituted an acceptably mild outburst and what was truly objectionable. "If we are fighting for democracy and freedom of speech," one censor noted after reading a short diatribe about the lack of food and ammunition, "can we take disciplinary action against the writer of this letter?" The following letter, however, was a prolonged rant the field censors believed might warrant serious attention.

Just a line and card to wish you all the best for Xmas and the New Year. How are you all keeping these days, just fine I hope. I'm feeling O.K.—no thanks to the damned army. I hav'nt been able to get home since Oct. but was hoping I'd be able to get home for Xmas but that is washed out as our unit (the 5th Gdn. Reg. R.C.A's colonel has decided that we shall not proceed farther than 40 miles from camp at Xmas on our 3 day leave—and we must not travel by train. The rotten old! x !! x We have 7 days leave coming to us—we are entitled to 7 days leave every

3 months in England and our time was up on 5th Dec.—and we can't get that. Other units have started their 10 day leave already—it is just a matter of getting the worst of a rotten bunch of officers I guess.

By the Great God above Win—I hate the army worse than I dreamt possible to hate anything. The army does everything humanly possible to break a man and talk about rotten—it is worse if that is possible— than the present day political set up. Can you imagine it—last Xmas they took us away from home 8 days before Xmas and now chaps who hav'nt been home for Xmas for years can't go now. Mark my words there will be a revolt or something of the kind in the army before this Winter is over. All the boys are completely dissatisfied. Now our rations have been cut 20 per cent and heaven knows the boys don't get <u>too</u> much to eat now. I'm cooking for the officers so I get all I can eat. We are living in quarters that have not been occupied for 10 yrs and were condemned years and years ago. They are damned lousy. There is no reason for it either. We are not needed over here—there is'nt food, accommodation or equipment for us.

There was a revolt so to speak in one outfit—comprised solely of Westerners—they have more guts than this Eastern trash. They were like us—fed up with the way things were going and when Gen. Odham came up for inspection they refused to go on parade. Conditions for them were improved in an awful hurry—believe me. If God and his almighty justice has anything to do with winning a war I don't see how the army can win it—it is too rotten and corrupt. Alice and her mother have given money, blankets, socks etc. to the red cross—another army racket and I have yet to see the first goods from the Red cross. A friend of one of our boys from Toronto received a letter from a trapper in Northern Ontario saying if she could let him have the same kind of socks for 55 c/s a pair—he'd take 6 pairs. She had donated the socks to the Red Cross, put her name on a paper in the toe of the sock—as I believe many women do—and that is how the soldiers get the Red Cross clothes and comforts. It is just a racket like it was in the last war.

The same with our mail. There are millions of cigarettes not reaching the addressee and thousands of parcels and they <u>don't</u> go down in the boat. There are too many light fingered guys handling the mail. Alice sent me a big parcel on Nov. 3rd and a letter on Nov. 4th and 11th. I received the letters but no parcel. Somebody figured they had more right to it than me. That is what is happening to thousands of the boys and the army doesn't do anything about it. They must know what's going on. I don't think even the army is that stupid. Thank God we have the

U.S.A. on our side—if it was'nt for her the war would have been over. When I get back I plan to stop at Montreal—buy a motorbike and see some of the U.S.A. and to see you before heading back for S'toon. Joan started kindergarten on Nov. 5th at a convent. I hope they don't try and make a catholic out of her. God help them and Alice if they do. I hear from Alice fairly often she has sent me money several times and some parcels. Her mother tho' can't do enough for me always sending me stuff and papers letters socks, eatables and sweaters. I've told her lots of time not to bother as I don't need them but you know her—she's got to have her own way. But still it's very good of her—she couldn't treat a son of her own any better.

How is the weather where you are? It is nasty here. Cold and frosty one night and raining and blowing the next. I sure don't like England or the people in it. What the hell Hitler wants this country for beats me and all the Canadians. I don't believe there are 20 men out of every 1,000 that are not sorry they ever came to this country. I know I am. I would'nt trade one square foot of Canada for this whole damned country. Jerry sure is making a mess of some of the places over here. Just wiping the places out. But he has'nt dropped many bombs near us yet. I guess he knows he does'nt need to bother about us with the quarters we have the kind of horse doctors we have. As long as one is able to walk they tell you you are not sick you're just swinging the lead. Several chaps have died of pneumonia already because the doc. said they were not sick. How is Ben doing—is he still working at Kohler? The Greeks sure are giving the Italians hell, I only wish we could get close to the jerries—we'd soon have them on the run. I've heard from Eric and Bert but hav'nt seen them. I saw Dolly, Tom, Conie and Jim besides Mum and Dad. I saw Vi—and she has grown to be a lovely girl. Not a bit course like Jim, Nell and young Jimmy. You'd hardly think she came from the same family. She works in a radio factory at a place call Woking—not very far from here, about 27 miles. We moved to this blasted plasted place on Oct. 10th from Mons barracks at Aldershot. Well I guess I'll ring off for now Win, be sure to write soon, Best of Luck and Wishes.

"Pigs is pigs and freedom of speech is freedom of speech," a censor wrote in his report, "but there are limits to both. We should pass this on to Corps for their necessary action."

—⚓—

The Parents of Private First Class William Lee Kyzer Receive a "Censored" Letter from Their Son

Censorship could also prove frustrating for family and friends desperate for information about their loved ones serving far from home. William Kyzer, a young farmer from Jacksonville, Arkansas, was drafted into the army after the outbreak of World War II and became an infantry rifleman in the Pacific. Kyzer's father and stepmother were eager to hear how William was faring, but they would mostly receive letters like the following, which appeared to have been cut up entirely by the censors:

Dear Dad & Carmilita
   I'm OK, days flies by here in

                                                 Well maybe it can be all again soon. I'm praying for it. Write soon Nothing like getting a letter from home. Here on

                                                       Love
                                                       Bill

P.S. They may censor this letter

In fact, Kyzer's mail was not edited at all; he simply hated writing letters and only penned the few sentences at the top and the bottom so that his folks would believe that the censors were responsible for slicing out the rest.

Stationed in Vietnam, Sergeant Gary Turnure Shares with His Family a Copy of "The Lifer's Prayer" & A US Soldier Sends a Strange, Watercolor-Painted Letter to a Friend Back in the States

Unlike in previous wars, letters by US troops in Southeast Asia were not censored. (Individual officers sometimes checked outgoing mail, but there was no official mechanism in place to review personal correspondences.) And while World War I and World War II letters were not without the occasional outbursts of biting humor, letters from Vietnam were consistently more sarcastic in tone. In his first message home from Marine Corps boot camp, an ordeal notorious for being psychologically and physically torturous, John Richard Ruggles expressed how absolutely thrilled he was with his new life and the kindness he was being shown by his superiors on a daily basis.

> *We have exactly 38 seconds to write this note. This is a real friendly and placid place. We are all enjoying it very much. Everyone on the staff, officers and sergeants alike are very patient to explain things which are confusing. Gotta go.*

Gary Turnure, who was in army basic training at about the same time, tried to be even more positive. "Hi Everyone," he wrote to his family in New Jersey. "I've finally realized this army will do me a lot of good. It's going to prepare me for a future in a variety of thriving occupations. In civilian life there's always a need for good howitzers cannoneers or scrub & buffing men, shoeshine boys, professional band marchers, and I will be most skillful in standing in line which will come in handy when I wait to collect my unemployment check." In a later letter, sent while he was in Vietnam, he enclosed the following ("Bennies" are perks or benefits given to the troops):

The Lifer's Prayer

The Army is my Shepard, I shall not think, It alloweth me to lie down on essential jobs. It leadeth me blindly, it destroyeth my initiative, It leadeth me in the path of parasites for my country's sake, Yea tho I walk through the valley of laziness, I shall fear no censure, for the Army is with me, It maketh me believe in great falsehoods. My inefficiency runneth over, I shall exist in fools paradise forever.

THE ARMY'S TEN COMMANDMENTS

1 THOU SHALT NOT THINK

2 THOU SHALT NOT PLACE THY HANDS IN THY POCKETS

3 THOU SHALT KNOW THY CHAIN OF COMMAND AND ALL
   ITS MISSING LINKS

4 THOU SHALT NOT LAUGH AT SECOND LIEUTENANTS

5 THOU SHALT NOT USE WORDS NCO'S CANNOT
   UNDERSTAND

6 THOU SHALT NOT DO THINGS IN A REASONABLE OR
   SENSIBLE WAY

7 THOU SHALT FEAR THOSE WHO HOLD A HIGHER RANK
   THEN THOU AND SCORN THOSE OF LOWER RANK

8 THOU SHALT NOT LAUGH OR MAKE OBSENE GESTURES
   AT RE-UP POSTERS

9 THOU SHALT NOT SPEAK WITHOUT USING PROFANITY

10 THOU SHALT BELIEVE IN THE NON-EXISTANT BENNIES
   FOR THIRTY YEARS

Another soldier, whose name is being withheld for reasons of privacy, lamented to a friend from home, "Not much else to say buddy except I'm sick as a dog. Last week my throat was bleeding. You know what they did for it. Nothing, absolutely nothing. Yes Sir there are some brilliant men in the service. Especially these guys with the stripes." As the war went on, his letters became increasingly eccentric.

"I'm seeing the war baby—The Death, The Mortors, The Panic—," he wrote several months later. "IT'S BAD! There are fire fights every night! DAMN!—If I seem to of changed any, you now know why! (To me I've changed an awfully lot!) Walked in naked! Why the hell not? . . ."

In the following "letter," the soldier took a more artistic approach to expressing himself. Blue and yellow watercolors were used to write JAP (for Just Another Private), which is surrounded by random exclamations—"Kill for Peace?", "I Quit!"—in red and blue ink. The barely legible text at the top reads: "You're a fink! Here I am, over in Viet Nam and I don't even get any word from the 'Voice of the Free'! Nice Guy! Just for that—I hope ya get drafted! (Not really—That's to shitty of a thing!) But I hope something bad happens, like you can't get any booze next Friday and Saturday night! So there—Fink!"

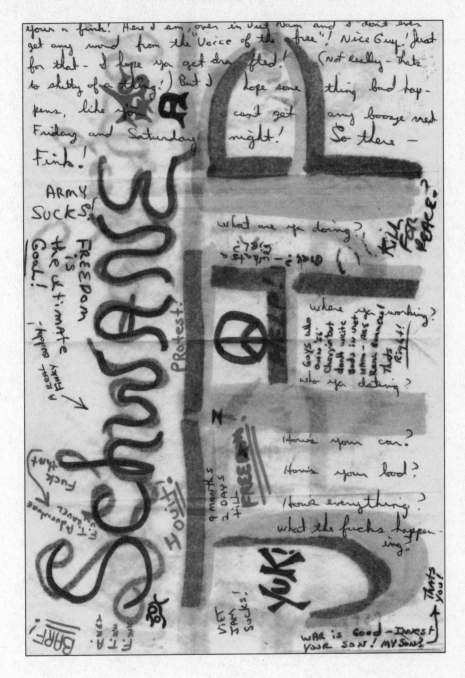

In a Package to His Wife, Sergeant Jerome H. Schumacher Includes Drawings of New Service Medals He Believes Are Needed in the Army

"Operation Desert Storm" represented the last major armed conflict before the widespread use of e-mail. (A nascent form of electronic communication existed, but few servicemen and -women had access to it.) Although not as rapid as messages zapped over the Internet, letters sent through regular mail offer a tangible, personal connection between those serving abroad and their family and friends back home. Recipients can see the handwriting of the sender and touch the same paper their loved one has held. Letter writers can also embellish their correspondences with sketches. A California National Guard platoon sergeant named Jerome H. Schumacher, who served with a military police unit in Saudi Arabia during the 1991 Gulf War, frequently wrote to his wife to assure her that he was fine and, despite the threat of Scud missiles, not in significant danger. Schumacher emphasized that, while he took his duties and the war situation seriously, he did not want her to worry, and in one letter home he included a series of lighthearted drawings that were inspired by assorted personality types he apparently encountered on a regular basis. Schumacher poked fun at his own unit, which he suggested was doing little more than checking ID badges.

"INK PEN" COMBAT DEVICE

PROPOSED

ALSO KNOWN AS THE ORDER OF FACE OR THE "I D" MEDAL

LIGHT GREEN W/DARKER GREEN HIGHLIGHTS

US ARMED FORCES

GONG IS RUGGED LAMINATED PLASTIC CONSTRUCTION W/LIKENES OF GEN SCHWARTZ KOPF.

Order #2x189 MP-270/13/u

THE 270th MP - DESERT SHIELD MEDAL
(Occasionally referred to as the "What did you do during the war, Daddy? Medal)

This proud medal is exclusively awarded to the brave men and women of
the 270th "Combat" Military Police Company.
The deeds of heroism and self-sacrifice by this small but proud unit
will go down in the annals of Army history and will be the standards by
which courage and devotion to dutyand country will, in the future, be
judged.
If the "Gong" portion of the medal somewhat resembles and ID card, it
may be because the checking of ID cards was 270th MP Co.'s primary
function in the war. Let it be said by all who look upon this medal,
"They accomplished their mission"

THE PRESTIGEOUS BROWN NOSE MEDAL

US ARNG ORDER 123-321-?/u.

This widely awarded medal is more and more difficult to present, as the supply is having a hard time trying to meet the demand. Roughly ½ of U.S. industry has been diverted to production of this coveted and richly deserved medla, but it just ain't enough.

In order to qualify for this fine decoration, the individual must meet one or more of the following critera: snitch on all or most of his/her fellow soldiers, badmouth others in front of first sergeant, give stupid orders in front of any/all authority figures, kiss ass in general.

Many, many awards to be issued.

NOTE: IF, IT PLEASES THE CAPTAIN, 1ST. SGT, LT. etc.

THE VAUNTED IDIOTIC DECISION MEDAL

US ARND MED.DEC I.D.1ea/u.

While often considered an "Officers" award, this medal now can and will
be awarded toall SNCOs of the 270th MP Co., particulary since officers
quit making any decisions.

Criteria for receiving this fine award are that, not some, not most, but
all decisions/orders must be absolutely and completely assinine and
counter-productive. The competition for this coveted medal is intense
and many will be awarded, or maybe not, but might be if the decision
can be made to mint them, and if a few bright individuals don't hog them
all up.

NOTE: E 5s MAY NOW QUALIFY.

**UN Worker Tom Shakow, in a Letter to His Parents,
Writes About the Challenges the UN Is Facing in Sarajevo
and Includes a Real (and Slightly Sarcastic) UN Memo About One
Critical Shortage in Particular**

*In June 1994, a twenty-one-year-old American named Tom Shakow left his
home in Washington, DC, much to the consternation of his mother, for the war-
ravaged capital of Bosnia and Herzegovina to work with the United Nations'
Office of the Special Coordinator. The UN had passed a series of resolutions
throughout 1994 to help restore quality of life in Sarajevo, and the Special Coordinator's staff was tasked with ensuring that essential needs and services (electricity, water, gas, etc.) were available to the public. They also spent considerable
time encouraging international donors to support critical projects that would
improve the safety, education, and housing of those living in the besieged city.
Millions of dollars had been pledged to pay for these efforts, but contributors were
reluctant to send the money until the war had come to a definitive end. In a letter home written soon after his arrival, Shakow updated his parents on the situation in Sarajevo, which was still dangerous, and included a photocopy of a
memo by an exasperated UN official emphasizing how the lack of resources was
affecting "essential needs" in their office as well.*

June 30th, 1994

Dear Mom and Dad, John and Peter,

 As I write, I'm listening to the OJ Simpson preliminary hearing live
on CNN from L.A. That should give you an idea both of how long it
takes a letter to reach you from Sarajevo, and also how incredibly
overblown this case is. But hey—it's better than the World Cup.

 Today was a <u>very</u> long day. It rained, and was humid and gloomy in the
city, which cast a pall over everyone's mood. On top of that, I disregarded
the second most fundamental rule I learned in college—never drink too
much coffee. (the first, incidentally, is "If you're going to ask, remember
to ask about <u>chlamydia</u>, too.") Anyway, once I drank my fifth cup, my
sense of humor went out the window. Then I had lunch with the acting
boss, Monsieur Rousselot, who is a very capable and friendly guy, but I
couldn't relax. And when I got back to the office, the toilets wouldn't
flush. And everyone around me was smoking like a chimney, and speaking
French, and generally going through a major crisis because the Pledging
Conference in New York only brought in nine million dollars for the
Trust Fund ($68m for Sarajevo overall), when we were asking for about
$500m. Such is the world of international development, I guess. I see now,
Dad, why you prefer the Bank to AID. The Bank controls its own money.

Anyway, all that said, it's hard not see the humor in the situation. An office in Sarajevo, where logically people should be worried whether they'll get home without being shot (sorry, Mom—it's not <u>that</u> dangerous, I'm just proving a point), is prone to the same bureaucratic crises as any place else. And people get tied all in knots over it. As for me, I just see the money issue as requiring that we do more coordinating and less disbursing. But then, they won't be laying me off, will they?

Just to give you an idea how things get here, I am enclosing a copy of memo written before I arrived . . .

UNITED NATIONS

Office of the
SPECIAL COORDINATOR FOR SARAJEVO

To: Ms. Marlene Leggott, Administrative Assistant, SAO Sarajevo

Subject: <u>Toilet Paper Needs for the Office of the Special Coordinator, Sarajevo</u>

With reference to my telephone conversation with you this morning, I hereby wish to place an order for off-white, rolled, pre-cut, soft hygienic paper.

As you can see from the attached list, there are 36 healthy persons, working from 08.00 to 17.30 hours at a minimum, all of whom are inclined to use toilet paper at least once a day; this may of course be influenced by cultural traditions, so we have included the nationality of our staff members to assist in your verification of our calculations.

Bearing in mind the following:

    a. at least 30 people participate twice a month in our Coordination Committee meeting and many others participate in countless smaller meetings; since a certain number of our many visitors will inevitably feel urgent needs, their requirements must also be met;

    b. our staff members residing at the Holiday Inn often experience an acute shortage of subject item which, unfortunately, does seem not to be on sale locally as yet;

    c. the security guard position we asked for two months ago has not been staffed yet, so we have no protection against the disappearance of a certain number of rolls;

    d. because of shortages of other commonly used items, toilet paper is not restricted for use only for its intended purpose; it also serves to dry one's own hands, clean dusty desk surfaces and coffee tables, etc.

Despite our lack of experience in this matter, and discounting the innovative use of alternative materials (such as correspondence from Zagreb), we came to the conclusion that we need 8 rolls of toilet paper per working day, 240 rolls per month, 1440 rolls for 6 months and 2880 per year.

Hoping that this request will meet the understanding of the supply Unit in Zagreb, and hoping also that the storage of this amount of paper will not block the only one toilet we have at our disposal in the Hidrogradnja Building, we would kindly appreciate an urgent response to this vital requirement. Thank you very much for your kind attention to this matter.

A few minutes later; I've just taken a shower, since I'm about to go out to dinner. The power went off here at the Holiday Inn, so I had to take a shower in near-total darkness, with just a candle to keep from smashing my head against the bathroom wall. I brought the radio John and Peter gave me into the bathroom, because the station I was listening to was playing a good jazz song. All in all, it was pretty romantic, despite the fact that I was showering alone. So there are things you learn in odd situations that could prove useful in normal times . . . that's really why I'm here.

I hope you are all doing well—I am looking forward to getting your first letter, you don't know how much. I miss you all a lot.

Much love,
Tom

—∞—

Lieutenant Commander JJ Cummings Describes His Missions Over Afghanistan and the Inevitable Rivalries Between US Navy Pilots and Their USAF and RAF Counterparts

Just over one month after the September 11, 2001, terrorist attacks on the United States, a multinational force was deployed to southwest Asia to battle al-Qaeda and Taliban forces and hunt down Osama bin Laden. Operation Enduring Freedom, as the mission was called, represented the first major American conflict where e-mail was utilized by the troops—perhaps with even greater frequency than traditional mail. (Owing to concerns about biological contaminants, it was also the first conflict in a generation that prohibited "To Any Soldier" letters—i.e., messages of support written by total strangers and mailed to servicemembers abroad. In September and October 2001, envelopes containing weaponized anthrax were sent through the US mail, killing five people and infecting many more.) The tone of the e-mails and letters by the troops who were serving in and around Afghanistan was reminiscent of messages sent in the early days of World War II—defiant, determined, and fiercely patriotic. But they were not without humor. No matter how unified the different services and nations involved in Operation Enduring Freedom were, high-spirited and time-honored rivalries could not be easily overcome. A Navy pilot aboard the USS Theodore Roosevelt, *Lieutenant Commander JJ Cummings, wrote the following e-mail to his family back in the States, updating them on his activities and adding a comment, here and there, about other pilots in the US and British air forces. (The ellipses are in the original text.)*

Happy Thanksgiving (belated) everybody!

For Thanksgiving, the ship dressed up the wardroom, dimmed down the lights and put out a nice T-day spread and, for a brief moment, it was almost like being home. Sure it was. I don't know too many folks who live in a gray tin can with 5,500 other roommates but what can you do! We had flights later in the day scheduled, so scores of aircrew had to fight off the triptofan nods during their 6 hour flights over Afghanistan. Can you see the headlines now? "US Fighter Down Over Afghanistan. Turkey Overdose Suspected. Should Have Gone For The Dry Ham." I was able to call home and chat briefly with Mackenzie (and Sara and Delaney, of course) who filled me in on the untimely passing of her second fish. "It's OK Daddy. We'll get another one." It was a great day.

The flights over Afghanistan continue. The country's landscape reminds me of northern Nevada (without the casinos). As you cross over the southern border with Pakistan, you are met by hundreds of miles of desert. After the "Desert of Death" (as the charts call it), you get into rolling hills and occasional 2000' mountain ranges. From about mid-Afghanistan and north, the country turns into dark brown mountains that max out around 13,000 feet. Snow tops a majority of these peaks which remind me of the area surrounding Fallon, NV (one of our training areas). As you near the northern border by the -stans (Uzbeki and Turkmeni), the mountains start easing off and work down back into light brown, sandy plains. Off to the northeast are big snow-capped ranges that reach up to 25,000 feet. Overall, extremely rugged looking terrain in Afghan. To date, I have not seen one tree. The rural areas are littered with villages that are filled with collections of roofless, four walled structures that appear to be abandoned. The "cities" are completely unremarkable and colorless with no structure being any taller than 2 stories. The only color I've seen in these cities besides the ever present light brown hue is the occasional red streak coming from the Taliban gunners as they open up with their anti aircraft artillery. There is some farm land present, but it is infrequent and minimal. In a nutshell, Afghanistan is a giant pile of brown to light brown rocks that is bordered to the south and north by huge deserts and bordered to the east by an even bigger pile of rocks. The only signs of life that I have seen are vehicles (Toyota appears to be the SUV of choice) moving on one of the country's three main highways, some lights in the smaller towns at night and Taliban tough guys running from their convoy of military vehicles right before multiple weapons impacts.

The bombs keep falling on the Taliban. Sometimes you get in country and drop, sometimes you can't. As you can gather from all of the news coverage, the ground picture is changing radically and as a result, the air strike players are a bit more restrained. That's OK though because it serves to further cut the Air Force out of the picture. Designed to fight a war against an immobile enemy with fixed targets, the USAF is having a hard time with this fluid battlefield stuff, scenarios to which the USN/USMC routinely train. I'm sure they'll do fine when they get their 13,000 foot runways built in . . . . . oh, that's right they don't have any runways nearby. Guess those boys should have invested in some carrier decks a few years back. Realize that the previous statements are heavily biased and ridiculously true.

A few funny stories for you before I sign off. Talked previously about the air to air refueling that goes on over here. Over time, you get a feel for who the cool tanker drivers are and who the dolts are. The dolts? Air Force guys, of course. Love all the gas they carry, but they have no personality whatsoever (big shocker there). Cool tanker guys? The Royal Air Force! Love these guys. They will always go the extra mile (literally) to make sure you get your gas when and where you need it. The RAF tankers are ALWAYS on station and on time. Apparently, the F-14 is their favorite platform so as an added benefit post tanking, you can pull up along side the pilot's window and he'll shove some literature up against the window for your perusal (your guess on the type of literature displayed).

A few days ago, we were directed to hang on this RAF tanker's wing until we received mission tasking. After about 10 minutes, I decide to strike up a conversation with the crew (we monitor the same frequency while getting gas) to kill time. Thus began the comedy. After a 30 minute exchange of good hearted jabs, the pilot delivered a challenge to our flight of two.

But first, let me explain a little bit about inflight refueling. As I have mentioned earlier, to get gas airborne we have to put out a refueling probe which extends out from the right side of the jet about 2 feet outboard and forward of the pilot's head. The tanker is dragging a 20 foot hose which ends in a basket that looks similar to a badminton "birdie". The basket is about 2 feet in diameter. Now the hard part of tanking at 300 MPH is getting in the basket, because as you near the basket, the air disturbance created by the nose of your jet causes the basket to move up and away from you. Also thrown into the moving basket equation is general air turbulence, as well as the "ham fist" of the pilot who is flying the tanker.

Sometimes you get in the first time, sometimes it takes a couple of stabs. Where was I? Oh yeah, so this RAF guy says, "If you F-14 chaps are truly America's Finest Fighter Aircraft (my quote from a previous discussion), then you should have no problem getting into the basket first time, right?" I respond with, "Yeah, I usually bat about .900 with these poorly designed Brit baskets. The problem is that when I get in close, I find myself thinking about Margaret Thatcher naked, get sick to my stomach and miss the basket. Tell you what, we'll put a case of beer on both Tomcats getting in the first time." Did I mention that he's flying a DC-9 type tanker where a basket comes off of each wing tip which exacerbates (thankyou thesaurus) the turbulence problem by virtue of the rough air flow over the wingtip? Screw it. Bet's on.

The call finally comes for us to go hit some targets and it's time to get topped off. Pressure's on. I head over to the tanker's left wing, my wingman over to his right and as we are closing in I tell my wingman, "Now Moses, as you get in close, try not to think about all of the great English warriors of the past: the Spice Girls, Boy George, Wham UK, and Dame Edna. Just free your mind and be the basket." A couple of corrections later and just as I plug (on the first attempt) I scream over the radio, "Revolutionary War, baby!" "Moses" was good on his first attempt so the final score was US-2, England-0. I doubt we'll see the beer but who would want a case of shitty warm Brit beer anyway.

Speaking of beer, somewhere in the Navy regulations it's written down that for every 45 consecutive days that you spend at sea without a port call, you rate two beers. Two weeks ago, they broke out 10,000 beers for the crew to tear into for this deployment's first of many "beer days". With beer day fast approaching, multiple discussions erupted in the Ready Room over how to best maximize the beer day allotment. Do you starve yourself for two days to increase the "buzz" potential? How about giving blood 2 hours prior to assist in decreasing the amount of blood in your alcohol system? Do you nurse your two beers over a two hour span or just chug 'em and ride the wave? Which type of beer gives you the most bang for the buck? Fosters? Yengling? MGD? All very important and crucial questions. After much mental anguish and repeated calls to the flight surgeon inquiring about blood donor opportunities, I decided on the "full fed, Fosters chug" gameplan. Rumor has it that over 22,000 beers were killed. Hmmm . . . . 5,500 person crew, 2 beers per person . . . . hey . . . . . . someone went through the line more than once! No comment. Only 20 days until our next beer day, so I will take inputs on any improvements to my gameplan!

One last thing before I complete my novella . . . . . . Please remember in your thought and prayers every single enlisted Sailor that is slugging it out here on the USS TR. The aviator types have it easy in that we get to leave this ship for 6 fun filled hours to fly into a foreign hostile land and blow stuff up. We have variety and excitement in our days. Think of that 19 year old kid up on the flight deck 17 hours a day, fixing the same jets day in and day out while maintaining the same daily routine. Imagine doing that for over 70 days straight (only two days off in the last 6 weeks). He looks forward to 4 things: 1) getting off his feet for 5 minutes, 2) eating bland Navy chow, 3) sleeping in a cluttered space shared by 239 other Sailors and 4) port calls. His variety and excitement comes mainly during inport visits and, to date, we have had none and oh, by the way, there isn't one in the near or even distant future. They are the real heroes of Operation Enduring Freedom because it is through their efforts that we are able to launch and ultimately defend American shores. Through it all, you rarely hear one complaint from these kids despite the fact that they are working harder than anyone on this planet in the most dangerous "office space" on Earth, the flight deck of an aircraft carrier.

Hope this email finds you all safe and having a great Holiday Season. Don't worry about us, we are doing great out here. I can honestly say that there is no other place in the world I'd rather be than right here, right now, sticking it to the Taliban.

Later, JJ

Featured Series

"Animals in Wartime"

**In a Letter to His Cousin Martha Williams, Robert E. Lee Extols
the Many Virtues of His Beloved Horse, Traveller**

&

**Dr. Neblett Tells His Son About Their New Mascot,
Which They Have Named After Their Commanding Officer**

&

**The Carrier Pigeon Valiant Delivers a Final Plea
from Trapped French Troops at Fort Vaux in Verdun**

&

**In a Letter Home, General John Monash Writes from France
About a German Messenger Dog That Deserted His Platoon
to Join the Australians**

&

In Two Memorandums, a Group of US Scientists in World War II Report on Their Experiments to Employ a Certain Animal as a Weapon Against the Japanese
&
Lieutenant Junior Grade BJ Armstrong Sends an E-mail to His Family About Two Military Dolphins That Have Gone AWOL

After being notified by an aide-de-camp that some of the troops were abandoning the army on horseback, General George Washington replied, in a January 8, 1777, letter, that his officers needed to be vigilant about preventing these desertions—because they couldn't spare the animals. "[T]he loss of a worthless soldier," Washington stated bluntly, "will occasion less regret when it is not accompanied with that of a Horse." Since the first warriors clashed thousands of years ago, animals have played an integral role in the defense and conquest of armies and entire nations. Among many other duties, they have served as sentries and alarms, hauled munitions and men across seemingly endless and insurmountable terrain, parachuted into enemy territory, traveled hundreds of miles to deliver urgent messages, detected buried explosives, and assisted in search and rescue missions. In a pinch, some have had the added bonus of being edible. ("This day Capt Goodrich's Company Kill'd my Dog, and another Dog, and Eat them, [and] I remain unwell," a starving and heavy-hearted Captain Henry Dearborn wrote while on the brutal 1775 march to Quebec during the American Revolution.) But for the most part, military animals are valued for their service and sacrifices, not their nutritional benefits. General Robert E. Lee spoke with generous praise about those with whom he fought, but few of his letters conveyed as much warmth and affection as the one he wrote to his cousin, Martha "Markie" Williams, about his faithful horse Traveller. Williams, an artist, had asked for a description of Traveller so that she could paint his picture, and the general responded with the following.

Lexington, VA. 22, Decr 1866

My Dearest Markie

If I was an artist like you, I would draw a true picture of Traveller ; representing his fine proportions, muscular figure, deep chest, short back, strong haunches, flat legs, small head, broad forehead, delicate ears, quick eye, small feet & black mane and tail. Such a picture would inspire a poet, whose genius could then depict his worth & describe his endurance of toil, hunger, thirst, heat & cold & the danger & suffering through which he has passed. He could dilate upon his sagacity & affection & his invariable response to every wish of his rider. He might even imagine his thoughts through the long night marches & days of battle through which he has passed. But I am no artist, Markie, & can therefore only say he is a Confederate <u>grey.</u>

To your other questions, I can give more definite answers. I purchased him in the mountains of Virginia in the Fall of 1861 & he has been my patient follower, ever since, to Georgia, the Carolinas & back to Virginia. He carried me through the seven days battle around Richmond & the second Manassas, at Sharpsburg, Fredericksburg, the last day at Chancellorsville, to Penn'a, at Gettysburg & back to the Rappahannock. From the commencement of the Campaign in 1864 at Orange till its close around Petersburgh, the saddle was scarcely off his back, as he passed through the fire of the wilderness, Spottsylvania, Cold Harbor & across the James River. He was almost in daily requisition in the Winter of 1864–1865 on the long line of defenses from the Chickahominy North of Richmond to Hatchers Run South of the Appomattox, 35 miles in width & in 1865 bore me to the final day at Appomatox Ct. House.

You know the comfort he is to me in my present retirement. He is well supplied with equipments. Two sets have been sent to him from England; one by the Ladies in Baltimore & one was made for him in Richmond, but I think his favorite is the American Saddle from St. Louis. Of all his companions in toil, Richmond, Brown Roan, Ajax and quiet Susy Song, he is the only one that retained his vigour to the last. The two first expired under their onerous burden & the two last failed.—You can, I am sure from what I have said, paint his portrait.—

I am very sorry to hear of Gertie's sickness. Tell her she must get well & come over & see my Cat, <u>Tom Nipper.</u> He has been reared in the stable & had the advantage of Traveller's company & has acquired the most refined manners. You omitted to enclose Mrs Lawrence's letters. All unite in much love to yourself & the children. Thank Mr Shepherd for his kindness & tell him not to trouble himself about the Erie bds: Mildred is in the E.S. of Md: The rest of the family are here & as usual.

Your Cousin

R.E. LEE,

Enlisted men and women on the front lines have written with equal fondness about dogs, cats, monkeys, and other animals they have rescued from battle zones. (Most armies prohibit servicemembers from keeping wild or domesticated animals as pets, but troops regularly violate the rule.) Amidst the hardships and *furious devastation of war, many combatants find solace in caring for something small and vulnerable, especially if the animals are a reminder of a family pet back home. They are also thought to bring good luck. Some of these "unsanctioned" animals became quite famous in their day, from Simon the rat-catching feline aboard the HMS Amethyst (the only cat to receive the Dickin Medal—the animal equivalent of Great Britain's Victoria Cross or the American Medal of Honor) to Lucky the dog, an injured stray found in Kuwait in 2003 by an American soldier who spent more than $1,000 of his own money to have the puppy flown to the US. In early January 1945, Dr. Robert A. Neblett, serving with the Thirtieth Evacuation Hospital in the southwest Pacific, wrote to his son back home in Texas about a beloved new mascot one of the soldiers had adopted. He called it Vernon, which, not coincidentally, was the name of their commanding officer. Considering the animal, it was not intended as a compliment to the officer.*

Dear Charles Robert,

I have wanted to write you for quite a few days. I received the shirt you made for Butch. I think it was a very nice shirt and if it had been a little larger it would have been a nice Christmas present for ole Butch.

Sometimes ago, one of our soldiers who works in the hospital went out in the jungle, with some of the natives who have been helping us in the hospital, to get some bananas and pineapples. While they were out there they found a baby pig. Now this little pig was so small the soldier brought him home and kept him in a box the size of a shoe box. He could not eat anything but milk and he had to be fed with a medicine dropper.

He named his little pig "Vernon". Vernon will go to his owner when he is called or when he is whistled for. Vernon will follow his owner around the hospital like a dog and grunts instead of barking. He can and does wag his tail. The soldier works on one of the wards at night so he keeps his pet in a box in his tent each night. In the morning when he gets back to his tent the pig will squeal and jump up on his hind legs and is so glad to see him. Vernon will not follow anyone but his owner. Vernon eats dehydrated potatoes, hash and bully beef. He is real thin and long and black with brownish stripes running lengthwise along his body. I took some pictures of him the other day. All of us are crazy about the little pig.

I do hope that you had a nice Christmas and know that you did for you have always been a little gentlemen and being such everyone loves you and wants to do nice things for you. Remember to be good and thoughtful to Mother and Sister. You are to look after them until I get home, you know. Hug them both for me and whisper in their ear that Daddy Bob is "so lonesome and that he loves them with all his heart." This holds also for you, my son. I will not write more tonight for I want to write Dotty a letter.

Love,
Daddy Bob

Some animals who began as mere pets went on to prove themselves heroically in battle. In October 1917, Private J. Robert Conroy, with the Twenty-sixth "Yankee" Division, smuggled his adopted bull terrier, Stubby, aboard the SS Minnesota in an overcoat and brought him to the trenches of war-torn France. Stubby displayed a unique knack for anticipating both gas attacks and incoming artillery. He would, almost comically, drop flat on his belly and put his front paws over his ears. By November 1918, Stubby had endured seventeen battles, cornered a German spy, and earned more decorations than any other war dog in history. Twenty-five years later another unofficial mascot would obtain leg-

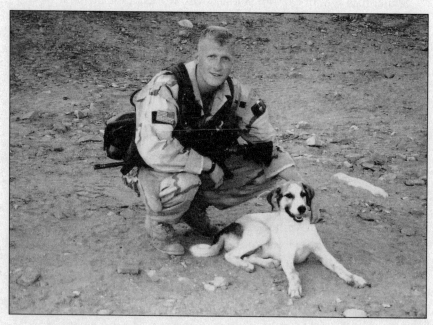

An American soldier, Captain Jason Ritter, with "Turbo," a stray dog Ritter and his platoon adopted while they were fighting in Afghanistan.

endary status for his service to the Allied cause. Voytek, a six foot six Syrian bear initially found as a cub by Polish soldiers, was so docile and intelligent that by the time he was full-grown he had learned to carry supplies and munitions to frontline troops in Italy. Notorious for seeking attention, he would bring much-needed humor to the men by doing somersaults and, while swimming in the ocean, mischievously popping up between unsuspecting bathers to scare the wits out of them. Animals officially trained for a military function were not, however, provided for amusement or companionship, and their missions were— and remain—exhausting and perilous ones. In World War I alone, an estimated eight million horses were shot or blown apart in combat or died of disease, overwork, or neglect. Messenger pigeons were gunned down in midair or torn to pieces by hawks specially trained to find and destroy them. And some literally flew themselves to death. Trapped inside Fort Vaux during the ferocious, ongoing battles in Verdun, France, during World War I, Major Sylvain Eugene Raynal and his men had reached the limits of human suffering. There was no clean water to drink. Raynal had shut off the fort's ventilation to prevent the Germans from gassing them, and the air became saturated with the stench of human waste and the decaying bodies of men who had been killed during the relentless bombardments. The Germans breached sections of the fort and sent streams of fire into the narrow passageways with flamethrowers. Realizing defeat was all but imminent, Raynal tied a desperate note to a homing pigeon named Valiant and released him into the sky. The message read:

We are holding, but are under a very dangerous attack of gas and smoke. Relief is urgently needed. Send a visual signal through Souville, which is no longer answering our calls for help.

This is my last pigeon.

Wounded and nearly asphyxiated by poison gas, Valiant nevertheless made it to a command post in Verdun—and then dropped dead on the spot. Although Fort Vaux would ultimately fall, Valiant was lauded as a symbol of courage, posthumously receiving the prestigious Legion of Honour. (Almost forty years later another carrier pigeon, Gustav, would become a national celebrity for bringing back one of the first reports of the D-Day landings in Normandy on June 6, 1944. An English "grizzle cock," Gustav flew 150 miles in about five hours, earning him the Dickin Medal. Unlike Valiant, Gustav survived the flight. Ironically, though, he met a tragic fate after the war, when his breeder, while cleaning the pigeon's loft, accidentally stepped on Gustav, killing him instantly.) Dogs have also been used as messengers, darting through minefields, destroyed towns, and dense forests, all the while trying to avoid being shot or captured. In World War I, a German dog named Roff became famous for "switching sides" in early May 1918. Just days before he would be promoted as commander of the entire Australian Corps, General John Monash sent the following short letter from Villers-Bretonneux, France, where his men were locked in a fierce battle with German forces trying to march on Paris. (It is not known for certain who Susan is, but she is believed to be a young friend.)

May 26, 1918

My Dear Susan,

In France here the weather has been very warm, and this has brought out all the beautiful wild flowers. The other day we took prisoner a beautiful German messenger dog. He is a beautiful Alsatian wolf hound, and he is very friendly. He has learned to speak and understand English, and is very faithful to us, and we all pet him so much.

In fact, Roff was a Doberman, and he was not taken prisoner by force; he voluntarily trotted over to the Australian side. The container in his collar still held the note intended for a platoon of German troops cut off from food and other necessary supplies. They had asked for relief, and, had Roff continued with his mission, they would have received the following snippy reply from their commander: "Weber has been in longer than you and he does not complain. We will send you food tonight. Give Roff any further messages—he does not complain." To the dismay of many an animal lover, creatures large and small have been "weaponized" in times of war to attack military and civilian populations alike. In World War II, Soviet troops regularly tied explosives to dogs that had been trained to run toward enemy soldiers and tanks, with fatal consequences for the targets—and, of course, the dogs. (If their letters home are any indication, the use of dogs in this manner unnerved and outraged German soldiers on the Eastern Front more than almost any other Soviet tactic.) Attempts to transform harmless animals into forces of destruction have, at times, veered toward the ludicrous. In World War II, a serious recommendation to drop bomb-wielding cats with tiny parachutes over enemy warships was entertained, the thinking being that since most cats dislike getting wet and always land on their feet, they would aim for the ship. Probably from sheer terror, the cat used to test the feasibility of the idea immediately blacked out after being dropped and was, therefore, unable to maneuver itself with any accuracy. The plan was scrapped. But another equally fantastic scheme was outlined in the following letter by a respected Harvard scientist named Earl P. Stevenson. Dr. Lytle S. Adams, who first advanced the proposal being considered, was not a professor or government official but a slightly eccentric dentist/inventor from Irwin, Pennsylvania, who had written directly to the White House with his concept. (The NDRC is the National Defense Resource Council.)

July 10, 1942
Office of the Coordinator of Research and Development
Navy Department
Washington, D.C.

Dear Sir:

When last in Washington the writer called at your office and presented an idea which has been brought to NDRC for its consideration and action. This idea, as will be evidenced by the attached correspondence, was first presented to the President of the United States last January and has since been brought to the attention of various individuals and organizations without, however, being finally disposed of in one way or another.

Briefly stated, the concept is to use the common American bat as a carrier for small incendiaries. The original proposal was to release these bats, for example, some hundreds of miles off the shores of Japan and at such a time as would permit the bat to travel to land, arriving shortly before daylight. The habit of the bat is such that with light it would seek a refuge by crawling into crevices under roofs, thatching, and generally into small places where conceivably fires could be very easily started by means of a bat-borne incendiary weighing approximately one ounce.

The inventor of this idea is Mr. Lytle S. Adams, who has consulted many authorities on the habits of bats and has partly thought through the problems incident to their use, including the development of certain suggestions as to the exact type of incendiary that could be used.

Dr. Conant, in assigning this problem to my Section, requested me to determine in the first instance whether there would be any conceivable tactical interest in this idea. Conceivably bats could be released from either submarines or planes, and my purpose in addressing this letter to your Office is primarily in connection with the first of these alternatives. In such a use the bats would have to be shipped at temperatures below 50 degrees F., where they hibernate and can be, I am told, packed in cases like any other inanimate objects. This, however, is one of the points that would have to be determined, and others are as follows:

Dr. Davis is probably taking considerable for granted in the assumption that there is no serious problem in designing an incendiary for this use. There are admittedly several ways of doing the job, but each would have to be made the subject of some investigational work. Then it is assumed, so far as I can read the record, that bats would be capable of seeking land if released at a considerable distance therefrom. From the migratory habits of some of these species this is indicated, but here, again, it would have to be proved.

Just how we could proceed experimentally to explore this idea is quite a problem. Doubtless there are many of the questions that could be answered by consulting the proper authorities, but NDRC has not thus far pursued the matter, as the first point to be determined is whether any of the Services would be interested in the idea. Obviously, this is not a major incendiary. From the standpoint of destruction it cannot be reckoned in the same class with other incendiaries now available. On the other hand, the use of such means might be very demoralizing, especially against a superstitious people. It cannot conceivably have any value as an incendiary for use against purely military objectives, as the chances are that the bats would seek the countryside rather than urban districts.

In submitting these papers to your Office it is my understanding that there is a group within the Navy which considers ideas originating within the Service, and that this suggestion might properly be submitted as having that origin. NDRC is prepared to go into this matter in whatever detail may be desired. The writer expects to be in Washington some time during the week of July 20 and will then follow up this letter by getting in touch with your Office.

Very truly yours
Earl P. Stevenson

The experiments were not a total flop, but in a July 2, 1943, memo, one of the technical aides on the project, Warren C. Lothrop, explained to his superiors the significant problems they encountered. (WCL is Lothrop himself; LFF is Dr. Louis F. Feiser, a Harvard colleague of Earl P. Stevenson; and CWS is the Chemical Warfare Service, which was tasked with creating the incendiary devices.)

July 2, 1943

On June 23rd, WCL interviewed Dr. Feiser on the bat tests.

LFF reported that a cooperative group of the Air Corps, CWS, Dr. Adams and himself had spent several days in the far West testing out the Adam's plan. These tests had shown that the bats were not as easy to catch as had been supposed, that they were more delicate than had been supposed, that they were much more difficult to cause to hibernate than had been supposed and that once in hibernation they were not as easily aroused as had been supposed. Furthermore, release of the bats from aircraft was an item which would require considerable experimentation. Some bats, if sluggish, plummeted to the ground, others if put out of the plane at high speed apparently had their wings broken. Lastly the bats were not able to carry the load expected (18 g) but would carry successfully a load of 11 g.

On the other side of the ledger, the bats, once properly gotten into the air, would act as gliders and covered a vast area, many of them not being located afterwards. Moreover they were found in some cases to have entered barns and to have climbed under the eaves of buildings. Because of the wide dispersion, the group did not try to run actual tests using an incendiary for fear of damaging private property.

In the latter stages of the experiment, there was a disaster in which the hangers and outlying buildings of the small airport used burned down. The cause of the fire was never ascertained, but it served to discourage the group.

A report prepared by Captain Wiley Carr and a Colonel at CWS, it was understood, had been sent to the Air Corps. This report more or less coincides with LFF's own opinion and recommended that the experiments be dropped and that the idea was probably impractical. No final decision had yet been made so far as LFF knew.

WCL will inquire of Colonel Aldrin in the matter and on the Air Corps decision LFF thought would depend the need for further work on the 17-hour delay.

Warren C. Lothrop

Less than two weeks later, the Army Air Force deemed "X-Ray," as the project was being called, impractical. But X-Ray still had its supporters, including Admiral John Sidney McCain (grandfather of Senator John McCain from Arizona), and testing went on for several more months. Adams, the dentist/inventor, was becoming increasingly demanding and intrusive as the experiments continued, at one point almost coming to blows with a US Marine named Lieutenant Charles J. Holt. "Everyone in the project seems to be in agreement that Adams cannot accept responsibility for the project and have it function," wrote Dr. W. G. Young, another advisor with the effort. Adams, he continued,

> *ordered Lieutenant Holt to prepare for a test to be held in the desert in which ten thousand assemblies [i.e., bats] were to be used. When Holt pointed out the tremendous hazard involved to the whole of Southern California by such a program, Adams was most indignant, and the Lieutenant finally had to tell him that such an experiment would not be performed even if he, Holt, had to stand in front of the Arsenal with a machine gun.*

By March 1944, after spending millions of dollars on the project, the government finally shut it down, focusing its efforts instead on a much more promising device—a nuclear weapon. Adams would contend after the war, with great disappointment, that if his plan had been pursued, it would have inflicted much greater damage on Japan than the atomic bombs. (As farfetched as X-Ray might have seemed, it is not entirely without precedent. After discovering that birds sought shelter in the thatched houses of a village he was attacking, an eleventh-century Norwegian warrior captured some of the birds, covered their backs with a smear of wax and sulfur and then set them on fire. As he had hoped, they returned to their roosts in panic and ultimately ignited fires throughout the town.) Winged and footed creatures are not alone in being called into service; aquatic animals are employed as well. Bottlenose dolphins, first used in Vietnam, hunt for mines, retrieve equipment fallen to the ocean floor that is inaccessible to military divers, and serve as guards to protect warships from attack by enemy agents armed with underwater explosives. (Sea lions and other marine mammals are being trained to perform similar feats.) Extremely intelligent, play-ful, and social, dolphins exhibit many humanlike characteristics; they can also be mischievous, aggressive, moody, and stubborn. In the buildup to Operation Iraqi Freedom, a team of dolphins was sent to the Middle East with Commander Task Force (CTF) 55, a group of American, British, and Australian sailors and Marines whose mission was to clear the northern Persian Gulf, which the US military refers to as the Arabian Gulf, of mines. The dolphins accomplished their assignment admirably, but in a few cases they demonstrated that they had minds of their own. Twenty-six-year-old Lieutenant junior grade BJ Armstrong, an HH-46D Sea Knight pilot stationed on the USS Kearsarge as part of a search and rescue (SAR) detachment, sent the following e-mail back to his family about one such incident. (EOD stands for Explosives Ordnance Disposal.)

Just wanted to drop everyone a note and say hello. Things are going out here. I wouldn't say going well, or badly, they are just going. The sandstorm has hit us after a frontal passage yesterday and even inside the skin of the ship our noses are filling with dust. No flying today but its just the kind of day that we need to be ready for SAR work. Nobody ever seems to go for a swim during good weather. I'm on the Alert Crew most of the day so I'll probably take in a lot of CNN while we sit around waiting (Ed . . . Alert 15, not bad since we don't have to be in the bird and we can even access one of the det's computers).

Just a funny story to pass along. A little over week ago, before this had all started getting real, we got a funny call from Tower while we were out flying. We were told to report all Dolphin sitings. We didn't see any for the couple hours I was up but we did think the call was rather odd. When we hotseated the bird to the next crew we asked about it and they had been briefed more specifically on what to look for. Apparently the EOD guys had lost one of their male mine hunting dolphins. It had just swum away. They had sent out a couple others, trying to lure it back (presumably females) with no luck. All the SAR birds out here in the Gulf were alerted in case we saw a lonesome dolphin swimming around. Apparently there was a happy ending, flipper showed back up a couple days later. I guess even our finned friends get a little weary of life on (and around) the boat.

Love to all,
BJ

The search for innovative ways to employ animals in both combat and peace-keeping efforts continues. In Mozambique, Gambian giant pouched rats are being trained to sniff out land mines left over from the country's vicious civil war. (Dogs are commonly used, too, but the rats' sense of smell is just as perceptive, and the rats themselves are cheaper, easier to care for, and lighter—and therefore less likely to set off a mine accidentally.) Bees are also being tested for mine-hunting activities; their bodies pick up all types of airborne particles, and if residual TNT is found mixed in with whatever pollen they are carrying, it can confirm the presence of land mines in a specific area. Similarly, entomologists are researching if bugs can be used as tiny sentinels that can be collected and then tested for toxins in the air, water, or soil during a possible bio-terror attack. Insects are not new to warfare. Glowworms were used in World War I to help soldiers read maps and other documents at night. Even plants are being enlisted. Biologists are working to determine whether it is possible to create genetically engineered plants that will quickly change colors upon detecting poison gases or other life-threatening agents. And these, of course, only represent the ideas that the military is able to make public.

Second Lieutenant Barbara "Heiny" Demetria, USMC, Serving in Operation Iraqi Freedom, Explains to Her Family How She Got Her Call Sign

No different than a civilian nickname given to a close friend, family member, teammate, or coworker, a military servicemember's informal "call sign" can be inspired by any number of factors. It can be an abbreviation of or play on someone's name, or a reference to a physical characteristic, personality trait, or military specialty. And in some cases, as twenty-three-year-old US Marine second lieutenant Barbara "Heiny" Demetria discovered, it can be prompted by a single unfortunate incident that draws the attention of the chain of command, from top to bottom—literally. (MOPP refers to chemical-protection suits,

DASC is the abbreviation for Direct Air Support Center, and COC is Combat Operations Center. The ellipses are in the original text.)

Hi everyone,

I was sitting on crew today and realized I hadn't shared the tale of my callsign with you. It is one of danger and embarrassment. I will try not to be too lengthy, but it takes some explaining . . . Everyone knows that all pilots have a callsign. Well we work pretty closely with the air officers and pilots so we all eventually get a "callsign", usually inspired by something you have said or done. Well I didn't waste any time in getting mine. I think it was our third location where Liza and I had to share a tent. There was a terrible sand storm that day—the worst one we've seen so far. The sky was orange in the hours before it started and we were sleeping before our crew. The wind was so violent it woke me up. It wasn't until I felt my face and realized there was a thick layer of dust on it. The sand was so fine and the wind blowing so hard that it went through the rain cover over our tent, through the actual tent walls and covered EVERYTHING in the tent—including us! It was absolutly disgusting. We were thinking it couldn't possibly get any worse . . . and then it did.

The torrential downpours ensued shortly after and completely drenched everything that was covered with dirt. What was great about this was that all of my gear (helmet, flak, MOPP boots, camelbag) was outside. Normally you put all this gear on to walk over to the system, but my flak vest was actually one with the ground and my helmet filled with mud. So I left it behind and hoped that day wasn't the day we took mortar rounds. Turns out we were located right in the middle of a dried out river bed—great place to be when it rains. So we all trudge over to the DASC in ankle-deep mud in the middle of the night with hardly any illumination from the moon. We get to the DASC and the tent is a total mess. Mud had been tracked all over the place. I was a liason that day between the DASC and COC. The COC tent was a big round tent we called the "Thunderdome" and it had several small off-chute tent (the DASC being one of them). So there is a little passage way that connects our tent to the Thunderdome and it was particularly slippery with all the mud that had been tracked in by traffic and I had come close to slipping several times . . . . *You probably think you know where this is going and you may be partly correct but it is much worse*

Shall we continue? OK, so the admin folks have a table set up in the COC just to the right of the passage way. General Mattis, as in the Commanding General of the entire 1st Marine Division, was using the phone at this table. I need to give the Air Officer in the COC some information so I start heading through the passageway and I felt myself slip. At this point one of those slow motion moments began and I thought "Noooooooo!" . . . I could feel myself falling and knew I couldn't stop. I was trying not to completely fall so I was on my hands and feet tumbling full force into the COC. The General's back was to me and I couldn't stop myself I went head-first into his butt. Yes, my head; his butt. Thus marked the birth of "Heiny". Since then I think I have heard about every joke there is about "kissing the General's ass" not being taken literally. Luckily the man was talking on the phone and was kind enough not to berate me. Everytime I see him and say good morning he smiles (Thinking, "Yup, that's the girl") and returns the greeting and I'm positive I blush (Thinking, "All he's thinking is 'that's the girl who rammed my butt with her head, I mean there are other ways of getting my attention'"). No he's really very nice. When we were back at Matilda I also used to put the frozen slices of butter under my leg to thaw while we ate, and they always used to joke that one day I would forget I put it there and get up to walk out of the chow hall with butter on my butt. So I think this one is going to stick :) I've gotta go for now but I thought you would enjoy that one. I'll write more as soon as I get a chance.

I love you guys,
Deme

—⁂—

Dayna Kennison Receives an E-mail from Her Husband, a USAF Major, Enumerating What Family Members Can Do to Help Returning Troops Adjust to Civilian Life

Long before the advent of e-mail, servicemen and -women composed amusing and satirical letters that lampooned military life and were copied (usually on mimeograph machines) and then widely circulated to friends and loved ones. One of the earliest of these parodies was an official-looking document instructing World War II combatants on what to expect and how to behave when they returned to their normal lives. "The United States is composed of land," begins the memo for American troops finally heading home in 1945, millions of whom had been away for years. The letter continues:

Bisecting the center is the Mississippi River. Everything east of the river is known as New York, while everything west is simply called Texas. There are a couple of other states, but they are not important. . . . Food is gen-

erally plentiful [and in] many restaurants you will see an item called "steak" on the menu. This dish is to be eaten with knife and fork. Steak has a meaty taste and isn't too revolting after one gets used to it. Of course, it doesn't come up to the luscious delectability of our own Bully Beef. . . . One must be very cautious when ordering drinks in bars and saloons. Bartenders try to sell old, aged stocks of Scotch and Bourbon. Don't be taken in by such practices. Some of the whiskey is twenty or even thirty years old, and obviously spoiled. . . . The country is run by Republicans, Democrats and Frank Sinatra. It's a big place because it stretches all the way across the country. Keep on your toes and you will get along alright.

German soldiers on the brutal Eastern Front fighting the Russians had their own version, titled "Notes for Those Going on Leave," which was considerably darker.

Curfew: *If you forget your [house]key, try to open the door with the round-shaped object. Only in cases of extreme urgency use a grenade.*
Defence against Partisans: *It is not necessary to ask civilians the password and open fire on receiving an unsatisfactory answer.*
Defence against Animals: *Dogs with mines attached to them are a special feature of the Soviet Union. German dogs in the worst cases bite, but they do not explode. Shooting every dog you see, although recommended in the Soviet Union, might create a bad impression. . . .*
General: *When on leave back in the Fatherland take care not to talk about the paradise existence in the Soviet Union in case everybody wants to come here and spoil our idyllic comfort.*

During the Vietnam War, the "coming home" advice was addressed to friends and family back in the States who were about to receive a returning serviceman: "[S]how no alarm if he insists on carrying a weapon to the dinner table. . . . If it should start raining, pay no attention to his joyous scream as he strips naked, grabs a bar of soap, and runs outdoors for a shower . . . Pretend not to notice if at a restaurant he calls the waitress 'Numbah One Girl.'" Despite the coarser language, the mock instructions end on a rather poignant note:

Above all, keep in mind that beneath that tanned and rugged exterior there is a heart of gold (the only thing of value he has left). Treat him with kindness, tolerance, and an occasional fifth of good liquor, and you will be able to rehabilitate that hollow shell which was once the happy-go-lucky guy you once knew and loved.

More good-natured than bitter, "Instructions for a smooth homecoming" was written just before the first rotation of troops began returning from Operation Iraqi Freedom. Dayna Kennison received the following version via e-mail from her husband, a major in the United States Air Force, Air National Guard. ("FNG," mentioned at the end of the letter, stands for "F——ing New Guy.")

These instructions are intended for the spouses and loved one's of deployed troops to help provide a smooth transition back to civilized life.

1. Leave a flashlight near your spouse while they are sleeping. It is possible the returnee may need to use the bathroom in the middle of the night. While they are walking around your backyard trying to find the bathroom, they may need a flashlight. Don't be alarmed if your returnee is more comfortable walking to the nearest gas station to use the restroom.

2. While your returnee is sleeping, it is imperative you make as much noise as possible. You have many options on what kind of noise to make. For instance run the lawn mower just outside the bedroom door. Hold conversations with people within 2 feet of the sleeping person. Play recordings of jet engines taking off at the highest volume your home stereo will allow. Your loved one is not used to sleeping in complete silence and could possibly suffer from severe insomnia if extreme noise is not maintained during the hours they try to sleep. Also keep the shades on all windows in the bedroom open. If the individual is sleeping at night, keep the lights on. Your loved one is not used to sleeping in the dark and may be very disoriented without a blinding light in their eyes.

3. Keep several boxes of bottled water near every water faucet in your house. The returnee will be scared out of their mind to drink or use the water from the faucet for brushing their teeth and will need the bottled water.

4. Under no circumstances is your returnee allowed more then 2 boxes of cereal. This could potentially lead to violence. However, they will adjust.

5. Be sure to place a cup of sand in front of an oscillating fan on high . . . enough said!

6. You might notice obsessive-compulsive behavior in your returnee due to the ever-present Hennessy Disease rampant at their deployed location. Simply provide your loved one with antibacterial lotion and they will be fine.

7. Don't be embarrassed if at your local bar your returnee pulls out his/her beer card. This will pass. If your returnee sneaks off to the bar and tries to bribe the bartender for a fourth beer, let them go—they need it.

8. Twice a week your returnee will be looking for the laundry turn-in point. Set up a tent in your backyard where laundry can be dropped off. Make sure not to use any type of laundry detergent or fabric softener, as the good clean smell and the softness of the clothing may confuse and frighten your returnee and cause them not to wear those articles of clothing. Also, be sure to put stickers on your returnees clothing. Ensure they are placed where they will irritate the hell out of them.

9. Only offer meals at certain times of day and ensure they sign for EVERYTHING. DO NOT under any circumstances allow the individual to eat at a time when the "chow hall" is not open. If they are permitted to eat during these times, it is very possible that the feeling of not being hungry could cause their bodies to go into shock. Additionally, ensure they stand in a line for at least 10 minutes and give them a large tray that you cleaned off with dirty dishwater to set their plates on. Find at least 10 or 15 of your friends, dress them in blue coveralls, and ask them to talk incoherently while they act unhappy to slop the food on the dishes ensuring to give them twice what they've asked for. Pile the food together in the middle of the plate—they'll think it tastes better that way.

10. With every meal ensure that there is plenty of fluffy steamed white rice. If this is not provided, your returnee will be unsure exactly what to do, and could possibly starve to death. Always offer salad, but sometimes don't use lettuce—instead substitute old cabbage and limit their selections of dressing to 1000 Island, Ranch, and Italian if you decide to provide it. Additionally, you must buy all plastic silver wear and Styrofoam plates.

11. Have your loved one bag the trash and then explain where you want it taken. It might be easier and preferred by your loved one to drop it off on the way to the gas station for a bathroom break.

12. Finally, your loved one may count the days he's been home and call everybody that visits the house "FNG". If this occurs, tell him he's leaving every few weeks and to keep counting—remind him he's making history.

These instructions are meant to help ease your returnee back into life at home. It will take some time and extra care on you part, but after 30–60 days, your loved one should be good as new. Just in time to return. Good luck.

—m—

At the Memorial of Caen in Normandy, France, a young girl (far right) looks at a wall-size photograph of two teenage Polish civilians being hanged by a German officer.

CAUGHT IN THE CROSSFIRE

Letters by and About Civilians

In place of a dutiful and grateful return to your King and Parent state, you have been guilty of the most unpardonable Rebellion, Supported by the Ambition of a set of designing men, whose insidious views have cruelly imposed on the credulity of their fellow creatures, and at last have brought the whole into the same Dilemma, which leads me to feel not a little for the Innocent of them, in particular on the present occasion, having it in orders to execute a just Punishment on the Town of Falmouth.

> —*British Navy Captain Henry Mowatt,*
> *ordering the citizens of Falmouth, Maine,*
> *on October 16, 1775, to evacuate their town*
> *before he burns it to the ground*

On the 18th Octbr last a Fleet under the command of Capt Mowatt burnt the Town of Falmouth as you've undoubtedly heard—. Your House Barn Out Houses, Fences & Office are all in Ashes.—I was obliged to flee for my Life—and my wife & I were were forced to foot it with large Bundles on our Arms about 6 or 8 Miles & abused as we passed the Road . . . am Still in the Woods, where if I cant get off either to London, Boston or Hallifax, I intend to remain till Peace be restored to this infatuated, this distracted Country—

> —*A citizen of Falmouth reports to a friend*
> *that the town is destroyed.*

283

Dear Ning: It is my greatest regret that I failed in my duty to provide you with the education and upbringing you deserve. I will never see you again in this life, my dear son. I hope you will grow up fast so that you can comfort your mother at her grave. I cannot teach you with my words anymore, but I can educate you with what I have done, which you will better understand when you are older. Please remember always that your mother sacrificed her life for the future of our country.

—Zhao Yi Man, one of millions of Chinese women
who assisted the army in resisting the Japanese,
sending a final farewell from prison to her young son
before her execution. The full-scale Japanese invasion
of China in 1937 was a harbinger of the devastation that
would be inflicted throughout Asia during World War II.

We hardly ever see coyote here though unless they are trapped somehow. There are snakes here, too. Rattlesnakes. I saw one about the 3rd day after we came to Ariz. in Camp I. There were scorpions too but not so many now. Few people got bitten by them but they didn't die yet. Boy it sure was awful when we first came here. Hot, dusty, half dead. The train ride was awful! Nothing but desert outside and boy was it hot! Before we evacuated from Watsonville to Salinas, I got an attack of appendicitis two days before the evacuation. They were going to give an operation but since we had to evacuated they didn't have to. Boy! it sure did hurt tho. Well, I guess I'll fold up now. Could you get me the address of Emily Noller? Does Mr. Bertognolle still teach? Give my regards to him if he's still teaching. Thanks. Write if you have time. Yours very truly, Toyoko Alva Nakata. P.S. People say we're better off than outsiders. I think so too.

—Toyoko Alva Nakata, age sixteen, writing from Poston, Arizona,
to her friend Captola Saunders. Nakata was one
of an estimated one hundred and twenty thousand Americans
of Japanese ancestry placed in internment camps
during World War II. The US government
officially apologized for the policy in 1988.

We have passed a couple of hot points initially, the first one is right when we crossed the border for the first time. The city is called Safwan and 50% of the population are children who are starving. The rest are men and women who might snap at any time. The city is now under the protection or security of the Brits. The Brits are doing an outstanding job. Now we don't travel through the city, instead we have to travel through an alternate road which is much safer. Basarah is not far from the road we travel on. On the sides of the road there are kids who beg for food. We give them our MRE's and water. I have had poverty stare at me dead in the eyes, these eyes that stare are from kids who do not deserve these harsh conditions. They are beautiful kids who need love, need shelter, and freedom. It breaks my heart to see them begging, soon they will be free. I've taken pictures of their faces to remind me that there are places in this world where people suffer, especially children.

—US Marine Corporal Denis Silva Torres,
writing from Iraq in early April 2003
to his future parents-in-law,
Ovidio and Isabel Diaz

It is hard to tell you the situation here, it is bad, very bad. I can't even get out with my own car, as I may be killed by the robbers, or by a mine put to the side of the road, or by a firefight between Americans and some people. Death is not an accident here, no, it is the only real, stable, possible thing here. I was trying to find a job, but no work is available. You know that I was forced to leave working with Americans. My home had become a target for those who are pretending to resist the invasion, and they had kidnapped my brother, sent me a message to quit or they would kill him, so I did. I don't know what to do. I think I will work as a taxi driver, but it is not easy, you know the traffic problems, the dangers of being robbed by someone. Write to me about you . . . I need to hear from you.

—Iraqi citizen Khadum A., writing from Baghdad
to a relative in August 2004

**Phoebe Morris, in an Emotional Letter to Her Father,
Describes the Attack on the Nation's Capital
&
Morris Notifies Her Father That She Fears Baltimore Might Be Next
&
After Fleeing to Philadelphia, Which Is All but Deserted,
Morris Informs Her Father of the Withering Assault
on Baltimore's Fort McHenry**

*Targeting the city was not, from a purely military standpoint, absolutely criti-
cal. But symbolically, a massive assault on Washington would humiliate the
United States and strike fear into the hearts of its people. In August of 1814, two
years after the US declared war on Great Britain, British forces approached the
American capital seeking retribution for their loss to the Colonies thirty years
before, and, more recently, for the burning of York, Canada, which was ruled
by the British. Often referred to as the second American Revolution, the War of
1812 erupted over several grievances, including accusations that the British were
arming the native population against white settlers in the Northwest Territories,
engaging in widespread trade violations, and clashing with US ships on the high
seas, mostly as a result of British-imposed blockades against commercial vessels
heading to Europe. There was particular outrage that the British were "impressing" thousands of American sailors; essentially, capturing them, claiming they
were still British subjects—even if they had become naturalized US citizens—
and forcing them to serve in the Royal Navy. (Critics of the war believed that
these offenses could have been resolved diplomatically, and some even argued that
the conflict was motivated by a desire to wrest control of Canada from the
British.) Despite the increasing threat of an invasion of Washington in the summer of 1814, President James Madison's secretary of war, John Armstrong,
adamantly opposed mustering additional troops to protect the city. It was a mis-
calculation with disastrous consequences. "They were ringing and twisting and
screaming, caling the lord, 'What is to Becom of us all'," a slave named
Michael Shiner later wrote about hysterical residents as the British approached
the defenseless capital. Shiner continued:*

[As] soon as We got sight of the British armmy raising that hill they look like flames of fier, all red coats and the stoks of their guns painted with red vermilon, and the iron Work shined like a Spanish dollar.

President Madison evaded capture by dashing to neighboring Virginia. Earlier in the day, Secretary of the Treasury George Campbell handed him two pistols to be used in the event that the president was forced to protect himself. First Lady Dolly Madison had already abandoned the executive mansion, but not before saving a copy of the Declaration of Independence and Gilbert Stuart's magnificent, eight-foot-tall portrait of George Washington. Led by General Robert Ross and Admiral George Cockburn, the British troops marched into the city on August 24, 1814. Phoebe Pemberton Morris, a twenty-three-year-old woman from Pennsylvania, had been visiting friends in Washington when the city fell into a state of panic. Morris began sending her father in Madrid a series of letters narrating with growing urgency the ongoing crisis. Phoebe's father was Anthony Morris, a close friend of the Madisons who was in Spain on the president's behalf secretly negotiating the purchase of Florida. (The "Palace," as Morris refers to it, was the President's House, which would later be renamed the White House. British soldiers had entered the mansion, found food hastily left uneaten in the opulent dining room, toasted to their conquest, and then looted and torched the building. Residents of Baltimore, Maryland, more than forty miles away, could see the red glow of the fires raging throughout the nation's capital.)

My dear Papa,

I hope before the conclusion of this letter to be able to insert some intelligence more agreeable than that with which it will commence—

On the 23rd instant 6 of the Enemy's frigates moved up the Potomac, being towed by 13 barges—The next morning they were at the mouth of Port Tobacco river—Before noon they had reached Bladensburg when an action commenced between the american troops under General Winder & the British under General Ross—The americans engaged did not exceed 2000, the main body being at Washington—The force of the enemy estimated at not less than 8 or 9000—The americans were overpowered by numbers. The 5th. regt. consisting of the flower of the Baltimore troops fought with great bravery & suffered severely. General Stansbury & Major Pinckney were wounded & taken—The americans retreated & were pursued by the British into Washington which they entered almost without impediment—The Navy yard, the Capitol & the Palace are destroyed! The explosion of the latter was heard at the distance of 16 miles, & the light of the conflagration was visible in Baltimore for many hours—It is supposed they are before now in that city—A Town meeting has been held to resolve upon some measures for the defence of Phila—We await the event with great anxiety—General Winder is said to have retreated across the long bridge into Virginia—The President & Secretary of State had taken the field—

Having rushed from Washington to Pennsylvania, Morris wrote to her father on September 6 that she was now in Philadelphia. As major cities along the East Coast braced for a British takeover, Morris was both fearful and defiant. (The lines of Spanish poetry at the end of the excerpt state: "To die for one's country, what a beautiful way to die!")

> *It is uncertain what city is next destined to be attacked by the enemy, who have proclaimed, that unless we withdraw our forces from Canada, they will destroy every Town which is assailable— . . . We are extremely anxious, indeed it requires the utmost exertion of my spirits to be composed under such various disturbances—Some gentlemen think it will be madness for any Ladies to remain in Phila should the enemy enter the City; & others think that it will be safer than those retreats in the vicinity which are frequently the resort of foraging companies, whose impertinence would be most annoying— . . . the Patriotism of America is roused, but many fear in vain—The enemy receive daily reinforcements and their troops are all disiplined while the greater part of our army consist of volunteers & militia—I believe no one has an idea that we shall be finally conquered, but we shall probably suffer severely*

> "Morir por la patria
> Que bello morir!"— . . .

On September 13, the Royal Navy launched a furious assault on Fort McHenry, which guarded Baltimore. If the star-shaped fort capitulated, the ships could then sail into the harbor and bombard the city, allowing thousands of British soldiers at nearby Hampstead Hill to charge in for an almost certain victory. With Washington crippled, the loss of another major city would have proved catastrophic to the United States. Like many Americans, Phoebe Morris believed the country's survival was at stake, and Fort McHenry was the linchpin.

Phil.a Wednesday Sept. 14th 1814

My dear Papa

This day has been one of the most anxious and I think among the most unhappy of my life—A suspense of 48 hours has been endured by all the inhabitants of Phil.a relative to the fate of Baltimore upon which

ours depends—the stages are all stopt & not even an express arrives.
Baltimore is so much more ably fortified than our city that should she
fall Phil.a will not attempt a defence—at least such is the opinion &
determination of almost all parties—the only accounts we receive are
from Videttes & the latest intelligence was that the Enemy had gained
possession of the heights, of the York & Lancaster roads & were
surrounding the city—a terrible cannonading has been heard for two
days General Smith commands; they are making the bravest resistance,
but a letter has been recieved by Mr. Dallas which says that Baltimore
must fall!—the result will most probably be known tomorrow
morning—We are preparing to remove to Montgomery—I have had
the satisfaction of knowing that you were in good health on the 7th of
June & in Seville—Mr. Latimer arrived in Phila from Liverpool, I have
not yet seen him as he left here immediately to join Mrs. Latimer who
is in Baltimore—The intelligence of your health and safety arrived
while we were in that gloomy state of despondency which nothing else
could have roused—I bless God that neither you or our dear Brother
are at home—

The British force is now immense—General Ross, Admiral Cockrane
etc carry desolation wherever they go—During the reign of Napoleon
when he conquered almost the whole European World there has never
been committed one single act of such wanton & savage tyranny as
that exercised by the British in burning the beautiful buildings of the
Capitol & the President's house—except in the days of the Goths &
Vandals, all fine edifices particularly those adapted to Civil purposes
have been carefully preserved—These ruffians tore down Mrs.
Madison's picture & said they would "keep Dolly safe & exhibit her
in London"—

Certainly we have been most unfortunately mistaken in the talents of
some of our rulers, Genl Armstrongs vindication is very feeble & the
conduct of General Winder who commanded our forces at Bladensburg
totally inexcusable, he ordered a retreat which was so unexpected, that it
was probably the cause of the confusion which prevailed—General Ross
said that he wished it would <u>rain militia</u> as they only created disorder in
the american troops & rendered their conquest the more easy—
tomorrow I shall be obliged to write the sad account of the Defeat of
Baltimore—Every man old & young of all political opinions are
indiscriminately engaged in this contest—

*At the time that Morris wrote her letter, the fate of Baltimore—and of the
nation—had already been decided. Morris learned the news the next day.*

(Almost nothing is known of Phoebe Morris's own fate after the war except that she never married and died in 1825.)

Thursday Morning 15

My dear Papa what a change from despair to joy the British are defeated! General Ross is killed! about noon we heard a loud huzza in the streets & throwing open the windows heard the glad the unexpected shout of Victory! Victory! Ross is killed! The Enemy are driven back to their Ships! a handbill was printed to this effect "Under the protection of Providence to whom all honor & glory should be ascribed the inhabitants of Baltimore assisted by the adjoining districts have done their duty to themselves & to their country—The enemy after severe loss decamped suddenly in the night & embarked with great precipitation—General Ross is killed. We cannot as yet describe the particulars of this tremendous conflict—how unexpected was this intelligence—We may yet be able to repulse the enemy & not as I have heard the Federalists say be obliged in less than three months to take the oath of allegiance to great Britain—As Philadelphia is generally supposed will be the next place to which the enemy will resort, we expect to leave it in a few days—

An estimated fifteen hundred to eighteen hundred shells rained down on Fort McHenry over a period of twenty-five hours. Francis Scott Key, a thirty-five-year-old American lawyer who had opposed the war from the beginning, watched the bombardment from the British frigate HMS Surprize. *(Key and a US officer named John Skinner, who negotiated prisoner exchanges, had appealed in person to British commanders on September 7 for the release of a well-respected American doctor who was being detained. The British accepted their terms but would not allow Key and Skinner to leave for the time being, as they had overheard the plan of attack on Fort McHenry.) As Key paced the deck of the* Surprize *during the thunderous barrage, both his sympathies for the besieged soldiers inside the fort and his anxiety for the future of his country grew with every passing moment. And then at dawn on September 14, everything went still. Key wasn't certain if the fort had surrendered or if the British had yielded. Dark, intermingling clouds of smoke and mist obscured the view of Fort McHenry. Suddenly, a massive American flag—thirty by forty-two feet—unfurled in the breeze. Key was ecstatic. The fort had miraculously survived, and, as it would later be reported, with relatively minor casualties. (Four soldiers were killed and twenty-four were wounded.) Key quickly pulled a piece of paper, an old letter, out of his pocket and immediately began scribbling a poem celebrating the "Defense of Fort M'Henry." It would, of course, later become immortalized as*

"The Star Spangled Banner," and in 1931 it was officially adopted as the nation's anthem. While the lyrics are Key's, the tune itself is "To Anacreon in Heav'n"—an old English drinking song.

—⁓—

Overwhelmed with Grief, Martha Barnett Tells Her Brother Daniel How Her Family Was Victimized by Federal Troops & Williamson Simpson Oldham Proposes to Confederate President Jefferson O. Davis an Attack on the Civilian Population in the North That Will "Fill [the] People with Terror"

Like the previous major conflicts fought on American soil, the Civil War exacted enormous suffering on civilian men, women, and children. But the scale of the devastation was like nothing the nation had ever experienced. Throughout the country, farms and orchards were razed, homes were ransacked by bullying soldiers and often burned to the ground, and, although rare, some civilians were killed or maimed in battles that broke out in their own backyards. On May 25, 1862, only a year into what would be a four-year conflict, Captain E. John Ellis, with the Louisiana Sixteenth Infantry, wrote to his sister about the plight of Southern civilians and how it was only fueling his resolve to defeat the Yankees.

> This war will close before long. By the 1st of August next we will be a free people and at peace. . . . God only knows what misery the war is inflicting. Sons, brothers, fathers are killed and wounded but this though bad enough is not all—as the Yankees advance through the country families are driven from their homes and these homes, Great-God! What a wreck they become—I have seen helpless women peeping through our camp, with helpless babes in their arms and four or five little children following along behind, hurrying forward to seek charity—beyond Corinth away from the scene of strife. . . . This contest on our part is just, and I am willing for me to wear out in the service or to die in the field before submitting to Yankee rule. Rather than this, I would be willing to live on the mud of the lake swamp, to pillow my head upon the Cypress Knee, to sleep with the dull eye of the alligator glaring on me & the slimy hissing moccasin coiled over my heart. God help the Yankees if our men get to close quarters with them.

Even Federal troops were stunned by the degree of destruction they encountered at the hands of their comrades. David Henry, who would go on to fight and ulti-

mately die for the Union in 1864, was eleven years old when he came to the United States from Newry in Northern Ireland. After settling in Armstrong County, Pennsylvania, Henry enlisted in the Union Army in August 1862. During his two years of service, Private Henry survived some of the bloodiest campaigns of the war, including the battle of Fredericksburg. With nearly thirteen thousand casualties to the Rebels' fifty-three hundred, the December 13, 1862, engagement was a horrendous defeat for the North as well as for General Ambrose E. Burnside, who had just been appointed commander of the Army of the Potomac. Two days before the battle, Fredericksburg endured an overwhelming bombardment and was then looted by Union troops. "If you had been in Fredericksburg and seen the way things were smashed up . . ." Henry wrote to his two daughters, Mary and Sarah, on Christmas Eve of the surreal spectacle of ruin. "I never saw the likes, houses, furniture, beds and everything strewed about the streets. There must have been a great many little boys and girls have had to fly for their lives from the ill fated city." He continued:

> *About 5 in the morning of the 11th as our engineers were busy lay the bridge across opposite the city, the rebel sharpshooters were hid in the houses along the bank in the town. They fired on our men killing a number of them. Then our cannon opened on the town about noon. There was several houses burning as our guns poured in a tempest of iron and lead. Never did I see such a sight as the city presented on Friday. The houses that escaped the fire were riddled from top to bottom. Furniture of the most costly kind was smashed up and scattered over the streets. Piano parts and settees were lying around. At one place a soldier would be seen sitting on a splendid rocking chair. Another would be seen carrying a bed, while here is one with a nice clock under his arm. Down by the corner another with a doll baby on a horse before him as large as life and others with whole arms full of cups and saucers and plates and still others with beautiful vases and books in any quantitys while tobacco and cigars that before had been very scarce were passing around in abundance. . . . [A] city of 12 to 15,000 inhabitants was laid in ruins in few hours and yet this is only one spot in the great desert of this wicked rebellion.*

While physical intimidation and the theft or destruction of property were the most common results of encounters between armed troops and civilians, there were incidents of rape, killing, and other horrific acts of violence. It is not known what specifically caused the confrontation between William J. Barnett and members of the Thirty-ninth Missouri Volunteers marching through Audrain County in Missouri, but it escalated terribly after the soldiers attempted to press his young sons into service and demanded from Barnett a "single tree"—a large, wooden, y-shaped device that connects a wagon to its horses. Writing in October 1864, Mrs. Barnett reported to her brother and sister-in-law the shocking turn of events.

D. A. Ellington
    dear brother

        I take the present opportunity of letting you know of my sad and bereaved condition. it falls to my heavy task to inform you of my misfortunes of late.

I have lost my husband one of my children and a third one is in a critical condition Last Monday evening just before sundown a few men belonging to the 39th Mo Volunteers came out keeping horses and wagons to go off on. Two of them rode up to the house and asked Mr Barnett his name they then asked him about the team he told them he had one but was not able to drive it they then asked how about his boys and while they were in the house Joe and Tommy started to run from the kitchen to keep from driving the wagon. the men come to the door and saw the boys running got on their horses and took after them and shot them both

Tommy was shot three times and Joe twice Tommy died in about 18 hours after he was shot. Joe we think will get well They then came back to the stable and shot Mr. Barnett killing him almost instantly he was shot in the head twice and in the arm once. O my brother and sister you have no idea of the sorrow and afflictions I have had to undergo during the past week yet I can say that I lack for no kindness which neighbors can bestow

Mr Barnett and Tommy were buried on Wednesday evening side by side in the same grave You cannot imagine my distress at seeing my dear husband and one of my darling children thus torn from my embrace by the rude hand of death and consigned to the narrow limits of the tomb there & await the final summons of Judge of all the earth at the final day of judgement when it shall be said come ye blessed of my father inherit the kingdom prepared for you before the foundation of the world. Then I hope to see my loved ones who have gone before me and I now trust are ranging the bright fields of Elysian glory. Pray for me and seeing my dear brother and sister how much I want to see you all come and see us if you can let Mary see this letter as we have not written to her thinking the mail was not going to where she lived farewell for the present your affectionate

                        sister Martha E. Barnett

Despite being shot several times, nineteen-year-old Joseph Barnett survived. The Barnetts' third son, William, escaped without injury. (William had been running back from a neighbor's house when he heard the gunfire and immediately hid himself.) Thomas Barnett was seventeen when he died, and he and his father were buried under a single gravestone with only five words for their epigraph: "Both murdered by Federal Troops." At the time that Martha Barnett wrote her letter, the Confederacy was rapidly disintegrating. Robert E. Lee's forces had not enjoyed a clear victory since Cold Harbor in June, Atlanta had been reduced to smoldering ruins after Sherman's infamous invasion, and Ulysses S. Grant was fortifying his entrenchments around Petersburg, Virginia, where the final major battle of the war would take place. With a growing sense of urgency and desperation, a band of Southerners conspired to terrorize the civilian populations in the North by spreading smallpox and Yellow Fever, blowing up buildings, and poisoning municipal water supplies. (Union troops were known to engage in a crude form of biological warfare by tossing animal carcasses in public wells to contaminate them.) On November 25, 1864, eight Confederate agents slipped into New York, the country's most populous city, and lit a series of fires they hoped would set all of Manhattan ablaze. Although they were successful in sowing panic, they failed to cause significant damage. Two and a half months after the New York attack, a Confederate senator from Texas named Williamson Simpson Oldham wrote to Jefferson Davis to inform him of a chemical weapon he believed would wreak even greater havoc on the city. (Richard McCulloh, alluded to as the inventor of the lethal substance, had been a science professor at Columbia University in New York before he joined the Southern cause.)

Richmond, February 11, 1865

His Excellency Jefferson Davis,
    President of the Confederate States of America:
    SIR: When Senator Johnson, of Missouri, and myself waited on you a few days since in relation to the prospect of annoying and harassing the enemy by means of burning their shipping, towns, &c., there were several remarks made by you upon the subject that I was not fully prepared to answer, but which, upon subsequent conference with parties proposing the enterprise, I find cannot apply as objections to the scheme.
    First. The combustible material consists of several preparations and not one alone, and can be used without exposing the party using them to the least danger of detection whatever. The preparations are not in the hands of McDaniel, but are in the hands of Professor McCulloh, and are known but to him and one other party, as I understand.
    Second. There is no necessity for sending persons in the military

service into the enemy's country; but the work may be done by agents, and in most cases by persons ignorant of the facts, and therefore innocent agents.

I have seen enough of the effects that can be produced to satisfy me that in most cases without any danger to be the parties engaged, and in others but very slight, we can (1) burn every vessel that leaves a foreign port for the United States; (2) we can burn every transport that leaves the harbor of New York or other Northern port with supplies and gunboat on the Mississippi River, as well as devastate the country of the enemy, and fill his people with terror and consternation.

I am not alone of this opinion, but many other gentlemen are as fully and thoroughly impressed with the conviction as I am. I believe we have the means at our command, if promptly appropriated and energetically applied, to demoralize the Northern people in a very short time. For the purpose of satisfying your mind upon the subject, I respectfully, but earnestly, request that you will have an interview with General Harris, formerly a member of Congress from Missouri, who, I think, is able, from conclusive proofs, to convince you that what I have suggested is perfectly feasible and practicable. The deep interest I feel for the success of our cause in this struggle and the conviction of the importance of availing ourselves of every element of defense must be my excuse for writing you and requesting you to invite General Harris to see you. If you should see proper to do so, please signify the time when it will be convenient for you to see him.

I am, respectfully, your obedient servant,

W.S. Oldham

Relatively few documents outlining such tactics survived the war; Simpson's letter was found on the floor of the Richmond statehouse after Union troops stormed the city in April 1865. New Yorkers had been unaware that their city was once again a major target of a strike, and an editorial writer for the New York Times *feared that citizens had become too complacent in the aftermath of the November 25th attack. "[I]t becomes us to see to it that we are not put off our guard by relapsing into somnolent indifference," he warned. "It is when we have got to fancy ourselves perfectly secure, that the pestilence will break out with new and accumulated force."*

—∞—

The Brother of a German Soldier Fighting in Belgium Advises Him to "Have No Compassion for These Cut-Throats," Referring to Belgian Men, Women, and Children

&

An Irish Woman, Alice S. Green, Shares with a Friend Stories About German War Crimes Against Both Allied Soldiers and Civilians

Hand-delivered on August 2, 1914, to the Belgian Minister for Foreign Affairs, M. Davignon, the letter from the German government was as cordial as a friendly note passed from one neighbor to the next about a potentially troublesome matter. Marked "Very Confidential," the message claimed that France was plotting to invade Germany through Belgium, a neutral country. The Germans asserted that they "cannot but fear that Belgium, in spite of the utmost goodwill, will be unable, without assistance, to repel so considerable a French invasion." The Germans offered a solution: they would strike France first. A preemptive attack, however, would require allowing the Germans to march through Belgium, and they hoped the government would turn a blind eye and grant free passage. The Germans would, they added, "feel the deepest regret" if Belgium rejected their proposal. And then for a brief moment, the open hand of brotherhood clenched tightly. "Should Belgium oppose the German troops," the message warned, "Germany will, to her regret, be compelled to consider Belgium as an enemy . . . [and] the relations between the two States must be left to the decision of arms." With that unpleasantness out of the way, the letter concluded on a genial note:

> *The German Government, however, entertains the distinct hope that this eventuality will not occur, and that the Belgian Government will know how to take the necessary measures to prevent the occurrence of incidents such as those mentioned. In this case the friendly ties which bind the two neighboring States will grow stronger and more enduring.*

Belgium had twelve hours to respond. At 9:00 P.M. that same evening, King Albert met with the Council of States and declared emphatically what the country's answer would be—"'No,' whatever the consequences." His military advisers and ministers agreed, and a reply was drafted. Like the German message that prompted it, the letter was not entirely perfunctory. "This note has made a deep and painful impression upon the Belgian Government," it began. But nor was it timid.

> *The Belgian Government, if it were to accept the proposals submitted, would sacrifice the honor of the nation and betray its duty towards Europe. . . . [The] Belgian Government is firmly resolved to repel, by all the means in its power, every attack upon its rights.*

The Germans were incredulous. Belgium had no formidable army to speak of, and to confront German troops would merely incur their wrath, inevitably costing innumerable Belgian lives while accomplishing little more than temporarily slowing down the German advance. Belgium was not, of course, alone in the struggle. Great Britain was bound by treaty to come to its aid, France had been preparing for a confrontation with Germany since their last war ended in 1871, and Russia—a French ally—would be pressing Germany from the east. The growing tensions were all part of a larger drama unfolding throughout the region. On June 28, 1914, just over a month before Germany's appeal to Belgium, a nineteen-year-old Bosnian Serb named Gavrilo Princip had shot Archduke Franz Ferdinand, the heir to the Austro-Hungarian empire. When Austria-Hungary threatened Serbia because of Ferdinand's assassination, the Russians vowed to protect their fellow Slavs, with a larger aim of expanding their influence over the Balkans. Germany, an ally of Austria-Hungary, declared war on Russia. With its defiant refusal to let German forces cross its borders, Belgium—along with England—was now drawn irrevocably into the escalating conflict. (The United States would not send troops for almost another three years.) True to their word, and less than a day after their ultimatum was rejected, German forces bore down on their tiny neighbor, clashing with outnumbered Belgian soldiers and terrorizing civilians in every town and village they trespassed en route to France. The burning of Louvain on August 25, 1914, and its world-renowned library, with almost a quarter of a million volumes and 750 medieval manuscripts, provoked international outrage. A Paraguayan priest named Manuel Gamarra, who was studying in Louvain, wrote to the Belgian Minister in Buenos Aires:

> *The burning began at half-past seven in the evening of the 25th August. Whilst the town was burning on all sides the Germans shot the unfortunate people as they fled from their burning houses. It was a night of unimaginable horror. . . . At Héront, five kilometres from Louvain, I saw in a corner of the wall the body of a little girl of 12 or 13 years of age burned alive.*

But for each accusation, the German military, from Kaiser Wilhelm II on down, responded that their troops were fired on first or that every Belgian was a potential franc-tireur—*a guerilla fighter—and needed to be dealt with mercilessly. (Thousands of the Belgians killed by the Germans in the opening days of the war were indeed soldiers, but many were also women, priests, and children.) The Kaiser even sent a telegram to President Woodrow Wilson lamenting the destruction of Belgium, but blaming it on the resistance of its "bloodthirsty" citizens. German propaganda pervaded deep into its own population. Afraid for the safety of his brother, a soldier marching into Belgium, a young German named "Willi" sent him the following advice. (A "Lazaretto" is a hospital that cares primarily for patients with contagious diseases.)*

Schleswig, 25.8.14.

Dear Brother,

I lately obtained your address through Frederick, and I trust that you will receive the present letter in good time before your regiment leaves for Brussels. No doubt should you have already started my letter will be forwarded.

As you know I am attached to the Lazaretto here and I shall remain here for a long time yet, perhaps altogether, although I should much like to go with a field ambulance, as an Inspector of ambulances. But I shall certainly remain here until the middle of September.

You will shortly go to Brussels with your regiment as you know. Take care to protect yourself against these Civilians, especially in the villages. Do not let anyone of them come near you. Fire without pity on every one of them who comes too near. They are very clever, cunning fellows these Belgians, even the women and children are armed and fire their guns. Never go inside a house, especially alone. If you take anything to drink make the inhabitants drink first, and keep at distance from them.

The newspapers related numerous cases in which they have fired on our soldiers whilst they were drinking. You soldiers must spread around so much fear of yourselves that no civilian will venture to come near you. Remain always in the company of others. I hope that you have read the newspapers and that you know how to behave. Above all have no compassion for these cut-throats. Make for them without pity with the butt-end of your rifle and the bayonet.

You will have learnt the news of the great victories. When you arrive in Belgium our soldiers would probably have crossed the Franco-Belgian frontier. Keep well. I hope that you will come back to the house in good health. May you prosper. Best greetings.

Your brother,
Willi

In a long, somewhat rambling diatribe to an English friend, the German mother of a soldier (Franz, mentioned in the letter) expressed similar disgust with the British, whom she now considered "vile traitors" for siding against Germany in a war that was spreading swiftly throughout Europe and other regions of the world.

We do not hate and despise the French, for they are in their right when they seek revenge from us, and try to reconquer Alsace and Lorraine; we do not hate the Russians, a poor, misguided people, who are led like sheep to the slaughter without knowing why; but we hate and despise the English who make war against us from mere mercenary reasons; a brother-people, who have been lying and intriguing against us for years, while, to our face, they are making believe friendship, desire for peace, good-will and what not. . . . I, for my part, I have to strike out something in my life; my love and respect and gratitude for the English, amongst whom I've lived and been happy. Never again will I seek their society, as I have done all my life. I shall shun them like dirt and poison. . . . And now, dear Bessie, good-bye. After this, you will not want to have anything to do with me again; and I don't blame you, for I will neither have anything to do again with an English person, if I can help it. Thank you again and again for your life-long friendship, for which I've ever been very, very grateful. If Franz falls, you shall know of it. My existence is terror, fear, anxiety, yet, if I could gain my country's victory by my boy's death, I would sacrifice him ten times over again, and so every woman thinks with me in Germany.

The feelings were mutual; English soldiers who had been fighting in Belgium and France came home with horrifying tales of German cruelty against innocent civilians and Allied soldiers alike. The British were aghast that a so-called civilized nation could commit such acts, especially a country so enamored of its supposedly advanced culture (or Kultur, as the Germans called it). The following letter, believed to have been written by a respected Irish author and scholar named Alice S. Green, articulated the sentiments of many in Great Britain whose contempt for the Germans was absolute. (Regarding several allusions in the letter: Theobald von Bethmann-Hollweg was the German chancellor; the Emden was the German light cruiser SMS Emden, renowned for both its proficiency at sinking Allied ships and its crew's humane treatment of enemy POWs; and Hermann Sudermann, who penned the poem from which Green quotes at the end of the letter, was a noted German playwright and novelist. There is no salutation or signature to the letter, which appears to be a typed transcript of the original.)

I am glad you thought my last letter fair and above racial prejudice. But I don't wish you to think that my small trumpet gives any uncertain sound as regards the German principles of warfare, and principles of conquest. No words would be strong enough, condemnatory enough, to say what I think of those principles; and the seal of "Kultur" with which the Germans seal their atrocities, makes those atrocities worse. The

Frederician tradition that the conqueror must subdue a people by all kinds of horror, torture, and cruelty,—that he must terrify and enslave it into submission,—before he <u>begins</u> to be kind and fatherly to it: it is <u>this</u> tradition and principle that Europe is up against. It is to Germany's eternal disgrace that she has allowed her "Kultur" to be identified with such a system; she will and must reap the reward. I suppose for a century or so, no one outside the Fatherland, will mention "Deutsche Kultur" without a smile! One really can't help smiling a little even now, when each fresh batch of attested horrors, or exactions on little towns already bled white, coincides with some swaggering remark by Bethman-Hollweg or others, about establishing "unsere Kultur" among poor ignorant foreigners. The indictment against the Germans is steadily growing in gravity; it is no question of horrors such as are committed by the scum of every army in every war, even the most civilized. It is something worse than that.

I don't want to speak of the enormous number of atrocities attested by witnesses, and certified by inquiry, that fill the documents of investigation by State authority; you have all, no doubt, seen Lord Bryce's report. But I wish to tell you of things I have heard privately from my relations and friends who are in active service. My own nephew has just been at home on leave from the French trenches for a few days, and came to see me. I hoped he would reassure me about German atrocities, but alas! no. He told me many horrible things which I will not write down. Among other things he told me of an incident which took place in a German trench which he and others afterwards took; he had bomb-throwers (people who carry bombs, grenades, and throw them,— otherwise unarmed), and those men were about to throw their bombs on to the Germans in the German trench, which would have killed them all, of course, when the Germans threw up their hands to capitulate; whereupon our bomb throwers desisted, did not throw, and came quickly forward to take the Germans prisoners; as they approached, several German bomb throwers sprang up from behind, threw their bombs on to our men, and killed nearly all of them. Can you wonder that my boy says, "I don't want to take German prisoners now; I don't believe it when they hold up their hands, nor when they show a flag of truce. You can't trust them."

He told me that when the Germans took some of our men prisoners, they in cold blood, stripped them naked, and then bayoneted them to death. The only comment my nephew made was, "I can't understand Germans, Aunt—; I can't understand a civilized people doing such things."

A friend of his in another regiment after the battle of Mons missed his sergeant, and went to look for him; he found him inside a farm-house, dying crucified against a wall with a nail through each hand. He was told of half a dozen Highland soldiers who were going through a ruined Belgian village at dusk; they saw a child looking out from a cottage window; they saw that there was something queer about the child; it was so stiff and still, with its arms stretched out; they went into the cottage and found the child was dead; it had been impaled and stuck up in the window to terrorize the inhabitants, I suppose. On the floor lay the dead naked body of the mother, mutilated. These Highland soldiers were so moved, that they stood in a ring around the body of the dead woman, clasped hands across it, and swore to each other never to take a German prisoner.

A Belgian lady to whom I talked, replying to some one who said, "The Germans may come here," said excitedly, "If the Germans came to this town, I would fly and go anywhere to escape from them; they are terrible." Her hostess was present and tried (I tried too) to reassure her, we saying, "Oh, no, you would stay with us; it would be unsafe to fly; you would suffer for want of food and shelter; you might die of starvation." She answered, "I would risk all that; I would leave you and go into the wilds of Wales, anywhere, anywhere, if I heard the Germans were coming." Why did she speak so? Because she had experienced a German occupation.

The brother of my chief friend here, who is just home from France on a few days leave, says that English reprisals on the things that the Germans do would be impossible,—that when he marches his troops through villages where the Germans have been, the sights are such in the houses (mutilation of the bodies of helpless victims, etc) that his roughest and coarsest Tommies are revolted. He says the Germans set fire to all churches,—that he has been through villages with all the churches blazing. He says English instructions are a great contrast; they are not allowed to set fire to a church; they do not do so, even if the church is being used by an enemy.

These things I have written down have come directly to my knowledge; you could multiply them a thousand times by interviews with English or French soldiers, or with Belgians throughout the country. The cruelty has been systematic, organised cruelty and ruthlessness, not accidental. I consider that the Kaiser is unfitted for his post; in war time he cannot control his impulsiveness, which in peace time is part of his charm. When just before Mons, in a moment of tense excitement among his soldiers, they listened for a message from their Emperor, and received a vindictive message from the Kaiser that they must "annihilate the English miserable little army"; when he said this and other foolish things, he did not mean "crucify the prisoners". No doubt he would regret that this was done, but the fact that he was so careless and heedless and given over to the fierce impulse of the moment, or knew his men so little as not to know that the effect of vindictive messages from their Kaiser would be to make the coarsest of them wreck tortures on helpless prisoners,—this quality of ignorance of his subjects on the part of the Emperor has repeatedly shown him unfitted for his post as war-lord. How different the really great leaders are! Such as Nelson, who in a moment of equal excitement, said, "England expects every man to do his duty." I think the German officers are worse than the soldiers, especially the Colonels, who could have stopped the cruelties and murdering.

Now I must end, and I don't wish to moralize or comment, but if the Germans had fought on other and nobler principles, how we should all have admired them. Especially we English, who are so ready to admire an enemy. (We lavished so much praise on the Captain of the Emden, that the Germans thought we couldn't mean it). Do you remember what Sir Philip Sidney called France years ago: "that sweet enemy"? We cannot call Germany that.

What do you think that all this Deutsche Kultur amounts to? I think it amounts to a great power of scientific organisation. But one of its worst sides is, that it enslaves its subjects to such an extent that they obey orders to do evil as readily as they obey orders to do good. "Obedience may be a spiritual virtue, but only if you still keep a will beyond the will to obey. The vice of the German obedience and its terrible power is that there is no will in it beyond the will to obey." In any case Deutsche Kultur can never attain to civilisation; it is too cramped, too caged, by the irons of its own making. If we want justice and refinement in its truest sense, we must look for those things where they grow. We look in vain for them inside the fence of Deutsche Kultur. Did you see Sudermann's Hymn? That wonderful poet of better things!

> O God, I pray
> That the Briton
> Like Judas perish.
> Let mine eyes see him
> Before I die,
> Grey in a hempen ring
> Dangling from on high.
> And as he swings

Let him descry
The German eagle
Wheeling in the sky.

In more than four years of fighting, approximately eight to ten million troops were killed in World War I. Estimates of civilian deaths vary widely, from the low millions to numbers that exceed military fatalities. Some historians suggest as well that since the increased poverty and deprivation caused by the war hastened the spread of the influenza virus near the end of the conflict, the tens of millions who died in the 1918 to 1919 pandemic should also be considered casualties of World War I.

—⁓—

An American Missionary Named James H. McCallum Writes to His Family from Nanking About the Vicious Treatment of Chinese Civilians by Invading Japanese Soldiers

Before the surprise attack on Pearl Harbor, before the brutal invasion of the Philippines and Malaya, before the Bataan Death March and the "hellships" that transported countless Allied POWs to Japan as slave laborers, there was Nanking (now known as Nanjing). After waging a fierce battle to capture Shanghai in November of 1937, an estimated fifty thousand Japanese troops stormed the Chinese capital of Nanking one month later and, with unrestrained savagery, began murdering and raping Chinese civilians until the following March. "It has been just one week now since the collapse of the Chinese Army in its Nanking defense," an American named James Henry McCallum began a letter to his family on December 19.

> *It is a horrible story to relate; I know not where to begin nor to end. Never have I heard or read of such brutality. Rape: Rape: Rape: We estimate at least 1,000 cases a night and many by day. In case of resistance or anything that seems like disapproval there is a bayonet stab or a bullet.*

Contemporaneous journals, photographs, correspondences, and other materials, both private and official, all attest to the enormity of the tragedy, and many of the most detailed firsthand accounts come from the letters by the more than two dozen Western missionaries, like James McCallum, who stayed in the city despite the urgent appeals of their embassies to evacuate immediately. (All of the missionaries would survive. Wilhelmina "Minnie" Vautrin, however, would take her own life a year to the day after she left Nanking to return to America. Many believe her suicide was caused by the trauma of having witnessed the massacre.) The missionaries put their own lives at grave risk, sometimes literally placing themselves between drunken, belligerent Japanese soldiers and trembling Chinese citizens. They also helped to create a Safety Zone within the city that offered some protection for residents who had no other means of escape. James McCallum, a forty-four-year-old American missionary working in Nanking, sent the following to his family, who were living in Kuling, China. (Please note: the letter, which does not have a salutation and ends abruptly, contains graphic descriptions of civilian deaths that might be unsettling for some readers.)

Have been so busy every day and five nights of the week that I've had no time to write. A foreigner must be on duty 24 hours here at the hospital in order to deal with the Japanese visitors. It is snowing and bitterly cold; our hearts ache for the thousands who have poor shelter and who are cooped up in such close quarters. Our hospital is full and the lighter cases fill the University Dormitory building. Some we cannot dismiss for they have no place to go. Have had fifteen or twenty babies within the last week; six on Christmas Day. It is easy to find Miss Hynds; she is always in the nursery mothering the whole crowd of babies.

Thought of you all on Christmas Day and hoped it was a happy time for you. We presumed you were still in Kuling. The rumors are reaching us that Kuling may be evacuated. We have been completely out of touch with the rest of the world. No one can get into Nanking and it seems very difficult to get out. We have talked of sending some one of our group out to carry the news of the terrible things that have been and still are happening here, but know that person would never get back if he once left.

I have been living with Mills, Fitch, Smythe, Sone, Wilson, Bates, and Riggs here in the Buck house. All of us have been doing double duty. We scarcely sit down to our meals without someone coming in every other five minutes or so to call for help. Food is swallowed whole and hurried exits are made to save a truck from being stolen or more often to protect women from soldiers. Seldom do we all sit down to eat at the same time. We dare not go out alone after dark but go in twos or threes.

Every day or two I have gone out for an inspection of our mission property. I have found visitors in our house at Peh Hsia Rd. Every time I have gone there. Every foreign house is a sight to behold; untouched until the Japanese army arrived, nothing untouched since. Every lock has been broken; every trunk ransacked. Their search for money and valuables has led them to the flues and inside pianos.

Our phonograph records are all broken; the dishes are in a broken mess on the floor along with everything else that was discarded after each

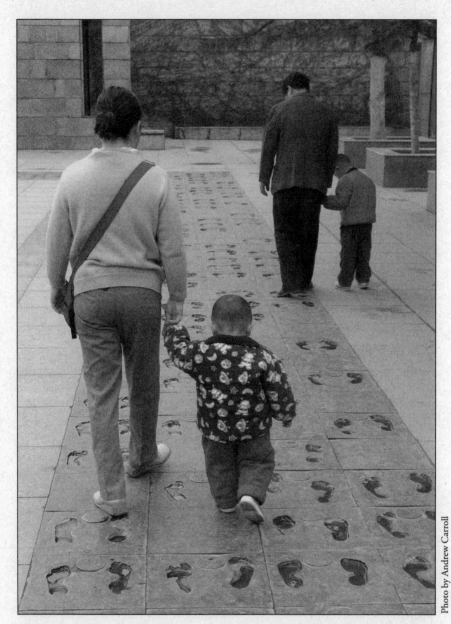

A Chinese mother walks with her young son down the Copperplate Passage of Footprints at the Nanjing Memorial. The 222 footprints represent, according to a nearby plaque with both Chinese and English text, the "eyewitnesses of the Nanjing Massacre, in which some 300,000 innocent people were killed."

looting. The front of the piano was removed and all the hammers struck with something heavy. Our house being outside the Safety Zone, this was not to be unexpected but houses within the Zone have shared a like fate. Two of our boys' school buildings were set fire to, one a complete loss. Nanking presents a dismal appearance. At the time the Japanese Army entered the city little harm had been done to buildings. Since then the stores have been stripped of their wares and most of them burned. Taiping, Chung Hwa and practically every other main business road in the city is a mass of ruins. In south city much of the area back of the main street was also burned. We see new fires every day and wonder when such beastly destruction will cease.

But far worse is what has been happening to the people. They have been in terror and no wonder. Many of them have nothing left now but a single garment around their shoulders. Helpless and unarmed, they have been at the mercy of the soldiers, who have been permitted to roam about at will wherever they pleased. There is no discipline whatever and many of them are drunk. By day they go into the buildings in our Safety Zone centers, looking for desireable women, then at night they return to get them. If they have been hidden away, the responsible men are bayonetted on the spot. Girls of 11 and 12 and women of fifty have not escaped. Resistance is fatal. The worst cases come to the hospital. A woman six months pregnant, who resisted, came to us with 16 knife wounds in her face and body, one piercing the abdomen. She lost her baby but her life will be spared. Men who gave themselves up to the mercy of the Japanese when they were promised their lives would be spared,—a very few of them returned to the Safety Zone in a sad way. One of them declared they were used for bayonet practice and his body certainly looked it. Another group was taken out near Ku-ling Sz; one who somehow returned, lived long enough to tell the fate of that group. He claimed they threw gasoline over their heads, and then set fire to them. This man bore no other wounds but was burned so terribly around the neck and head that one could scarcely believe he was a human being. The same day another, whose body had been half burned over, came into the hospital. He had also been shot. It is altogether likely that the bunch of them had been machine-gunned, their bodies then piled together and then burned. We could not get the details, but he evidently crawled out and managed to get to the hospital for help. Both of these died. And so I could relate such horrible stories that you would have no appetite for days. It is absolutely unbelievable but thousands have been butchered in cold blood—how many it is hard to guess— some believe it would approach the 10,000 mark.

We have met some very pleasant Japanese who have treated us with courtesy and respect. Others have been very fierce and threatened us, striking or slapping some. Mr. Riggs has suffered most at their hands. Occasionally have I seen a Japanese helping some Chinese or pick up a Chinese baby and play with it. More than one Japanese soldier told me he did not like war and wished he were back home. Altho' the Japanese Embassy staff has been cordial and tried to help us out, they have been helpless. But soldiers with a conscience are few and far between.

Now it is time to make the rounds of the hospital. There are a hundred on the staff. When we have water and lights again it will be much easier, for the lamps to look after and water to pump each day increases our labour considerably.

Many ultra-nationalist Japanese politicians and their supporters still strenuously deny that widespread atrocities and killings occurred in Nanking, insisting that the numbers have been exaggerated by China and the United States, allies in World War II, to justify the use of atomic weapons against Japan in 1945. The Chinese—and most historians, American and otherwise—have well documented that an estimated two hundred to three hundred thousand innocent people were butchered and tens of thousands of women were raped. The issue remains a source of tension between China and Japan to this day.

—〜〜—

**The Parents of Beryl Myatt Send Their Daughter
a Cheerful Letter as She Begins Her "Big Adventure" to Canada
(and Away from German Air Raids on England)
&
Elizabeth P. Hudson Reports to Her Parents in South Africa
the Courage and Resolve of Her Fellow Londoners After Months
of Bombings
&
Hans Schröter Informs the Daughter of His Neighbors How His Family
and Her Parents Died in One of the Worst Air Attacks on Germany
&
After Almost Five Months as a POW, an American Soldier Writes
to His Father About Being Imprisoned by the Germans
and Surviving the Firebombing of Dresden**

"Dear Mummy & Daddy how are you getting on[?]," six-year-old Leila Rothstein wrote to her parents on March 24, 1941, from the English countryside. Rothstein had exciting and undoubtedly surprising news for her parents:

I have got a husband and his name is Keneth Farrow, when I come home do you think There will be any room for my ~~hub~~ husband, Please send me a scarf because it is verry cold. Pamala Portuies has moved because she was unhappy. my birthday is the same day as my husband's brother's birthday, his name is Ronny. When I am reddy to marry kenneth he'll be 27 and I will be twenty. Kenneth is a nice looking boy love to all Leila

Rothstein was one of millions of children temporarily evacuated from England's major cities during World War II to safeguard them from incessant bombing campaigns by the German Luftwaffe. (Rothstein would survive the war and, later in life, get married—but not to Kenneth Farrow.) Two days after the German invasion of Poland, Great Britain and France declared war on Germany, and Prime Minister Winston Churchill repeatedly warned the British people that a massive bombardment of their country was imminent. On May 19, 1940, in his first speech as prime minister, Churchill sought both to embolden the French—already being hammered by the Germans—and to prepare his own countrymen for the adversity to come. "This is one of the most awe-striking periods in the long history of France and Britain," Churchill stated.

> Side by side, the British and French peoples have advanced to rescue not only Europe but mankind from the foulest and most soul-destroying tyranny which has ever darkened and stained the pages of history. Behind them—behind us—behind the armies and fleets of Britain and France— gather a group of shattered States and bludgeoned races: the Czechs, the Poles, the Norwegians, the Danes, the Dutch, the Belgians—upon all of whom the long night of barbarism will descend, unbroken even by a star of hope, unless we conquer, as conquer we must; as conquer we shall.

France surrendered a month later. Relishing the opportunity to humiliate the French as he believed his own country had been more than twenty-one years earlier at the end of World War I, Adolf Hitler ordered the June 22 armistice-signing to take place in the very railcar in which Germany had capitulated on November 11, 1918. Operation Eagle, the Luftwaffe's effort to dominate the skies of Great Britain, commenced less than three weeks later, on July 10, and would last for almost four harrowing months. Although vastly outnumbered, the tireless Royal Air Force pilots—with a little help from the recently developed radar system—thrashed the Luftwaffe, preventing them from gaining air supremacy and, it is believed, ultimately staving off a full-scale ground invasion of England. (Questions remain as to whether Hitler ever intended to carry out such an operation, which the Germans had code-named Sea Lion, or was merely engaging in one of the greatest bluffs of the war. Regardless, had the Luftwaffe gained control of the British skies, the Allied cause in Europe would have sustained a crippling, if not fatal, blow.) The RAF could not stop all air raids, however, and on September 7, 1940, Hitler ordered major residential areas to be pounded almost without interruption for nearly two months. Tens of thousands of British men, women, and children were blown up or burned to death in the ensuing fires during what would become known as the Blitz, the German word for lightning. (Aerial attacks would continue throughout the war but dropped off significantly after the Germans invaded the Soviet Union in June 1941 and concentrated their forces in the east.) Many parents feared that their children would be casualties of such a widespread assault, even outside of the cities, and they felt the safest course of action was to send their children to Allied countries far from danger. For the parents of Beryl Myatt, relief came just two days after the Blitz began. "I have to inform you that your child, _Beryl Myatt,_ has been accepted for the evacuation overseas," began the September 9, 1940, letter to Myatt's parents from a local government official. Their young daughter would be allowed entry into Canada, where she would stay with relatives, and Mr. and Mrs. Thomas Myatt were instructed to arrange for her departure immediately. (A variety of obstacles, including immigration quotas, prevented entire families from joining their children.) The confidential letter continued:

> I have enclosed two labels for your child's luggage and a tie on label which should be fixed on an outer garment. . . . She should carry a sufficient supply of food and thirst quenching fruit to last 12 hours. No bottles should be carried. No chocolate should be included. It will be appreciated that it is the utmost importance in the interests of the children that the least possible publicity should be given to the port of embarkation and commencing date of the voyage.

It was an excruciating decision for the Myatts—or any parents—to make, but one with the best interests of their daughter in mind. Hoping to keep her spirits high through what would undoubtedly be a difficult separation for a young child, Myatt's mother and father sent her enthusiastic letters about the new home she would soon be visiting and emphasized how much they loved her. But their daughter would never receive the letters; Beryl Myatt and almost three hundred other passengers (including more than eighty children) on the SS City of Benares perished in the waters of the Atlantic six hundred miles from land after being torpedoed by a German U-boat. On September 21, Mr. and Mrs. Myatt wrote the following letter to their nine-year-old daughter, unaware that she was already dead.

Our Dearest Beryl,

This is our second letter to you since you, set out on your big adventure Dear, and we suppose you were very surprised when you arrived at Auntie Emmies to find a letter and your Dandy and Sunny Stories waiting there for you. We will send them each week.

We expect that you enjoyed your voyage on the boat across the wide Atlantic Ocean, and your long journey on the train to Winnipeg. We don't suppose you saw any icebergs during your voyage across, as it would hardly be quite cold enough at this time of year. How would you like to be a nurse on a big Ocean Liner when you grow up Dear?

Now, sweetheart, don't forget what we told you. We want you to let auntie and uncle see that you can be a great help to them about the house by helping to the best of your ability, such as running errands, & helping auntie with her housework and her baking, and above all dear, keep your bedroom tidy and always hang your clothes up in their right place, and this will show Auntie and uncle that you really appreciate the opportunity they have given you to have a grand holiday in one of the most interesting countries in the World—CANADA—the home of the Maple Leaf. You haven't forgotten, have you, "The Maple Leaf for Canada, The Rose for England, The Leek for Wales, The Thistle for Scotland, and the Shamrock for Ireland."

You remember the photograph you had taken at Christchurch School, Killburn—well, Mummy wants to know if you would like us to send it on to you. Let us know Dear, will you?

How are Pat and Sue. We hope they are O.K. and that they were not seasick or in any way upset by their journey.

The weather here is still fairly nice—what kind of weather are you having?

Well Dear, please give our Love to auntie & uncle & when you write you must tell us all about what you are doing.

Everybody at home sends their Love. Must close now with Tons of Love and Heaps of Kisses. God Bless You.Mummy & Daddy.
XXXXXXXXXXXXXXXXXXXXXXXXXXXXX

Far from regretting the "collateral damage"—as civilian deaths resulting from military actions are euphemistically called—their troops were causing, the German high command welcomed these casualties as integral to their overall strategy. "The Fuerher declared that he would repeat these raids night after night until the English were sick and tired of terror attacks. He shares my opinion absolutely that cultural centers, bathing resorts, and civilian cities must be attacked now; there the psychological effect is much stronger," Joseph Goebbels, Adolf Hitler's diminutive, almost skeletal minister of propaganda, wrote in his personal diary. He added:

> *The English, I suppose, will have occasion to be surprised when this undertaking is launched on a big scale. There is no other way of bringing the English to their senses. They belong to a class of human beings with whom you can talk only after you have first knocked out their teeth.*

The bombings, however, would have the opposite effect. Despite the relentless explosions, fires, blackouts, and food shortages, the English civilians—especially those who did not have country homes to escape to and slept in subways ("tubes") and makeshift bomb shelters—demonstrated extraordinary grit and perseverance. Elizabeth Pritchard Hudson, a South African woman residing in London, was awed by the resilience she encountered throughout the city. On May 1, 1941, she sent the following to her parents in South Africa. (Hudson frequently used "wd." for "would," and the "[?]" and other parenthetical additions in the text are her own. Jan Smuts, whom Hudson refers to, was a prominent South African statesman. The account below represents the bulk of a two-part letter, and there is no signature for the first section, which is printed here in its entirety.)

My darlings,

  <u>More</u> letters from home today, one from each of you. This has been a rich week for mail. They were both written in March, Dad's on the 17th & Mom's on the 26th & talked about such recent things that they sounded quite normal. It was delicious. The box you are sending me is causing an anticipatory stir in our house, you know I have always enjoyed food—well everyone is as bad as I am now—in fact it has quite replaced the weather as the Englishman's topic of conversation. You overhear at bus-stops & in tube trains snippets such as: "Have you tried the new eggless cake made with honey instead of sugar & oil instead of butter?"—to which the reply is: "Well, my children eat my honey ration & my grocer can't get any oil"—or house-wives exchanging gossip about the latest discovery on the kitchen front (I believe they all enjoy it enormously)—instead of the old: "Unusual weather for the time of year, isn't it?" To which the reply should be: "Yes, it always is." I have never before heard so many people, or been myself so thankful for this country's climate: it rains (as tonight) & you say: "Thank God, there won't be a big blitz." It wd. be hell at home with those long, lovely, clear nights. Fog means no siren at all & even very great cold & frost, & of course wind, will keep them away.

I have just come back from Potten End today leaving Harley & Little Wilf in fine health & spirits in spite of our second evacuation. Winston's recent speech cheered everyone up about it, he is a wonderful old man to make such a heartening tirade out of such unpromising material, isn't he. I imagined you listening to him just before going to bed as we were doing at 9 o'clock. We also listened to Smuts, who went down very well too.

You both keep saying things about the air-blitz being such an ordeal. Well, it sometimes is, but you know these things sound much worse than they are. I am continually thankful that I don't have to sit & listen to reports of raids on you, & see pictures which show only damage & fire & leave out (naturally) the masses of untouched houses. I think you are the brave ones to write so cheerfully & sweetly. I am sure I should get querillous (?) & nerve-shattered in no time. Things happen to people & unthinkably horrid they are, but it is roughly localized & very seldom are there more casualties than there are from ordinary road-accidents. That is how you must think of it—for a shorter period the danger is greater—there is no danger, so to speak, of being run over in the day time. Proportionately blitz-life is only as dangerous to us as this world of motors <u>wd.</u> have seemed to are great-grandfathers. A motor accident seems horrid when you're there but there are such millions of people who don't have them. Remembering this perhaps you can bear to read the report of a taxi driver given at our post police station. I think it is most wonderfully typical of the Cockney at his laconically matter-of-fact best, & shows how simply & unmelodramatically they take these things—comically so, & I don't think it's callous to find comedy in the tragedies because we have adjusted our minds to the fact that the tragedies do happen we accept them & look at them in the same light as we do the rest of life. Thank God for the adaptability of the human mind, for to continue to be overwhelmed by (or even to allow oneself to examine) each horror would most certainly lead to insanity. If you continued to think of each motor accident as a ghastly & horrible thing you wd. soon be a nervous wreck.

Well, our Wardens have not yet traced the body of Dr. Snaith's house-keeper. Everyone else has been accounted for in our area. Because of this, our rescue-squad is compelled to continue digging in the wreckage of Ebury Street, where she lived, until they are sure she is not there. It is over two weeks now since the bomb fell there & it wd. be a waste of time to go on digging if she wasn't there, so we are trying every ally to trace her body somewhere else. We found one unidentified one in the street, but the Doctor, her employer, cannot definitely say this is ~~her~~ she. One

Warden heard a taxi-driver mentioned in a conversation & traced him up to Kennington, near Fulham, & brought him here to be questioned. I will now copy for you the report he wrote:—

"Statement taken from John H. Davies (No.1116) taken at Gerald Rd. April 26th 1941. 20.00hrs. On the morning of the 16/17 April between 12:00 & 12.15 hrs. my cab was stationary at the corner of Eaton Terrace & Chester Row. I was preparing to change a wheel. (This was in the midst of fire & brimstone hailing all round him) This necessitated me going into the back of my cab to get the jack out. At the precise moment of lifting the back seat the explosion of the bomb took place, throwing me out into the middle of the road. Recovering, I decided to carry on changing the tyre & did so. (!!!) I then replaced my tools carelessly (!!!!) into the back of the cab, having decided to take my cab home (he means instead of going on cruising about for passengers as he had been doing; God knows who he expected to find hailing a taxi at that hour in the hell that was going on, but, as you will see, he found the only passenger he might have expected)! On stepping forward towards the Driver's seat, my right foot came in contact with human remains. I then proceeded home to Kennington to my garage, which had been bombed & was burning at the time. I then looked into the back of the cab with more care & discovered the pelvis section of a human body I then decided to go home feeling rather exhausted (this is beyond comment). The following day I reported the matter to the district Inspector Fury, Kennington Lane Police Station. The section was taken to the mortuary in Kennington & there I was told the matter ended. Hanging on to the rear no. plate were the light under-clothing usually worn by an elderly person (female). Signed by John M. Davis, we believe that this "section," as he calls it, is part of another "section" found in the bombed street because his cab was just outside the street, & that the two together make Dr. Snaith's house-keeper, if we can prove this we can stop digging. She might easily have been blasted into his cab as he was blasted out (that he is alive is a miracle & he must have been badly wounded in spite of the fact that he continued to look after his cab & his livlihood instead of dashing to the nearest shelter as one might expect) because blast does the most extraordinary things, such as killing many people by the impact & force of air in the stomach, through the mouth, without doing them any visible damage except that it <u>always</u> removes their shoes. One doctor was blown out of his bed-room, with his bed, right out of his house, over the next row of houses & into the gardens beyond. It sounds fantastic but is quite true because he was seen, in that bed, a couple of hours earlier by his maid, & the next morning was found quite near it in the gardens. Blast can also shred a pair of curtains to ribbons & leave them hanging. It is unpredictable & uncanny.

Darlings, I hope these things will not sicken you. I don't know whether being at a distance from them will make you more or less sensitive about it. Having had my bad shock & recuperated I can & must now find them interesting. If you don't, just forget it as you forget the motor accidents. Or regard it as impersonally as one does a murder story. The memorable thing is the impeturability of that taxi-driver. Needless to say that story is not for publication & I'm not even sure whether I ought to send it to you. Our log-book will make some reading after the war!

As enemy warplanes killed their people and destroyed their towns and cities, the British did not merely stay on the defensive. Much to the surprise of Air Marshal Hermann Goering, who had assured Hitler that the British were not capable of infiltrating so deeply into their territory, the RAF bombed Berlin in late August 1940. Two and a half months later, they hit Munich, the birthplace of the Nazi Party. On November 14, Hitler retaliated by ordering Operation Moonlight Sonata, a ferocious nighttime raid on Coventry. Wave after wave of German planes, nearly five hundred in all, swarmed over the city, dropping bombs and incendiaries specifically orchestrated to ignite a firestorm. The barrage would continue without pause for almost eleven hours. The RAF struck back—and hard, attacking Hamburg, Cologne, Hanover, and Berlin multiple times. Their most devastating and, indeed, controversial raid came near the end of the war. Churchill would deny that the firebombing of Dresden was revenge for Coventry (which suffered more than forty raids in all) or any other British city, but for Air Marshal Sir Arthur Harris, vengeance was justification enough:

> *The Nazis entered this war under the rather childish delusion that they were going to bomb everyone else, and nobody was going to bomb them. At Rotterdam, London, Warsaw, and half a dozen other places, they put their rather naïve theory into operation. They sowed the wind, and now they are going to reap the whirlwind.*

The whirlwind descended on Dresden the night of February 13, 1945, less than three months before the war was over, and lasted for fifteen hours. Emulating the attack on Coventry, British and American warplanes carpeted the city with thousands of tons of high explosives and incendiary bombs, and Dresden—a pearl of architectural beauty—was soon engulfed in an ocean of fire. Residents of the city, including countless refugees, were burned alive, crushed by falling debris, killed by shrapnel, or suffocated in a thick, all-encompassing shroud of smoke. Some who sought relief from the scorching heat in water fountains were boiled alive. (Approximately one hundred to two hundred thousand people were initially believed to have died in the attack, and the name Dresden has since become synonymous with the wartime slaughter of innocent civilians. Recent scholarship, however, based on newly released British and German documents, argues that Dresden was a legitimate military target and the estimated number of casualties has been wildly inflated, with twenty-five to forty thousand fatalities being a more realistic count. A final consensus is unlikely ever to be achieved.) In the following letter to a female acquaintance whose mother and father were killed in the attack, a native of Dresden named Hans Schröter described in obvious despair how her parents and his own family members had died. (The "20th of July" refers to the failed assassination attempt in 1944 on Adolf Hitler led by Colonel Claus von Stauffenberg and other high-ranking members of the German military.)

August 5, 1945

Dear Mrs. Ganze,

I only just received your letter with its sad contents—my belated, heartfelt sympathy to you. But so many are experiencing the same. Fate's turn was the worst for me. I don't have any interest in living longer. I stand completely alone in a miserable world—no purpose or sense anymore—because what is there to work for? I have had to sacrifice my family and seven friends to Hitler's crazy idea. If only the 20th of July had been successful! But you are happy—you still have your husband, your child, your home—I wish you the best from all of my heart, but now I want to describe the events on February 13th and 14th to you. It was terrible and I will never forget it for the rest of my life.

Saturday evenings and Sundays, I was at Marienstraße 38–42. This brings up powerful memories of my loved ones—hopefully, I will be taken soon—all I am lacking is opium. I will tell you the story: we were all in the cellar, we in 38, your parents with Eulitz in 42, had all survived two attacks successfully and thought we would live through this one. But that would unfortunately not be the case. With the second attack, the door of #38 was destroyed, so that only the emergency exit for 40 and 42 was left. As we got to #40, the flames from the stairwell hit us in the face, so to save our lives we had to move quickly. Everyone acted very calmly. The electric lighting failed, but we had flashlights and petroleum lamps at hand. To get through the exit required great courage, which many could not seem to muster, and perhaps this was the case with your parents. They thought, perhaps, we would survive in the cellar, but they didn't factor in running out of oxygen. When I ran out, I saw my wife and son standing in Marienstraße 42 so helplessly, but I had an older aunt from Liegnitz, and I wanted to save her, so I said to my wife, I'll be back in 2 minutes. But when we came back in just that amount of time, my loved ones had disappeared, and I searched for them in the cellar, on the street—they were nowhere to be found. Everything was in flames, and it was almost impossible to go anywhere. Since I couldn't find my family, I summoned once more the little bit of courage that I had and went over to the Bismarck memorial and waited an hour across from the little house until the roof caved in. Then I went 30 meters along the Ringstraße and waited there until daylight, and everything that you saw was so grotesque that you can hardly describe it, everything was covered with burned corpses.

I went with great haste to my home and office, hoping to find my loves still living, but that didn't happen. They lay on the street in front of house 38, so peaceful, as if they slept. You can imagine what I was going through. At that point, I determined to go where my in-laws and close friends were and help them get out of the cellars. For this, I summoned two men from the Wehrmacht since none of my associates were there. When we opened the emergency exit to #38, such a tremendous heat came out that it was impossible to go inside. So we went in the entrance to #40, through the bathroom, and down into its cellar to get to #42. The cellar in #42 was full of corpses. I counted 50 of them. Eulitz was there, but I couldn't recognize your parents since everyone was on top of each other. Just seeing it was terrible.

Afterwards, I described everything to the local commando in the Leskästen on the street. Then I got sick with a respiratory infection and couldn't be present at the burials, so I cannot write to you about what happened there. One more thing remains to tell you. The cellar stairs of #42 had caved in, so the people couldn't get out. I am certain you can imagine for yourselves how gruesome this was. I greet you and your family,

Yours,
Hans Schröter

Ironically, a group of US prisoners of war being detained in Dresden lived through the firestorm virtually unscathed. When the air raid sirens began to blare, the Americans and a handful of German guards were hurried into a giant meat locker underneath a Schlachthof (slaughterhouse), which protected them first from the bombs and then from the raging inferno above. One of these prisoners, a twenty-two-year-old army private first class from Indianapolis, sent the following letter to his father back in Indiana chronicling his time as a POW.

Dear people:

I'm told that you were probably never informed that I was anything other than "missing in action." Chances are that you also failed to receive any of the letters I wrote from Germany. That leaves me a lot of explaining to do—in precis:

I've been a prisoner of war since December 19th, 1944, when our division was cut to ribbons by Hitler's last desperate thrust through Luxemburg and Belgium. Seven Fanatical Panzer Divisions hit us and cut us off from the rest of Hodges' First Army. The other American Divisions on our flanks managed to pull out: We were obliged to stay and fight. Bayonets aren't much good against tanks: Our ammunition, food and medical supplies gave out and our casualties out-numbered those who could still fight—so we gave up. The 106th got a Presidential Citation and some British Decoration from Montgomery for it, I'm told, but I'll be damned if it was worth it. I was one of the few who weren't wounded. For that much thank God.

Well, the supermen marched us, without food, water or sleep to Limberg, a distance of about sixty miles, I think, where we were loaded and locked up, sixty men to each small, unventilated, unheated box car. There were no sanitary accommodations—the floors were covered with fresh cow dung. There wasn't room for all of us to lie down. Half slept while the other half stood. We spent several days, including Christmas, on that Limberg siding. On Christmas eve the Royal Air Force bombed and strafed our unmarked train. They killed about one-hundred-and-fifty of us. We got a little water Christmas Day and moved slowly across Germany to a large P.O.W. Camp in Muhlburg, South of Berlin. We were released from the box cars on New Year's Day. The Germans herded us through scalding delousing showers. Many men died from shock in the showers after ten days of starvation, thirst and exposure. I didn't.

Under the Geneva Convention, Officers and Non-commissioned Officers are not obliged to work when taken prisoner. I am, as you know, a Private. One-hundred-and-fifty such minor beings were shipped to a Dresden work camp on January 10th. I was their leader by virtue of the little German I spoke. It was our misfortune to have sadistic and fanatical guards. We were refused medical attention and clothing: We were given long hours at extremely hard labor. Our food ration was two-hundred-and-fifty grams of black bread and one pint of unseasoned potato soup each day. After desperately trying to improve our situation for two months and having been met with bland smiles I told the guards just what I was going to do to them when the Russians came. They beat me up a little. I was fired as group leader. Beatings were very small time:—one boy starved to death and the SS Troops shot two for stealing food.

On about February 14th the Americans came over, followed by the R.A.F. their combined labors killed 250,000 people in twenty-four hours and destroyed all of Dresden—possibly the world's most beautiful city. But not me.

After that we were put to work carrying corpses from Air-Raid shelters; women, children, old men; dead from concussion, fire or suffocation. Civilians cursed us and threw rocks as we carried bodies to huge funeral pyres in the city.

When General Patton took Leipzig we were evacuated on foot to Hellendorf on the Saxony-Czechoslovakian border. There we remained until the war ended. Our guards deserted us. On that happy day the Russians were intent on mopping up isolated outlaw resistance in our sector. Their planes (P-39's) strafed and bombed us, killing fourteen, but not me.

Eight of us stole a team and wagon. We traveled and looted our way through Sudetenland and Saxony for eight days, living like kings. The Russians are crazy about Americans. The Russians picked us up in Dresden. We rode from there to the American lines at Halle in Lend-Lease Ford trucks. We've since been flown to Le Havre.

Photo by Andrew Carroll

More than sixty years after the bombing of Dresden, Germany, many buildings remain blackened by the firestorm that engulfed the city.

I'm writing from a Red Cross Club in Le Havre P.O.W. Repatriation Camp. I'm being wonderfully well fed and entertained. The state-bound ships are jammed, naturally, so I'll have to be patient. I hope to be home in a month. Once home I'll be given twenty-one days recuperation at Atterbury, about $600 back pay and—get this—sixty (60) days furlough!

I've too damned much to say, the rest will have to wait. I can't receive mail here so don't write.

May 29, 1945

Love,

Kurt Jr.

Kurt Jr. is, in fact, Kurt Vonnegut Jr., who had been captured by the Germans during the Battle of the Bulge and returned to the United States in the summer of 1945. Vonnegut went on to become one of the world's most esteemed and influential writers, and his experience in Dresden inspired the literary classic Slaughterhouse-Five. *Fourteen years after the war, Dresden and Coventry became "sister cities" (also referred to, especially in Europe, as "twin towns") promoting cross-cultural events and exchanges with one another to foster reconciliation and mutual understanding.*

—⁂—

A Doctor Serving with the Polish *Armia Krajowa* Explains to His Fiancée the Grave Challenges They Are Facing but Assures Her That "Warsaw Will Be Free of Germans" & In Letters to Loved Ones, Two Dutch Resisters Reflect on Faith and Forgiveness Before Being Executed & Danae Vagliano, the Mother of a Member of the French Resistance, Recounts to a Family Friend How the Nazis Treated Her Daughter After They Captured Her

Many civilians fought back. Regardless of age, gender, or ability, and lacking military training and stockpiles of weapons, average citizens in nations conquered by Germany and Japan employed both nonviolent and lethal means to destabilize the occupation of their towns and cities. They created underground radio programs to keep morale high and disseminate essential information. They served as spies, providing critical updates to Allied intelligence on enemy troop levels and movements. They cut communication lines, disabled military vehicles, and sabotaged railroads, airfields, and ports. They assassinated high-ranking officials and collaborators. And in some cases, they even launched large-scale, coordinated offensives. After German troops blitzed into Poland on September 1, 1939, Polish citizens battled the highly trained German soldiers throughout the war. Armia Krajowa (the Home Army), also known as AK, was the largest underground resistance army of World War II. Beginning on August 1, 1944, the AK waged a ferocious counterattack against the Germans in what would become known as the "Warsaw Uprising." The AK was led by Polish military officers, but much of the fighting was done by civilians. Tadek J. (his last name is not identifiable) was a twenty-one-year-old medical student who offered his expertise to treat wounded members of the AK—a "crime" punishable by death. In a letter to his fiancée written at the beginning of the Uprising, Tadek conveyed the threats they were facing, but also their sense of determination to counter the Nazi invaders. (Jurek is his younger brother, and PASTA refers to Warsaw's telephone exchange building.)

Dearest Dzidziunia!

I am terribly worried about you, but the fact that your home is on our territory brings me some solace. I tried to reach you three times already, but failed. Once I was forced to turn back as my comrade was shot as we were crossing a street. It is supposedly safer to cross there now, but unfortunately I cannot leave my post at the hospital. I have been made (imagine that) the commander of a military hospital, a small one, which only has 25 beds, but I am the only one here who knows anything about surgery.

The first three days of the Uprising were the most trying for us (that is for me and Jurek, as we failed to reach Zoliborz). Jurek is a member of a detachment assigned to capture the PASTA building.

Don't worry about me, as for the past two days I have not left the hospital and have no need to be close to the front line. Jurek miraculously survived the collapse of a building. Bombs keep falling all around us, but our spirits are high. The horrors I saw are difficult to imagine. There are huge numbers of injured. Only recently have I been able to sleep 4–5 hours a day, which is more than before. In Wola I saw an American airdrop.

The fervor among our soldiers is tremendous. All we need is more weapons, as ammunition is plentiful, and Warsaw will be free of Germans.

I have to end this letter now and go back to my duties.

I kiss you dearly and love you so much

Tadek

Bolstered by the assumption that the Allies would come to their aid, the Poles, outgunned and surrounded on all sides, fought aggressively. But the desperately needed support did not come. Joseph Stalin, intending to dominate Poland for his country's own territorial purposes, wanted the AK and Germans essentially to wipe each other out before his troops marched into the city. Soviet soldiers on the other side of the Vistula River from the Uprising were ordered to stand down, and Stalin refused Prime Minister Churchill's persistent appeals to allow Allied warplanes to refuel in the Soviet Union and provide the Poles with ongoing assistance. (British and American warplanes nevertheless attempted airdrops, but the missions were extremely hazardous and the containers often fell into German hands.) On the ground, the outlook grew bleaker with every passing day. Writing again to Dzidziunia, Tadek was candid about the precariousness of their situation and the scarcity of clothing and other essential supplies.

Dearest Dzidziunia!

I received your letter. It gave me lot of joy. I would like to see you as early as possible. I was planning to visit you tonight (because I am to busy during the day), but never left because an injured soldier who was brought in from Aleje, said that the passage would be to dangerous. I may possibly visit you tonight if I find somebody to fill in for me. I have missed you so much that when I see you I will embrace you like never before. It is peaceful here now, bombing has stopped. Jurek has been assigned to a company protecting the General Staff. They are being fired upon by tanks and grenade launchers. When I was there yesterday, a grenade exploded and injured three soldiers.

We have just received new underwear and socks. I also have a raincoat and one that belonged to a German military policeman. I got hold of it at a hotel on Widok Street. The German was shot in the head and the raincoat was blood stained but the rain washed it down and now it is first-class. The German died on me when I was changing his dressing.

I will try to see you as soon as I can. In the meantime I send you a long and passionate kiss. I love you so much.

Tadek

Without the air or ground support from the Allies the Poles had anticipated, the Warsaw Uprising was crushed with brutal finality sixty-three days after it started, leaving an estimated quarter of a million civilians dead. The AK was, however, successful in killing upwards of one hundred and fifty thousand Wehrmacht and SS soldiers during the war. Tadek and Dzidziunia both survived and married, but Jurek was fatally wounded during the Uprising and, after being rushed to Tadek's hospital, died in his brother's arms. (As Stalin had hoped, Soviet troops swept into Poland the following winter and soundly routed the Germans. Poland would be oppressed by the Soviet Union for more than five decades; the country's first free elections would not be held until 1990.) Although not as organized or extensive as the Polish resistance movement, tens of thousands of Dutch citizens also banded together to undermine the occupation of the Netherlands after the May 10, 1940, German invasion. The German files on individual Dutch resisters condemned to die, which were preserved during and after the war, include copies of their last letters, many of which emphasize the profound sense of religious conviction that influenced their actions. One Dutch resister facing death, Henk (last name unknown), seemed truly at peace in his final moments—even to the point of forgiving his captors. "When you receive this letter, I will not be alive anymore," he began a letter to his father.

> *This evening at 8 o'clock I was informed that I will have to depart this earthly life tomorrow at seven-thirty. Do not be sad, it just has to be. We mortals often cannot understand it and rebel against it, but we have to realize that "God has given, therefore God also has the right to take away". A German priest came to see me tonight and we have talked for several hours. He is a fine man, even if he is someone who belongs to the people of our enemies. Therefore, I ask you as my last wish: do not bear hate, even if that will sometimes be hard for you, and be tolerant. Perhaps he will visit you in a while, receive him hospitably and amicably. That will give me great pleasure. . . . [I]t is regrettable that I will not live to see the peace, as I had always hoped to be able to participate with all my strength and energy in the reconstruction, not only materially but also spiritually. Our real work will not actually begin until after the war. We must take away the hatred between the Nations, because only if that disappears can there truly be peace.*

The details surrounding the sentence of a Dutchman known only as Harmen are unclear, as civilians could be executed for anything from hiding Jews and protecting them from persecution to reading unsanctioned newspapers. When writing from his prison cell to his pastor, Harmen's thoughts seesawed between different emotions as he struggled to maintain his faith through an agonizing delay. (The letter, which was in fact Harmen's last before being executed, has been edited slightly in the interests of privacy. "Br." is his abbreviation for the name of a cellmate.)

Dear Pastor and Friend,

The things we have gone through! Last Friday, the four of us were first transported to Amsterdam and we were extremely cheerful in the car. One of us had been told that we would be interrogated again and that could be favorable after the death sentence. So the blow came all the harder. We had three hours to live and could start writing our farewell letters. I did so, while awaiting your visit. I had a brief talk with Father Ferwerda and could assure him that I was doing fine. I couldn't have said otherwise; I was incredibly peaceful and courageous. That was God's work, where else could I have gotten such cheerfulness? I could peacefully say farewell to everyone and everything—only, that broke the last tie with this earth.

Then, fifteen minutes before the time, there came the news: postponement. That completely shattered me. While I was looking Death in the face, I did not have a single rebellious moment; my trust in God remained strong. When I was locked up in that horrible death cell with its heavy bars, there was even a moment that I felt the urge to start singing. I looked at that mass of iron with a smile. When the door slammed shut, I thought: that's the door to earthly life closing for good. But this was followed immediately the clear and steadfast thought: "If He so desires, God can even redeem this", but not the slightest sadness or disappointment in that, not the slightest desire that He would actually do so. Only when I was plunged back from the certainty of death into doubt and fear, into having to wait again, my faith gave out. I remained assured of God's unfathomable goodness in Jesus Christ, of his forgiveness for sin, I remained certain that He knows better than I, but I had to appeal for His special aid, weeping and sobbing, to be able to bear this new shock. I suffered for two days, with my cellmate; at times we could talk about God's rich mercy, but my own certainty about salvation was gone. I did not rebel against God about this—I just fought that last battle to the end in that first sleepless night from Friday to Saturday and only now have learned, before all else, to pray: Thy will be done. I have said: Lord, I can't go on anymore, here I am, utterly powerless and beaten. Now, I await only Your mercy. . . .

Dear friend, in this miserable prison there is really only one thing we can do with great, liberating conviction with our hearts and mouths: to praise God for His miracles. The daughter of Br. wrote to him: as God wants it, so it is good. How does the child come up with that? he said. God plows the world deeply. Let us pray that after these horrible times, the New Order come closer to God's light, closer than our dead, saturated past. Give my regards to your wife, the members of the Church Council and the Congregation and accept my, perhaps next-to-last greeting in Jesus Christ our Lord from

your loving
Harmen

Four days after German troops rolled into Paris on June 14, 1940, and only weeks after vanquishing the Netherlands and Belgium, a lone voice broadcasting from BBC Radio in London beseeched the French people not to yield without a fight. "Has the last word been said? Must hope disappear? Is defeat final? No!," he exclaimed. "Whatever happens, the flame of the French resistance must not be extinguished and will not be extinguished." The speaker was General Charles de Gaulle, the former French undersecretary of war who would emphatically reject the armistice that ceded half of France to Nazi Germany. (Ironically, the new French prime minister appointed to lead the Vichy regime, which would collaborate with the Nazis to rule occupied France, was Marshal Henri Philippe Pétain—the "Hero of Verdun" who had defended his country so tenaciously in World War I.) Encouraged by de Gaulle's words, countless French citizens risked their lives over the next four years to subvert the Vichy government and aid the Allied effort as it prepared for the liberation of France in June 1944. Born to Greek parents who had homes in both France and England, Elaine Vagliano was inspired by de Gaulle's call to arms and joined the Resistance. After the Germans had been driven from France by the Allies, when it was safe to write freely about the occupation, Elaine's mother, Danae, wrote a long and intensely emotional letter to a friend in Great Britain about what the past four years had wrought. She focused particularly on the barbarity of the Gestapo soldiers (the Nazi secret police), and the fierce courage of the men and women, including her daughter, who actively served in the Resistance.

Dear Mr. Andrews,

With all our hearts we want to thank you for your wonderful letter and Mrs. Andrews. We are so touched by your great and sincere sympathy. Please thank your daughter from me for her dear, beautiful letter! I hope that a friend will send you this letter for I cannot write to each one of you yet! It would take six weeks at least by post and I should like you to know the details now! Will you also thank Miss Norman for her kind nice letter and Ellen Wicks and Florence. I want them to know quickly how <u>much</u> we appreciate their sympathy and their thought of us. Later, I shall write to them all by ordinary post as I cannot trouble too often this kind friend of mine, who is doing such fine work in Paris. She is English and has a heroic husband who is "somewhere" near the front lines. They are a fine pair. I need not repeat to you all our agony and suffering. We were luckily arrested the same day as our daughter, though not at the same place. We had the great luck of seeing Elaine three times during our arrestation. Once in the courtyard outside the Grasse Prison before leaving for Nice and twice in the cellar at the Gestapo's Headquarters at Nice or rather at <u>Cimiez</u> above Nice.

In the Nice prison we were separated and each of us were pushed into different cells with three other occupants. No murderers and criminals in England would be put into such filthy places; full of bugs and with hardly any food. No one could endure such treatment for long and many prisoners died after a couple of months. The Gestapo knew that we were pro-English and pro-de Gaulle and perhaps they knew that we did propaganda work. The real reason for our arrest I think was to torture my daughter still more and hurt us to make her breakdown. We were beaten in front of her and though she adored her father and me, she never gave away the names of her comrades. Even now I can see her poor little shrunken face with two big burns on it, and the anguish in her eyes. Tears rolled down her cheeks but she was silent. I prayed that she would not give way through her love for us. She never did for you see, if she had betrayed the names of her fellow workers or indicated where their Headquarters were, most of the Resistance groups would have been found and tortured and shot. She told me this very quietly and simply in the Gestapo cellar at Cimiez. We spoke in whispers for we knew that the Germans kept us all together and had microphones in the place. It happened so at the Cannes prison.

She told me also the name of this "great friend" who had denounced her. Elaine was so loyal to her friends and could not believe this fact, until she saw this woman's signed statement and a list of names. I was also given this list of the people on it who had come to see me on Sunday and this woman had also come on that day! I refused to sign it and denounce them of course. This cost me four teeth because the Gestapo man thought I could give details concerning them which this vile woman did not know, though she knew that they were violently anti-German. But she gave away those she knew. Luckily she was not aware of the Resistance organizations (their headquarters) and some of the agents' names. She gave away those she was acquainted with and said that Elaine had sent her twice to various places with letters. Elaine trusted her, but she never told her of her "Big Work".

On the 25th of July my daughter became anxious and burnt all her papers and warned her fellow workers. (She told me this in prison and added "Nothing could ever have been found or used against me, for no proofs existed. It was only through Antoinette R.C. that the Gestapo found out that I had sent these letters. It was only through Antoinette that they knew that I had helped people to escape. She had begged me to save her son from the Germans and I had him sent away. This was the first thing Antoinette put on her deposition and she added (to impress the Germans, I suppose) that her son's departure had been against her

<u>wish</u>!!!) Then my darling cried and said to me "Oh Mamma, I was fond of her! <u>Why</u> did she do such a thing to me?" I could answer that Judas still exists and has some followers on this earth.

This horrible woman is now in prison in Cannes since the end of August. She is to be judged one day. She told the French Interrogator that she had denounced my daughter (after she (Mme.R.C.) had been taken by the Gestapo, on a minor charge) because she was "Mentally tired" (!) She added that she had not been tortured. Some of her family say: "Poor Antoinette"! She was so tired—"<u>mentally</u>"! It's not a good excuse, for Mme. R.C. is a very strong woman and not a tender rosebud! Through her I have lost my darling and without her our house is empty. Poor Stephen is sweet, but he is a man, and young, so he is gradually getting over it. It's natural but for Marino and I it is different. Elaine was the mainspring in our house. She was so full of life, so unselfish and for us more than a daughter—a <u>friend</u>, who always helped me and kept me alive during these last four dreadful years. My husband has suddenly become an old man and I feel a hundred! I shall never forget those awful days, my child's torture, her last words! "Goodbye, Mamma darling" and her gallant little smile. She told the lady in her cell that she was so happy, so relieved, that we had been released, but she sobbed all night. We were not allowed to stay in Nice. On our return to Cannes we moved Heaven and Earth to get her out of prison. We even offered bribes, sometimes money tempts these Nazis! I was very ill on my return as my face was in a mess and had been cut open, so blood poisoning set in and reached my eyes. All this did not bother me, for I kept thinking of my darling, alone with those Nazis! I kept on hoping that Elaine would return; that it was all a German bluff; that they could not hurt her any more, as no proofs existed (even then, I could not believe that they could murder her!)

The landing took place (it's all over so I hope I can mention it <u>now</u>). We were cut off from everything. We had no light (only 4 candles!) no water, not much food and we lived in our cellar—but we were so thrilled! We kept on saying how delighted Elaine would be. She wanted so much to see <u>all our</u> flags on the roof of our house! The bridges were down, the roads were bombed. No news came through at all. We waited and Nice was taken! We waited, but Elaine did not arrive. The police knew the truth and some of our friends too—until on the 22nd Stephen came in sobbing and told us that Elaine had been shot! On the 3rd October her body was brought back as it is against the law in France to transfer bodies from one place to another. (We had to fight the police and at last they gave way and we got our child back. It was dreadful!) We had to wait even for <u>that</u>!

She was brought back like a soldier on a gun carriage and her coffin was covered with a French flag. (It still is, as she is lying in a vault!) She never came home <u>to us</u>. She was taken to the Mairie and all night she had a guard of honour around her and soldiers stood at attention. Next day she had a State funeral, so grand and they gave her "tous les honneur". "Un salut d'honneur" and the "Last Post" and so many, many flowers! We all stood near her like stone statues, for we could not even cry. Cannes had taken her from us. She was <u>their</u> heroine. "Notre Helen!" (A street near the rue d'Antibes is called "rue Helene Vagliano—Herione de la Resistance"). The <u>only</u> person who helped me was a woman of the Resistance, when she came to see me after Elaine's funeral. She had fought <u>with</u> the soldiers and she had, earlier, hidden arms. She was arrested, but escaped by a miracle. Her husband was taken, tortured and killed. On the day before Elaine's funeral, she heard that her only son had been shot by the Germans. She told me all this so simply and, when I tried to condole and said she was so brave, she answered "C'est affreux—mais je n'ai pas le temps de pleiner"! (It's dreadful, but I have no time to cry!) I saw the anguish in her eyes! We became great friends. She belongs to "Les Femmes de France". I am their President, as they call it over here. We have to find clothes, etc. for the families of the Resistance; for the families or only the children of the victims of the Gestapo and for the families of the men who were forced to go and work in Germany. It's good work, for these women are wonderful! For Christmas we arranged parties and a Christmas tree for all these children, over a thousand; one for Elaine's pets (the Prisoners' children). (She had worked so hard for them.) and a party for the children of the soldiers who are "somewhere" in the mountains. It is good to be occupied, but when one returns home the wound re-opens!

We were asked to send the photos of the victims who were killed by the Gestapo to England. We had to collect these. First of all we went to the Mont-fleury prison in Cannes. There, on the 14th of August, these creatures of Himmlers, had a champagne party—(one of them is now arrested and confessed) then these <u>Herrenmensch</u> took off their coats and went into the basement. There they shot down all the helpless prisoners, amongst others, two young girls of 19 and of 20 years old. We saw blood on the floors—on the mattresses (the one I had occupied on July 29th, 30 and 31st was steeped in blood!). We saw over-turned stools, bloody fingerprints on the walls. On the 15th of November, we went to L'ariane, near Nice, where my child had been murdered! We found the farmer who had been the only witness as the land belongs to him. On the 15th of August he saw a lorry drive up. He saw prisoners descend from it. He saw the Gestapo agents and German soldiers push these prisoners over the high bank on to the strip of land by the river edge. He heard these brutes laugh as these helpless people fell. He rushed over the bridge leading to his house on the other bank. Near it he saw two machine guns. Before he shut his shutters he saw all the prisoners in a row facing these machine guns across the narrow river. He heard the guns fire three times, and soon after the sounds of revolver shots. Much later a neighbour came to him and said a dreadful tragedy had taken place and both men rushed across the bridge. There they saw a horrible sight. Bodies of men and women all over the place. Some had tried to escape and had been horribly murdered and even stamped upon as they lay!

My daughter had not tried to escape for she lay on her side. Her face was covered in blood (even her pretty hair!) and at the back of her head there was a huge hole made by a revolver. (When she was put into her coffin her little head was detached!) To return to the horrible photos, amongst them we found my daughter's, taken after death! When she left my room on the 29th of July at 10.30 a.m. she looked so fresh and gay. Her pretty hair was especially arranged; she had a new dress on and she asked me if I liked it! I only recognised the <u>dress</u> in her last photo, for the Germans had destroyed her face! We <u>had</u> to see all these horrors, because in this way we can tell the truth and not be accused of exaggerating these things. If any man and woman in England ever see these photos let them think that <u>this</u> girl—<u>this</u> boy might have belonged to them if Germany had won the war! These horrible murders would have happened over there in towns and villages, too! One does not need to exaggerate in France and I suppose in all countries which the Germans occupied.

The people here do not ask only for sympathy. They want to be believed, because what they have suffered happens to be true! We hear on the radio people make speeches on "We must be kind to the Germans after the War". "There must be no hate!" After all, the Germans are human!" I can answer <u>No</u>! I am not a hysterical woman, mad with hate because my child was murdered by the Germans! I simply state that if you do not and have not lived in towns <u>occupied by the Germans</u>, you cannot understand what it means! "Be kind to the Germans" sticks in our throats!!! These Germans are not human! They voted for Hitler; they did not protest against the Gestapos even in their country! They shouted with joy when Hitler told them in his speeches that he meant to burn every town and village in England! Kindness to them, even beaten—is weakness. When they left the towns over here and in Cannes, they deliberately fired in each window they passed. In ours too, and we hid in our cellars! They fired on civilians and burnt houses and entire villages. They behaved like savages. We still look over our shoulders when we speak to a friend and still shake when the door bell rings too loudly! The German cars came often to our house. Twice to arrest us. (The first time they pretended that my husband was a <u>Jew</u>!!! The charge was too ridiculous and he returned, but how we suffered until he did so.) They came twice to take the house and tramped all over it and said they would return. Luckily, next day they found houses near us which suited them better. They became our neighbours—all around us and down the road. The German soldiers prowled in our garden night and day. They cut down our trees; stole our fruit; broke stone benches and <u>we could not complain</u>!

The German women were as bad; they used to roar with laughter when they saw prisoners in lorries! I know that suffering exists in every country. In England you were bombed, and everyone was so brave. It must have been awful and yet you all stood up to it. All honour to England. What you do not know, thank God, is to be tortured <u>slowly</u>, to be dying and to see, at the last, sneering German faces, or laughing ones as you die! My daughter was always called the "sale Anglaise" (the dirty English girl) by the Germans. She had a strong English accent when she spoke French and that infuriated them. It was owing to her English upbringing and to her English education that Elaine learnt self-control, determination and the courage that leads to endurance and to sacrifice. I should like people in <u>England to know about her</u>, and to understand why she "stuck to it" (her job) up to the end! She would not want honour or decorations, only the remembrance of her friends. She told me, to please give you <u>all</u> her music; and especially Bach's (as Mr. Andrews admires him so much). She had collected lots of old musical scores! For Sue Harvey she said to me "Please give her my silver fox skin—<u>in case</u>! I answered "of course I will—<u>in case</u>"! We never finished the sentence.

On the 13th of August she smuggled out two letters from her prison by a released prisoner. One was to us <u>and frantic</u>! She wrote to say that the Germans were coming to fetch us and keep us till the end of the war, as we had complained! (We had not done so, or seen friends or left the house, but people in the bus had seen our faces and talked about us in Cannes). Luckily the roads were being bombed and the Boches did not come for us. The other letter was sent to her "Chief". She wrote "Do not be anxious I shall <u>never</u> speak"! When he showed it to me, he cried like a child.

Would you send a copy of my letter to Sue Harvey, 46 Godfrey Street,

London, S.W. 3., and say I thought that the details about Elaine might interest her, as she loved my child. I should like to hear from her too, as she was my daughter's friend. (Please ask Sue Harvey to show this letter to <u>Uncle Bill</u>—Marino's Uncle.)

Would it trouble you too much to send some details to Ellen and to Wicks? Where is Cliffe? He used to be so fond of Marino! We were so sorry to hear that you had both been so ill. What bad luck you had!

We send you both our best wishes for a Happy New Year and the best of health. <u>When</u> shall we meet? Our best and most affectionate regards.

Danae Vagliano

P.S. Mamma is well and was as courageous as a lion even with the Germans!! Shall we ever get <u>books</u>? How we long for them!!

Please excuse this badly written letter, but memories come back when I mention these events! <u>I do hope you will get it soon</u> as you knew Elaine since her birth—so these things will interest you I hope!

Six weeks after Charles de Gaulle transmitted his rallying cry to the French population, he was tried in absentia for treason by Vichy France and condemned to death. When Paris was liberated more than four years later, General de Gaulle triumphantly marched into the city with Allied troops and became head of the provisional government. Marshal Pétain fled the country weeks after de Gaulle's arrival, but returned to France in April 1945. He defended his collusion with the Nazis as an effort to save France from being destroyed (as Poland was), but the argument proved unconvincing, and the almost ninety-year-old Pétain was sentenced to be shot before a firing squad. De Gaulle commuted the judgment to life in prison, and Pétain died behind bars in 1951.

—ᴍ—

**A Russian Boy Named Slavik Provides His Aunt Natasha
with an Account of How Wretched Life Has Become
During the Blockade of Leningrad
&
Slavik's Sister Galia Begs Her Aunt to Come and Find Her,
Now That Everyone in Her Family Is Gone
&
Private First Class Harry Zaslow Depicts for His Parents
the Hellish Existence of a Group of Girls He Met
Who Had Been Enslaved by the Nazis**

Of the more than fifty million people killed in World War II, the majority were believed to have been civilians—a substantial percentage of whom were chil-

*dren. Russian boys and girls fared among the worst. Rural and peasant fami-
lies were either massacred by invading German troops or expelled from their
homes only to perish from exposure, and those trapped in the cities of Moscow,
Leningrad (now St. Petersburg), and Stalingrad (now Volgograd) suffered
through some of the most punishing bombardments and blockades of the war.
The siege of Leningrad alone lasted nearly nine hundred days, from September
8, 1941, until the end of January 1944, extinguishing the lives of at least six
hundred thousand Russians. Some estimates put the number at over one million. (Subsisting each day on, at best, one small loaf of "bread" made of flour,
sawdust, and paper, hundreds of thousands died of hunger alone. Starving the
Russians to death was precisely what Hitler had intended.) Two young siblings,
Slavik and Galia (last names unknown), were orphaned during the assault
and, in March 1943, they pleaded to their aunt to come and care for them.*

Hello dear Aunt Natasha. A salute from Leningrad.

Oh, aunt Natasha, Galia and I have lived through so much in this
war. Bombings, hunger and again, filth and epidemics. If I wrote about
them all, I doubt you would believe me. 27 September Uncle Lyosha is
wounded. 24 November Papa is buried. 15 January we buried Liza. 28
February we buried mommy. Kostya was killed. Sashka is in shell-shock.
Galia and I are alone together with no relatives. Oh it's lonely, aunt
Natasha. All hope lies with you—please come soon, we are waiting for
you.

I kiss Aunt Natasha warmly. Slavik.

Weeks later, Galia wrote to her aunt with news of a terrible development.

10 April.

Greetings from Leningrad. Hello dearest Aunt Natasha.

This morning we received a letter from you dated 1 March. You write
that you have no letters from us. After mother's death I gave you 2
telegrams—and Slavik and I wrote four letters—this is already the fifth.
They say that the letters do not reach their destinations. So here:

16 February mother died

16 November father died

10 January grandmother died and

15 January Aunt Liza died

21 March our room was destroyed and Slavik received a wound to the
head.

23 March he died in the hospital at 9 o'clock in the morning.

And I found myself alone.

Dearest Aunt Natasha my hope now rests on you and I wait for you to come like a guardian angel. I think that you will not abandon me. I am left all alone, without neither relatives, nor relations. Mother's and father's acquaintances have all been either evacuated or won't show their noses. The streetcars have not been running all winter. And there is not a single person who could really take pity on me and help me out.

It's true, Uncle Lyosha came as soon as he heard about these horrors. But he was allowed in for only fifty hours, worse still he did not make it onto the train and had to walk to Alexandrovka on foot. He and I met for only a few hours, but I was so glad (you must understand this yourself, dearest aunt Natasha).

He brought me some groceries. They were not much to be honest, but still, they helped me out greatly. My mood, aunt Natasha, is very grim. The large room is destroyed. All our things are covered in filth. Everything is covered in slaked lime from the walls. And that is the kind of dirt that you cannot clean up without water—and there's no water. And it's far to go and get water, and to stand around an hour for one pail, and then to carry the dirty water out to the dumpster is also not easy. So, I have not the energy to clean.

As soon as it is warm and the water is running again and I am still alive, I will clean up everything. Now the letters travel better—you will probably receive this one. But for now, good bye. Warm kisses to you.

Galia

It is not known what happened to Galia during or after the siege. Young girls of any nationality—Russian, Polish, French, Dutch—captured by the Germans faced the possibility of a fate worse than any other except death. Two weeks before V-E Day, a nineteen-year-old private first class from Philadelphia named Harry Zaslow wrote a letter to his parents from Germany after a heartbreaking encounter with teenaged victims of Nazi depravity. (Zaslow's father, himself, was a Russian immigrant, and the "blue envelope" Zaslow refers to was a special letter servicemembers could write that allowed them to bypass their unit censors. The letter would still be checked before being posted to the United States, but only by a total stranger, enabling the troops to raise personal matters they did not want, for whatever reason, revealed to buddies or commanding officers who might have access to their mail.)

Thursday, April 26, 1945

Dear Mom & Dad,

I havn't written you in the past three or four days simply because I have been moving around so much. I wrote a letter to you in a blue envelope about five days ago and just now I got a chance to mail it with this letter. So you can see how busy I am. But incoming mail is coming in pretty good. I received letters steadily from Dorothy and Norm, from Sam Mills, a nice letter from Lorraine and one from Stanley. It usually takes from 10 to 15 days for your letters to reach me.

Its an easy life now Mom, believe me. All this war is in my estimation is mopping up operations. I do expect to get into one more big fight before this war is over. We are headed for that place now. Where, I cannot tell you but by the time you receive this letter it will be all over. I imagine its going to be the last big fight too. But don t worry about it because I have been in them before and I know the art of war.

The other day I walked into a slave camp. They were still living in there, Russian girls. They had no other place to go. No sight of pity ever hit me so hard as when I entered that door. It was not the filth because there was none, they kept the place pretty clean. It was not the crude furniture and beds because one sees that all over Europe. What made me and a score of other fellows boiling mad was the condition of the women, girls and—babies. Babys, babys, all over the place. Their mother's faces were weary and tired and they were feeding their babies with what they had left of themselves. One Polish girl, she must have been about 15, 16 years old told me the same story that I have been hearing since I crossed the Rhine. They worked hard during the day with not much food and at night, German soldiers. She said, "Look what a German soldier gave me." I asked her if the baby was just born. "NO, five days ago" and it was no bigger than a kitten. "Ten babies died in the past week," she said. I was glad to get out of that sad and gloomy maternity. It's not like America. Yet I wonder if American woman appreciates their high morals and respect given to womankind. The Germans don't.

I received two letters from you dated April 5, and 7th. Take advantage of staying at Aunt Annie's place for awhile. It will do you and Jerry some good. Did you become a citizen yet Dad? I hope you make the grade because it will help you a lot if you do become a citizen! Nothing more to write.

All my love,
Harry

—∞—

**Army Medic Sergeant Arthur I. Wallace Relates His Impressions
of the Dachau Concentration Camp and a Poignant Memorial Service
Conducted by a Polish-American Priest**

&

**Lisa Rosenblum, a French Jew Being Deported
to Auschwitz-Birkenau, Bids Her Family Good-Bye
&
A Polish Teenager Sends a Message from the Pustkow Labor Camp
Informing His Parents That He "Won't Get Out of Here Alive"
&
In a Letter to Her Husband, a Hungarian Doctor
Named Anna Koppich Relates What Happened to Her
and Their Young Son at the Auschwitz-Birkenau Extermination Camp**

*In letter after letter after letter, the sentiments—the utter disbelief, rage, sorrow,
and desire to communicate what they had seen—were remarkably similar. On
April 13, 1945, Major Malcolm Leon Downs wrote the following to his wife:*

> *I have heard and read of things like these but you cant believe it till you
> see it and I have seen some awful things but this is past belief. We came
> right into this city on the heels of the Army with orders to hit the Gestapo
> Political Prisoner Camp. We went there about noon. We got up at 4 AM
> and drove hard all morning for nearly a hundred miles when we hit the
> Camp it took your breath away. People lying on the floors in Barns
> shriveled up. Just skin and Bones. Absolutely starved to death and tortured.
> Hundreds were dead in their beds, just skeletons . . . Another Camp on the
> other side of town has about 900 Hospital Cases but only a few bodies
> because they have a large Crematorium and they burned the dead and
> sometimes the live ones. There were 40 bodies piled up waiting and the
> ovens were full. There were huge pits in back filled with ashes and parts
> of bones. A Polish Doctor told me that the ashes in the Pits represented
> 13,000 People . . . I thought for awhile that maybe the people were not
> all bad but they are a race of madmen and not fit to live. The longer I stay
> here the worse I hate them and I dont believe I will ever be able to have
> any use for them again.*

*On June 28, 1945, a British soldier named Ralph Walsh sent the following to
his family in Headley, England.*

> *About 2 miles from the camp were notices "Typhus area" and before you
> reached the camp itself you could smell "death". However we "rolled" into
> No 3 and a half of the blocks were barbed-wired off labelled "Typhus" and
> the poor devils at the windows were full grown men & women weighing
> no more than 4 or 5 stone . . . just bones covered with parchment, eyes
> open sunk 1 1/2 inches into their heads, sores in most cases over their bod-*

*ies. . . . One poor devil still clutched a lovely crucifix & another had tried
to end it by cutting her throat . . . It's a pity everyone couldn't have seen
those bodies then I don't think there would be a chance of any more wars.*

*Writing on a "liberated" German typewriter, Sergeant Arthur I. Wallace
described for his family in Dayton, Ohio, not the worst extermination or concentration camp built by the Nazis—that was an infamy reserved for Auschwitz-
Birkenau, where an estimated 1.1 to 1.5 million individuals, mostly Jewish,
were murdered—but the first: Dachau. Constructed just outside of Munich in
March 1933 (more than six years before the outbreak of World War II), it
became known, with chilling irony, as the "Mother Camp." It served as a model
for the hundreds of camps and subcamps to come, as well as the initial training
ground for senior commandants and low-level guards alike, most of whom represented the misfits, ex-criminals, and sociopaths of the German military
deemed unfit for action at the front. They were instructed on how to impose discipline with savage efficiency and separate the weak inmates from the strong. The
former, in many camps, would be exterminated immediately, and the latter were
either worked to death or succumbed to starvation, exposure, forced marches, or
disease. Tens of thousands of men, women, and children were murdered within
Dachau's walls and electric fences before Allied troops arrived on April 29, 1945.
Sergeant Wallace, a thirty-six-year-old medic with a mobile hospital unit,
typed out the following letter to his family depicting the revolting confines and
sadistic treatment of the inmates. (The many spelling errors throughout were due
to the unfamiliar German typewriter keyboard, which, as Wallace noted with
some frustration, had "more gadgets on it than a dashboard of a P51." There is
no salutation or signature to the letter.)*

We have taken over the Dachau Concentration Camp,the largest area of
it"s kind in all Germany. All the pictures you have seen depicting
German brutality are true but they dont tell the whole story—far from
it.A word picture can not adequately describe the horror and conditions
which confronted us when we came in. This area was manned by the
German SS troops (**SS**—they even have their official insignia on this
typewriter) and their methods are,no doubt, familar. The whole area
comprises about one half square mile. which is made up of two huge
three story buildings probably for administration and barracks for the
SS troops. xxxxxxxxx This was also quite a German ordinance depot
but more about that later. I would say their own area consummed
about6/8 of the total, the remaining was the infamous "Compound."
To continue from this pointa feeling of nausea comes over me. The odor
and stench was indescribale.You really have to expierence some thing like

this to get the true effect. Starved scrawny human bodies werelittered all over the camp. (As we learned later when they heard the Germans were leaving they broke out of the compound and were shot by the ⚡⚡ troops) The real xxxx horror greeted us in the compound and the adjacent railroad tracks.Bodieswere stacked, perhaps piled would be a better word, like so much coal. Nothing but skin and bone. Their arms and legs no larger than a silver dollar. It was terrific. There was"nt one pile but they were spread all over. Then there was the crematory. Seeing those poor starved people of all nationalities was bad enough but here was something one read about it books or a bad dream. Some of the furnaceswere still under fire. others with doors openwhere in full view were more bodies actually stuffed in like paper. Some of personnel took one look with the resultantheaves. It was ghastly. But it was all ghastly.One thing seemed to be worse than the other. There were ten huge furnaces in this building for the soul purpose of burning the bodies. The gas chamberwhich was also in this one buildinghad more bodies. The box cards held more bodies loaded to top. There must have beenten ot twelve cars. We still cant figure out the box car idea but when yous ee all this reaseoning departs and you run for the nearest corner to vomit. The next"scene" was their shooting gallery. One wonders where they conceived all the ideas. Here were more bodiesstrewn about. They would line up these peopleagainst a wall of dirt and fire away. Target practice, no doubt. Then there was the ditch with grill work . For the people who were too weak to stand up, they would place them on this grill work and shoot them, the blood running into the ditch. You know now why I mention that nauseated feeling. There arexxxxx means of torture they employed. Did you ever see a man with his head slashed wide open with an ax or beaten to death by clubbing. You"d run for the nearest latrine too. During the time these people were in the xxxxx compound they must have presented qite a problem. The quarters were far from sanitary and obviously the Germans did"nt care. They were packed into these long wooden xxxxx shacks. Beds were triple xxxxx decked and pushed together so the could sleep crosswise. Intwo of these beds six to nine people would sleep. Their rationswere small, very small. If one of them would die the others would not report it so as to get his rations. Finally after the stench would become so great he would be discovered by the attendant. These patients would kill one another for food and just leave the body lay or strip him of all identification and throw him out. Without exception all those in the compound have xxxxx xxxx typhus and we are treating them. They have shown a world of improvement sine our hospital moved in. Soon as they are classified they are removed from

the compound into our hospital . When we came in there must have
been twenty to thirty thousand people in the compound but graduall
this number is decreasing. We have a lot of help now with German
doctor and nurses and medics. Shortly they will take overand run the
hospital under supervision of Military Government.

To get away from the gruesome to a more favorable vein, their ordnance
depot herewas quite elaborate.,very completeboth in tools and supplies.
Drill presses, punch presses in great numbers. Guns all over and xxx
various supplys. We have taken advantage of all this for our own benefits.
This was really a haven for souvenir hunters if they can get the stuff into
the states. The SS had the best of everything Their own living conditions
were replete with all modern conveniences, and wehave taken over all of
it to our own advantage. Might seem strange to all of you reading this
that the SS troops could live in just splendor when a short distance away
people were dying from starvation and disease but those of us who know
the SS can understand it. They were absolutely viscious and ruthless.
Living thru some thing like this always brings about an eventual brighter
side . The first Sundayxxxxxxxxx here we attended Mass xxxx which was
said by a Fr. Lewandowski who was born in New Haven Conn. When a
small boy he went to Poland to study for the priesthood and ultimately
ended up in the compound. Consequently he spoke English. At the end
of Mass he gave a short sermon which will always remain in my memory
when the horror is gone. To me it was the most stirring sincere and
heart felt rendition of a man" feeling of overwhelming joy and
happiness—being free again and being treated like a human being.
The metamorphises was too great. Here was this priest with tears
running down his bearded face thanking us for they never expected to
be liberated. He spoke only for a few moments but what he xxx said and
the way he said it left you in utter astonishment, sort of a mental abyss.
After we took over here we "xxxxx "solicited" the help of the German
civilians to clean up the mess. We were all glad of that as you can well
appreciate. Some of those in the compound helped too. They are now
segregated according to nationalities. Each area has a large banner
stretched over its entrance and in substance they say " We are ever so
grateful to the Americans for liberating us" When you pass one of these
banners it gives us a feeling of pride and satisfaction. Some of them are
fairly well recovered and to show their appreciation they will not let us
do a thing. (That is alright with us because prior to this we had a rough
time of it)

The foregoing just about winds up the story of Dachau Concentration
Camp near Munich except for one thing which I have purposely left

until the end in order that those of you reading this will be in a more acceptable mode. I spoke of dead bodies being all over the place and if I would have mentioned any figure you would not believe it, and if I have been successful in adequately painting the picture so as for one to grasp the slightest conception of conditions, multiply it a hundred fold then perhaps you will believe me when I say there were 13,ööö dead bodies to gxxxxx greet us and the death rate was 200 a day until we got things under control. Now it is about one or two a day.

Uncensored letters from those imprisoned by the Nazis are extremely rare. Some inmates were able to smuggle messages out of the camps or toss them from trains while being deported, but the risks were enormous, and the likelihood that their correspondences would reach their friends or loved ones was scant. Lisa Rosenblum was a French Jew arrested in Paris for not wearing the mandatory yellow Star of David patch designating that she was Jewish. In late October 1943, she was condemned to Auschwitz-Birkenau, where she would eventually be killed. On October 30, she scribbled the following note to her family while en route to the extermination camp. (How the message got to her husband, Henri, and their children, Bernard—a POW who had been serving in the French Navy—Paulette, and Edouard is unclear, but they received it at the end of the war.)

Photo by Andrew Carroll

Emil Slusarczyk, one of more than a million individuals killed at the Auschwitz-Birkenau extermination camp.

Wednesday

My Dearest,

The day before yesterday I received your letter. I have no more strength to cry. Tomorrow Thursday at 3 o'clock after midnight they will finish us up. We are here a 1000 people. Among us are many old people and small children. Where they are going to take us, we do not know.

My Dearest Henri, Paulette, son, and my elderly mother, I clasp you to my heart. All of you should pray to God for me. I would like to live to see all my children. I am kissing all my family and all our good friends. I plead with you, do not go out any place, because every day new prisoners will arrive. I do clasp you to my heart.

Do not forget Bernard. Żalman and Esther and their son are also on the same train.

Lisa

A fourteen-year-old boy named Chaim (last name unrecorded), confined at the Pustkow labor camp in Poland, was able to slip a short message addressed to his mother and father through the camp's barbed-wire fence and into the hands of a local peasant. The note made it to them, but, tragically, Chaim's prediction at the end came true. (With the exception of the last line, which cuts off abruptly, the ellipses throughout the letter are believed to be in the original.)

My dear parents, if the sky were paper, and all the seas of the world an inkwell, I could not describe my suffering and all that I see around me. The camp is located in a clearing. From the morning they make us work in the forest. My feet are bleeding because they took away our shoes . . . We work all day almost without eating and at night we sleep on dirt (they took our cloaks away too). Every night drunk soldiers come and hit us with wooden sticks, and my body is black with bruises like a piece of burnt wood. Sometimes they throw us a raw carrot or a beet and it is shameful: We fight over a little piece or even a leaf. The other day two boys escaped, so they lined us up and every fifth person was shot . . . I was not fifth, but I know that I won't get out of here alive . . . Chaim

For many who did survive the camps, freedom came at a devastating emotional cost. They would be plagued by depression, lose their faith, or become unable to establish lasting relationships—for fear that these, too, would end in tragedy. (The converse was also true: some discovered that their belief in God and their connections to friends and loved ones only deepened.) In the worst cases, solace from the haunting memories could only be found in suicide. Others experienced "survivor's guilt," convinced that they should not have lived when, from their per-

spective, so many stronger or nobler or kinder souls did not. The degree of pain may have varied, but no one came through the camps entirely unscathed. Little is known of Antoni Kropielnicki, the Polish writer of the letter below, or the recipient, Helena Lubke, except that she was a family friend who lived in Switzerland. On May 9, 1945, Kropielnicki wrote to Lubke of that unforgettable day when he was released from the Murnau concentration camp in Germany, and he asked Lubke to inform his wife that he was still alive:

> On April 29, 1945 at 16:30 hours, a Polish-American soldier drove his tank through our gate and machine-gunned a group of SS officers who were just arriving at the camp. What an irony of fate that an SS general— Brigadefuhrer Fink and three of his officers—lay dead for half a day at the gate to the Polish camp, killed by bullets aimed by a Pole who arrived from across the ocean. . . . We still sleep in barracks without sheets and pillows, bitten by bed-bugs. Please let my wife know, since I don't have her address, that I am healthy and free, but this barbed wire is still mangled into our hearts.

Two months after the Nazis evacuated Auschwitz-Birkenau as Soviet troops advanced into Poland, a Hungarian physician named Anna Koppich, who had been deported to the camp for being a Jew, wrote a series of letters to her husband, Ferri, recounting all that had transpired since he had left home. (Like many of the country's Jews, Ferri was forced by the Hungarian military into providing manual labor for the army.) She began by describing how their young son, Gyurika, had been distressed by his father's departure.

> We tried to play act, make believe that somebody brought news from you. We didn't spend too much time together except after lunch. He asked lots of questions, and he did not mind if sometimes I didn't have answers. He loved to eat at Mother's or at the Hausmann's, and claimed that kosher food is better. He even wrote to the relatives in Vasarhelj that he would only come to visit if they would cook kosher. He was a devout little soul, and he blamed me for not lighting candles on Friday night. . . . He was happiest when we ate at Mother's on holidays. If we had noodles with poppy seeds, he didn't want to eat; he wanted to save his share for you. It took a lot to convince him that we had plenty left before he was willing to have some. If we made cookies to send to you, he wouldn't even touch them, since it was "more important for Daddy."

On May 9, 1944, Koppich and her son were forced from their home and into the Ghetto. Six-year-old Gyurika was almost paralyzed with fear.

In the ghetto, the Nazi (SS) murderers reigned. We stood in line for medical examinations, and when one SS killer kicked an old Jew who fell, Gyurika was squeezing my hand, kept his eyes looking at the ground, and his entire little body was shaking. I was only afraid of what we would have to see and witness before our own death. I managed to send word to Buchler to try to help us. The ghetto was in the brick factory. There was a roof but no walls on two sides, only dirt and dust and cold wind. Somehow we built our tent and got settled. I tried to prepare our darling before we left our house. I told him that the soldiers needed our house and we'd just go camping. Didn't he love excursions? He said no, not this kind.

Their situation, however, was about to change dramatically for the worse. Koppich, her parents, and Gyurika were all loaded into a cattle car and taken to Auschwitz. Within moments of arriving at the camp, Koppich was separated from her family and, because of her profession, ordered to work in the camp's "hospital." This led to an extraordinary brush with one of the vilest members of the Third Reich—Dr. Josef Mengele. The senior physician at the camp, Mengele became infamous for his heinous experiments on inmates, especially children. On March 12, 1945, Koppich wrote to her husband:

The number of sick people increased every day, the first dysenteries appeared, an epidemic of scarlet fever started. We did not know how to deal with all the illnesses, and at that time, we still did not believe the horror stories that the Blockalteste [barracks elder or leader] told us. Our chief murderer, Mengele, appeared, thirty-nine years old, good looking, elegant with pleasant features. He was so kind and considerate; he was concerned about everything. He came because the first death occurred; a young girl who committed suicide in the bathhouse at her arrival died a day later.

In one of her final letters to Ferri before they were reunited, Koppich summarized her final days at Auschwitz before being moved to a woman's concentration camp or "FKL" (Frauen Konzentraton Lager), as she referred to it. And with enormous difficulty, she shared her anguish about the suffering her only child, who had turned seven while at Auschwitz, had to bear in a place more sinister and frightening than any nightmare. (Rozsa was her twenty-four-year-old relative who died from an illness Koppich does not name. The letter, dated March 19, 1945, and translated years later by a cousin, Agnes Kun, does not include a salutation or signature. Eva, alluded to at the end, is another cousin.)

Today is the anniversary of Rozsa's death and also of the German invasion of Hungary. I have to finish my letter for now, since the Red

Army is leaving, and I don't want to stay behind. I have two important jobs to do: one, to give a physical checkup to all the women; and two, to gather some more data that will be useful for us in our future fight against fascism.

My dear, the following is strictly for you. I'd like to describe to you my horrible suffering for a period of three months, without actually relating all the chronological events. On October 13 they "liquidated" the hospital. In two hours, they loaded 530 of a total of 600 patients on the "death trucks." These were mainly strong, recovering young girls and women, since the ones that were really ill were "liquidated" previously. I had to just stand there and observe how all those for whose lives I fought, all those whom I managed to save several times from being taken away, all those whom I managed to heal were gone. We were taken to the FKL, and here I lost my last glimmer of hope the same way as all my work in the hospital went down the drain. This was the end of the camps—the "other side." There was nothing beyond it. So all the stories that there are huge camps beyond were untrue. I had to face the horrible reality that my darling child and my good parents are no more. Please forgive me for causing you so much pain, but you are the only one I can be weak with, you are my only solace, you're the only one I can lean on. Everybody else, family and friends, always expected me to be the strong one. My only consolation is that you are there and I can talk to you about my feelings.

And now I have a confession to make. For many, many years, even after I gave birth, I thought that being in love is the most formidable, the strongest feeling in the world. Later I realized, however, what being a mother means. I found out that motherly love is way above any other kind, a kind of love that is so little talked about, so little written about.

When I finally found out with certainty what happened, the world just stopped existing. I myself felt like I stopped living. Husband or sister could not make a difference in my state of mind. I did my work mechanically; the patient and her illness, life or death, didn't mean anything to me. Luckily I was assigned to a ward that only contained old Polish women, most of them suffering of rheumatism or just old age. I only lived for my sorrow. I cried all day long, I stopped eating, and didn't even have the energy to wash up. I couldn't even keep the appearances up. My patients liked and understood me even though I neglected them, but the staff despised me because of my desperate attitude. I envied those mothers who died with their children. I did not want to live any longer, and a death wish was my only emotion. On November 20th they took Eva to Germany. This was the last straw. I totally collapsed. I could not stop crying any more. I cried while I worked; I cried all day and all night. I relived every mistake that I made raising my child. I did nothing but torture myself. My left hand got infected; that caused physical pain for weeks.

I thought I was stronger and more resistant emotionally (mentally). People coped better with the loss of their loved ones in the camp. Only I, who was stronger than the average person, broke down totally. I was on a roller coaster that seemed infinite. My dear Gyurika, my child that meant life and joy and sorrow to me, was no more. Everything ceased to exist. I stopped existing myself. When I was at the end of my rope, I came down with a very serious case of hepatitis. I had no strength left, but I welcomed death; I was happy that I'd share his (Gyurika's) fate. When I thought the end was approaching and I thought of you, my darling, and my dear Eva, all of a sudden I realized that both of you will need me. So I started to fight for my own life, and as I improved physically, my mental and emotional balance started to improve too. And now that I am free, I thank you, dear heart, that you saved my life.

So now I started to worry about you and Eva, but I hope that we'll be reunited. I am not broken anymore. I have energy and goals, my dream came true: the Red Army liberated me. I want to live and work for you and Eva, but the loss of my dear child left such a tremendous vacuum that can never be filled.

—⁂—

Survivors of the Japanese Takeover of the Philippines Share with the Honorable Emmet O'Neal Personal Stories of Terror and Abuse During the Three-Year Occupation

After five months of intense fighting against Japanese troops, Filipino and American soldiers (initially led by General Douglas MacArthur and then by General Jonathan M. Wainwright) surrendered the Philippines on May 6, 1942. For those forced to live under Japanese occupation for the next three years, even their worst fears could not prepare them for the unrelenting brutality to come. Writing letters or any other accounts that recorded Japanese atrocities was punishable by death, and very few contemporaneous journals or correspondences by Filipinos exist. But after the war, the newly appointed American ambassador Emmet O'Neal actively encouraged Filipinos to write to him about their experiences. Almost everyone in the country had been scarred by the occupation, and Ambassador O'Neal received thousands of letters describing everything from mass executions of innocent civilians to isolated acts of humiliation and torture. The following letter is just one example of the latter. (The texts, which were transcribed for the ambassador, do not include salutations.)

Cotton growing was forced among the people of Calumpang and other neighboring barrios. There were Japanese inspectors who went around to visit the cotton fields. The people worked from early morning to late afternoon. In spite of this the people were not properly treated.

There was a poor worker, Timoteo de Gracia, a thin man of 41 years of age. He was a lone worker for he was a widower. When Okada, a cruel Japanese inspector visited this poor man's cotton field, he found that a few plants were not yet sprayed with insect poison. Very early the next morning he was called to the office. He was sent to a dark room with his son, the inspector following him. He trembled because of the danger before him. At the command of Okada, Timoteo lifted a bar of iron about fifteen centimeters in diameter and three feet long. He held it high in the air with his straight, slim arms while his eight-year-old son with tears in his eyes looked pitifully at his father. Because of the steady weight of the iron bar, Timoteo lowered his arms a bit, but Okada whipped him with a piece of wood that forced the poor fellow to raise the bar again. The punishment lasted for a day with tears in the eyes of both father and son. Since that time Timoteo remained silent, dull and stupid but worked hard due to fear perhaps. After a month he became insane always calling the name of Okada.

When the Americans arrived a year after, he was sent to Mandaluyong Psychopathic Hospital where he spent his last days.

Crispina de Garcia

Many Filipinos discovered that trivial misunderstandings could have horrifying consequences, as evidenced in a letter by Genciana Paipan. (The guerillas were native Filipinos fighting the Japanese.)

San Luis, Batangas

One early morning on August 28, 1944, a man by the name of Esco was assigned as a "Segidan" or a Japanese guard post at Tang, a barrio of Lila. In the afternoon he went home to Calvario, on his way near Sacsac spring, he met a troop of Japanese soldiers. The head of the troop asked him where he came from. Esco with fear and respect replied that he came from his duty as a "Guardia". Esco did not know the meaning of Guardia and segidan. Guardia means a Bohol Guerilla Guard and a Segidan means a Japanese Guard. The Japanese troop upon hearing that

Esco have been a Guardia seized him, beat him and took him to a lone place. There he was tied to a tree and was beheaded.

Children, too, were the victims of barbaric punishments, no matter how insignificant the matter.

A boy about twelve years old was caught stealing nails in a factory in Grace Park. The factory was managed by the Japanese. The boy was tied and brought to the cemetery. While a Japanese was digging his grave, the boy did not stop saying bad words to the Japanese soldiers. He even spit on their faces. The Japanese beheaded him. But before they buried him they got his heart because they said he was a brave boy.

J.N. Falcon

—⁓—

Masao Yamaguchi Writes to His Sister Explaining How Her Mother, Brother, Sisters, and Nephew All Died in the Attack on Nagasaki
&
After a Tour Through What Was Once the City of Yokohama, Commander Walter C. Michels Urges His Young Daughter to "Not Forget the Capacity for Destruction that Exists in Man"

Nagasaki was not the primary target. Three days after Hiroshima had been all but wiped off the face of the earth by a four-ton atomic bomb nicknamed "Little Boy," President Harry Truman ordered an additional strike on Japan. Critics have argued that President Truman authorized the use of the weapons not only to compel an unconditional surrender, but to intimidate the Soviet Union, which, although an ally of the United States at the time, was threatening to become its principal opponent after the war. Truman was a veteran artilleryman from World War I and familiar with the horrors of combat, and he remained adamant throughout his life that his aim was to end the war as swiftly as possible. Truman also contended that the tremendous American and Japanese casualties on Iwo Jima and Okinawa, two islands vastly smaller in size than mainland Japan, vindicated his belief that the atomic bombings prevented a full-scale invasion of the country and saved innumerable lives—on both sides. When no immediate word of surrender came after Hiroshima was hit on August 6, 1945, Truman gave the word to proceed with the second attack. Early on the morning of August 9, a B-29 Superfortress piloted by twenty-five-year-old Major Charles Sweeney approached the city of Kokura, the site of one of the country's largest munitions plants. Thick clouds and smoke, however, hampered visibility, and the crew could not locate the designated target point. They tried several more times before heading to their alternate city—Nagasaki, home to weapons factories and the Mitsubishi shipyards. One facility was believed to have produced the torpedoes used on Pearl Harbor. Nagasaki, too, was obscured by haze, and with fuel running low, Sweeney and his crew were close to aborting the mission. Suddenly, there was a break in the clouds. At 11:02 A.M. local time, a plutonium bomb nicknamed "Fat Man" dropped through the air and detonated fifteen hundred feet over the heads of the city's two hundred and forty thousand residents. Approximately a third of them were killed, and another third were critically injured. Those closest to the blast were literally vaporized. Twenty-nine-year-old Masao Yamaguchi was the only member of his family living in Nagasaki who did not perish in the attack itself or from radiation poisoning. After the Japanese surrendered on August 14, 1945, Yamaguchi wrote to his sister Yae, who lived in Chigasaki to inform her that their entire family, including his three-year-old son Masakatsu, was gone. (Tadao was their brother, and Ine, Kie, and Yoshi were their sisters. There is no greeting to the letter.)

I must tell you about what happened in Nagasaki on August 9th. At the time, people were constantly anxious because of the threat of daily air raids by the enemy. That's why I decided to evacuate Mother and Masakatsu on the 8th to Kie's place in Katabuchi, but they didn't feel comfortable there, so they came back home to Takenokubo that evening. I sent them to Katabuchi because they have a secure air raid shelter there, and I had heard that the enemies had announced at the time that they were going to burn down Nagasaki on the 8th, so I took them there early morning on the 8th.

Also, the 8th was the day when Tadao was going to get married into the Tani family in Inasa (the Tani family had a daughter who was 19 and a mother) but Mother was busy taking care of Masakatsu who was sick, so Ine and I took Tadao to Tani family's place, and the wedding took place at around 8pm. An air raid siren started blaring, and the lights went out, but everything went smoothly, and after celebrating their wedding, we arrived back home in Takenokubo at around 9:30 pm.

The following day was the 9th. Since Masakatsu was ill at the time, I had taken a day off of work, so I woke up at around 7 am on the 9th. As always, the preliminary alert was issued starting at 6:30 am that day.

On August 1st, the shipyard that I was working for in Akinoura was attacked. Luckily, I wasn't killed, and since then, I've been very careful about listening for the the warnings. Whenever the preliminary alert was issued, I changed into the air defense clothes. And because Mother forgot to bring Masakatsu's medicine with them when they returned from Katabuchi, I left for Katabuchi at 7:30 am.

In the meantime, the air raid warning had stopped, so I left Katabuchi a little before 11am, and took the train to Uragami. When the train was around Hamanomachi, there was a flash and a crashing sound, so I jumped off the train and lay down on the ground. When I got up after a while and looked around, I saw a massive fireball that was coming up from Uragami, and all the houses along the roads had been completely destroyed. I couldn't go further toward Uragami from Gotouchou, so I went back to around the prefectural office, and I'm not sure how I arrived there, but before I knew it, I was at the top of Tateyama. When I looked down, the waterfront to Chikuchou, Uragami was engulfed in flames. Because of the winds, the fire was spreading toward the top of Tateyama. I couldn't keep my eyes open, so I followed a path to the top of Zenza School. The school was incinerated. The blaze started to die down, so I left from there and came out by the Honren temple.

In the midst of all this, I stepped over several dead and injured people. The parts of the body that were exposed were bright red and burnt very badly. There were people screaming, "Help" from everywhere, but I was concerned about getting home, so I dared not to stop for them and dashed through the fire to get to Takenokubo.

There was nothing there. Our house, which was by the middle school, had been completely blown away. I had followed the road as best I could, and when I came across the area that I thought was our house, I found Mother and Masakatsu lying in agony. I didn't see Ine around, and when I picked up Mother, her injury was so severe that her spine was exposed, and her face was swollen. There was dirt in her eyes, mouth and nose. I can't even describe what I saw. As for Masakatsu, he just lay there motionless. When I picked him up, his body was stiff and his eyes were caked with dirt. The only thing he was able to do was to close and open one of his eyes, but he didn't say a word. Mom kept repeating, "Give me water, give me water," but if I gave her water at that moment, I was afraid she was going to choke, so I carried her to the side of the road, and took just Masakatsu to Katabuchi.

When we got to Katabuchi, the sun had set, and the enemy planes were flying endlessly above us. The bell announcing the attacks rang incessantly. While we were in the air raid shelter, I worried about Mother, but there was nothing I could do. Masakatsu was suffering and kept asking for water. His condition was getting worse, and on the third day, the 12th, as he called out for Mother, his short life came to an end. There was no place to cremate him, so I buried him in the ground, in the Kie family's grave.

Also, Tadao, who had just got married the day before the bombing, came to visit me clinging a pillow. Yoshi had just come by from Shimabara, so I decided to stay in the care of Yoshi's family with Tadao. After four days, Tadao developed a fever and diarrhea, and he died on the 18th. The only thing we were able to do for him was to help him find a doctor and have prayers read for him.

I was concerned about Mother, since I had left her, so I took the first train out to Nagasaki on the 19th, and went to Takenokubo, but she was nowhere to be seen. The only thing I saw was the cloth she uses as a pillow, and one rice ball that the rescuers had given her. I didn't find Ine either. I searched the shelter and Inase School, but it was no use.

Going back to Tadao, according to what he had told me before he died, he, his wife and his Mother-in-law were visiting Takenokubo on the 9th. Because it was so hot, he had taken off some of his clothes and was in his underwear when everything started crashing down. He escaped from underneath the house and rescued his Mother-in-law, wife, sister Ine, Mother, and nephew Masakatsu. At that time, there was blood coming out from Ine's mouth and nose, and she was mumbling something, but she started running around hysterically as she suffered, and then she died. I found out that Mother had passed away in the street, so the rescuers most likely cremated her. Tadao had found Mother and was giving her water until the afternoon of the third day, the day when Tadao visited me in Katabuchi. Mother thought he was me, and kept calling him "Masao, Masao."

It is all so tragic. Even as I write all this, my hands shake and my heart aches; the scenes of that day appear before me. They're driving me crazy. Images of Mother lying on the road covered with dirt and blood as she groaned, of Masakatsu, of blades of grass dyed in red, tree after tree torn from the ground, countless people injured and killed. I really thought that the world was coming to an end.

Shimo no gawa area was the worst of all. Many people inhaled poisonous fumes. Even though they didn't have any wounds, a lot of people died. That was the case of Tadao. In the place of Mother and Ine's bones, I took back the burnt dirt of our house and buried it. Tadao's wife and Mother-in-law were able to go back to their home in Inasa, but they did not survive.

What a tragedy. I heard you were injured by the bombing, but keep your spirits high. Rest well, and I hope you will recover soon. I'd like to visit the doctor at your hospital and thank them, but it's not that easy right now, so I send all my love. Take care.

Masao

For the American pilots and crews who had, throughout the war, watched from miles above as bombs demolished Japanese towns and cities below, there was a feeling that justice was being served—not only for Pearl Harbor, but for the millions of lives lost in the war resulting from Japanese aggression throughout the Pacific. "These pilots are all young kids, comparatively speaking," a Life magazine war correspondent named Jack Wilkes wrote to his wife, Sara Jane, on April 4, 1945, while he was covering the China-Burma-India theatre. (The twenty-eight-year-old Wilkes had wanted to be a soldier, but he was disqualified because he had a missing thumb.) He continued:

> It's quite a thrill listening to them over the radio and inter-phone on the plane . . . They act like a bunch of freshman at their first football game. Not all the crew can see their results so it's up to someone who can observe to tell the results . . . And they really sing it out—"You've got a beautiful BEAUTIFUL fire down there" . . . "Right down his throat" . . . Then a circling job for a better look and you go back home in a wreath of smiles. The Japs have been bombed and the accounts are being squared away.

Paul A. Reitz, who actually flew in raids over Japan, echoed these comments in his letters home to Rowan, Iowa. "We went on our 25th mission the evening of August 1st," the twenty-six-year-old first lieutenant told his mom on August 4, 1945.

> It was the largest aerial assault in the history of the war. More than 800 B-29's poured more than 6,000 tons of fire on four more Jap cities. This raid was larger than the greatest ever put over Germany. Our target was the city of Mito, located sixty miles northeast of Tokyo. When we got there the pathfinders had already been there and the city was burning nicely. These Jap towns make such _lovely_ fires.

But when some of these servicemen were able to see the extent of the damage on the ground firsthand, their reactions were more tempered. (For Reitz, the human cost of the air strikes came to him after the war and in his very own hometown; by an incredible coincidence, a Japanese woman who had lived in one of the cities he had bombed moved into a house just a few blocks from his. After the two realized their extraordinary connection, they talked at length about the war and eventually developed a strong friendship. Reitz remained proud of his contribution to the Allied victory, but later expressed regret about the deaths of innocent civilians.) Servicemen who visited Hiroshima and Nagasaki were especially thunderstruck by the enormity of the destruction. "Hiroshima is *something I never hope to see again,"* Colonel Hubert A. Schneider wrote to his wife, Mary, on September 6, 1945, after a visit to what remained of the city.

> *The damage there is so extensive, so complete, that it frightens you. They say Hiroshima was Japan's most modern city and very much like an American city with American type office buildings, apartment houses, etc. Today not more than 5 or 6 of these are standing and every one of these is completely burned out . . . The whole place looks just as if a giant hand had pressed down on the place and then set fire to it. Houses way out of town have caved in roofs and trees in the same area lean away from the city having been pushed over by the blast. A few people poke around among the ruins but even these are taking a chance of being burned by the radio activity which still remains. Hiroshima burned for 8 hours after the bomb fell and people who went in after the fire for rescue purposes died days later from the effects of the rays.*

Photo by Andrew Carroll

Left almost exactly as it was after the atomic bomb obliterated Hiroshima at 8:16 A.M. on August 16, 1945, the "A-Bomb Dome" is one of many reminders and memorials throughout the city that focus on the blast, which killed an estimated seventy thousand Japanese civilians. Those closest to ground zero essentially evaporated.

Serving on a hospital ship that arrived in Nagasaki's harbor just weeks after the city was obliterated, Pharmacist's Mate Second Class Donald West related to his wife, Elizabeth, his experiences treating victims of the radiation. (The long-term effects were still unknown to doctors and scientists at the time.) On September 15, 1945, West sent the following to his wife:

> The radio activity of the atomic bomb hasn't been positively identified. That's one reason we were to take x-rays, to see if we could find anything on the film that would throw any light on the cause of death. The other doctors with us were specialists, too. While we were upstairs they were else-where in the building, watching a post mortem of one of the victims that had just died (a fifteen year old boy), and getting slides and samples and other things for study. The victims of that mysterious energy, whatever it is, just wilt away and die very quickly, once the symptoms begin to assert themselves. These were all injured with that one bomb—the second one—but the symptoms are just now showing up. It's apparently very much like a radium or x-ray burn, but it's so much more widespread that it's very nearly 100 percent fatal, or at least is proving so here. The victims look weak and ill, they aren't visibly injured at all, but the effect is there, and there is no cure. . . . The women and children stared at us with frank curiosity and some bowed politely to us as we passed. But the men, apparently mostly discharged soldiers, ignored us, or looked at us out of the corner of their eyes. We took the opportunity of looking out of the vacant windows to where the town had been around us, but there was nothing there but a rubble of broken bricks and concrete. All the wooden things had been burned up when the fire swept through in the wake of the bomb. I have never seen such complete and thorough destruction before and hope I never do again.

While the almost apocalyptic force of the atomic weapons that exploded over Hiroshima and Nagasaki stunned the world, conventional and incendiary weapons dropped on Japan in the latter part of the war ultimately killed and wounded more civilians. The March 10, 1945, firebombing of Tokyo alone claimed more lives than Nagasaki. On September 9, exactly one week after the Japanese surrender was signed on the USS Missouri, an American commander named Walter C. Michels had the opportunity to visit Yokohama, which had been decimated by aerial bombings. Michels, thirty-nine years old at the time, was so shocked by what he encountered that he felt compelled to write the following letter to his twelve-year-old daughter, Leslyn, back in Strafford, Pennsylvania. (Nan was his wife and Leslyn's stepmother.)

Aboard the U.S.S. Teton
in Yokohama Harbor

Dear Leslyn,

It isn't often that I ask you to save one of my letters, but I am going to ask that you save this one. The reason is that I took time this afternoon to walk about Yokohama for a couple of hours, and what I have to say tonight may be useful to show to someone else in some future day when war again threatens the world and it is up to your generation to stop it.

I don't know whether to be glad or sorry that you weren't able to see the city with me. I'm sorry because the shear awfulness of it all is something that is worth burning into the memory of everybody; I'm glad because I would hate to have you feel as dejected and sick with the human race as I felt when I finished.

Here is a city, or rather was a city, comparable in size with Philadelphia or Baltimore,—one of the leading ports of the world,—so nearly completely destroyed that it will take months just to clean it up, to say nothing of starting reconstruction. Around the edges of the city something is left and looks pretty decent, but in the center nothing but a few buildings stands. And the ones that are still there have been so thoroughly gutted by the intense heat that they will probably be useless.

When I say nothing stands I mean exactly that. It isn't a matter of roofs gone, or broken walls, for all that is left is a pile of the metal parts of the buildings, scattered over the original sites. One can walk down a street and say, "This must have been a pottery shop" because of the broken masses of china left, or, "This was a store," because of the quantities of burnt and scorched tin cans. But those are the only remnants of what were once, houses, offices, work shops, and stores.

I think I felt most depressed when we passed through the remains of a stone wall, of which parts of the gateposts still remained. It had obviously been built around a private residence and the owners name "SENZAKI" was still readable to our interpreter. Inside there were just enough things left to indicate the presence, at one time, of a walled garden, one of those gardens of minature trees and plants, with little pools carved from stone, of which the Japanese people were so fond. Even in its present state there was something about the place that carried the idea of loving care and of a happy family. I could only think of how I would feel had the same thing happened to Strafford!

You understand, dear daughter, that I'm not saying that the incendiary bombing should not have been done. Once the horrible inhuman and ungodly war had started, the consequences could not be avoided. That is why I'm writing to you so seriously tonight. I believe that my generation can help peace for awhile, if we work at it hard enough, but your generation must not forget the capacity for destruction that exists in man, and must somehow see that neither you nor your children face this again. I don't want your sons, if you have any, to look upon the sight that I saw today, or on the even worse sights which another war may bring, with improved technical means of killing and maiming the bodies and souls of other men.

In order to accomplish that, you, I, and everyone else who believes in the Christian ideals by which we supposedly live must get into the political race and fight for right, even though it inconveniences each of us and interferes with the things that we want to do. That thing that appears on your report card at Baldwin "Good Citizenship" is very, very important.

I hope that you'll show this letter to Nan and that you won't think that your Daddy is being too impersonal and serious in writing this way, but I feel very keenly tonight that we all have a big job ahead, which we must tackle in the spirit of my favorite quotation from Lincoln, "With malice toward none, with charity for all, and with a firm determination to do the right as God gives us to see the right."

Love and goodnight to a dear daughter from,

Daddy

The impact of Michels's trip to Yokohama was not fleeting; after the war he converted to Quakerism, a denomination of Christianity that advocates nonviolence as one of its fundamental tenets.

— ᴍ —

Lieutenant Colonel W. L. Larson Tells His Daughter Antoinette About a Horrific Accident Involving Several Korean Children

Although servicemen and -women usually refrain from sharing vivid depictions of violence in correspondences to younger family members, they will occasionally—perhaps for cathartic reasons or to remind their children of the realities of warfare—detail gruesome incidents with surprising bluntness. Letters written by troops during the Korean War, in particular, tended to be more candid than those from World War II because there was virtually no censorship. In a short, jarring letter to his ten-year-old daughter in Fredericksburg, Virginia, Lieutenant Colonel W. L. Larson described the awful outcome of the discovery by some inquisitive Korean children of unexploded artillery. (The letter, apparently handwritten in haste or under duress, is missing words in several places.)

Dear Toni:

How's my big pretty girl this evening?

Some small Korean children picked up a live ammunition on our test range which hadn't gone off or exploded. These children took large shell home and started hammering on it with a rock and it exploded. It killed one or two and wounded about three other children. We expect none of them to live. One piece of shrapnel went right through ~~her~~ stomach of one of young girls. The Air Force and other unit used this range so we don't know whether it was our ammunition or some one elses.

Such things are terrible particularly when they are young children.

A Big Hug & Kiss,

Daddy

———

Cecilia Reed, Serving as a Nurse in Vietnam, Sends a Note to Relatives About Attacks on US Army Hospitals by Pro-Communist Collaborators Pretending to Be Civilians & The Younger Sibling of a North Vietnamese Soldier Implores His Brother to Avenge Their Family Members Killed by Enemy Bombings

From British soldiers battling ragtag American minutemen in the late eighteenth century to Coalition forces clashing with insurgents in Iraq more than two hundred years later, it is a dilemma that confounds and infuriates almost all troops who fight in a foreign land: how does one distinguish between harmless civilians and enemy combatants, who often wear no uniforms and can instantly blend into the native population after hiding or discarding their weapons? American troops have faced this threat in many conflicts, but during the Vietnam War, the confusion proved especially tragic for both sides. "Let me tell you what goes on around here," a US soldier wrote to a buddy back in the States, "over here you have to watch everbody." (The letter has numerous misspellings and almost no punctuation.)

One of my friends was walking through the jungle and a women picked up her skirt and fired him twice She was up in a tree hiding my friend saw her—shot back once and killed a little kid about 5 year old—We were fighting so one sargent pulled out a [grenade] and through it at some soldier The little kid ran out picked it up and threw it back at the sargent and blew up the sergeant. . . . When you fight over here ~~most of~~ a lot of time these Viet Congs will bring there wives and children and walk

*behind them and at the same time shoot at you. . . . The only people I feel
sorry for is the little kid because the don't know better.*

*Even medical facilities, which treated both Americans and Vietnamese, were tar-
geted by the pro-Communist forces with makeshift explosives carried or planted
by presumedly innocent citizens. Cecilia Reed, a forty-nine-year-old nurse
from Milroy, Montana, updated family members about her service with a US
Army evacuation hospital near Pleiku. "Everyone has great respect for these people," Reed said of relations between her staff and the Vietnamese. "There is a very
extensive program going on in helping the people as well as the war." But several months later a flurry of bombings would make it impossible for the Americans to help the locals who depended on their care. (Reed's letter contains many
typos, which are likely the result of—as indicated in other correspondence—the
poor quality of the typewriter she was using. The reference to "svcm" is an abbreviation for serviceman, and CO is commanding officer.)*

Sunday morning 8/24/69

This is a nice Sunday morning, beautiful weather and a good rest last
night. Was talking to a young svcm who was down at the 6th convalesc
ent Center the day after the attack and he said that it was an inside job as
well as from outside and that there were sachel charges planted all over
the place. and at least twelve wards and other bldgs blown up. Almost a
hundred injuries and two deaths. So guess we are not being any too
careful. IN fact the CO told me the other day that they found on one of
the visitors, Vietnamese, the making of one and when they found it on
her, the patient who, she had been visiting departed the hopsital the next
day. Our CO is gradually weeding out all of the Viet. and Montonyards
patients from the hosp. which is very sad in one way because it is the
only medical care available to them. On the other hand, we must prtect
our own US patients and staff. In deed, it is a strange type of war. The
gate between us and the Air Base is now open and it is just about two
blocks to their club which makew everyone happy again. Should wind
this up and beleive I'm at the bottom, about.

Love, Ceil

*As with any major conflict, determining the exact number of civilian casualties
in Vietnam is nearly impossible. Estimates for the "American period" of the war
range from hundreds of thousands of deaths to 5.1 million, a figure announced
by the Vietnamese government in 1995. (This number is significantly higher
than what the pro-Communist forces reported twenty years earlier, but in
1995 Vietnamese officials conceded that a lower number had been manufactured*

during the war so as not to demoralize their people.) There is little debate, however, over the fact that the war inflicted widespread suffering on civilian men, women, and children throughout North and South Vietnam, as well as in Cambodia and Laos. Civilian deaths also, not surprisingly, fueled hostility toward the enemy. With the exception of his first name (Thoa) and the fact that he was later killed in battle, little is known about the North Vietnamese soldier who received the following letter from a younger brother living at home. Much of the letter concerns everyday family matters and clearly reflects the sentiments of a sibling longing for the safe return of a beloved brother. But it is also an impassioned reminder as to why he is fighting.

Vinh Yen, Nov. 1967

My dear brother,

This is your little brother! Do you miss me? Since I was back in the country and met you while you were on leave, I have not received any letters from you. I am working hard and time passes by quickly. I am also helping with the re-construction of many collapsed bridges. I have transferred to a Middle Transport Professional and Technical School. Today, I am taking time to write a letter to you.

My dear brother, our grandparents, aunts, and I are all well. Our family is okay. I want to inform you briefly about my job and I hope that you will not worry about me, "All to serve our country." I also want to tell you to revenge our father!

Regarding my job, I am teaching at the Middle Transport Professional and Technical School of Ha Noi. There are 120 instructors and 1,257 students in my school. I am responsible for training 120 students in technical skills. My students are all different ages, the eldest is 30 years old and the youngest is 18; they are staff officers. Also there are some international students from Laos. I am helping 5 Laotian students in studies.

Life at my school is relatively poor. As you know our country is at war; the American army is losing, so they have gone crazy and have been dropping bombs everywhere. Therefore, my school has had to evacuate to a forest location at the Vinh Phu province. As a result, our accommodations and classrooms are in need of improvement.

Regarding my studies, I am now in school till June-1968 and I am planning to study at a University after that. Now, my salary is VND 50 per month including 0.5 kg sugar, 18 kg rice; it relatively good for me.

My dear brother, I have traveled to many places and many cities. Every time I go to either Ha Noi, or Hai Phong, or back to our town, I always think of you—I miss you so much. How wonderful it would be if you would have accompanied me on those trips. Oh! I would like to share with you my good news; our grandparents and parents will buy me a bike either in coming May or June-1968. I hope that you will be happier knowing this news.

Next I must tell you the bad news, that on 22-August-1966, an American airplane bombed the city of Ha Noi, and they killed our uncle's wife. She dies leaving behind four children for uncle Can. Our grandmother has to help him to look after his children. She is exhausted.

Regarding uncle Do, uncle Ha, and their wives, they are doing well. They love to share the happiness with you. And Mrs. Ngoat has graduated, but she is not sure which school she will be assigned to for teaching. She is doing fine though.

Dear brother! Living at this time, we need to strive for the ideals of our youth; I am also serving our country diligently.

My brother, this letter is quite long already. I promise that I will write you more next letter. Now try to focus on your job: kill more American soldiers to revenge our father and for many other people who have died.

With the love from the bottom of my heart, I wish you health, and happiness. Remember to write a letter to our grandparents so that they are not so worried about you. Once again, I wish you all the best, and more successes in fighting against the American empire invading our country.

Hope to see you soon. In a warm and welcoming home.

Love your younger brother.

How the North Vietnamese soldier was killed is uncertain, but a US service-man who came across his body noticed the letter and kept it as a souvenir, a common practice in wartime. American soldiers were encouraged to destroy their letters from home so that the enemy could not glean essential information from them or determine the state of American morale—either in Vietnam or in the US. Although there is no indication that such a thing ever happened, a twenty-year-old young private first class named Dan Wagenaar described in a July 1969 letter home a devious ploy involving discarded letters.

> *I'll just jot down a few lines. We're at Dau Teing after three nights in the field. We're going to Tay Nihn for awhile apparently. I'll be glad to see what it's like up there although I like this place we've been at. Also, I might caution you and Mom and Dad if you get some letter that says the VC have got me or killed me don't pay any attention to it as VC pick up our old envelopes and have letters sent to the families to worry them. It's very unlikely that such a thing would happen, but it's possible. Well, I'd better close, we have a lot to do.*

Several days later—and before they had even received his brief letter—Wagenaar's family was officially notified that Dan had been killed in Vietnam.

—⁓—

**Sarajevo Resident Mevlida Pekmez Expresses to Her Sister
and Mother the Anxiety She Feels as the Siege of
Their Beleaguered City Continues
&
As Serbian Troops Assault the "Safe Haven" of Srebrenica,
a Dutch Army Medic Named André Dekker Tells His Girlfriend Ingrid
That This Might Be His Final Message to Her
&
In a Terse, Fragmented Letter, Dekker Shares
with Ingrid His Impressions of the Fall of Srebrenica
&
As NATO Warplanes Bomb Belgrade, Patricia A. Andjelkovic E-mails
Family and Friends Abroad About the Degree to Which She
and Her Neighbors Are Trying to Maintain a Sense of Normalcy**

On November 2, 1991, a group of Serbian soldiers entered a hospital in the town of Vukovar, Croatia, and rounded up approximately two hundred and sixty patients, both civilian and military, along with doctors and members of the hospital staff. The Croats were taken to the neighboring town of Ovcara, where many were beaten. (A small number were released.) Under cover of darkness, the Serbs then drove the Croats to a pig farm, lined them up side by side, and mowed them down with machine guns and automatic rifles. The corpses were tossed into a mass, unmarked grave. The Vukovar massacre, as it would be remembered, was merely a prelude to the bloodshed that would envelop the Balkans in the years to come. After Yugoslavia's Communist ruler Josip Broz Tito died in 1980, tensions flared between the republics that constituted Yugoslavia, and in 1991, Slovenia and Croatia officially proclaimed their separation from the federation. Slobodan Milosevic, the Serbian president of Yugoslavia at the time (Serbia was home to the Yugoslav capital, Belgrade, and was the largest of the republics, both geographically and in terms of population), dispatched ground and naval forces to halt the secession as aggressively as possible. Dubrovnik, considered one of the most picturesque cities on the Adriatic coast, sustained a three-month bombardment from the sea—a display of brute force by Milosevic intended both to intimidate Croatia into submission and to serve as a cautionary example for other republics considering a move toward autonomy. Refusing to be threatened, Bosnia and Herzegovina declared independence in March 1992. Bosnians of Serb ethnicity began to fight with

Bosnian Muslims, with the most volatile area being the nation's capital, Sarajevo, a multiethnic city of almost half a million people. Thousands of peace demonstrators spontaneously took to the streets in the beginning of April 1992, only to be gunned down by Serb militants. Milosevic and Radovan Karadzic, leader of the Bosnian Serbs, blockaded all roads leading in and out of the city and closed down the international airport. The citizens were trapped, and no outside aid—including food and medicine—could come in. Serb artillery and sniper units moved into position on the hills and mountains that surrounded the city, and by mid-April, the thunder of incoming shells announced that the siege of Sarajevo had begun. As the Serb stranglehold tightened, residents assumed that the world would be outraged and press Milosevic to withdraw his forces. (Bosnia's own army was no match for the Serbian troops.) Week after week, they waited. No help came. Months turned into a full year, and then another. United Nations resolutions were passed, an arms embargo on all of the republics was imposed, as were economic sanctions, but little of it staunched the violence. Thousands of people were dying—shot by snipers on their way to work or school; killed in the daily mortar attacks on apartment buildings, busy thoroughfares, parks, and even cemeteries where families had gathered to bury a loved one; or became victims of malnutrition and cold. The number of miscarriages and deaths by suicide soared, while birthrates plunged. Traveling anywhere in the city, even just a few blocks, could be fatal, and people depended on letters either carried by loved ones or delivered through the Red Cross to check in on each other's well-being. The following message was sent by Mevlida

Photo by Andrew Carroll

An elderly man walks through a cemetery in Sarajevo.

Pekmez to her sister Raza Durakovic, who was caring for their mother. Like many letters of the time, it accentuates the despair experienced by so many residents of Sarajevo as the siege wore them down mentally and physically. (Although not everyone mentioned in the letter is identifiable, Enes is their brother, Selma is his daughter, and Avdo is Mevlida's husband. The paper is in poor condition, making the text illegible in parts.)

My Dear ones,

I am losing hope that I will ever see you. My dear mother, I cry every day. Every day, every moment. . . . These letters are very slow in getting to you. I see that you have written on January 3rd but I got it only on April 2nd. I have no idea what is going on with you. I know mom is ill, I know you are desperate, I know you don't have anything, like us, but all this can be overcome if these atrocities would stop so we can get together again. My dear mother, I beg you to hold on, don't give up. The children dream about you all the time. I don't dream about you, I'm with you twenty-four hours a day. . . .

I've moved three times so far. You can survive for only five days from the humanitarian aid. We went into this war without money. . . . Mubera has made the children very happy. She has sent them 200 marks, and Ajko 100. One relative sent me 100 marks. That's all I have for this year. A pack of eggs costs 50 marks. Sugar is 80. Imagine how happy the kids are when I'm able to get that for them. They're wonderful. They're not kids anymore, but old people. They don't go to school. It's too far away and it is dangerous to take them. Also, they don't have any clothes or shoes to put on to go to school. What can I tell you about Enes? Should I write to you about what he has been through? Selma has unsurprisingly taken the whole thing well. . . .

Avdo has changed drastically for the worse. He is fighting like a lion, but this situation seems an eternity. He's dreaming to take us somewhere out of here. Where?! There are no roads around us. Some cry to come back, while others try to run away through the airport and die like chickens. Oh God, you have loved all these people for all of us. There's no space in this letter for Emir to write you. He will write you through the Red Cross.

I love you and kiss you. Say hello to Nada, Jelha, Dzemo.

As Serbian atrocities against Bosnian civilians escalated, pressure on Europe and the United States, in particular, to end the siege was also mounting. But there was still reluctance to get involved (or, in the words of some anti-interventionists, "entangled") in the Balkans crisis. Everything changed after Sre-

brenica. Located in the easternmost part of Bosnia and Herzegovina, Srebrenica was designated a UN "safe haven" and protected by Dutch peacekeepers. The lightly armed troops were ordered not to engage the Serbs except in self-defense. On July 7, 1995, thousands of Serb forces descended on Srebrenica. The Dutch urgently requested air support but none came. As the sound of gunfire and shells exploded all around them, death seemed a certainty. André Dekker, a twenty-year-old army medic, frequently updated his girlfriend, Ingrid, on the rising tensions in the region. On the evening of the 6th, fearing for his life, Dekker dashed out a final letter to his girlfriend. In the heat of the moment, he addressed her as his wife. They were not married. (OP is an abbreviation for Observation Post, and QRF stands for Quick Reaction Force.)

20:00
To my dearest wife

During this moment of great uncertainty, I am writing you a farewell letter. Since four-thirty this morning, our enclave has been under fire from tanks, artillery, and mortars. Since then we have been cooped up in the bunker, allowed only to go out sporadically and in full gear. OP Foxtrot, which was closest to OP Echo, took three direct hits. No casualties, only damage to the OP. There were several detonations of unclear origin. The question is whether OP Foxtrot has to leave now or not.

At any rate, I told Alex that I wanted to go with him on the YPR in case something went wrong, but Willem came up to me and told me I was to take over the QRF from Jasper, whose grandfather had just passed away. Stands to reason, and I didn't mind, but the situation is growing steadily more threatening, and combined with the fact that my rotation has been moved up again and it is not clear what is going to happen next, there are a few things I must tell you. On TV they say that Foxtrot was only hit once and that we are not under fire ourselves. However, the opposite is true.

I am a medic with the QRF (1900) until the day after tomorrow. Two whole days. Things may change then, but I'll cross that bridge when I come to it. It's just that the feeling I have now is not good. And with the threat of an attack, I am fearing for my life for the first time. It may be because the tour is coming to an end. It doesn't matter what brings it about, I'm having a bad premonition. I'm hoping that I am not good at this sort of thing and everything will turn out all right, but it's very depressing.

I will sleep in the bunker with my colleagues of the QRF as well, so we'll be the first to know if something happens. For now, enough of this.

My point actually is that I have come to the conviction that you were the woman I wanted to marry. I am eternally grateful to you for all the support you have indirectly given me and my family these past months. So grateful that I would turn the world upside down if I ever had to go and look for you. Perhaps you received some comfort from me, as I certainly got it from you. You're everything to me, my confidante, my shoulder to cry on, my love nest, and everything you give to me exceeds my expectations. I feel good when I'm with you, I can be myself and together we are invincible.

Ingrid, you really were my wife.

Do not be sad for what has happened
Think with pleasure of all that we were able to do
And the good times we had.
Look ahead with your head held high
And set course for your future
You, the strongest, the most joyful and loving woman in the world
Find peace within and go on.
Do this for me, then I will have done this for you.
André

The Dutch troops were taken hostage by the Serbs but later released, and Dekker made it through the attack uninjured. The remaining residents of Srebrenica were not so fortunate. Beginning on July 10, the Serbs surrounded an estimated twelve thousand five hundred Bosnian Muslims, almost all of whom were men, including many young boys. Over five thousand were able to escape to safety, but the remaining seven thousand or so were enfiladed with machine gun fire, mortared at close range, and positioned in groups directly in front of tanks, which then fired on them point blank. Almost two weeks after his farewell letter, Dekker was far from Srebrenica and able to inform Ingrid he was alive. But he was deeply shaken, and on July 19 he composed a somewhat disjointed letter that listed images and observations that had stuck in his memory. "I couldn't write in the last few weeks, it was just too much, too terrible to put into words," he began. "Therefore, I will use catchwords and try to clarify everything a little more. . . ." (The initials YPR refer to an armed personnel carrier.)

I am writing this letter to you on one of the evenings preceding our departure.

The planned itinerary is to go to Split and next to Belgrade, but all of us prefer Zagreb.

The reason is very simple. We do not want to run the risk of having to cross through Muslim territory and to come under fire again as yet. Having to pass along sniper alley south of Sarajevo and to put our lives in the balance. Not only that, but it's also a three-day drive and all we want, when we go, is to get home as quickly as possible. Isn't this what the politicians wanted as well: "We want to get our Dutch military personnel home as quickly as possible." Of course.

Both of us will have learned plenty, and certainly the fact that waiting in uncertainty supercedes the facts as established by either the politicians or Defense or any other agency, and certainly in view of the past half year.

As it turns out, the reunion with family and friends is not all that important, as evident from the TV news, where it was said that hundreds of family members were still waiting for their returning soldiers. Luckily, we haven't had all that many bad experiences here and so we don't want to go home yet.

No, the decision was made that we can leave with all materiel we have here. Because relocating by convoy would be far to slow, we need transport materiel which should arrive tomorrow.

- Under fire at Foxtrot, seized the next day
- Multiple o.p.'s threatened and seized subsequently
- Foxtrot colleague killed during retreat
- Nights, days in the bunker
- Stood in the middle of town for one day with the YPR, Alex and Willem
- Mortar and rocket strikes at 50 meters from the YPR
- The next day, hundreds, thousands of refugees in and around the compound
- Horrible scenes
- Cowardly enemy fighters scream like everybody else
- Another day later, thousands of refugees in compound after the town came under fire
- Hysteria
- Request for air support
- Mortar / rocket on compound
- Wounded people in our buildings, boy with injured arm, girl with injured leg, both wounded by grenades; old woman with hole in hip
- total hysteria
- Keep head cool, am the last returning medic
- Signal to take down compound, ran to the YPR under fire and unprotected
- Drive to Potocari

- emergency aid refugees, wounded
- coffee in bunker, then slept
- had to burn letters
- tending to the wounded
- half of the wounded transported Kladanj, Tuzla, crippled people, dead people
- had to leave behind lad with broken pelvis in Bratunac
- Doc Shouten remained with the Serbs voluntarily
- Girl with injured leg, and old woman in truck
- Saw refugees pass by during traffic jam. Familiar faces
- Had a break-down with Willem
- Maximum engagement for taking care of the wounded and the sick
- Little guy with smiling eyes, man with black eye and stick, man with cigarette and aching back, the two gals, the woman who had just had an abortion, the singing man, the boy without parents, the foul-smelling man next to the screaming woman, I.V.s, catheters and injections.
- Farewell?
- TV images arrival in Tuzla
- Rest, talk, sleep and come to our senses, think a lot and hope for a speedy return to The Netherlands.

Considered the worst wartime atrocity in Europe since 1945, the massacre at Srebrenica, and subsequent mortar attacks on marketplaces in Sarajevo itself, triggered the US and its allies to launch NATO airstrikes against the Serbs. Now facing the military might of the West and a rebuilt Croatian army (which Milosevic denounced for committing atrocities against Serbs), Milosevic agreed to a cease-fire. In December 1995 a peace treaty, based on negotiations the month before in Dayton, Ohio, at the Wright-Paterson Air Force Base, was signed by Milosevic, President Alija Izetbegovic of Bosnia and Herzegovina, and President Franjo Tudjman of Croatia. (NATO forces were then dispatched to the region to implement the agreement.) Just as the Balkans were struggling to establish a semblance of calm and stability, another region of the former Yugoslavia was disintegrating into turmoil. The ethnic Albanians who lived in Kosovo, a province of Serbia, were now pushing for autonomy as well. (Most Kosovars were ethnic Albanians, and although ethnic Serbs represented a minority of the population, they controlled the government and the military.) During the mid-1990s, the Kosovo Liberation Army began clashing with Serb forces, and by 1998 President Slobodan Milosevic was accused of once again initiating a campaign of ethnic cleansing to crush the independence movement and to make Kosovo ethnically "pure." Exasperated with Milosevic and the orders emanat-

ing from his administration in Belgrade, NATO began an intensive air war against Serb positions in Kosovo. But this time NATO warplanes also struck Belgrade, itself, hammering military and government installations in the Serb capital. Patricia A. Andjelkovic was a teacher in Belgrade who began to send e-mails to family and friends abroad after the first bombs began to fall on March 25, 1999. Andjelkovic loathed Milosevic (as did many Serbs), but was furious about the air raids, convinced that while what was happening in Kosovo to the ethnic Albanians was an injustice, the crisis was an internal matter in which the world had no right to meddle—and one that potentially could have been averted if the West had supported Serbs who demonstrated en masse against Milosevic in 1996 and 1997. What especially angered Andjelkovic was the NATO tactic of knocking out bridges, factories, power grids, and other facilities on which the people of Belgrade as a whole relied. "Before I lost the lights this morning, another satellite reporter literally gloated over the strikes on power plants," Andjelkovic wrote on May 25.

> *I think strikes against targets which heavily affect the civilian population cannot, in any terms, be condoned. They are cruel, inhumane, and show a definite lack of respect for human life. Do they care how many people have already suffered or died because there's no current or water? . . . There are people who depend on dialysis machines, those who must use absolutely sterile equipment, and those being otherwise cared for in hospitals.*

Her outrage culminated on April 12, when a precision-guided missile struck a train dead-on as it crossed a bridge, killing or wounding about two dozen pas-

Postcard from
Belgrade,
Serbia.

sengers. A NATO spokesperson expressed regret over the loss of life, but insisted the bridge itself was a legitimate military target and the train was not meant to be hit. Andjelkovic had her own views on the subject. (The pronunciations added parenthetically are Andjelkovic's own.)

> *Just a few minutes ago I heard on the news (local and foreign) that an international passenger train, bound for Greece, was bombed around noon as it passed over a bridge near Leskovac (LES-ko-vahts), about three hours south of Belgrade. Eight people or so were killed, some apparently children. These lives, unsuspecting passengers, people like you or me, were the "collateral damage" (sounds so much better than "deaths", doesn't it?) that NATO speaks of. Why, for God's sake, would a pilot bomb a bridge with a train on it in broad daylight? . . . What in God's name went on in the pilot's head? I imagine that even with high-tech warfare, it still comes down to a human being to push the button.*

Andjelkovic tried to focus on positive stories, too, most notably the efforts of the city's residents to band together and persevere during the blackouts, water shortages, deafening explosions, and constant fear of being in the wrong place at the wrong time. Three and a half weeks into the NATO campaign, Andjelkovic related an annual event in Belgrade that she had assumed was going to be cancelled under the given circumstances.

April 19, 1999
Monday

Dear Family/Friends,

I hope my several days silence hasn't troubled anyone. We are still here, relatively safe and sound. I spent Saturday continuing to do spring cleaning around the house, interspersed with long dog walks, and cruising the grocery stores for things I may need. There are still no shortages, but to the trained observer (i.e. anyone who survived the sanctions imposed on Yugoslavia during the Bosnian War), it's obvious that there will be. Grocery stores are beginning to rearrange items on the shelves, spreading them out, rows of products are no longer 3–4 rows deep, and more expensive, imported items are more predominant, the local ones having been all but bought up. I don't have the natural instinct to lay in great amounts of necessities. Some people are buying large sacks of flour, liters and liters of cooking oil. Perhaps I should.

A few letters back, I mentioned that I had noticed that the city's white traffic lines and pedestrian crosswalks had been repainted, and that this was usually done in April because of the yearly Belgrade Marathon, open to runners from all over the world. I had doubted that this event would take place this year, but sure enough, last Saturday, 15,000 runners from Yugoslavia and 10 foreign countries, including the US, braved a torrential downpour worsened by hail, to complete a shortened route of the marathon's 46 km regular course. If they had run the full course, the participants would have passed in front of our building, but this year I had to watch on tv.

Usually, the Belgrade Marathon offers a cash prize and a car to the winner, but because of the exceptional circumstances this year, Belgrade's 12th marathon was transformed into a "fun run". Indeed, the theme was "Stop the Bombs, Run the World". Before you read too much of the last part, know that it is a poor translation of "Trcite Svet" (run around the world). No double-entendres intended; the other meaning would have required a different verb. Instead of an official number, the participants, ranging in age from 70's to babies in pushcarts, had targets pinned to their shirts. Because of the pouring rain, onlookers didn't have to offer water to the runners, but encouraged them by waving peace flags and cheering. The circuit was not only shortened, but also slightly rerouted to show television viewers the damage done to several of the city's buildings.

I am a strong walker, but I've always admired the stamina of runners, and I always watch the marathon both on tv for the downtown part, and often outside my building or by the river park where I can watch in person. This year, the marathon meant something more to me and, I'm sure, to all of those watching and participating. Gone were the cash and the flashy car prizes, gone were the fame and glory of winning, but people ran as if the laurels still awaited them. (Again, it's the teacher in me, but in the past few years, it's hard to get kids to do anything above and beyond the call of duty without their asking, "Do we get candy/stickers?" Gone is much of the intrinsic value of "just for fun".)

To be truthful, I had to admit that running a marathon in the midst of war, be it a de facto one as if that makes it any less of a war, appeared to me at first as absurd. However, as I watched these people, Yugoslav and foreign, running their hearts out, the race made more and more sense. For both participants and spectators, it was a chance to do more than run or cheer. It was an opportunity to show the world in some small way their opposition to the bombing. Physically for them and for the spectators, the race purged their anxiety, frustration, and anger in a healthy, non-violent way. Their enthusiasm was not dampened by the rain, which beat down for a greater part of the race. Nevertheless, I had to suppress a fleeting thought about the rain, which still emerges as I watch local vegetable and flower gardens grow each day—what's in the rain?

Bombs have fallen on chemical factories in nearby Pancevo (PAHN-cheh-vo), releasing amounts of chlorine, ammonia, and other chemicals into the air. The rain falls onto earth and whatever's on it, in it. Don't talk to me about using or not using chemical warfare. It's the same thing to drop a bomb with dangerous chemicals as it is to hit factories that produce chemicals, and allow them to spread. And spread they do, far and wide.

A few days back, President Clinton spoke to the nation, reiterating that he had nothing against the Serbian people, and that we Americans shouldn't either. I don't think the Serbian Americans believe that, nor do the Serbian people here. As the cliché goes, actions speak much, much, louder than words. It's hard to believe the President's statement when your husband has lost a leg, your son has been called up, when your house no longer exists, when you jump when a car backfires, or when you have to explain to small children why they are being bombed.

On Saturday during the day they ran in Belgrade for fun. At night, many flee to the shelters. In Kosovo, villagers run for their lives. All of this could have been prevented, resolved in a peaceful, humane manner, and long before it came to this humanitarian and ecological catastrophe, which directly affects not only Serbia (and I'm including Kosovo, which is part of Serbia), but all of Europe.

Until next time.

On June 9, after seventy-eight days of bombing, Milosevic relented and agreed to allow UN peacekeepers into Kosovo. Sixteen months later, he lost the presidential elections to Vojislav Kostunica. Milosevic initially refused to accept the results and holed up in the presidential compound, where he stayed for six months. He finally surrendered himself in April 2001 and was later taken to the Hague to stand trial for war crimes. Despite the seeming irrefutability of his guilt, Milosevic remained a hero to many Serbs, and only two and a half years after his arrest, while he was still in jail awaiting trial, he was elected to a seat in Serbia's parliament.

—⚬—

Safely Back Home, Anna Miller Tells Her Loved Ones About an Unprecedented Act of Violence That Occurred Right Before Her Eyes

"First, let me say that I would not have or be making it through experiencing this trauma without all of the incredible support, care, concern, and love I have felt poured on to me," twenty-two-year-old Anna Miller began a deeply heart-

felt "thank you" letter to her family and close friends. "I realize this letter is arriving to you all almost a month late," Miller went on to say,

> *but it has taken me time—time to express my thoughts and emotions— sometimes I would start to write and just get too emotionl, or feel like I needed a break. So I apologize—but here it is . . .*

Miller had returned home to North Carolina several weeks before from what was supposed to have been a routine business trip, and she wanted everyone close to her to know exactly what had happened and that their thoughts and prayers were truly appreciated. In ten handwritten pages, Miller went on to describe how, while attending a business seminar in a Lower Manhattan hotel, she and her coworkers suddenly became eyewitnesses to—and almost victims of—one of the most catastrophic attacks in United States history. (The letter is uncut; the ellipses are in the original.)

My hotel room was on the 30th floor; therefore, waiting on the elevator seemed like an eternity. I walked to the window and looked at this beautiful building next door to us that was having all of this construction and rennovations done to it. We started our meeting just after 8:30—after telling everyone that when we had our lunch break at noon, the best place to go was across the street to the world trade center—they had a great food court. My co-worker Paige & I were sitting in the back of the room and she was telling me how good the shopping was there & that we also <u>had</u> to go eat at the Windows on the World restaurant at the top of the w.t.c. At this point, I remember hearing this really loud noise, which I now realize was the first plane flying overhead, and then <u>loud</u> crashing sounds. I remember thinking to myself "Oh gosh—some of the construction from the building next door has fallen & hit our building." Bob, my other co-worker who was instructing the class at the time, thought/said the same thing and we continued on with business. Because we were on the 3rd floor & almost directly under the W.T.C. we could not see/realize what had happened. There was a gap in the curtains and I couldn't help but peering out to see if I could determine what had happened. I saw people beginning to gather on the street corner & noticed that they were all looking & pointing up. Bob was having to raise his voice because suddenly all you could ~~wh~~ hear were sirens.

At that point, I tried to subtely motion to Bob that something was definitely going on out there & a man in our class said, "I don't mean to be rude, but can we stop for a second and look out the windows to see what's going on?" At that point, everyone rushed to the windows. I remember looking down and seeing <u>no</u> cars on this normally busy NYC street except for a few scattered down the street, stopped in their tracks, pan caked by the fallen debris; And every kind of emergency vehicle you can image coming from every direction. More and more people were gathering on the street, but because we were directly below it, we still could not tell what had happened. Paige & I went down to the lobby to try & figure out what was happening and that's when I realized it was something major. They were not letting anyone out of the hotel and the lobby was becoming a medical station. People were coming in or being brought in off the streets, some were what seemed to be going into shock, others covered in blood, others even worse—EMS people were setting up medical stations and I decided we'd better get back up to the room, get Bob (our other co-worker—older man—Paige & I are both in our 20's) and figure out what we should do. We got back up to the conference room where everyone was, still faces plastered to the window. Just as I got to the window to look out again someone screamed Holy Shit, (sorry) I could hear another loud noise, and looked up to realize that it was a commercial airliner swerving around a building in front/diagonal of us. Then it disappeared. Then another boom & our building shook. Still, no idea that the WTC had been hit—just very aware that something terrible was happening and having no idea what to do.

I remember as I was looking out the window I turned to the guy Brian beside me & said "Brian, I really think that's blood & flesh, in the street." After which, I ran for the pay phones outside of our room to call my family and tell them I loved them because I had no idea what was about to happen to me. No luck—not a single phone—regular or cell, was working. Then an emergency intercom system came over and said that the New York City police department was evacuating the building. I was petrified to go out there. After a team of Marriott grey-suited workers led us through stairways, offices, a kitchen, and I couldn't really tell you where else, we made it to a back emergency exit. None of the normal exits/entrances were open because the debris was falling there, blood/flesh was in the street, rescue cars were everywhere, etc. So, we got to this exit and another Marriott worker, who obviously had not heard NYPD announcement said "you musn't go out there—it's terrible, you don't want to see what's in the streets." Someone yelled to him that we had been told to evacuate & he commanded that we all keep our heads up, <u>don't look</u> at what is in the streets, and <u>RUN,</u> RUN in the same direction as everyone else. We got out & did exactly that. (At this point I was with Paige, and 3 men from our class Bryan, Jack, and Gier—who I will never forget as long as I live) We held hands & ran with the screaming masses of paniced people. I noticed though that everyone kept turning around & looking up—we all did too—And that's when I saw both WTC bldgs above me in flames and someone jump from I have no idea what floor.

I didn't look back again until we got to the point where we couldn't run any further, Battery Park. We figured it was the safest place because if they were going to attack again, there were no buildings in the park. I stood there in absolute shock, terror, and disbelief as I watched the towers burn. Black smoke was billowing out from the buildings and more & more people were running into the park for safety. It was so petrifying to be in the middle of it all because all that you know of what is happening is what you're seeing right before your eyes—which is horrific—and what all of the paniced people are screaming. "America's under attack." "All of New York is going to be blown up." "We've gone to war." and on and on. . . . I was frantic to get in touch with anyone in my family because I knew they probably knew by now what was happening and that I was in the middle of it. I wasn't sure if I was going to live through that day and wanted to be able to let anyone and everyone know how much I loved them. I was afraid it was going to be my last chance. Every time I tried a cell phone all I could get was a busy signal . . . No one could get a cell phone, or any phone for that matter, to work. But I was bound & determined to get through to someone. I was shaking so badly I could barely dial the numbers. Finally I was able to get through to my Dad and the sound of his voice, while it was exactly what I wanted to hear, made me all the more afraid. Afraid it was the last time.

Just as I hung up the phone, ~~and start~~ I watched the first building fall. There was so much commotion, screams, noise, confusion—that even though I had known the building had just fallen and that's what was filling the city air with the overhead intense sounds—I couldn't make clear reasoning and I thought it was more planes flying over to wipe out New York. The air around us was starting to get darker and massive herds of screaming people starting running—I realized they were running from this black wall that was quickly approaching—I remember thinking "This is it. This wall of I don't know what that is moving towards me has poison in it that will kill us all." All 5 of us got down and put our faces to the ground and the men covered us with their jackets/shirts I just broke down into tears, so terribly frightened, And although we couldn't look at each other, Paige grabbed for my hand and said "Anna, this is not our time to die. We will make it through this." We stayed in that huddle for I don't know how long—what seems like forever, until finally we realized that people had begun to move around us. I stood up to a shower of soot. Literally, it was pouring soot. We couldn't really open our eyes and I had covered my mouth and nose with the man Jack I was with's jacket. ~~That's when~~ We were all huddling there, I guess just stunned not knowing <u>what</u> to do and that's when I saw Bob (our co-worker we had left at the Marriott) I started screaming his name. I wouldn't have recognized him if he hadn't of taken his shirt off & wrapped it around his face. It was a distinctly patterned shirt—he was maybe 3 feet away and I still had to call his name (first & last) 5 times before he registered. Everyone was in such disbelief and shock—nothing was registering or making sense. Out of no where emergency vehicles were pulling up with water & masks to breathe through. Men were shirtless every~~one~~where because they had taken them off to give to people to breathe through.

The six of us just stood there holding each other not really knowing quite what else to do. I remember planting my face into Bob's chest because it was so hard to hold my eyes open they burned so badly & I really couldn't breathe—but he just wrapped his arms around me and when he did it—his strength made me realize how terribly I was shaking; my entire body just shook in his arms. Then came the next set of intensely loud crashing noises booms, bangs, screams and each of us grabbed each other by the hands and ran for better shelter. I wasn't even thinking about what was happening—just keeping focused on holding onto hands and each other staying away from the paniced seas of people, and breathing through my mask. We found a restaurant patio and all of us closed one of the huge table umbrellas over us and we watched the pile of soot grow around us and listened to people shouting out the names of what I assume to be people they could not find. A man & wife came and got under an umbrella next to us with their baby in it's stroller. I had a little of the water I had gotten from a rescue worker left and reached out from under our umbrella to hand it to them. The wife grabbed my arm and said Oh, we were so desperate for water for our baby. I think that maybe this was the point that I told myself—Anna, you must not panic. Everyone is so frightened, but if we remain calm, we can help each other. We made our way into the restaurant where they were shredding their table clothes into squares for people to breathe through. It was still very difficult to breathe in there because so much had come in through the doors.

~~A~~ I looked around at all of us packed into this restaurant with grey hair, bloodied clothes, masks on our faces—we all looked the same, I just recall thinking—everyone looks the same and we're all going through the same thing—Each of us—black, white, Japanese, business persons, daughters, mothers, children—we're all the same right now.

And everyone was trying to get through to their loved ones on cell phones. I think we all just felt—there's no words to appropriately convey it—the preciousness of life, the importance of expressing of love, the desperateness to be with those who we care about—I know ~~I kept thinking~~ all I wanted to do was hear the voices of those that I love. I'd never ~~thought~~ felt so real ~~seriously about~~ the thought/feeling/fear of never speaking to them again. Jennifer is the next person that I got a hold of and I remember when I said "Jenny"—the impact of love, relief, fear, I felt when she said "Oh my God Anna" as we both burst into tears. (I had many memorable, unforgettable phone conversations that day and since that day which I won't write to each of you about—but please everyone know that they are all ingrained in my heart and soul and are so special and I have written them down in my own personal journal.)

~~Th~~ We were at the water and could see boats coming from all around to get people out of the city. Finally I guess sometime around 1 we took a ferry over to Jersey City. They packed as many people as they could onto the boat, yet it was stunningly quiet. We all stood and looked towards New York City—a smoldering cloud of ~~of black smoke & devastation~~ catastrophe and devastation,—in disbelief. ~~and~~ As we got off the ferry onto the dock in Jersey City, ~~the~~ it was lined with first emergency medical workers to take those in shock or injured, then a row of police men & women and volunteers with trash cans of bottled water and buckets of rubber gloves—for those of us who wanted to help others, but to protect ourselves from diseases transmitted through blood. There was a large office building there that had opened it's doors to everyone coming in from the city. They were bringing desks, phone lines, phones, chairs, food, water coolers,—anything they could into the lobby to help us coming in from the city. The had their employees taking people upstairs to use restrooms, phones, etc.

I remember going to the bathroom where many women all stood soaking paper towels and trying to clean off all the soot from our hair, faces, and necks because it was so irritating to the skin. My skin itched so terribly it felt like it was on fire. I volunteered to call our office and let them know we were okay & try to figure out what we were going to do next. I had pulled out a notepad & pen out of my purse in Battery Park and gotten the first/last names of everyone we were with, our room # at the Marriott, our company names, and emergency family #s—so it made sense that I be the one to go use the phone. Now what made me think to do all that in the midst of such a crisis—I have no idea—good parenting, life experiences? I was calm at this point—so calm I was surprising myself—and spoke with our office to deliver the message. I remember I was on speaker phone with our CEO, VP, CFO, and office manager and Keith—our CEO said to me—"Anna you sound remarkably calm." I told him that I just knew that now was not the time to allow myself to become emotional. I had to remain focused so that we could help each other and get through this. I felt so proud of myself—if you can believe it, during the middle of everything—but Keith said to me "Young Lady, I am certainly impressed with and appreciate your maturity and we will do everything in our power to get you back to us safely."

I met my group back at the meeting pole in the lobby and tried to figure a plan of what to do next. The room was packed with people. I helped a woman who came in with blood dripping down her face & her baby in her arms. This old man, ~~came~~ struggling to walk & even had soot in his eyelashes came in & I had paper towels & water and helped him. What was so beautiful at such a horrendous time was that everywhere you looked, that's what you saw . . . People helping people. No matter who, what—I think everyone there just loved each other like each stranger was a family member. I always had my pen & notepad in hand just because I felt like we were all too stunned to think clearly, so anything important that we/I needed to remember, I was writing down. At least 3 people came to me in that lobby asking if I was a reporter! The word was already widespread that all flights were grounded and hotel rooms booked. All nearby streets, even in New Jersey were closed to all traffic except emergency vehicles. The sound of sirens was constant. The six of us walked to a location where the busses were operating to pick people up and help them get away from the wreckage.

On the street masses of people were lined up, caked in soot or blood, some without shirts, or shoes, all of us trying to get further away from the city. We decided to make our way towards Newark because our company was trying to get us rental cars there and also my co-worker Paige had family friends that could pick us up there. We finally got a bus to the train station. ~~Wh~~ We were standing as a group trying to figure out which train to get on and I realized there were men in orange vests helping everyone. Since I had my notepad and was writing all of our directions down, I said y'all wait right here under this pole and I'll go ask one of these men what the best route for us to take is. As I was writing down directions, the police came rushing through screaming for everyone to evacuate. Terror more than ever rushed through me—I thought—"how smart—they new everyone would come to the train stations and now they're going to blow them all up." I just covered my head and ran as fast as I could, along with thousands of other terrified people out onto the streets. I got pretty far, to the next street corner, and they were shouting it was a scare and for everyone to come back. I couldn't move—I just stood there, exhausted of fearing for my life so many times. And I was by myself—I had lost my group members. Just as the tears started gushing, I remember a rescue worker—and I honestly couldn't tell you if it was a man or a woman—I just remember their blue outfit—coming and holding me and walking me back to the train station to help me find my co-workers/family. I remember saying to look for blue shirts b/c almost all of us were wearing blue shirts and that's when I heard them yelling out my name.

To quickly summarize the rest of the day because I do now realize I've written you all a book—We got on a train & finally made it to Newark where this incredible family helped us & took us to their home. We stayed the night there. Even though they had many bedrooms, Paige and I slept together and held each other the entire night through. We were able to get a rental car and drove the whole 13 hrs. back to Charlotte on Wednesday.

"It is weird now the way that everytime I hear a plane fly overhead, I stop and feel a quick jolt of fear. Or everytime I hear a siren—it triggers a flashback for me. But I realize now that it will take time," Miller concluded her letter of gratitude. "I appreciate so very much the constant network and outreaching of support and love I have felt. My Love to each of you—Anna."

—⁓—

———— **Featured Series** ————

"Iraq"

**Commanding Officer Abdul-Mohsen Salman Kazem,
with Iraq's Sixty-fifth Special Forces Brigade, Outlines
the "Burn and Destroy" Tactics His Troops Must Employ
Against Kuwaiti Civilians
&
Another Iraqi Officer, Shawai Helu Shamkhi,
Instructs His Comrades to Take "Appropriate Measures"
Against a Boy Caught Carrying the Kuwaiti Flag
&
Before His Hand Is Cut Off, Nazaar Joudi, Detained in the
Abu Ghraib Prison, Assures His Wife That "Something Good"
Will Come from This Punishment
&**

**Nine Years Later, an Elated Joudi Once Again Writes to His Wife
with a New (Prosthetic) Hand Attached in the United States
&
An Eleven-Year-Old Iraqi Girl Named Sana Begs Her Aunt
Overseas to Help Her Leave Baghdad as Soon as Possible
&
An Iraqi Student in Baghdad Sends an E-mail to a Friend in the US
to Convey to Him What Life Is Like in Baghdad
After Operation Iraqi Freedom**

What shocked so many who arrived at the scene after the shooting had stopped was the span of the carnage, a seemingly endless procession of scorched vehicles, dead bodies, and millions of dollars worth of plundered goods scattered in every direction. There was also the smell—a nauseating, sickly sweet combination of smoke, decay, and perfume, tons of it (all stolen from Kuwait), saturating the desert air. The "Highway of Death," as it became known, was the result of a massive bombardment by Coalition warplanes on Iraqi troops fleeing from Kuwait in the last days of February 1991. But despite the casualties, there was little pity from some of the observers. "We got there after the inferno," one US Army staff sergeant wrote on March 22 to a friend named Laurie Frost back in the States.

> *Everything was burned black, The metal of the vehicles and guns rusted where the fire melted the paint and the Humid Gulf air hit the Naked metal. Amid all this was color. Suitcases had burst and bright clothing was scattered everywhere. It's almost impossible to describe. It's something you had to see. They're cleaning it up now. I took some Arab head Scarves off the bodies. I don't know why. But I felt revenge I guess.*

At another point in his letter, which recalled his conversations with Kuwaitis about the Iraqi occupation, the soldier explained to Frost the reason for his anger. (Please note: the following excerpt describes acts of torture in extremely graphic detail.)

> *Saw a lot of horror. Kuwaitis brought pictures to me. Horrible pictures. I saw bodies in the hospital morgues where the Iraqis dumped them—There was NO Refridgeration—NO electricity—I saw thing I will never forget. Things that will be with me forever—Such horror. The IRAQIs were Animals. Not at all human. They'd torture women in the most perverse, sick, ways and then kill them and children—They'd torture babies in front of thier parents—Then kill the parents by torture—What's the point? For*

what?! They took a little girl about 3–5 years old . . . took a drill and drilled holes into her starting at the feet, a hole every 2 inches. The final hole was through the forehead. That one is with me. In my dreams. And I cry for her—even NOW. I don't think I'll write anymore about this cause it hurts too much.

Thousands of Kuwaiti citizens were killed, tortured, raped, and imprisoned by Iraqi troops (primarily the elite Republican Guard), all of which President Saddam Hussein dismissed as lies and propaganda. Some accounts of atrocities disseminated early in the war were disproved, but the photographs and documents—many by Iraqis themselves—discovered in the detritus of the almost seven-month occupation attested to the sanctioned brutality inflicted on the Kuwaitis. Postwar interviews with returning civilians provided further confirmation. Less than a month after the Iraqi invasion in August 1990, as protest rallies and declarations of national pride by the Kuwaitis continued, one Iraqi commanding officer, Abdul-Mohsen Salman Kazem, instructed his troops in no uncertain terms how the citizens should be treated.

In the Name of God, Most Gracious, Most Merciful
Secret and Personal
65th Special Forces Brigade
Date: 1 September 1990

In accordance with the instructions issued by the authorities, please take the measures required by the items below:

1. Burn and destroy all the homes on which there are slogans hostile to our leadership, the pictures of the defunct al-Sabah dynasty, or Kuwaiti flags. This is to be done after evicting the inhabitants.
2. Burn and destroy every district in which any military, security, or Popular Army individual is martyred.
3. Arrest any person who owns, or keeps at his home, a weapon. Post him, along with the weapon, to our headquarters.
4. Annihilate any hostile demonstration.

Notify all officers and fighters of this matter.
Brigadier SF Staff
Abdul-Mohsen Salman Kazem

A message by another officer, Shawai Helu Shamkhi, reveals that Kazem's orders were being followed, regardless of the age of the "perpetrator."

Popular Army Command in Kuwait
Kerbelaa II Command
Date: 1/11/1990
To: Sulaibikhat Section
Subject: Information

Comradeship greetings,

At 5:30 p.m., the guards of our HQ gate saw a child carrying a flag of the defunct regime. He was arrested as he was trying to fix it at the Main Street. The flag is fit to fix. We therefore post to you Najiya Hemeid Selim, the child's mother, who lives at a house close to the Main Street. Kindly take them over and take the appropriate measures.

Comrade

Shawai Helu Shamkhi

No one suffered more at the hands of Saddam Hussein, however, than the Iraqi people themselves. He raided Iraq's treasury as his citizens starved; he built palaces as hospitals, schools, and electricity and water treatment plants fell into disrepair; and he dragged his country into two major wars during the 1980s and 1990s. (Ten years before Hussein ordered the annexation of Kuwait, he declared war on Iran, leading to an almost eight-year conflict with millions of casualties.) An estimated two to three million Iraqis in all were killed by Hussein's dictatorial regime, and hundreds of thousands of these slain men, women, and children were discarded in unmarked mass graves throughout the country, many of which were unearthed by Coalition troops during Operation Iraqi Freedom. Countless videotapes and documents detailing the executions of Iraqi citizens were also found in captured government offices during the OIF invasion. After learning about one such discovery, a twenty-seven-year-old US Army sergeant named Mark Rickert sent the following e-mail from Iraq to his girlfriend, Jennifer, in Tennessee.

A few months ago, [a major with the 490th Public Health Team and his men] explored a building once owned by a special Iraqi police force from the old regime. In this building, the soldiers found a room as big as a movie theater with shelves lining the walls from top to bottom, filled with jars of bundled paper. The old regime evidently used these jars as a filing system. The civil affairs team had a translator with them at the time, and so the major pointed out a jar, opened it, and read the paper inside. The document had a detailed account of one interrogation. Apparently, during the Iran/Iraq war, they captured an Iraqi accused of selling information. The Iraqi police couldn't get any information out of the guy, so they brought in his brother and put a gun to his head. The suspect still refused to talk, so they shot his brother in the head. While his brother lay bleeding on the floor, they brought in his sister. The guy remained silent, and so they sent her to an adjacent room with three or four others where they raped her just in earshot. After that, they brought in the man's mother and little brother. One by one, the Iraqis killed the suspect's entire family, until finally putting a bullet through the suspects head. The fact that they documented this account is disturbing, but the true horror is that this jar was pulled from thousands of others. The whole place was filled wall to wall, floor to ceiling, with these jars, and each contained a documented case of torture, murder and rape. The major said that this was his defining moment, and he knew he was doing a good thing by being here.

Before the 2004 scandal involving American soldiers abusing inmates at Abu Ghraib, the prison was notorious within Iraq as a symbol of everything savage and tyrannical about Hussein's dictatorship. Vicious beatings, lynchings, and many other forms of torture and execution were conducted on a daily basis. Amputations of hands, feet, tongues, and ears were also common, and eyes were frequently extracted as well. In 1995 an Iraqi money exchanger named Nazaar Joudi was arrested for dealing in foreign bills (Hussein had decreed that only Iraqi dinars, although practically worthless, could be used as currency) and sent to Abu Ghraib. While confined there, Joudi's right hand was removed and his forehead was marked with a black cross to identify him as a criminal. Joudi was then charged the equivalent of fifty US dollars to cover the cost of the procedure. On the night before the amputation, Joudi wrote his wife Um Furqaan the following letter. (There is no salutation.)

To every believer there is a sacrifice and there is a price to every sacrifice. The price for this is my right hand. Freedom also has a price and freedom is more valuable than anything. Do not be sad because of what happened to my hand. Hopefully Allah will replace it with an even better one.

I hope you understand that this is Allah's will, so bear with this. God will reward you for standing next to your husband and being my right hand. Behind every great man there is a great woman. Hopefully, something good will come out of this amputation for me and you.

Nazaar Joudi

Miraculously, Joudi's wish would be realized. In June 2003, a journalist and independent documentary producer named Don North was working in Baghdad when he heard about nine businessmen, including Joudi, whose right hands *had all been cut off. (One of the men had since died and two had emigrated to Europe.) After a tip from a Texas oil engineer who overheard North talking about the story in a Baghdad café, North contacted a prominent reporter named Marvin Zindler in Houston, Texas, who was known for his philanthropy. Zindler promptly called two local surgeons, Dr. Joe Agris and Dr. Fred Kestler, who agreed to donate their services. Houston's Methodist Hospital volunteered their facilities. The Coalition Provisional Authority, which was governing Iraq at the time, and the Pentagon secured the Iraqis' exit from Baghdad to an airbase in Germany; Continental Airlines let the men fly from Europe to America for free; the Otto Bock Co., which produces prosthetic limbs, provided the men with highly sophisticated bionic hands that normally cost $50,000 each; and Dynamic Prosthetics helped the men learn how to use their new hands. After the operations and two months of physical therapy, the Iraqis traveled to Washington, DC, and Arlington, Virginia, where Joudi placed flowers on the Tomb of the Unknown Soldier. While still in the nation's capital, he wrote the following letter to his wife.*

In the name of God, the compassionate, the merciful.

After more than nine painful years, I am able again to use my right

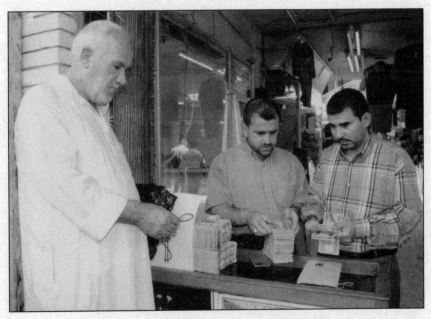

*Nazaar Joudi, far right, at his shop in Baghdad, Iraq,
before having his new hand attached.*

hand to write those words to my dearest wife, Um Farqaan. However, this time it is different. I wrote my first letter at Abu Ghraib prison, a few hours before my hand was cut off. That bleak and horrific place. This time I am writing my letter from the most beautiful place in the world, Washington, D.C, the capital of the United States of America. I wrote my first letter back in 1995, full of sorrow and pain. I asked God to provide me with another hand. God responded to my prayer and gave me a new hand. Actually God has given me more than one new hand. He has given me the hands of American friends who offered their friendship, hands of the people in Houston, who assisted us, and the endless care and kindness provided by the best physicians in the world.

Now I am writing these words with happiness, where grief has been converted into joy and gladness. This happiness was provided to me by the people and the government of the United States. Moreover, by their removal of that tyrant Saddam Hussein. So look my wife to the justice of God, how I was in the worst place in the world, and now I am in the most beautiful.

Thank you God.
Nazaar Joudi
May 28, 2004

Nazaar Joudi at Arlington National Cemetery in the United States,
after his surgery.

At almost the exact same time Joudi was composing his letter to his wife in Iraq, an eleven-year-old girl in Baghdad was writing to her aunt living in the United States. "Greeting to the smell of the spring flowers and the beauty of lilies," the young girl, Sana, began her handwritten letter. But despite the young girl's anticipation of spring, her world—as indicated in the very next line—was one of fear and violence.

I need you to help us move from here because we are dying here and bomb blasts are taking place every day in our neighborhood. The other day there was a bomb blast in front of my school and I almost got killed.

I need for you to save us, and I beg you and if you really love us and care for us as relatives, then you will save us from here. Please call us; it has been days or months that we haven't talked on the phone.

Please, don't come back here because bombings are everywhere. Save us, save us and don't even think about coming back here and stay where you are. For the sake of our family please save us.

Best regards and hoping to hearing from you soon.

Sana

Love you

For countless civilians like Sana (whose fate is unknown), life had become both hopeful and terrifying after Saddam Hussein was forced from power in April 2003. Gone was the ruthless Baathist regime that had murdered millions. Electricity, water, and other utilities were gradually being restored and even improved upon over their pre-invasion levels. Schools and hospitals were being rebuilt and repaired. But while the blanket of oppression had been lifted, bombs, shootings, kidnappings, and other dangers were becoming everyday occurrences. The most conservative estimates have reported that thousands of innocent Iraqis have been accidentally killed during Operation Iraqi Freedom, and many human rights groups counter that, beginning with the Shock and Awe airstrikes that preceded the ground invasion, the number is in the tens of thousands and possibly over 100,000. Even Iraqis who supported the removal of Hussein were nevertheless frustrated with the multinational Coalition's inability to establish security in the major cities. "I think you have heard about the bombing in Kerbala and Al-Kadhim," an Iraqi high school student e-mailed a friend in the United States named Mark von Sponeck, "those were the most horrible terrorist actions ever." (His e-mail was written in English and is printed here verbatim. The ellipses are also in the original.) He continued:

[W]hen we saw the victims on TV, I could see tears in Mom's eyes . . I remained silent and filled with anger . . I was worried about all my friends

*who could be there too . . our neighbor was worried about her husband
who luckily didn't get hurt. One thing is that those attacks failed to start
violence between Shia and Suna . . in fact it has caused them to unite . .
because everyone realized that this wasn't resistance at all . However many
people including me blame the Coalition for all this . . where were they
when it happened?!*

*The student, who wishes to remain anonymous, voiced his fiercest resentment,
however, for the Iraqi insurgents and foreign terrorists coming into Iraq through
neighboring countries. In a message rife with anguish and bordering on resignation,
he vented about another series of attacks that prompted him to wonder
if there would ever be an end to the chaos.*

Dear Mark ,

This week has been a week full of pain , difficulty , terrorism and anger .

This week was one of the hardest weeks , probably the hardest of
them all .

We have been taking our first quarter exams , in which our teachers
are trying to give us questions with a level higher than the other schools,
to make us final grade students study hardest .

My daily studying routine starts with returning home at 3 pm because
of all the traffic mess . . . and then I would have a nap , watch TV a little
. . . then I would study from 7 pm to late night times exceeding 2 am .

The situation has become more tense in Baghdad than ever . . . all I
hear is the consequent explosions that come from either Iraqi or
American sides against each other.

The worst started on Sunday , when electricity was off , and came
after 2 days and a half , leaving Baghdad in darkness all this time .

What made all that was when some "bastards" hit an oil tube feeding
Baghdad with oil , including both fuel for its power plant and its gas
stations .

The blackout had a terrible effect on our studying for the exams . I
and many other students had to study using oil lamps when our
generators are off(because of the lack of fuel , the have to lessen the work
hours), while others went to mosques , which have generators .

My school even cancelled an exam on Tuesday because of the
students' situation , and because they couldn't copy the exam papers .

The lack of fuel caused the black market of fuel jump with its prices
crazily . . .

But the meanest of all these terrorist operations , was putting a
bombed bag in a primary school in Karbala (in the south) which

exploded killing two children and injuring many . . . is this going to free us ? is it going to let the ones who did go to heaven? Did it at least touch the Coalition ?! No . . they are a group of ignorant , infidel , wicked and cowardly murderers who love blood and pain. Who refuse to let us live without their master , Saddam Hussein , who is no less than them .

Another thing was putting explosives near the main communication tower in Baghdad. Luckily it was discovered before exploding .

All these attacks ensure that Iraq is becoming a "Terrorist Hole" in which terrorists are a mixture of Saddam's guys , Foreign extremers and others .

And after all this suffering , still some "people" are considering all this as resistance ! I wonder how could hurting us all that bad is going to "free" us ! and after all that , the Arab news channels stay silent , not wanting to confess that this is not the resistance they keep talking about , like they did during all the terrorist attacks .

The power finally came on Tuesday , at a bad , yet better than nothing , rate .(2 hrs on—4 hrs off) .

The traffic mess is more and more terrible , my school's minibus was even hit by another car , and you should have seen the peaceful me yelling at the driver of the car which hit us , in a manner that I couldn't believe . . but I and our driver kept ourselves from saying any bad things , or quarreling , until the IP (Iraqi Police) came . . they finally took our side and the car is still unrepaired

The traffic mess is partly caused by the huge number of cars bought and taken to Iraq , and because many of them were bought by people are unqualified for driving , who don't know any driving rules but taking the wrong side , and yelling ! Not to forget the blocks put by the troops for security .

All this has made getting to school very difficult . . it takes the driver an hour and half to come and take us , and the same time to take us home . while it took half an hour to come or to take us home .

The situation been having a very negative effect on us . . people now would keep wondering about the future , and how will all this end ? what will come out of it? When will we have a day with no explosions , no power off , bad traffic and no lack of security . When will we look at all this and say " that was in the past" ?

We are all waiting for the Festivals following Ramadan . . which are going to be a good rest for us . . I hope.

Elaine Lucille Banks

Aftermath

Postwar Letters

You have come to a world full of great problems. With many vexations and sad conditions. And at a time when great and momentous questions fill the minds of all mankind and War Horrible War is filling the nations with Desolation and Sorrow. Yet, 'tis a good old World. All about us in nature so much that is grand and beautiful. I sincerely hope that as your young life expands you may be able to grasp and retain with unusual power in your life a large measure of the Beauty, Pleasure and happiness all about you. And live to see these great problems which vex us so at present, settled on principles of justice and right. And men shall learn to War no more.

—Nathan B. Moore, writing to his newborn
great-granddaughter, Elaine Lucille Banks,
on May 20, 1916, fifty-one years after he
fought in the Civil War

Towards the end of the War in the Pacific, we were taken out of the classroom under the Student Mobilization Act and sent to a war plant to build balloon bombs. After defeat, we were told that only some of the balloons reached the United States and were useless as weapons having caused but a few forest fires. Then, 40 years after the war, we learned for the first time about what is known as "The Oregon Tragedy," involving the loss of six lives. We who at the time were school girls, only 16 years of age, were nevertheless full participants in the war, bringing pain and hardship to others. Such a realization truly sent a chill down my spine. My heart pains to learn that the six victims were Sunday school children on what was meant to be a joyful picnic with a newly-wed minister's wife. These 1,000 cranes were folded one by one by some of us who made the balloon bombs, seeking forgiveness and with a prayer for peace and a vow that the error of the past shall never again be repeated. We pray from afar in Japan that the six victims rest eternally in peace.

> —*Tetsuko Tanaka, writing in 1987, to the surviving members*
> *of the Mitchell family. In May 1945, Mrs. Archie Mitchell*
> *and five children were out picnicking on Gearhart Mountain,*
> *near Bly, Oregon, when out of curiosity one of the children picked up*
> *a "balloon bomb." The incendiary devices were built by the Japanese*
> *and floated across the Pacific to start forest fires in the United States.*
> *All five children and Mrs. Mitchell died when the bomb exploded*
> *in the child's hands.*

On the 26th of April 1937, Guernica was the victim of an aerial attack by the Condor Legion squad, which converted the name of this town into an emblem of belligerence and caught the defenseless population by surprise, turning them into victims of a terrible atrocity. The day of Guernica and the human suffering that its name symbolizes since then form part of the collective memory of our peoples. I want to acknowledge this past and recognize expressly the fault of the German planes involved. To the survivors of the attack and witnesses of the horror, I offer my message of condolence and sorrow. I wish to remember those people whose happy lives were shattered on that day in Guernica, whose families were massacred, whose homes were destroyed, whose surroundings were stolen. I share your mourning for the dead and the injured. I offer to you all, those who still carry the wounds of the past within them, my open hand as a prayer for reconciliation.

> —Dr. Roman Herzog, president of Germany, writing to the survivors
> of Guernica, Spain, sixty years after German airplanes bombed
> the defenseless city, killing and wounding thousands of men, women,
> and children. With the encouragement of Spain's fascist leader
> Francisco Franco, Adolf Hitler used the attack as training for his
> nascent Luftwaffe, which would go on to terrorize millions
> of innocent civilians in World War II.

Sixty years ago we in Guernica had an unexpected visit. Many of us were still children when men from other lands came, and they dropped a rain of fire, shrapnel and death. And they destroyed our town. That unbelievable act did not leave with us a feeling of hate or vengeance but an enormous, an immense desire for peace that such incidents should never happen again. And that from the ruins of what was our town should surge a symbol of peace for all nations of the world. Today we have another perspective. Once again people from other lands have come to us. They come from the front and with hands extended. Although we speak different languages, we can understand each other. And we are able to do now what then we could not—open our arms and say to them: "Welcome to Guernica, let us walk together in peace. Ongi etorriak."

> —Luis Iriondo, representing the survivors, in reply

Lots of very bad people here coming in from other countries with no other purpose than to kill Americans. It is good that they are here and we are keeping them busy so they don't feel that they need to come to the U.S. and kill innocent people. Every military person here is a volunteer and knew (or should have known) what they signed up and were getting paid to do. I am glad that we are here and able to grab some of these creeps before they can do more damage to innocent civilians. Whatever the news says about Weapons of Mass Destruction and lack of evidence, bears little relevance on the dangers that this country posed(s) in the war on terrorism. The focus is misplaced by people who have no idea what is really going on over here. Sorry to wax political. . . . we are doing good stuff here. Getting creeps off the streets and making the world safe for Starbucks. Gotta go babe. . . . Thinking of you Love you!

> —*Tyler (last name withheld), a US Navy Seal*
> *in Iraq, writing to his wife back in the States*

After Helping to Liberate a Foreign Country from Oppressive Rule, Lieutenant George F. Telfer, with the Oregon National Guard, Writes Home About a Growing Insurgency Against US Troops
&
With Casualties Mounting, Telfer Complains That It Is Impossible to Distinguish Between "Friendly" Civilians and Potential Enemies
&
As the Postwar Peace Descends Into Full-Fledged Combat, Telfer Describes the Constant Dangers They Must Face

With strong public and congressional support, the president of the United States sends armed forces to a foreign land to topple its corrupt, dictatorial government. Facing minimal resistance, the Americans prevail decisively and are welcomed enthusiastically by the liberated citizenry. Victory is announced. But when the native population realizes that the United States is not withdrawing its troops and intends to maintain a strong presence in the region, the once-embraced American soldiers soon find themselves the targets of fierce guerilla attacks. "We are not waging war against the inhabitants," the US president assures his fellow Americans, some of whom are questioning the invasion and accusing the administration of imperialistic aims. "A portion of them," he continues,

> *are making war against the United States. By far the greater part of the inhabitants recognize American sovereignty and welcome it as a guaranty of order and of security for life, property, liberty, freedom of conscience, and the pursuit of happiness. To them full protection will be given. They shall not be abandoned . . . Order under civil institutions will come as soon as those who now break the peace shall keep it. Force will not be needed or used when those who make war against us shall make it no more. May it end without further bloodshed, and there be ushered in the reign of peace to be made permanent by a government of liberty under law!*

The president is William McKinley, the time is the end of the nineteenth century, and the country under occupation is the Philippines, which the US had just liberated—along with Cuba—from Spanish authority. Until the Gulf War in

1991, the Spanish-American War in 1898 was the shortest major conflict in US history. Numerous factors caused the war, including American sympathy in the late 1890s for rebels in neighboring Cuba trying to overthrow Spanish rule. The newspapers of the day, each trying to outdo its competition, reported with growing frequency and sensationalism on Spanish atrocities against the Cubans. Americans were further outraged when, on February 15, 1898, more than 260 US servicemen were killed by an explosion on the USS Maine *in Cuba's Havana Harbor. (A Spanish mine or, perhaps, torpedo was initially blamed as the cause; later investigations suggested the explosion was the result of an accident from within the ship.) The US declared war in late April 1898, and by August Spanish forces in Cuba and the Philippines—where a squadron of Spain's Pacific fleet was anchored—were soundly defeated. Under the Treaty of Paris, Spain surrendered control of Cuba, the Philippines, and other territories on December 10, 1898. The "splendid little war," as the statesman John Milton Hay famously referred to it, was over. But the American annexation of the Philippines infuriated the native population, who were not even allowed representation in Paris. Minor clashes erupted, along with isolated raids on American ammunition stockpiles. On January 7, 1899, a lieutenant in the Oregon National Guard named George F. Telfer wrote to his daughter Grace back in Portland about one such incident that proved fatal. (Hazel is his youngest child.)*

From "somewhere in the Philippines," American troops write home.

Dear Grace,

I have just learned that there will be a mail at 10 A.M.—& it is now 9
I will have to rush.

The news of Sgt. Morses death will reach you & you may worry
some. It happened, for a wonder, that I was in bed at the time so did not
even know of the affair until this morning.—There is a Magazine on the
wall—in sight of our quarters. There is a strong guard there. There has
also been a great deal of trouble on account of insurgents trying to steal
ammunitions. Our sentrys know that in a fight with natives they must
shoot quick—or the native will knife them. Capt. Wells & some other
officers heard shots there last night and ran over to see what was up.
Morse went with Wells. The party scattered out around the buildings &
parapet—for the purpose—of catching the man who had been seen by
the sentry. Morse left Wells & went a short distance—outside the
parapet—to see if the native was skulking outside. He sprang up onto
the parapet & down on the inside within 30 feet of the sentry. The latter
naturally supposing the attack was coming from that way—& having no
time for identification—in the dark—fired. The shot was fatal & poor
Morse died within a very short time. He was not acting under order,—
nor was he under arms. The officers saw him come over the wall &
recognized him—but not in time to warn the sentry.

I feel worse about his death than I would if it had been anybody else.
For I thought a great deal of his mother & father—as well as himself.
They were among the last to bid me good bye at McKinley & I was with
Morse when he said good bye to his mother. He was very bright &
would have been 2nd Lieut. if we could have got Povey out. I was
coaching him up, & letting him drill the company in order to fit him for
examination. A great amount of company detail that would have fallen
on me was performed by him. He is to be buried this afternoon.

I am pretty well—but my stomache gets off a little now & then. Court
work keeps me at my desk a great deal—so I do not have to get heated much.

The Presidents proclamation to the inhabitants printed in English,
Spanish & Tagalog was posted up last night. The inhabitants don't know
what to make of it.—Neither do we. Of course we have not seen the
original text—only a translation of a cypher telegram.

We are so disheartened at our treatment by our friends at home, and the
disagreeable duty we have to perform here,—that we have lost all interest
in everything and are simply killing time until we can be sent home.

Tell Mama that the payments from Crocker-Woolworth bank will
cease with January 1—I expect. The arrangement has terminated & we
will have to send drafts from here. In case she does not hear from San F.

she will understand the reason. Mr. Newhall will probably let her draw just the same. There will be no trouble except the uncertainty of the mails.

I will send drafts as soon as paid. I have lost Hazels picture. Had it on a screen by my desk—& I think somebody took it.

With love to all,
Your affectionate father,
Geo. F. Telfer

The presidential proclamation Telfer alluded to emphasized that:

> *the paramount aim of the Administration [is] to win the confidence, respect, and affection of the inhabitants of the Philippines by insuring to them in every possible way the full measure of individual rights and liberty which is the heritage of a free people, and by proving to them that the mission of the United States is one of beneficent assimilation.*

Less than a month later, US troops and Filipino insurgents clashed in Manila, sparking the official commencement of hostilities. After sending out an order to his army that "friendly relations between the Philippine force and the American forces of occupation are broken, and the latter will be treated as enemies," Emilio Aguinaldo, the new president of the Philippine Republic, released his own proclamation:

> *I know that war has always produced great losses; I know that the Philippine people have not yet recovered from past losses, and are not in the condition to endure others. . . . Be not discouraged. Our independence has been watered by the generous blood of our martyrs. Blood which may be shed in the future will strength it. Nature has never despised generous sacrifices.*

The day after Aguinaldo issued his statement, Lieutenant George Telfer described to his daughter the threats and dangers he and his comrades were now encountering. (The following is the first of a two-part letter, and there is no signature at the end.)

Manila, P.I.
Feby 6 1899

Dear Grace,

Am somewhat tired out tonight. Got back to quarters at 11 o'clock this morning after two days steady duty. At 10:30 Saturday night heavy firing was heard out at the insurgent line, and shortly after, the call to arms was sounded at our barracks. In a few moments we—-Co. "L" was out at our assigned position by the south gate.—And the greatest battle of the present war was under way. The fight lasted until dark last night Sunday. All night long we heard the firing in an uninterrupted line around the city. Rifle fire, cannon—large guns and small. The roar was terrific.

In the morning the Charleston on the North East & the Buffalo & Monadnock on the South, commenced firing into insurgents camps. This of course added greatly to the uproar. We came in for breakfast, and as the fighting was several miles away we were allowed to go to quarters. Got a short nap and then packed a few necessarys articles in my pockets. Then came another call and we moved out again. Stood around in the sun for several hours. Then came an order for Cos. "L" and "D" to go toward the front. We went about two miles out and stood in the sun two hours more and watched the ambulances bringing in the wounded—a cheerful sight.—The ambulance men looked like butchers, with their hands and arms covered with blood. Every now and then a gang of prisoners would be brought in. There was a great deal of excitement of course. Ammunition carts coming in empty and going back loaded, messengers dashing in and out—refugees bringing their belongings— some in carriages & some walking. Every village or church occupied by insurgents was burned by our troops as soon as reached. Nothing was spared,—so of course the women, children & aged people had to come into the city.

The only work our company did was Sunday—after we stood in the road long enough to feel the sensation of Mauser bullets going over our heads & now & then dropping in the road around us,—was to go to a large monestery & capture 1000 natives who had taken refuge there. Genl. Hughes had been informed that these people would break out that night & set fires throughout the city & plunder the neighborhood. So Co. L was sent to hold them. It was rather a tame affair. I took half the company around to the back entrance & Capt. Wells to the front. The people were in the courtyard in the center of the building. The priests told them that if they would behave themselves they would receive no harm. So they were very quiet. We put a sentinel at each corner of the room & at the doors—on the outside. My platoon slept on the floor at the back vestibule & the others in the front. I tried to sleep the early part of the night—but between the cold (I don't know when I have been so cold before) and the mosquitos I could not. So I spent the night going from sentinel to sentinel & in among the sleeping natives. Listening for shots on the outside, & watching for a possible rush from the inside. The crowd was composed mostly of women & children & old men. There were perhaps 300 fighting men in the lot.

There was very little fireing at the outer lines during the night—so we knew the Phillopenos were retreating & that those inside would turn "friends" by morning. Sure enough every mothers son of them were bowing to the earth & smiling sweet enough to melt butter. Early in the forenoon people came to look for their cooks & servants who had left them on Saturday—to join their countrymen in the fight. First they would assure us that the servant was not a fighting man & had nothing to do with the insurectos, then turn & abuse him for deserting them. At noon Monday we were ordered to let the whole lot go & return to our quarters.

Eastwicks battalion—consisting of Cos. C,—K—& G. are with Hales Brigade out at the water works & had a little fighting yesterday—we hear.

The fighting is so far away now that we don't hear it, and have settled down to the dull routine of police work. I have my court martial work to look after & don't have much time to think. It was a great battle & the volunteers fought as well as the regulars—and there was no "Teddy" Roosevelt—Rough riders or other cheap candidates for newspaper notoriety to show off.

You will have full accounts long before this so I will not attempt any description. Some of our officers who staid in the walled city during the fight went out & had their pictures taken, standing among the dead on the battlefield,—N.B.—we keep "tab" on some of these people & there will be a "hot time" in Oregon if they attempt to spring any thing of that sort when we get home.

During March and April, American troops swept through the countryside, fighting a more coordinated rebellion. On April 14, Telfer wrote to his family about the expanding conflict—and the army's increasingly harsh tactics, which were deemed necessary to crush the insurrection.

Apl 14 1899

Dear Family,

We are still guarding railroad. Also it is still hot. All efforts to induce the natives of the Province of Bulacan seem to be of no avail. The commissioners sent out proclamations, printed in Spanish and Tagalog offering every inducement for them to return to their homes and occupations. They returned—but. The fun commenced about 5 days ago. I went out with 13 men to scout toward the east. I found a very rich country—thickly settled. I treated the people nicely & they were very friendly—and had nothing to do with the insurrection. Having gone 8 miles & turned north & crossed the Rio Marilao intending to return on the other side. The water was very deep & we had to cross on a bamboo raft two at a time. When the last two were about to come over, the natives opened fire from a trench on our front. I dare not retreat on the raft—could not advance & the river bank was a jungle of tangled bamboo and trees. There was nothing to do but crawl through. We found a caribou trail & forced our way along as fast as we could—keeping the timber between us & the natives. After a two mile scramble we came to a stone dam & were able to cross back. As soon as a habitation was reached—we stopped to rest. I was so used up that I laid down & took a nap.

In little less than an hour we started home. Just as they last man started, the pursuing party crossed the dam & opened fire. We could not stop to fight as we were enclosed by timber on 3 sides. We retreated until we came to an open then turned on them & soon forced them to cover. Then we resumed our march homeward. There was about 40 against our 14. That night the insurgent forces moved on to our lines & made a concerted attack.—I had fallen onto the left of their advancing line. We heard firing north of us during the night. As it was not near us we went to bed & to sleep. At 3:30 am we were aroused by the cracking of rifles & zip of bullets. Our outposts had not given us warning & we were surprised. We tumbled out behind the rice dikes & fired where we could see flashes. It was pitch dark & the racket was so great that it was very hard to direct our fire. The rice dikes here are about 10 inches high & we had no other protection. We laid on our faces when not shooting. The thing lasted about two hours when the insurgents withdrew. In the mean time they had cut the wires on either side of us so we could not communicate with headquarters. Four men who were patroling the track were cut off & 3 killed. One played 'possum & escaped—badly wounded.

The next day we proceeded to devastate the country. We burned every house within two miles of our camp—& drove the natives away. At noon Col. Summers & balance of regiment came up on train & picked up A & L. We went about 10 miles where we camped for the night with the 13th Minnesota. Genl, Wheaton arrived & took command. Some artillery also arrived At daybreak we started for Sta Marie—an insurgent strong hold. Aguinaldo was there with about 1000 troops. They made slight resistance & then retreated. We burned the town & every house or rice stack near their. We marched back to the railroad leaving a trail of smoke such as this country has never seen before. We shot at every human being that came within range—paying not attention to white flags. We took train at 3 P.M. & returned here. Yesterday we commenced fortifying the camp. Our company is on one side. A on the other & M on the track. I am bossing trench building on our side. The men think it pretty hard work. We have plenty of chickens to eat in consequence.

The men who kicked at not being allowed to go out & fight are getting their stomachs full. War is nice to read about—but is not enjoyable.

We get little news out here. Cannot get away long enough to go to Manila. I don't know whether Mr. Lewis has arrived or not. Presume he would remain sometime in Hong Kong.

I received letters from you dated Mch 6,—last week. Will try & answer some day.

Affectionately,

Geo. F. Telfer

Less than two months later, Telfer safely returned home with thousands of other troops whose tour had expired. (Telfer eventually moved to Washington state, where he lived until October 1930, and died peacefully at the age of seventy-five.) In May of 1900, a hero of the Civil War named Arthur MacArthur, who had also led the capture of Aguinaldo's makeshift capital of Malolos, was appointed the military governor of the Philippines. MacArthur allowed even more punitive actions against the insurgents, which critics in the US argued merely aggravated the violence. MacArthur would be replaced in 1901 by future president William H. Taft, who was considered less draconian than his predecessor. Despite Taft's "softer approach," reports of abuses by American soldiers, including the torture of prisoners of war, would undermine support for the war back in the States. Defenders of the troops countered that the Filipinos were also committing atrocities and that the US army was gaining ground. By the spring of 1902, most of the guerilla leaders had been captured or killed, and on July 4, Theodore Roosevelt—who had assumed the presidency after McKinley was assassinated—proclaimed that the war was over. (Scattered rebel activity would continue for more than a decade.) Almost forty-three years later, Arthur MacArthur's son, Douglas, would liberate the Philippines from Japanese occupation. The country became a politically independent republic on July 4, 1946.

—ɯ—

The Assistant Adjutant General Informs the Mother of Private Robert Parnell How Her Son Died During the Occupation of the Philippines

&

British Commander in Chief Guy Carleton Writes a Short Note of Condolence to the Mother of One of the Last Casualties of the American Revolution
&
A French Woman Who Cared for a US Soldier Felled by Disease at the End of World War I Assures His Mother He Will Not Be Forgotten

In the four years following the victory over the Spanish in 1898, more than one thousand US troops—almost three times the number of soldiers killed in the Spanish-American War itself—would die in combat during the postwar occupation of the Philippines. (The Filipino death toll is unknown, but many estimates place the number in the hundreds of thousands, which also includes fatalities from disease.) On August 5, 1901, as the conflict between US troops and Filipino insurgents raged with seemingly no end in sight, Lieutenant Colonel Morris J. Foote received word that a soldier had deserted. Foote sent an official dispatch to the adjutant general on the matter:

> *Sir: I have the honor to report that Private Parnell, Company "G" 9th. Infantry, deserted yesterday, taking his rifle and belt full of cartridges. I thought at first he had been captured. I sent two parties out at once to look for him and one of the parties obtained information from two different natives at different places, that they saw him in a canoe with his rifle in his hand and three natives paddling the boat along the coast, to the south. I have notified the head men of all the barrios along the coast as far as Lepato that he must be brought back, and in a day or two I will offer a reward of sixty (60) pesos for the man and thirty (30) for the rifle. Very respectfully, Morris C Foote*

As it turned out, the soldier was not a deserter and had, in fact, met a tragic end. Private Parnell's mother was notified of her son's death, but was not given details, and on October 24th, 1902, she wrote to the government for information about her son. She received the following matter-of-fact reply from the office of the Assistant Adjutant General:

November 4th, 1902.

Mrs. E. Parnell,
    No. 30 Farragut Avenue,
        West Summerville, Massachusetts.

Madam:

    In reply to your letter of the 24th ultimo requesting full information as to the death of your son Robert I. Parnell, late Private, Company G,

9th Infantry, I beg to advise you that at first reports, the soldier was reported as having deserted August 5th, 1901, while on guard at Basey, Sama, P. I. At a later date, reliable information was received whereby it shows that instead of having deserted, the soldier was captured by insurgents on that date and taken by them to the mountains in the interior of the island where some time in October he was stabbed to death with a bolo held in the hands of one Nicholas Lobrio, a noted insurgent. The killing appeared to have been in retaliation, or revenge for the death of an insurgent officer who had been killed in action with the Americans some time previously.

On this information, which was derived from native sources, and on the recommendation of the soldier's former Company Commander, who stated that private Parnell's character while a member of his company was good, and that he was a man of intelligence and integrity, the charge of desertion was removed from the official records, and the same amended to show the soldier as having been killed as above set forth. The murder was committed in the mountains of Sulat, near the barrio of Cogboborac, Island of Samar, P. I.

Under date of August 30th, 1902, the Commanding General of the Department of Luzon informed the Commanding General Division of the Philippines, at Manila, by telegraph, that the body of this soldier had been reported by the Captain Bell, 1st Infantry, as having been recovered at Dolores, Samar, P. I. No further information with reference to the recovery of the remains or their disposition has been received. However, under date of August 4th, 1902, the Quartermaster General of the Army, this city, communicated with the Chief Quartermaster, Division of the Philippines, requesting that he cause a special search to be made for the remains, and it is suggested that if you desire their removal to the United States, you address a request to that effect to The Quartermaster General, this city, to whose jurisdiction the matter pertains.

Very respectfully,

Major of Infantry,
Assistant Adjutant General.

No letter, with the exception of the last message written by their son or daughter, causes more heartache for parents than the one notifying them that their child has died. But this grief is all the more compounded when it comes after major military operations have ended. Accidents, disease, and scattered fighting inevitably claim the lives of troops who had assumed that since they had survived combat, they would be heading home. General Guy Carleton, commander in chief of all British forces in the Colonies at the end of the Amer-

ican Revolution, is not likely to have known personally the soldier surnamed Freemantle who was killed in October 1782. Nevertheless, he was aware of how the young man's mother would feel upon learning that her son had died when the conflict was all but over. (Although the Treaty of Paris, in which Britain officially agreed to end all hostilities and remove its troops, was not ratified until January 1784, General Charles Cornwallis's surrender to American forces came more than two years earlier in October 1781.) On November 8, 1782, Carleton expressed himself with brief but sincere sympathy:

Camp at Long Island

Madam

It is with unfeign'd regret that I must convey to you the melancholy Tidings of your gallant Son's death on the 20th Ultimo. He was perhaps the last Victim of this unhappy Conflict, being slain in a skirmish by a band of Marauders near Charleston in South Carolina while guarding the King's Stores.

Your Son was a good Soldier & an exemplary Youth & the whole Regiment deplores his loss.

I am, Madam, with great
Respect, Your most Obedt Humble Servt
Guy Carleton
Commander-in Chief

The death of Corporal Carl C. Saunders, who served with the American Expeditionary Force (AEF) in World War I, was doubly tragic; it came soon after the war was over and was the result not of combat, but of a prolonged illness. Recognizing the overwhelming despair his mother would feel upon hearing the news, a French woman who had cared for the young man sent Mrs. Saunders a heartfelt assurance that his contribution was as meaningful as any other, and that his sacrifice would never be forgotten.

Vals-les-Bains, France

Dear Madam,

It is a mother who is writing to you, a mother who has been with your dear child in his last days; and it had seemed to me that to tell you a little of his last acts and gestures may soften the bitterness of your grief.

Your son came with the 310th Band to pass a few days at Vals-les-Bains, in the Paris Hotel, of which my husband and I are the proprietors.

The first week I noticed him but little, as they all wore the same uniform; I scarcely distinguished them one from the other. At the end of a week; as a result of an epidemic of grippe, there were many sick in the house who stood about the fireplace, for it was very cold at the time. Then I noticed the little blond, as we called him, not knowing his name. I made hot drinks for him and his comrades, but after two days he preferred to stay in bed. The doctor, at his first visit, did not consider his condition serious, but at a second visit, in reply to my question, he answered, "It is serious, very serious." It appears that your dear child had a fall two months before on getting upon a train (or truck) and very serious disorder in the vertical column resulted. After this second visit his condition grew worse, though he was without great suffering. The poor little fellow was drowsy and we had to shake him and talk to him to get him to take liquid.

His comrades were admirably devoted and cared for him as no nurse would have done. He was for them a little brother, whom they petted and spoiled to quiet his pain. He was never left alone day or night and when they saw him depart, they wept like children. How I have regretted that I did not speak English! The doctor having decided an operation was necessary, they decide to take him to Montelimar. His comrades put him into the conveyance, but the poor boy no longer knew what was going on about him so was spared the anguish of saying goodbye. An hour before he left, my husband and I went up to see him and I kissed his forehead in his mother's name, then cut off this lock of hair as a last remembrance, but he noticed nothing.

Well, one thing certain is that though your son was deprived of his mother's care he did not know the commonplaceness of a hospital bed and so long as he was conscious saw about him the faces of devoted friends. The chaplain came to see him before he left.

The American authorities had his body brought back to the cemetery of Vals-les-Bains, where he rests beside several of his comrades.

When I go to see the graves of my own family, I assure you, Madam, that he will have a visit for his mother's sake.

If I can be of any service to you I am entirely at your service. With all my sympathies, I am yours,

Mme. J. Armand
Hotel de Paris,
Vals-les-Bains
Ardèche

—⁂—

Lieutenant David Arthur Thompson Reports to His Father with Astonishing Candor About the Retrieval of His Brother Joseph's Body, Which Had Been Hastily Buried During the War

For four years after World War I, the American Graves Registration Service assumed the mournful duty of recovering the bodies of slain troops and, depending on the wishes of the family, burying them in American military cemeteries or returning them to the States for private ceremonies. Twenty-seven-year-old Lieutenant David Arthur Thompson was an executive assistant to the chief of the AGRS and was personally involved with identifying fallen soldiers in Europe. But the job became an intensely personal one when he sought out the body of his own brother, Joseph, who had been killed in the war. In an understandably emotional but extremely frank account, Thompson details for his father how his brother was retrieved and the personal effects found with the remains. (Please note, the middle part of the letter is particularly graphic and might prove disturbing for some readers. But, along with the more poignant expressions of grief and faith, it offers insight into how Thompson was coming to terms with the death of a beloved family member and fellow soldier.)

May 24, 1919

Dear Dad,

I intended to write mother, but I can't tell her as much as I can you. When you read this, you can explain to her everything that you wish.

I have just taken Joe from his grave in the woods to a lot in the national American Cemetery at Romagne, France. I had to supervise the work myself on account of the shortage of officers; therefore, made a personal inspection of the body, which as you might know, I'd rather die than do, but which had to be done.

I'm going to be very plain in telling you, and know it might hurt, but I know you will wish to know. I am awful glad that it was I that could do it, and not any of you, as it would have drove any of you insane.

With three colored boys given me as a detail and a Dodge light truck, I made my way over the hills 40 miles. Sometimes the road was so bad we had to cross fields, and at one place had to build a small bridge over a place where the road was destroyed.

We left Romagne at 7:30 and got to the grave at the Harmont woods at noon. I had the colored fellows dig down the side of the grave until we struck the body, or could see the clothes. I saw his feet and legs first, and then the rest of his body, just as he fell.

He was dressed in new clothes, and had on his rain coat, and full pack, with the exception of the rifle and helmet. He was not in a box, as I expected, but merely a blanket thrown over the top of his body, and some loose boards over that.

We removed the blanket, boards, etc. And of course, the body was badly decomposed. The head was blown from the body by a high explosive shell, but what was left of the skull was lying there. The face was entirely blown away. I then unbuttoned the coats and found his other identification tag about his neck, which then and there identified him without going further.

I then placed him in a coffin we had brought with us and placed it in the car. We then got the body of Carl Coombs out, as we did Joe. Coomb's body was also badly decomposed, and he was a heavy boy to lift out.

The odor from both was terrible and I had to forget for the moment who they were. I had rubber gloves, but could hardly touch the bodies without cleaving the flesh from the bone. Therefore, had to work carefully and slowly.

We then had both bodies in the car and drove back to Romagne by going away around through the rear of the German lines, and got back to the cemetery at Romagne about 5:00 p.m.

There I turned both bodies over the undertakers who were present. I had the clothes removed and carefully searched, with good results.

I found in his clothes: your last letter to him, a pocket knife, fountain pen, his diary, testament, Book of Psalms, another book with annotations of all mail received and sent, some small pictures he had received from home, about 10 Francs in money, two watches, one his own, the other a German watch, a few German coins, and German post cards.

His diary is very interesting, and his Psalm book is wonderful, and shows that he died with a clean soul. This little book is known as, "The Shepherd Psalm", and was given to him by Emily M. Rogers. In it he has written a little prayer which is as follows:

"I pray thee, O God, that I may be beautiful within. This is my most earnest prayer. Most of us I believe will see home and friends again. If we do, how many will curse every drink they have taken, every oath they have uttered, every shameful thing they have committed here, that they wouldn't at home.

It threatens my stripes, my discipline, my popularity, and my advancement. These four things are temporary. The clean within is permanent and is greater than all of these temporal things.

This war will last but a short time. I have 30 to 1 chances of coming out. What is one year of service to indulgence, to say, 50 years and one year of service; and a clean conscience for the other 50 years. Anyway, after, before, present, or anytime, I despise all ungodly things. My real inner self resents it.

Secondly, for the love of <u>Mother,</u> <u>Father,</u> relatives, and many friends, I despise them. Again for love of God who has kept all well at home, at training camp, at sea, and who has kept me in perfect health since my arrival, for this reason do I despise that which God despises."

Now, Dad, isn't that most wonderful. I wish you would tell Dr. Day of it. There are many other smaller verses, all of great interest. On the last day of the diary, written October 14th, as he was leaving Verdun, for the Harmont, he writes as follows:

"Oh, it's hard to realize peace when the shells of the enemy are tearing all around us. "Peace" Oh! I pray God it will come before morning, and Mother's prayer may be realized.

All kinds of disheartening reports of the work which lay before us. I send Xmas letter home, and a note to Art. Feel well and O.K. tonight. Storm seems to clear up at 2:30 a.m. Old French men take gas quite seriously."

The poor kid prayed for peace and God gave it to him, Dad. How thankful I am that God gave it instantly. He was prepared to die, and did not suffer. I am happy over the thoughts of it, but God only knows how I miss him. I loved him so much.

Dad, these things are worth the world to you. I shall preserve them carefully; although they are in pretty bad shape, owing to the dampness of the ground and body. Also, they are badly stained and smell bad. I have soaked them all in gasoline, and in a day or so, they will be O.K.

I shall bring them to mother, everything. But I ask you all for them to be kept in my family, when you leave us to join poor Joe. I have gone through a living hell to get them, and after you and mother, they are mine.

Joe now rests beside Carl Coombs in the Romagne Cemetery, with 35,000 others. It is a beautiful place and our national Monument in France. I pray that you will let his body lie there in peace. I know he would wish it.

He is now buried deep in a coffin; and on Memorial Day, his grave will be beautifully decorated. General Pershing will be there to pay his last respects to his men who fought under him and it will be a beautiful ceremony.

I thank God I have accomplished so much. Every minute I have stayed here, I have been well paid for. I expect a promotion shortly, and next week, I will give up my company to become camp adjutant.

We expect to finish here within the next few months. Then we will all be home. Most of the work now is on artillery, and very few small arms.

I have many pictures that I took, and I turned them in to the camp photographer yesterday, and should have them in a week. Luckily, as I looked through my trunk last night, I found several maps of Romagne, so can show you just where the cemetery is.

As I stay over here longer, and see how well our cemeteries here will be taken care of, I am more convinced that our Joe should remain here.

I have had one experience of moving his body, and it was so hard that I wish now that you all would allow it to remain here as a part of our country's great monument to the world war.

They have started a movement in France to have some girl look after each grave, or group of graves. There is a young girl here that will look after them both, that is, Joe's and Carl Coombs'.

She is the only girl that has ever visited their graves. She went there only under great risk and hardships. Just because she wanted to be the one that could have charge of the graves after we are all gone. She wrote to Ma and as she speaks and writes very good English, I know Ma will be glad to write her in the years to come. As this girl has the time and means to go there, she will do it gladly.

She has been reading Joe's diary, and Psalm book, and I tell you, it is enough to impress anyone. They have been very good friends to me here.

I know Ma will be pleased to have this stuff. To see his own writing will be more to her than his body. Please let it now Rest in Peace.

I feel now that I have accomplished everything possible. The grave location is: Section 9, Plot 3, Grave 155. Joe is buried in the <u>Northeast corner</u>. Write soon, Dad, and love to all.

Your Son,
Art.

One year later Joseph Thompson's body was disinterred and brought to the United States, where it was buried in the family plot in Watertown, Massachusetts. David Thompson remained in France until 1923 and would later assist the American Graves Registration Service with the selection of the "Unknown Soldier" at Arlington National Cemetery.

—◦◦◦—

West Point Superintendent Douglas MacArthur Describes to His Fiancée an Incident That Prompted Vivid Memories from World War I

To ensure the confidence of the men and women who serve with them, it is considered imperative for those who send troops into battle to project, at all times, a sense of calm and control. "An officer can <u>have</u> no feeling," one lieutenant explained to his family in a letter home. "It is awful to see men you like drop by your side and not be able even to feel sorry. You can't stop for mercy—as the greatest good for the greatest number must be thought of first. If you do stop to think, you become unnerved." Publicly, few military leaders exuded more strength and authority than Douglas MacArthur. Son of a famous American general, graduate of West Point, and combat veteran of World War I, MacArthur achieved the five-star rank of General of the Army in December 1944, governed the occupation of Japan, and led all American and United Nations forces in Korea from 1950 to 1951. (MacArthur's boldness—or, to many, brash arrogance—would get him fired by President Truman.) But privately, in the immediate aftermath of World War I, MacArthur confided to those closest to him that the horrible memories of combat haunted him. While still in his thirties, MacArthur served as Chief of Staff of the Forty-second (Rainbow) Division, and then commanded the Eighty-fourth Infantry Brigade as a brigadier general. After the war he became superintendent of the United States Military Academy.

In December 1921, Ferdinand Foch—the French general who, during the last seven months of World War I, led almost all Allied forces—paid a visit to West Point. Foch's arrival provoked a rush of emotions that MacArthur shared in the following letter to his fiancée, Louise Cromwell Brooks.

Winter, 1921

Dearest of Women:

Today Came France—and once more the echo of battle. As he stepped from his train and came forward with the old twist in his eyes, the old bristle in his hair, I felt the clutch at my heart, the thrill in my veins;—it almost seemed as though I could smell again the smoke and blood of my glorious Rainbow! He took me in his arms just as he did of yore,—and for a fleeting flash we were back again in the poppy fields of Flanders.

We have honored him—and he has gone—but my thoughts are back tonight around those stark white crosses where I left my children forever.

Douglas MacArthur (center)
and Ferdinand Foch (left)

Bitter, scalding thoughts of those men who were, who followed me to the end with dogged, patient eyes, with white scared faces, with shaking wobbling knees, but coming on, and on, and on to my shout until the red smear stretched them clawing in the mud with my name on their lips, my voice in their ears. How gladly would I lay down my own life if I could only bring them back! My poor, faithful, devoted men! I am on my knees tonight praying God that in His pity He will redeem their souls and bring them at last to that peace which passeth all understanding. And may He be merciful to me who took them to their death.

Douglas

—ᴍ—

A Staff Sergeant Named Joseph Portnoy Relates to His Wife a Memorable Encounter with a Group of Germans
&
In a Letter to Her Niece, Lieutenant Isabelle Biasini Reflects on the Impact the War Has Had on European Children and Shares Her Hopes for the Future

"You may as well begin to prepare for the next war," a private first class in the US Marine Corps named Richard Millin wrote to his uncle in Pennsylvania from Europe during World War I. Millin had seen firsthand the devastation caused by Germany and believed it was only a matter of time before it would be a menace to the entire world. Millin continued:

> *It is coming as sure as the sun rises and sets. And America must be prepared. It will not be possible for us to stay out of it. It is absolutely necessary that we be in it. We must. France to my mind has passed her zenith. She will not be able to stand another war like this one. . . . Germany has no sense of decency nor any conscience. She must be exterminated or rendered absolutely powerless. If it is not done now, it will have to be done after the next war. And if the next war goes to Germany God help the world.*

Millin's letter was written in 1919. Twenty-six years and fifty million dead later, another global war would be nearing its end, and the same outrage would be echoed in many of the correspondences by those who were eyewitnesses to the death and ruin caused by Germany throughout World War II. In a letter dated April 16, 1945, an American Red Cross nurse named Angela Petesch shared with family members in California her emotions as the war was drawing to a close:

We are in a real Nazi city now and for the first time I'm beginning to have a real feeling of hatred and antagonism for the German people as a whole. You can feel it in the air. The stories that have come back to us from the men who have visited the concentration camp nearby, where so many atrocities were committed, have done much to stir us up in all our Army papers and probably yours, too. Hundreds of bodies of slave laborers were discovered there, the bodies of three American airmen included—some burned, some starved, all emaciated, stacked up like cordwood. The German mayor or burgomeister and his wife were taken by force out to see the place after the Americans took over the area. They went home and hung themselves that night—whether from shame and remorse that they belonged to such a murderous race, or from fear that we might do the same to them, I don't know. Thousands of American soldiers have been taken to see it as a kind of exhibit A to help teach them to hate and fight.

With the memories of fallen comrades still fresh in their minds, Allied service-members were equally—if not more so—infuriated by the staggering enormity of pain and suffering the Axis powers had inflicted on the world. And the front-line combatants, in particular, felt passionately about ensuring that the generations to come would never again witness bloodshed on such a wide scale. A twenty-five-year-old US Marine captain from Massachusetts named Frank Rudert wrote the following to his parents after a restless night spent thinking of all his friends who had sacrificed their lives to bring the war to an end:

If we for one minute forget the price that these men paid, all we have fought for is of no value. [If only] the coming generations can learn from our experience, and not have to forfeit their youth as we have done; the price of war can never be put too strongly before them, and most of all the price of human life. I hope we never have cause to regret not having wiped out, to the last living being, both the people of Germany and Japan.

Despite the anger and hatred that existed on both sides, servicemen and -women found one reason in particular—expressed in letter after letter—not to despair entirely for the state of humanity. Just weeks before V-E Day, a twenty-three-year-old Jewish staff sergeant named Joseph L. Portnoy wrote to his wife from Germany about an incident that affected him profoundly. A residue of bitterness remained, but his hopes for a peaceful future were emboldened.

Darling Own,

Yesterday was terribly dreary. It rained all day, and the hours stretched endlessly. I noticed a group of children playing in the hay barn. They seemed to be having a heck of a lot of fun, I went to watch them. It wasn't long before I was the center of their games, and they were teaching me German tongue twisters.

They range in age from four to about nine, full of life. Three children are the children of a minister, three others belonged to a doctor. Naturally the fathers are away in the war, and the youngsters are hungry for the affections of a male adult.

They soon agreed on my name as uncle Haans, and we continued from there. It was interesting to hear stories that they'd learned about America. America is a place where enormous goblins swim in the rivers and streams, and they carry knives in their mouths, and eat little children. That's what happened to all the baby dolls in Germany. They swam to America, and were immediately eaten up by the goblins. I asked the children if they believed such stories. They said that they didn't. I think that we can believe them, that they don't believe these things, and also if they are treated fairly by the Americans, they will retain those young impressions that we, as soldiers, give them by our kindness; and the job of reeducating this new generation of German children will become a simpler job. I have no sympathy what so ever with the suffering of their elders, but it's the children that can be coddled a bit while they're still at this impressionable age. The children would vie for a chance to sit on my lap and hug me. It's pathetic how hungry they are for the love of a male adult, a father. At the same time, I realized how eager I was to have a youngster in my arms. I can just imagine dear how wonderfully sweet it will be to hold Bobby in my arms, and how completely beautiful it will be to be near your love again. Gosh darling, the floodgates of our emotions will burst right open once we are together again, and I'm quite willing to be drowned in the sea of our love.

We are anxiously waiting now for the link up between the Russians and Americans. Frankly I can't imagine how we can go much further now that the Russians are in Berlin. Darling there just isn't anything much to conquer in our vicinity except isolated pockets of resistance.

Things are going beautifully, and before long we will be wondering where we will go on our weekend passes, and how long it will be before we embark for home. It won't be too long now honey. The worst of this war is long past.

Today, Sunday, is peacefully quiet, and now that I've eaten a delicious dinner, I think I'll go out and see the children.

Send me letters soon dearest, and try to get pictures to me.

Your Ever Adoring
Husband

Thousands of miles away, a yeoman first class named Ted Steinkamp, stationed in Japan, would have a very similar encounter, which he described in a Christmas Day letter to his wife and daughter in Grand Island, Nebraska.

Just returned from downtown and had an experience I will never forget. The chaplain obtained about 3—20# boxes of hard mixed Christmas candy, which he decided should be distrubuted to the children of Yokosuka. Well, we goes down to transportation and obtains a weapons carrier, and seven of us get aboard and go to the "city". Honey, you have heard that it is more blessed to give than to receive—now I know the full meaning of it. Never in my life have I experienced such a thrill in giving. If you could have seen the expressions on these kids face when we gave them a handful of candy, you could never forget it. Apparently they have never had any in their life to speak of, and we were practically mobbed everytime we stopped. The mothers with children on their back would walk up, bow, hold out their hands and say "please" & with a very courteous "sank you" (they cannot pronounce "th") go on their way. It was impossible to move if we stopped in any particular spot for any time at all. So many people coming out of nowhere—we'd have to pull away gradually, one of us standing on the side to see that no one would get run over. Probably more good was done in the distribution of this candy than the State Department could do in a long time. Candy is more than candy to these people, it is food. They don't have much of it. Honey, I never before realized how well off we Americans are— we all have so much more than people on this side of the world. The things we call necessities are out of the question for them—I thought of Katherine and the nice Christmas she was having in our home & how I would hate to think that she'd have to chase after a truck to get a few pieces of candy.

Stationed in Europe to help relocate refugees, Lieutenant Isabelle Biasini did not have children of her own, so she wrote instead to her young niece, Joy Ellen Grigat, about her experiences in postwar Germany. The twenty-six-year-old Biasini had worked in the children's programming division of New York's WWOR radio station before the war, and then, to the shock of her family, enlisted in the Women's Army Auxiliary Corps. Biasini sent the following letter from Frankfurt, Germany, on November 4, 1945. Five-year-old Joy was just entering kindergarten back in New Jersey.

Dearest Joy—

I got your letter you wrote and had Daddy mail for you. It was very sweet of you to write me. My sakes you must be getting to be a big girl when you can write a letter all by yourself!

Mommy told me you had started to school and that you liked it very much. I'm glad you like it because school is a lot of fun—learning to read & write and draw pictures. I'll bet when I get home, you'll be able to read the funnies too me! A lot of the little German girls are going back to school now too. Thanks to the victorious Armies of the Allies, they all now have the same chances to learn the things you do—they also now have an opportunity to go to Sunday school and to learn about the Lord and may worship him instead of being forced to adore some fanatic who wanted merely to enslave the world.

Honey, I know this letter will probably be hard for you to understand. I have gotten into the habit of thinking you older than you are—not in years but in understanding. I have seen the youngsters of France & Germany some your age, some younger—whose faces and manner of speech show them to be far older mentally than their years. They have lost their childhood already before they have even reached their teens. Looking at them, I thank God that you & Sharon & Susan were born in a free country away from this endless strife. It will be you & them who will have to keep it that way—my most fervent hope for the future is that neither of you will ever have to don a uniform.

Darling, I know this is "over your head" but my pen has run away with me—perhaps some day you will be able to read this and understand what I am driving at. Just remember to practice love & tolerance but don't let yourself be blinded by high ideals. Think things out for yourself and don't let yourself be swayed by a lot of high sounding words or playing of bands, flag waving, etc.

I'm going to sign off now, honey, thank you again for the letter and the birthday present.

Love
Aunt Sis

—⚌—

Lila Oliver Writes to a Friend About the Attitudes of the Wounded Soldiers She Sketches as a Volunteer Artist with the USO

Along with the estimated twenty-five million troops killed in World War II, millions more were forever disabled. Although they made it home alive, they faced a difficult period of rehabilitation that often involved excruciating physical therapy and numerous operations, especially if they were blinded or paralyzed, severely burned, or had lost a limb (or limbs). Confined to a hospital bed for days, weeks, or months at a time, away from friends and loved ones, they also had to overcome constant boredom. Lila Oliver, a twenty-two-year-old graduate of the Philadelphia College of Art, recognized that there was nothing she could do to alleviate the physical suffering of the wounded young men, but through her skills she hoped she could at least help them pass the time more enjoyably. In 1943 she volunteered for the USO's "Sketching Unit," which traveled to military hospitals throughout the country to create portraits of the GIs. In a letter to a female friend named Terry, Oliver responded to the question of whether or not the patients appreciated her work.

> *I suppose they know little about its artistic value, and from that angle I might say no. They care little about a delicate, sensitive line. On the other hand, they do value my coming to the hospital and drawing them. They think the idea is "swell" and they enjoy the likeness as well as the fact that I draw them in uniform when they are really wearing pajamas. My favorite quip, "You know, I've dressed more GIs than anyone around here," always gets a laugh. That's what I am here for, not to be "arty" but . . . to give the kids an extra chuckle, take their minds off being sick, and maybe flatter them a bit. Nearly everyone confides, "You know, this is the first time I ever had my pitcher 'etched—hope I don't break the charcoal. . . ."*

Oliver was also moved by the way in which the men coped with their ailments. In a letter written just after the war to Terry, whose husband, Allan, was in the service, she commented on the different attitudes she encountered in the wards. She was especially taken by one young corpsman who had been a medic before getting shot in battle.

Dear Terry,

Time skips by. My work, photography, the canteen, and the local hospital sketching trips, all conspire to keep me busy.

That was a grand long letter. More of the same, please. You're thinking, of course, of Allan when you ask if the boys have changed much. Funny thing—but I don't think they do. Some, having had experiences enough for a lifetime, are older, even have gray hairs. They are a little older, yet have a greater zest for life. Sound contradictory? T''isn't. They've seen much, so they are older, but what they have lived through makes them appreciate each day and each hour. To be sure, I never before knew these individual kids, but among my models are the kind of people I knew. There are the students and jitterbugs, the smart kid, the man-about-town, the college smoothie, everybody's kid brother, the pessimist and optimist (more of the latter), and even Mamma's boy has retained his individuality.

You ask what I think of the boys' coming home changed and different, and, truly, I don't think it happens. They have new ideas, more mature outlooks, enough to make an adjustment a real consideration, but it's my conviction that most GIs bring back the same essential structure of character with which they joined the service. I s'pose others will disagree. Really, the reactions of their families when the boys first come home creates as many problems as the kids bring with them. They want to be treated as normal and left alone. They haven't forgotten what home is like, or how to act among civilians. From the time they shipped over, all the little memories they could gather were held carefully together. The kids haven't forgotten. They'll offer a woman a seat in the streetcar as quickly as some of the people who never left town, without lectures, books of instructions, or ten easy lessons in how to be a civilian. Most of them can't understand why people think they need hints on what to do on their first furlough in the States. They've told me so.

The disabled ones? They want to be treated squarely and honestly. Most of the boys have more courage than I knew existed. If we don't pity and stare sideways with long sad glances they'll be O.K. They need a chance. I say we shouldn't pity them; I didn't say we shouldn't help them; most assuredly we must not forget them. How can we repay the loss of a leg to a twenty-year-old?

I sketched a hospital corpsman, a patient in one of the Atlantic City hospitals, last Sunday. His two roommates had recently been transferred and he was lonely. That's why they sent me in. He was a youngster with the most wonderful disposition and bright red hair, with a cowlick in back that stood straight up. This kid was in the midst of a series of neuro-surgical operations. He told me how it was to be a medic in the European theatre.

"You stay behind the lines mostly. Then when the guys get hit, why, you just go help them, and then pull 'em out. If things get extra tough, you fight, too. Then there's always one guy who does some fool thing, goes out and gets himself hurt, and you go risk your neck to drag him out. Of course, you swear up and down that you won't do it again—isn't your fault if those guys want to take silly chances! But the very next time you go right after 'em and do the same damn thing all over again."

He told me how he got hit.

"We were taking a machine gun nest and there had been a lot of fire. I crawled out to take care of some of our men. Nearby was a wounded Jerry so I inched myself over to give him first aid. He was pretty bad. The Krauts saw me and ceased firing. They waited until I finished bandaging that guy up and then opened up on me—got me in the leg! Naturally, our guys were mad as hell 'cause they could see the whole thing. They took that whole gang and when the few Jerries that were left marched out with hands up they all waited for the one who got me. He was the last one to come out. Then all together our guys yelled to me, "Hey, look, kid!" and all together they gave it to him. We took the others prisoner."

When I had finished the sketch and he had approved he told me his name. It was Goldblatt. "Just call me Goldy."

This had been another long letter. You asked a question which I feel very strongly.

My wisdom tooth is making its presence known—the one on the upper right side. It hurts when I chew and cramps my eating style. I can't even enjoy a good yawn, but I am sleepy. Bedtime.

Love,
Lila

—⁓—

Shaken by His Combat Experiences in Korea, Private Al Puntasecca Asks His Family to "Be Patient" with Him When He Returns Home
&
Olwyn Green Writes a Final Love Letter to Her Husband Charlie, Who Served in Both World War II and the Korean War

Physical injuries do not yield the only scars of war. There can be internal afflictions as well that many—though certainly not all—combat veterans carry with them after their service, from spells of sudden, overwhelming sadness to persistent and life-threatening depression. Upon coming home, they are often confronted with a world that is radically different from the one they have just left. They might experience pronounced mood shifts, sharing feelings of helplessness and vulnerability one moment and becoming distant and uncommunicative the next. Only those who have been under fire can truly understand how searing the experience can be, and how deeply it can wound even the most resilient and mature individuals. After surviving a year of harsh conditions and bitter fighting in Korea from 1952 to 1953, a nineteen-year-old private from New Jersey named Al Puntasecca learned that he was finally returning to the States. Puntasecca had served in an artillery outfit with the Twenty-fifth Infantry Division, Forty-fourth Battalion, A Company, and the work was thunderously loud (he permanently lost part of his hearing) and extremely dangerous. Before embarking on the long journey back home, Puntasecca sent a letter to his parents and two siblings, Bud and Emily, forewarning them that he was—and probably would remain—a changed man.

Dear Everybody,

I'm coming home! It's official as of this morning. It will be some time before I crash in your door, a few weeks, maybe, but, I'm coming home! Remember I told you how seasick I was on the way over here? Well, I can't wait to do it again.

That little house is going to look like a palace to me and, you people like Kings, and, Queens. People who love you. A clean place to live. A clean place to live <u>life.</u> To sleep in a what do you call it, bed? yeah, that's it, bed. Running water. Hot meals. And, what's this I hear about people having private bathrooms, and, private showers? Really? Is it true some people eat three times a day, or, more? and, they sit on a <u>chair,</u> by a <u>table.</u> What's the matter, can't they dig a hole in the back yard like everybody else? A place where you can close your eyes any time you want to, no more 90 day wonders, no more Sargeants with Patton complexes, "All right, you bastards! Off, and, on." No more this! No more that! So, ma, put the spaghetti on right now. Plenty of sauce, and, a ton of sausage. And, Pepsi! A 50 gallon drum! Yeah, and, 10 lbs of cheese.

Bud, remember you beat me up everytime the Yankees lost? or, your horse lost? or, you lost? or, the day after Sunday was Monday? I think we'll get along much better from now on. Emily, you get busy on that brass band, and, ticker tape parade. Nothing fancy. What Ike had is O.K. It is going to be hard being civilized again. What the hell ever civilized means, so, don't be surprised if you think you have a savage in the house for a while.

Yeah. I'm looking forward to seeing you again, but I'm in no hurry to see the expressions on your faces when <u>you</u> see <u>me.</u> I want to see you try to hide the shock on your faces. You might even ask me for proof I'm your son. Don't feel bad. I see it in my own face every day. I have spent 12 months over here. The longest 30 years of my life. A short time ago I was 18, and, all I was worried about was cars, girls, and, how much beer a <u>real man</u> could drink. No more. Don't get me wrong. I still want a hot car, a hot girl, and, a cold beer, but, there were times I could have traded them all for a warm blanket. A wool hat. A pair of gloves, or, ear muffs. another pair of socks. A shoelace. A goddamned <u>shoelace!</u> There were times I would have traded my soul for a drink of cold water, or a cup of hot coffee. But, I am coming home now. Chuck isn't. He's listed M.I.A. If he's on this side of the line I hope he makes it. If he's on their side I hope he's dead. He'd wish the same for me. Leon is dead. His girlfriend killed him. Stabbed him in the back while he was facing the Gooks.

How many guys have been killed in wars? How many not born because they were killed? Did it start with Cain, and Able? The caveman? Who? Does it matter? And, for <u>what</u>? What? Has anything changed? Will anything change? No, Never. So what do we do? <u>Nothing!</u> If something could have been done I'm sure somebody would have done

Private Al Puntasecca

it. All we can do, all anybody can do is try to understand. I can't hear as well out of my left ear anymore. The 105 is no slingshot. Something about the big cells of the ear crushing the small cells of the ear further, and, further in until it makes a blockage. I hear what you're saying all right. It just takes time to get to where I can <u>understand</u> it, so, be a little patient, okay?

You know, it's almost funny, we see a guy in a wheel chair, a guy on crutches, one arm, hooks for hands, and, we break our backs trying to help him. But, what about the wounds you can't see? The phantoms, the nightmares, the ghosts in your head? I am going to tell you now. you'll need a lot of patience with me. Patience, and, understanding. We all will. See you soon. See you soon. See you soon.

Jr.

Regardless of whether their loved one is gone forever or returns home a notice- ably different person, the spouses, family members, and friends of servicemen and -women often undergo their own postwar healing and adjustment period as well. Born December 26, 1919, in South Grafton, Australia, Charlie Green joined the militia at the age of sixteen and went on to fight in World War II, first as an infantry officer and then as the commander of an entire battalion. His young

Charlie Green playing with his daughter Anthea and their dog Sandy.

wife, Olwyn, longed for his homecoming with great expectations after years of anxious waiting. Their relationship remained strong and loving, but Charlie, his wife soon discovered after his return, was not the same. The man who had written passionate love letters during the war was now taciturn and often seemed uncomfortable around other people. The battalion commander who earned the Distinguished Service Order found himself struggling to start a farm. He was restless. He missed the camaraderie of his mates and the life-and-death significance of their missions. In June 1950 the Korean War erupted, and, much to his wife's dismay, Charlie was eager to join the fight. "Racehorses will gallop," was his explanation. In September he was appointed the commanding officer of the Third Battalion, Royal Australian Regiment. On September 12, while in transit to Korea, Charlie sent his first letter home: "The trouble is not as bad as you would believe," he wrote to Olwyn, "in fact it's rather more like civil war and with our unit we will have little to worry about." Just over two weeks later he was in Korea, and the tenderness he had so frequently expressed in his World War II letters appeared once again. "How are you keeping my sweet and Bubby too of course," Charlie wrote on October 27, referring to their three-year-old daughter Anthea.

> I do hope you are well and as happy as can be. We have only about another twenty miles to go to our final objective and after that the thing should be over. . . . God bless you my darling and keep you well. I love you more than ever and hope that we are together again in a little while.

Before Olwyn received his letter, the local telegram boy came bicycling up to their house in Grafton carrying a pink envelope. She stood frozen on the front step. "Regret to inform you that your husband, 2/37504 Lieutenant Colonel Charles Hercules Green," it began, "was wounded in Korea Stop Suffering from shrapnel wound . . ." Although there was reason for hope—he was "only" injured—Olwyn knew that her worst fears had been realized. At about midnight the next evening, after an agonizing wait, she received the notification that her husband was in fact dead, killed during a Chinese artillery attack. He was thirty years old. Decades later, Olwyn Green sat down and relived their relationship through all of his letters that she had preserved, but, until that time, had not reread. In 1992, and living in Sydney, Olwyn Green penned one last letter to her husband.

Sydney 1992

My dearest Charlie,

It's a long time since I've written you. I didn't think you would get any messages. Now I am not so sure.

You see, I've been going over the past. I went back over your life before you met me. I loved doing that. That picture of you as a lad reminds me so much of what Anthea was like as she grew up. I've been dwelling on the short but rich time we had together. The good times were wonderful, weren't they? It all seemed like yesterday and you were so vividly present. Then I had a dream about you. That's why I felt I should write.

I think I have learned a lot, my darling. There's no point in questioning or regretting the past. It's gone. For years I worried about what happened to us. One thing doesn't frighten me any more. It is Time. Time doesn't exist. We make a big mistake in measuring it out in minutes or years, or in past or future. Our marriage was a lifetime. And the couple of frightening occasions when I saw into the future have made me realize that maybe, once in a while, we are permitted a glimpse of infinity. I think it is fear that prevents us from seeing into the future—or from seeing straight. It is forty odd years since I saw you, but they seem to have disappeared.

Lately, I've stopped having the bad dream that you were so far away and couldn't get in touch with me. I hated that dream I had over and over again. I could never understand it.

As I said, the other night I dreamt about you. It was a very different dream. You came close to me. Then a very strange, bright light shone down on the left side of your face, illuminating it so that I could see your eyes. The light showed me the tears in your eyes. That woke me up. I can't bear to think of you crying. Please don't cry. There must be no more tears—yours or mine. There is no need for us to cry. What we shared was too beautiful to cry about. And though we failed in a way, God knows, we tried.

I am not young any more, Charlie. I have wrinkles and grey hair. That youthful beauty you told me to preserve has gone. I still have a fair bit of energy, though. I've needed it when I have been minding those grandchildren of ours.

I feel a kind of mellowness now. And I don't have that physical ache for you that I used to suffer so strongly. In fact the way I feel keeps bringing a line from Keats to my head: "Season of mists and mellow fruitfulness." That is exactly how I feel. Remember how I love poetry. I can't stop it from running through my head. That's how we got Anthea's name.

I worked and saved to fill the years. Now I can enjoy these autumnal days. I feel content, and, yes, I feel rich, even though I've never filled the gap you left. It wasn't an empty gap. I've always had your love to sustain me.

What I look forward to is seeing our two grandsons grow into manhood. They are beautiful boys. The younger one is the image of Anthea when she was little, in looks and in a determination to carve an individual path in life. Anthea's path took many deviations before she resolved into her true, exceptional self. Your daughter has your strength. The elder one is like me in his ways, some people say. In appearance, he is like you—handsome.

In all those hundreds of letters I wrote to you, I always told you how much I loved you. I probably didn't tell you: You are the finest human being I have ever known.

Please be at peace and remember that I've always loved you.

Your loving wife,
Olwyn

—⁓—

Lieutenant Colonel Ty Smith, Commander of the JPAC Detachment in Hanoi, E-mails His Wife About Their Efforts to Locate Missing US Servicemen

In the mountains of the Korean peninsula, the fields and forests of Europe, the oceans and islands of the Pacific, the jungles and rice paddies of Southeast Asia, and many other corners of the earth where American troops have fought, the remains of almost ninety thousand soldiers, Marines, airmen, and sailors lie unrecovered and unknown. Their families have had no body to bury or even the solace of knowing with certainty the fate of their loved one. But for the past three decades, teams of highly dedicated investigators, translators, explosives technicians, forensic anthropologists, and many other civilian and military personnel have been working exhausting hours in brutal conditions to collect the remains of those listed as missing in action (MIA) and bring them home. Created in 2003 out of a merger between the thirty-year-old US Army Central Identification Laboratory, based in Hawaii, and the eleven-year-old Joint Task Force— Full Accounting, the new organization is called the Joint POW/MIA Accounting Command, or JPAC for short. (JPAC's highest priority, in fact, is to search for living Americans being held as prisoners of war. The issue of US combatants from past wars still being detained as POWs is an emotional and controversial one, but most experts believe that the possibility of finding surviving POWs in Korea, China, Vietnam, Laos, Cambodia, or—in the case of the 1991 Gulf War—Iraq is extremely unlikely.) The on-site work itself, is meticulous and painstaking, involving treks deep into secluded and treacherous areas. JPAC teams have had to rappel cliffs, hike glaciers, and dive into murky lakes and rivers. Accessing these remote places can be dangerous as well, and on April 7,

2001, JPAC suffered its worst loss when seven US servicemen, along with nine Vietnamese colleagues, died after their M1–17 helicopter crashed in the Quang Binh province of Vietnam while on a mission. Of JPAC's eighteen recovery teams, ten are dedicated to finding those missing from the fighting in Vietnam and surrounding countries. (Five teams focus on the Korean War, and three are responsible for World War II, the Cold War, and the Gulf War.) Like most JPAC personnel stationed abroad, Lieutenant Colonel Ty Smith went for months without seeing his family. Fifty-three years old and a veteran of the Vietnam War himself, Smith commanded the Hanoi-based JPAC Detachment Two, and he frequently e-mailed his friends and relatives about the colorful characters with whom he worked and, more importantly, how meaningful his job was to him and the fallen comrades he wanted to honor. Smith sent the following to his family on July 12, 2003.

Still in Danang where the six teams have gathered for a week of end of mission report writing from the thirty or so sites investigated and the five sites excavated this Joint Field Activity. It meant also I finally got a chance to meet the majority of folks in the command, minus the several hundred Vietnamese who work for us. I have always sort of collected eccentrics but I have to admit my collection would simply overload here. I do not think I have ever met in once place so many extraordinarily interesting and decidedly different individuals. My training as garrison commander at the Army War College came in good stead today, gave at least five speeches to different teams and events and did a promotion—a warrant officer to CW3, as far as anyone could tell it was an historic occasion, the first field promotion done in Vietnam since the war. I spent the evening with our science guys, the anthropologists assigned to each team who govern the science of the excavations. The dean of them, Dr. Moore, or "Hoss" has been here a decade. A six-foot-six Oklahoma cowboy, complete with Tony Llama boots, huge Texas Ten-gallon hat, Cambodian scarf around his neck, completely deaf, but a good lip reader in a multitude of languages, one of fifty board certified forensic anthros in the US. He became an immediate fast friend, he hugs me, a big bear hug. The science guys spent the evening drinking beer and arguing with fierce passion over the subtleties of taphonomic erosion. I let this go on for a half-hour before I asked what means taphonomic? After a fascinating one-hour lecture I now know it means the science of how various soils and environmental conditions degrade biological material, in this case the bones of our missing boys. The science guys get pretty animated about the subject so I won't ask that again. Combined with them are all sorts of unexploded ordnance specialists, field medicine doctors &

medics, linguists, intelligence analysts, team leaders, mortuary affairs specialist, and the life support crew. The life support analysts are probably the most uniquely trained folks in the entire military. Their job is to recognize or research and identify any and all equipment and parts associated with any of the dozens of variations of ejection seats, survival equipment, parachutes, or flight gear issued to military pilots between 1958 and 1973. They can look at a single scrap of harness or even a washer or grommet, get on their field computer data bases and chemistry sets and usually within a few hours tell you what type of aircraft and what years the piece of gear was used. Amazing. The more I see of the quality field work and the talent and the dedication and the hardship these folks endure to do their mission the more humbled I am by this privilege of command. Ty

In March of 2004, just a few months before his tour was over, Smith wrote to his wife from Hanoi.

Dear Holly,
Very interesting and emotional day. This morning I briefed the delegation from Vietnam Veterans Memorial Fund (VVMF), the guys who raised the money and oversee The Wall in Washington D.C. With them was Ann Sherman Wolcott the president of Gold Star Mothers, whose ranger son was KIA in Vietnam. Most of the group of twenty were veterans on their first trip back—day two—so the energy level was off the scale. The briefing went fine, except the part where they seemed astonished at the level of effort, the difficulty, the danger, and the complete commitment of the government and our fine young military men and women to the mission. I ended with the part about our son Miles serving in Iraq and now I had the perspective of a parent, rather than just another commander on a mission, it had become a personal quest. We now have twenty extra prayers for Miles every night. At the end they had a short memorial ceremony and Mrs. Wolcott made a little speech about this being her first trip here and suddenly how fortunate she felt because at least she had her son in the end to put in Arlington, and about all those mothers who did not, but can live in hope we will find the answers. I was so drawn to her, I hugged her and held her and we had some tears, and we held hands for the rest of the visit. I had lunch with Jan Scruggs, the President of VVMF, whom I had heard about for years, he was the Vietnam vet who started the whole Wall project. I finally told him I had tried to go there three or four times but always turned back, just couldn't face it, but I thought maybe now after

being here again, I at least wanted to go see the names of the guys we had found and sent home on my watch. He kindly offered to take me, just himself. I said maybe. Ty

—⁂—

A Vietnam Veteran Leaves a Posthumous Letter at the Vietnam Veterans Memorial for His Buddies Killed in the War & Another Veteran Assures His Friends That Their Sacrifice Will Always Be Remembered

When "The Wall" was created in 1982, its founder, Vietnam veteran Jan Scruggs, believed it should be a tribute not only to those who had given their lives in Southeast Asia, but also to those who had come home alive. The Vietnam Veterans Memorial, as it is officially called, has since become the most visited monument in the nation's capital, offering hundreds of thousands of veterans who travel to Washington each year a quiet, dignified space to remember their comrades and reflect on their own experiences. Millions of tourists from the United States and all over the world also come to honor those who have served and pay their respects to the 58,245 names carved on the massive black granite panels. What Scruggs and National Park Service staff who oversee the care of The Wall did not expect, however, was the enormous number of personal items that veterans, family members of the deceased, and total strangers would leave at the memorial. Many of the poems and letters, in particular, reveal both intense suffering and a desire to find peace by recalling memories and expressing emotions that have long been suppressed. "The things that I am going to say in this letter are about twenty years and a whole lifetime late, but maybe that won't matter once they've been said," one veteran began a long, handwritten letter to a close buddy killed in Vietnam.

A lot of the guys who were there say they feel like they lost something in-country. I know what I lost. I've always said that when you died, it was like killing the other half of myself. Maybe that's not necessarily true. What I did lose was youth . . . all of the idealism, trust, self-confidence, and personal power that we had, either inside or drilled into us. I'm scared, now, most of the time, and I hurt a lot. What happened to us has cost me a life as much as it cost you yours. I've never been able to get close to anyone since you died. My wife, step-daughter, my son. I live in the past, 'cause today hurts too much. I want out of the past. The war is over. I need _my_ war to be over, too. I never got to say goodbye. So I've come to this monument to have a little memorial service and to say goodbye and to let you go. I'll

never forget you, don't worry about that. . . . Goodbye, John. If there is a
caring, Christian God, I hope that he has forgiven both of us and taken
you with all of our brother warriors to a peaceful final reward.

Another veteran, who had apparently served as a medic, had greater success in
coming to terms with his grief, but he still wondered how future generations
would remember and learn from a conflict that would increasingly seem
remote and distant to so many of them.

Dear Timothy, Christopher, Frank, & John

I have journeyed again to this monument to pay tribute to those of us
who suffered and to offer my respects to you who left your bodies so
unexpectedly. My memories of your deaths are not involved with as
much pain or anger as was once the case. Time, thought, and maturity
have healed my emotional and physical wounds, but always within
myself there are those places which never forgets.

It is always difficult to obviously determine how the conditions
concerning the deaths and injury of so many can affect the current state
of consciousness of a new generation. Whether directly or indirectly
your passing has had significant affect on our culture today. I know that
as time travels forward the affects are less and less apparent, but future
youth will experience simular traumas distinctive to their own
generation. In their own painful realities perhaps your conditions will
not be forgotten.

Althougth I was not successful in healing your injured bodies as they
layed wounded in my arms I feel I have healed the wounds in my soul
that opened when you died. Peace be with you now and also for all of
those of our generation who must continue to heal their wounds, calm
their anger, and find solice with their memories.

A veteran from Chicago expressed his gratitude to his comrades for saving his
life, and he assured them that he would continue to let others know of their
heroism for as long as he lived.

Dear Brothers,

I know I am a little late in bringing you these words, but you have
been on my mind since the war and will always be in my heart. I have
tried to thank you, but no matter what I tried, there seemed to be no
significant way it could be done. You sacrificed your lives to pay me the
highest honor amongst men. There are no words that I can use to

possibly ever repay you. I can however, by letting this letter be read, let the world know of your bravery, courage, and care for your fellow man.

On September the seventh, nineteen hundred and sixty eight, without regard for your own safety and in the true spirit of brotherhood, you acted above the call of duty and honor, to save the life of a comrade you barely knew. A man who certainly would have died, without your committing of selfless acts on his behalf. Our country does not offer an award that ranks high enough to suit your actions. I thank you for my life and beautiful family. I have long commiserated with the fact that I have what you can not. You will never be forgotten nor will any aspect of my life have any meaning without your ever present sharing of my soul. I made a vow to myself to not let your deaths be in vain. I have a commitment to teach to the world the mistakes made, and the fruitlessness of war. I do this through the children. I teach them that your sacrifice was for them not me.

Your place on this wall, shows our future leaders and warriors that we can not repeat Vietnam. They have a choice in their future, and I know if you were able to give them direction and strength of conviction, your words would echo my own, and lead them away from the mistakes of the past. I miss you. I wish I might relate to your families, that you were the best. Maybe they'll read this and know I am talking about you. To anyone reading this letter who has loved ones on this most sacred of stones, I am also writing this to all of you, to the families and friends of all my brothers and sisters, whose names are etched in eternity on this wall. These names, these fallen soldiers are the best our generation had to offer. The world could never compensate for the great contributions you would have made. I can only hope that in some small way, you would be proud of the path I have taken in your honor.

— ⁂ —

Abdul Hameed Al-Attar, the Father of a Missing Kuwaiti POW, Sends a Message Through the Red Cross in a Final, Desperate Effort to Determine If His Son Is Still Alive

During the Iraqi occupation of Kuwait that began in August 1990, thousands of Kuwaitis were imprisoned for "crimes" as minor as joining a protest march or displaying the national flag. They were interrogated, tortured, and, in many cases, brutally executed, especially if they were believed to be members of Kuwait's armed forces. After the country's liberation in February 1991, the terms of surrender accepted by the Iraqi regime in March demanded the return

*of all POWs (or their remains). A month later, United Nations Resolution 687
stipulated specifically that*

> *in furtherance of its commitment to facilitate the repatriation of all
> Kuwaiti and third country nationals, Iraq shall extend all necessary
> cooperation to the International Committee of the Red Cross [ICRC], pro-
> viding lists of such persons, facilitating the access of the International Com-
> mittee of the Red Cross to all such persons wherever located or detained
> and facilitating the search by the International Committee of the Red Cross
> for those Kuwaiti and third country nationals still unaccounted for. . . .*

*Approximately six thousand Kuwaitis were repatriated in the weeks following
the cease-fire. But in April Iraq claimed there were no remaining prisoners and
refused to cooperate with the ICRC's efforts to account for every POW. In February 1993, Kuwait presented documented evidence that five hundred and seventy of their citizens, including more than one hundred and twenty students,
were still missing. (Thirty-five foreign nationals who had been living and working in Kuwait had also disappeared.) The family members of these prisoners held
out hope that, in time, they would be found alive in Iraq. The last time one
Kuwaiti man, Abdul Hameed Al-Attar, had heard his son Jamal's voice was
when the boy cried out for him while being held in a Kuwaiti police station,
which had been converted by the Iraqis into an "intelligence center." Four years
later, his father made one last attempt, through the ICRC, to get a letter to his
son, wherever he might be.*

Dear Son Jamal,

Today is September 13, 1994, and four years have already passed since
we lost your trace, exactly four years have gone since I received that
telephone call informing me about your arrest by the Iraqi soldiers on
that afternoon.

My Dear Son Jamal, four years have passed but your voice is still
shaking in my head from when I went to Rumaitheya police station
trying to get you out or at least know your condition, but the Iraqis
denied that you were there or knowing anything about you. Then
moments later you heard my heated argument with the Iraqi soldiers
and called me saying, "Father father I am here!" and then I heard you
screaming from the pain when they began lashing and hitting you, and
then your voice vanished to this day.

My Dear Son, so far the Iraqis are strongly denying the existence of
any Kuwaiti prisoner in Iraq, but they offered the possibility of some
missing Kuwaitis still wandering somewhere inside Iraq but afraid to

show themselves up, so I and members of the family are still hoping that this story is real, but yet if this is the case, how will this letter reach you?

Even so I must tell you that your mother is still keeping your personal belongings in your room, checking them every morning as if you will be coming soon (probably today or tomorrow) she says with tears pouring from her red eyes, and she always repeats your jokes which you used to tell us from time to time, but instead of laughing she cries and then weeps and wails, and we all share her sadness and sorrow for your long absence.

My Dear Jamal, if you receive this letter from the ICRC read it with full confidence in yourself and trust in mighty God that he is with you and with every person on earth all the time, and be assured that we and all of the Kuwaiti people will never, never forget you or any of your mates. Have confidence in yourself that you are great in all circumstances and even if you die—"May God forbid that"—you and your other missing or prisoners will forever be our national pride.

You will remain in our minds and hearts forever. May God be with you, dead or alive.

We miss you.

Your sad father on behalf of all the family.

When Coalition forces invaded Iraq in the spring of 2003, many family members of the missing POWs prayed that their loved ones would be discovered still in confinement—but at least alive—in Iraqi prisons. Tragically, not one was found.

—◊◊◊—

**Captain Peter Caddick-Adams, with the UN Peacekeeping Forces in Bosnia and Herzegovina, Describes Christmas Celebrations in Battle-Scarred Sarajevo to a Friend Back in England
&
US Army Captain Christine McNeff Reports Home About a Patrol Through an Albanian Town and Her Reaction to Meeting Kosovar Refugees**

Although their efforts tend to receive less attention than those of the frontline troops who charge into battle, the role of United Nations, NATO, and other peacekeeping soldiers is equally critical to the world's security. They, along with civilian aid workers, are responsible for maintaining the often fragile cease-fires in nations plagued by violence, thereby ensuring that the hard-won peace does not unravel in the months and years to follow. In addition to sta-

bilizing the region, by force if necessary, they provide medical assistance and sup-
plies to the sick and wounded, monitor elections, prevent human rights abuses,
train native police forces, rid the area of land mines, and assist with countless
other duties to bring humanitarian relief and protection to those in desperate
need of both. Casualties are rare, but they do occur. Hostile acts represent the
second most common cause of death after accidents, which are frequently the
result of vehicle-related fatalities on battered and unsafe roads. During the
forty-two months of warfare in the Balkans, which began in 1991, hundreds
of thousands of Bosnian Muslims and Croatians were killed by Serbian troops,
and a million more became refugees. The 1995 Dayton peace agreement
brought a tenuous cease-fire, and tens of thousands of NATO troops were sent
to serve, first as an "implementation" force—known as IFOR—and later as a
"stabilization" force, SFOR. One of the SFOR soldiers, a captain with the
British Army named Peter Caddick-Adams, wrote vivid accounts detailing his
experiences in Bosnia and Herzegovina. The following letter, addressed to a
friend in London two days after Christmas in 1996, is laced with humorous
observations about military life and the inevitable clash of cultures when
international forces work together, but it also accentuates the heartbreaking con-
ditions the citizens of Sarajevo had endured for almost four horrific years.

Dear Nigel

Christmas morning dawned with not a flake of snow in sight. We'd
had some earlier in December, & plenty of the white stuff was forecast,
but so far, our gathering of the world's most qualified military
meteorological experts had failed to come up with the goods. I had
reasoned that if there was one place on earth that could guarantee a
white Christmas, it would be Sarajevo. First call of the day was to our
headquarters on the far side of the city for a Festival of Nine Lessons and
Carols. Organised by our transatlantic cousins, the service was in fact a
competition to cram in as many carols as possible—the final tally was
fourteen, at which point my voice gave out. The cousins changed the
tunes of several favourites, & introduced a carol new to me, to the tune
of *Greensleeves* (thumbs down). The congregation were the English
speakers of SFOR, & included a few brave Germans & Dutch.
Americans have a thing about singing holding lighted candles, so we
provided a fair rendering of *Silent Night* to the accompaniment of
burning hymn-sheets, treading the hot wax into the carpet. Events like
this have to be recorded by US television, & I must admit I got rather
irritated by the pop of flash bulbs in my face as I tried to put meaning
into *See Amidst the Winter's Snow,* but a glance outside confirmed that
there was still none of the white stuff.

The carol service in Sarajevo Cathedral on Christmas Eve was one to remember. This was organised by the Wehrmacht &, although advertised as an English-German service, only two words of English in fact surfaced—*Hape-ey Cvist-mase.* They'd have done better to stick to Latin. The Wehrmacht had been ordered to attend 'in a voluntary capacity', & neat rows of them appeared in full kit, as though hot foot from Nuremberg Torchlight Prayer Meeting. These days, they wear a leopard-spot camouflage uniform with matching field cap, looking for all the world like an earlier generation who distinguished themselves so well in Normandy, Arnhem, & in *The East.* I sat next to Oberfeldwebels Steiner, Kruger & Heinrich. This is, of course, their first operational deployment since 1945; perhaps it is fitting that they should return to a campaign 'where the iron crosses grew'. Some of them are excellent coves, if humourless. I seem to have found a fellow soul in one of their majors, the second in command of a battalion in the 10th Panzer Division, who has just completed a history of his division *'in the old days'.* ("The only scrap we missed was Poland, until you captured us in North Africa in '43. You know, von Stauffenberg was one of our staff officers.") Christmas Eve's service was memorable by some excellent Handel and Mozart on the Cathedral organ, & singing *Still Nacht, Heilige Nacht,* in candlelight. It's one carol that sounds so much better in its original German, and has echoes of communal singing in the trenches, during the 1914 Christmas Truce. German camera crews recorded the service & I gather I made an appearance on Christmas day television in the Fatherland, alongside the singing Oberfeldwebels. The standard of celebratory fire (point your gun in the air & empty the magazine) is not what it used to be in Sarajevo. Time was, a year or two ago, when you could sit on the rooftops and watch the most spectacular fireworks modern armies could buy. Tracer arching up to the heavens, artillery rounds and signal flares popping all over the place. Last year I gather Christmas Eve was spectacular. This year, I counted fifteen rounds fired from a machine gun nearby, and that was it—bit of a damp squib, if you ask me. Expecting better on New Year's Eve.

Time for Christmas lunch. First, in time honoured tradition, serve the chaps—not many of them, as this HQ is all chiefs and no indians. Then the generals (no shortage of them) served us. Catering for so many nationalities, the menus were rather mixed up, and I ended up a plate of roast beef, turkey, ham, mint sauce, and chips . . . Onto pudding, and the (Bosnian) chefs had made an outstanding effort with the *British* Christmas pud—done to a crisp . . . A pneumatic drill required to tackle the outer case, and a drinking straw the interior, which was as molten lava. A glance outside, and yes, the white stuff was tumbling down, and by evening a very respectable four inches had accumulated. Her Majesty's annual broadcast being sadly unavailable, I made do with a showing of *Independence Day,* & a bucket of pop corn, courtesy of the cousins, in the office next to mine—yes, we carried on working, and in uniform. Being predominantly Muslim, the city carried on too. I spotted just one Christmas tree, and two festively-dressed shop windows in a walk around town on Christmas Eve; rather a refreshing change from an English high street at this time of year. No invitations to challenge the national debt, or over-consume. Unfortunately, the Christmas spirit did not dissuade some fundamentalist Muslims in Sarajevo from deciding that Santa Claus threatened Islam, and that the solution was to mug any Croat Father Christmases they encountered. We at the Residency have all received greetings cards from American primary school children. Delightful creations in crayon and pencil, mine from Amy (six-and-a-half), contained a picture of a man with a gun (me, I presume) & the message 'Hpaay Crsmas Sowder, Com Hoame Safe'. As I write, the snow has accumulated to a very ski-able fourteen inches, with the overnight temperatures plunging to minus seventeen. I'm sure the novelty of so much of the stuff will soon wear off, but for now, Sarajevo is a vignette from a Brothers' Grimm fairy tale—some pretty, winding cobbled streets, a jumble of ancient, half-timbered houses, with steep pitch roofs, all laden with snow, glistening icicles & snow-dusted pine trees on the hills beyond. This is the first Christmas the Sarajevans will enjoy since 1991. Last year, although at peace, they were still suspicious that the fragile Dayton Peace Agreement would fail, and were just recovering form the siege, lifted in October. One of our interpreters told me the story of her sister & the camel hair coat. Sister gave birth to her second child in the winter of 1993. She ran out of fuel to heat her house, and wood was too expensive. Spare furniture & every nearby tree or bush had already been sacrificed to the hungry stove. To provide warmth, she decided to burn her best camel hair coat. It burned slowly, but well enough to provide warmth all one weekend, & long enough to bake a week's supply of bread. The coat meant a lot to her, & her face was wet with tears all weekend whilst it burned—it was her last luxury, the final ink with civilisation. She doesn't want another, because it will remind her of the four-year siege, & of the child who died of hypothermia afterwards. On a lighter note, I discovered that our (four-star) general, commanding SFOR, has only brought two books with him, to last for the whole of the operational tour—& he's already coloured one of them in! We had a major scare the other day. One of our jet pilots reported he had a 'lock-on' from a ground radar. Such events in a pilot's life are rare, for they're usually followed by a ground-to-air missile, & instant death. Our chap took evasive action, and escaped. We shouted at the Serbs, threatened the Muslims & swore at the Croats, but all claimed innocence. Then we found the culprits: two military policemen who'd got bored with zapping speeding Landrovers with their radar gun, and pointed it at a passing jet. I must extend my thanks to those of you who sent me Red Cross parcels. The files in the Christmas cake will be most useful, as would have been the miniature compass in the mince pie, had I not eaten it. I'm looking forward to experimenting with the sewing kit to turn my issue blanket into a guard's dress uniform, but unfortunately, the ink of the escape map printed on the silk handkerchief ran, and I now have obscure parts of Hungary over my nose. Please, are the fake identity papers & bank notes in the Gentleman's Relish, Belgian chocolates or the marmalade?

With the very best wishes for Christmas and the New Years.

Back Feb. 5th.

Hope all is well.

Peter

As Bosnia and Herzegovina struggled to keep the powder keg of animosity between different religious and ethnic groups from reigniting, the Yugoslav province of Kosovo was descending into chaos. Serbian military and security forces clashed with increasing frequency against the Kosovo Liberation Army, and Serbian President Slobodan Milosevic—who would later be captured and tried for war crimes—began ordering punishing reprisals against virtually all of the Albanian Kosovars. (The ethnic Albanians living in Kosovo represented the majority of the population. The Serbs were the minority, but controlled the army and the government.) Innocent men, women, and children were killed or forced from their homes by Serb troops, and in 1998, the United States and other powers threatened Milosevic with a massive bombing campaign if he did not order an immediate stop to what many observers considered to be "ethnic cleansing." Milosevic indicated he would cooperate to some degree, but by the following year it was evident that he had no intention of halting the violence. On March 24, 1999, a US-led NATO air offensive was launched against the Serbs that included strikes against the Yugoslav capital, Belgrade. After more than two and a half months of bombing, Milosevic finally relented, calling for the withdrawal of Serbian troops and allowing peacekeeping forces in. Three weeks before the cease-fire, an American soldier named Christine McNeff, a twenty-

four-year-old first lieutenant in the US Army (1st Armored Division, 501st Military Intelligence Battalion, Bravo Company), was stationed in neighboring Albania, where so many Kosovars had fled to for safety. Overwhelmed by both the suffering and resilience of the people she encountered, McNeff wrote the following on May 22 to her parents in Pennsylvania. (The ellipses are in the original text.)

Dear Mom and Dad,

Hope all is well on the homefront . . . things are progressing day by day here. Like Dad always says . . . the days go by quickly, but the minutes drag painfully. I honestly have no clue when we will be out of here, but my gut feeling tells me late summer or early fall. Like I said . . . save that beach tag . . . it gives me hope!!

If you think that you are confused about what the heck is happening here, you should be here! The feeling and the focus change daily, sometimes hourly. It makes for a bit of stress, to say the least. That is why your letters and e-mails mean so much to me. After concentrating on this stuff for 16–18 hours, those little reminders of home make my day. I do apologize for keeping in "sporadic" touch, at best. The environment here is a bit tense and stressful, and sometimes if you are on the phone or e-mail, you feel like you are not doing the "right thing," or that you are not doing all you can to potentially save lives . . . I know that sounds strange, but that is the attitude that permeates this place . . . and probably for a very good reason.

On Friday, I went out with a patrol of 82nd Airborne Infantry guys on a mission. They gave me a hard time when I first showed up to go out, say that Congress would not allow them to take a woman on a combat patrol. I told them to stuff it. It was good to get outside the wire and see what this country is all about. First of all, it is an absolutely beautiful country . . . with mountains similar to those in Arizona, but green and lush. People say it reminds them of Northern California with a Mediterranean climate. Unfortunately, this place is dirt poor . . . much worse than Bosnia, at least what I have seen of both countries. We visited a local town to assess the local populace attitude toward NATO and US Forces in the area. As we drove through the village, children swarmed the vehicle, reaching in it, and shouting, "MRE, MRE", and "chocolate". The people as we drove by would also say, "Please don't leave Albania," and "Serbia is that way!" (I like that one) The town itself was decrepit and filthy . . . animals wandering the streets . . . trash everywhere. The buildings and houses had no windows and appeared to be crumbling at the seems. No one really spoke decent English, which is why we had an interpreter with us. She was a student at the university in Tirana studying English and her English was excellent. We asked around and finally found the village elder/schoolteacher/ doctor/mayor. He was a distinguished older man with impressive charisma. The best part of the experience was talking with this man and realizing the plight of these people. These people are not stupid, as sometimes I think that we consider them. They have families just like us, and they simply want the best for them. There is no difference whatsoever between us and them. He spoke of his appreciation for the US, ever since WWII. He also spoke of communism and its impact, and what the situation has been like since communism has disappeared. His eyes teared when he spoke. He thanked us for being here, and asked if we could employ the many jobless people in his town. There are also about 300 Kosovar refugees living in his town, which puts a strain on everything. He told us that they would riot if Brown and Root hired from another town instead of his. (This is common) Then we went to a little coffee shop in town and we drank turkish coffee (it was beyond disgusting, but it is rude not to finish what they serve you). We chatted (through the interpreter) about everything from the States and how he dreamed of someday going there, to how strange it was for them to see a woman in the Army. It was a truly eyeopening experience. As we left the coffeeshop, all of the schoolchildren had gathered outside. I could have closed my eyes and been in Mom's class. They were all dressed like American kids and behaved similarly. They were light and dark and had different color hair, and they were all good spirited. Children are children, I suppose.

I thought you might enjoy the above debrief of my very first combat patrol. ☺ For the first time since I have been here, I felt the impact of our presence here. I felt the overwhelming impact of throwing people out of their homes for no good reason and what it feels like for the people of their heritage. It sounds silly, but these victims became real to me, and so did the local Albanians, the people who come onto base each day to clean the porta-potties and collect the laundry and trash . . . they are just trying to make it.

It makes me all the more grateful for what I have and all the more humble for all that I take for granted. God has blessed me with so much, the best of which is my family. Please pray for the victims over here, because they are much more our brothers and sisters that I think we know.

I love you and miss you very much.

Chris

Separated from His Mother in South Korea for Fifty Years, a North Korean Man Named Kim Sung Ha Is Given Permission to Write Her a Single Letter

What was remarkable about the short, sweet love letter by a husband to his wife was not only its lyricism and beauty, but that it represented their first communication in five decades. "I wish I could meet you my sweetheart," seventy-nine-year-old Kim Kyong Bin wrote to Song Il Soon. "If I were a bird, I would fly and sit on a branch of a tree in our garden and pour out my heart." In one of the most terrible legacies of the Korean War, which destroyed countless lives, an estimated seven to ten million family members were permanently separated from one another during the chaos of the fighting. North Korea's Communist regime prevents its citizens, like Song Il Soon, from traveling where they choose or communicating with whom they want, regardless of whether it is a spouse, child, or parent. They are trapped in their own country. Kim Sung Ha, the second oldest son of a family with ten children, was a young man studying for his postgraduate degree in Seoul when the North invaded the South in June 1950. One day during the war, he simply vanished. His family later learned that Communist troops had taken him by force. Two other siblings, Chang Ha and Ok Hee, disappeared as well. As time passed—months, years, then decades—the family feared the worst. And then, in January 2001, the Kims were notified that Sung Ha and his brother and sister were, in fact, still alive and had been in North Korea all these years. In March, the two Koreas negotiated an agreement allowing several hundred people to exchange letters with a loved one on the other side, and Sung Ha was granted permission to write to his mother, who lived in South Korea and was 101 years old. (The South Korean participants were chosen by a computer lottery; the North would not reveal its process.) North Koreans fortunate enough to be selected for this mail exchange had to include enthusiastic praise for the "love and generosity" their Dear Leader, Kim Il Sung (who ruled from 1948 to 1994) and his son and successor, Kim Jong Il, had bestowed on them. (The fact that Kim Sung Ha, whose underlying anguish is evident throughout the letter, has not been able to communicate with his own mother for half a century speaks to how loving and generous the Dear Leader was, in fact, toward his citizens. Kim also did not know he had three other siblings, born after he was taken to the North.) On March 5, 2001, Kim, now in his seventies, wrote the following.

Dearest Mother,

The much-awaited, but unbelievably surprising news came today that you are still alive. Until now, I have worried day and night. Last night I couldn't sleep because I was thinking of you. For the first time in 50 years, my heart is beating so hard as I write this letter to you.

We have been apart for 50 years! I can't even describe how much I have missed you. I can only imagine your pain of not knowing the whereabouts of your children.

Among seven children, you loved me dearly. I vividly remember as a kid following you everywhere from one room to another, wanting to be with you all the time.

I have been living comfortably under the warm care by our leader Kim Il Sung. Words cannot describe the love and generosity I have received from him.

I always thought of you when I had a joyous occasion in my life, such as meeting our great leader Kim Il Sung in college, receiving a watch engraved with the name of the great leader, and receiving a Ph.D. I wish I could make you proud of me in those moments. The nation took good care of me.

Mother, please forgive this son who couldn't even send you a letter for such a long time or buy you nice clothes and warm meals on your birthday.

I miss you Mother.

My two siblings in North Korea are living comfortable lives under much love and care of our great leader Kim Il Sung and Marshall Kim Jong Il. Do not worry about us.

Photo by Andrew Carroll

Kim Min Ha

Ok Hee, Chang Ha, and I each have several children who all went to college and have decent jobs. We all get together in one house and spend time together during national holidays and vacations. I always feel great sorrow because of you and my other brothers and sisters in the South.

I am already over seventy years old and have grey hair, but I am healthy and currently working as a professor. I have the great leader Marshall Kim to thank for that.

How are Min Ha, Ok Nae, Ok Leo, Ok Hwa, and Shin Ja doing in South Korea? No matter how much time goes by or how things change over the years, I can never forget the days in your arm with my siblings. Thanks to the great leader Kim Jong Il, I received the opportunity to write you this letter. Now I firmly believe that I will be able to meet you in person in the very near future.

As your son, I will continue to live honestly in the North. I promise you won't be disappointed in me when I finally see you in person, as our two nations become one.

I don't know where to begin and what to start with. There are so many things to tell you and fill you in on.

Today, I will end here. Please take care of yourself and be healthy. I also wish health and happiness for my younger siblings in the South. I enclose two photos.

From your son,
Kim Sung Ha

Kim Min Ha, one of Sung Ha's younger brothers, received the letter and read it to their mother. She died the following month. Kim Sung Ha never had the opportunity to see her again.

—∽—

A Refugee from Afghanistan, Masuda Anna Mohamadi, Returns to Her Homeland and E-mails Her Friends Her Impressions of the War-Torn Country

When tens of thousands of Soviet troops invaded Afghanistan in December 1979 (the Soviets claimed they were "invited" by the existing Communist government to crush a growing insurgency of Muslim fundamentalism), the ferocious bombardment of Afghan towns and villages sparked a refugee crisis of astonishing proportions. Millions of Afghan men, women, and children fled to neighboring Pakistan and Iran. A six-year-old girl named Masuda Anna Mohamadi escaped from Afghanistan with her family and made it to the United States, ultimately settling in Virginia. After the US-led Operation Enduring Freedom top-

pled the Taliban regime, which had been ruling Afghanistan since 1996 (the Soviets left in 1989), Mohamadi decided to return to Afghanistan and become a teacher. Twenty years of ceaseless violence had devastated the country, and Mohamadi, in e-mails to friends back in the States, chronicled the range of emotions she experienced after returning to the country of her birth. The following is dated November 14, 2002.

Dear friends,

Satar is one of the men who guided us through the mountains 23 years ago. He is handsome with dark eyes, a thin tan face, and a peaceful and gentle disposition. He ate dinner with us at my uncle's house. After he left us at the border of Pakistan in 1979 he began fighting with the mujahedin. I asked him to tell me stories about his life and he leaned back and began speaking.

He told me about the night the soviets were bombing Jaji daily and the villagers fled to the mountains. They set up camp in crevices along the rocks and used logs and leaves for shelter. It began to rain one night and the mountain streams flooded their hideouts. Satar had been shot in the arm and his elbow was shattered. He held onto his children with one hand while his broken elbow rested against his chest. By morning dozens of people were missing swept away by the water but the villagers couldn't go down to the fields in the daylight because of the bombings. They waited until the next night to search for their relatives and bury them in the dark.

Satar's elbow ached and he went to find the village doctor. The doctor told him to find some fish and hold the meat against the wound until the bones softened a bit and then the doctor would set the arm in place. Satar replied, "How am I going to catch a fish when bombs are falling from the sky?" Satar walked to Pakistan where a doctor took an x-ray and fixed his arm.

During another battle Satar was with my uncle Abdul, who had been shot in the thigh. Satar tried to carry Abdul but he was too heavy. He hid my uncle in the mountains and he went to look for a donkey to carry Abdul out. As he was walking past a field he saw hundreds of dead bodies. He had to be careful not to step on them. They were Afghan soldiers employed by the Soviets. He said the dogs were eating the bodies because they lay rotting for so long.

I asked him if he had nightmares from the war. He said, "When I first started fighting all the spit in my mouth went dry from fear but after a few years it was just a part of life. Nothing scared me. I fought the soviets but after they left I stopped. I am at peace with what I have done."

My uncle Abdul (Zahir's younger brother) had been sitting in the room as we talked along with four women and six children. We had all eaten dinner together on the floor, digging into the same bowls and plates of rice, spinach, kidney beans, and salad with our hands. After dinner we drank tea and ate baked chickpeas sprinkled with red pepper and I listened to more stories. The men, women, and children sit with each other and they listen to each other, make fun of one another, yell at the children, eat, tell stories, hug and pinch, and so much cursing. They share a love that is real and raw. In the house they don't have a television, furniture, beds, electricity, or toys or books for the children but they laugh so much and with so much life. I am so fortunate to sit with them.

Abdul always ends the night with a few sarcastic remarks. This one is his favorite, "I almost lost my life trying to save Afghanistan and all anybody wants to know now is if I can speak English and work a computer. God damn all of you."

much love,
maso

Ten days later, Mohamadi described her visit to the prison where her father, who had worked in the government, had been confined after the Soviet invasion.

Dear friends,

We started our English classes today but mine won't start until Saturday because there isn't any heat in the room. We sent out notices to the students this morning at 8 to show up at 8:45 so you may guess that not too many showed up today but tomorrow is another day. The bathroom in the hallway doesn't work, the toilets are dry and dirty with missing seats, faucets caked with mud, trash on the floor, no running water but there is a beautiful sign on the front door that says toilet.

I'm hungry and I still have ten more days to go until the end of Ramadan. When I get hungry I get cranky and irritable and when I go home at 2 I sit in front of the oven and eat until I feel like passing out.

On Friday I went for a drive with my mom and sister. Our driver is a sturdy man named Abdullah who carries an automatic rifle at all times. We headed to pul-i-charki, the place where my father was imprisoned for 8 months 23 years ago. We followed a paved road that led us out of the city for a long time and then turned right into a narrow dirt road lined with market stalls filled with radishes, long spring onions, and fat cauliflowers. It's the end of November but the days are still warm, the sky blue and sunny. As we neared the prison it looked as I had imagined it. It's strange to visit places that I have written about but never seen. The walls were lower than I thought, all stones, with the watchtowers crumbling.

At the front gate five soldiers stopped us. My mother rolled down her window and said that her husband was imprisoned here and that her daughter wanted to see the place. They looked at each other with strange glances and one of them even smirked. They said usually we don't let anyone in but since you are women and you have traveled from so far we'll give you a tour. The driver was hesitant because they wouldn't let him drive in and he didn't want to leave the car alone. My mother and sister stayed in the car and the driver, his rifle, and I walked in with four soldiers.

The prison was emptied out after the fall of the Taliban. My father had been kept in block 2, which was at the far right end, and the driver didn't want to go that far so we went into the first building on our path. There was a mile long heap of rusted buses, cars, and metal. Once inside the building, we went up three flights to a hallway with tiny individual cells which had metal bars for doors. There was also a large room with huge metal bins that were used for washing clothes. Water dripped in through the walls and the floors were wet, the ceilings low. We went into another hallway lined with cells and I stared out the thin, triangular window. On the cell window I saw a rusty lock. I grabbed it and held onto it. I asked them where the torture room was. They said those rooms were hidden in places they couldn't even find and once they found them they couldn't get out.

We walked outside again and the entire place was eerie. During my father's time close to 60,000 men were imprisoned here and many of them killed. The prison is in the middle of a dusty field and if you look out you see huge dents in the ground possibly from the massive graves.

A heavy energy rested inside of me as soon as I arrived there and it hasn't quite left. I think there are thousands of ghosts in and around pul-i-charki seeking justice or peace.

I was disappointed I didn't see the exact room my father was held in but I was nervous about my mom and sister being alone in the car. At first I was nervous about the soldiers but they spoke in pashtu with us and they seemed harmless. It's so hard to imagine my father surviving in that prison because he's such a gentle man. He'll chase an ant around the room and take it outside rather than kill it. He was never tortured but many of his friends were. Two of his friends were beaten so badly that they couldn't walk and he had to watch them drag their bodies from place to place.

They are slowly rebuilding the prison but I wish they'd make a memorial instead for the lost lives. I'm not usually one for memorials but this time I think it would be healing, not only for the land, but also for those people whose family members disappeared in the surrounding fields.

much love,

maso

Amidst the widespread poverty, lingering oppression of women, virtually non-existent health care, hostilities between tribal factions, daily fears of terrorist attacks by those loyal to Osama bin Laden and al-Qaeda, and a vast array of other problems and threats, Mohamadi was reminded of the richness and beauty of her native country during her frequent trips to smaller towns and villages outside of her home in Kabul. The following was written on January 26, 2003. ("Mazar" is Mazār-e Sharif, located in northern Afghanistan.)

dear friends,

I returned from mazar on Friday after an eleven hour drive, through the solang pass, a one mile tunnel that took us half an hour to get through because two looray's (big colorful trucks) moving in the opposite direction were stuck to each other. We sat in our 4x4 white UN car inhaling fumes. Then one of our cars got stuck driving across a metal bridge and it took three hours to pull it out, bang the rim back into shape, and drive slowly to a mechanic. Some men from the village crowded around the bridge. When I got out of the car to assess the situation and a group of young boys circled around me staring so hard that I quickly climbed back into the car.

One boy came by my window and peered in, his cheeks red from the cold. He had beautiful brown eyes and I smiled at him and he smiled back. I felt like we had been friends for a long time and he became my protector keeping the others away.

I didn't know what to expect in mazar except that it was dangerous with frequent kidnappings so I took my mace just in case. We had traveled to Mazar to choose about twenty government employees to take part in our capacity building program, a three-year program geared to teach them English, computers, management skills, procurement, and everything else needed to run a government. When our work was done we were ready for some sight seeing and we were taken to the ziarath, the supposed burial place of the fourth caliph Ali whose tomb rests inside.

The Ziarath is a blue gem in an otherwise muddy, drab city of crumbling buildings littered with the remains of old, rusted cars and tanks. White pigeons have made the place their home resting along the ledges and flying from one minaret to the other. As soon as I walked past the front gate I was filled with a warm energy. A group of children ran up to me begging for money which I was told not to give them or else I'd be mobbed so I took their picture instead.

I was a bit nervous as I walked in because I wasn't sure what to do inside. I followed my traveling companion who walked up to a wooden box in front of the room, which was the tomb. A woman in a white burqa was kissing it. I sat down on the burgundy rug and lifted my hands to my chest and cupped them open and I prayed for peace in Afghanistan. Behind and around us sat more old men with copies of the Quran in front of them accepting money. When I walked back outside the swarm of kids ran up to me so I quickened my pace to the car but they kept up, begging for money, telling me they were orphans. They were professionals.

From the car I stared out at the structure, so startlingly blue and beautiful, amazed that it had survived, and I could see and feel how such a place could sustain the hopes and prayers of the people.

I had left Kabul with two images swirling around inside me. One was of a man who was missing the bottom half of his body. He had wrapped a rice sack around his waist and he was lifting himself up and forward with his fists rhythmically moving down the street, the top half of his body strong and sturdy. On the same day I saw a little girl sleeping on the side of the road with a stone under her head for a pillow and a lime green scarf covering her face. I desperately wanted to replace these images or balance them out with something beautiful and I found that something in Mazar.

much love,
maso

Three months later, after suffering a sudden, horrible loss, Mohamadi wrote to her friends: "In the Afghan people, I found love and beauty and hope, and I couldn't imagine being anywhere but with them. But it was always by my father's side, doing all these things as his daughter, taking pride in his name and his work. And now he is lost and I'm crippled without him." Mohamadi's father was President Hamid Karzai's minister of mines and industry. In late April 2003, his plane mysteriously vanished over the Arabian Sea. No one knows if the plane experienced mechanical failure or if sabotage was involved. On March 31, Mohamadi wrote:

Nothing hurts more than looking at my mother, her face long and sad, white streaks grown in over her auburn hair, pools of tears welling up in her eyes everytime she looks at me, knowing I remind her of my father, of the past four months we spent together. She doesn't know if we are the fortunate or unfortunate family. Would it be better to be grieving over a gravestone right now or trapped in the not knowing, stuck somewhere between madness and hope. I imagine this is how my people have felt most of their lives and now I am no different.

As heartbreaking as the loss remains, Mohamadi continues to create positive and lasting change in Afghanistan; in 2003 she created a nonprofit organization called Support Education in Afghanistan, which is working to build primary schools in rural areas of the country.

—⁂—

Lieutenant Kathy McConkey Laments to Her Family That, with War Raging in Iraq, Many of the Troops in Afghanistan Feel That They Have Been Forgotten

"By the way, if you want to do some real good back home," an American soldier named James F. Wilson wrote to his wife, Marjorie, *"every time you hear somebody say that the war will be over soon, look them straight in the eye and tell them that a lot of people are still dying over here."* The letter was written in May 1944, more than a year before World War II was over, and the sentiment was not unusual. Another serviceman, a pilot who had trained in Florida, grumbled to a friend in December 1945:

[A]ll through the war when government officials were pleading with the civilians not to travel [in order to save gas and other necessities], I saw train after train each day come down from New York to Florida resorts, crowded with people who didn't give a damn about the war . . . but just wanted to travel South and spend their money and have a good time.

Reports of factory laborers refusing to work long hours provoked outrage as well. *"We're all mighty fed up with the strikes that are going on back home,"* a medical officer named Frederick McIntyre wrote to his wife, Kay, from Europe. *"I believe they should send some of our fighting outfits home to patrol the factories and take care of the picketers and strikers. I'm sure there would be no more strikes. . . ."* Regardless of the war, the justness of the cause, or the fanfare accorded to departing troops, there comes a time in virtually every conflict when the interest and attention of the general public begins to wane, and it can be demoralizing to the spirits of those on the front lines. In the aftermath of 9-11, American forces in Afghanistan were lauded enthusiastically for their swift *defeat of the Taliban. But in the ensuing years, as the eyes of the world turned to Iraq, military personnel in Afghanistan who were hunting down Osama bin Laden, protecting President Hamid Karzai and members of his administration from assassination, and fighting isolated pockets of al-Qaeda resistance—and getting killed and wounded in the process—began to feel as if their efforts were being neglected. Kathy McConkey, a firefighter paramedic and member of the US Army Reserves, was sent to Afghanistan in early February 2003 to begin a six-month tour of duty as a nurse at the Kandahar Airfield. On April 1, McConkey e-mailed her family in Ohio with a grim reminder that while many in the States believed that the war in Afghanistan was over, the fighting continued.*

Hello!

My time here is like nothing I can describe. Losing U.S. soldiers is like losing a fellow firefighter. The first memorial service was an incredibly sad experience. Hearing grown men speak with wavering voices, some shedding tears, was more than I could bear. I cried for all of them. It was strange to actually be talking with the para-jumpers and then see them run off to attempt to save others, only to hear of their death hours later. One of them married five days before coming here, two had June weddings planned, one had a three year old at home, the other had an 11yo and 14 yo sons. I hoped it was my last memorial . . . it wasn't. On Saturday a Special Forces team went into a village to meet with the leader to discuss humanitarian aid. They were ambushed; three critically wounded. One soldier died in flight and the other shortly after arriving. His injuries too severe to even try to resuscitate him. The third went through extensive surgery and woke during the night. Still on the vent, he tearfully asked for his friends. His commander told him "they did their duty". He understood. The S.F. teams sat with their dead comrades for hours in our triage area. It was terrible. I tried my best to avoid the area because of the utter sadness there. During surgery I would step out to give updates. The men would soak up every word that I said and I could sense their desperation that this man live. He had to live, for their sake. Today was the memorial for the S.F. A sad event again. This was not something I was prepared for when I deployed. Seeing the caskets draped with the American flag as they were loaded onto the C-130 was very moving. They again played the bagpipes and taps. In the end, they played the Green beret theme song. They make 8 U.S. soldier deaths in 10 days.

The fighting in the area has increased. Most people expected this. I don't watch CNN too often because the coverage of Iraq becomes too much of the same thing. I can't imagine what the soldiers there in the field are going through. There loses are much greater than ours. Soldiers here become frustrated that Afghanistan isn't mentioned more often on CNN. They feel people think they are fighting "last years war" and that they are being forgotten. They are not satisfied with the little blerb that scrolls across the bottom of the screen.

I was sent outside the wire last week to exam female Afghans. It is supposed to be done by a female doctor but there are none here. I was nervous and excited about this. I went into a small village where the women collected into one mud house. They dress very colorfully and became very excited about my presence. They know that I bring food and medicine. They had me sit on a beautiful pillow and surrounded me being very talkative. I could not understand a word they said and this amused them even more. When the male interpreter came in it was amazing. The women scattered immediately against the walls and covered themselves, some covered completely with blankets. If I needed to examine them the interpreter would step out and the women immediately uncovered and became very talkative again. When he came back they quickly covered again. They were like light switches, covering and uncovering in record time. I was able to photograph two younger females. A female cannot have her photo taken once she reaches puberty. If you take her picture and a male family member finds out she is beaten. Each man is allowed to have four wives, and they usually are married by age 16. The people in this village suffer from dehydration and malnutrition. Almost all have stomach worms.

I have been sick all day today with the "Kandahar crud". Gastroenteritis is a serious problem here and I guess it was my turn. I try to run after the sun sets (way too hot during the day). I have gotten used to running with my 9mm. Most have much heavier weapons to carry. I am even used to the porta-jons . . . although I will probably forget to flush when I get home. I doubt I will want to stay in a tent anytime soon after this.

I hope everyone is doing well at home. I miss everyone and continue to look forward to coming home! I appreciate your emails, you would be surprised at how the little things mean so much.

Love,
Kathy

**After Losing Her Son in Afghanistan,
Terry Ward Appeals for Help from a Woman Named Gloria Caldas,
Who She Believes Will Understand Her Pain
&
Caldas Replies**

As with the war in Iraq, the majority of US casualties in Afghanistan came after it appeared major combat operations were over. (By December 2001, the Taliban authority had all but collapsed.) On September 20, 2004, Terry Ward was unloading groceries outside of her home in Westminster, South Carolina, when a family friend rushed over to the house and told her to go inside and wait for an urgent phone call. When Ward asked if something was wrong, the friend repeated, "Just get to the phone, get to the phone." Soon after she walked in the door the telephone rang and her daughter-in-law, Tammy, told her the terrible news: Ward's thirty-year-old son, Staff Sergeant Tony B. Olaes, had been killed in Afghanistan. A few minutes later several US Army vehicles pulled into the driveway, and a military chaplain and casualty officer confirmed to Ward that her son was dead. Olaes was a Green Beret combat medic, and he and another soldier, Robert S. Goodwin, were shot during an ambush in Shkin, Afghanistan. Unbeknownst to Ward, a website honoring fallen troops created a memorial page that paid tribute to her son. Ward learned of the site about a month after her son died, and she came across a message posted by a total stranger:

> To Tony's Family and Friends:
> On behalf of the Blanco-Caldas family, we send our sincerest condolences. We share the same loss . . . the same pain. Our prayers are with you in this most difficult time and we thank you for your soldier's bravery and sacrifice.
> Sincerely,
> The Family of Capt. Ernesto M. Blanco-Caldas, 82nd Airborne
> KIA Iraq 12/28/2003.
> Gloria Caldas (The Big Ern's Mom) of San Antonio, TX

Ward was deeply moved by what Gloria Caldas had written and felt an immediate connection with a mother who was experiencing the same sense of despair. Ward sent Caldas the following e-mail:

DEAR GLORIA,
 THANK YOU SO MUCH FOR THE CONDOLENCES ON THE FALLEN HEROES SITE FOR MY SON. MAY I ALSO

EXPRESS MY CONDOLENCES ON THE LOSS OF YOUR OWN
SON. I AM SO DEVASTATED AND I CANNOT FIGURE OUT
HOW TO GO ON. HOW DO YOU MANAGE EVERY DAY?

MY SON HAD 3 YOUNG SONS, 11, 10 AND 7. HOW DO I
HELP THEM? AND HIS WIFE, WHO LOVED HIM SO MUCH. I
KNOW I NEED TO BE STRONG FOR THEM ALSO, BUT I AM
SO SAD MYSELF.

SO SORRY TO ASK YOU THESE QUESTIONS, BUT YOU
HAVE BEEN THERE ALSO, SO I KNOW YOU UNDERSTAND.

PLEASE FORGIVE THE CAPITALS, BUT I AM LEGALLY
BLIND AND HAVE A HARD TIME ON THE COMPUTER, IF
THE LETTERS ARE NOT BIG.

I HOPE YOU DON'T MIND ME WRITING YOU, BUT I
FIGURED THAT IS WHY YOU GAVE YOUR EMAIL ADDRESS.
HOPE I AM NOT RAMBLING.

I LOOK FORWARD TO HEARING FROM YOU, AND HOPE
MAYBE YOU CAN GIVE ME SOME INSIGHT.

YOURS TRULY,

TERRY A. WARD

MOTHER OF SSG. TONY BRUCE OLAES

KIA SEPTEMBER 20, 2004

Caldas responded right away.

Oh Terry! I know so well the pain you are going through. I wish no one
else would have to go through what our families have experienced.
During the first several weeks after Ernie's "Homegoing," I fell into a
black hole.

I guess this was the Lord's way of protecting me from the horror of
the unthinkable. Losing a child is a bad thing. In my anger, the Lord and
I had quite a few very lively discussions! But little by little, I began to
climb out of the despair with the loving support of family, friends and
my faith. Ernie was not married yet, but he did leave a grieving fiancee
who has not yet recovered. They were scheduled to marry on June 12th.
It's now been 9 months since he was killed, I am finally able to provide
support and comfort to those around me . . . his sister, grandparents,
aunts, uncles, cousins and all those who have also been deeply affected
by his loss.

Normal will never be what it was before . . . we've all had to redefine
"normal." Nothing will ever be the same, but you learn to just take one
day at a time. Sometimes there are bad days, sometimes worse days. But

I know that as long as I have a breath in my body, my son will live in my heart. I'm sure you feel the same. My faith sustains me and I know that I will be reunited with him when I too go Home. I know I'm rambling, Terry.

My heart aches for you. Please get back to me. Tell me more about Tony. I'm sure your extremely proud of him, as I am of Ernie.

By His Grace,
Gloria

Gloria Caldas and Terry Ward continued to e-mail one another words of support and encouragement after their initial exchange. "JUST WANTED TO LET YOU KNOW THAT I AM THINKING OF YOU AT THIS DIFFI-CULT TIME," Ward wrote to Caldas after Christmas 2004. "I AM ALSO KEEPING YOU IN MY THOUGHTS AND PRAYERS AS THE ANNIVERSARY DATE OF ERNIE'S DEATH APPROACHES. JUST KNOW THAT YOU ARE NOT ALONE."

Featured Series

"Reconciliation, Confrontation & Dialogue"

**Lois Hoffman, the Widow of an American Veteran,
Receives a Stunning Letter from a Man Who Had Known
Her Husband in World War II
&
A Japanese Woman, Takako Yamakawa, Writes
to an American World War II Veteran, Jerry Yellin,
About Her Feelings for His Son
&
Yellin and Takako's Father, a Japanese World War II Veteran,
Correspond About Their Children's Desire to Marry One Another
&
A Vietnam Veteran, Chuck Theusch, Exchanges E-mails
with a Vietnamese Woman, Tran Thi Anh Thu, About the
Changing Nature of America's Relationship with Her Country
&
Khaled Al-Maeena, a Saudi Arabian Editor, Initiates
a Written Dialogue with a Reader Who Had Sent Al-Maeena Hate Mail**

Dated January 2, 1992, the letter began like so many of the other messages of condolence Lois Hoffman received from veterans who had known her husband,

George, before he passed away at the age of eighty. "The new year 1992 was not yet one and a half hours old when William Dutton called to inform us that George had died," wrote the longtime friend who had first encountered Hoffman when they were both navy commanders in World War II. "Although I was aware of the fact that George had been a very sick man owing to his lung problems, I was shattered by the news of his demise. With him a very short, but intensively experienced period of our mutual past was borne to his grave." Unlike Hoffman's fellow veterans, however, this man, Gunter Leopold, was Hoffman's enemy in 1944; Leopold was the Austrian commander of a submarine in the German navy that Hoffman's destroyer, the USS Corry, had sunk. As the letter continues, Leopold expresses the grief that he and his wife are feeling because of Hoffman's death, and he recalls Hoffman's extraordinary decency and the unique relationship the two men began during the war. (The minor mistakes are the result of Leopold's attempt to write in English, which he understood very well but did not speak fluently.)

I am mourning for a very good friend. Indeed, true friendship it was, although we found ourselves in a war against each other—he, the American destroyer commander, and I, the German submarine commander. But this war was only the dreadfully loathsome setup which compelled us to fight against each other, but in our hearts we naval men never felt hatred against each other. As soon as one of us was no longer able to fight, all so-called enmity ceased and was replaced by the awareness of the always existing solidarity among Atlantic navies. Therefore it had seemed to be just a matter of course that the American pilot of the plane that we shot down while it dropped the fatal bomb on our submarine, who had not been scratched, helped me, the seriously wounded "enemy", into his liferaft and rendered first aid. And when after two or three hours George's destroyer "Corry" came up, an American sailor climbed down into the water up to his chest, in order to bundle me up within the liferaft, so I could be pulled up aboard for owing to the loss of blood I had been to weak to climb aboard by myself. Although it was midday-time on a Sunday, and in the officers' mess the table had been set for lunch, George ordered all dishes to be removed, and though I was smeared with diesel oil from top to toe I was put on the table in order to be operated. I was cleaned off oil, and before the young doctor Anderson of Swedish descent started surgery, George welcomed me as his guest aboard his ship, addressing me as "captain", and offered me for the duration of my stay his bunk in the captain's room. When the doctor was about to take off my right leg just above the knee, warning of the danger of gangrene, I protested, and the admirable physician willingly took great pains to save my leg, by removing dozens of fragments, by taking care of severed tendons, muscles and nerves and by heaping lots of penicillin onto the wound, before he devoted himself to the other injuries. When George was informed that I had to come round, he came to "my" bunk and advised me to pray that there would be no gangrene.

I have the most pleasant memories of my stay aboard the destroyer "Corry", because it was marked by the chivalrous way of thinking by George, the American commander, who looked after me day by day, sitting at my bedside and devoting many hours to tell me about America, his family and his service in the navy. He never made me conscious of the fact, that meanwhile I had the status of a prisoner of war. I was, as he time and again emphasized, his guest. (Secretely I was not at all sad about my fate, since I was fed up to the brim with this kind of war, when German submarines were hunted like hares on account of the American superiority in radar and sonar, and I would have been even happy about the change in my fortune, if not so many of my crew had died.) With his great tactfulness George never asked me a military or political question. When after a few days I was able to hobble about with my leg in thick plaster (and with a turban-like head bandage), George dragged me to sunny places on the upper deck and he insisted that I put my arm round his shoulder, not allowing anybody else to heave me about. Twice I was invited to have the evening meal in the officers' mess, where I was assigned the seat of honour next to him. When subsequently a motion picture was shown, George bent underneath the table to push a cushion under my foot and kept inquiring about how I feel. In my lifetime I have respected and admired George in view of his personality and his humanity. During manoeuvres I also got to know him as an extremely proficient mariner and as a man of courage to stand up for his humanitarian beliefs. When the admiral aboard the aircraft carrier "Block Island" ordered my transfer to his ship, George declined to execute this order with reference to my "critical condition". When the "Corry" entered the harbour of Boston in the afternoon of March 29th, 1944, I, the German prisoner of war, stood next to the captain on the bridge and was even allowed for a short while to act as his helmsman. Saying goodbye to George I was on the verge of tears since we had become pretty close. I had forebodings that in the forthcoming custody of the army I would in all probability have to go without this unique quality of George's warmheartedness. (My premonitions proved true: at the Fort Devens army hospital I was referred to as the "Nazi subcommander", ended up in a padded cell of "Section eight" for loonies and had to eat chops with a spoon, until I was "rescued" by naval intelligence officers.) On parting George gave me one of his khaki-uniforms, in which I looked very much American. When, lying on a stretcher, I left the "Corry" and his captain, the sailors showered masses of chocolate, cigarettes, chewing gum and other goodies upon me. While being carried over the gangway, all men on deck saluted to me, the German PoW. This generosity symbolizing a spirit of decency of mind was doubtlessly the result of George's splendid example as a commander. To the best of my recollection I have told the story of George Hoffman a thousand times as that of a knight in shining armour in a heroic epic.

Dear Lois, at our age we are especially affected by the death of someone whom we love, becoming conscious of how quickly human life may come to an end. From my own sorrowful experience I know that the confrontation with the finality of death produces deep emotions which tend to brighten up the memories of the deceased in our heart. In my view the image of George cannot grow brighter than it has been up to now. He will always rank foremost among those few whom I consider an exceptionally good friend.

Very affectionately yours

Gunter and Katinka

Just months after Hoffman had rescued Leopold, the USS Corry *was destroyed when it struck a German mine off the coast of Normandy during the June 6, 1944, Allied invasion of France. More than two dozen of Hoffman's men were killed, and he himself barely survived; Hoffman was the last to leave the ship, which sank in only eight minutes, and he was pulled out of the water unconscious. After being sent to England, Hoffman returned to the United States on the* Queen Mary *in July 1944. Leopold, who was being treated in a US military hospital, was able to find Hoffman's address and the two began a regular exchange of letters for almost fifty years. (They were not, however, ever able to meet again after the war.) Friendships between veterans who were once adversaries are not uncommon—and the connection can become a strong one, as they have shared, albeit from opposing sides, traumatic experiences that even their closest friends and family members might not be able to understand. But these relationships are not always initiated voluntarily. For an American veteran named Jerry Yellin, recollections of his World War II service in the Pacific, where he flew bombing missions against the Japanese, provoked intense emotions and lingering anger. Forty-two years after he returned to the United States, Yellin found himself back in Japan—sitting in his youngest son Robert's home in Mishima, meeting Robert's girlfriend, Takako Yamakawa, for the first time. (Robert had gone to Japan to teach English three years earlier.) Yellin and his wife, Helene, knew that their son was in love, and Yellin suspected that Robert was intending to stay in Mishima with Takako. "We're really pleased to be here, and to meet you," Yellin said to Takako, trying to be polite. "I don't know what Robert's plans are, but I want you to know that whatever Robert decides to do, including living in Japan, will be all right by me." But the memories of the war, of close buddies losing their lives during raids over Japan and the stories of atrocities committed against American POWs, could not be erased overnight. Yellin, who later wrote of the conversation in his memoirs, then said to Takako in absolute candor:*

> *I have many concerns, however, about my ability to accept [Robert's having] a serious relationship with a Japanese woman. I flew over your country several times as a young man. Many of my friends were killed. I have not resolved all of that in my mind yet. As a father, I will not stand in the way of my son's decisions. But as an American, I am not sure I can accept his decision whole heartedly. I also don't know anything about your father and his feelings about Robert, about America, about the war.*

Takako's father, Taro, was indeed a veteran with his own very painful memories from the war, and he disapproved of the relationship entirely. Takako expected her mother, Hatsue, to be sympathetic; Taro's parents had objected to his marriage to Hatsue because she came from a class they deemed lower in status than their own. But when Takako handed her parents a bottle of brandy the Yellins had offered to the Yamakawas as a gesture of goodwill, her mother's immediate reaction was severe: "I know you are interested in [that] gaijin," she exclaimed, using a derogatory word for outsiders. "I want you to know you can marry any Japanese man that you choose, but you will not bring a foreigner into our family." Over time, however, Takako was able to encourage her parents to at least meet with Robert, and in a letter to the Yellins, she described the result of that encounter.

Dear Mr. and Mrs. Yellin,

I was very happy to meet you and Jerry last March. I am sorry to have taken so much time to write to you and thank you for your encouragement. I wish my parents felt as you do. My mother was against my involvement with Robert, but I am set on my plans to marry him. I needed time to find the courage to tell my father. My mother is the type of woman who would agree with any decision my father would make, so he is the one I had to convince. But it has taken me much longer than I ever thought it would to speak to him about Robert. Robert is an American who, I thought, couldn't speak Japanese too well. He wore a full, heavy beard. That alone seemed bad enough, but on top of it, his father had actually attacked Japan from the air during the war, even strafing the very town where I had been born. I couldn't see Robert making a good impression. I cried a great deal and became far too upset and afraid to say anything. Instead of acting to clear the air, I just became more and more depressed.

Finally in August, with my friend Kiyo's encouragement, I did speak to my father. I told him I had someone I wanted him to meet.

"I see," said my father. "You must mean that foreigner. Give me some time to think about it."

Days passed with no conversation about our talk. Then, with no warning, my brothers arrived. One came from Kanazawa, seven hours away, and the other from Yokohama, a three-hour journey. The emergency family council took place. I was asked many questions from all sides. What kind of a person is Robert? Why is he in Japan? Does he intend to return to his country soon? What kind of school did he graduate from? What is his religion? And more. Most of the questions were asked by Tadashi and Kiyotaka, my brothers. My father kept his mouth closed and watched the scene out of the corner of his eyes, and just listened. My brothers finally gave their permission to arrange a meeting with Robert.

When the day of the meeting arrived I was apprehensive and nervous. My father had arranged for us to have lunch in a private room at a Japanese family restaurant with a lovely garden. The meeting went much better than I had expected. In fact, now that I think about it, I wonder how my father was able to hold back all the emotion I knew he felt. He always had dreams for his only daughter, and they did not include marrying a foreigner, especially an American, his old enemy!

That night, I sat down with my father and talked with him about the meeting with Robert. He told me, "The day you showed me the picture of all of those foreign men and said you wished to marry one of the men in the picture was a difficult day for me. I knew that some day I would have to let my 'treasured daughter' go, and I knew you were now reaching a marriageable age, but I was astonished by the suddenness of the proposition.

"In the picture were several foreign men, but of all the choices, the heavily bearded American one was your choice! Again I was shocked. My feelings towards America and the war were frozen deep within me. I was just beginning, after forty-three years, to accept the changing times. For all those years, I was pretending to be flexible and adaptable. But now you, my daughter, wanted to marry an American, out of all the choices available to you among Japanese men. To marry the son of my enemy!

"I had brought up my children without interfering in their lives. I always believed in the child's independence as much as possible. I only forbid actions that would interfere with other's wellbeing. I encouraged my children to strive for whatever they believed in; but this? It seemed that you had thought through your decision very well. I knew that you had talked to your mother and that she had been quite adamant. 'No gaijins in our family,' your mother said.

"If I said no, it would go against my philosophy. Your mother and I put our heads together and finally decided that the least we could do was to meet your young man.

"I was quite surprised to find that Robert was accustomed to the Japanese language, as well as the Japanese lifestyle. Moreover, I found, he was a likable person with a keen interest in wabi and sabi (the taste for simplicity and tranquility the Japanese consider the ultimate state of being), even beyond the level a Japanese man might show. He also possessed a stillness that has become rather rare in modern-day Japan. I liked him very much. Then, in the ensuing conversation, I learned that his father and I had a lot in common, both in age and in our life experiences. When I heard that Robert's father had been an ace pilot in the war, I had a premonition of the decision that I would make regarding your marriage.

"For myself, even though I sought the path of a pilot in the war, I never realized my dream. But I steadfastly held to the firm belief that there were no enemies in 'the ones who flew in the sky.' Although in the past we were enemies, there is an affinity between all fellow fliers, just from the experience of flying; regardless of being a friend or foe.

"Robert also mentioned that his father had flown a P-51 Mustang over Japan. My emotion changed from simple admiration to overwhelming wonder. The P-51 had been the object of adoration of all Japanese student pilots. I imagined that anyone flying that plane would be an extraordinary person, and I was convinced that this young man had, in his blood, much of what I admired. It was all I could handle to keep my composure, suppressing my desire to shout for joy that my only daughter would pick such an excellent counterpart. I did not say anything to you about my thoughts, because I wanted to speak to your mother first. When I told her about my feelings, that I thought your young man was suitable for you to marry, she quickly agreed to my decision. So, Takako, I am very happy for you, and most anxious to meet your new parents."

I cried with joy at what my father had told me.

That conversation cleared the air between my mother and me so we began to look for a place to have the wedding reception. We already knew that I would have the ceremony at the Mishima shrine, that is where all of our family occasions are held. We hope to get the Skylight Room at the Mishima Plaza Hotel for the dinner reception after the wedding ceremony. Robert will call you as soon as we have set a firm date.

Takako Yamakawa

The Yellins were extremely touched by the letter, and Jerry decided it was time to write to the family that would soon, through Robert and Takako's wedding, become part of his own.

My Dear Yamakawa Family:

It is with great pleasure that I send you greetings from America. We were very pleased when Robert phoned us last night and informed us of his plans to marry Takako in March of next year. We think it is exciting for them. You can be assured that Takako will be welcomed into our family by Robert's brothers and my wife and me, with love and respect.

We were told by Takako in April that you Yamakawa-San, and I share a lot in common. It seems we were born in the same month of the same year, shared similar experiences in our youth, and then devoted the rest of our lives to what we felt was most important of all, raising our families. Both of us have four children, all of whom have good education and futures. You and I have strong marriages, and now, these two families will be joined together by the marriage of our youngest children.

I can fully understand that you might be upset by Takako's decision to marry a man other than a Japanese because of the differences in tradition and culture. We, too, had some doubts as to the wisdom of the decision. However, the more we examined your traditions and culture, we saw that there were many more similarities than differences. Truly what matters to us is the respect that two people have for each other and the fact that they want to be with each other as a family, much as we have led our lives.

We want you to know that we are all happy for Takako and Robert and we wish them a long and happy life together.

We look forward with great enthusiasm to meeting you and your family in February and being part of the wedding on March 5th.

Signed,
Jerry and Helene Yellin

A few weeks later, the Yamakawas replied—both in English and Japanese, in the form of an elegant scroll handwritten on beautiful paper.

Dear Mr. And Mrs. Yellin:

Here the season of autumn is beginning to appear in the trees and in the air. It seems that fate has brought your warm letter to us from so far away. We are grateful that Takako is welcomed into Robert's family with such a warm feeling. We would like to thank your family.

When Takako told us of Robert and their plans it was like a bolt out of the blue. But after we met Robert and saw his quietness and consideration, we found that our daughter's eyes were correct. After Robert told us about his father, it seems we are of the same age and shared similar backgrounds. We feel happy to see your pictures and know that Takako will be accepted into such a good and healthy family.

Although our customs and lifestyles are different, in these modern times, they may be interchangeable. I expect that Robert and Takako will be able to do this. Our family is not so well off, but our hearts and feelings are like the sky. We always want to have that feeling, plentiful, and wide like the blue sky. Our distance is far but we are happy to be family and relatives, distance cannot change these situations. We are very happy.

March 5th is a lucky day for marriage at the Mishima Shrine. It will soon be here. At that time you will be here, we look forward to that day and are glad to think of it now. We answer your letter in happiness and wish you health and happiness in your life and work.

Signed,
Taro and Hatsue Yamakawa

Yellin was so moved by their words that he wrote one more time to the Yamakawas before the wedding.

Dear Yamakawa-San:

I am writing to you today with a wonderful feeling of happiness, respect and gratefulness to you and your family. Your letter expressed, in poetic terms, a beautiful sentiment that could only come from a man of depth and great understanding. Both Helene and I are deeply touched by your words and your thoughts.

Even more, it has given us an insight into Takako's background and upbringing and strengthened our feelings about the coming wedding. Only you and I, Yamakawa-San, can know about the soul-searching we both had to go through to reach this level of complete acceptance. We are soon to be family and share in the joys of that which families experience. This is all the wealth that I believe a man needs. We indeed are both fortunate to have reached this stage of life.

We will be arriving in Japan on Saturday, February 27 and plan to stay two weeks. We look forward to meeting you and your family and spending time getting to know you.

Please give my warmest regards to your wife, your sons, and my future daughter.

Signed,
Jerry Yellin

Robert and Takako remain happily married to this day. (The Yellins and the Yamakawas are also now the proud grandparents of three children.) Just as individuals who fought against one another have worked to create bonds of friendship, so have nations. Less than two decades after the last American troops left Saigon in 1975, the government of the United States tentatively began to normalize its diplomatic ties with Vietnam. One of the most significant developments came in February 1994, when President Bill Clinton ordered an end to the nineteen-year-old US trade embargo against Vietnam. Three years later, Douglas "Pete" Peterson became the first US ambassador to Vietnam since the end of the war. Incredibly, Peterson was a former air force captain who had flown bombing missions over North Vietnam and was shot down in 1966. He ultimately spent six hellish years as a prisoner of war. Peterson's personal experience muted some of the American opposition to improving, in any way, the country's relationship with Vietnam. At a 1999 press conference, Ambassador Peterson was asked by a reporter, "Here it is, twenty-five years after the war and the president of the United States is here dealing with the communist government of Vietnam, trying to establish cordial relations. With all due respect, sir, to you and to others who have served in the war, might not the families of those who perished in that war ask what did their loved ones die for?" The ambassador replied:

Well, each of those families would have to answer that for themselves, of course. I would never try to pre-empt their feelings, because I know—I know—how they feel. My family, too, suffered greatly. In fact, I personally suffered every imaginable hurt and problem that one could, short of death. But I am convinced that those who lost their lives, those who suffered here would be among the first to stand up and say, we don't want this to happen again. And that by constructive effort and engagement on our part, the United States can make sure that we do not have a circumstance arise that could give the opportunity for misunderstanding, and then therefore an opportunity for the renewal of a conflict either here or in the region. And I know that those people who served here, I think every single one, even though they have painful memories, would engage with me and others to prevent any similar conflict in the future. And that's why I'm here.

With economic sanctions lifted and a spirit of reconciliation beginning to thrive, American veterans started traveling to Vietnam in increasing numbers. Many wanted to show their wives and children the country that had affected them so profoundly when they were young servicemen. Others went alone or with war buddies, often as a cathartic experience or simply out of curiosity to see how much had changed. And some went to launch community projects that would strengthen the fledgling relationship between America and Vietnam. Francis J. "Chuck" Theusch, a successful businessman and former Republican candidate for Congress, was an eighteen-year-old kid from Wisconsin when he was sent to Vietnam in December 1969 with the American Division, 11th Brigade, 4/3 Infantry. Exactly thirty years later, he returned to the land that had claimed the lives of so many of his friends and had become an integral part of his own personal history. Theusch fell in love with the country and wanted to demonstrate the depth of his affection in a lasting and tangible way. He began by supporting a nine-year-old Vietnamese orphan, Le Ngoc Diem My, through a charitable program. And when he noticed the scarce educational facilities for Diem My and other impoverished children, especially in rural areas, Theusch embarked on a more ambitious effort—funding the construction of libraries throughout Vietnam. Most of the Vietnamese community leaders and residents Theusch met with were delighted to work with him on the project, and on October 13, 2001, they celebrated the opening of the first library funded by Theusch. Not everyone, however, welcomed Theusch with open arms. During a visit to the district of Son My, one woman he was introduced to named Tran Thi Anh Thu would barely speak with him. Thu made it clear she was suspicious of his motivations because he was an American, and her mistrust was understandable; Son My was where the My Lai massacre occurred in March 1968, when US troops killed hundreds of defenseless villagers, including women and children. Thu worked at the My Lai Memorial. Theusch convinced Thu to at least begin a dialogue with him, and gradually, through their correspondence, she began to trust him. He returned to Son My several times and a genuine friendship blossomed. After writing to Theusch in one e-mail mostly to say hello, she mentioned in passing that she was tired and physically unwell. Theusch thought it might have something to do with the nature of her job. "Dear Mrs. Thu, I am so happy to hear from you, but so sad that you feel bad," he e-mailed her in November 2002. (It is customary for some Vietnamese to drop articles when speaking English, and Theusch often did the same when he wrote to Thu.)

I believe you have hard job to tell sad story every day over and over. You are a very special woman to do very special job. When you first give me tour I could see in your eyes a sensitive sadness that I shall never forget. But you have helped me understand the deep pain we left behind. It is part of why I come back to Vietnam and feel desire to work in Viet Nam the rest of my life.

A month later, Thu, who was feeling better, sent Theusch the following e-mail, recalling a story from the war that involved her aunt. (These correspondences have been edited slightly in the interests of privacy.)

Mr Chuck, You are okey when you returned to America? Why didnot you go back to Wisconsin but to Chicago? You know I did not think I met a good American. Many years ago, I hear my grandmother told me that when U.S troops based in Quang ngai, my arnt who was [sick]. While she went to market, she met some G.Is on the way they took her

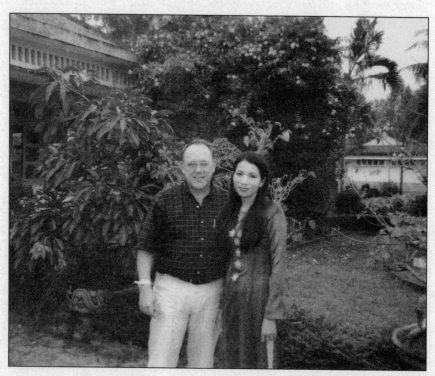

Chuck Theusch and Tran Thi Anh Thu in Vietnam

on helicopter.she thought they will do some bad things and kill her, she didnot think they flew her to hospital at CHU LAI and operated [on] her, then they tookcare her until she very weel and flew her back.Although I know there are many G.Is killed my people in Duc Pho and Son My but there are some try to help my people.So when I met you at the first time I couldnot smile. That is a question in your mind,isnt it?Talking with you some times, I recornized that We cannot live in past and I donot wake up that painful. We must look toward the future and try to do good things. Vietnam and America shake hand in hand to become good friends.No enemies and Vietnam will live in peace forever

In the following letter, Theusch expressed how important their friendship had become for him as well, and how symbolic it was of the larger dynamic between their two nations. He hoped that both relationships would flourish. (The phrase "hanh phuc," which Theusch uses near the end of his letter, is essentially an offering of best wishes for a happy and prosperous life.)

Dear Miss Thu,

   I am happy to hear from you. There is sadness in you. Please tell me of the difficulty in your life. I am not sure how I could help, but I would try to do the best for your and your family.

   Your are a special person to me. Somehow after all the pain of your life and history of Son My you have found kindness for me, an American, in your heart. You have inspired me and moved me in many ways someday I will explain to you.

   Each trip to Viet Nam I feel the depths of sadness over the darkness of the past, but then in the children I find the joy and hope for the future. Maybe it is why I need Vietnamese children in my life so much—they beam with bright light of better tomorrows for all of us.

   There is a man in American who has funded a library in Ha Noi. I have a meeting with the Hanoi People's Committee this week about it. I hope to get more money to build more libraries, and I want to do more in Quang Ngai. Duc Pho has been so very good to me.

   I was only in Quang Ngai a day and so sad I could not see you. I miss that sunny smile of yours.

   I may try to get to Da Nang this week yet before I go home—I miss my daughter, Diem My very much. Having no wife or children in the USA I guess she has special meaning to me. Imagine, Viet Nam has given me a daughter! Now if I find a good mother for her my life circle will be complete, and my future be clear.

One thing has been clear to me since my return to Viet Nam in 1999—Viet Nam is and always will be my life.

I will call you soon. Sometimes in life it is good to talk to a friend. You have one forever in me. Thu, you are a better person than I am, I try to make myself a better man. But I stand in your shadow, and that of the people and country I have come to respect and love so much.

The weather in Ha Noi is cool but I like it. I wish I could spend 3–4 days in Quang Ngai. I told Quyhn and Houng at the Central I would like to go Karaoke sometime in Quang Ngai.

Please write soon. I wish you hanh phuc with all me heart and soul. I pray for you and your family.

Most Sincerely,
Chuck

The Library Project of Vietnam continues to grow significantly, and Theusch's goal is to build six hundred libraries by 2015, one for every district in Vietnam. (They are expanding into Cambodia and Laos as well.) In the years preceding and following the Vietnam War, the United States had only one formidable opponent—the Soviet Union. No other power in America's history had the ability to bring about the nation's total annihilation. But that threat was mitigated by the fact that the United States could retaliate with equal, if not greater, force. The collapse of the Soviet Union in 1991 heralded an age of near invulnerability for the United States. The bombings of the World Trade Center in 1993 (which killed "only" six people), the Oklahoma City Murrah Federal Building (an act of homegrown terrorism) in 1995, the US embassies in Tanzania and Kenya in 1998, and the Navy destroyer USS Cole *in 2000 rattled but did not destroy that sense of security and confidence. And then came 9-11. Suddenly the United States was confronted with an agile, almost invisible enemy consumed with the desire to kill as many innocent civilians as possible, decapitate the nation's government, and, in targeting its financial infrastructure, bring about America's economic ruin. President George W. Bush was emphatic, from the very beginning, that even though all of the 9-11 terrorists were Muslims, the US was not at war with Islam. Nevertheless, relations between Americans and Muslims in the US and abroad deteriorated rapidly. One man caught between these two worlds is Khaled Al-Maeena, a Saudi Arabian journalist, who had been educated as a young man in America, and sent most of his children to college there as well. He still travels to the US frequently to visit close friends and participate in educational events created to foster mutual understanding and dialogue between Muslims and people of other faiths. Because of his role as the editor in chief of the English-language daily* Arab News, *he personally receives letters and e-mails voicing a wide range of reactions to current affairs covered in either the paper's news section or editorials. Many are carefully reasoned, well-articulated criticisms of opinions expressed in the paper. But some are pure venom. "F——— you, Towel headed camel jockey . . . son of a pig and monkey," read one. "There are NO civilized countries in the muslim world," began another. It went on to call for the incineration of the Middle East. (The typos are in the original.)*

> *If you people want to turn back the clock to 800 years ago, then I think we should help to turn back the clock even more . . . ALL THE WAY BACK TO THE STONE AGE. I think that my country should just NUCK you bastards and get it over with!!!*

Arab-Israeli relations were fodder for countless messages:

> *You Arabs are the biggest losers. Israel with a population of 5 Million kickes your ass. you have like what?? 300 Million Arabs and 3000 times bigger countries?? haha you are the joke of the hole world : -)*

Another reader offered the following menacing e-mail with a gleeful tone: "Congrats to U, my little buddy and to your fabulous country, your #3 on the list, hehehe: 1) Iraq . . . . 2. Iran . . . . 3. Saudi Arabia . . ." And along a similar theme:

> *God, I really hope we go to war with your country—I look forward to the day we destroy your country and those of Syria, Iran, and Iraq. Your playing with fire you jerkoffs, in continuing to taunt and embarrass the United States—my sincerest wish is that we takeover your country, open up a Club Med in Mecca, complete with Strip Joints . . . and 24-Hour bars and taverns for our military, and let the Israelis govern the rest of your country as military dictatorship—now that would be poetic justice.*

Al-Maeena tried to respond to every message, no matter how vituperative. Many did not care or were unwilling to engage in a rational discussion about whatever issue had inspired them to write, but some did, prompting candid exchanges between Al-Maeena and his readers. Soon after the 9-11 attacks, a Montana resident named Ray, who had come across Arab News *on the Internet, sent the following combative message. (Ray included his full name with the e-mail, but his last name and other information has been deleted here in the interests of privacy.)*

This American thinks that ALL Arabs, Muslims, and Islam in total should be sent to dwell in hell at the hands of Christian warriors. And God would view this as a good fight to rid the world of evil and send them to hell where they belong. You people are nothing but filthy, hateful, cowardly, pigs. You are lower than swine.

Where is the sanity in some stupid, jack ass Imam accusing "Zionists" of state terrorism—Why does he not talk about the thousands of innocent people that bin Laden the ARAB Muslim has killed, the children he has orphaned, and the widows he has created!? I have never felt such true hatred until recently—when I saw all the swine Muslims dancing in the street rejoicing the death of thousands of people. My hatred continues to run deep and extends to Saudi Arabia. The Islam religion is built on a foundation of hatred, intolerance, and violence—which will beget the same from Christians—one hundred-fold, and lead to it's downfall—the end of Islam. I hate you people so much. You filthy, murderous, satanic pigs. I HATE YOU ALL—THE Q'URAN IS THE BOOK OF SATAN THE DEVIL, THE TEACHINGS OF EVIL, THE BOOK THAT IS USED TO JUSTIFY MURDER. ANYONE WHO WORSHIPS ISLAM IS THE DEVIL'S CHILD. THERE WILL BE A GREAT CONFLICT IN THE FUTURE, A CONFLAGRATION BETWEEN ISLAM AND CHRISTIANITY AND THE CRUSADERS OF CHRISTIANITY WILL RID THE WORLD OF THE SATANIC HELL THAT IS ISLAM—YOU SHALL PERISH FROM THE EARTH!!!! GOD WILL SEE TO IT FOR THE DEEDS THAT YOU HAVE DONE!! I ABSOLUTELY HATE ALL OF YOU IN THE MOST PURE FORM OF HATRED.

Ray

Recognizing there was probably little he could do to change the mind of someone so beset with rage, Al-Maeena sent back a simple message, emphasizing that, "Instead of such vitriol, I would request you to join us in a prayer for world peace. Sincerely, Khaled A. Al-Maeena." Perhaps taken aback that he received a reply offering even a semblance of cordiality, or possibly already feeling remorseful for his outburst, Ray sent the following, remarkably conciliatory e-mail:

Sometimes, during the course of human events, when tragedies occur, our minds and souls can be so stirred as to evoke great emotions. These emotions are not always pleasant. Indeed, emotions can become quite strong enough as to cause people to do things that come from the emotional mind rather than the heart. This is what happened to me.

Recent events caused me to write the very nasty email that you received, with the intent to provoke you into an argument so I could "vent" my feelings, and make myself feel better at your expense. This was wrong, very wrong. I believe that God let me do this to teach me a lesson. The lesson I have learned is that making others mad does not, in the end, make one feel better about themselves. Rather, it makes one feel bad about themselves. I have learned a good lesson, but I must express my most sincere apologies for directing my anger at all of you. I am not the kind of person that my messages would indicate. And I already knew that people can't carry around hatred, but I needed to learn again. I have found that I can not hate people, I was not raised that way, and it is much too heavy a burden to carry. If my father read what I wrote, I would not be able to type any letters as he would have broken my fingers. I will not offer any excuses for my actions, because the way I have been effected by recent events is not at all your problem.

I have never seen nor have I read the Q'uran—where I live, it would be hard to find such a book. Anyway, I'm sure the Holy Q'uran is a good book full of words of goodness, love, and peace. I hope you will find it in your hearts to forgive me for my outburst of false emotions, and except these words from my heart: please forgive me, and may we all be blessed so that we may one day live in peace—if not for us, then for our children.

If any of you ever come to Montana, I would welcome you in my home so that I may gain a greater understanding of Islam.

God Bless You Everyone,
Ray

Al-Maeeena responded almost immediately:

Greetings and peace from Saudi Arabia.

I was overwhelmed by your letter. God Bless you and all Americans. I would like to welcome you as my personal guest any time you wish to come.

As for the Qur'an or other books you need please let me know and I shall send it to you.

Hopefully you and I will be part of the "dialogue of civilizations".

As the father of five children, four of whom studied in America, I am determined that the evil acts of some depraved people, be they of any race, not spoil the strong relation between America and us.

If there is anything else you need to know please feel free to ask.

Respectfully,
Khaled A. Al-Maeena

On December 24, just a few weeks after they had begun their correspondence, Al-Maeena sent Ray a special gift—a transcription from the Qur'an of the story of Mary and the birth of Jesus Christ. Al-Maeena's new pen pal was moved by the gesture.

Dear Mr. Al-Maeena:

On the eve of Christmas, I have received a wonderful gift. Tonight when I retire, in that time when thoughts pass through one's mind before sleep comes; I shall pray to the Lord and thank him for the understanding and forgiveness you have shown to me. And, I will thank him and ask that his blessings be bestowed upon you for the wonderful gift you sent me. The story of the birth of Christ from the Qur'an was beautiful.

Merry Christmas to you and your family, and a wish that the coming New Year, be full of goodness, health, and prosperity.

Maybe we will be one year closer to world peace.

Season's Greetings,
Ray

Several months later, Ray, a World War II veteran in his seventies, passed away. Al-Maeena heard the news from Ray's son, Jeff.

I am sending you this message at my father's behest. Last Friday he had a heart-attack and he seemed to know that he was not long for this world. He would have been 76 in July. He told me of the first e-mail he sent to all of you and how he regretted that his anger had gotten the better of him. He also told me of the respect he had for all of you for your forgiveness and continued messages.

My father was a warrior. I suspect his brief encounter with all of you helped give him some peace of mind. My father had obtained a copy of the Holy Qur'an and had been reading it. In one of my last conversations with him, he told me that he believed no matter a man's faith, we are all children of God and therefore we are all brethren. With that in mind, I shall end this letter to you by saying, based upon his beliefs, he will be looking forward to meeting you.

Go in Peace,
Jeff

EDITOR'S NOTE

"What, specifically, are you looking for?" This is often the first and most understandable question people ask me when I appeal to them for extraordinary war letters, and to this day I am unable to formulate a succinct response. The problem is that whenever I try to come up with a definitive list of themes and topics, someone surprises me with a letter that is unlike anything I have read before.

A quick example: in Belgrade I visited the Archives of Serbia and Montenegro to search for letters written by Serbian soldiers during World War II, a time when our two nations were united in fighting the Nazis. A very gracious curator, Predrag Krejik, showed me a letter by a Serbian prisoner of war named Branislav Popovic and began translating it aloud in English. Addressed to Popovic's son, it offered little more than a perfunctory update on his situation and a brief mention of family friends (or possibly old neighbors)—the Zmijovics, the Stakorics, and the Gladovics—held in the same camp. I thanked Predrag for letting me see the letter and asked if Popovic had possibly written something a little more candid. Predrag smiled, recognizing that I didn't understand the significance of the message. Zmijovics, Stakorics, and Gladovics, he explained, were the words "snakes," "rats," and "hunger" manipulated to look like Serbian last names. This was Popovic's way of evading the censors to inform others that, despite German assertions to the contrary, the prisoners were starving and confined in wretched circumstances. It was the first coded POW letter I had ever seen. (Due to space limitations I was unable to include the letter itself in this book, but the story is what is relevant here.)

Determining what makes a letter "extraordinary" is of course subjective, but overall I'm partial to correspondences that accentuate the individual human drama within the vast sweep of history. They are less about the size and scope of warfare—casualty estimates, troop movements, military strategy—than the singular, dirt-under-the-fingernails experience of what it feels like to plunge headfirst into battle. These letters pack an immediate visceral punch and reveal the distinct voices and personalities that make the larger stories more accessible and real.

Although I was initially only interested in combat-related material, I discovered that some of the most emotionally intense war letters ever written make no references to battle. They are heartfelt messages by parents and spouses writing home about missing the birth of a child or a wedding anniversary or a family reunion. Some are letters by teenaged soldiers who have matured considerably since they left for the front lines and are now apologizing to their parents for their past rebelliousness. Or they are letters full of wry humor, emphasizing to those back home that there is nothing to be anxious about. And in so many cases, their words represented the last ones they would ever write. These letters are not as dramatic as brief messages hurriedly penned in foxholes as bullets kicked up dirt just inches away. But written in the life-and-death context of war, their quiet, reflective sentiments are as potent as any description of hard fighting.

Before embarking on my trip around the globe, I made up an extensive inventory of "must find" letters that related to topics and historical events significant to each country. (From the outset I had decided to concentrate only on wars in which Americans had put a substantial number of "boots on the ground," even if our involvement came years after the conflict had started. To expand the focus beyond this would have been too unwieldy, although it did mean having to forgo pursuing stories from some of the world's most fascinating confrontations. One of the most intriguing, to me, is the 1896 clash between Great Britain and Zanzibar, considered the shortest war in history. The whole affair clocked in at about forty-five minutes.) In England I wanted letters about the Christmas Truce in 1914 and the Luftwaffe air raids during World War II, among many others. In Seoul I sought out letters by South Korean troops who had served with the Americans in Vietnam. In Amsterdam I hoped to find letters by Dutch soldiers who had been at Srebrenica. In Baghdad I asked the few Iraqis I had the chance to meet where I could find any letters or e-mails written since the March 2003 invasion. The final "must find" list I compiled was more than a dozen pages long, single-spaced.

With the indispensable assistance of first-rate guides, I pored over thousands of letters, many of which I copied and mailed back to the States where I later cataloged them by country and by topic (love, combat, humor, etc.). If they required translating and seemed destined to be included in the book, I often had them checked by a second and even third party to ensure I was being faithful not only to the words, but the tone and spirit of the text. Combining these foreign letters with the American ones I had already collected (after having traveled throughout the US for almost two years) was the next challenge.

The main question was whether to arrange the letters by war or by theme. I settled on the latter; what I had found so intriguing about these correspondences was how people from vastly different backgrounds over hundreds of years articulated strikingly similar emotions—yet each from their own unique cultural perspective. Within the chapters, and to impose some semblance of order on the book, I decided to arrange the letters chronologically. I made some exceptions for the "Featured Series" sections, which focus on a particular subject as expressed in related letters from many conflicts. And these letters, although designated as "featured," are not necessarily any better or more interesting than others in the collection. They simply worked well as a self-contained group.

The vast majority of the book's approximately two hundred primary letters and e-mails (i.e., the correspondences set in roman font and introduced by italicized headnotes) are unedited and transcribed exactly as they were initially written. Misspellings, typos, grammatical and syntactical mistakes, curious asides in the middle of otherwise gripping stories, and everything else have been left intact so that each letter reads as true to the original as possible. There are a few exceptions to this, and in most cases they relate to deleting personal information or changing a name to protect an individual's privacy. Any such alterations are indicated in the headnotes. In several instances regarding letters with minimal or no punctuation, I have added a space or two in appropriate places to indicate the end of a sentence. Due to the shortage of available paper, some writers covered every inch of their letters, front and back, with writing and made no indentations to mark the beginning of new paragraphs. This can make for arduous reading, so when it appeared to me that a writer was beginning a new thought, I took the liberty of starting a new paragraph.

Throughout the headnotes I have interwoven excerpts from letters I could not use in their entirety but that nevertheless offer insights and observations that reinforce the primary letters immediately before or after them. (Unlike the primary letters that represent the core of the book and are extremely rare or previously unpublished, a handful of the excerpts in the headnotes come from other well known anthologies and sources.) Similarly, at the beginning of each chapter there are several epigraphs that relate to the larger theme of the section that follows. Some of these epigraphs have been edited for length, and they have been done so without adding ellipses to maintain an aesthetic simplicity. Needless to say, no words have been added to these texts, nor has the essence of the correspondence been changed.

A final note about the editing process: while fact-checking the headnotes, I was struck by the degree to which there are wide discrepancies in the casualty estimates used even by respected historians regarding certain battles and attacks on civilians. I made every effort to obtain the most accurate data, and I have tried to indicate where the largest differences among scholars exist. Inevitably people will disagree about these statistics, and I welcome feedback from those who have reliable and updated information.

Although I believe I was successful in tracking down the letters I most wanted to find, some ultimately proved elusive. I regret, for example, not being able to locate letters by African soldiers who fought side by side with Allied troops during the world wars and in other major conflicts. Also, although I had uncovered some remarkable correspondences pertaining to the Cold War for my last book, *War Letters*, this time I came up empty-handed. I am enormously grateful to the American troops who shared with me their letters and e-mails from Iraq, but my single greatest frustration was my inability to obtain anything by other coalition forces who were deployed to the region. Along these lines, I was disappointed that I could not find more correspondences by men and women who serve in the US military but who are not originally from America. (Approximately one out of every forty people in our armed forces is foreign-born.)

In Mexico my wonderful guides, Angelica Morales Carballo and Pablo Mondragon Silva, and I had a lead on a fascinating story about Irish soldiers who served with US troops during the Mexican-American War but eventually began to sympathize with the Mexicans and switched sides. Letters by these Irish soldiers did not seem to be archived anywhere in Mexico—or in Ireland, which I visited as well. I also was unable to unearth *any* letters written by Mexican troops during the war with the United States.

While in France I had hoped to locate previously unpublished letters by several of its most famous citizens: the pilot and children's author Antoine de Saint-Exupéry, Marguerite Duras (who I was told had interrogated Nazi collaborators during World War II), and famed sea explorer Jacques Cousteau, who also served in the Resistance. In each case, nothing. In Berlin and Munich I hunted for World War II pen-pal letters by German children writing to English boys and girls to promote friendship in a time of conflict. Except, as the story was told to me, the whole effort was part of a German intelligence operation to determine British morale during the war. In Australia I held in my hands a sensational World War I letter by an aboriginal soldier, but much to my dismay one of his descendants did not want the letter published under any conditions, even anonymously. It was heartbreaking to have to relinquish such a find, but respecting the wishes of those who own the letters is paramount, so that was the end of that.

There were some misses in the US as well. The grandniece of a World War I serviceman told me that when her great-uncle died in the war, the family feared that his mother—who was terribly sick—would lose the will to live if she learned her son had been killed. One of the man's siblings decided to write letters as if they were from the soldier himself, forwarding them first to a friend in Paris who then mailed them (so they would be properly postmarked) back to the States. The mother died peacefully some time later, but was comforted by the thought that her son was alive and well in France participating in the country's reconstruction. All of these letters have since been lost. In a somewhat similar vein, during his service in the Coast Guard, a gifted young wordsmith ghostwrote love letters for his buddies to send to their spouses or girlfriends. What makes the story especially appealing is that the sailor was Alex Haley, who would go on to write *Roots* and become one of our nation's most influential authors before his death in 1992. I pursued every possible lead I could think of to locate "Haley's" letters, but with no luck.

The publication of *Behind the Lines* does not, however, represent the end of my search for these and other letters. This book is part of a larger mission to ensure that wartime correspondences are preserved for future generations. Hopefully it will inspire others to recognize the value of their wartime letters, show them to their families, and, ideally, share them with the rest of the world.

My terrific guides in Mexico City, Pablo Mondragon Silva and Angelica Morales Carballo, at the Santa Domingo Plaza, where a row of typists for hire are available to help people write business and personal letters on any subject.

Nguyen Van Thanh, one of my translators in Ho Chi Minh City, reading through old letters (most of which were written during the time of the Vietnam War) we found at a small antiques shop.

Christian Scharnefsky, now a close friend who served as my guide in Berlin, looking at a photograph of the great anti-Nazi theologian Dietrich Bonhoeffer.

Jared Wells, holding down the fort in Washington, DC.

ACKNOWLEDGMENTS,
PERMISSIONS, AND SOURCES

From the time *Behind the Lines* was little more than a faint glimmer of an idea to the moment it became a completed, tangible creation, this book has benefited from one small miracle after another. Whenever help was most needed, someone stepped forward to lend a hand, track down specific letters, or extended their hospitality as I traveled throughout the United States and abroad. I doubt I will ever be able to express to them all the depth of my gratitude for their kindness and generosity.

My good fortune began on November 11, 1998, when Abigail Van Buren ("Dear Abby") and her daughter Jeanne Phillips profiled the Legacy Project in their column. Everything that has happened since is thanks to them (we are now up to an estimated seventy-five thousand war letters from every conflict in the nation's history), and I will be forever indebted to Jeanne and her mother for bringing attention to this little effort from the start. I also want to thank Olivia "Newt" Vis, who works in their office, for all of the consideration she has shown me over the years.

I am grateful beyond words to Miriam Altshuler, who is everything an author could ask for in an agent and everything a person could want in a friend. Miriam is one of the most genuinely caring individuals I have ever met, and I would be lost without her. No matter what crisis or problem emerges, Miriam is there with a shoulder to lean on, words of support, and indispensable guidance and advice. I also want to thank her assistant, Sara McGhee, who is incredibly gracious regardless of how many times I pester her with questions or concerns about some matter.

I am also indebted to Miriam for helping me find first-rate editors for both this book and my earlier ones, each of which was a labor of love. It was a joy to work with Deborah Baker on *Letters of a Nation*, and then with Gillian Blake on *War Letters*, and I adore them both.

I am now extremely lucky to be working with Colin Harrison, the editor of this book and a brilliant author in his own right. Colin understood my vision of *Behind the Lines* from the outset, and he has provided impeccable editorial insight throughout this process. He is truly one of the best in the business. Due to the staggering amount of work required and the nature of the material, which can be emotionally overwhelming, there were some very hard days while writing this book. But despite my nerve-wracking delays and failure to complete chapters on time, Colin responded with empathy and understanding (and the occasional gentle nudge), and it has been a pleasure and a privilege to work with him every step of the way. Colin's assistant, Sarah Knight, deserves recognition for everything she has contributed to this book as well.

Sarah is one of the hardest-working and most all-around stellar people I have encountered in publishing, and she has my deepest appreciation.

Along with Colin and Sarah, there is a team of people at Scribner who invested a tremendous amount of their time and energy in this project. First and foremost is Susan Moldow, the publisher, whose support from the beginning has been truly phenomenal. Susan, along with Nan Graham and Roz Lippel, sees *Behind the Lines* as something more than just an anthology of wartime letters, and I cannot express how grateful I am for all that they have done for me and this book. Every author should be so fortunate as to have such a publisher, and it is a true honor to be part of the Scribner family. I also want to extend my thanks to Suzanne Balaban, Lucy Kenyon, Kate Bittman, and Sue Fleming, who, along with many other extremely talented and creative people, are responsible for publicizing and marketing the book. John Fulbrook, Mia Crowley-Hald, Erich Hobbing, and Aja Shevelew have all worked countless hours to see this book through a very intense production schedule, and I know I've caused them all many headaches.

Because I was away traveling for so long to research this book and then deeply immersed in the writing process after I came home, I have been appallingly delinquent in spending time with family and friends. They, in return, have been nothing but loving and supportive. I am truly sorry to them for being absent for so long, and more grateful to them than they can know for putting up with me throughout all of this. I am particularly indebted to my parents (especially considering that I fibbed to them when I said I was not going to Iraq and Afghanistan, although it was only because I didn't want them to worry), who took in all the packages of research material I sent home, and simply kept me going through it all with their prayers, inspiring messages, and phone calls along the way.

Perhaps the greatest of the "small miracles" came after a phone call I received from Nate Mick in Senator Chuck Hagel's office the summer before I left on my journey. Nate and I had worked briefly together on a project that distributes free books to our troops overseas, and Nate asked if I was in need of an intern. "His name is Jared Wells, he's just out of college, and he's a first-rate guy," Nate assured me, and indeed he was— and still is. Jared worked with me for more than six weeks on a volunteer basis before I headed overseas, and I was so impressed with his intelligence, integrity, humanity, maturity, and sense of humor that I asked him if he would be interested in working with me on a full-time basis when I returned. He agreed, and there is no more direct way for me to say this: without Jared, this book could not have been written. Jared is responsible for finding some of the best letters in the book, including those by the Iraqi civilians and the Guernica exchange at the beginning of "Aftermath." He spent weeks poring through previously unpublished letters at the Library of Congress and National Archives, he helped edit every draft of the manuscript I wrote (and he did so with a deft touch), and he has simply been there—no matter how grueling the hours or challenging the assignment—whenever the need was most critical. He and his girlfriend, Deanna Durrett, who is equally amazing, helped me maintain my sanity through some of the most stressful periods as deadlines loomed. Jared also happens to speak three languages, which, considering the nature of this project, came in handy on numerous occasions. Jared is going to go far in life, and I will be proud to say "I knew him when . . ." after the rest of the world sees how much he has to offer as well.

Most importantly, there would be no Legacy Project if it were not for the tens of thousands of people who have sent us letters (and now e-mails) of great personal significance. For those of us who are civilians, it is difficult to understand fully how much military life demands of the men and women who serve in the armed forces, and I hope these correspondences will give us a glimpse into what they and their loved ones sacrifice both on and off the battlefield. The names of those who have contributed letters and e-mail featured in this book, as well as those who have helped me regarding the trip around the world in other essential ways, are acknowledged below. Again, I cannot express how grateful I am to them for everything they have done to help make this book a reality. I am mortified at the prospect that I have forgotten to mention people integral to the trip, this book, or the Legacy Project in general, and, if I have, I truly apologize. (Not all of the countries I traveled to are listed here, as in some cities, especially those I stayed in only briefly, I was able to get around on my own and made the visit more to see a war memorial or military cemetery than to find letters. Conversely, I discovered letters along the way written by soldiers from countries that I did not visit. These are mostly correspondences that were picked up after a battle by either comrades or enemy troops and eventually made their way to archives and museums in nations other than the fallen soldier's homeland.) Here we go:

United States of America: Christine Albert and Richard D'Abate, at the Maine Historical Society; Ted Alexander with the National Park Service; JoAnn Ballard, Joe Carbo, and Michele Mendez, at our building, who kept the office safe and secure while I was away; Rick Baillergeon, who has been a great friend and supporter of the Legacy Project from its earliest days; Scott Baron, one of my heroes, who is responsible for finding the Demetria Barber and Toyoko Alva Nakata letters, and is the author of several terrific books, including *They Also Served: Military Biographies of Uncommon Americans* (MIE Publishing, 1998) and *International Stars at War* (Naval Institute Press, 2002); Terry Baxter, who sent me a copy of the Tetsuko Tanaka letter; Laura E. Beardsley and Max Moeller, at the Historical Society of Pennsylvania, who are responsible for finding the Thomas and Percival Drayton letters; Judy Bellafaire and Britta Granrod, at the Women in Military Service for America Memorial at Arlington National Cemetery; John Bernard, who got me onto the USS *Kitty Hawk,* which was, without question, one of the greatest experiences of my life; Stephen Brengle; Paul Brockman, at the Indiana Historical Society, who kindly sent me a photocopy of the Kurt Vonnegut letter from their archives; my revered mentor/guru/sensei, Chris Buckley; Bruce E. Burgoyne, who is America's foremost expert on Revolution-era Hessian soldiers and the author of many books on the subject, and who provided me with the Christian von Molitor letter; Dorothy Butchko; Dr. Nic Butler, Dr. Eric Emerson, and Karen Stokes at the South Carolina Historical Society; Parker Calvert, for introducing me to Lois Hoffman, who shared with me the Gunter Leopold letter (coincidentally, Lois's daughter, Constance Phelps, had sent me the same letter years before, but I was only focusing on American letters at the time); G. Wade Carmichael Jr., who first told me about the Kurt Vonnegut letter; Marjorie H. Carne, for sending me the Angela Petesch letter (and I am also grateful to Kristin Gilpatrick, who wrote *The Hero Next Door* [Badger Books, 2000], and Todd Hunter of Hunter Halverson Press, LLC, who will be publishing a book of Angela Petesch's letters, *War Through the Hole of a Doughnut*); Mary Carter, who is constantly keeping an eye out for great war letters for me; Emily Catherman, who is one of the people most responsible for making the trip possible at all. Just days after Scribner accepted the idea for this book, I was suddenly seized with panic at the enormity of the task ahead of me. Emily, whom I had met in North Carolina while I was traveling throughout the US looking for American letters, called me out of the blue and asked if I needed assistance with anything in particular. I told her I appreciated the offer, but the main chore ahead of me—finding contact information for hundreds of military-related institutions around the world that might have war letters in their archives—was not something I presumed she or anyone else would be terribly interested in doing on a volunteer basis. Not only did she do it enthusiastically, but she was absolutely meticulous in her work, and I simply cannot thank her enough; Tim Chesser, who kindly provided me with information on the Drayton brothers; Chan Chrisman, who found the Samuel Bard letter; Charlotte Cole, who has always gone out of her way to help with the Legacy Project's mission; Dave Cooke, who has also been extremely supportive over the years; Dr. Kazimiera J. Cottam (one of the foremost experts on Russian women who fought in World War II), who very considerately shared with me dozens of letters from her own files that she took not only the time to select, but to translate for me as well; Kevin Coyne, who wrote a terrific article on Eddie Grant for *Smithsonian* (October 2004) and put me in touch with Karen Kubara, Grant's grandniece; Lynda Crist at Rice University, for help finding the Williamson Oldham Simpson letter; Sharon Curry, who generously forwarded me e-mail by her son Scott, who served in Iraq; Richard Danzig, who provided me with numerous first-rate contacts around the world; the entire Davidson family, and especially Tommy, who is single-handedly responsible for the fact that the manuscript for this book was late; Frank Davies, who has gone beyond the call of duty to help the Legacy Project bring in letters; Alvin Deutsch, who is my lawyer and a wise and gracious friend; John F. Di Virgilio, in Hawaii, who went out of his way to help me find Pearl Harbor veterans—both American and Japanese; Isabel and Ovidio Diaz, who forwarded me a copy of Denis Silva Torres's incredible letter about Iraqi children; Terry Dorman with the National Park Service; Jono Drysdale, a close friend and my resident Canadian expert (and I am also grateful to his girlfriend, Meredith Margaret Henne, for putting me in touch with Margaret Tilley, who reviewed the American Revolution letters); everyone at the Eisenhower Center, particularly Doug Brinkley, Kevin Willey, and Michael Edwards; John Elko, who put me in touch with Max Young and has been a steady and supportive friend throughout this process; Clay Feeter, who contributed great Civil War letters to the Legacy Project; Duery Felton Jr., curator of the Vietnam Veterans Memorial Collection, who has always been generous with his time and assistance; Nate Fick, a US Marine who was one of the first combatants to share with me his letters from Iraq (and I am also indebted to Denise Gitsham for introducing me to Nate); Pearl Harbor survivor Dick Fiske; Merrilee A. Foley, for sending in David A. Thompson's letter; Nessa Forman, who initiated an effort similar to the Legacy Project in Pennsylvania and shared with us some of their best letters; Christopher J. Fox, at Fort Ticonderoga, who provided me with letters from numerous eighteenth- and nineteenth-century conflicts, particularly the French and Indian War; Roger France, who provided the BJ Armstrong letter; Brad Fultz, a US Marine who helped me catalog some of the German letters; James Gaines, who delivers the mail at my building and always looks out for me; Shawna Gandy and Lucy Kopp, at the Oregon Historical Society, for all of their help with the George P. Telfer letters and photograph from the Philippines; everyone at the Gilder Lehrman Institute of American History, especially Jim Basker, Karina Gaige, Richard Gilder, Lesley Herrmann, Lew Lehrman, Susan Saidenberg, and Sandy Trenholm; Dan Gillcrist; Caroline Gluck with the BBC, who put me in touch with Kevin Kim (who led me to the Kim Min Ha letter); Chris Goddard, who wrote about Roff, the German messenger dog, and provided me with all of the information used in the profile of Roff; Bill Groniger, who is one of the most patriotic Americans I know; Ilana Greenstein, who has assisted the Legacy Project over the years in numerous ways; Emily Grosvenor, who translated many of the German letters and has simply been a joy to work with; Erin Gruwell, who is one of the most amazing and inspiring individuals I met on the entire journey and is now a dear friend; Sylvia Helene Hairston, who kindly provided me with the Oscar Mitchell letter; Joyce A. Hallenbeck, whose constant love and support is always appreciated; Shane T. Hamilton and Megan McLaughlin at Miller & Chevalier, who have offered indispensable legal assistance over the years; Greg Henry, who provided me with much-needed travel information before I embarked; Nancy Manring Holman, who shared the Maschil Manring letter; Linda Howell, who helped track down letters from several wars; Paula Huntley, author of *The Hemingway Book Club of Kosovo* (Jeremy P. Tarcher/Putnam, 2003); Karen Hurd, who put me in touch with her son, Chris, who wrote a profoundly moving letter about the death of a friend; Pearl Harbor survivor Everett Hyland, who gave me the best tour a visitor could hope for at the USS *Arizona*; Sunil Iyengar; Jake Jeppson, who researched embassies around the world for me and had been my assistant on *War Letters* before he went off to college; Alan and Sue Johnson-Hill, for taking so much time to help me include Kenelm Clifton Johnson-Hill's letters/journals to his wife; Terry A. Johnston Jr.; David Jones, who advised me on where to go in Vietnam; Mary Karcher at *Leatherneck*, who has done more to help me find letters and e-mail by marines than anyone; Garrett Kasper, who was my excellent host and guide in Bahrain; David Kennedy with Dan Curtis Productions; Courtney King, who has assisted me in many ways, particularly with my trip to the Middle East; Brian Knowlton, at the *International Herald Tribune*, who wrote about my (at the time) planned trip to find war letters around the world; Yumi Kobayashi, who read through stacks of barely legible war letters found at a flea market in Japan on my behalf and earned my undying gratitude; Brian J. Lang, at Dumbarton House/The National Society of the Colonial Dames of America, who provided the Phoebe Morris letters; Yvonne Latty, who wrote the sensational *We Were There: Voices of African American Veterans, from World War II to the War in Iraq* (Amistad, 2004), and who found the Waverly Woodson letter; Chris Lillie, at the Pentagon, who helped me with the book distribution project for the troops; Brian Lipson, my fellow history buff and agent extraordinaire in Los Angeles; Jan Lorys and his staff at the Polish Museum of America, who provided me with a copy of a book they self-published, Metchie J.E. Budka's *Autograph Letters of Thaddeus Kosciuszko in the American Revolution* (1977), which contains a facsimile of the Kosciuszko letter in this book; Pam McDonough, my technical adviser extraordinaire who advised me to film and photograph the trip (and Brad Smith at Penn Camera who set me up with the equipment); Pat McGhee at Fort Hood; James P. McInerney, for submitting the Frank Rudert letter; Flo and Harold McKenzie; Ross McMullin, who is the world expert on Harold "Pompey" Elliott and essentially ghostwrote the introduction to Elliott's Gallipoli letter; Kathy McNeeley and Christopher Purdell, who found the James Williams letter; my pre-trip medical team, Drs. Alex Chester, Marc Doctors, and Arnold Miller, as well as Jennifer Dunphy, who advised me on health issues before I traveled around the world; Douglas Osama Meehan, for assistance with my trip to Vietnam, and his amazing wife, Caroline Suh, for her advice on camera equipment; Richard Mei Jr., who set up the small gathering in Belgrade that led to my meeting Patricia A. Andjelkovic (Richard also put me in touch with the staff at the US Embassy in Tokyo, where he worked, and he has since become a dear friend whom I admire greatly); Mike Meyer, at the VFW, to whom I am eternally indebted for everything he has done for me and the Legacy Project over the years (and I am also grateful to Becky Curtis, who works with Mike); Allen Mikaelian, who assisted me early on with finding war museums and archives around the world; Harry Miller, at the Wisconsin Historical Society, who once again saved me by sharing first-rate letters from their collection; Marja Mills, a dear friend who has also been instrumental in helping us spread the word about the Legacy Project; Lynn Mooney, who helped shape the focus of this book; Conrad J. Netting IV, who kindly shared with me his mother's incredible World War II letters and is writing his own book, *Delayed Legacy*, about the courage and heroism of both his parents (Maverick Publishing Co., 2005); Larry Ng; Zabih U. Noori at Print Time; Tom O'Sullivan; Florence Ochi at the Japanese American National Museum; Kate M. Ohno at the Yale University Library, who quickly found and sent to me the letters by Benjamin and William Franklin as my deadline approached; T. Michael Parrish, who provided me with the Robert E. Lee letter; David Pelizzari, who not only seems to be fluent in every language spoken on this earth but is also one of the most generous souls I've ever met; Nancy Pope, my epistolary comrade-in-arms at the National Postal Museum; Alice Leccese Powers; Pam Putney, for her love and travel advice; Nadia Rawls; John Rees, who generously shared with me numerous letters from the American Revolution, including the letters by Henry Johnson; Bonnie Reich, who found a copy of the stunning Pearl Harbor letter by William Czako in her house, left behind by the previous tenants; Danielle and Jason Ritter, for sending in the great photo of Jason with "Turbo"; Ken Robinson and his brother Steve, both of whom I admire enormously; Joe "Buck" Rogers, a true American patriot; Nikki Roth-Stiles, who assisted me in finding the Jonathan S. Mosby letter; Lorraine Sais and Elana Samuels at the Museum of Tolerance in Los Angeles; Susan Salm, who is one of my favorite Texans and put me in touch with Alisa Johnson at the Daughters of the American Revolution National Society, who helped me find great War of Independence letters; Barbara Schneider, who generously shared with me letters by her son Stephen Webber; Rye Schwartz-Barcott, a US Marine whose friendship and advice throughout the years I value enormously; Jan Scruggs and everyone else at the Vietnam Veterans Memorial Fund (especially Holly Rotundi and Alan Greilsamer), for their support and for making my trip to Vietnam so memorable; Lottchen Shivers; Alex and Pat Shakow, who first shared with me their son Tom's letters from Sarajevo; Jane Singer, who very generously shared the Civil War terrorism information and correspondence with me and is doing her own book on the subject, *The Confederate Dirty War: Arson, Bombings Assassination and Plots for Chemical and Germ Attacks on the Union* (McFarland & Company, 2005); Ilene and Sid Slagter, who have been helpful in numerous ways and edited *Chicken Soup for the Veteran's Soul* (HCI, 2001); Martha Smalley at the Yale University Divinity School, for sharing the James H. McCallum letter; Corey Smathers and everyone else at Lincoln Action Program who assisted us with finding letters and e-mail from the current war; Megan Smolenyak, editor of *Honoring Our Ancestors* (Ancestry Publishing, 2002), who helped the Legacy Project get its message out to the genealogical community; Mark von Sponeck, executive director of the extraordinary Global Nomads Group, who helped me locate e-mail by Iraqi civilians; Joel Swerdlow, for providing invaluable help with this book and so many other projects; Alex Thomas at Travel Documents; Margaret Tilley, who helped review the American Revolution letters; Liza Tobin, whose support through this whole period of travel and writing was more appreciated than she will ever know; Tim Todish, author of *America's First First World War: The French and Indian War, 1754–1763* (Purple Mountain Press, 2002), who, along with Chris Fox, helped me find French and Indian War correspondences; Sheri Travillian, who shared with me the incredible e-mail by her nephew Gary Chandler who is serving in Iraq; Olga Tsapina, Curator of American Historical Manuscripts at the Huntington Library, who went out of her way to find for me copies of the Francis Lieber and Robert E. Lee letters; Martin Vigderhouse; Pearl Harbor survivor Herb Weatherwax; Don Wilson, who put me in touch with Masuda Anna Mohamadi; Greg Wessel, a stamp and letter collector who was one of the first to suggest that I search for foreign war letters; Rob Wilson, whose selfless work with the Veterans Education Project is an inspiration to me and so many others; Ellen Wingard, for her love and support; Mariruth Leftwich Wurdeman, at the Charlotte Museum of History, who helped me find the F.M. Desha letter; Jerry Yellin, who graciously allowed me to publish his postwar letters, and is the author of a powerful memoir titled *Of War and Weddings: A Legacy of Two Fathers* (SunStar Publishing, 1995); Ann Sherman York, former president of the American Gold Star Mothers; Massimo Young, about whom I cannot rave enough—Max is one of the smartest and most remarkable young individuals I have met, and he assisted Jared Wells and me with research, translating letters, organizing the Legacy Project collection, and in countless other ways; James W. Zobel at the MacArthur Memorial Archives, who, once again, provided me with an extraordinary, never-before-published letter by Douglas MacArthur; I'd also like to extend a word of thanks to the good people at Expedia.com. Seriously. I planned almost the entire trip on the Internet, primarily using Expedia, and in seven months of travel to more than thirty countries, not one thing went wrong. That, in itself, is a miracle. *Afghanistan*: Masuda Anna Mohamadi, who very generously shared with me her extraordinary e-mail; Khatera Atayee; Haroon Gharzai; Mustafa Merzazada; and the staff of the Intercontinental in Kabul. Despite the bombing, the hotel remains one of my favorites from the entire trip. *Australia*: Lynette Aitchison, David Jolliffe, Margaret Lewis, and Ian Smith at the Australian War Memorial, and I am particularly indebted to Emma Jones, who helped me locate many terrific letters while I was in Canberra and has endured a barrage of e-mails since I returned to the States. *Austria*: Dr. Christoph Tepperberg, at the Austrian State Archives/War Archives in Vienna. *Belgium*: In Ypres—my guide Kristof Demey; Dominiek Dendooven at the In Flanders Fields Museum Documentation Center, who provided me with numerous first-rate World War I letters; and General James Jones, Supreme Allied Commander, Europe, to whom I am especially grateful for taking the time to meet with me during my visit to NATO Headquarters in Mons. (Paul Whitfield and Shirley Richardson were also very kind in helping to set up the meeting.) *Bosnia and Herzegovina*: Dalila Sinanovic and Nidzara Beganovic, in particular, at Veterans and Invalids of the Patriotic War, for providing me with letters by residents of Sarajevo written during the siege; Fatima Sirucic, who put me in touch with Amir Telebecirovic. As I mention in the introduction to this book, Amir was not only one of the best guides I had on the trip, he has become a dear friend whose compassion and love for his country, along with his desire for reconciliation with those who viciously attacked it, affected me deeply. *Canada*: Wayne Abbott, whose Northern Sky Entertainment did a fantastic documentary based on World War II letters (*From a Place Called War: 1939–1945*), several of which he and his very gracious sister Laura Abbott shared with me; Timothy Dubé and Andrew Horrall at the Library and Archives, Canada, who were extremely generous with their time and expertise (and Andrew is responsible for helping me find the Canadian censored letters in the humor chapter). I am also grateful to Tim for putting me in touch with Stephen Fochuk, a freelance researcher who tracked down letters after I left Canada. Despite the fact that they were closing their archives in a matter of days (in preparation for a move to a new building), Carol Reid, Patricia Grimshaw, Dean Oliver, Maggie Arbour-Doucette, and their colleagues at the Canadian War Museum were incredibly helpful in directing me to promising collections in their archives. Most of all, I am indebted to my good friend Dr. Stephen Davies at Malaspina University-College. Stephen started an effort similar to the Legacy Project, called The Canadian Letters and Images Project, and he has preserved thousands of Canadian war correspondences and photographs. The Hart Leech and William Mayse letters are both from Stephen's collection. *China*: Charlie Chi in Beijing, who assisted with some of the initial research; Malia DuMont; Lucia Buchanan Pierce; Benjamin Kostrzewa, who was living in Beijing at the time and, being fluent in Chinese, offered to serve as one of my guides (and who also enlisted the support of three exceptional translators to go through the letters he found, Tang Hanjie, Zhang Huyue, and Yi Xiaojie); Vivian Lee, who, along with Ben, was indispensable and a joy to work with, served as my main translator and is responsible for finding the Zhao Yi Man letter, for which I am extremely grateful; Wang Yi at the National Museum of China; Sandy Zhang, who volunteered to serve as my guide and translator in Nanjing (and I am also grateful to Ying Shen and Shen Tao for putting us in touch); and Zhu Cheng Shan, director of the Nanjing Massacre Museum. My trip to Nanjing was an especially profound one, primarily thanks to Iris Chang. Iris wrote the international bestseller *The Rape of Nanking*, and despite the fact that we had had no previous connection, she promptly answered a rather lengthy e-mail from me asking all sorts of questions about where I should go and whom I should visit on my trip to China. She could not have been more supportive and thoughtful. This began an all-too-brief friendship, and Iris, who took her own life in November 2004, will be missed dearly by everyone who knew her personally or indirectly through her work. *Czech Republic*: Milada Hladikova, who went out of her way to help me plan my trip to Prague, and Major Eduard Stehlik at the Historical Institute of the Army of the Czech Republic, who was responsible for finding the Jan Kubic letter. Major Stehlik is, himself, the author of an incredible book titled *LIDICE: The Story of a Czech Village* (available in English through the Lidice Memorial), which focuses on the massacre of innocent Czech citizens that took place after the assassination of Heydrich Reinhart. *Egypt*: Marwah Afifi, who essentially (and flawlessly) organized my entire trip to Alexandria, El Alamein, and Cairo. *England*: Vicky Britton, who helped with research after I left England; Justin Clegg and Tim Thomas, at the British Library; Richard Davis and other staff members at the Leeds University Library; the brilliant literary agent Sara Fisher; at The Second World War Experience Centre in Leeds, I am indebted to Claire Harder and especially Dr. Peter Liddle, the director of the Centre, for allowing me to go through their archives and use some of their best letters (Dr. Liddle has probably done more to preserve British wartime letters than anyone alive); Alison Miles and Emily White at the Tate Library and Archive in London; Christopher Miller, who did an enormous amount of research for me at the Imperial War Museum; journalist Chris Redman, who helped me try to get in touch with British troops in Iraq; Anthony Richards and Roderick Suddaby at the Imperial War Museum, which is quite simply one of the best war museums in the world, went out of their way to help me find stellar letters in their extraordinary archives. I truly cannot emphasize enough how hospitable and generous Anthony and

Roderick were, and I am enormously grateful. *France*: In Normandy—my guide Catherine Mennesson; Françoise Passera, who shared with me letters from the Memorial of Caen, one of my favorite museums; Lucien Tisserand at the German Military Cemetery; and Thomas Schlich, who is passionate about preserving wartime correspondence as well. In Paris—Marie-Jeanne Badault, an incredible teacher who gave me the opportunity to come and speak at her school; Jean-Pierre Gueno, who has brought enormous attention to the importance of saving wartime letters in France, and who has edited several first-rate books, including the sensational *Paroles de Poilus 1914–1918*, published by Librio in cooperation with Radio France; Nicole Guillou at the US Embassy in Paris; Chaibong Hahm and Gillian Whitcomb at UNESCO; Patrick Jarreau with *Le Monde*, who put me in touch with Annick Cojean, who did an incredible article for the newspaper on the Legacy Project. In Lyon—Caroline Gurret and Chantal Lorro at the Museum of the Resistance. In Verdun—my guide Ingrid Ferrand; Catherine Jung at The World Center for Peace; Isabelle Remy at the Verdun Memorial; Corentin Seznec at the Alliance Française de Washington, DC; Major General Pascal Vinchon at the French Embassy; Drew Tarlow; and Ann Kordahl, who introduced me to Gail Noyer, Lisa Aidan, Tama Carroll, and Janet Lizop in Paris to help me in my efforts. Janet, in particular, has been my lifeline to France since I returned to the States, and she has gone out of her way to help me track down essential contacts and is single-handedly responsible for finding the Jacques Aulong letter. I also wish to thank Pierre Lescault for assistance with finding the Vietnam letter written by the French soldier in 1949. *Germany*: Dr. Peter Jahn, at the German-Russian Museum Berlin-Karlshorst, for providing me with extraordinary letters by German and Russian veterans; and Dr. Klaus A. Lankheit, at the Institut für Zeitgeschichte, one of my earliest and most helpful German contacts. Dr. Gerhard Bauer, Jan Hoffman, and Harald Schindler at the Militärhistorisches Museum der Bundeswehr in Dresden; Ewald Behrschmidt; Friedrich Richter at the Dresden Stadtmuseum; Dr. Irmtraud von Andrian-Werburg at the Germanisches National Museum; my exceptional guide and translator Sally Slenczka, who put me in touch with Michael Kaiser; and Von Hartmut Voight at the *Nürnberger* newspaper, who helped us spread the word about the project; I am especially grateful to Dr. Katrin Kilian and Dr. Clemens Schwender at the Feldpost-Archiv Berlin, who provided me with several of the best German letters in this book. Their efforts with the Feldpost-Archiv have helped preserve countless German wartime letters, and they are providing an invaluable service to history. They could not have been nicer or more cooperative. The person most responsible for making my visit to Germany, and especially to Berlin, a success is Christian Scharnefsky. When we met, he presented me with a meticulous schedule for my week in Berlin that, he assured me, was planned so that all outdoor tourist activities would take place on sunny days and all indoor research would be conducted on gloomy ones. Considering he had confirmed the schedule weeks before I arrived, I assumed he was joking. As it turned out, he was not. In spirit (and somewhat in looks), Christian reminds me of a younger version of the great theologian Dietrich Bonhoeffer; Christian is a man of integrity, humor, and conviction, and spending time with him and his wife, Katrin, was a highlight of the entire trip. *India*: David Omissi, who edited *Indian Voices of the Great War: Soldiers' Letters, 1914–18* (MacMillan Press, 1999). We have never met or communicated, but it is his incredible work that inspired me to go to the British Library to find more of these letters in their collection. Information I quoted about the Indian troops came primarily from Omissi's book; and Shyam Singh Saklani, Kirit Singh Rathore, and Amit

Majumdar, my guides in New Delhi. *Iraq*: Eric Clark, Dave Farlow, David Gercken, Andy Meissner, Mark Rickert, and Chris Stannis, who hosted me in Iraq, and Muammal Jaafar, who helped me find letters and e-mail by Iraqi civilians. *Ireland*: Ciara McDonnell, at the National Library of Ireland, who could not have been more helpful both during my stay in Dublin and after I returned to the US. *Italy*: Maria Teresa Tringali, whom I found serendipitously through a friend of a friend of a friend, was one of the best organizers and guides I encountered on my trip. (And I am indebted to Alice Power and Mike Dolan for helping me find Maria Teresa.) When it seemed like we were going to have trouble finding war letters in any Italian museum, Maria Teresa located the Fondazione Archivio Diaristico Nazionale, which has been collecting letters and diaries for years. I am extremely grateful to Loretta Veri and Andrea Franceschetti for sharing with us material from their collection. Maria Teresa and I also traveled to Anzio, and Silvano Casaldi, curator of the Museum of the Allied Landing, was very generous in providing me with letters from his archives as well. *Japan*: In Hiroshima—Kahori Wada and Minoru Hataguchi at the Hiroshima Peace Memorial Museum. In Nagasaki—Nobuko Kamata, with the Nagasaki A-Bomb Testimonial Society, who shared with me the extraordinary letter by Masao Sakai; my guide, Joji Nakamura, and Takashi Morita at the Nagasaki Atomic Bomb Museum. In Okinawa—Dave Davenport, who runs the Battle of Okinawa Museum; Futenma Choukey at the Himeyuri Peace Museum; Takayasu Fuji and Hirokatsu Tamatsu at the Okinawa Prefectural Peace Memorial Museum; Professor Hiroshia Hosaka at the University of the Ryukyus; and my trusty guide, Ueda Shoji. In Tokyo—Kitano Ryuichi at the *Asahi Shimbun* newspaper; Lee Hyon Suk at the Foreign Correspondents Club of Japan; Naomi Shin, her father Zenji Abe, and the rest of their family for taking the time to come and meet me during my all-too-brief stay in Tokyo; Chikara Ishii, Fusako Watanabe, Okada Hiroyuki, Sakae Tani, and Shigeru Ishii at the Japan Memorial Society of the Students Killed in the War (Wadatsumi Society), who share a passion for preserving wartime letters and whose letters were used to create a phenomenal book titled *Listen to the Voices from the Sea*, translated by Midori Yamanouchi and Joseph L. Quinn (University of Scranton Press, 2000); Iki Hiroshi and Takahashi Daisuke, as well as the Yushukan and Public Relations Office of the Yasukuni Jinja, who provided many of the Japanese letters in this book; and my incredible guide and translator Amiko Nobori, who also continued to serve as my link to Japan once I left. The US Embassy was extremely helpful, and I am especially indebted to Mark Davidson, Margot Carrington, and Erika Wada. They are three of the most amazing people I met on my journey. *Kuwait*: Dr. Youssef Abdul-Moati, who generously shared letters from the Center for Research and Studies on Kuwait; Yacoub Abdulla, who was the perfect host and is responsible for helping me find all of the Kuwait-related letters in the book; Dr. Fatma Al-Khalifa; and Tahani Al-Terkate, Sarah Deyyain, and Tory Randall at the Kuwait Information Office, who helped me plan my trip. I also wish to thank Anna Maria Slemp, my military contact in Kuwait, who helped me get into (and, most importantly, out of) Iraq. *Malta*: John Galea, a taxi driver who, in one day, rushed me around the island at a breakneck pace to show me one extraordinary war-related site after another. *Mexico*: Although we had difficulty finding Mexican war letters, primarily because very few seem to exist, my guides Angelica Morales Carballo and Pablo Mondragon Silva made my trip to Mexico City one of the most enjoyable of the entire around-the-world journey. I am indebted to my friend Abigail Seymour for helping me find Angelica and Pablo. I also want to thank Aida Flores at the US Embassy for her assistance as I was planning my visit, and Maria Eugenia Sevilla for profiling the search for Mexican war letters in *Reforma*. *Netherlands*: In Amsterdam—Hubert Berkhout, René Pottkamp, and Erik Somers at the Netherlands Institute for War Documentation, where I found the letters by Dutch resisters; Frits van Suchtelen at the Dutch Resistance Museum; Hans Masselink at the *Trouw*; and Alissa Ede. At the Veterans Institute's Centre for Research and Expertise, I cannot thank Gielt Algra enough for all of his assistance and hospitality during my stay in Holland. (Joanne Mothaan and Martin Elands, also at the Institute, were very helpful.) I am especially grateful to Gielt for putting me in touch with André Dekker, who shared with me his letters regarding Srebrenica. *New Zealand*: Dr. Alistair Carlile, Diane Gordon, and, in particular, Bruce Ralston, at the Auckland War Memorial Museum, who helped me find letters in their collection. I was extremely fortunate to meet Rob Bailey at the Museum; he was researching a similar topic and told me about letters he had already located, copies of which he very kindly shared with me. Due to time constraints I did not have a chance to visit one of New Zealand's best resources, the Kippenberger Military Archive at the Army Museum Waiouru, but the archivist there, Dolores Ho, went out of her way to send me material from their collection. I am also grateful to Scott MacLeod at *The New Zealand Herald* for profiling the search for Kiwi war letters. *Northern Ireland*: Amanda Moreno, at the Royal Irish Fusiliers Museum in Armagh, who shared letters from their collection and also put me in touch with Jaki Knox at the Royal Ulster Rifles Museum in Belfast. Jaki, too, was immensely helpful, especially in suggesting the Charles Sweeney correspondence. *Philippines*: Gerard Alolad, who lives in the US but has family in the Philippines and did initial research for me during one of his college breaks; Ramon Alonso Jr., who served as the tour guide during my visit to Corregidor; Elissa and Lysander Canlas for their advice as I prepared for my trip to Manila; Waldette M. Cueto, the librarian at the American Historical Collection, Ateneo de Manila University; Maita Oebanda at the University of Santo Tomas Museum of Arts and Sciences, who helped me find other archives and collections. Maita pointed me in the direction of the Filipinas Heritage Library, where I found the Marcial Lichauco letters. Through a wonderful bit of good luck, my contact at the US Embassy, Joe Mussomeli, was—only weeks before my arrival—vaulted into the position of, essentially, the acting US ambassador to the Philippines. (My profound thanks go out to my old friend John Meyers for putting me in touch with Joe.) Joe and his wife could not have been more welcoming, and it made the whole trip to the Philippines that much more special. *Poland*: Aleksandra Bukowska and Zdistaw Zajdler, at the Muzeum Wojska Polskiego; Eva Gryk and her father Jan Niebrzydowski, who so generously went through his personal archives and offered many remarkable letters; Andrew Koss at the US Embassy; Anna Kowalczyk, who helped me try to find letters and e-mail by Polish troops in Iraq; Magdalena Kowalska, my initial contact and now dear friend in Warsaw, who helped me plan my trip to Poland, and Joanna Kowalska, who helped us spread the word about the project through *Newsweek Poland*; Edyta Kurek at the Jewish Historical Institute in Warsaw, and the Institute's director, Dr. Feliks Tych, who could not have been more gracious or generous with their time; Krzystof Molenda, who put me in touch with Rafal Nowakowski at the Muzeum Literatury; Lynne Olson and Stanley Cloud, who wrote a phenomenal book called *A Question of Honor: The Kosciuszko Squadron* (Knopf, 2003) about the Polish pilots who flew with the RAF during World War II. Lynne and Stanley were extremely helpful, and I am especially grateful to them for putting me in touch with Ewa Sobotowski, who has gone to heroic

lengths to help me find letters from Poland and is a joy to work with; Beata Czekaj-Wis-
niewska, Malgorzata Gwara, and Andrzej Wesolowski at the Centralna Biblioteka
Wojskowa, who provided Zbigniew Janicki's letter; Krzysztof Piotr Starzecki, my
guide in Warsaw; and Marzena Weidrzyk-Kaszuba, my guide at Auschwitz-Birkenau.
Russia: Elizabeth Adams, who has, without question, contributed more to helping me
find Russian war letters than any other person, and she has my eternal thanks for her
seemingly boundless generosity. After hearing about the Legacy Project, Elizabeth contacted me before I left for Russia and was instrumental in setting up my trip, finding
guides and translators, tracking down archives with letters, translating letters with
impeccable skill, and simply being of assistance whenever a problem or crisis came up.
I want to say a special word of thanks to Alexey Rumyantsev, who first communicated
with me after I left Russia and, along with Elizabeth Adams, is one of those essential
contacts without whom I would not have found the Russian letters that ended up in
this book. I am also grateful to Leonid Frolov, one of my neighbors here in the US, who
kindly did some last-minute translations for me. In Moscow—Boris Semyonovich
Ilizarov, a kindred spirit who has been collecting letters by "common" Russian soldiers;
Diana Kondratenko at the State Historical Museum; Dr. Andrey A. Lebedev, deputy
chief of Izvestia; Colonel Alexander Konstantinovich Nikonov at the Central Armed
Forces Museum, which provided the majority of the Russian letters in this book; Jeremy
Weinberg, my old high school classmate, who put me in touch with reporters at the
Moscow Times (Oksana Yablokova) and *St. Petersburg Times* (Irina Titova); and Dr.
Nikolai Yakuba at the Central Museum of the Great Patriotic War. The US Embassy
was extremely helpful while I was in Moscow, and I especially appreciated the advice
and assistance offered by James P. Sonborn, Michael Allen, Yuri Boguslavsky, David
Hasenauer, Thomas Shipp, and Ralph T. McCall. In St. Petersburg—Dr. Sergei Efi-
mov and Colonel Alexander Sergeevich Monaenkov at the Military-Historical Museum
of Artillery, Engineer, and Signal Corps; and at the State Memorial Museum of the
Defense and Blockade of Leningrad, director Anatoliy Alexandrovich Shishkin and senior research assistant Nikolay Petrovich Dobrotvorskiy provided me with the exceptional letters by the young Russian children writing during the siege. In Volgograd—I
am grateful to my guide Tamara V. Fyodorova. *Scotland:* Dr. Iain Gordon Brown and
Colm McLaughlin, at the National Library of Scotland; Edith A. Phillip, at the
National War Museum of Scotland, who went out of her way to help me find Scottish
letters in their collection; and although I was not able to find letters or e-mail by Scottish troops in Iraq, Gethin Chamberlain and Lieutenant Colonel Hugh Blackman both
very kindly assisted me in my search. *Serbia and Montenegro:* Zermen Filipovic, for
helping with translations; Vesna Injac-Malbasa, at the National Library of Serbia; Mil-
ica Jovanovic, at *Danas*, for helping to spread the word about the Legacy Project; and
Predrag Krejic and Dragos Petrovic, at the Archives of Serbia and Montenegro, for sharing letters with me. At the US Embassy in Belgrade I am indebted to Jasna Kunic, Allen
Docal, and Richard Mei Jr. for their kindness, hospitality, and support before, during,
and after my trip to the Balkans. *South Korea:* Michele M. Cenzer and Kim Su Nam
at the US Embassy, who helped me plan my trip to Seoul and put me in touch with
Kim Hoo-ran at *The Korea Herald*; Kevin Kim at the BBC in Seoul, who, despite the
fact that the South Korean government was in the midst of a major presidential crisis,
took the time to help me find Kim Min Ha. Most importantly, I am indebted to Lee
Kyu Young (a.k.a. "Shawn") for being my primary guide, translator, and researcher
before, during, and after my stay in South Korea. His persistence and humor made the

trip a resounding success. *Spain:* Iratxe Momoitio Astorkia, director of the Gernika Peace Museum, and Ana Teresa Nuñez Monasterio, who works in the Museum's documentation center; Tom Hare, who found and translated the Guernica letters; and Amanda Olivia Guglieri Lillo, who helped me with my search for letters and e-mail describing the March 11, 2004, bombings in Madrid. *Thailand:* I am grateful to my guide Pramai "Mike" T. West, who took me out to Kanchanaburi. I am especially grateful to Rod Beattie at the Thailand-Burma Railway Centre, for telling me about the Kenelm Clifton Johnson-Hill letters/journals. *Vietnam:* Huynh Ngoc Van at the War Remnants Museum; Nguyen Quang Hoa, my guide in Hanoi; My Hang, who assisted me with spreading the word about our efforts through the media; Nguyen Van Thanh, my temporary guide in Ho Chi Minh City, who had the terrific idea of visiting antiques shops that sold old envelopes to see if there were wartime letters inside (there were); Nguyen Huu Viet, my primary guide in HCMC, who was tireless in contacting museums and archives throughout Hanoi and HCMC and is responsible for finding the "Dear Tan" letter; Robert Kulp and Dr. Phan Minh Hien, both of whom assisted me with my search for Dien Bien Phu letters; Chuck Searcy, who helped me find so many of the contacts I depended on during my trip; and Tran Dinh Song, who put me in touch with Hoa and Viet.

The homefront translators: Many of the individuals who assisted me with translations live in the countries listed above, and others, like David Pelizzari and Ewa Sobotowski, were previously mentioned because they helped in numerous other ways. The following translators, who all live in the US, went above and beyond the call of duty (most either volunteered to work for free or reduced their fees substantially), and needless to say, without them, there could not have been a book: Chie Berkeley, Megumi Furukawa, Radwan Hakim, Sammy Kim, Daniel Lautenslager, Julia Leikin, Luu Pham, Tamar van Raalten, Armend Reka, and Ivana Ticha. Listed below are the individuals and institutions that either granted me permission to use their respective letters (or e-mails) or, particularly in the case of museums, libraries, and archives, granted me access to their collections.

Considerable efforts have been made to trace and acknowledge the ownership of letters under copyright listed below. If, however, there are any mistakes or omissions, please contact the publisher so that these errors can be corrected in future editions. (Several of the letters are, in fact, e-mails, but all correspondences are referred to as letters.) In some cases, a copyright holder's identity is withheld below due to privacy concerns. The designation "courtesy of"—used primarily to indicate letters archived in a museum, historical society, or library or privately held by someone with no connection to the letter-writer or his/her family—indicates only that these institutions or individuals have provided physical access to the respective letter. Once again, many thanks to everyone who shared or submitted a letter.

John Abrams letter © Ellen Abrams Blankenship, reprinted by permission of Ellen Abrams Blankenship; Khaled Al-Maeena exchange with Roy and Jeff reprinted with permission of Khaled Al-Maeena and Arab News; Abdul Hameed Al-Attar letter © Abdul Hameed Al-Attar, reprinted by permission of Abdul Hameed Al-Attar; Khadum Al-Hilli letter courtesy of Muammal Jaafar; Patricia A. Andjelkovic letters © Patricia A. Andjelkovic, reprinted by permission of Patricia A. Andjelkovic; "Mme. J. Armand" letter courtesy of Paul A. Saunders; BJ Armstrong letter © B.J. Armstrong, reprinted by permission of BJ

Armstrong; James Arnold letter © Dovie Stewart, reprinted by permission of Dovie Stewart; Heather Ashline letter © Heather Ashline, reprinted by permission of Heather Ashline; Jacques Aulong letter © Jacques Aulong, reprinted by permission of Jacques Aulong; Demetria Barber letter © Demetria Barber, reprinted by permission of Demetria Barber; Samuel Bard letter reprinted by permission of the American Antiquarian Society; Martha Barnett letter © Marjorie Jones, reprinted by permission of Marjorie Jones; Maurice Barnett letter © Rande & Cynthia McCabe, reprinted by permission of Rande & Cynthia McCabe; Elizabeth Barton letter © Karen Duncan, reprinted by permission of Karen Duncan; John "Jack" Bateman Beer letter courtesy of the Imperial War Museum (London), Department of Documents (86/19/1), reprinted with permission of J.E. Overall; David Bellon letter © David Bellon, reprinted by permission David Bellon; Roy F. Bergengren letter courtesy of the Wisconsin Historical Society (Don Anderson Papers, Box 12); Isabelle Biasini letter © Joy Grigat, reprinted by permission of Joy Grigat; Gaston Biron excerpt courtesy of Jean-Pierre Gueno at Radio France; Christian Brodeching excerpt courtesy of Jean-Pierre Gueno at Radio France; Ted Brush letter © Cheryl Brush, reprinted by permission of Cheryl Brush; Peter Caddick-Addams letter courtesy of the Imperial War Museum (London), Department of Documents (03/20/1); Gloria Caldas letter © Gloria Caldas, reprinted by permission of Gloria Caldas; Guy Carleton letter, from the manuscript collection (IR 7106–1), courtesy of the National Army Museum (London); Robert Carver letter © Robert O. Carver, reprinted by permission of Robert O. Carver; Gary Chandler letter © Gary Chandler, reprinted by permission of Gary Chandler; Alfred Dougan Chater letter © Simon D. Chater, reprinted by permission of Simon D. Chater; James O. Cherry letter © Janet Fahrenbruck-Lynch, reprinted by permission of Janet Fahrenbruck-Lynch; Jim Colman letter © Mary Colman, reprinted by permission of Mary Colman; Fiorgio A. Contro letter reprinted by permission of Fondazione Archivio Diaristico Nazionale (Santo Stefano AR), "Caro Marco"/Luca Rossi, E/T2 ADN; Joseph Ball Cralle' letter © David Cralle, reprinted by permission of David Cralle; H.W. Crowle letter courtesy of Australian War Museum; JJ Cummings letter © JJ Cummings, reprinted by permission of JJ Cummings; Scott Curry letter © Scott Curry, reprinted by permission of Scott Curry; William Czako letter © Sandra Cook, reprinted by permission of Sandra Cook; Shed Karn Das letter courtesy of the British Library, from the "Reports of the Censors. Indian Mails in France" (L/M/5–825 through 828) in the Oriental and India Office Collections; Benjamin O. Davis letter courtesy of the US Army Heritage and Education Center, US Army Military History Institute (Carlisle, PA); Corbin Davis letter courtesy of Carolyn Curtiss; André Dekker letters © André Dekker, reprinted by permission of André Dekker; F. M. Desha letter from the Mary G. Sledge Collection (PC 1441), courtesy of the North Carolina Office of Archives and History; Andrew DeVilbiss letter © Brian J. Tucker, reprinted by permission of Brian J. Tucker; Malcolm Leon Downs letter © Dot Essex, reprinted by permission of Dot Essex; Percival and Thomas Drayton letters reprinted by permission of the Historical Society of Pennsylvania; Thomas A. Edwards letter © Thomas A. Edwards, reprinted by permission of Thomas A. Edwards; John Eggleston letter reprinted by permission of the Daughters of the American Revolution National Society, Americana Collection; Yanagida Eiichi letter reprinted by permission of the Yasukuni Jinja (Tokyo); Harold "Pompey" Elliott letter courtesy of the Australian War Museum; E. John Ellis letter © Steve Ellis, reprinted by permission of Steve Ellis; J.N. Falcon and Crispina de Garcia letters courtesy of Mary O'Neal; Bill Fant letter © Mrs. Joel Fant Trout, reprinted by permission of Mrs. Joel Fant Trout; P. Thomas Ferck letter courtesy of Laura Allwine; Hans Fleischer letter from Kriegsbriefe Deutscher Studenten, edited by Dr.

Philipp Witkop (Verlag Friedrich Andreas Perthes A.-G., Gotha 1916); J. W. Foster letter © J. W. Foster, reprinted by permission of J. W. Foster; L. Vincent Francese letter © L. Vincent Francese, reprinted by L. Vincent Francese; Karl Fuchs letter excerpts from Sieg Heil!: War Letters of Tank Gunner Karl Fuchs, 1937–1941 *by Karl Fuchs (Archon Books, 1987); Margaret Gage letter excerpt from the "Calendar of Home Office Papers of the Reign of George III. 1773–1775," edited by Richard Arthur Roberts (printed for Her Majesty's Stationery Office, London, 1899; preserved in the British Public Record Office); Sergei Galkin letter reprinted by permission of the Central Armed Forces Museum (Moscow); Joseph Goebbels diary excerpt from* The Goebbels Diaries 1942–1943 *edited, translated, and with an introduction by Louis P. Lochner (Doubleday & Company, 1948); Kotka Gofman letter reprinted by permission of the Central Armed Forces Museum (Moscow); Eddie Grant letter © Karen Kubara, reprinted by permission of Karen Kubara; Horace Greeley letter © Jeanne C. Thayer, reprinted by permission of Jeanne C. Thayer; Alice S. Green letter, from the AS Green Papers (MS 15, 120), reprinted by permission of the National Library of Ireland (Dublin); Moses Hall letter from the Microfilm Room (RG 15), courtesy of the National Archives (Washington, DC); Johanne Haas letter excerpt from* Kriegsbriefe Gefallener Studenten *edited by Dr. Philipp Witkop (Georg Müller Verlag, 1928); Josh Harapko letter © Pat Moran, reprinted by permission of Pat Moran; Ichizo Hayashi letter reprinted by permission of Japan Memorial Society of the Students Killed in the War (Wadatsumi Society); Albert Heath letter © Arthur and Barbara Munzig, reprinted by permission of Arthur and Barbara Munzig; David Henry letter © Pat Pehrson, reprinted by permission of Pat Pehrson; Dr. Roman Herzog letter courtesy of Del archivo del centro de documentación de Gernika GoGoratuz, Centro de Investigación por la Paz, Fundación Gernika GoGoratuz; Jerry Hill letter © Jerry Hill, reprinted by permission of Jerry Hill; Theodore Hodgkins letter from the Microfilm Room (RG 107 [L-45]) courtesy of the National Archives (Washington, DC); August Hopp excerpt from* German Students' War Letters, *edited by Philipp Witkop and translated by A. F. Wedd (Pine St. Books, 2002); Lawrence Hoppner and Lorraine Howard letters © Lawrence and Lorraine Hoppner, reprinted by permission of Lawrence and Lorraine Hoppner; George Huckle wartime log entries © The Second World War Experience Centre, reprinted by permission of Dr. Peter Liddle, Director of The Second World War Experience Centre; Robert Hughes letter © Pat Hux, reprinted by permission of Pat Hux; Thomas Hunt letters © Marion Jean Berger, reprinted by permission of Marion Jean Berger; Elizabeth Pritchard Hudson letter courtesy of the Imperial War Museum (London), Department of Documents (03/20/1); Chris Hurd letter © Chris Hurd, reprinted by permission of Chris Hurd; William Hutchinson letter from the Microfilm Room (RG 15), courtesy of the National Archives (Washington, DC); Luis Iriondo letter courtesy of Del archivo del centro de documentación de Gernika GoGoratuz, Centro de Investigación por la Paz, Fundación Gernika GoGoratuz; Zbigniew Janicki letter reprinted by permission of the Centralna Biblioteka Wojskowa; Henry Johnson letter courtesy of the Monmouth County Historical Association (New Jersey); William Johnson letter from the Microfilm Room (RG 15), courtesy of the National Archives (Washington, DC); Kenelm Clifton Johnson-Hill letters/journals © Alan Johnson-Hill, reprinted by permission of Alan Johnson-Hill; Nazaar Joudi letters courtesy of Don North, reprinted by permission of Don North and Nazaar Joudi; Michael Kaiser letter © Michael Kaiser, reprinted by permission of Michael Kaiser; Bruno Kaliga letter reprinted by permission of the Feldpost-Archiv Berlin; Abdul-Mohsen Salman Kazem letter courtesy of the Center for Research and Studies on Kuwait; Jan Kubis letter courtesy of Historical Institute of the Army of the Czech Republic; Tadamichi Kuribayashi letter reprinted by permission of Yasukuni Jinja (Tokyo); Kim Kyong Bin letter quoted from a BBC News report on March 15, 2001; Kim Sung Ha letter courtesy of Kim Min Ha, reprinted by permission of Kim Min Ha; Harold E. Kipp letters © Norma Kipp Avendano, reprinted by permission of Norma Kipp Avendano; Henry Kircher letters reprinted by permission of the Illinois State Historical Library; Burton Klein letter © Burton Klein, reprinted by permission of Burton Klein; Anna Koppich letter (RG-04.048) courtesy of the United States Holocaust Memorial Museum Collections Division, Archives Branch (Washington, DC); Tadeusz Kosciuszko letter courtesy of the Polish American Museum (Chicago); Natalya Kovshova letter reprinted by permission of the Central Armed Forces Museum (Moscow); Antoni Kropielnicki letter courtesy of Jan Niebrzydowski; William Guy Lamont letter courtesy of Jane Jenkins; W.L. Larson letter © Antoinette L. Dooley, reprinted by permission of Antoinette L. Dooley; William Lee Kyzer letter © Ernie Kyzer, reprinted by permission of Ernie Kyzer; Lee Jung Ho letter reprinted by permission of The War Memorial of Korea; Robert E. Lee letter (HM 8838) reprinted by permission of the Henry E. Huntington Library; Hart Leech letter courtesy of the Canadian Letters and Images Project; Gunter and Katinka Leopold letter courtesy of Connie Phelps and Lois Hoffman; Marcial Lichauco letters © Jessie Coe Lichauco, reprinted by permission of Jessie Coe Lichauco; Francis Lieber letter (LI 3756) reprinted by permission of the Henry E. Huntington Library; Ronald "Butch" Livergood letter © Ronald "Butch" Livergood, reprinted by permission of Ronald "Butch" Livergood; Maitland Livsey letter © Maitland Livsey, reprinted by permission of Maitland Livsey; Warren C. Lothrop letter courtesy of the National Archives and Records Administration ("Office of Scientific Research and Development," RG 227, Division 19 Records, SAC-6, T, BAT-X-RAY); Bernard Paul Lyons letter © Mary Jo Meloy, reprinted with permission of Mary Jo Meloy; Douglas MacArthur letter courtesy of the MacArthur Memorial Archives (Norfolk, Virginia); Ian H. Macdonnell letter from the Brotherton Library Special Collections (Liddle Collection) courtesy of the University of Leeds, Leeds, United Kingdom; Robert P. Mackey letter © Robert P. Mackey, reprinted by permission of Robert P. Mackey; John Madden letters © John Madden, reprinted by permission of John Madden; Maurius Maillet letter courtesy of Jean-Pierre Gueno at Radio France; Maschil Manring letter © Ed Manring, reprinted by permission of Ed Manring; William Mayse letter © Susan Mayse, reprinted by permission of Susan Mayse; James H. McCallum letter courtesy of the Yale University Divinity School Library and Professor Herold J. Wiens; Kathy McConkey letter © Kathy McConkey, reprinted by permission of Kathy McConkey; Frederick McIntyre letter © Frederick McIntyre Jr., reprinted by permission of Frederick McIntyre Jr.; Christine McNeff letter © Christine McNeff, reprinted by permission of Christine McNeff; Russ Merrell letter © Pam Merrell, reprinted by permission of Pam Merrell; Justin Merhoff letter © Justin Merhoff, reprinted by permission of Justin Merhoff; Erma Meyers letters © Ralph Aarons, reprinted by permission of Ralph Aarons; Roger Micault letter courtesy of Pierre Lescault; Walter C. Michels letter © Leslyn Michels Goodrich, reprinted by permission of Leslyn Michels Goodrich; Anna Miller letter © Anna Miller, reprinted by permission of Anna Miller; Frank Charles Miller letter courtesy of the Canadian War Museum; June Clevenger Miller letter © Gaylo Conner, reprinted by permission of Gaylo Conner; Richard Millin letter © Peggy Millin, reprinted by permission of Peggy Millin; Masuda A. Mohamadi letters © Masuda A. Mohamadi, reprinted by permission of Masuda A. Mohamadi; Christian von Molitor letter reprinted by permission of the New York Public Library; General John Monash letter courtesy of the Australian War Memorial; Melville Montgomery letter © Elizabeth Dowey, reprinted by permission of Elizabeth Dowey; Edward J. Moore letter © Edward J. Moore, reprinted by* permission of Edward J. Moore; Nathan B. Moore letter © Linda Manion, reprinted by permission of Linda Manion; Phoebe Morris letters reprinted by permission of the Morris Family Papers, Dumbarton House/The National Society of the Colonial Dames of America, Washington, DC; Jonathan Singleton Mosby letter courtesy of J Leyburn Mosby Jr.; Henry Mowat letter reprinted by permission of the Maine Historical Society; letter by Mr. and Mrs. Tomas Myatt, the parents of Beryl Myatt © The Trustees of the Imperial War Museum (London), Department of Documents (67/280/1), reprinted by permission of the Trustees of the Imperial War Museum; Toyoka Alva Nakata © Alva Wirth, reprinted by permission of Alva Wirth; Paul Nash letter (TGA 8313/1/1/162) © Tate Archives London, 2005, reprinted by permission of the Tate Archives; Robert A. Neblett letter © Dorothy N. Perkins, reprinted by permission of Dorothy N. Perkins; Gerald I. Nelson letter © Victoria Nelson Eliot, reprinted by permission of Victoria Nelson Eliot; Conrad J. Netting III letter © Conrad J. Netting IV, reprinted by permission of Conrad J. Netting IV; Jim Norton letter © Jim Norton, reprinted by permission of Jim Norton; John Ogilvie letter courtesy of the Fort Ticonderoga Museum; Williamson Simpson Oldham letter from the Microfilm Room (RG 153), courtesy of the National Archives (Washington, DC); Lila Oliver letters and sketches © Lila Oliver Asher, reprinted by permission of Lila Oliver Asher; Ula Owen letter courtesy of E.C. Victorsen; Genciana Paipan letter courtesy of Mary O'Neal; William Paterson letter courtesy of the Trustees of the National Museums of Scotland; Mevlida Pekmez letter © Mevlida Pekmez, reprinted by permission of Mevlida Pekmez; James R. Penton sketches and letters © Anita Stewart and Marjory A. Penton, reprinted by permission of Marjory A. Penton; Max Peters letter © Max Peters, reprinted by permission of Max Peters; Angela Petesch letter © Rutledge Parker Hazzard, reprinted by permission of Rutledge Parker Hazzard; Lewis Plush letter © Gary Lee, reprinted by permission of Gary Lee; John Pohlman letter courtesy of Carolyn Barber-Long; Joseph L. Portnoy letters © Joseph L. Portnoy, reprinted by permission of Joseph L. Portnoy; Naubat Rai letter courtesy of the British Library, from the "Reports of the Censors. Indian Mails in France" (L/M/5–825 through 828) in the Oriental and India Office Collections; the Sylvain Eugene Raynal message is inscribed on a plaque at Fort Vaux in Verdun, France; Cecilia Reed letter © Kathleen McGarry, reprinted by permission of Kathleen McGarry; Paul A. Reitz letter © Julie Mangold, reprinted by permission of Julie Mangold; Mark Rickert letter © Mark Rickert, reprinted by permission of Mark Rickert; William Rigby letter © Bernadette Gentry, reprinted by permission of Bernadette Gentry; Jason Ritter letter © Jason Ritter, reprinted by permission of Jason Ritter; Leila Rothstein letter © Leila Hoffman, reprinted by permission of Leila Hoffman; Lisa Kouchelevitz Rosenblum letter (RG-10.054*01) courtesy of the United States Holocaust Memorial Museum Collections Division, Archives Branch (Washington, DC); Frank Rudert letter © Bruce Rudert, reprinted by permission of Bruce Rudert; John Richard Ruggles letter © Christine Ruggles Smith, reprinted by permission of Christine Ruggles Smith; Travis Russell letter © Travis Russell, reprinted by permission of Travis Russell; Sana letter © R. Ali, reprinted by permission of R. Ali; Neil Schmelz letter © Tom Schmelz, reprinted by permission of Tom Schmelz; Hubert A. Schneider letter © Pete Schneider, reprinted by permission of Pete Schneider; Hans Schröter letter courtesy of Stadtmuseum Dresden (from "Verbrannt bis zur Unkenntlichkeit"), reprinted by permission of the Stadtmuseum Dresden; Jerome H. Schumacher letter © Jerome H. Schumacher, reprinted by permission of Jerome H. Schumacher; John C. Sellars letter courtesy of Norman Schwarz; Tom Shakow letter © Tom Shakow, reprinted by permission of Tom Shakow; Shawai Helu Shamkhi letter courtesy of the Center for Research and Studies on Kuwait; Shayma letter courtesy of Muammal

Jaafar; Philip H. Sheridan letter excerpt from The War of the Rebellion: A Compilation of the Official Records of the Union and Confederate Armies, *Series 1, Vol. 43, Part II, p. 671. (Government Printing Office: Washington, DC, 1880); Robert Sherrard letter © Barbara L. Sherrard, reprinted by permission of Barbara L. Sherrard; Michael Shiner diary excerpt from the Library of Congress (Manuscripts Room); Denis Silva Torres letter © Denis Silva Torres, reprinted by permission of Denis Silva Torres; Thakur Singh letter courtesy of the British Library, from "Reports of the Censors. Indian Mails in France" (L/M/5–825 through 828) in the Oriental and India Office Collections; Eddie Slovik letter courtesy of Edward Woods; Ty Smith letters © Ty Smith, reprinted by permission of Ty Smith; William H. Smith letter © Mary Jewel Hester, reprinted by permission of Mary Jewel Hester; Sebron Sneed letter courtesy of A. Jack Jernigan; Ted Steinkamp letter © Kathy Menter, reprinted by permission of Kathy Menter; David R. Stevenson letter © William Stephenson, reprinted by permission of William Stephenson; Earl P. Stevenson letter courtesy of the National Archives and Records Administration ("Office of Scientific Research and Development," RG 227, Division 19 Records, SAC-6, T, BAT-X-RAY); Andrew Osborn Stoan letter © Joan Violante, reprinted by permission of Joan Violante; Noel Streatfeild letter © W.H.C. Streatfeild, reprinted by permission of W.H.C. Streatfeild and the Noel Streatfeild Estate; Ray Stubbe letter © Ray Stubbe, reprinted by permission of Ray Stubbe; Charles Sweeny letter reprinted by permission of the Royal Ulster Rifles Museum (Belfast); William Taylor letter © Edith Lenart, reprinted by permission of Edith Lenart; Tetsuko Tanaka letter courtesy of Professor Yuzuru J. Takeshita; William D. Taylor letter © Edith Lenart, reprinted by permission of Edith Lenart; George F. Telfer letters (from the George F. Telfer Papers, MSS 2635) reprinted by permission of the Oregon Historical Society Research Library (Portland, Oregon); Chuck Theusch letter © Chuck Theusch, reprinted by permission of Chuck Theusch; David Arthur Thompson letter © Howard Thompson, reprinted by permission of Howard Thompson; Tran Thi Anh Thu letter © Tran Thi Anh Thu, reprinted by permission of Tran Thi Anh Thu; Jean Thuiller letter courtesy of the Canadian War Museum; Frederick C. Trenne letter courtesy of the Auckland War Memorial Museum; Thomas Tuckhorn letter © Thomas Tuckhorn, reprinted by permission of Thomas Tuckhorn; Gary Turnure letter © Gary Turnure, reprinted by permission of Gary Turnure; Danae Vagliano letter © The Second World War Experience Centre, reprinted by permission of Dr. Peter Liddle, Director of The Second World War Experience Centre; James Van Veen letter courtesy of Elise Kerlin; Robert M. Wada letter © Robert M. Wada, reprinted by permission of Robert M. Wada; Gene Vance Jr. letter © Lisa Vance, reprinted by permission of Lisa Vance; Dan Wagenaar letter © Elaine Wagenaar, reprinted by permission of Elaine Wagenaar; Arthur I. Wallace letter © Mary Wallace, reprinted by permission of Mary Wallace; "Werner Walti" letter courtesy of the National War Museum of Scotland; Ralph Walsh letter (1995.A.1138) courtesy of the United States Holocaust Memorial Museum Collections Division, Archives Branch (Washington, DC); Terry Ward letter © Terry Ward, reprinted by permission of Terry Ward; Stephen Webber letter © Stephen Webber, reprinted by permission Stephen Webber; David Welch letter from the Microfilm Room (RG 15), courtesy of the National Archives (Washington, DC); Josef Wenzel excerpt from* German War Students' War Letters, *edited by Philipp Witkop and translated by A. F. Wedd (Pine St. Books, 2002); Donald West letter © Elizabeth West, reprinted by permission of Elizabeth West; Jack Wilkes letter © Jackie Hinkston, reprinted by permission of Jackie Hinkston; James Williams letter reprinted by permission of the South Carolina Historical Society; Jimmie Wilson letter © Marjorie N. Wilson, reprinted by permission of Marjorie N. Wilson; Waverly B.*

Woodson Jr. letter © Waverly Woodson Jr., Reprinted by permission of Waverly Woodson Jr.; Masao Yamaguchi letter courtesy of Nobuko Kamata, reprinted by permission of Nobuko Kamata and the Nagasaki A-Bomb Testimonial Society; Takako Yamakawa letter © Takako Yamakawa, Jerry Yellin letters © Jerry Yellin, and Taro and Hatsue Yamakawa letters © Taro and Hatsue Yamawaka. All letters reprinted by permission of Jerry Yellin; Harry Zaslow letter © Harry Zaslow, reprinted by permission of Harry Zaslow; David Zehden letter © Margery Galluzzi, reprinted by permission of Margery Galluzzi; K. Zehmisch letter courtesy of the In Flanders Fields Museum; Davydovych Zemchenkov letter reprinted by permission of the Central Armed Forces Museum (Moscow); Zhao Yi Man letter courtesy of the National Museum of China.

Anonymous letters (and, again, please note that there are other anonymous letters in the book for which a donor cannot be cited for reasons of privacy and are not listed here, but the letters are still under copyright): **"Forever Yours" (Chapter 1):** *"French mother from St. Pierre" epigraph is from* Letters from Armageddon: A Collection Made During the World War *by Amy Gordon Grant (Houghton Mifflin Company, 1930); letters by the father of Mohemad Feroz Khan and "Hindu soldier" heading "off to Paris," both courtesy of the British Library, from the "Reports of the Censors. Indian Mails in France" (L/M/5–825 through 828) in the Oriental and India Office Collections; excerpt of letter by "Pam" to "Major Martin" from* The Man Who Never Was: World War II's Boldest Counterintelligence Operation *(Bluejacket Books, Naval Institute Press, 2001), written by Ewan Montagu; "Ivy" letter to John "Jack" Bateman Beer letter courtesy of the Imperial War Museum (London), Department of Documents (86/19/1); letter by "Charlie" to Gertrude "Trudel" Geschwill courtesy of Gertrude Kempe; letter by Iraqi soldier to his mother courtesy of the Center for Research and Studies on Kuwait;* **"Lines of Fire" (Chapter 2):** *British officer letter from the Periodical Room (Microfilm 3284), courtesy of the Library of Congress; Confederate soldier letter ("We must fight to the death . . .") © Steve Ellis, reprinted by permission of Steve Ellis; Union captain letter ("I long for the day . . .") excerpted from James M. McPherson's* For Cause and Comrades: Why Men Fought in the Civil War *(Oxford University Press, 1997); Indian soldier "Maganlal" letter courtesy of the British Library, from the "Reports of the Censors. Indian Mails in France" (L/M/5–825 through 828) in the Oriental and India Office Collections; Turkish soldier letter courtesy of the Australian War Museum; "French officer" letter excerpt about Verdun from* Letters from Armageddon: A Collection Made During the World War *by Amy Gordon Grant (Houghton Mifflin Company, 1930); "Dear Tam" letter by "Kien" reprinted by permission of the South Vietnam Women's Museum;* **"Laughing Through the Tears" (Chapter 3):** *Russian soldier to his "Dear and Beloved Wife!" letter courtesy of the State Historical Museum, Moscow, reprinted by permission of the State Historical Museum; "My (dear, (dearest, (darling," letter courtesy of the Imperial War Museum (London), Department of Documents [Misc 4 (46]); "Dear Leader of the Company!" letter dated January 2, 1917, courtesy of the In Flanders Fields Museum; "Willi" letter dated July 10, 1943, reprinted by permission of the Feldpost-Archiv Berlin; Letters intercepted by the Canadian Field Censors courtesy of the National Archives of Canada; "Notes for Those Going on Leave" letter is excerpted from page forty-six of Antony Beevor's* Stalingrad *(Penguin Books, 1999) and, according to Beevor's endnotes, comes from Tsentralnyy Arkhiv Ministerstva Oborony (Central Archive of the Ministry of Defence, Podolsk (206/294/48, p. 346); and "Instructions for a smooth homecoming" courtesy of Dayna Kennison.* **"Caught in the Crossfire"(Chapter 4):** *"A citizen of Falmouth" letter reprinted by permission of the Maine Historical Society; the material relating to the August 25, 1914, letter by "the* *brother of a German soldier fighting in Belgium"* is from Belgium and Germany *by Henri Davignon (T. Nelson & Sons, 1915), in which a facsimile of the letter also appears; the excerpt from the letter by the "German mother of a soldier (Franz)" to her "English friend"* is from Letters from Armageddon: A Collection Made During the World War *by Amy Gordon Grant (Houghton Mifflin Company, 1930); Dutch resistance letters courtesy of the Netherlands Institute for War Documentation (Amsterdam); letters written by the Russian children "Slavik" and "Galia" during the siege of Leningrad courtesy of the State Memorial Museum of the Defense and Blockade of Leningrad, reprinted by permission of the Museum; "Chaim" letter courtesy of the Jewish Historical Institute (Warsaw); the letter by a "US soldier" writing to "a buddy back in the States" from Vietnam is courtesy of David M. Rosenthal; "US Army staff sergeant" letter to Laurie Frost courtesy of Laurie Frost; Iraqi student letter to Mark von Sponeck courtesy of Mark von Sponeck. "Aftermath" (Chapter 5): "Assistant Adjutant General" to the mother of Robert Parnell and Morris J. Foote letter courtesy of the American Historical Collection, Rizal Library, Ateneo de Manila University; letters left at the Vietnam Veterans Memorial courtesy of the Vietnam Veterans Memorial Collection, National Park Service; "Murray" letter to Judith Herman courtesy of Judith Herman Keller.*

INDEX

ABOUT THE AUTHOR

ANDREW CARROLL is the editor of several *New York Times* bestsellers, including *War Letters* and *Letters of a Nation.* He is also responsible for bringing back the "Armed Services Editions" (ASEs), which were pocket-sized editions of national bestsellers and literary classics handed out to US troops stationed abroad during World War II. Carroll revived the ASEs in 2002, and he has distributed hundreds of thousands of the books to American servicemen and -women in Iraq, Afghanistan, and other places around the world.

THE MISSION CONTINUES . . .

The Legacy Project is a national initiative that works to honor and remember those who have served this nation in wartime by seeking out and preserving their personal letters (and now e-mails). We are looking for letters from all of our nation's conflicts and on any subject matter, including expressions of love, descriptions of combat, humorous anecdotes, eyewitness accounts of historic events, reflections on faith or the subject of war itself, and, above all, any well-written letter that describes an incredible story or offers insight into the nature of war and its effect on those involved. We are also interested in letters written by the family members and loved ones of those who serve.

Although we appreciate the generosity of those who have offered, the Legacy Project does not accept monetary donations. Nor do we solicit or accept grants, government funds, or any other form of financial assistance. If you would like to contribute war letters to the Legacy Project, please send a legible photocopy or typed transcript of the material to:

> The Legacy Project
> Attn: Andrew Carroll
> PO Box 53250
> Washington, DC 20009

E-mails can be forwarded to: WarLetters2004@yahoo.com.

We prefer that you not send us original letters, unless you are planning to dispose of the material otherwise and/or do not want the originals returned. We are a very small organization, and due to the overwhelming volume of mail we receive, it can take us several months and possibly longer to respond. We would be grateful if you would include your address and phone number so we can reach you.

For additional information about the Legacy Project, as well as free information on how to preserve your family's letters, links to additional organizations preserving historic materials, and many other military-related resources, please visit our web site: www.WarLetters.com.